'This is an outstanding and innovative book from one of the UK's leading academic insurance lawyers. The relationship between climate change and insurance is much discussed but this is the first comprehensive study, covering the international regime governing climate change, the liabilities that may arise and their insurability, the development of new insurance products and the incidence of public-private solutions to large scale losses. Fascinating reading for insurers, lawyers, brokers, academics and indeed scientists.'

Prof. Robert Merkin KC, *Professor of Law, University of Reading and Special Counsel, Duncan Cotterill, UK*

'This book is an essential and comprehensive reference guide for anyone in the insurance industry who is interested or involved in the intersection of insurance and climate change. It provides thought-provoking views on the role of the insurance industry in addressing the global threat of climate change.'

Julian Enoizi, *Chief Executive Officer, Guy Carpenter Europe, UK*

'Dr. Arnold-Dwyer's book is one of those for which the reader has been urgently waiting. For the first time, the triangular relationship of insurance, law and climate change is comprehensively discussed. With scholarly thoroughness, the interplay of these three elements is fundamentally examined. On this basis, important impulses are given for combating climate change through insurance. Quite simply, a must read.'

Prof. Dr. Dr. h.c. Helmut Heiss, *Professor of Private Law, Comparative Law and International Private Law, University of Zürich*

'Insurance is both an underlying engine of many economies and also a key financial market for tackling climate change. This book lays out how insurance companies can act upon climate change both through the policies they write and the investments they make. Importantly the book is grounded in a legal framework that explains how the contractual relationships and regulatory obligations of insurance companies can also be used to leverage action on climate change. I expect it to be an important resource for scholars and policymakers on this very topical issue.'

Prof. Paula Jarzabkowski FBA, *Professor of Strategic Management UQ Business School, University of Queensland and Bayes Business School (formerly Cass), City, University of London*

INSURANCE, CLIMATE CHANGE AND THE LAW

LLOYD'S INSURANCE LAW LIBRARY

Series Editors: Robert Merkin and Malcolm A. Clarke

Directors' and Officers' Liability Insurance
Adolfo Paolini and Deepak Nambisan

Insurance Law and the Financial Services Ombudsman Service
Judith P. Summer

Reinsuring Clauses
Ozlem Gurses

Insurance Disputes
Third Edition
The Right Honourable Lord Mance, Iain Goldrein QC and Robert Merkin

The Law of Liability Insurance
Malcolm A. Clarke

Lloyd's
Law and Practice
Julian Burling

Systemic Risk and the Future of Insurance Regulation
Edited by Andromachi Georgosouli and Miriam Goldby

Chinese Insurance Contracts
Law and Practice
Zhen Jing

The Law of Liability Insurance
Second Edition
Malcolm A. Clarke

Good Faith and Insurance Contracts
Fourth Edition
Peter MacDonald Eggers QC, Simon Picken and Patrick Foss

The Law of Compulsory Motor Vehicle Insurance
Özlem Gürses

Directors' and Officers' Liability Insurance
Adolfo Paolini and Deepak Nambisan

The Global Insurance Market and Change
Emerging Technologies, Risks and Legal
Edited by Anthony A Tarr, Professor Julie-Anne Tarr, Maurice Thompson and Dino Wilkinson

Insurance, Climate Change and the Law
Franziska Arnold-Dwyer

For more information about this series, please visit: www.routledge.com/Lloyds-Insurance-Law-Library/book-series/LILL

INSURANCE, CLIMATE CHANGE AND THE LAW

FRANZISKA ARNOLD-DWYER, LL.B., LL.M., PH.D.

Senior Lecturer in Insurance Law, Contract Law and Sustainability at the Centre for Commercial Law Studies, Queen Mary University of London

Solicitor of the Senior Courts of England and Wales

informa law
from Routledge

First published 2024
by Informa Law from Routledge
4 Park Square, Milton Park, Abingdon, Oxon OX14 4RN

and by Informa Law from Routledge
605 Third Avenue, New York, NY 10158

Informa Law from Routledge is an imprint of the Taylor & Francis Group, an informa business

British Library Cataloguing-in-Publication Data
A catalogue record for this book is available from the British Library

Library of Congress Cataloging-in-Publication Data
Names: Arnold-Dwyer, Franziska, author.
Title: Insurance, climate change, and the law / Franziska Arnold-Dwyer, LL.B., LL.M., Ph.D., Senior Lecturer in Insurance Law, Contract Law and Sustainability at the Centre for Commercial Law Studies, Queen Mary University of London, Solicitor of the Senior Courts of England and Wales.
Description: Abingdon, Oxon [UK] ; New York, NY : Routledge, 2024. |
Series: Lloyd's insurance law library | Includes bibliographical references and index.
Identifiers: LCCN 2023044626 (print) | LCCN 2023044627 (ebook) | ISBN 9781032289595 (hardback) | ISBN 9781032333069 (paperback) | ISBN 9781003319047 (ebook)
Subjects: LCSH: Climate change insurance--Law and legislation. | Climatic changes--Law and legislation. | Climatic changes--Risk assessment. | Liability for environmental damages.
Classification: LCC K3585.5 .A965 2024 (print) | LCC K3585.5 (ebook) | DDC 368.1/22--dc23/eng/20231005
LC record available at https://lccn.loc.gov/2023044626LC ebook record available at https://lccn.loc.gov/2023044627

ISBN: 9781032289595 (hbk)
ISBN: 9781032333069 (pbk)
ISBN: 9781003319047 (ebk)

DOI: 10.4324/b23081

Typeset in Times New Roman
by Deanta Global Publishing Services, Chennai, India

CONTENTS

ACKNOWLEDGEMENTS

I am grateful to all my colleagues in academia and the insurance industry who encouraged me to pursue the study of *Insurance, Climate Change and the Law*, shared their insights, and provided valuable feedback on my work, over the long gestation period of this book. I am especially grateful to my research assistants, Megan Latham, Poorva Kumar, and Sofiya Mhaisale, who helped me at various stages and with different aspects of my research. The funding I received from Queen Mary University of London, and their sponsorship of my COP27 attendance, was much appreciated and contributed to the successful completion of this book. I also thank my family for all their support.

Unless otherwise stated, the opinions expressed in this book are my own and any errors or oversights remain mine. While every care has been taken to establish and acknowledge copyright and to use materials within the scope of the fair dealings exception, I tender my apology for any accidental infringement.

The law is stated as at 1 July 2023.

TABLE OF CASES

Cases from England and Wales and House of Lords / Supreme Court decisions

Cases from European Union courts

Cases from other jurisdictions

Germany

Netherlands

USA

TABLE OF LEGISLATION

UK primary legislation

UK secondary legislation

UK financial services binding regulatory materials

PRA

PRA Rulebook for Solvency II Firms

FCA

FCA Handbook

FCA Instruments

EU legislation

Directives

Regulations

Commission Delegated Regulations

Legislation from other jurisdictions

France

New Zealand

United States

TABLE OF INTERNATIONAL TREATIES AND INSTRUMENTS

Treaties

United Nations instruments

ABBREVIATIONS AND DEFINITIONS

1992 CCC	1992 United Nations Framework Convention on Climate Change
ABI	Association of British Insurers
ARC	African Risk Capacity
BoE Climate and Capital Frameworks Report	Bank of England, 'Report on Climate-Related Risks and the Regulatory Capital Frameworks' (March 2023)
CCA 2008	UK Climate Change Act 2008
CCC	1992 United Nations Framework Convention on Climate Change
CCR	Capital Requirements Regulation – Regulation (EU) No 575/2013 of the European Parliament and of the Council of 26 June 2013 on prudential requirements for credit institutions and investment firms and amending Regulation (EU) No 648/2012
CCRIF	Caribbean Catastrophe Risk Insurance Facility
CCUS	Carbon capture, utilisation, and storage technologies
CDM	Clean Development Mechanism
CDRFI	Climate and disaster risk finance and insurance
CER	Certified emission reduction credits
Client's best interest rule	An insurer who offers IBIPs must act honestly, fairly, and professionally in accordance with the best interests of its policyholders

Climate change risk	Climate change risks are risks caused by or associated with climate change. In the insurance context, it has become customary to adopt a classification of climate change risk with three broad categories: (1) physical risks; (2) transition risks; and (3) liability risks
Climate risk	Acute physical risks associated with climate change, such as windstorms, droughts, flooding, wildfires, and extreme weather
COBS	FCA Handbook, Conduct of Business Standards (COBS)
COP	The Conference of Parties (country signatories) established under the 1992 United Nations Framework Convention on Climate Change
CRA 2015	Consumer Rights Act 2015
CRD	Climate resilient development
CRD Bond	Climate Resilient Development Bond
CSDDD	Corporate Sustainability Due Diligence Directive – currently at proposal stage: Proposal for a Directive of the European Parliament and of the Council on Corporate Sustainability Due Diligence and amending Directive (EU) 2019/1937 COM/2022/71
CSR	Corporate social responsibility
CSRD	Corporate Sustainability Reporting Directive (Directive (EU) 2022/2464 of the European Parliament and of the Council of 14 December 2022 amending Regulation (EU) No 537/2014, Directive 2004/109/EC, Directive 2006/43/EC, and Directive 2013/34/EU, as regards corporate sustainability reporting)
EBA	European Banking Authority
EFRAG	European Financial Reporting Advisory Group

EIOPA	European Insurance and Occupational Pensions Authority
EIOPA Adaptation and Insurance Report	EIOPA, 'Impact Underwriting – Report on the Implementation of Climate-Related Adaptation Measures in Non-Life Underwriting Practices' EIOPA-BoS-22-593 (February 2023)
EIOPA Non-Life Underwriting and Climate Change Report	EIOPA, 'Report on Non-Life Underwriting and Pricing in Light of Climate Change' EIOPA-BoS-21/259 (July 2021)
ERU	Sinks measured in emission removal units
ESG	ESG stands for 'environmental, social and governance' and refers to criteria, factors, and attributes considered, measured, and reported in relation to corporate governance and investments
ESG integration	As an investment approach, ESG integration means that ESG issues are incorporated into the consideration of sustainability-related risks, opportunities, and impacts in the investment processes to assess their implications for enterprise value creation and hence financial returns
ESMA	European Securities and Markets Authority
ESRS	European Sustainability Reporting Standards
ETF	The implementation of the Paris Agreement relies on 'an enhanced transparency framework': each party is required to provide regularly information on its GHG emissions, its progress in achieving its NDC, and its adaptation measures, and the financial support, technology transfer, and capacity-building support provided or received. This information will undergo a technical review and multilateral

	consideration and then feeds into the 'global stocktake' which will assess the collective progress towards the long-term climate goals
EU	European Union: the EU's current members are Austria, Belgium, Bulgaria, Croatia, Cyprus, the Czech Republic, Denmark, Estonia, Finland, France, Germany, Greece, Hungary, Ireland, Italy, Latvia, Lithuania, Luxembourg, Malta, the Netherlands, Poland, Portugal, Romania, Slovakia, Slovenia, Spain, and Sweden. The UK left the EU in 2020
EU Action Plan	European Commission 'Action Plan: Financing Sustainable Growth' (COM (2018) 97)
EU Finance Strategy	Communication from the European Commission to the European Parliament, the Council, the European Economic and Social Committee, and the Committee of the Regions, 'Strategy for Financing the Transition to a Sustainable Economy' (COM (2021) 390)
EU MAR	Regulation (EU) No 596/2014 of the European Parliament and of the Council of 16 April 2014 on market abuse (market abuse regulation) and repealing Directive 2003/6/EC of the European Parliament and of the Council and Commission Directives 2003/124/EC, 2003/125/EC, and 2004/72/EC
European Climate Law	Regulation (EU) 2021/1119 of the European Parliament and of the Council of 30 June 2021 establishing the framework for achieving climate neutrality and amending Regulations (EC) No 401/2009 and (EU) 2018/1999
EU Taxonomy	Regulation (EU) 2020/852 of the European Parliament and of the Council of 18 June 2020 on the establishment of a framework to

	facilitate sustainable investment, and amending Regulation (EU) 2019/2088
FCA	Financial Conduct Authority
FCA Sustainability Disclosure Proposals	FCA, 'Sustainability Disclosure Requirements (SDR) and Investment Labels' CP22/20 (October 2022)
FEMA	Federal Emergency Management Agency
Flood Re	Flood Re Limited
FRC	Financial Reporting Council
FSB	Financial Stability Board
FSMA 2000	Financial Services and Markets Act 2000
FSMA 2023	Financial Services and Markets Act 2023
GFANZ	Glasgow Financial Alliance for Net Zero
GHG	Greenhouse gases include water vapour, carbon dioxide (CO_2), methane (CH_4), nitrous oxide (N_2O), and fluorinated gases
GIIN	The Global Impact Investing Network
Global Shield	Global Shield against Climate Risks
Green Claims Directive	Currently at proposal stage: Proposal for a Directive of the European Parliament and of the Council on substantiation and communication of explicit environmental claims COM/2023/166 final
Green reinstatement	Green settlement of claims terms that mandate or encourage the beneficiary to apply settlement proceeds towards the reinstatement or repair of property with low-carbon materials and lower GHG emissions, or the replacement of personal property with recycled or lower emission alternatives
GWP	Gross written premiums
IBIP or insurance-based investment products	An insurance-based investment product is a contract of insurance which offers a maturity or surrender value and where that maturity or

	surrender value is wholly or partially exposed, directly or indirectly, to market fluctuations, and does not include: (a) non-life insurance products; (b) life insurance contracts where the benefits under the contract are payable only on death or in respect of incapacity due to injury, sickness, or disability; (c) personal pension products; (d) officially recognised occupational pension schemes; and (e) stakeholder pension products (FCA Handbook, Definitions)
ICOBS	FCA Handbook Insurance Conduct of Business Sourcebook (ICOBS)
ICPs	IAIS Insurance Core Principles
IDD/Insurance Distribution Directive	Directive (EU) 2016/97 of the European Parliament and of the Council of 20 January 2016 on insurance distribution (recast)
IDF	Insurance Development Forum
InsuReslience	InsuResilience Global Partnership for Climate and Disaster Risk Finance and Insurance Solutions
Inward impact	The impact of climate change risks on an insurer or the insurance industry
IPCC	Intergovernmental Panel on Climate Change
IPCC 2014 Synthesis Report	IPCC, 'Climate Change 2014: Synthesis Report' (Fifth Assessment Report, Core Writing Team, R.K. Pachauri and L.A. Meyer (eds.) Geneva, Switzerland 2014)
IPCC 2021 Physical Science Report	IPCC, 'Climate Change 2021: The Physical Science Basis' (Masson-Delmotte, V., P. Zhai, A. Pirani, S.L. Connors, C. Péan, S. Berger, N. Caud, Y. Chen, L. Goldfarb, M.I. Gomis, M. Huang, K. Leitzell, E. Lonnoy, J.B.R. Matthews, T.K. Maycock, T. Waterfield, O. Yelekçi, R. Yu, and B. Zhou (eds.) Cambridge University Press 2021)

IPCC 2022 Adaptation Report	IPCC 2022 Mitigation Report; IPCC, 'Climate Change 2022: Impacts, Adaptation and Vulnerability' (H.-O. Pörtner, D.C. Roberts, M. Tignor, E.S. Poloczanska, K. Mintenbeck, A. Alegría, M. Craig, S. Langsdorf, S. Löschke, V. Möller, A. Okem, B. Rama (eds.) Cambridge University Press 2021)
IPCC 2022 Mitigation Report	IPCC, 'Climate Change 2022: Mitigation of Climate Change' (P.R. Shukla, J. Skea, R. Slade, A. Khourdajie, R. van Diemen, D. McCollum, M. Pathak, S. Some, P. Vyas, R. Fradera, M. Belkacemi, A. Hasija, G. Lisboa, S. Luz, J. Malley (eds.) Cambridge University Press 2022)
IPCC 2022 Sixth Assessment Report	IPCC, 'Synthesis Report of the Sixth Assessment Report' (Sixth Assessment Report – Longer Report, Hoesung Lee, Katherine Calvin, Dipak Dasgupta, Gerhard Krinner, Aditi Mukherji, Peter Thorne, Christopher Trisos, José Romero, Paulina Aldunce, Ko Barrett, Gabriel Blanco, William W.L. Cheung, Sarah L. Connors, Fatima Denton, Aïda Diongue-Niang, David Dodman, Matthias Garschagen, Oliver Geden, Bronwyn Hayward, Christopher Jones, Frank Jotzo, Thelma Krug, Rodel Lasco, June-Yi Lee, Valérie Masson-Delmotte, Malte Meinshausen, Katja Mintenbeck, Abdalah Mokssit, Friederike E.L. Otto, Minal Pathak, Anna Pirani, Elvira Poloczanska, Hans-Otto Pörtner, Aromar Revi, Debra C. Roberts, Joyashree Roy, Alex C. Ruane, Jim Skea, Priyadarshi R. Shukla, Raphael Slade, Aimée Slangen, Youba Sokona, Anna A. Sörensson, Melinda Tignor, Detlef van Vuuren, Yi-Ming Wei, Harald Winkler,

	Panmao Zhai, and Zinta Zommers, Cambridge University Press 2022)
ISSB	International Sustainability Standards Board
KID	A key information document under Regulation (EU) No 1286/2014 of the European Parliament and of the Council of 26 November 2014 on key information documents for packaged retail and IBIPs (PRIIPs) art 5, as onshored into UK law by the European Union (Withdrawal) Act 2018. Regulation (EU) No 1286/2014 – as onshored – is revoked by the FSMA 2023, s 1, but s 1 has not yet come into force
KPIs	Key performance indicator
Long-term temperature goal	The objectives of the Paris Agreement to strengthen the global response to the threat of climate change by substantially reducing global GHG emissions to limit the global temperature increase to well below 2°C while pursuing efforts to limit the increase to 1.5°C above pre-industrial levels
LR	FCA Handbook Listing Rules Sourcebook (LR)
MCR	Minimum capital requirement
NDC	Parties to the Paris Agreement submit every five years national climate action plans – which are referred to as nationally determined contributions – in which they undertake and communicate 'ambitious efforts' to achieve the Paris Agreement's objectives
Negative screening	An investment approach that excludes certain investments on the basis that they fail to meet certain sustainability-related criteria
NFIP	National Flood Insurance Program
NFSIS	Non-financial and sustainability information statement
NZIA	Net-Zero Insurance Alliance

OECD Insurance and Adaptation Paper	Organisation for Economic Co-operation and Development (OECD), 'Enhancing the Insurance Sector's Contribution to Climate Adaptation,' OECD Business and Finance Policy Papers (OECD Publishing 2023)
ORSA	Own risk and solvency assessment
Outward impact	The external impact of an insurer's or the insurance industry's operations and value chains on the climate and climate change
Paris Agreement	Paris Agreement under the United Nations Framework Convention on Climate Change (adopted 12 December 2015; entered into force 4 November 2016) TIAS 16-1104
PCRAFI	Pacific Catastrophe Risk Assessment and Finance Initiative
PGE	Protection Gap Entity
PPP	Prudent Person Principle as set out in the PRA Rulebook, Solvency II Firms, Investments, 2.1
PPPart	Public-private partnership
PRA	Prudential Regulation Authority
PRA Role of Capital Requirements Report	PRA, 'Climate-Related Financial Risk Management and the Role of Capital Requirements: Climate Change Adaptation Report 2021' (October 2021)
PRA SII	PRA Rulebook, Solvency II Firms
PRA SS3/19	PRA, 'Enhancing Banks' and Insurers' Approaches to Managing the Financial Risks from Climate Change,' Supervisory Statement SS3/19 (April 2019)
PRI	Principles for Responsible Investment
PRIN	FCA Handbook, Principles of Business (PRIN)
PROD	FCA Handbook Product Intervention and Product Governance Sourcebook (PROD)
PSI	UNEP FI Principles of Sustainable Insurance

RMU	Removal units
s.172 duty	The duty of directors of a company under s.172 of the Companies Act 2006
SARHA	Social Action, Responsibility and Heroism Act 2015
SASB	Sustainability Accounting Standards Board
SCR	Solvency capital requirement
SDGs	The 17 sustainable development goals contained in the 2030 Agenda for Sustainable Development for 2016–2030
SEADRIF	Southeast Asia Disaster Risk Insurance Facility
SFCR	Solvency and financial condition report
SFDR	EU Regulation (EU) 2019/2088 on sustainability-related disclosures in the financial services sector
Shareholders Rights Directive	Directive (EU) 2017/828 of the European Parliament and of the Council of 17 May 2017 amending Directive 2007/36/EC as regards the encouragement of long-term shareholder engagement; adopted into UK law through the Occupational Pension Schemes (Investment and Disclosure) (Amendment) Regulations 2019 and the Pension Protection Fund (Pensionable Service) and Occupational Pension Schemes (Investment and Disclosure) (Amendment and Modification) Regulations 2018
SHIP	UN Framework Convention on Climate Change, Sharm el-Sheikh Implementation Plan (adopted at COP27 in 2022) Decision 1/CP.27
SIF	Sustainable Insurance Forum
Sinks	Processes and activities that remove GHG from the atmosphere

Solvency II Directive	Directive 2009/138/EC of the European Parliament and of the Council of 25 November 2009 on the taking-up and pursuit of the business of Insurance and Reinsurance (Solvency II) (recast)
Sustainable focus	A 'sustainable focus' investment approach means that investments are selected on the basis that they fulfil certain sustainability criteria and/or deliver on specific and measurable sustainability outcome(s)
SYCS	FCA Handbook Systems and Controls Sourcebook (SYSC)
TCFD	Task Force on Climate-Related Financial Disclosures: set up by the Financial Stability Board in 2015 to improve and increase reporting of climate-related financial information
TCFD products	IBIPs and any in-scope pension schemes business provided by an in-scope life insurer subject to the FCA ESG Sourcebook
TFEU	Treaty on the Functioning of the European Union
TTA	The New Zealand Earthquake Commission which will become the Toka Tū Ake – Natural Hazards Commission
UK	United Kingdom of Great Britain and Northern Ireland
UK insurer	An insurer who carries on insurance business in the UK
UK MAR	EU MAR which had direct effect in the UK until 31 December 2020 when it was onshored into UK law by the European Union (Withdrawal) Act 2018. Changes to EU MAR were made by the Market Abuse (Amendment) (EU Exit) Regulations 2019, to ensure that the onshored legislation operates effectively in the UK
UNEP	The United Nations Environment Programme

CHAPTER 1

Introduction

Less than a decade ago, Mark Carney, the then-Governor of the Bank of England and now UN Special Envoy on Climate Action and Finance, called climate change 'the Tragedy of the Horizon.'[1] But climate change is no longer a horizon problem that will only impact future generations or distant places – it is now a tragedy unfolding presently and in front of people's eyes across the world. The average global air temperature broke a new record on 4 July 2023 with 17.18°C (62.9F),[2] prompting António Guterres, Secretary General of the United Nations, to warn that 'climate change is out of control,' and that the current generation must act now to limit climate change and its harmful effects: '[i]f we persist in delaying key measures that are needed, I think we are moving into a catastrophic situation.'[3] Climate change is recognised by many of the world's governments, large parts of civil society, corporations, and the scientific community as a major global threat that requires a collective response at a global scale.

The projected impacts of climate change on the environment and communities cannot be halted unless we reduce greenhouse gas ('GHG') emissions.[4] The 2015 Paris Agreement seeks to curb the threat of climate change by setting goals to keep the global temperature rise below 2°C and to pursue efforts to limit the temperature increase to 1.5°C, compared to pre-industrial levels.[5] In furtherance of the Paris Agreement goals, the UK Government

1 Mark Carney, 'Breaking the Tragedy of the Horizon – Climate Change and Financial Stability' (Speech at Lloyd's of London, September 2015) <https://www.bankofengland.co.uk/speech/2015/breaking-the-tragedy-of-the-horizon-climate-change-and-financial-stability> accessed on 1 June 2023.

2 According to data collated by the US National Centers for Environmental Prediction, as reported by *The Guardian*, 'UN Says Climate Change "out of Control" after Likely Hottest Week on Record' (7 July 2023).

3 *The Guardian*, 'UN Says Climate Change "out of Control" after Likely Hottest Week on Record' (7 July 2023).

4 Intergovernmental Panel on Climate Change ('IPCC'), '2018 Special Report – Global Warming of 1.5°C' (Masson-Delmotte, V., P. Zhai, H.on-O. Pörtner, D. Roberts, J. Skea, P.R. Shukla, A. Pirani, W. Moufouma-Okia, C. Péan, R. Pidcock, S. Connors, J.B.R. Matthews, Y. Chen, X. Zhou, M.I. Gomis, E. Lonnoy, T. Maycock, M. Tignor, and T. Waterfield (eds.), Cambridge University Press 2018), Summary for Policymakers.

5 Paris Agreement under the United Nations Framework Convention on Climate Change (adopted 12 December 2015; entered into force 4 November 2016) TIAS 16-1104 (the 'Paris Agreement'), and see Chapter 2.

DOI: 10.4324/b23081-1

has set itself a legally binding target to reduce UK net GHG emissions by 100% by 2050,[6] and a 78% reduction target for 2035[7] (compared to 1990 levels).

Aims of this book: this book examines the legal and regulatory issues arising from climate change for insurance companies and the legal framework that governs what insurance companies are required or permitted to do to take climate action. The purpose of this book is threefold: first, it systemises the emerging area of climate change-related regulations and other areas of law that have implications for climate-related decision-making as they apply to insurance companies. Secondly, the book considers how and to what extent the insurance industry can take climate action by instrumentalising insurance contracts and investments within the existing legal and regulatory framework, and it addresses normative questions about whether and how laws and regulation could support insurers in doing so. Thirdly, the book puts forward proposals for insurance products and risk transfer and loss resilience structures that can support policyholders to take climate action. All three objectives break new ground.

The public discourse on the extent to which corporations should pursue social or environmental, social, and corporate governance goals has not side-stepped the insurance industry. Insurance companies across the world have found themselves at the front line of climate change challenges providing insurance cover in relation to risks associated with climate change. As risk carriers, insurance companies pay claims for climate change-related losses – such as property damage caused by windstorms, flooding, and wildfires – which have been increasing in frequency and severity. Liability insurers are called upon to cover environmental liabilities and defence costs. As major institutional investors, insurance companies invest in assets that may be increasingly vulnerable to climate risks. Insurance regulators across the globe have therefore started to require insurance companies to identify, manage, and report on climate change risks that could pose a threat to their financial stability and ultimately a risk to their ability to provide cover for climate change risks and pay claims.

However, the focus on an insurer's balance sheet is an inward-looking perspective that does not address the main cause of climate change: anthropogenic GHG emissions. Providing insurance cover to consumer and business policyholders for climate change-related physical losses and liabilities improves their financial resilience to those risks but does not limit or reverse climate change and does not improve physical resilience to climate change impacts. Arguably, the availability of insurance cover for climate-related risks contributes to the status quo: policyholders are less likely to be incentivised to engage with climate change mitigation and adaptation in the knowledge that they have insurance protection against the financial consequences of those climate change-related risks.

To make a positive contribution to combatting climate change, the insurance industry must consider what steps it can take to reduce and remove GHG emissions and to adapt to climate change effects that are already having harmful impacts. Such steps can be implemented at the operational level of an insurance company, but action can also be directed at

6 Climate Change Act 2008, s 1, as amended by the Climate Change Act 2008 (2050 Target Amendment) Order 2019, s 2.

7 The 78% reduction target was set in the UK's sixth Carbon Budget (2021).

Department for Business, Energy and Industrial Strategy, 'UK Enshrines New Target in Law to Slash Emissions by 78% by 2035' (20 April 2021) <https://www.gov.uk/government/news/uk-enshrines-new-target-in-law-to-slash-emissions-by-78-by-2035> accessed on 1 June 2023.

stakeholders in the insurance value chain. For the insurance industry, the key components of climate action through its value chain are 'impact underwriting' and 'impact investment.' While some insurance companies are already investing in projects and activities that reduce or remove GHG emissions and are gradually withdrawing from providing insurance to certain fossil fuel enterprises or for carbon-intense projects, there has yet been little research on how insurers can use their 'products' – namely insurance policies – to shift their customers' behaviour and processes from generating GHG emissions to reducing GHG emissions and to encourage them to invest in measures that shore up resilience to climate change impacts. This book addresses that gap. Anchored in the contractual relationships between an insurer and its policyholders, there is enormous potential for insurance companies to provide practical support to their consumer and business policyholders for making better-informed choices on energy sources and efficiency, to incentivise them to take adaptation measures to make their properties more resilient to climate change-related weather risks, and to empower them to take ownership in their transition towards a net-zero economy.

The Companies Act 2006 already requires the directors of a (UK-incorporated) company to have regard to 'the impact of the company's operations on the community and the environment' in discharging their duty to promote the success of the company.[8] Yet, implementing impactful climate action is more ambitious and, arguably, more controversial: it requires impact underwriting strategies and impact investment policies with clear climate objectives setting out the scope for the reduction or removal of GHG emissions and/or for meaningful adaptation measures. If insurance companies are to take on the double challenge of impact underwriting and impact investment, this will have conceptual, legal, and societal implications. This book considers all three, with a focus on legal and regulatory issues arising from impact underwriting and impact investment.

Conceptually, the role of insurance in modern society needs to be (re)examined in light of the global response to the threat of climate change. Is it desirable and appropriate for insurance companies to promote a climate agenda and to act as 'silent regulators' through private contractual arrangements? The international community recognises that sustainable and just solutions to the climate crisis require collective action from states and private actors, in particular from financial institutions. Yet, political backlash against environmental, social, and governance ('ESG') issues sees a conflict between insurers pursuing environmental and social objectives on the one hand, and maximising profits for their shareholders while keeping premiums low for policyholders on the other. In this book it will be argued that insurers' role should be re-cast as 'enablers': insurers can empower other actors in the insurance value chain to take climate action within the theoretical frameworks of stakeholder capitalism and environmental stewardship. While the insurance industry cannot replace the government's role in regulating climate impact through carbon pricing, taxes, and emission trading systems, it can raise awareness of climate-related risks and exert influence over policyholders and investee companies shaping their responses to the global threat of climate change to enhance their own welfare and for the benefit of society as a whole.

If insurers are to take an enabling role, it needs to be considered to what extent existing legal and regulatory frameworks permit, prohibit, or (dis)incentivise insurers to do

8 Companies Act 2006, s 172(1)(d).

so. This book examines rules and regulations from different fields of law that determine what insurance companies are required, (not) permitted, or (dis)incentivised to do to take climate action. A successful adoption of impact underwriting and impact investment practices can be fostered by setting disclosure and reporting standards to ensure consistent approaches and practices. Divergent practices can distort competition and make it difficult to compare effectively different insurance companies (and different financial services providers more generally) and their products, thus creating an uneven playing field. Customers and investors will only be able to trust corporate and product disclosures if they can rest assured that certain labels and descriptions relating to environmental impact, objectives, and outcomes are meaningful and are not used to green-wash products and corporate identities. This book maps the emerging disclosure standards as applicable to insurance companies and insurance products.

Enabling policyholders and investee companies in their transition to a sustainable net-zero economy comes at a cost and at the risk of creating insurance protection gaps. Impact underwriting could be more expensive for insurers and policyholders as a result of risk pricing, additional risk management costs, higher reinsurance premiums, and higher indemnity costs under 'build-back-better (greener)' schemes. Impact investment could result in comparably lower returns on green investments and increased cost of capital for investee companies in the fossil fuel industry. Both impact underwriting and impact investment are likely to generate additional transaction and governance costs. Additional costs can exacerbate insurance protection gaps that are already expanding as a result of catastrophic weather events that are linked to climate change. On a societal level, consideration must be given to who should bear those costs and how insurance protection gaps can be minimised. The UK Government's 'Net-Zero Strategy' is seeking to implement a fair transition to a net-zero economy and to 'make it easier and fairer for individuals, businesses and households to decarbonise.'[9] The Paris Agreement requires the implementation of its temperature goal and its adaptation and climate resilience objectives to reflect equity and notes the concept of 'climate justice' when taking action to address climate change.[10] A key finding from the 6th IPCC Synthesis Report is that climate action that 'prioritise[s] equity, climate justice, social justice and inclusion lead[s] to more sustainable outcomes, co-benefits, reduce trade-offs, support transformative change and advance climate resilient development.'[11] The international community has started to address these issues with the establishment of a Loss and Damage Fund.[12] This book is not the place to consider

9 HM Government 'Net-Zero Strategy: Build Back Greener' (October 2021) 10 <https://assets.publishing.service.gov.uk/government/uploads/system/uploads/attachment_data/file/1033990/net-zero-strategy-beis.pdf> , accessed on 1 June 2023.

10 Paris Agreement art 2 and Recitals.

11 IPCC, 'Synthesis Report of the Sixth Assessment Report' (Sixth Assessment Report – Longer Report, Hoesung Lee, Katherine Calvin, Dipak Dasgupta, Gerhard Krinner, Aditi Mukherji, Peter Thorne, Christopher Trisos, José Romero, Paulina Aldunce, Ko Barrett, Gabriel Blanco, William W.L. Cheung, Sarah L. Connors, Fatima Denton, Aïda Diongue-Niang, David Dodman, Matthias Garschagen, Oliver Geden, Bronwyn Hayward, Christopher Jones, Frank Jotzo, Thelma Krug, Rodel Lasco, June-Yi Lee, Valérie Masson-Delmotte, Malte Meinshausen, Katja Mintenbeck, Abdalah Mokssit, Friederike E.L. Otto, Minal Pathak, Anna Pirani, Elvira Poloczanska, Hans-Otto Pörtner, Aromar Revi, Debra C. Roberts, Joyashree Roy, Alex C. Ruane, Jim Skea, Priyadarshi R. Shukla, Raphael Slade, Aimée Slangen, Youba Sokona, Anna A. Sörensson, Melinda Tignor, Detlef van Vuuren, Yi-Ming Wei, Harald Winkler, Panmao Zhai, Zinta Zommers, Cambridge University Press 2022) ('IPCC 2022 Sixth Assessment Report') [4.4].

12 UN Framework Convention on Climate Change, 'Decision -/CP.27: Sharm el-Sheikh Implementation Plan' (22 November 2022) s VII, art 46 <https://unfccc.int/documents/624441> accessed on 1 June 2023.

distributive justice in the delivery of the UK Government's net-zero policies and climate justice at an international level, but it examines how public-private partnerships between the insurance industry, government authorities, and other stakeholders could be used to minimise protection gaps and to harness the opportunities of impact underwriting supported by government policies and public and private finance.

This book is structured as follows: Chapter 2 provides an overview of the causes and effects of climate change and the international treaties that set expectations and targets to address climate change. Chapter 2 also positions climate action as a subset of environmental protection measures and explores the relationship between climate action, climate resilient development approaches, sustainability, and 'ESG.' Chapter 3 provides a brief introduction to the nature of insurance and insurance concepts such as insurability and protection gaps. It describes the different types of climate change risk which have been conceptualised in a classification distinguishing between physical risk, transition risk, and liability risk and explores by reference to the concept of 'double materiality' the inward impact of climate change risks on an insurer's business and the outward impact that an insurer's operations and value chain can have on the environment. Chapter 3 also introduces a new 'enabling conception' of insurance that serves as a theoretical basis for the insurance industry providing support to policyholders, investee companies, and other stakeholders in their net-zero transition.

Chapter 4 explains why climate change is a regulatory issue and maps to what extent insurance regulators have integrated climate change risks and combatting climate change into their regulatory regimes. It compares the regulatory approaches to climate change issues of the International Association of Insurance Supervisors ('IAIS'), the UK Prudential Regulation Authority ('PRA'), the Financial Conduct Authority ('FCA'), and the European Insurance and Occupational Pensions Authority ('EIOPA'). It also examines anti-ESG legislation developments in the US. Chapter 5 systemises the existing and emerging disclosure frameworks that require disclosing entities to make publicly available information on the climate change risks they are facing and their impact on the environment. It critically examines the recommendations of the Task Force on Climate-Related Financial Disclosures, the International Sustainability Disclosure Standards, the emerging UK sustainability-related disclosure regimes, and the EU sustainability-related disclosure regime and taxonomy framework, as they apply to insurance companies.

Chapters 6 and 7 are concerned with how insurers – in their capacity as risk carriers – could take an enabling role by engaging in climate-related impact underwriting. Chapter 6 puts forward a definition of, and justifications for, climate-related impact underwriting. It examines legal issues that can arise when insurers insure 'green' by providing insurance cover for technologies and infrastructure projects aimed at climate change mitigation and adaptation, and when they cease to insure 'brown' by withdrawing from underwriting fossil fuel projects and assets. Chapter 7 is concerned with 'greening insurance' – insurance products and services that shift policyholders' behaviour and processes towards taking climate change mitigation and adaptation measures. It analyses the legal and regulatory issues that can arise when features to incentivise policyholders to take climate action are integrated at different stages in the insurance value chain.

Chapter 8 examines the enabling role of insurers in their capacity as investors. They can take this role by engaging in climate-related impact investment and stewardship. It identifies definitions and rationales for 'climate-related impact investment' and 'climate-related stewardship' derived from a critical examination of the literature and considers the regulatory requirements that apply to, and legal issues that may arise in respect of, an insurer's own investments and insurance-based investment products. Chapter 8 also proposes two potential insurance solutions that combine climate-related impact underwriting and investment. Chapter 9 examines how public-private partnerships between the insurance industry, government authorities, and other stakeholders could be used to minimise protection gaps and knowledge gaps and to support climate-related impact underwriting with public and private finance. It does so by reference to case studies of the UK's Flood Re, the US National Flood Insurance Program, New Zealand's Toka Tū Ake – Natural Hazards Commission, and regional risk pools. Chapter 10 summarises the main findings on why and how insurers should take an enabling role through climate-related impact underwriting and investment and how the existing legal and regulatory frameworks can be harnessed, or could be improved, to support the development of green insurance products and green investment while creating safe and fair market conditions, ensuring the protection of policyholders and maintaining broad access to insurance.

While regulatory aspects have been covered for all types of insurance, the insurance product focus of this book is on consumer and business property insurance and insurance-based investment products, driven by the overriding theme of the enabling role of insurers in supporting their policyholders and other stakeholders with taking climate action. Climate change is, of course, one of the biggest health threats facing humanity, and this will have repercussions on health and life insurance. Space limitations have meant that these aspects have not been covered in this book and the author hopes to pursue separate research on the impact of climate change on life and life-related insurance products and the life insurance sector in the future.

Methodology: this book is the product of a combination of legal research methodologies, reflecting that the confluence of 'climate change,' 'insurance,' and 'the law' is terra nova as a research topic and that the constituent parts are grounded in different disciplines (and in different legal subjects within 'law'). The politicisation of climate change issues makes it appropriate to study the relevant law in its social and jurisdictional context.

The physical understanding of the climate system and climate change is based on climate science which itself integrates multiple lines of evidence and specialisations. For climate science aspects, Chapter 2 relies on the climate change assessment carried out by the Intergovernmental Panel on Climate Change ('IPCC'). The IPCC is the United Nations body for assessing the science related to climate change. The IPCC does not conduct its own research but expert volunteers from all over the world prepare assessment reports that provide comprehensive summaries of what is known about the drivers of climate change, its impacts and future risks, and how adaptation and mitigation can reduce those risks, based on an open and transparent review of thousands of scientific papers published each year.[13] In addition to the physical science behind climate change and climate change mitigation and adaptation, climate change has an international law dimension which reflects that climate change does not respect national boundaries and is a global problem that must be addressed through international co-operation. The author draws on doctrinal legal research and analysis as a means of ascertaining the international

13 IPCC, 'About the IPCC' <https://www.ipcc.ch/about/> accessed on 1 June 2023.

law, rules, and principles applicable to climate change that set the baseline for national climate goals and targets.

Chapter 3 considers insurance as a legal and economic construct: in legal terms, insurance is based on a series of contractual relationships between an insurer and its policyholders, overlaid by laws and regulations. The economic functions of insurance are to transfer and spread risk. An actuarial understanding of insurance – based on a risk assessment by calculating the likelihood of financial loss – presents challenges in relation to complex climate risks. Informed by the socio-legal conceptions of insurance as a risk transfer product or service and as a tool for risk governance, and by corporate social responsibility scholarship, it is hypothesised that insurers could and should act as climate action enablers. This hypothesis is tested against the legal and regulatory framework throughout the remaining chapters with doctrinal research methods. It is also tested from social, historical, and (behavioural) economic perspectives, using secondary data from a wide variety of documentary sources.

Chapters 4 and 5 draw on doctrinal legal research and comparative legal analysis as a means of (1) ascertaining the law in relation to climate change risk assessment and disclosures respectively, and (2) systemising the law within the wider framework of insurance regulation and corporate reporting laws. Comparative legal analysis between the UK and the EU insurance regulatory and disclosure regimes in relation to climate change risks, and an evaluation of the law in the context of the UK's net-zero targets, provides normative answers as to how laws and regulation could support insurers in their enabling role.

Chapters 6 to 8 combine fundamental research on the enabling role of insurers with applied research to provide specific insurance solutions for climate change mitigation, adaptation, and resilience building delivered through climate-related impact underwriting and investment. Innovatively, Chapter 7 also uses a value chain approach to examine legal issues that can arise at different points in the insurance value chain when insurers engage in climate-related impact underwriting. Emerging scholarship is expanding the narrow understanding of environmental law as prescriptive public law rules to private environmental governance and to 'the fields of law governing the corporation and markets' that interact with a corporation's environmental decision-making.[14] This book builds on this scholarship and examines rules and regulations from different fields of law that determine what insurance companies are required, (not) permitted, or (dis)incentivised to do to take climate action. This is not a book on environmental law (nor indeed on climate science or on insurance law) but it seeks to contextualise the climate-related laws that apply to insurance companies and considers whether and how legal and regulatory barriers to impact underwriting and impact investment could be addressed.

Chapter 9 examines case studies of the UK's Flood Re, the US National Flood Insurance Program, and New Zealand's Toka Tū Ake – Natural Hazards Commission to identify different design features for insurance public-private partnerships. The observed design features were evaluated by reference to efficiency and good governance criteria, and those deemed to be 'good design features' were used to build a model for a climate risk public-private partnership structure to address protection gaps, knowledge gaps, and funding gaps in relation to climate risk losses. This is another example of solution-focused applied research.

14 Sarah E. Light, 'The Law of the Corporation as Environmental Law' (2019) 71 Stan L Rev 160.

At the planning stage of this book in late 2020/early 2021, the author had hoped to conduct a series of interviews with climate change, ESG, and sustainability professionals from the insurance industry, but there was very little appetite to go on record at that time. The lack of positive responses was due to the fact that, at that time, climate-related risk assessments were regarded as a largely non-public and sensitive regulatory matter between an insurance company and its regulator, the outward impact of an insurance company's operations and business on the environment had not yet fully crystallised into public disclosure requirements, and insurance companies were prioritising COVID-19 related matters. The author therefore decided to abandon interview-based data collection and to rely instead on publicly documented statements, reports, interviews, data, and statistics (which incidentally have exploded in volume over the last two years). Nevertheless, the author's main propositions and findings have been informed by many conversations with, and feedback received from, market participants at meetings and conferences and in response to prior publications on the topic. The Climate Resilient Development Bond discussed in Chapter 8 has already received a significant amount of insurance press and social media attention.

Who should read this book: this book has been written for a diverse audience. It is a clarion call addressed to the insurance industry to engage in climate-related impact underwriting and investment. The book puts forward proposals for insurance products and risk transfer structures that can support policyholders to take climate action and explores the complex legal and regulatory landscape to be navigated and provides a conceptual basis – that of insurers as climate action enablers – for doing so. This book should be of interest to insurance lawyers and compliance and legal advisers to the insurance industry, as a comprehensive source of existing and forthcoming climate change-related laws and regulations and other areas of law that have implications on climate-related decision-making and compliance matters as they apply to insurance companies. It offers a comparative analysis of UK and EU sustainability-related disclosure regulations and provides the scientific and international law background to set insurance-specific laws and regulation in context. To regulators and policymakers, this book offers a holistic study of legal and regulatory barriers to climate-related impact underwriting and investment, including some suggestions as to how laws and regulations could be more supportive of these activities within their regulatory mandates. This book should also be read by academics and researchers in the field of corporate social responsibility as it contributes to the stakeholder model within corporate social responsibility theories. It puts forward a conception of insurance that sees insurers as enablers of policyholders and other actors in the insurance value chain empowering them to take climate action. Environmental and sustainability lawyers and professionals may be interested in this book as it explores the role of the insurance industry in addressing the climate emergency. Key insurance concepts are explained so as to make the book accessible to readers who do not have an insurance background. Finally, this book should also be read by professionals in climate disaster risk management, such as professionals in government departments, non-governmental and intergovernmental organisations, environment agencies, philanthropic foundations, and financial institutions, as it provides an understanding of and suggestions for the contribution that the insurance industry could make at a local, regional, and global level to risk transfer and resilience building solutions.

CHAPTER 2

Climate change

The science, the international stage, terminology, and boundaries

Before the role of insurance in the global fight against climate change can be explored, it is necessary to consider some key concepts relating to climate change, the science behind it, and the efforts of the international community to respond to the threat of climate change. This chapter sets the scene for the discussion in the following chapters and provides an overview of the key literature and international treaties on climate change. Section 2.1 defines 'climate' and 'climate change.' Section 2.2 sets out the main evidence-based findings of the IPCC on the causes of climate change, climate change impacts, and its projections for different GHG emission reduction pathways and their temperature impacts. Section 2.3 outlines the international treaties – the most prominent of which is the Paris Agreement – that have sought to address climate change, and how these treaties have been implemented in the UK and the EU. Section 2.4 positions climate action as a subset of environmental protection measures and explores the relationship between climate action, climate resilient development approaches, sustainability, and 'ESG.'

2.1 Climate and climate change

'Climate' has been defined as 'the average course or condition of the weather at a place usually over a period of years as exhibited by temperature, wind velocity, and precipitation.'[1] 'Climate' is different from 'weather' as the former represents a temporal average of weather conditions, whereas the latter refers to the temperature, humidity, windiness, and cloudiness at a certain place and time.[2] Broadly speaking, 'climate change' signifies a change in the Earth's weather patterns and weather variables that persists for an extended period, typically decades or longer, due to external or internal natural processes, or human activities.[3] However, 'climate change' has also acquired a narrower meaning referring specifically to human-induced (anthropogenic) climate change. For example, the 1992 United Nations Framework Convention on Climate Change (the '1992 CCC') defines 'climate change' as 'a change of climate which is attributed directly or indirectly to human activity that alters the composition of the global atmosphere and which is in addition to

1 *The Merriam-Webster Online Dictionary* <https://www.merriam-webster.com/dictionary/climate> accessed on 1 June 2023.

2 Arthur P. Cracknell and Costas A. Varotsos, *Understanding Global Climate Change* (2nd ed, CRC Press 2022) [1.1.1].

3 Ibid [1.1.4].

DOI: 10.4324/b23081-2

natural climate variability observed over comparable time periods.'[4] It is the anthropogenic climate change that the international community seeks to stop and reverse.[5]

2.2 The IPCC and climate science

The IPCC is the United Nations body for assessing the science related to climate change, climate change impacts and future risks, and options for adaptation and mitigation. With its assessment reports, the IPCC provides governments at all levels with scientific information that they can use to develop climate policies. In their 2014 Fifth Assessment Report, the IPCC found that human (anthropogenic) GHG emissions 'are extremely likely to have been the dominant cause' of the observed warming since the mid-20th century,[6] but more recently the IPCC concluded more firmly that it is 'unequivocal' that 'human activities,' principally through GHG emissions, have caused global warming, with global surface temperature reaching 1.1°C above 1850–1900 in 2011–2020.[7]

2.2.1 Drivers of climate change

GHG include water vapour, carbon dioxide (CO_2), methane (CH_4), nitrous oxide (N_2O), and fluorinated gases. When coal, oil, and natural gas are burned to generate electricity, power transportation, or provide heat, they produce CO_2. CH_4 emissions are attributable to cow and sheep farming (caused by fermentation of food in their stomachs) and are caused by coal mining, oil and gas extractions, and waste landfills. Anthropogenic N_2O emissions largely arise from using fertilisers for agricultural purposes. Fluorinated gases deplete the stratospheric ozone layer.[8] Economic and population growth have increased anthropogenic GHG emissions since the pre-industrial era, leading to unprecedented concentrations of CO_2, CH_4, and N_2O in the atmosphere.[9] Although the global COVID-19 pandemic led to a slow down in CO_2 emissions from fossil fuel and industry, GHG emissions continued to rise across all sectors.[10]

The increased concentration of CO_2 in the atmosphere changes the balance between the incoming short-wave solar radiation and the long-wave (infrared) outgoing radiation from the Earth. The incoming solar radiation interacts with the Earth's surface where much of the energy is converted into infrared radiation. This infrared radiation is then blocked by the CO_2 concentration near the Earth's surface.[11] CH_4 and N_2O emissions have a similar

4 United Nations Framework Convention on Climate Change (adopted on 9 May 1992, entered into force on 21 March 1994) 1771 UNTS 107, art 1.

5 See Section 2.3.

6 IPCC, 'Climate Change 2014: Synthesis Report' (Fifth Assessment Report, Core Writing Team, R.K. Pachauri and L.A. Meyer (eds.) Geneva, Switzerland 2014) ('IPCC 2014 Synthesis Report') [SPM 1.2].

7 IPCC 2022 Sixth Assessment Report [2.1].

8 United Nations Environment Programme, 'How Do Greenhouse Gases Actually Warm the Planet?' (5 January 2022) <https://www.unep.org/news-and-stories/story/how-do-greenhouse-gases-actually-warm-planet> accessed on 1 June 2023.

9 IPCC 2014 Synthesis Report, Summary for Policymakers [1.1] 4.

10 IPCC, 'Climate Change 2022: Mitigation of Climate Change' (P.R. Shukla, J. Skea, R. Slade, A. Khourdajie, R. van Diemen, D. McCollum, M. Pathak, S. Some, P. Vyas, R. Fradera, M. Belkacemi, A. Hasija, G. Lisboa, S. Luz, J. Malley, (eds.), Cambridge University Press 2022) ('IPCC 2022 Mitigation Report'), Summary for Policymakers [B1].

11 Cracknell (n 2) [1.1.6.1].

effect. This is also referred to as the 'greenhouse effect' because the infrared radiation trapped by a GHG blanket is comparable to heat being trapped in a glass greenhouse. An ozone layer depleted by fluorinated gases can absorb fewer ultraviolet rays from the incoming solar radiation. As well as being harmful, ultraviolet radiation also leads to a warming in the affected areas on Earth.[12] The scientific evidence is clear that anthropogenic GHG emissions have warmed the atmosphere, the oceans, and land.[13]

2.2.2 Observed changes in the climate system

The IPCC has noted 'widespread and rapid changes in the atmosphere, ocean, cryosphere and biosphere,' including the following:

- each of the last four decades has been successively warmer than any decade that preceded it since 1850. Global surface temperature in the first two decades of the 21st century (2001–2020) was 0.99 [0.84 to 1.10]°C higher than 1850–1900. Heatwaves have become more frequent and more intense across most land regions since the 1950s;
- globally averaged precipitation over land has likely increased since 1950, with a faster rate of increase since the 1980s. The frequency and intensity of heavy precipitation events causing flooding have increased since the 1950s;
- glaciers have retreated globally since the 1990s and the Arctic Sea ice area retreated significantly between 1979–1988 and 2010–2019 (decreases of about 40% in September and about 10% in March);
- ice loss on land and thermal expansion from ocean warming has caused sea levels to rise faster since 1900 than over any preceding century in at least the last 3,000 years. Rising sea levels contribute to the flooding of coastal areas and low-lying lands;
- the global proportion of major (Category 3–5) tropical cyclone occurrence has increased over the last four decades, and it is very likely that the latitude where tropical cyclones in the western North Pacific reach their peak intensity has shifted northward;
- compound extreme climate events have increased since the 1950s. This includes increases in the frequency of concurrent heatwaves and droughts on a global scale, fire weather in some regions of all inhabited continents, and compound flooding in some locations;[14]
- generally, vulnerable communities that have historically contributed the least to current climate change are disproportionately affected by its impacts.[15]

12 Ibid [1.1.6.2].

13 IPCC, 'Climate Change 2021: The Physical Science Basis' (Masson-Delmotte, V., P. Zhai, A. Pirani, S.L. Connors, C. Péan, S. Berger, N. Caud, Y. Chen, L. Goldfarb, M.I. Gomis, M. Huang, K. Leitzell, E. Lonnoy, J.B.R. Matthews, T.K. Maycock, T. Waterfield, O. Yelekçi, R. Yu, and B. Zhou (eds.), Cambridge University Press 2021) ('IPCC 2021 Physical Science Report'), Summary for Policymakers [A.1].

14 Ibid [A.2] and [A3].

15 IPCC 2022 Sixth Assessment Report [2.1].

All of these observed changes have been scientifically linked to the warming of the climate system as a result of human activity and in particular anthropogenic GHG emissions.[16] The IPCC has confirmed that there is a near-linear relationship between cumulative anthropogenic CO_2 emissions and the global warming they cause: each 1,000 $GtCO_2$ of cumulative CO_2 emissions is likely to cause a 0.27°C to 0.63°C increase in global surface temperature.[17]

2.2.3 Climate change emission scenarios

The IPCC Working Group has modelled temperature changes for five illustrative emission scenarios that cover the range of possible future development of anthropogenic drivers of climate change starting in 2015 and based on the assessment of multiple lines of evidence:

1. very high GHG emissions and with CO_2 emissions that would double from current levels by 2050 (labelled 'SSP5-8.5' by the IPCC Working Group);[18]
2. high GHG emissions and with CO_2 emissions that would double from current levels by 2100 ('SSP3-7.0');
3. intermediate GHG emissions and with CO_2 that stay at current levels until 2050 ('SSP2-4.5');
4. GHG emissions that would reduce to 1990 levels by 2050 followed by net negative CO_2 emissions ('SSP1-2.6');
5. GHG emissions that would reduce to 1990 levels by 2050 followed by net negative CO_2 emissions at a higher level ('SSP1-1.9').[19]

For each of the five emission scenarios, the IPCC has modelled changes in global surface temperature for selected 20-year time periods compared to the average global surface temperature of the period 1850–1900 (reported in °C).

Table 2.1 shows that the average global surface temperature will continue to rise until at least mid-century under all emissions scenarios considered. Unless GHG emissions – and in particular CO_2 emissions – are reduced significantly from current levels within the next few decades, the temperature rise is likely to exceed 1.5°C by 2050 and 3°C by the end of the 21st century. Even at current emission levels (SSP2-4.5 – shown in grey), a temperature increase of 2°C or more is very likely. At 1.5°C global warming, heavy precipitation and associated flooding are projected to intensify and be more frequent in most regions in Africa and Asia, North America, and Europe. Small low-lying island states are at risk of being flooded completely. Also, more frequent and/or severe agricultural and ecological droughts are projected in a few regions in all inhabited continents except Asia compared to 1850–1900. With every additional increment of global warming, extremes in the climate system, such as heatwaves, heavy precipitation, and droughts, are likely to become more frequent and intense.[20] An increase in the global temperature of more than

16 IPCC 2021 Physical Science Report, Summary for Policymakers [A.4].

17 Ibid [D1].

18 'SSP[number]' refers to the Shared Socio-economic Pathway or 'SSP' describing the socio-economic trends underlying the scenario, and 'y' refers to the approximate level of radiative forcing (in watts per square metre, or $W\ m^{-2}$) resulting from the scenario in the year 2100.

19 IPCC 2021 Physical Science Report, Summary for Policymakers [B1].

20 Ibid [C2].

Table 2.1 Estimated changes in global surface temperature

	Near term 2021–2040		*Mid-term 2041–2060*		*Long term 2081–2100*	
Scenario	*Best estimate*	*Very likely range*	*Best estimate*	*Very likely range*	*Best estimate*	*Very likely range*
SSP1-1.9	1.5	**1.2** to 1.7	1.6	**1.2** to 2.0	1.4	**1.0** to 1.8
SSP1-2.6	1.5	**1.2** to 1.8	1.7	**1.3** to 2.2	1.8	**1.3** to 2.4
SSP2-4.5	1.5	**1.2** to 1.8	2.0	**1.6** to 2.5	2.7	**2.1** to 3.5
SSP3-7.0	1.5	**1.2** to 1.8	2.1	**1.7** to 2.6	3.6	**2.8** to 4.6
SSP5-8.5	1.6	**1.3** to 1.9	2.4	**1.9** to 3.0	4.4	**3.3** to 5.7

IPCC 2021 Physical Science Report, Summary for Policymakers [B1]

2°C compared to that occurring in pre-industrial times is dangerous to human health and life and harmful to ecosystems and biodiversity.[21]

2.2.4 Limiting future climate change

In its 5th Assessment Report, the IPCC concluded:

> Without additional mitigation efforts beyond those in place today, and even with adaptation, warming by the end of the 21st century will lead to high to very high risk of severe, widespread and irreversible impacts globally (high confidence).[22]

Yet, according to the IPCC's recent 6th Assessment Report, there are still significant mitigation and adaptation gaps and finance flows fall short of the levels needed to meet climate goals across all sectors and regions.[23] It is unlikely that the temperature goal to limit the temperature increase to 1.5°C above pre-industrial levels will be met during the 21st century.[24] While the melting of ice sheets and ocean level rises caused by past GHG emissions are 'irreversible for centuries to millennia,' other changes in the climate system can be halted and could be gradually reversed if the average global surface temperature can be reduced.[25] Human-induced global warming can be slowed down, stopped, and reversed by climate change mitigation, namely the reduction of GHG emissions and the introduction and enhancement of processes and activities that remove GHG from the atmosphere ('sinks').[26] Mitigative interventions that limit warming to 1.5°C, and 2°C, require deep, immediate, and sustained GHG emissions reductions and the accelerated deployment of sinks and carbon dioxide removal strategies.[27]

According to the IPCC's modelling, scenarios with very low or low GHG emissions (SSP1-1.9 and SSP1-2.6) would lead within years to noticeable effects on GHG and aerosol concentrations and air quality and would slow down global surface temperature increase

21 IPCC 2014 Synthesis Report 13 (SPM 2.3) and 17 (SPM 3.2).
22 IPCC 2014 Synthesis Report 17 (SPM 3.2).
23 IPCC 2022 Sixth Assessment Report [2.3].
24 Ibid.
25 IPCC 2021 Physical Science Report, Summary for Policymakers [B5] and [D1.6].
26 IPCC 2014 Synthesis Report 17 [SPM 3.2].
27 IPCC 2022 Mitigation Report, Summary for Policymakers [C3] and [C11.1].

over the next decades.[28] By the end of the century, those low emission scenarios would decrease the global surface temperature gradually and limit the frequency of heavy precipitation and flooding, while limiting the number of regions where extreme heat can occur, relative to higher GHG emissions scenarios.[29] Only those pathways where global net GHG emissions can be reduced by 100% in the early 2050s can limit global warming to 1.5°C, and to 2°C if that reduction is achieved by the early 2070s, compared to 1990 levels.[30]

2.3 The international climate change architecture

Climate change does not respect national boundaries and is a global problem that must be addressed through international co-operation. Decision-making at the international level is characterised by consensus-building between states which can be difficult to achieve because of their different political and social systems, conflicting economic interests, and differences in the levels of their development. Until relatively recently, there were also diverging views on the scientific basis of climate change, and in some states 'climate change deniers' remain influential. The effectiveness of international measures depends on the available means of enforcement within the international legal order and their domestic implementation.

2.3.1 1992 Climate Change Convention

On the international stage, the 1992 CCC was the first treaty that sought to address growing concerns about climate change, acknowledging 'that change in the Earth's climate and its adverse effects are a common concern of humankind.'[31] Although there was limited scientific evidence at the time, the 1992 CCC linked climate change to anthropogenic GHG emissions.

The 1992 CCC entered into force on 21 March 1994 and has since been ratified by 196 countries and the EU.[32] Its main objective as stated in Article 2 is:

> stabilization of greenhouse gas concentrations in the atmosphere at a level that would prevent dangerous anthropogenic interference with the climate system. Such a level should be achieved within a timeframe sufficient to allow ecosystems to adapt naturally to climate change, to ensure that food production is not threatened and to enable economic development to proceed in a sustainable manner.

The 1992 CCC establishes Principles and Commitments. The Principles set out in Art.3 provide a framework for how the parties seek to achieve the main objective of reducing GHG emissions and protecting the climate system, including

28 IPCC 2021 Physical Science Report, Summary for Policymakers [D2].
29 IPCC 2021 Physical Science Report, Summary for Policymakers [D2].
30 IPCC 2022 Mitigation Report, Summary for Policymakers [C2].
31 1992 CCC.
32 United Nations Climate Change, 'Status of Ratification of the Convention' <https://unfccc.int/process-and-meetings/the-convention/status-of-ratification/status-of-ratification-of-the-convention> accessed on 1 June 2023.

- **equity**: recognising that parties should take action 'in accordance with their common but differentiated responsibilities and respective capabilities' and that the 'developed country Parties[33] should take the lead in combating climate change and the adverse effects thereof';[34]
- **the precautionary principle**: requiring the parties to 'take precautionary measures to anticipate, prevent or minimize the causes of climate change and mitigate its adverse effects' even if there is a 'lack of full scientific certainty';[35]
- **sustainability**: recognising that sustainable economic development is essential for adopting measures to address climate change;[36]
- **co-operation**: requiring parties to co-operate in combating climate change and not to take measures that 'constitute a means of arbitrary or unjustifiable discrimination or a disguised restriction on international trade'.[37]

The Commitments in Art.4 of the 1992 CCC are a mix of high-level obligations applicable to all parties and specific targets applicable to developed country parties. All parties are required to '[t]ake climate change considerations into account, to the extent feasible, in their relevant social, economic and environmental policies and actions,'[38] to formulate and implement plans for the reduction of GHG emission,[39] and to report on GHG emissions and their actions to address climate change and to adapt to its impacts.[40] The developed country parties committed to adopting measures to mitigate climate change with the aim of reducing GHG emissions jointly to their 1990 levels by 2000.[41] However, this 'commitment' – being the result of heavy negotiations and compromise – has been criticised for merely establishing 'soft targets with many loopholes.'[42] Developed country parties and other industrialised parties also agreed to provide financial support for climate change mitigation and adaptation action in developing countries under a system of grants and loans set up through the 1992 CCC and to share relevant technology with less-advanced nations.[43]

Perhaps most significantly long-term, the 1992 CCC established a 'Conference of Parties' (COP) as its supreme decision-making body to 'keep under regular review the implementation of the Convention and … make, within its mandate, the decisions necessary to promote the effective implementation of the Convention.'[44] Since the 1992 CCC came into force, the COP has met annually – except in 2020 because of the COVID-19 pandemic – most recently in Sharm El Sheikh in 2022 (COP27). The COP is the primary

33 Listed in Annex 1 of the 1992 CCC. Developed countries are countries belonging to the Organisation for Economic Co-operation and Development (OECD), the EU, and countries with 'economies in transition' from Central and Eastern Europe.

34 1992 CCC art 3(1).

35 Ibid art 3(2).

36 Ibid art 3(3) and (2).

37 Ibid art 3(4).

38 Ibid art 4(1)(f).

39 Ibid art 4(1)(a).

40 Ibid art 4(1)(a).

41 Ibid art 4(2)(a) and (b).

42 Philippe Sands and Jacqueline Peel, *Principles of International Environmental Law* (4th ed, Cambridge University Press 2018) 304.

43 1992 CCC art 4(3), (4), and (5).

44 Ibid art 7(2).

negotiation forum to progress the climate agenda and has been instrumental in reaching agreement on the Paris Agreement.[45]

2.3.2 Kyoto Protocol

The Kyoto Protocol was a protocol to the 1992 CCC that was adopted on 11 December 1997 following recommendations by COP1 that the GHG emission reduction targets in Art.4(2) of the 1992 CCC needed to be strengthened. Having met with considerable resistance by some parties to the 1992 CCC, the Kyoto Protocol finally entered into force on 16 February 2005 and was eventually ratified by 191 countries and the EU.[46] The Kyoto Protocol has now been superseded by the Paris Agreement,[47] but it constituted a major international milestone and introduced a number of concepts that have been retained in the Paris Agreement.

The Kyoto Protocol sets binding emission reduction or emission limit targets for developed country parties to the 1992 CCC and a timetable for their achievement.[48] These targets were expressed as levels of allowed emissions divided into assigned amount units ('AAUs'). They added up to an average 5% emission reduction compared to 1990 levels over the five-year period 2008–2012 (the first commitment period), and 18% over the eight-year period from 2013 to 2020 (the second commitment period).[49] While the developed country parties who ratified the Kyoto Protocol collectively reduced GHG emissions,[50] global GHG emissions have surged and, in 2019, resulted in the highest atmospheric GHG concentrations for at least 800,000 years.[51]

Controversially, the Kyoto Protocol contained 'flexibility mechanisms' and 'sinks' which allowed parties with emission reduction or limiting commitments to meet their targets:

1. **emission trading**: Art.17 allowed countries that have AAUs to spare (i.e. unused emissions units) to sell this excess capacity to other developed country parties. A party may buy AAUs because it cannot meet its national target or because it may be more cost-effective to do so rather than to reduce GHG emissions;
2. **Clean Development Mechanism** ('CDM'): Art.12 allowed a developed country party with an emission reduction commitment to implement an emission reduction project in developing countries. Such projects can earn saleable certified emission reduction credits ('CERs') which can be counted towards meeting a developed country party's national target;

45 See Section 2.3.3.

46 United Nations Climate Change, 'Parties to the United Nations Framework Convention on Climate Change' <https://unfccc.int/process/parties-non-party-stakeholders/parties-convention-and-observer-states?field_partys_partyto_target_id%5B512%5D=512> accessed on 1 June 2023. Notably, the United States is not a party.

47 See Section 2.3.3.

48 Kyoto Protocol to the United Nations Framework Convention on Climate Change (adopted on 11 December 1997, entered in force on 16 February 2005) art 3(1) and Annex 1.

49 The second commitment period (2013–2020) was established following the Doha Amendment to the Kyoto Protocol adopted on 8 December 2012.

50 Sands (n 42) 309.

51 IPCC 2021 Physical Science Report, Summary for Policymakers [A.2.1].

3. **joint implementation**: Art.6 allowed a developed country party with an emission reduction commitment to earn emission reduction units ('ERUs') from an emission reduction or emission removal project in another developed country party's territory which can be counted towards meeting the former developed country party's national target;
4. **sinks**: activities or mechanisms which remove GHG from the atmosphere are referred to as a 'sink.' Art.3(3) allowed a developed country party to set off against its emission reduction commitment any sinks – measured in so-called removal units ('RMUs') – resulting from direct human-induced land use change and forestry activities in its territory.[52]

Under the Kyoto Protocol's emissions trading scheme, AAUs, CERs, ERUs, and RMUs were tradeable and transferrable, and the transfer of these units was tracked through a registry system. This has turned GHG into a commodity with a thriving carbon offset market. Proponents of the flexibility mechanisms and sinks have argued that they encourage net GHG emission reduction in a cost-effective way, as well as stimulating green investment.[53] However, these mechanisms have been criticised as obstacles to further GHG emission reductions by allowing rich developed countries to buy their way out of their commitments and by implicitly allowing certain GHG emitters in key industries to carry on 'as usual' without searching for alternative solutions where it is cheaper to buy offset units.[54]

The Kyoto Protocol was also criticised for perpetuating the firewall created by the 1992 CCC between developed country parties with GHG emission reduction commitments and developing country parties with no specific targets even though some of them – like China – were at the time heavy and growing GHG emitters.[55]

2.3.3 Paris Agreement

After decade-long negotiations, the Paris Agreement was adopted by 196 parties at the Paris COP21 Conference on 12 December 2015, entered into force on 4 November 2016, and has now been ratified by 193 parties.[56] The objectives of the Paris Agreement are to enhance the implementation of the 1992 CCC and to strengthen the global response to the threat of climate change, including by

52 Further governing principles regarding eligible land use change and forestry activities were agreed in the UN Framework Convention on Climate Change, Marrakesh Accords (adopted at COP7 in 2001) Decision 11/CP.7 54 <https://unfccc.int/resource/docs/cop7/13a01.pdf#page=54> accessed on 1 June 2023.

53 United Nations Climate Change, 'What Is the Kyoto Protocol?' <https://unfccc.int/kyoto_protocol> accessed on 1 June 2023.

54 Clive Spash, 'The Brave New World of Carbon Trading' (2010) 15(2) *New Political Economy*, 169.

55 This was one of the main reasons why the United States refused to ratify the Kyoto Protocol. See Sands (n 42) 308.

56 Paris Agreement under the United Nations Framework Convention on Climate Change (adopted 12 December 2015, entered into force 4 November 2016) TIAS 16-1104. It is now widely accepted that the Paris Agreement has the legal character of a treaty under the Vienna Convention on the Law of Treaties 1969. See: D. Bodansky, 'The Legal Character of the Paris Agreement', (2016) 25(2) *Review of European Comparative and International Environmental Law*, 142; and Navraj Singh Ghaleigh, 'Aims, Objectives and Principles' in Geert Van Calster and Leonie Reins, *The Paris Agreement on Climate Change: A Commentary* (Edward Elgar Publishing 2021) [2.25].

1. substantially reducing global GHG emissions to limit the global temperature increase to well below 2°C while pursuing efforts to limit the increase to 1.5°C above pre-industrial levels (the 'long-term temperature goal,' also referred to as 'climate change mitigation');
2. increasing the ability to adapt to the adverse impacts of climate change and foster climate resilience;
3. provide financing to developing countries for climate change mitigation and adaptation.[57]

The Principles of Equity, Sustainability, Co-operation, and the Pre-cautionary Principle found in the CCC are recognised in the Preamble of the Paris Agreement. In addition, the Preamble acknowledges the concept of climate justice and that climate action should be consistent with human rights.

In contrast to the Kyoto Protocol, the Paris Agreement does not establish specific targets for developed country parties to achieve the long-term temperature goals but instead requires all parties to submit every five years national climate action plans (which are referred to as nationally determined contributions, or 'NDCs') in which they undertake and communicate 'ambitious efforts' to achieve the Paris Agreement's objectives.[58] Each party is required to 'prepare, communicate and maintain successive NDCs' and to pursue domestic mitigation measures that aim to achieve those NDCs.[59] While the extent of emission reduction targets is left to the discretion of the parties, developed country parties are expected to be more ambitious with their NCDs and take the lead by undertaking economy-wide absolute emission reduction targets,[60] developing country parties are to be supported in their efforts,[61] and the least developed countries and small island developing states may develop GHG emission reduction plans reflecting their special circumstances.[62] A key weakness of the Paris Agreement is that the NDCs are self-determined by each party and not binding.

Art.4(1) sets out the timeframe for the long-term temperature goal: the parties must aim to reach global peaking of GHG as soon as possible and undertake to achieve rapid reductions thereafter in accordance with the Principles 'so as to achieve a balance between anthropogenic emissions by sources and removals by sinks of greenhouse gases in the second half of this century.'[63]

In addition to climate change mitigation, the Paris Agreement puts emphasis on adaptation by referencing it in its objectives and recognising in Art.7(1) the need to enhance adaptive capacity, strengthen resilience, and reduce vulnerability to climate change. Parties are required to 'engage in adaptation planning processes and the implementation of actions, including the development or enhancement of relevant plans, policies and/or contributions,'[64] and must submit and update periodically an adaptation communication

57 Paris Agreement art 2(1).
58 Ibid art 3.
59 Ibid art 4(2).
60 Ibid art 4(4).
61 Ibid art 4(5).
62 Ibid art 4(6).
63 For the Principles, see above and see the Paris Agreement, Preamble.
64 Paris Agreement art 7(9).

to set out its adaptation plans and actions.[65] Further, the Paris Agreement also recognises loss resilience – 'the importance of averting, minimizing and addressing loss and damage associated with the adverse effects of climate change,' such as the impacts of extreme weather events and rising sea levels.[66] Art.8(2) references the existing framework for addressing climate change loss and damage in the 'Warsaw International Mechanism for Loss and Damage associated with Climate Change Impacts,'[67] and Art.8(3) encourages co-operation and mutual facilitation in relation to adaptation measures.

Co-operation between parties and financing for developing countries for climate change mitigation and adaptation are cornerstones of the Paris Agreement.[68] They were also two of the most contentious issues in the negotiation process, especially with regard to the contribution from wealthy developing countries such as China.[69]

1. **finance**: A provision that developed country parties should provide financial support for climate change mitigation and adaptation action in developing countries was already contained in the 1992 CCC[70] under a system of grants and loans set up through the 1992 CCC, and to share relevant technology with less-advanced nations. The Paris Agreement reaffirms that position but for the first time also encourages voluntary contributions by other parties and acknowledges that financing must be mobilised from a variety of sources, including public and private funding;[71]
2. **technology transfer**: Art.10 envisages mitigation and adaptation technology development shared and transferred by the parties. Collaborative approaches to research and development and facilitating access to technology to developing country parties are to be supported by the administrative and financial mechanisms of the 1992 CCC and the Paris Agreement;[72]
3. **capacity-building**: the Paris Agreement acknowledges that not all developing country parties, and in particular the least developed countries and those that are particularly vulnerable to the adverse effects of climate change (such as small island developing states), are able to take effective climate change action.[73] Accordingly, all parties are required to co-operate to enhance the capacity of developing country parties to implement the Paris Agreement, and developed country parties should support capacity-building actions in developing countries.[74]

---

65 Ibid art 7(10).

66 Ibid art 8(1).

67 UN Framework Convention on Climate Change, Warsaw International Mechanism for Loss and Damage associated with Climate Change Impacts (adopted at COP18 in 2013), Decision 3/CP.18 <https://unfccc.int/topics/adaptation-and-resilience/workstreams/loss-and-damage/warsaw-international-mechanism> accessed on 1 June 2023.

68 Paris Agreement Preamble, art 2(1)(c) and 9–11.

69 Sands (n 42) 327.

70 See Section 2.3.1 and Paris Agreement art 4(3).

71 Paris Agreement art 9(2) and (3).

72 Ibid art 10.

73 Ibid art 11(1).

74 Ibid art 11(3).

As most of the operative provisions of the Paris Agreement do not set hard or binding targets, its implementation relies on 'an enhanced transparency framework' ('ETF').[75] Each party is required to provide on a regular basis information on its GHG emissions, its progress in achieving its NDC, its adaptation measures, and the financial support, technology transfer, and capacity-building support provided or received.[76] This information will undergo a technical review and multilateral consideration and then feeds into the 'global stocktake' which will assess the collective progress towards the long-term climate goals.[77] The global stocktake is an innovation of the Paris Agreement to be undertaken by the COP, the first one being due at COP28 in Dubai in 2023 and thereafter every five years.[78] The outcome of the global stocktake may lead to recommendations for some parties to set more ambitious plans and to make better progress on implementing their NDCs. Yet, the ETF recognises the burden that reporting can place especially on the least developed countries and small island developing states and therefore expressly states that it should be implemented 'in a facilitative, non-intrusive, non-punitive manner, respectful of national sovereignty.'[79] Similarly, the Paris Agreement's compliance provisions in Art.15 are designed to be 'facilitative in nature' and 'non-adversarial and non-punitive,'[80] whereby an expert-based committee is charged with facilitating implementation and promoting compliance. The Paris Agreement is binding on its signatories but there are no enforcement mechanisms.

The Paris Agreement seeks to strike a balance between pursuing the twin objectives of climate change mitigation and adaptation and recognising the Principles of Equity and Sustainability. As a result, some of the parties' obligations – such as setting and achieving their own NDCs and adaptation plans – can be vague and voluntary and seemingly allow for low ambition and idleness, and there are no mechanisms for censure and enforcement. Critics have pointed out that the absence of hard targets and legally binding obligations undermines the Paris Agreement's effectiveness for a number of reasons: mere political commitments are taken less seriously by states than legally binding obligations because the risk of reputational damage is lower and no sanctions apply,[81] and voluntary commitments make it harder to rely directly on the Paris Agreement in litigation against national governments.[82] The latest UNEP Emission Gap Report found that current NDCs combined with other mitigation measures put the world on track for a global temperature rise of 2.4–2.6°C by the end of the century[83] – far above the Paris Agreement's long-term temperature goals. Yet, the Kyoto Protocol has shown that hard targets can be too inflex-

75 Ibid art 13(1).

76 Ibid art 13(7)–(10).

77 Ibid art 13(11) and (13) and art 14(1).

78 Ibid art 14(2).

79 Ibid art 13(3).

80 Ibid art 15(2).

81 Daniel Bodansky, 'The Legal Character of the Paris Agreement' (2016) 25(2) *Review of European Comparative and International Environmental Law*, 142.

82 See e.g. *R. (on the application of Friends of the Earth Ltd) v Heathrow Airport Ltd* [2020] UKSC 52, 105–111 (Lord Hodge and Lord Sales); *R (on the application of Friends of the Earth Limited) v The Secretary of State for International Trade/Export Credits Guarantee Department (UK Export Finance) ('UKEF'), Chancellor of the Exchequer v Total E&P Mozambique Area 1 Limitada, Moz Lngl Financing Company Limited* [2022] EWHC 568 (Admin), 119–122 per Stuart-Smith LJ (appeal dismissed in [2023] EWCA Civ 14).

83 United Nations Environment Programme, 'Emissions Gap Report 2022: The Closing Window' Climate crisis calls for rapid transformation of societies (2022) [4.4] <https://www.unep.org/resources/emissions-gap-report-2022> accessed on 1 June 2023.

ible. It would have been impossible to negotiate binding targets for all parties that attract sanctions for non-compliance. The Paris Agreement has gained almost universal support because it is a voluntary pact and thus enables all participating states, including developing countries, to take co-ordinated but self-determined climate action, 'motivated by mutual self-interest' and, to a lesser extent, altruism.[84]

The Paris Agreement has also been criticised for letting off lightly wealthier developing countries, in particular China and India. In fact, this was one of the main criticisms of the USA under the Trump administration leading to the US's temporary withdrawal.[85] China remains the largest GHG emitter, its emissions continue to rise, and it has set itself a far-off net-zero goal in 2060.[86] India has submitted an NDC that does not meet the Paris Agreement mitigation objective in Art.2(1)(a) and has set itself a delayed net-zero target in 2070.[87]

Perhaps most significantly, the Paris Agreement's own objectives and long-term temperature goals have been criticised for being not nearly ambitious enough to avert dangerous global warming and extreme weather.[88] Emission trading allows polluters to meet their emissions reduction targets by buying carbon off-sets which can have the effect of lowering their ambitions. Climate Action Tracker[89] reports that progress on fresh and more ambitious 2030 climate targets and participation in sectoral initiatives have stalled since COP26 in Glasgow in 2021.[90] The Paris Agreement remains controversial but at least a baseline has been set. The annual COP and the ETF provide opportunities for scrutiny, review, and soft pressure on the international stage. The United Nations Environment Programme ('UNEP') promotes the coherent implementation of the Paris Agreement objectives and serves as an advocate for climate action on the international stage.[91] As a matter of fact, the Paris Agreement has led to the wide-spread adoption of domestic climate action legislation and policies and, in an increasing number of states, the Paris Agreement objectives have been enshrined in domestic law.[92]

84 Navraj Singh Ghaleigh, 'Aims, Objectives and Principles' in Geert Van Calster and Leonie Reins, *The Paris Agreement on Climate Change: A Commentary* [2.31].

85 US Department of State, On the U.S Withdrawal from the Paris Agreement Press Statement (Press Statement, 4 November 2019) <https://2017-2021.state.gov/on-the-u-s-withdrawal-from-the-paris-agreement/index.html> accessed on 1 June 2023.

86 Climate Action Tracker, China <https://climateactiontracker.org/countries/china/> accessed on 1 June 2023.

87 Climate Action Tracker, India <https://climateactiontracker.org/countries/india/> accessed on 1 June 2023.

88 See the IPCC's climate change emission scenarios in Table 2.1; Dana Nuccitelli, 'Climate Scientists Debate a Flaw in the Paris Climate Agreement' (*The Guardian*, 29 March 2018).

89 Climate Action Tracker is an independent scientific analysis that tracks government climate action and measures it against the globally agreed Paris Agreement aim of 'holding warming well below 2°C, and pursuing efforts to limit warming to 1.5°C.' It is run as a collaboration of two not-for-profit organisations, Climate Analytics and NewClimate Institute. Climate Change Tracker <https://climateactiontracker.org/about/> accessed on 1 June 2023.

90 Climate Action Tracker <https://climateactiontracker.org/publications/despite-glasgow-climate-pact-2030-climate-target-updates-have-stalled/> accessed on 1 June 2023.

91 United Nations Environment Programme, 'About the United Nations Environment Programme' <https://www.unep.org/about-un-environment> accessed on 1 June 2023.

92 Ghaleigh (n 84) [2.39].

2.3.4 *Implementation of the Paris Agreement in the UK*

The following is a high-level overview of the UK's climate change legislation and key policies that address the objectives of the Paris Agreement. The UK government ratified the Paris Agreement on 17 November 2016. However, ratification of an international treaty only gives rise to obligations of the UK in international law; it does not incorporate the treaty obligation into domestic (UK) law – they 'are not part of UK law and give rise to no legal rights or obligations in domestic law.'[93] To give treaty obligations effect in domestic (UK) law, they need to be incorporated with domestic legislation. Moreover, the Supreme Court in *R. (on the application of Friends of the Earth Ltd) v Heathrow Airport Ltd* said that the mere ratification of the Paris Agreement is not itself a statement of 'Government policy.'[94]

Preceding the Paris Agreement by several years, the UK Climate Change Act 2008 (the 'CCA 2008') established a framework for the UK to achieve a reduction in GHG emissions and adapt to the impact of climate change. The CCA 2008 sets the UK government a legally binding national carbon target and imposes a duty to establish carbon budgets for the UK.[95] Amongst other matters, the CCA 2008 also establishes an independent advisory body (the Committee on Climate Change) tasked with advising on climate action,[96] sets up national GHG trading schemes,[97] and addresses the impact of and adaptation to climate change.[98]

The original carbon target in the CCA 2008 was an 80% net reduction of GHG emissions by 2050 compared to a 1990 baseline. Following new IPCC scientific evidence on meeting the objectives of the Paris Agreement,[99] the UK Committee on Climate Change reported that the aim of the Paris Agreement for emissions to reach net-zero in the second half of the century was likely to require the UK to revise its 2050 carbon target to seek greater reductions and advised that 'it is therefore essential that actions are taken now to enable these deeper reductions to be achieved.'[100] Accordingly, using the carbon target amendment mechanism, the UK government adjusted the target to reduce GHG emissions to 100% by 2050.[101] The UK government also announced a 78% reduction target for 2035

93 *R (Miller) v Secretary of State for Exiting the European Union* [2017] UKSC 5, [55] (Lord Neuberger, Lady Hale, Lord Mance, Lord Kerr, Lord Clarke, Lord Wilson, Lord Sumption, Lord Hodge).

94 *R (on the application of Friends of the Earth Ltd) v Heathrow Airport Ltd* [2020] UKSC 52, [112] (Lord Hodge and Lord Sale). Whether the Paris Agreement constitutes a 'Government policy' was considered in the context of the Planning Act 2008, s 5(8).

95 Climate Change Act 2008, ss 1 and 4.

96 Ibid Part 2.

97 Ibid Part 3.

98 Ibid Part 4.

99 IPCC, '2018 Special Report – Global Warming of 1.5°C' (Masson-Delmotte, V., P. Zhai, H.-O. Pörtner, D. Roberts, J. Skea, P.R. Shukla, A. Pirani, W. Moufouma-Okia, C. Péan, R. Pidcock, S. Connors, J.B.R. Matthews, Y. Chen, X. Zhou, M.I. Gomis, E. Lonnoy, T. Maycock, M. Tignor, and T. Waterfield (eds.), Cambridge University Press 2018), Summary for Policymakers.

100 Committee on Climate Change, 'An Independent Assessment of the UK's Clean Growth Strategy, from Ambition to Action' (2018) 21 <https://www.theccc.org.uk/wp-content/uploads/2018/01/CCC-Independent-Assessment-of-UKs-Clean-Growth-Strategy-2018.pdf> accessed on 1 June 2023.

101 Climate Change Act 2008, s 1, as amended by the Climate Change Act 2008 (2050 Target Amendment) Order 2019, s 2.

(compared to 1990 levels), and this has fed into a recommendation by the Climate Change Committee in its Sixth Carbon Budget.[102]

The UK government's commitment to reducing GHG emissions is incorporated in 'The Ten Point Plan for a Green Industrial Revolution' (November 2020)[103] and in the 'Net-Zero Strategy: Build Back Greener' (October 2021),[104] two strategy documents which aim to deliver net-zero emissions in the medium term alongside economic growth and investment in innovative green technologies. Climate Action Tracker has noted that, while the 'Net-Zero Strategy' measures are expected to result in significant GHG reductions, their impact has not yet been fully quantified and it remains uncertain whether they will achieve the UK's carbon targets for 2035 and 2050.[105] The funding committed to climate action in the 'Ten Point Plan' is insufficient to implement the measures needed for achieving those targets.[106] Lord Deben, Chairman of the UK Climate Change Committee, said that:

> [The UK] Government has been too slow to embrace cleaner, cheaper alternatives and too keen to support new production of coal, oil and gas. There is a worrying hesitancy by Ministers to lead the country to the next stage of Net-zero commitments.[107]

After its withdrawal from the EU, the UK Emissions Trading Scheme (UK ETS) commenced on 1 January 2021,[108] to replace the UK's participation in the EU Emissions Trading Scheme (EU ETS). It applies to energy-intensive industries, the power generation sector, and aviation.[109] The design and coverage of the UK ETS is almost identical to the EU ETS and operates on the 'cap and trade' principle,[110] where the total amount of GHG that can be emitted by sectors covered by the scheme is capped and, subject to this cap (which reduces over time), emission 'allowances' are allocated for free to qualifying operators (on application to the UK ETS regulator).[111] The EU-UK Trade and Co-operation Agreement[112] commits the UK and the EU to consider such a linkage between the UK ETS and the EU ETS but this has not happened yet.

Climate Action Tracker rates the UK's overall climate action – measured against the objectives of the Paris Agreement – as 'almost sufficient.' This rating reflects the fact that

102 The 78% reduction target was set in the UK's sixth Carbon Budget (2021) but no implementing legislation has been passed. See: Department for Business, Energy and Industrial Strategy, 'UK Enshrines New Target in Law to Slash Emissions by 78% by 2035' (2021) <https://www.gov.uk/government/news/uk-enshrines-new-target-in-law-to-slash-emissions-by-78-by-2035> accessed on 1 June 2023.

103 Department for Energy Security and Net-Zero, 'The Ten Point Plan for a Green Industrial Revolution' (2020) 7 <https://assets.publishing.service.gov.uk/government/uploads/system/uploads/attachment_data/file/936567/10_POINT_PLAN_BOOKLET.pdf> accessed on 1 June 2023.

104 HM Government, 'Net-Zero Strategy: Build Back Greener' (October 2021) 10 <https://assets.publishing.service.gov.uk/government/uploads/system/uploads/attachment_data/file/1033990/net-zero-strategy-beis.pdf> accessed on 1 June 2023.

105 Climate Action Tracker <https://climateactiontracker.org/countries/uk/policies-action/'> accessed on 1 June 2023.

106 Ibid.

107 Climate Change Committee, 'Better Transparency Is No Substitute for Real Delivery' (Press Release 23 June 2023) <https://www.theccc.org.uk/2023/06/28/better-transparency-is-no-substitute-for-real-delivery/> accessed 24 June 2023.

108 Established under the Greenhouse Gas Emissions Trading Scheme Order 2020, s 16.

109 Ibid, sch 2.

110 See Section 2.3.5.

111 GHG Order (n 109), Pt 2 ch 1.

112 The EU-UK Trade and Cooperation Agreement concluded between the EU and the UK sets out preferential arrangements in a number of trade-related areas. The EU-UK Trade and Cooperation Agreement (adopted on 30 December 2020, entered into force on 1 May 2021) TS No.8/2021.

some aspects of the UK's contribution 'are world-leading, like its domestic emissions reduction targets, while others, like its contributions to global climate finance, remain inadequate' and that it needs "clearly quantified and funded policies to meet its targets.'[113]

2.3.5 Implementation of the Paris Agreement in the EU

The EU's first climate action package pre-dated the Paris Agreement. The Treaty on the Functioning of the European Union, Art.11 requires the '[e]nvironmental protection requirements must be integrated into the definition and implementation of the Union's policies and activities.' The EU set itself and its member states three key targets that were enacted into legislation in 2009: a 20% cut in GHG emissions (compared to 1990 levels); for 20% of EU energy to come from renewables; and a 20% improvement in energy efficiency.[114] In 2014, the EU also introduced a 2030 target to cut GHG emissions by at least 40% (compared to 1990 levels).[115]

The EU was instrumental in negotiating the Paris Agreement and advocated, not always successfully, more ambitious commitments.[116] The EU is a party in its own right, having ratified the Paris Agreement on 5 October 2016.[117] Following the Paris Agreement, the European Council and the European Parliament called on the European Commission to prepare and maintain a strategy for long-term EU GHG emissions reduction in accordance with the Paris Agreement,[118] and this request is now enshrined in Art.15(2) of the Regulation on Governance of the Energy Union.[119] The strategy has become the 'European Green Deal'[120] and has been passed into law with the European Climate Law.[121] Thus, there are now revised targets to reduce net GHG emissions by at least 55% by 2030,[122] and by 100% (net-zero) by 2050[123] (compared to 1990 levels). The European Commission

113 Climate Action Tracker <https://climateactiontracker.org/countries/uk/> accessed on 1 June 2023.

114 European Commission, '2030 Climate & Energy Framework' <https://ec.europa.eu/clima/eu-action/climate-strategies-targets/2020-climate-energy-package_en> accessed on 1 June 2023.

115 Ibid.

116 Pete Betts, 'The EU's Role in the Paris Agreement' in Henrik Jepsen, Magnus Lundgren, Kai Monheim, and Hayley Walker (eds), *Negotiating the Paris Agreement: The Insider Stories* (Cambridge University Press 2021), ch 6.

117 United Nation Climate Change, 'Paris Agreement – Status of Ratification' <https://unfccc.int/process/the-paris-agreement/status-of-ratification> accessed on 1 June 2023.

118 Communication from the Commission, 'A Clean Planet for All: A European Strategic Long-Term Vision for a Prosperous, Modern, Competitive and Climate Neutral Economy' (2018), COM/2018/773, s 2.

119 Regulation (EU) 2018/1999 of 11 December 2018 of the European Parliament and of the Council, OJ L328/61(11 December 2018) on the Governance of the Energy Union and Climate Action, amending Regulations (EC) No 663/2009 and (EC) No 715/2009 of the European Parliament and of the Council, Directives 94/22/EC, 98/70/EC, 2009/31/EC, 2009/73/EC, 2010/31/EU, 2012/27/EU, and 2013/30/EU of the European Parliament and of the Council, Council Directives 2009/119/EC and (EU) 2015/652 and repealing Regulation (EU) No 525/2013 of the European Parliament and of the Council.

120 The European Green Deal is a wide-ranging set of measures adopted by the European Commission to gear the EU's climate, energy, transport, and taxation policies towards improving the well-being and health of citizens and future generations. See: Communication from the Commission, 'The European Green Deal' (2019) COM/2019/640.

121 Regulation (EU) 2021/1119 of the European Parliament and of the Council of 30 June 2021 establishing the framework for achieving climate neutrality and amending Regulations (2021) OJ L243/1(EC) No 401/2009 and (EU) 2018/1999.

122 Communication from the Commission to the European Parliament, the Council, the European Economic and Social Committee, and the Committee of the Regions, 'Stepping up Europe's 2030 Climate Ambition – Investing in a Climate-Neutral Future for the Benefit of Our People' (2020) COM/2020/562.

123 European Climate Law, art 2(1).

has put forward further proposals for delivering the European Green Deal[124] and has published a 2030 Climate Target Plan[125] and, most recently, the REPowerEU Plan.[126] If implemented, according to Climate Action Tracker's assessment, this would result in emission reductions of around 57–58% and thus meet the 2030 target of 55%.[127]

The EU ETS was the world's first international emissions trading system when it was set up in 2005.[128] The system operates in trading phases (current trading phase 2021–2030) and has been revised several times to maintain its alignment with the EU's evolving climate strategy and consistency with the Paris Agreement. The EU ETS works on the 'cap and trade' principle. A cap is set on the total amount of eligible GHG that can be emitted by the installations covered by the system. The cap is reduced over time so that total emissions fall. Within the cap, installations buy or receive annual emissions allowances (the total number of which is limited), which they can trade with one another as needed. There are heavy fines for installations that cannot match their emissions with sufficient allowances at the end of the year.[129]

Climate Action Tracker rates the EU's overall climate action – measured against the objectives of the Paris Agreement – as 'Insufficient.' While its emission reduction targets are 'acceptable,' the EU policies already implemented to date fall just short of achieving the 2030 target,[130] but more significantly, the EU's international climate finance contributions are rated as 'Insufficient' as contributions to date have been low compared to its fair share to the global efforts in reducing GHG emissions.[131]

2.3.6 Implementation of the Paris Agreement worldwide

A growing number of countries, regions, and cities have set themselves net-zero GHG emission targets.[132] In the United States, the Inflation Reduction Act,[133] signed into law in August 2022, puts the US back on a path towards meeting its Paris Agreement commitment. By setting out a programme for building a 'Clean Energy Economy' and reducing harmful pollution, the Inflation Reduction Act aims to reduce GHG emissions by 40% compared to 2005 levels.[134] The COP26 Glasgow Climate Pact for the first time explicitly links fossil fuels and coal to the climate emergency, requiring parties to 'accelerat[e]

124 Communication from the Commission (n 121).

125 European Commission (n 115).

126 Communication from the Commission to the European Parliament, the European Council, the Council, the European Economic and Social Committee, and the Committee of the Regions REPowerEU Plan (2022) COM/2022/230.

127 Climate Action Tracker, EU <https://climateactiontracker.org/countries/eu/> accessed on 1 June 2023.

128 Directive 2003/87/EC of the European Parliament and of the Council of 13 October 2003 establishing a system for greenhouse gas emission allowance trading within the Union and amending Council Directive 96/61/EC.

129 European Commission, 'EU Emissions Trading System (EU ETS)' <https://ec.europa.eu/clima/eu-action/eu-emissions-trading-system-eu-ets_en> accessed on 1 June 2023.

130 Climate Action Tracker, EU <https://climateactiontracker.org/countries/eu/policies-action/> accessed on 1 June 2023.

131 Ibid.

132 For a current overview of countries with a legally binding net-zero target, or proposed legislation, and a 'performance tracker,' see 'Net-Zero Tracker' <https://zerotracker.net/> accessed on 1 June 2023.

133 The White House, 'By the Numbers: The Inflation Reduction Act' (Press Release 14 August 2022) <https://www.whitehouse.gov/briefing-room/statements-releases/2022/08/15/by-the-numbers-the-inflation-reduction-act/> accessed on 1 June 2023.

134 Inflation Reduction Act 2022 (U.S), Subtitle D Pt 1.

efforts towards the phasedown of unabated coal power and phase-out of inefficient fossil fuel subsidies.'[135]

Yet, there remains an 'emission gap': current NDCs combined with other mitigation measures and pledges put the world on track for a global temperature rise of 2.4–2.6°C by the end of the century.[136] In addition, the UN Adaptation Gap Report 2022 highlights that ongoing adaptation actions are not keeping pace with accelerating climate risks and impacts.[137] Climate action finance provided to developing countries remains insufficient.[138]

The COP27 Sharm el Sheik Implementation Plan ('SHIP') notes the emission, adaptation, and financing gaps and urges all country parties to take, accelerate, and scale up their climate mitigation and climate adaptation actions.[139] SHIP, for the first time, recognises that funding arrangements must be set up to respond to loss and damage for developing countries associated with the adverse effects of climate change.[140] Moreover, SHIP affirms that sustainable and just solutions to the climate crisis require 'social dialogue and participation of all stakeholders,' and in particular finance from financial institutions and institutional investors for a global transition to a net-zero economy.[141]

2.4 Climate action, the environment, sustainability, and ESG

The media, government policies, and business reports often mention 'climate action,' 'environmental (protection/issues/objectives),' 'ESG,' and sustainability together and, frequently, it is not clear where the boundaries between these different concepts are, what they have in common, and how they interconnect. As will be discussed in Chapter 5, creating a common terminology remains one of the challenges of regulating, and giving disclosures, on these matters. There is no universally agreed understanding of environmental issues or sustainability standards. This section does not attempt to provide definitions but seeks to explain 'climate change' and 'climate action' within the wider context of protecting the environment, ESG, and sustainability.

2.4.1 Environment, climate action, and climate resilient development

The environment is the land, water, air, and atmosphere in or on which people, animals, and plants live. Environmental harms caused by human anthropogenic activities can manifest themselves in different ways, including air pollution, deforestation, the depletion

---

135 UN Framework Convention on Climate Change, 'Decision 1/CMA.3/CP.26 Glasgow Climate Pact,' art 3.

136 United Nations Environment Programme, 'Emissions Gap Report 2022: The Closing Window – Climate Crisis Calls for Rapid Transformation of Societies' (2022) <https://www.unep.org/resources/emissions-gap-report-2022> accessed on 1 June 2023.

137 United Nations Environment Programme, 'Adaptation Gap Report 2022: Too Little, Too Slow – Climate Adaptation Failure Puts World at Risk,' (2022) pt 15 <https://www.unep.org/resources/adaptation-gap-report-2022> accessed on 1 June 2023.

138 Climate Action Tracker, 'Glasgow's 2030 Credibility Gap: Net-Zero's Lip Service to Climate Action' (2021) 7 <https://climateactiontracker.org/documents/997/CAT_2021-11-09_Briefing_Global-Update_Glasgow2030CredibilityGap.pdf> accessed on 1 June 2023.

139 UN Framework Convention on Climate Change, 'Decision 1/CP.27: Sharm el Sheikh Implementation Plan' (22 November 2022) s VII, sec IV, V, IX <https://unfccc.int/documents/624441> accessed on 1 June 2023.

140 SHIP art 46.

141 SHIP s 8 cl 28 and s IX cl 30–31.

of fresh water and land resources, and the destruction or reduction of biodiversity and ecosystems. Climate change is the result of the increased concentration of anthropogenic GHG emissions in the atmosphere[142] and, as such, used to be classified as a sub-category of atmospheric or air pollution in the past.[143] It now appears almost always as an environmental harm in its own right,[144] although there is a recognised interdependence of climate (change), ecosystems, and biodiversity.[145]

Conversely, the protection of the environment includes the protection of the atmosphere and combating climate change. However, taking 'climate action' has acquired an extended meaning: under the Paris Agreement responding to the threat of climate change is not limited to climate change mitigation,[146] but also includes climate change adaptation[147] and strengthened climate change resilience.[148] Similarly, the environmental objectives in the EU Taxonomy Regulation include climate change mitigation and climate change adaptation,[149] and the IPCC has a separate working group reporting on 'Mitigation of Climate Change' and 'Impacts, Adaptation and Vulnerability.'[150]

Climate change mitigation is the process of achieving the long-term temperature goal as set out in the Paris Agreement, to hold the increase in the global average temperature to well below 2°C and pursuing efforts to limit it to 1.5°C above pre-industrial levels, by reducing GHG emissions and enhance sinks.[151] In contrast, climate change adaptation means the process of adjustment to actual and expected climate change and its impacts in order to moderate the harm of climate change, or to exploit beneficial opportunities arising from climate change.[152] Climate change resilience is the capacity to avert, minimise, and cope with loss and damage associated with the adverse effects of climate change.[153] Climate change adaptation and resilience are not processes that stem climate change as they do not reduce GHG emissions and enhance sinks. Yet, they are included in 'climate

142 See Section 2.2.1.

143 See e.g. United Nations, 'Report of the United Nations Conference on Environment and Development' (Rio de Janeiro, 3–14 June 1992) agenda 21, cl 9.6.

144 See e.g. United Nations General Assembly, 'Resolution Adopted by the General Assembly on 25 September 2015: Transforming Our World: The 2030 Agenda for Sustainable Development' (21 October 2015) A/RES/70/1; Communication from the Commission, The European Green Deal (2019) COM/2019/640, and Department for Energy Security and Net-Zero, 'The Ten Point Plan for a Green Industrial Revolution' (2020) 7 <https://assets.publishing.service.gov.uk/government/uploads/system/uploads/attachment_data/file/936567/10_POINT_PLAN_BOOKLET.pdf> accessed on 1 June 2023.

145 IPCC 2022 Sixth Assessment Report 4.

146 Paris Agreement art 2(1)(a) and 4.

147 Ibid art 2(1)(b) and 7.

148 Ibid art 8(1).

149 Regulation (EU) 2020/852 of the European Parliament and of the Council of 18 June 2020 on the establishment of a framework to facilitate sustainable investment, and amending Regulation (EU) 2019/2088, art 9(a) and (b).

150 IPCC 2022 Mitigation Report; IPCC, 'Climate Change 2022: Impacts, Adaptation and Vulnerability' (H.-O. Pörtner, D.C. Roberts, M. Tignor, E.S. Poloczanska, K. Mintenbeck, A. Alegría, M. Craig, S. Langsdorf, S. Löschke, V. Möller, A. Okem, B. Rama (eds.) Cambridge University Press 2021) ('IPCC 2022 Adaptation Report').

151 IPCC 2022 Mitigation Report, Glossary; and see Regulation (EU) 2020/852 of the European Parliament and of the Council of 18 June 2020 on the establishment of a framework to facilitate sustainable investment, and amending Regulation (EU) 2019/2088, art 2(5).

152 IPCC 2022 Mitigation Report, Glossary; and see Regulation (EU) 2020/852 of the European Parliament and of the Council of 18 June 2020 on the establishment of a framework to facilitate sustainable investment, and amending Regulation (EU) 2019/2088, art 2(6).

153 IPCC 2022 Mitigation Report, Glossary; and see Paris Agreement art 8(1).

action' as they reduce the exposure and vulnerability of human and natural systems to climate change impacts. In his seminal paper 'Resilience and Stability in Ecological Systems,' Holling introduced the idea of ecological resilience as a measure for an ecological system to absorb change and disturbance which should be considered alongside the idea of 'stability' which is focused on returning an ecological system to its former state of equilibrium after a disturbance.[154]

The IPCC has adopted the concept of 'climate resilient development' ('CRD'), which is a strategy of co-ordinated and integrated implementation of adaptation and mitigation solutions, to support sustainable development[155] for all and to achieve better results by leveraging their interdependence.[156] There is no single preferred pathway or the best combination of adaptation, mitigation, and other sustainable development strategies, rather:

> All pathways involve complex trade-offs and synergies among different actions. The climate resilient development concept helps assess the extent to which solutions currently exist to meet societal goals or the extent to which an expanded solution space is required. The concept also helps assess the role of various actors, including governments, citizens, civil society, knowledge institutions, media, investors and businesses as well as assessing the need for arenas of engagement in which they can interact.[157]

CRD approaches are founded in recent interdisciplinary research[158] and have been accompanied by a shift in international policies as evidenced in the Paris Agreement which explicitly links its objectives of climate change mitigation, adaptation, and resilience to 'the context of sustainable development.'[159] The discussion will return to the interlinkage of CRD and sustainable development in the next section, once the terms 'sustainability' and 'sustainable development' have been explained.

CRD is not without challenges: climate action can be constrained or delayed by CRD implementation which takes into account social, economic, and geographic inequities, and, vice versa, CRD interventions that focus on climate action alone can exacerbate inequality and economic vulnerabilities.[160] Moreover, as CRD implementation is based on negotiation and consensus between many diverse actors and actions, agreement reached on the lowest common denominator can seem unambitious and ineffective.[161]

2.4.2 Sustainability

A recent discourse analysis shows that there are different perceptions of 'sustainability' typified by ideological positions on the limits of economic growth, the ability of technology to solve environmental issues, and the substitutability of natural capital with human or financial capital.[162] However, a common starting point is the 1987 Report by the United

154 Crawford S. Holling, 'Resilience and Stability of Ecological Systems' (1973) 4(1) *Annual Review of Ecology and Systematics*, 1, 23.

155 See Section 2.4.2.

156 IPCC 2022 Adaptation Report ch 18.

157 Ibid [1.5.3].

158 For a comprehensive literature review, see IPCC 2022 Adaptation Report [18.1].

159 Paris Agreement art 2(1).

160 IPCC 2022 Adaptation Report [18.1.4].

161 Ibid, and see discussion of Paris Agreement in Section 2.3.3.

162 Peter Ferguson and Linda Wollersheim, 'From Sustainable Development to Resilience? (Dis)continuities in Climate and Development Policy Governance Discourse' (2022) 31(1) *Sustainable Development*, 4.

Nations Brundtland Commission which defined 'sustainability' as 'meeting the needs of the present without compromising the ability of future generations to meet their own needs,'[163] and 'sustainable development' as 'a process of change in which the exploitation of resources, the direction of investments, the orientation of technological development, and institutional change are made consistent with future as well as present needs.'[164] The IPCC defines 'sustainability' as:

> ensuring the persistence of natural and human systems, implying the continuous functioning of ecosystems, the conservation of high biodiversity, the recycling of natural resources and, in the human sector, successful application of justice and equity.[165]

In June 1992, at the Earth Summit in Rio de Janeiro, Brazil, more than 178 countries adopted the Rio Declaration on Environment and Development which states that at the centre of sustainable development is a right of 'human beings to a healthy and productive life in harmony with nature,'[166] and that sustainable development must 'equitably meet developmental and environmental needs of present and future generations.'[167] The Rio signatories also adopted Agenda 21, a comprehensive plan of action to build a global partnership for sustainable development to improve human lives and protect the environment, which, since then, was superseded by the 2000 Millennium Development Goals,[168] which in turn have now been replaced by the 2030 Agenda for Sustainable Development.[169] The 2030 Agenda for Sustainable Development is a shared route map for peace and prosperity for present and future generations and contains 17 sustainable development goals ('SDGs') for 2016–2030:

- Goal 1. End poverty in all its forms everywhere;
- Goal 2. End hunger, achieve food security and improved nutrition, and promote sustainable agriculture;
- Goal 3. Ensure healthy lives and promote well-being for all at all ages;
- Goal 4. Ensure inclusive and equitable quality education and promote lifelong learning opportunities for all;
- Goal 5. Achieve gender equality and empower all women and girls;
- Goal 6. Ensure availability and sustainable management of water and sanitation for all;
- Goal 7. Ensure access to affordable, reliable, sustainable, and modern energy for all;
- Goal 8. Promote sustained, inclusive, and sustainable economic growth, full and productive employment, and decent work for all;

163 United Nations, 'Report of the World Commission on Environment and Development, Our Common Future' (1987) [27].

164 Ibid [30].

165 IPCC 2022 Adaptation Report, Glossary.

166 United Nations, 'Report of the United Nations Conference on Environment and Development' (Rio de Janeiro, 3–14 June 1992) Principle 1.

167 Ibid art 3.

168 UNGA, 'Resolution Adopted by the General Assembly: United Nations Millennium Declaration' (18 September 2000) A/RES/55/2.

169 UNGA, 'Resolution Adopted by the General Assembly on: Transforming Our World: The 2030 Agenda for Sustainable Development' (25 September 2015) A/RES/70/1.

- Goal 9. Build resilient infrastructure, promote inclusive and sustainable industrialisation, and foster innovation;
- Goal 10. Reduce inequality within and among countries;
- Goal 11. Make cities and human settlements inclusive, safe, resilient, and sustainable;
- Goal 12. Ensure sustainable consumption and production patterns;
- Goal 13. Take urgent action to combat climate change and its impacts;
- Goal 14. Conserve and sustainably use the oceans, seas, and marine resources for sustainable development;
- Goal 15. Protect, restore, and promote sustainable use of terrestrial ecosystems, sustainably manage forests, combat desertification, and halt and reverse land degradation and halt biodiversity loss;
- Goal 16. Promote peaceful and inclusive societies for sustainable development, provide access to justice for all, and build effective, accountable, and inclusive institutions at all levels;
- Goal 17. Strengthen the means of implementation and revitalise the global partnership for sustainable development.

The SDGs recognise that ending poverty is interlinked to globally shared strategies that improve health, education, equality, inclusivity, and security; give access to natural resources; promote economic growth and innovation; stem climate change; and preserve biodiversity and ecosystems.

How do sustainability, sustainable development, and the SDGs relate to climate change, climate action, and CRD? The 2030 Agenda for Sustainable Development explicitly references the global threat of climate change to achieve sustainable development:

> Climate change is one of the greatest challenges of our time and its adverse impacts undermine the ability of all countries to achieve sustainable development. Increases in global temperature, sea level rise, ocean acidification and other climate change impacts are seriously affecting coastal areas and low-lying coastal countries, including many least developed countries and small island developing States. The survival of many societies, and of the biological support systems of the planet, is at risk.[170]

Taking climate action to combat climate change is one of the SDGs. The targets within that goal include strengthening climate change adaptation and resilience, as well as integrating climate change mitigation measures.[171]

The SDGs are 'integrated and indivisible'[172] which are accorded 'equal priority in our implementation efforts,'[173] but the 2030 Agenda is silent as to how to balance the economic, social, and environmental dimensions of sustainable development if they are in conflict. On a textual analysis, given the order of the SDGs (with 'climate action' being Goal 13 out of 17) and the strong focus on eradicating poverty and strengthening human rights in the 2030 Agenda text, there seems to be a higher prioritisation of anthropogenic sustainability over eco-centric sustainability. However, it is also arguable that recognising

170 Ibid [14].
171 Ibid [13.1] and [13.2].
172 Ibid [55].
173 Ibid [61].

that each country faces specific challenges to achieve sustainable development, whether the focus is on the economic, social, or environmental dimension, is part of each national government's discretion in setting its own national targets for achieving the SDGs and deciding how these should be incorporated into national planning processes, policies, and strategies.[174] The IPCC employ the concept of CRD to identify conflicts, balance trade-offs, and make progress on achieving the SDGs.[175]

There are diverging views on whether 'sustainable development' and CRD are different albeit connected concepts. For some commentators, CRD merely constitutes an extension of the language of sustainable development to give greater emphasis to the role of climate action and environmental protection in enhancing human and ecological well-being.[176] Other commentators suggest that CRD is an enabling condition or process to achieve sustainable development,[177] and some view CRD and sustainable development as separate concepts with different objectives.[178] This ongoing debate, coloured by ideological positions on economy theory, is beyond the scope of this book. It will therefore adopt the IPCC's current perspective of CRD as a process for identifying pathways for the co-ordinated and integrated implementation of climate change adaptation and mitigation solutions on a fair and equitable basis, which will improve social, economic, and environmental outcomes in line with the SDGs.[179]

2.4.3 ESG

ESG stands for 'environmental, social and governance,' and refers to criteria, factors, and attributes considered, measured, and reported in relation to corporate governance and investments. ESG could be thought of as non-financial information flows that aid decision-making.[180] Thus, the directors of a company may take into account ESG factors when they take decisions on behalf of the company, and investors may consider a company's ESG attributes alongside financial performance considerations when deciding whether or not to invest in or divest from the company. Regulators may be interested in a company's ESG performance from a risk perspective, and other stakeholders, such as customers and suppliers, may also have ESG-related expectations regarding the company's activities and products. The idea behind ESG is for businesses to be accountable for their negative externalities, and any negative impact of the production and consumption of their products and services, and thus be incentivised to address any adverse impacts.[181]

---

174 Ibid [55] and [56].

175 IPCC 2022 Adaptation Report ch 18, and see Section 2.4.1.

176 Peter Ferguson, Linda Wollersheim, 'The World Bank's Resilience Discourse: Reactive Environmental Norm Diffusion and the Crisis of Global Climate Governance' in Viktor Jakupec, Max Kelly, and Jonathan Makuwira, *Rethinking Multilateralism in Foreign Aid: Beyond the Neoliberal Hegemony* (Routledge 2020) 160.

177 See e.g. IPCC 2022 Adaptation Report ch 18.

178 See e.g. United States Agency for International Development, 'Climate-Resilient Development – a Framework for Understanding and Addressing Climate Change (2014)' <https://pdf.usaid.gov/pdf_docs/PBAAA245.pdf> accessed on 1 June 2023.

179 IPCC 2022 Adaptation Report [1.5.3] and ch 18.

180 UK All-Party Parliamentary Group on Environmental, Social, and Governance Report, 'Defining ESG,' Figure 1 (April 2023) <https://appgesg.org/wp-content/uploads/2023/04/20230425-APPG-Defining-ESG-report-final-web.pdf> accessed on 1 June 2023.

181 H. Tricks, 'In Need of a Clean up' (*The Economist – Special Report on ESG Investing*, 23 July 2022) 3.

ESG factors are usually broken down into different risks and opportunities in the three component areas. As there is no universally applicable ESG framework, the individual ESG risks and opportunities can vary significantly but may include:[182]

- **environmental**: pollution prevention and control; environmental impact from energy use; GHG emissions; use and protection of natural resources (e.g. water, land) and related protection of biodiversity; waste management; environmental impacts from transportation or from the use and disposal of products and services; development of green products and services;
- **social**: implementation of international employment standards; diversity, inclusion, and anti-discrimination issues; working conditions; health and safety; consumer relations and protection; community relations and engagement;
- **governance**: corporate ownership structure; leadership and board diversity; decision-making processes; business environment and main trends and factors that may affect future development; business objectives and strategies; implementation and review of policies and risk management strategies; non-financial key performance indicators relevant to the particular business; respect for human rights; anti-bribery and anti-corruption policies and controls.

As will be discussed in Chapter 4, the effect of climate risk on a company's business and a company's outward impact by taking climate action are examples of the 'E' within 'ESG.' 'ESG' is frequently used interchangeably with '(corporate) sustainability,' but there are differences:

1. **application**: ESG consideration applies in the corporate and investment context, whereas the United Nations have asked all countries and all stakeholders, acting in collaborative partnership, to implement the 2030 Agenda plans for sustainable development and pursue the SDGs;
2. **scope**: the corporate governance issues that fall within the 'G' of 'ESG' have no direct equivalent in 'sustainable development' and the SDGs. For example, 'transparency' which is the basis for corporate disclosures is not captured by 'sustainability.' Some of the more specific corporate 'social' responsibility issues also fall outside the scope of 'sustainability.' Present and future economic needs are a 'sustainability' consideration but not part of 'ESG';
3. **transformation**: ESG factors give a snapshot of a company's activities, governance, and impact at a particular point in time. In contrast, sustainable development is an ongoing process to 'equitably meet developmental and environmental needs of present and future generations';[183]
4. **measurability**: there are emerging frameworks for the disclosure of ESG information which provide metrics that measure and systematically record ESG factors.[184] ESG factors are becoming increasingly data driven and detail oriented so

182 Breakdown based on: UK All-Party Parliamentary Group on Environmental, Social, and Governance Report (n 181).

183 UNGA, 'Report of the United Nations Conference on Environment and Development' (Rio de Janeiro, 3–14 June 1992) Principle 3.

184 See Chapter 5.

that evidence-based disclosures and informed decisions can be made. In contrast, 'sustainability' is a more fluid concept closely linked to strategy covering multiple topics.

The overlap of 'ESG' and 'sustainability' is most prominent in relation to disclosure obligations and recommendations. As will be seen in Chapter 5, sustainability-related disclosure frameworks frequently reference 'sustainability' in their name or title, but the specific disclosures made tend to focus on environmental and social factors evidenced by data and metrics, as well as information on sustainability strategy and objectives. ESG data is used to benchmark a company's performance in achieving its sustainability strategy and objectives.[185]

There can also be tension between the 'E' and the 'S' and 'G': for example, as the war in Ukraine and its impact on energy security have magnified, prioritising energy security (a social goal) by reinstating coal consumption over climate policies to reduce GHG emissions creates a conflict between the 'S' and the 'E.'[186] Conversely, prioritising the 'E' by imposing a climate change levy on all households can have negative 'S' consequences by putting additional pressure on low-income households that are already struggling financially.[187] The CRD approach discussed in Section 2.4.1 recognises the potential conflicts and trade-offs and assesses climate action in the context of sustainable development. The 'realpolitik' of governments accountable to their electorate is also more likely to favour addressing immediate social issues over more long-term environmental objectives.

2.5 Conclusion

Human activities, principally through GHG emissions, have unequivocally caused global warming. The CCC, the Kyoto Protocol, and the Paris Agreement are supporting rising levels of national ambition and encouraging the development and implementation of climate policies at all levels but current climate change mitigation and adaptation policies and their implementation are not sufficient to meet the long-term temperature goal set in the Paris Agreement and to adapt adequately to the adverse impacts of climate change. The terminology surrounding climate action, CRD, sustainability, and ESG is still developing and concept boundaries are not yet settled. The following chapters will explore the role of insurance and the insurance industry in this emerging landscape of climate action and CRD.

185 UK All-Party Parliamentary Group on Environmental, Social, and Governance Report (n 181).

186 Valentina Romei and Martin Arnold, 'Germany Turns to Coal for a Third of Its Electricity' (*Financial Times*, 7 September 2022).

187 The UK government had been proposing a climate change levy of £120 on all households to fund the hydrogen industry but this proposal has now been abandoned in light of rising interest rates and inflation. See: *The Telegraph*, 'Households Will Be Spared £120 Net-Zero Levy, Says Grant Shapps' (23 June 2023).

CHAPTER 3

Climate change risks and the role of insurers

This chapter introduces key insurance concepts and provides the theoretical frameworks for considering risks associated with climate change, and for the role of insurers in the fight against climate change and the transition to a net-zero economy. It also advances one of the key theses put forward in this book: that, leveraging their contractual relationships, insurers can engage with and support their policyholders and other stakeholders to take climate mitigation action and to adopt climate change adaptation measures.

Section 3.1 provides a brief introduction to the nature of insurance, and the law and economics of insurance contracts. Section 3.2 describes the different types of climate change risk which have been conceptualised in a classification distinguishing between physical risk, transition risk, and liability risk. Section 3.2 also describes key technical concepts such as insurability, complex risks, and protection gaps and analyses how they apply to climate change risks. The interaction between climate change, climate change risk, and insurance is explored in Section 3.3 by reference to the concept of 'double materiality': the inward impact of climate change risk on an insurer's business, and the outward impact that an insurer's operations and value chains have and can have on the environment by contributing to or counteracting climate change. In Section 3.4, different conceptions of insurance are considered as a theoretical framework for exploring the societal role of insurers and insurance in relation to climate change, and as justification or normative choices that support impact underwriting. It will be argued that a new 'enabling conception' can be a theoretical basis for the insurance industry providing support to policyholders, investee companies, and other stakeholders in their net-zero transition.

3.1 Nature of insurance

The legal relationship between an individual policyholder and an insurer is based on a contract of insurance which is an agreement to transfer risk from the policyholder (the insured) to the insurer. There are two basic types of insurance: indemnity insurance and contingency insurance. In indemnity insurance, the insurer undertakes to pay the insured an indemnity (or to provide a corresponding benefit) upon the occurrence of the insured event that is adverse to the interests of the insured, in return for the payment of a premium by the insured.[1] In contingency insurance, the insurer provides for the payment

1 *Prudential Insurance Co v Commissioner of Inland Revenue* [1906] 2 KB 658, 663 (Lord Chanell).

DOI: 10.4324/b23081-3

of a predetermined sum of money upon the occurrence of a contingent event.[2] A policyholder can insure with respect to risks affecting property, life, health, and liabilities. The policyholder transforms his or her risk of a large financial loss resulting from the loss of, or damage to property or the risk of incurring liability to a third party, into the certainty of 'losing' a relatively small amount by way of premium payments. In return for paying premium, the policyholder gains peace of mind that, in the event of a loss covered by the insurance contract, it will be indemnified for that loss by the insurer.[3] In first party (life, life-related, and property) insurance, policyholders buy insurance to protect themselves and their families. In third-party insurance, policyholders buy protection against financial loss suffered as a result of being held liable for injury or loss caused to third parties. The insurance protection is not against the insured risk itself – the insurer cannot prevent the loss of property by fire or the death of a person – but the financial impact of the insured risk.

The insurer is able to absorb the risk more efficiently (1) as a result of the law of large numbers, (2) because it can diversify its portfolio with different risks (different assets, time horizons, locations, insured perils), and (3) because an insurer can pool and invest the premium income more profitably compared to an individual or business investing its premium savings if it does not buy insurance for a particular risk.[4] Thus, insurance is a mechanism for transferring and pooling risk. Ewald sees the effectiveness of insurance in the idea of solidarity: the collective risk-sharing of the community of policyholders who pay into a fund administered by the insurer to provide financial help to those policyholders who have suffered a loss, while the fund gives rise to yield for the insurer.[5]

The process of assessing risks to be transferred and calculating a premium that is reflective of the specific risk and the underwriting pool as a whole is called 'underwriting.' There is an overall social gain as the aggregate exposure to the risk of all policyholders participating in that pool is mitigated.[6] Insurance also has a wider societal benefit in that it provides fast compensation to victims of disasters, accidents, and torts, and income security in retirement or ill-health, easing the burden on tax-funded benefits and compensation schemes.[7] The transfer of risk to insurers means that insurers are liable to pay claims to policyholders if the insured event occurs. It is therefore also referred to as the 'liability side' of the insurance business, and insurers involved in insurance activities on the liability side of their business are also referred to as 'underwriters' or 'risk carriers.' An insurer can on-transfer the risk it has assumed by buying reinsurance.

2 *Medical Defence Union Ltd v Department of Trade* [1980] Ch 82, 89 (Lord Megarry).

3 Behavioural economics theory has it that most people are 'risk averse.' In the insurance context that means that they have a preference for the certainty of paying a (small) premium over the uncertainty of a large future financial loss. See: Ronen Avraham, 'The Economics of Insurance Law – A Primer' (2012) 19 *Conn Ins LJ*, 29, 37.

4 Eric A. Posner and E. Glen Weyl, 'An FDA for Financial Innovation: Applying the Insurable Interest Doctrine to the 21st Century Financial Markets' (2013) 107 *Nw U L Rev*, 1307, 1314.

5 F. Ewald (trs J.-M. Dautrey and C.F. Stifler), 'Risk in Contemporary Society' (2000) 6 *Conn Ins LJ*, 365, excerpted in John Lowry and Philip Rawlings, *Insurance Law: Cases and Materials* (Hart Publishing 2004) 101.

6 Ibid. See also: Lloyd R. Cohen and Michelle E. Boardman, 'Methodology: Applying Economics to Insurance Law – an Introduction' in Julian Burling and Kevin Lazarus (eds.), *Research Handbook on International Insurance Law and Regulation* (Edward Elgar Publishing 2011) 19, 22–23.

7 Avraham (n 3).

Most types of insurance are voluntary in the sense that a person or business can choose whether or not to buy insurance-based on their risk appetite which may be shaped by their vulnerabilities, their risk attitudes, the level of premium, past experience, and professional advice received. For some activities, third-party liability insurance is compulsory: laws and regulations mandate that insurance is in place as a means of ensuring that the policyholder can access insurance funds to pay compensation for specified injuries and losses that she has caused to others. In the UK, for example, a person using a motor vehicle on a road or other public place must have third-party liability motor insurance in place,[8] and employers must insure against liability for bodily injury or disease sustained by their employees arising out of and in the course of their employment in Great Britain.[9] Professional indemnity insurance is frequently indirectly compulsory as a licensing or membership requirement under the rules of an industry regulator or professional body.[10]

Insurance companies also act as investors: to protect the value of the premium income against inflation, the pooled premiums become part of a fund or funds which insurers invest in assets – such as bonds and shares – or in funds investing in assets, that generate additional income. This additional income can be used to enhance an insurer's ability to pay claims to its policyholders. Depending on the duration and predictability of their exposure, insurers will adopt different investment strategies. Standard property insurance contracts tend to be for a duration of twelve months and provide cover for losses that occur during that twelve-month policy period. Accordingly, premium investments tend to be more short-term but need to be relatively liquid. Liability policies may provide cover for liabilities that arise during the policy period but do not crystallise until much later. Some of the premium may therefore be invested more mid- or long-term. In contrast, for life insurance and annuity products, the time elapsing between an insurer receiving premiums and paying claims can span over many years, and therefore premium tends to be invested in matching long-term assets. For certain life insurance products, the investment return on the premium is a core component of the pay-out to the policyholder or its beneficiaries ('insurance-based investment products' or 'IBIP'). In those instances, insurers act as asset managers: the insurer invests (some of) the premium on behalf of the policyholder or beneficiary in specified investment funds which are managed by the insurer. The pay-out on maturity varies according to the investment performance of the fund (and the underlying assets) in which the premium has been invested.

The investment and asset management activities of insurers are frequently referred to as the 'asset side' of their business. Their investment activities in equities and bonds provide a key link into the financial and capital markets and ultimately underpin the real economy. In 2021, the assets of insurance companies globally amounted to approximately US$40.3 trillion.[11] The UK insurance industry is one of the biggest institutional investors

8 Road Traffic Act 1988, s 143(1).

9 Employers' Liability (Compulsory Insurance) Act 1969, s 1(1).

10 E.g. solicitors' firms must have professional indemnity insurance under the SRA Indemnity Insurance Rule, r.3s; and insurance broker firms must have professional indemnity insurance under the FCA Handbook, Prudential Sourcebook for Mortgage and Home Finance Firms, and Insurance Intermediaries (MIPRU), 3.2.1R.

11 Statistica, 'Total Assets of Insurance Companies Worldwide from 2002 to 2021' <https://www.statista.com/statistics/421217/assets-of-global-insurance-companies/#:~:text=In%202020%2C%20the%20assets%20of%20insurance%20companies%20globally,by%20around%2024%20trillion%20U.S.%20dollars%20since%202002> accessed on 1 June 2023.

in the London stock market and across other asset classes; in 2021 it was managing over £1.7 trillion worth of assets – equivalent to approximately 25% of the UK's net worth.[12]

3.2 Insurability of climate change risks and protection gaps

3.2.1 Insurability

In their dual role as underwriters and investors, the insurance industry is well-placed to understand risks and their financial impacts. On the liability side, insurers must assess the size of the risk by reference to the probabilities with which one or several losses are expected to occur during the policy period and the amount of loss expected upon its occurrence. Not all risks are insurable, and some risks previously insurable can become uninsurable. Uninsurable risks display characteristics that make them unacceptable or unsuitable for insurance. Insurability is a fluid and multi-dimensional concept, and there are degrees of insurability on the spectrum ranging from high insurability to uninsurability. The following criteria usually indicate that a risk is insurable:[13]

1. the loss is accidental – the event that triggers the loss must be fortuitous;
2. the loss is definite – the time, place, and cause of loss must be identifiable;
3. the loss is calculable – the maximum exposure, the average loss per occurrence, the likely number of occurrences, and the associated costs of settling a claim can be assessed by actuarial-mathematical methods. This will usually be the case if there is historic claims data from a large number of similar exposure units;
4. limited exposure to catastrophic losses – the insurer's maximum exposure for one loss and for the totality of losses should be limited to what the insurer can pay without endangering its financial stability. Where the risk is correlated to other risks, the loss-spreading effect does not work well because the pooling effect is undermined.[14] The insurer itself will become risk averse;
5. affordable premium – even if the first four criteria are met, if the premium charged by the insurer is too high, potential policyholders are unlikely to buy insurance cover and will prefer to retain the risk of loss. The level of premium is a commercial criterion;
6. no legal and public policy restrictions – some losses cannot be insured as a matter of law and public policy. For example, under English law, a policyholder who does not have an insurable interest in the insured subject matter cannot insure.[15] The liability for criminal law fines and certain regulatory penalties cannot be insured for public policy reasons: the *ex turpi causa non oritur actio* maxim

12 Association of British Insurers ('ABI'), 'UK Insurance & Long-Term Savings Key Facts' (December 2022) <https://portfolio.cpl.co.uk/ABI-KeyFacts/2022/end/> accessed on 1 June 2023.

13 Baruch Berliner, 'Large Risks and Limits of Insurability' (1985) 10 *The Geneva Papers on Risk and Insurance – Issues and Practice*, 313, 325.

14 Ibid.

15 Marine Insurance Act 1906, s 4 (for marine insurance contracts); Life Assurance Act 1774, s 1 (for life insurance contracts); and common law for non-marine non-life insurance (see most recently *Western Trading Limited v Great Lakes Reinsurance (UK) Plc* [2015] EWHC 103 (QB), [2015] Lloyd's Rep IR 561; reversed in part on a different issue [2016] EWCA Civ 1003, [2016] Lloyd's Rep IR. 643).

holds that a person cannot recover damages or claim compensation caused by their own illegal acts.[16]

Conversely, risks that are catastrophic, too unpredictable in occurrence and effect, difficult to quantify and price, or that cannot be priced at an affordable level are uninsurable. In addition, there is a nascent trend for insurers to withdraw from underwriting carbon-intense activities in order to transition their underwriting portfolios to net-zero emissions.[17] For example, insurers who are members of the UN-convened Net-Zero Insurance Alliance ('NZIA'), a group of the world's leading insurers, have pledged to transition their underwriting portfolios to net-zero GHG emissions by 2050.[18] As more insurers and reinsurers will do so, the pressure on the remaining insurers who still underwrite carbon-intense activities will increase to follow suit: they will face reputational risk, litigation risk, and shareholder pressure for failing to do so, and they may find it difficult to reinsure.[19] As a result, premium levels charged for carbon-intense activities by the remaining insurers may increase, and some commentators have predicted that coal projects will soon become uninsurable.[20]

3.2.2 Climate change risks

Climate change risks are risks caused by or associated with climate change. In the insurance context, it has become customary to adopt a classification with three broad categories that was first introduced by Mark Carney, the former Governor of the Bank of England and UN Special Envoy on Climate Action and Finance and the UK Prime Minister's Finance Adviser for COP26, in his seminal speech 'Breaking the Tragedy of the Horizon – Climate Change and Financial Stability' at Lloyd's in 2015:[21] (1) physical risks, (2) transition risks, and (3) liability risks.

Physical risks: physical risks encompass losses from physical phenomena associated with climate change, such as windstorms, flooding, wildfires, and extreme weather.[22] Insurers differentiate between acute climate risks (e.g. floods, droughts, extreme weather, wildfires) and chronic climate risks (e.g. longer term shifts such as temperature rises, sea level rises, and coastal erosion). Loss can be direct (e.g. destruction of property) and indirect (e.g. business interruption and disrupted supply chains). Physical risks are not limited to property; they can also cause harm

16 *Safeway Stores Ltd v Twigger* [2010] EWCA Civ 1472, [2011] 2 All E.R. 841; also see: FCA Handbook, Enforcement Guide (EG), 7.5.3.

17 See Chapter 6, Section 6.4.3.

18 NZIA, 'Statement of Commitment by Signatory Companies' <https://www.unepfi.org/psi/wp-content/uploads/2021/07/NZIA-Commitment.pdf> accessed on 1 June 2023.

19 See Section 3.3.1.

20 See e.g. Insure Our Future, '2022 Scorecard on Insurance, Fossil Fuels and the Climate Emergency' (October 2022) 14–16 <https://insure-our-future.com/wp-content/uploads/2022/11/SP-IOF-2022-Scorecard-v0.8-online-1.pdf> accessed on 1 June 2023; John Quiggin, 'Coal Is on the Road to Becoming Completely Uninsurable' (*The Conversation*, 19 August 2019).

21 See: Mark Carney, 'Breaking the Tragedy of the Horizon – Climate Change and Financial Stability' (Speech at Lloyd's of London, September 2015) <https://www.bankofengland.co.uk/speech/2015/breaking-the-tragedy-of-the-horizon-climate-change-and-financial-stability> accessed on 1 June 2023.

22 Ibid.

to human life and health. The Geneva Association draws a distinction between climate change risks (including physical, transition, and liability risks associated with climate change) and a narrower sub-category of 'climate risk' which only encompasses acute physical risks,[23] and this distinction shall be adopted for this book.

Transition risks: counteracting climate change requires a substantial reduction of global GHG emissions to limit the global temperature increase to well below 2°C while pursuing efforts to limit the increase to 1.5°C above pre-industrial levels (the Paris Agreement 'long-term temperature goal').[24] This process of transitioning can cause disruption, affect the value of assets, and result in additional transaction costs and other costs associated with adjusting to a lower carbon economy. Key examples of transition risks, as identified by the IAIS, are policy changes, law reforms, changes in investors' attitudes towards carbon-intense assets, societal activism posing a risk of reputational damage to enterprises that do not engage sufficiently in the transition process, new renewable energy technologies (such as wind and solar power) entering the market, and the disruption of supply chains that were dependent on carbon-intense industries and materials.[25]

Liability risks: liability risk arises from climate-related litigation. A party who has suffered a climate-related loss may seek compensation from another party who can be held responsible for that loss, including for action or inaction relating to climate change mitigation and adaptation, or insufficient or inaccurate disclosure in relation to climate risks. Over 2,000 climate change cases are currently being litigated in more than 40 jurisdictions.[26] The types of lawsuits brought include:

1. administrative cases against governments and public bodies challenging decisions on the grounds of failure to mitigate or adapt to climate change (e.g. *Urgenda* litigation in the Netherlands[27] and the constitutional claim against the German government by BUND and Greenpeace[28]);
2. tortious claims in nuisance, product liability, trespass, misrepresentation, or negligence by members of the public, pressure groups, or public bodies against corporations active in the carbon sector (e.g. *Lliuya v RWE AG* in the German courts[29]);

23 The Geneva Association, 'Anchoring Climate Change Risk Assessment in Core Business Decisions in Insurance' (September 2022) 14 <https://www.genevaassociation.org/publication/climate-change-and-environment/climate-change-risk-3-report> accessed on 1 June 2023.

24 See Chapter 2, Section 2.3.3.

25 IAIS and the Sustainable Insurance Forum ('SIF'), 'Issues Paper on Climate Change Risks to the Insurance Sector' 15 (July 2018) <https://www.iaisweb.org/page/supervisory-material/issues-papers> accessed on 1 June 2023.

26 Sabin Center for Climate Change Law (January 2023) <http://climatecasechart.com/about/> accessed on 1 June 2023.

27 Decision of the Supreme Court of the Netherlands dated 19 December 2019 in *State of the Netherlands (Ministry of Economic Affairs and Climate Policy) v Stichting Urgenda*, Case No. 19/00135 (English translation available on <https://www.urgenda.nl/wp-content/uploads/ENG-Dutch-Supreme-Court-Urgenda-v-Netherlands-20-12-2019.pdf> accessed on 1 June 2023).

28 Decision by the Bundesverfassungsgericht dated 24 March 2021 – BVerfG, Beschluss des Ersten Senats vom 24. März 2021, 1 BvR 2656/18 -, Rn. 1-270 <http://www.bverfg.de/e/rs20210324_1bvr265618.html> accessed on 1 June 2023.

29 Decision of the 5. Zivilsenat des Oberlandesgerichts Hamm dated 30 November 2017 in *Lliuya v RWE AG*, Case No. Az.5 U 15/17 OLG Hamm) (English translation available on <https://climatecasechart.com/wp

3. shareholder/investor actions against corporations and their boards for failing to account for possible risks to carbon-intensive assets or for failing to account for or disclose risks to business models and value chains in financial reporting (e.g. *In re Exxon Mobil Corp. Derivative Litigation* in the US[30]);
4. stakeholder actions against corporations and their boards for 'green-washing' their corporate information by misrepresenting their climate impact, level of climate action, or environmental standards[31] (e.g. Deutsche Bank DWS has been sued by consumer groups in relation to a statement in marketing material that it invests 0% in controversial sectors such as coal[32]);
5. regulatory investigations in relation to inadequate or inaccurate disclosure of climate risks and benefits in public corporate documentation or product information (e.g. BNY Mellon's investment adviser division was fined $1.5 million by the US Security Exchange Commission (SEC) in 2022 to settle allegations that it had misstated and omitted ESG information for mutual funds under its management[33]).

Chronic physical risks are not insurable as they happen gradually over a longer time horizon and, therefore, lack in definition (criterion 2). They arguably also lack in fortuity (criterion 1) as the shift in climate patterns, and the impacts on natural and human systems, are already in the process of happening.

Some acute physical risks are, or could become, uninsurable. Acute physical risks associated with climate change are increasing in frequency and severity.[34] The effect of these acute physical risks can be compounded by the exposure (e.g. hurricanes cause more damage in urban and industrialised areas) and the vulnerability[35] (e.g. the lack of capacity to respond to droughts and wildfires) of affected communities and ecological systems.[36] Insurers are already using climate-conditioned weather-related catastrophe models by adjusting the catalogue of events either by selecting events that are more likely under future climate conditions or by adjusting the attributes of the events (e.g. in terms of frequency or severity) to reflect future climate conditions.[37] As insurance pay-outs for

-content/uploads/non-us-case-documents/2017/20171130_Case-No.-2-O-28515-Essen-Regional-Court_order.pdf> accessed on 1 June 2023).

30 *In re Exxon Mobil Corp. Derivative Litigation*, Case No. 3:19-cv-16380 D.N.J. (Complaint filed available on <http://climatecasechart.com/case/saratoga-advantage-trust-energy-basic-materials-portfolio-v-woods/> accessed on 1 June 2023).

31 Climate risk is a sub-set of environmental risk which also include risks associated with the damage and pollution of water and marine resources and the degradation of biodiversity and ecosystems – see Chapter 2, Section 2.4.1.

32 *Reuters*, 'Deutsche Bank's DWS Sued by Consumer Group over Alleged Greenwashing' (24 October 2022).

33 SEC, 'SEC Charges BNY Mellon Investment Adviser for Misstatements and Omissions Concerning ESG Considerations' (Press Release 22 May 2022) <https://www.sec.gov/news/press-release/2022-86#:~:text=The%20Securities%20and%20Exchange%20Commission%20today%20charged%20BNY,Adviser%20agreed%20to%20pay%20a%20%241.5%20million%20penalty> accessed on 1 June 2023.

34 See Chapter 2, Section 2.2.2.

35 Vulnerability is defined as the 'propensity or predisposition to be adversely affected and encompasses a variety of concepts and elements, including sensitivity or susceptibility to harm and lack of capacity to cope and adapt' in the IPCC 2022 Adaptation Report [5, fn 8].

36 IPCC 2022 Adaptation Report, Summary for Policymakers [5].

37 Organisation for Economic Co-operation and Development (OECD), 'Enhancing the Insurance Sector's Contribution to Climate Adaptation,' OECD Business and Finance Policy Papers (OECD Publishing 2023) ('OECD Insurance and Adaptation Paper') <https://doi.org/10.1787/0951dfcd-en> accessed on 1 June 2023.

weather-related losses have grown significantly over the last 50 years – with US$105 billion in 2021, the fourth highest since 1970[38] – premiums increase and could potentially render insurance unaffordable (criterion 5), and/or insurers could withdraw insurance cover from particular perils or geographical areas because losses have become incalculable (criterion 3) and/or too catastrophic and correlated to other risks (criterion 4). For example, following the 2019/2020 bushfires in Australia, two of Australia's biggest insurers – Suncorp and IAG – temporarily suspended selling insurance in fire-affected areas of Victoria and New South Wales.[39] Australia's Climate Council has found that 'one in 25 Australian properties will be effectively uninsurable by 2030, due to rising risks of extreme weather and climate change.'[40] In California, some homeowners can no longer buy any property insurance covering wildfires, while others can no longer afford to buy insurance because of spiralling premium prices.[41] US insurer State Farm has stopped writing California property business for a number of reasons including because of the 'rapidly growing catastrophe exposure.'[42] The Insurance Bureau of Canada estimated that 10% of Canadian homes are now uninsurable due to extreme weather.[43] A study by Tesselaar et al. on the impacts of climate change on EU flood insurance markets shows that, in the context of climate change, the gradual increase of premiums for flood insurance will result in a growing number of existing policyholders who will no longer be able to afford flood insurance in the future.[44]

Transition risks, such as regulatory, technological, reputational, and market risk, are generally not insurable as they lack specificity (criterion 2), calculability (criterion 3), and insurable interest (criterion 6). The scope of transition risk is difficult to define as market, technological, and regulatory changes and stakeholder attitudes affecting reputational risk intersect to trigger a change in business dynamics in the underlying sector. Different sectors and geographic locations are affected in many different ways. The changes may be gradual, rather than attributable to a specific event, and any harmful effects may be difficult to isolate from other macro- and microeconomic variables unrelated to transition risks.[45] The harm caused by transition risks is not the physical loss of or damage to assets

38 See Swiss Re Group, 'Global Insured Catastrophe Losses Rise to USD 112 Billion in 2021, the Fourth Highest on Record' (1 June 2023) <https://www.swissre.com/media/press-release/nr-20211214-sigma-full-year-2021-preliminary-natcat-loss-estimates.html#:~:text=Global%20insured%20catastrophe%20losses%20rise%20to%20USD%20112,given%20increases%20in%20wealth%2C%20urbanisation%20and%20climate%20change> accessed on 1 June 2023.

39 Ben Butler, 'Suncorp and IAG Temporarily Stop Selling Insurance in Fire-Affected Areas of Victoria and NSW' (*The Guardian*, 14 January 2020).

40 Climate Council, 'One in 25 Australian Homes Uninsurable by 2030: Climate Council Launches Cutting Edge Digital Climate-Risk Map' (Press Release 3 May 2022) <https://www.climatecouncil.org.au/resources/australian-homes-uninsurable-2030-climate-risk-map/> accessed on 1 June 2023.

41 Mary Williams Walsh, 'How Wildfires Are Making Some California Homes Uninsurable' (*The New York Times*, 20 November 2018).

42 Steve Evans, 'State Farm Stops Writing California Property, Cites Exposure & Reinsurance Challenges' (*Reinsurance News*, 29 May 2023).

43 Leyland Cecco, 'The Uninsurables: How Storms and Rising Seas Are Making Coastlines Unlivable' (*The Guardian*, 13 October 2022).

44 Max Tesselaar, W.J. Wouter Botzen, and Jeroen C.J.H. Aerts, 'Impacts of Climate Change and Remote Natural Catastrophes on EU Flood Insurance Markets: An Analysis of Soft and Hard Reinsurance Markets for Flood Coverage' (2020) 11 *Atmosphere*, 146.

45 UN Environment Programme's Principles for Sustainable Insurance Initiative, 'Insuring the Climate Transition – Enhancing the Insurance Industry's Assessment of Climate Change Futures' (January 2021) sec 3.1.2 <https://www.unepfi.org/industries/insurance/insuring-the-climate-transition/> accessed on 1 June 2023.

but would be a financial loss as reflected in a reduction in asset or share value. There is no insurable interest in speculative and unascertainable future profits.[46]

In relation to liability risk, the liability for compensation payable to third parties and defence costs are generally insurable, whereas specific legal rules and public policy may prohibit indemnification in relation to regulatory penalties and criminal law fines (criterion 6). At the time of writing, climate liability risk shows no signs of becoming uninsurable and instead is being embraced by insurers as a risk to be managed as well as presenting business opportunities for new products.[47]

3.2.3 Simple risks and complex risks

The insurance and sociology literature conceives of insurance as a governance tool to manage and control risk[48] and distinguishes between simple risks and complex risks. Simple risks can be assessed actuarily by calculating the likelihood of financial loss.[49] Financial losses associated with simple risks can be minimised by solutions designed and administered by technical experts (insurers and/or government agencies).[50] But many risks are not simple and cannot be calculated as a linear function of probability and effects – they are complex, because they display interconnected cause and effect relationships and cascading effects, they are uncertain because they are influenced by policy and subjective decisions, and they are ambiguous because there are different viewpoints on the extent to which these risks are tolerable and whether and how they should be addressed.[51] As acute physical risks associated with climate change are increasing in frequency and severity, and their effects can be compounded by the exposure and the vulnerability of affected communities and ecological systems,[52] they can no longer be assessed by actuarial means and reach the limit of insurability.[53] The degree and extent of climate action fighting climate change are dictated by political commitment, policy decisions, laws, and funding at multiple levels.[54] The severity of climate risk and climate change risk is influenced by the rate of global warming which in turn is dependent on policy decisions taken that determine the GHG emission reduction pathway.[55] The complexity of climate risk in conjunction with the high degree of

46 *Lucena v Craufurd* (1806) 2 Bos. & P. N.R. 269, 321.

47 See e.g.: Marsh, 'Delta Side D: Cover for Investigation Costs Related to TCFD Reporting' which provides liability insurance cover for investigations costs arising from a climate disclosure-related investigation <https://www.marsh.com/uk/services/financial-professional-liability/products/delta-side-d-cover-investigation-costs-tcfd-reporting.html> accessed on 1 June 2023.

48 Richard V. Ericson, Aaron Doyle, Diana Ericson. and Dean Barry, *Insurance as Governance* (University of Toronto Press 2003); F. Ewald (n 5); Tom Baker and Jonathan Simon, 'Embracing Risk' in Tom Baker and Jonathan Simon (eds.) *Embracing Risk – The Changing Culture of Insurance and Insurability* (University of Chicago Press 2002) and see Section 3.4.4.

49 See Section 3.1.

50 For an overview of the literature on simple and complex risk, see: Maureen Essen, Sarah McCaffey, Jesse Abrams, and Travis Paveglio, 'Improving Wildfire Management Outcomes: Shifting the Paradigm of Wildfire from Simple to Complex Risk' (2023) 66(5) *Journal of Environmental Planning and Management*, 909, Sec.2.1.

51 Marjolein van Asselt and Ortwin Renn, 'Risk Governance' (2011) 14(4) *Journal of Risk Research*, 431, Sec.4.

52 See Section 3.2.2.

53 Ulrich Beck, *The Risk Society: Towards a New Modernity* (SAGE Publications Ltd 1992).

54 IPCC 2022 Sixth Assessment Report [4.7].

55 See Chapter 2, Section 2.2.3.

concentration in climate risk exposures in some geographical areas and in some industries, exacerbated by existing vulnerabilities,[56] mean that climate risks could even pose a systemic threat to the stability of the financial system as a whole beyond the financial risks faced by individual institutions.[57]

Although SHIP, for the first time, acknowledges that a 'Loss and Damage Fund' must be set up to respond to the negative consequences that arise from the unavoidable risks of climate change,[58] the protracted negotiations relating to the fund show that there is no firm consensus as to whether, how, and by whom these risks should be addressed. There continue to be influential climate change denial theories.[59] Conceptually, given that physical climate risks are characterised by complexity, uncertainty, and ambiguity, they can be classified as 'complex risks.'[60]

3.2.4 Protection gaps

Uninsurable climate change risks give rise to 'protection gaps.' 'Insurance protection gaps' have been defined as the difference between the amount of insurance that is economically beneficial and the amount of coverage actually purchased, whereas 'risk protection gaps' are defined as the difference between total economic losses and insured losses.[61] Thus, the 'insurance protection gap' focuses on what insurance should be in place, whereas the 'risk protection gap' is a mere mathematical calculation of the uninsured losses. Feiman argues that the insurance protection gap – to what extent insurance should be in place but is not – must discount uninsurable risks as those risks could never be insured.[62] This however disregards the fluidity of the boundary between insurability and uninsurability when it comes to affordability: a risk that is inherently insurable can become commercially uninsurable if premium levels rise above what policyholders can afford. There are a number of causes for protection gaps, including buyer-side reasons such as behavioural biases, social and cultural factors, and lack of trust in insurers or insurance products, but the main concerns in relation to protection gaps for physical climate risks are uninsurability and the lack of access to relevant insurance products.

Between 2011 and 2021, total economic losses from natural catastrophes were US$2,419.5 billion of which only US$890.9 billion was insured (37%), leaving a protection

---

56 See Section 3.2.4.

57 PRA, 'Supervisory Statement: Enhancing Banks' and Insurers' Approaches to Managing the Financial Risks from Climate Change' SS3/19 (April 2019) [2.5]–[2.6]; Domenico Curcio, Igor Gianfrancesco, and Davide Vioto, 'Climate Change and Financial Systemic Risk: Evidence from US Banks and Insurers' (2023) 66 *Journal of Financial Stability*, 101.

58 UN Framework Convention on Climate Change, 'Decision -/CP.27: Sharm el-Sheikh Implementation Plan' (22 November 2022), art 46.

59 See e.g. Damian Carrington, 'The Four Types of Climate Denier, and Why You Should Ignore Them All' (*The Guardian*, 30 July 2020).

60 Physical climate risks have been described as complex risks in the IPCC 2022 Sixth Assessment Report, Figure 4.3.

61 The Geneva Association, 'Understanding and Addressing Global Insurance Protection Gaps' (April 2018), 8 <https://www.genevaassociation.org/sites/default/files/research-topics-document-type/pdf_public/understanding_and_addressing_global_insurance_protection_gaps.pdf> accessed on 1 June 2023.

62 Jay Feiman, 'What Is a Protection Gap? Homeowners Insurance as a Case Study' (2020) 27(1) *Conn Ins LJ*, Pt II(C).

gap of US$1,528.6 billion (63%).[63] Protection gaps vary between geographical locations: for example, in the UK the protection gap has been 25% (US$3.3 billion), from 2011 to 2021.[64] The explanation for this comparatively small protection gap is that, in the UK, where flooding is the most prevalent weather-related risk, homes located in areas prone to flooding have remained insurable due to a statutory scheme – Flood Re – funded through cross-subsidies from properties not exposed to flood risk.[65] In contrast, China, which is vulnerable to flooding and storms, has had a protection gap of 95% (US$283.4 billion) for the same period.[66] In lower middle- and lower-income countries natural catastrophe risk protection gaps persisting are in excess of 95%.[67]

Some of the least developed but most vulnerable countries do not have mature insurance markets through which relevant insurance products can be distributed and administered, and a significant proportion of individuals and small businesses may lack risk awareness and the financial literacy to understand what insurance has to offer.[68] Concerns about an unstable legal environment and the prospect of small uptake may not justify the set-up and transaction costs for insurers.[69] Although new technologies (such as selling insurance via apps) and new insurance products (micro-insurance and community-based natural catastrophe cover)[70] have helped to give access, insurance protection remains unavailable and out of reach for many in lower middle- and lower-income countries.[71]

Protection gaps in relation to property exposed to climate risk can result in a significant financial burden for uninsured losses on affected individuals and enterprises. Without insurance, they are less likely to have the financial resilience to withstand a negative shock to their assets and income and to absorb increased expenditure. The IPCC Report Climate Change 2022 Report on 'Impacts, Adaptation and Vulnerability' highlights that, across sectors and regions, the most vulnerable people and systems are disproportionately affected by physical climate risks:

> Regions and people with considerable development constraints have high vulnerability to climatic hazards (high confidence). Global hotspots of high human vulnerability are found particularly in West-, Central- and East Africa, South Asia, Central and South America, Small Island Developing States and the Arctic (high confidence). Vulnerability is higher in locations with poverty, governance challenges and limited access to basic services and resources, violent conflict and high levels of climate-sensitive livelihoods (e.g., smallholder farmers, pastoralists, fishing communities) (high confidence). Between 2010–2020, human mortality from floods, droughts and storms was 15 times higher in highly vulnerable regions, compared to regions with very low vulnerability (high confidence) … Present development challenges

63 Swiss Re Institute, 'Natural Catastrophes: The Protection Gap' (interactive tool for protection gaps in natural catastrophe risk) <https://www.swissre.com/risk-knowledge/mitigating-climate-risk/natcat-country-profiles-infographic.html#/> accessed on 1 June 2023.

64 Ibid.

65 See Flood Re <https://www.floodre.co.uk/> accessed on 1 June 2023 and see Chapter 9, Section 9.4.2.

66 Swiss Re Institute (n 63).

67 The Geneva Association (n 61) 6, 10–12.

68 Ibid 26.

69 Ibid 29–30; Ceres, 'Inclusive Insurance for Climate-Related Disasters: A Roadmap for the United States' (January 2023) 8–9 <https://www.ceres.org/sites/default/files/reports/2023-01/Inclusive%20Insurance%20Report.pdf> accessed on 1 June 2023.

70 See e.g. some of the projects led by the UNCCC Munich Climate Insurance Initiative <https://climate-insurance.org/> accessed on 1 June 2023 and also see Chapter 8, Section 8.5.1.

71 The Geneva Association (n 61) 6, 10–12.

causing high vulnerability are influenced by historical and ongoing patterns of inequity such as colonialism.[72]

> Future human vulnerability will continue to concentrate where the capacities of local, municipal and national governments, communities and the private sector are least able to provide infrastructures and basic services (high confidence). Under the global trend of urbanization, human vulnerability will also concentrate in informal settlements and rapidly growing smaller settlements (high confidence) … Vulnerability will also rapidly rise in low-lying Small Island Developing States and atolls in the context of sea level rise and in some mountain regions, already characterised by high vulnerability due to high dependence on climate-sensitive livelihoods, rising population displacement, the accelerating loss of ecosystem services and limited adaptive capacities (high confidence).[73]

The April 2022 floods in South Africa exemplify the interaction of climate risk with many of the vulnerabilities noted by the IPCC: marginalised communities living in informal settlements on land prone to flooding, who had been forcibly relocated there as a legacy of Apartheid, were the most severely affected by the flooding.[74] However, the disproportionate effect on vulnerable people and communities is not limited to the least developed and developing countries. A recent report by Ceres highlights that in the US, people with low and moderate incomes and people of colour are disproportionately harmed by loss and damage caused by coastal storms and hurricanes, extreme rainfall, flooding, and wildfires.[75] This is driven by many factors, including that they may live in areas more prone to those risks and in housing stock that is not sufficiently resilient to withstand those risks, they may face barriers to receiving the necessary information and resources for preparedness and evacuation, and they have no financial safety net to cope with the loss of property, unexpected expenses, and a coinciding reduction in income.[76]

Where protection gaps lead to hardship and have cascading effects on economic activities, supply chains, and the performance of loans and investments across the financial system,[77] governments will be under pressure to step in to offer financial relief. This may have indirect consequential effects on taxation or budgetary constraints in other areas.[78] Developing countries may have insufficient funds to respond to loss and damage associated with the adverse effects of climate change. As a result, natural catastrophes can escalate into humanitarian crises, compounding food and water insecurity, displacement, and the precarity of the livelihoods of local communities,[79] as well as contributing to the growing debt burden of those countries.[80] These protection gaps and their consequences

72 IPCC 2022 Adaptation Report, Summary for Policymakers [B.2.4].

73 Ibid [B.2.5].

74 World Weather Attribution, 'Climate Change-Exacerbated Rainfall Causing Devastating Flooding in Eastern South Africa' (13 May 2022) <https://www.worldweatherattribution.org/climate-change-exacerbated-rainfall-causing-devastating-flooding-in-eastern-south-africa/> accessed on 1 June 2023.

75 Ceres (n 69) 8–9.

76 Ibid 1.

77 IAIS (n 25) 14.

78 ECB and EIOPA, 'Policy Options to Reduce the Climate Insurance Protection Gap – Discussion Paper' (April 2023) [1.1–1.3] <https://www.eiopa.europa.eu/system/files/2023-04/ecb.policyoptions_EIOPA~c0adae58b7.en_.pdf> accessed on 1 June 2023.

79 SHIP sec VI, art 44.

80 SHIP sec VI, art 45.

have been acknowledged by the international community[81] and in the literature[82] for many years. While regional risk pools have been set up to address some of these protection gaps,[83] it was only at the COP27 meeting in Sharm el-Sheikh in 2022 that the international community acknowledged for the first time that a 'Loss and Damage Fund' must be set up to respond to the negative consequences that arise from the unavoidable risks of climate change.[84]

Although the mechanisms for and contributions to the Loss and Damages Fund are still being negotiated, the role of insurance is already crystallising: the insurance industry will contribute with their expertise and potentially further funding, including through the 'Global Shield against Climate Risks'[85] and the 'InsuResilience Global Partnership Vision 2025'[86] initiatives for climate and disaster risk finance and insurance. These initiatives will be discussed further in Chapter 9.

Protection gaps can also arise as a result of climate action: some insurers have started to withdraw from underwriting carbon-intense activities in order to transition their underwriting portfolios to net-zero emissions.[87] Decreased underwriting capacity could push up premium levels charged, or even impact the availability of insurance cover, for carbon-intense activities. While this may look like a welcome development, there is increased transition risk to other industries that are still reliant on coal and fossil fuels, which in turn could impact other businesses along supply chains, and ultimately consumers. Therefore, when designing insurance strategies to combat climate change, one consideration should be the avoidance of new protection gaps where insurance portfolios are transitioned to net-zero too rapidly or where the costs of transitioning to net-zero are too high. This will be considered further in Chapters 6 and 7.

3.3 The interaction between climate change, climate change risk, and insurance

Having considered the insurability of climate change risks, this section (1) examines how climate change risks have already impacted, and can affect, an insurer's business ('inward impact'); and (2) sets the scene for exploring how an insurer's operations and value chains have and can have an external impact on the climate and climate change ('outward impact'). Together, inward and outward impact are referred to as 'double materiality,' a concept that derives from 'materiality' in climate-related reporting and which

81 UNFCCC, 'Conference of the Parties Decision 3/CP.18: Approaches to Address Loss and Damage Associated with Climate Change Impacts in Developing Countries That Are Particularly Vulnerable to the Adverse Effects of Climate Change to Enhance Adaptive Capacity' <https://unfccc.int/documents/7643#beg> accessed on 1 June 2023; Warsaw International Mechanism for Loss and Damage Associated with Climate Change Impacts, established at COP19 (November 2013) in Warsaw, Poland <https://unfccc.int/topics/adaptation-and-resilience/workstreams/loss-and-damage/warsaw-international-mechanism> accessed on 1 June 2023.

82 For a summary, see: The Geneva Association (n 61).

83 See Chapter 9, Section 9.5.1.

84 SHIP sec VII, art 46.

85 Partnership of the V20 Concept for Consultation and German G7 Presidency, 'Global Shield against Climate Risks' (November 2022) <https://www.bmz.de/resource/blob/127498/global-shield-against-climate-risks-concept-barrierefrei.pdf> accessed on 1 June 2023.

86 InsuResilience Global Partnership, 'InsuResilience Global Partnership Vision 2025' (July 2021) <https://www.insuresilience.org/wp-content/uploads/2022/10/vision2025_211022-1.pdf> accessed on 1 June 2023.

87 See Chapter 6, Section 6.4.3.

was first formally proposed by the European Commission in 2019.[88] As will be discussed in Chapter 5, double materiality has already become a central building block of the EU legislative architecture on sustainability reporting and disclosures for companies and financial firms. Inward and outward impact are themes that are introduced at this juncture and are then developed in the following chapters.

3.3.1 Inward impact: the impact of climate change risk on insurers

Climate change risk poses a threat to an insurer's financial stability, and ultimately its ability to provide insurance cover and pay claims. Table 3.1[89] shows how physical risk, transition risk, and liability risk can have negative financial impacts on both the liability side and the asset side of an insurer's balance sheet.

3.3.2 Outward impact: the impact of insurers on the climate and climate change

As explained in Chapter 2 (Section 2.2), anthropogenic GHG emissions are the dominant cause of a warming of the atmosphere, the oceans, and the land leading to changes in the climate system. An insurer's outward impact therefore needs to be considered in relation to GHG emissions it directly or indirectly generates, any other harmful impacts on the climate system, and processes and activities it engages in to reduce GHG emissions or remove GHG from the atmosphere. Following the introduction of the Greenhouse Gas Protocol in 2001 which sets reporting and accounting standards for GHG emissions,[90] it has become customary to classify GHG emissions from an organisation within three 'scopes':

- Scope 1 – direct GHG emissions: refers to the direct emissions from a company's own or controlled operations, such as from generating electricity, chemical processes, transportation, and fugitive emissions from equipment leaks;
- Scope 2 – electricity-related indirect GHG emissions: refers to indirect emissions from purchased or acquired electricity, steam, heat, and cooling;
- Scope 3 – value chain-related indirect GHG emissions: refers to all other indirect emissions that are not caught in Scope 2 and are generated throughout an organisation's value chain.

Scope 3 includes GHG emissions from (1) purchased goods and services (office supplies – e.g. plastic paperclips); (2) capital goods (equipment, machinery, buildings, facilities, and vehicles); (3) fuel- and energy-related activities to the extent they are not captured in Scopes 1 and 2; (4) upstream transportation and distribution (delivery of products and

88 Communication from the Commission, 'Guidelines on Non-Financial Reporting: Supplement on Reporting Climate-Related Information' (June 2019) 2019/C 209/01.

89 This table has been adapted, and developed further, from: IAIS (n 25) 16–17 Table 1; and The Geneva Association, 'Climate Change Risk Assessment for the Insurance Industry' (February 2021) 16–19 <https://www.genevaassociation.org/publication/climate-change-and-environment/climate-change-risk-assessment-insurance-industry> accessed on 1 June 2023.

90 The World Business Council for Sustainable Development and the World Resources Institute, 'The Greenhouse Gas Protocol: A Corporate Accounting and Reporting Standard' (2004) <https://ghgprotocol.org/corporate-standard> accessed on 1 June 2023.

Table 3.1 Inward impact of climate change risk on insurers

Climate change risks	*Liability side/underwriting business*	*Asset side/investment activities*
Physical risks: potential negative financial impacts that could arise from direct physical effects on assets and property and in indirect impacts such as business interruption and interrupted supply chains due to extreme weather events (acute risks) and long-term shifts in climate patterns (chronic risks) caused by climate change.	*Pricing and underwriting risk*: in non-life insurance, pricing and underwriting risks arise from changing risk profiles to insured assets and property. If the insurer does not assess the risk profile of the insured asset correctly, the premium charged may not be sufficient to cover its liability for claims and expenses, and to make a profit. Although risk exposure can be adjusted via annual premium pricing, limited historical data makes it difficult to isolate what impact physical climate risks will have compared to other loss drivers, and to what extent they can coincide with other uncorrelated events and loss factors in non-linear ways. If premium has been under-priced, this could inhibit claims payments (see: claims risk – below). If risk-based premium pricing rises beyond demand and customers' willingness to pay, assets and property exposed to physical climate risks can become uninsurable. This can create protection gaps (see above). In life-related insurance, there may be pricing risk due to changing mortality profiles and demographic trends (life and health). For example, heat-related health issues associated with extreme weather events can compound pre-existing health conditions or vulnerabilities. Climate-related catastrophic weather events can also increase mortality. At the reinsurance level, the availability and cost of reinsurance cover for weather-related risks may become prohibitive for smaller insurers in certain markets – potentially leading to reinsurance gaps (which in turn is likely to result in underwriting capacity constraints and lead to further insurance protection gaps).	*Investment risk*: the profitability of insurer investment portfolios may be affected if invested in sectors, property portfolios, or financial assets which may be at risk from physical climate risks such as flooding, wildfires, and windstorms. Physical climate risks, such as extreme weather, may affect the credit ratings of sovereigns and the credit quality of municipal bonds, through direct losses to infrastructure, as well as impacts on economic activity and revenue base.
	Claims risk: the effects of physical climate risk risks, especially the confluence of extreme weather events (e.g. hurricane and flooding at the same time and in the same location) and the increased frequency and severity of such events (e.g. multiple hurricanes in short succession in the same location), are likely to manifest in a worsening claims experience, or an unexpectedly high claims burden, for weather-related perils. A volatile claims experience can cause liquidity issues. Increasing claims will require insurers to re-assess and adjust their technical provisions and solvency capital requirements which in turn may lead to the need for further matching asset or limiting their underwriting capacity (see Chapter 4 and Chapter 8).	

(Continued)

Table 3.1 Continued

Climate change risks	*Liability side/underwriting business*	*Asset side/investment activities*
	Strategic/market risks: if only a few insurers increase premium to adjust to increasing physical climate risks, these insurers may become uncompetitive. This could result in significant portions of an insurer's underwriting business falling away due to lack of demand, affect its market share, and create a strategic risk to overall business viability. If premium pricing increases beyond what customers are willing to pay or can afford to pay, assets and property exposed to physical climate change risks can become uninsurable, creating protection gaps (see above).	
	Operational risk: insurers' own assets (property, IT systems, human resources) and supply chains may be affected by physical climate risks, leading to increasing operational costs which could restrict underwriting capacity or interrupt operations.	
Transition risks: potential negative financial impacts that could result from the process of transitioning towards a low-carbon economy.	*Pricing, underwriting, and claims risks*: transition climate risks can have an effect on the risk profile of insured assets. If the insurer does not assess the risk profile of the insured asset correctly, the premium charged may not be sufficient to cover its liability for claims and expenses and to make a profit. If premium has been under-priced, this could inhibit claims payments.	*Investment risk*: the profitability of an insurer's investment portfolios may be affected if invested in sectors, property portfolios, or financial assets which may be at risk from transition climate risks, such as regulatory risk, market risk, technology risk, and reputational risk (see below).
	Regulatory risk: increasingly, there will be national and regional policy and regulatory measures to limit emissions and to promote climate-friendly adaptation. This could impact the insured value of assets (e.g. in the fossil fuel sector, and for real estate that does not meet environmental performance factors).	*Regulatory risk*: increasingly, there will be national and regional policy and regulatory measures to limit emissions or promote climate-friendly adaptation. This (together with technological changes and changes in societal attitudes – see below) could result in stranded assets (assets which no longer have a market to be traded) in the high carbon/fossil fuel sectors.
	Strategic/market risk: climate change risks are likely to affect the insurance demands and needs of individuals and enterprises. If an insurer does not/cannot respond with appropriately designed products to satisfy new customer demands and needs at an affordable premium level this could significantly affect its market share and create a strategic risk to overall business viability. Insurers also face market risk when developing new 'green' insurance products: insufficient customer demand, potentially high research and development costs, and the risk of free riders (other insurers adopting the same or similar products once developed but without incurring the research and development costs).	*Market risk*: as the high carbon/fossil fuel sectors become vulnerable to regulatory risk, technological innovation in renewable energy and reputational pressures, these sectors may become less productive or even unviable. As a result, the value of investments in those sectors could become more volatile, decrease, and even result in stranded assets. Sectors that heavily rely on fossil fuels (e.g. transport, steel production) may experience supply chain issues as a result of the fossil fuel sector becoming less productive, impacting on their own productivity, and consequently the value of investments in those sectors. Life insurers who offer life and annuity products where the investment return on the premium is a core component of the product are likely to see demand for products that pursue green or sustainable investment strategies. If that demand cannot be met, this will eventually affect their market share.

(Continued)

Table 3.1 Continued

Climate change risks	*Liability side/underwriting business*	*Asset side/investment activities*
	Technology risk: innovations in energy technologies can create new opportunities for insurers (e.g. new types of cover targeting renewable energy-specific risks, such as shortfall). Insurers who do not respond in a timely manner to market demands could miss out on market share (see above). The risk assessment and premium pricing for insurance cover for new energy technologies may however be based on limited historical data which can create pricing and underwriting risk (see above). New energy technologies can also be vulnerable to sudden policy changes which affect risk profiles of insured assets or affect market growth. New technologies may have physical characteristics that pose higher risks than their conventional equivalents (e.g. location in vulnerable geographies, materials used are more susceptible to physical damage, and reliance on emerging technologies).	*Technology risk*: technological innovations can disrupt existing business models, markets, and supply chains. This can have a negative effect on the value of investments in conventional structures – in extreme cases, rendering the underlying business obsolete and turning it into a stranded asset. Innovative technologies can present investment opportunities, but prototypical technologies with little track-record can also be volatile investments. Innovative technologies themselves are vulnerable to becoming obsolete as and when better and more cost-effective technologies in the same field are developed.
	Reputational risk: as awareness levels of climate change increase, it is becoming a civil society issue and there are increasing numbers of social movements calling for limits on emissions and for climate-friendly adaptation. Insurers who fail to put in place strategies for impact underwriting (see below – e.g. withdrawing from underwriting carbon-intense/fossil fuel projects) may suffer reputational harm. They will compare unfavourably to their peers who have such strategies and may be the subject of negative publicity, resulting in loss of market share, and create a strategic risk to overall business viability. Premium increases or previously insured risks becoming uninsurable may also lead to reputational harm. Withdrawing from underwriting carbon-intense activities is likely to affect existing relationships with customers in affected industries.	*Reputational risk*: insurers who fail to put in place strategies for impact investment (see below – e.g. divesting from carbon-intense/fossil fuel projects) may suffer reputational harm. They will compare unfavourably to their peers who have such strategies and may be the subject of negative publicity, resulting in loss of market share, and create a strategic risk to overall business viability. Increased scrutiny as result of emerging disclosure standards (see below) is likely to increase reputational risk for those insurers who do engage with outward impact.
Liability risks: climate-related litigation claims	*Liability cover claims risk*: insurers are exposed to liability risk and defence costs if their policy wordings provide cover under specialist environmental liability policies or silent cover under more general liability policies. The insured's liability can arise from being held responsible for contributing to climate change, or failing to mitigate or adapt to climate change, or non-compliance, non-disclosure, and corporate governance failures in relation to climate change. The frequency and diversity of legal actions concerned with climate change are increasing (see above).	*Direct litigation risk* (actions against insurers): can arise from actions brought against insurers directly relating to the consideration of climate change in investment decision-making, or inadequate disclosure of climate change risks in public documents or product information.

supplies); (5) waste generated in operations; (6) business travel; (7) employee commuting; (8) upstream leased assets; (9) downstream transportation and distribution (e.g. sending marketing materials to insurance distributors and policy documentation to customers); (10) processing of sold products; (11) use of sold products; (12) end-of-life treatment of sold products; (13) downstream leased assets; (14) franchises; and (15) investments.[91]

How does this classification apply to insurers? Insurers' Scope 1 emissions include GHG emissions from using any vehicles owned by the insurer. Scope 1 emissions could, but are unlikely to, be relevant to insurers in relation to substantial equity investments in companies that generate GHG emissions in their operations, e.g. in energy and transport sectors or the chemical industry: any GHG emissions associated with an equity investment where the insurer obtains financial control (50%+ of shareholding) or significant influence (20–50% of shareholding), or enters into a joint venture, would fall into Scope 1. Insurers' Scope 2 emissions would be GHG emissions generated by heating or cooling offices and storage facilities and their own use of electricity. The Scope 2 emissions of an insurer whose energy needs are met by fossil fuel energy sources will be higher compared to the Scope 2 emissions of an insurer who uses green or renewable energy.

With regards to Scope 3, there are a number of sub-categories that will have no or only marginal application to insurers: e.g. upstream and downstream leased assets (8 and 13); processing and end-of-life treatment of sold products (10 and 12); and franchises (14). Some of the sub-categories are relevant to the operational side of an insurance company: for example, sub-category (1) applies to the purchase of office supplies; sub-category (2) applies to an insurer's equipment, IT hardware and machinery, facilities, and vehicles; sub-categories (6) and (7) – business travel and employee commuting – are likely to be relevant; and sub-category (9) could apply to sending marketing materials to insurance distributors and policy documentation to customers.

To the extent they do not fall within Scope 1 (via a substantial equity investment – see above), GHG emissions associated with an insurer's investment activities are captured by Scope 3 sub-category (15). However, under the Greenhouse Gas Protocol Scope 3(15), an insurer would only need to account for debt investments where the use of proceeds is known, and for equity or debt investments in project financings.[92] Accounting for debt investments where the use of proceeds is unknown, for investments in managed funds and other investments and financial services – including 'insurance contracts' – is optional.[93] The reasons advanced for not attributing any GHG emissions from those types of investments and insurance contracts to insurers are (1) without ownership interests or direct control over the customer's activity the insurer cannot influence the customer towards reducing the associated GHG emissions,[94] and (2) the possibility of 'double-counting' (i.e.

91 The World Business Council for Sustainable Development and the World Resources Institute, 'The Greenhouse Gas Protocol: Corporate Value Chain (Scope 3) Accounting and Reporting Standard' (2011) ch 5 <https://ghgprotocol.org/sites/default/files/standards/Corporate-Value-Chain-Accounting-Reporing-Standard_041613_2.pdf> accessed on 1 June 2023.

92 Ibid.

93 Ibid.

94 Partnership for Carbon Accounting Financials, 'Insurance-Associated Emissions' (November 2022), 8 <https://carbonaccountingfinancials.com/files/downloads/pcaf-standard-part-c-insurance-associated-emissions-nov-2022.pdf> accessed on 1 June 2023.

the same GHG emission being accounted for by the customer/emitter and the insurer).[95] The Partnership for Carbon Accounting Financials has recently proposed reporting and accounting standards for 'insurance-associated emissions,'[96] and this recommendation has been adopted as an in-scope emission in the Target-Setting Protocol[97] published by the NZIA to transition their underwriting portfolios to net-zero GHG emissions by 2050.[98]

There are strong arguments for taking into account GHG emissions associated with underwriting activities when assessing outward impact: underwriting is the core business of insurance companies and the insurance cover they provide is their 'product.'[99] The Greenhouse Gas Protocol under Scope 1 sub-category (11) clearly envisages the capture of GHG emissions associated with the use of 'sold products.' Moreover, an insurer can influence a customer's activities even without ownership interest because they can enable business activities by providing insurance (or hinder them by limiting or declining insurance cover).[100] Double-counting can be addressed by allocating a share or using an attribution factor to the GHG emissions attributed to the insurer.[101] Accounting for GHG emissions associated with an insurer's underwriting business will increase transparency in relation to net-zero targets set by insurers, such as the commitment by NZIA members. Finally, as a matter of consistency in reporting and accounting, insurers should only be given outward impact credit for climate-related 'impact underwriting' and 'impact investment' (i.e. processes and activities they engage in that directly or indirectly reduce GHG emissions or remove GHG from the atmosphere), if in return they accept an (adjusted) attribution of GHG emissions associated with their underwriting and investment activities.

3.3.3 Outward impact: climate-related impact underwriting and impact investment

Insurers can have a positive outward impact by contributing to the transition to a net-zero economy through 'impact underwriting' and 'impact investment,' as well as reducing GHG emissions in their own operations. 'Impact underwriting' generally refers to using insurance to promote sustainability and the SDGs for the benefit of a wider group of stakeholders or society as a whole. Chapters 6 and 7 contain a detailed examination of climate-related impact underwriting which can include different approaches: (1) supporting climate change mitigation and adaptation activities and technologies by providing insurance cover (insuring green); (2) reducing underwriting activities that have harmful impacts contributing to climate change (not insuring brown); and (3) by developing insurance products and services that shift policyholders' behaviour and processes towards reducing their GHG emissions (greening insurance).

'Impact investment' is concerned with a range of investment approaches that, in addition to financial returns, pursue ethical goals or SDGs for the benefit of a wider group

95 Kenza Bryan and Ian Smith, 'Activists Criticise Insurance Industry's First Attempt to Measure Carbon Emissions' (*Financial Times*, 17 January 2023).

96 Partnership for Carbon Accounting Financials (n 94).

97 NZIA, 'Target-Setting Protocol 1.0' (January 2023) <https://www.unepfi.org/industries/insurance/launch-of-nzia-target-setting-protocol-version-1-0/> accessed on 1 June 2023.

98 NZIA (n 18).

99 Also see Section 3.4.3.

100 Partnership for Carbon Accounting Financials (n 94) 8, and also see Chapter 6, Sections 6.3 and 6.4.

101 Partnership for Carbon Accounting Financials (n 94) 6.

of stakeholders or society as a whole. Reference is made to Chapter 8 which examines climate-related impact investment and stewardship.

3.4 Role of insurers and the insurance industry

This chapter started with a consideration of the nature of insurance and will conclude with some observations on the societal role of insurers and the insurance industry in relation to climate change. Thinking about their role is relevant to the reasons why, and the extent to which, insurers should engage in climate-related impact underwriting and will thus set the scene for the following chapters.

Expectations have been set, and public pressure on insurers is mounting, to take an active part in advancing the objectives of the Paris Agreement. For example, the SHIP affirms that sustainable and just solutions to the climate crisis require 'social dialogue and participation of all stakeholders,' and in particular finance from financial institutions and institutional investors for a global transition to a net-zero economy.[102] The UNEP FI Principles of Sustainable Insurance ('PSI') expect insurers to embed in their decision-making environmental issues relevant to their insurance business.[103] The Principles for Responsible Investment ('PRI') require that investors incorporate environmental issues into investment analysis and decision-making processes.[104] The Glasgow Financial Alliance for Net-Zero, a global coalition of leading financial institutions committed to accelerating the decarbonisation of the economy, asks '[e]very … insurer, and investor … to adjust their business models, develop credible plans for the transition to a low-carbon, climate-resilient future, and then implement those plans.'[105] The most forceful challenge yet to engage with climate-related impact underwriting was set by António Guterres, Secretary General of the United Nations: 'We need net-zero commitments to cover your underwriting portfolios, and this should include the underwriting of coal – and all fossil fuels.'[106] As will be discussed in Chapters 6 to 8, there are not yet, however, any substantive norms that set standards of behaviour in relation to climate-related impact underwriting and investment.

There are cogent public policy reasons why the private sector should participate in combating climate change and its effects:

- climate change is a global emergency that requires international co-operation and co-ordinated solutions at all levels;[107]

102 SHIP sec VII, art 50 and s IX, art 61 and 62.

103 UNEP FI, 'Principles for Sustainable Insurance' <https://www.unepfi.org/psi/wp-content/uploads/2012/06/PSI-document.pdf> accessed on 1 June 2023, and see Chapter 6, Section 6.1.

104 PRI in partnership with UNEP Finance Initiative, 'Principles for Responsible Investment', Principle 1 <https://www.unpri.org/about-us/about-the-pri> accessed on 1 June 2023, and see Chapter 8, Section 8.1.2.

105 Glasgow Financial Alliance for Net-Zero, 'Accelerating the Transition to a Net-Zero Global Economy' <https://www.gfanzero.com/> accessed on 1 June 2023.

106 António Guterres, 'Closing Remarks to Insurance Development Forum' (Speech at the 2021 Insurance Development Forum Summit, 8 June 2021) <https://www.un.org/sg/en/content/sg/speeches/2021-06-08/closing-remarks-insurance-development-forum> accessed on 1 June 2023.

107 See Paris Agreement, Preamble and art 6(8)(b).

- climate change risks are complex risks that require multi-directional collective action not only to make such risks more manageable, but also to legitimise the actions taken to address such risks;[108]
- climate change risks exacerbate protection gaps;[109]
- there is no time to rely on international agreement alone and momentum must be built around the transition to a net-zero economy;[110]
- to send governments 'a resounding signal' that they must strengthen their contributions to the Paris Agreement;[111]
- society is turning to corporations, investors, and financial institutions for solutions to climate change because governments are failing to achieve effective policies and meaningful results.[112]

These reasons set the emerging normative agenda for climate action by private actors but they do not explain within a conceptual structure the proper influence of public policy – advancing the objectives of the Paris Agreement – over the scope of private insurance coverage and the societal role of insurers and insurance in relation to climate change. In relation to climate-related impact underwriting, insurers are called upon to limit their freedom to contract, with whom to contract, and on what terms to contract, for providing insurance, and to use the contractual framework to exert influence over their policyholders.[113] For insurers, there is considerable transition risk (regulatory, market, technology, and reputational risks – see above) involved in doing so. From the perspective of policyholders, impact climate-related underwriting could be seen as an abrogation or delegation of governmental responsibilities and the assumption of quasi-regulatory functions by insurers.[114] Adopting Abraham's 'Four Conceptions of Insurance,'[115] justifications for normative choices and the role of insurers in relation to climate-related impact underwriting can be tested by reference to the contract conception, the public utility/regulated industry conception, the product conception, and the governance conception.

3.4.1 Contract conception

The contract conception of insurance perceives a contract of insurance as a voluntary agreement between an insurer and one or more insureds. This is the prevalent conception in legal analysis and market practice (and the one which has been adopted above to explain what 'insurance' is). It assumes that the contract parties have autonomy with full freedom of contract, and that the contract alone governs their relationship. Therefore, whether their

108 Van Asselt (n 51) sec 5.

109 See Section 3.2.4.

110 Glasgow Financial Alliance for Net-Zero, 'Our Mission' <https://www.gfanzero.com/about/> accessed on 1 June 2023.

111 United Nations, 'Race to Net-Zero Campaign' <https://unfccc.int/climate-action/race-to-zero-campaign> accessed on 1 June 2023.

112 See e.g.: Jonathan R. Macey, 'ESG Investing: Why Here? Why Now?' (2021) Yale Law and Economics Research Paper Forthcoming, Law and Economics Center at George Mason University Scalia Law School Research Paper Series No. 22-013 <https://papers.ssrn.com/sol3/papers.cfm?abstract_id=3942903> accessed on 1 June 2023.

113 See Chapters 6 and 7.

114 See Section 3.4.4.

115 Kenneth S. Abraham, 'Four Conceptions of Insurance' (2013) 161 *Univ Penn Law Rev*, 653.

contract of insurance advances the objectives of the Paris Agreement, and how rights and obligations in relation thereto are allocated, is a matter of agreement between the parties. Under this hermetic view of their contractual relationship, there is no room for policy agendas and regulation prescribing climate action to overlay the terms of the contract.

As Abraham has pointed out, one issue with this analysis is that 'most actual insurance transactions do not involve subjective assent' since many policyholders lack understanding of, and real choice and bargaining power in relation to, standard form issuance contracts.[116] Merkin and Steele have criticised the contract conception for being too limited: insurance is more than just the contractual relationship between the insurer and the insured and should be considered in the context of relations to other (re)insurers, other parties providing indemnities, contract parties of the insured, and third parties to whom the insured owes tortious duties.[117] Modern contract law recognises that there must be limits on freedom of contract to protect weaker parties and third parties, to introduce principles of fairness and reasonableness in contract,[118] and to prohibit or discourage parties from contracting out from areas where the legislator has intervened in the public interest.[119] Legislative interventions are relevant to the public utility-regulated industry conception.

3.4.2 Public utility-regulated industry conception

The public utility-regulated industry conception of insurance understands the insurance industry as a highly regulated industry with cartel-like characteristics providing a fundamental service used by a large proportion of people. This conception has gained currency in the US where the insurance industry operates under a grant of immunity from federal anti-trust law.[120] Given the perceived quasi-public nature of insurance and the anti-trust privileges the insurance sector enjoys in the US, the regulated industry conception of insurance considers it to be in the public interest to regulate contracts of insurance in relation to the general availability of insurance products and service, their contractual terms, and pricing.[121] Abrahams notes that, outside the health and motor insurance markets, the public utility-regulated industry conception is not an accurate description because the US insurance market is competitive and diverse, and there is no 'take all comers' requirement as there is for utilities companies.[122]

Insurers carrying on insurance business in the UK are comprehensively regulated under the Financial Services and Markets Act 2000 ('FSMA 2000') framework. Insurance product terms and pricing are regulated in general terms through duties imposed on insurers,

116 Ibid Sec. I.

117 Robert Merkin and Jenny Steele, *Insurance and the Law of Obligations* (OUP 2013), ch 2 and 3.

118 John Adams and Roger Brownsword, 'The Ideologies of Contract Law' (1987) 7 *Legal Studies*, 205, 206–213.

119 E.g. in relation to motor insurance, the Road Traffic Act 1988, s 145 mandates specific coverage and terms, and s 148 renders certain kinds of terms ineffective.

120 K.S. Abraham (n 115) Sec IV; The World Business Council for Sustainable Development and the World Resources Institute, 'The Greenhouse Gas Protocol: Corporate Value Chain (Scope 3) Accounting and Reporting Standard' (2011) ch 5 <https://ghgprotocol.org/sites/default/files/standards/Corporate-Value-Chain-Accounting-Reporing-Standard_041613_2.pdf> accessed on 1 June 2023. See also: McCarran-Ferguson Act (15 U.S.C.) §§1011–1015.

121 K.S. Abraham (n 115) Sec II.

122 Ibid.

including the 'consumer duty' to deliver good outcomes,[123] and product governance regulations requiring insurers to assess whether a product provides good value and good outcomes to the target market.[124] The UK insurance market too is diverse and competitive – a factor which would militate against a public utility-regulated industry conception, according to Abrahams. In any event, the scope of insurance regulation is circumscribed by the statutory functions and objectives of the insurance regulators, the FCA and the PRA.[125] Their authority has been extended under the Financial Services and Markets Act 2023 ('FSMA 2023') so that both regulators will need to take into consideration 'the need to contribute towards achieving compliance with section 1 of the Climate Change Act 2008 (UK net-zero emissions target).'[126]

3.4.3 Product conception

The product conception of insurance sees insurers as selling a product to the insured to cover him against the financial consequences of specified risks. Like goods, insurance policies should be of 'satisfactory quality' and 'fit for the purposes' for which they are supplied.[127] This translates into requiring (1) the policy to satisfy a degree of utility to the policyholder and (2) the insurer to provide information about key features of the policy at the pre-contractual stage.[128] Under the product conception of insurance, the insurer should be held liable either on the basis of a 'defective warning' by the insurer as to the features of the policy, or on the basis that the policy is 'defective in design' on the grounds that it is unsuitable or has impaired utility to the policyholder.[129]

The product conception is reflected in the FCA's 'ICOBS Insurance Conduct of Business Sourcebook' ('ICOBS') and 'PROD' which use the language of '(insurance) product' for the insurance policy, 'manufacturer' for the insurer, 'customer' for the insured, and 'distributor' for insurance brokers and intermediaries. ICOBS contains rules and guidance about ensuring that an insurance product is suitable to the customer's demands and needs,[130] and that the customer is provided with appropriate information about the key features of the product at the pre-contractual stage.[131] PROD contains rules about the product design, testing, and approval process for insurance products before they are launched.[132] The product conception also explains the requirements for disclosing and reporting on outward and inward impact in the EU and UK sustainability-related disclosure regulations (discussed in Chapter 5) and is also evident in the FCA's approach to green-washing (discussed in Chapter 5).

123 See Chapter 7, Section 7.4.5.

124 FCA Handbook, Product Governance Sourcebook (PROD) ('PROD'), 4.2 and 4.5.

125 FSMA 2000, ss 1B-1E for the FCA; and ss 2AB-2C for the PRA.

126 FSMA 2023 s 27 and see Chapter 4, Section 4.3.2.

127 K.S. Abraham (n 115) 674–675. The relevant UK legislation is the Consumer Rights Act 2015, s 9 and the Sale of Goods Act 1979, s 14.

128 Daniel Schwarcz, 'A Products Liability Theory for the Judicial Regulation of Insurance Policies' (2007) 48 *Wm & Mary L Rev*, 1389, 1436–1438.

129 Ibid 1436–1438; also see: J.W. Stempel, 'The Insurance Policy as Thing' (2009) 44 *Tort Trial Ins. Prac LJ*, 813, 828–829.

130 ICOBS 5.2.

131 Ibid 6.1.

132 PROD 4.2.

The product conception pivots on a policy's purpose which is determined by reference to the policyholder's ex ante intention or (presumed) preferences on the scope and extent of coverage for a given price. The Insurance Development Forum noted that 'insurance is not simply a commodity that is bought on price … but is a service solution that is bought on perceived value to reduce risk and manage loss.'[133] As more policyholders become 'climate-conscious,' there may be growing expectations and demand for 'green' insurance products that not only provide cover for specific perils but also seek to reduce climate change risk.[134] However, the product conception cannot explain why insurers should reduce underwriting activities that have harmful impacts contributing to climate change when there is still market demand for coverage for coal and fossil fuel assets (where the intention is to have coal/fossil fuel coverage); and why they should develop insurance products that shift policyholders' behaviour and processes towards reducing their GHG emissions where there is no established market demand for such products (and consequently no intention or preference). These aspects of climate-related impact underwriting can be better explained with the governance conception.

3.4.4 Governance conception

The insurance and sociology literature conceives of insurance as a governance tool to manage and control risk.[135] The governance conception recognises that insurers can perform quasi-governmental functions. They regulate their policyholders' behaviour in relation to the risk and deliver welfare benefits in addition to, or instead of, governmental social security protection. Ericson, Doyle, and Barry[136] identify several dimensions of how insurers 'govern':

> First, it attempts to produce knowledge of risk by objectifying everything into degrees of chance of harm. Second, it makes everything it objectifies calculable and thereby subject to commodification. It uses actuarial techniques to convert the concrete facts of objective risks it produces into probability classifications. Each classification is then assigned its respective cost so that prices can be set and compensation for the effects of chance can be paid. Third, actuarialism creates a risk pool, a population that has a stake in the identified risks and the specific harms they entail. This stake transforms the population into a collective with an interest in minimizing loss and compensating those who have suffered loss. Fourth, insurance protects against loss of capital. What is actually insured is not the particular event that causes harm to a member of the risk pool, but the capital against which the insurer offers indemnification. Fifth, insurance is managerial. It manages risks on the basis of surveillance and audit for a population dispersed in space and time but nevertheless bound together by the collective interests noted above. Sixth, the population is also bound legally. Insurance objectifies risk by making it subject to contract and adjudication. At the same time, it helps the law to assign liability to the party most able to distribute the loss through insurance. Seventh, in providing a futures market in security, insurance offers a cultural framework for conceptions of time, destiny, providence, responsibility, economic utility, and justice. Eighth, insurance is a social technology of justice. It bridges individual and social responsibility through distributive

133 Insurance Development Forum, '2022 in Review: A Year of Influence and Implementation' (February 2023) <https://www.insdevforum.org/4118-2/> accessed on 1 June 2023.

134 See Chapter 7.

135 Ericson and Doyle (n 48); F. Ewald (n 5); Tom Baker and Jonathan Simon, 'Embracing Risk' in Tom Baker and Jonathan Simon (eds.) *Embracing Risk – The Changing Culture of Insurance and Insurability* (University of Chicago Press 2002).

136 Ericson and Doyle (n 48).

> justice (collective sharing of loss) and restorative justice (financial indemnification). Ninth, insurance is therefore political, combining aspects of collective well-being and individual liberty in a state of perpetual tension.[137]

The existing scholarship on the conception of insurance as governance has focused on insurers as 'quasi-regulators'[138] where insurance is conceived as a tool to control policyholders' behaviour or achieve specific outcomes to mitigate the risk insured and prevent loss. Through risk-based pricing, partial coverage (exclusions), and risk mitigation terms, insurers can incentivise or obligate policyholders to mitigate the insured risk. For example, insurers may give better coverage terms and better premium rates (1) in motor insurance to policyholders who drive safely (as evidenced by a clean driving record) and (2) in health insurance, to policyholders who lead a healthy lifestyle (in health insurance, the pre-contractual questionnaire often includes questions on smoking, alcohol consumption, and exercise). Many cyber insurers will refuse cover if basic cyber hygiene and protection protocols are not met.[139] Just like governments make laws that set standards for behaviours, the contract of insurance imposes obligations on policyholders that set standards for their conduct in relation to risk for the duration of the contract, and, like law enforcement agencies, the insurance industry uses sophisticated inspection and audit systems to ensure that policyholders comply.[140]

The governance conception can explain the dynamics of withdrawing from underwriting coal and fossil fuel assets: by declining cover to a coal mining company, the insurer signals that it considers coal mining activities harmful and potentially causes the coal mining activities to cease if operations legally or economically depend on insurance cover being in place. It could therefore be argued that the insurer exercises a quasi-licensing function in respect of the coal mining company's activities.[141] In this example, the insurer contributes to the reduction of risk to the public at large (in this case the risk of harmful effects from climate change) which, as Abrahams points out, is a function that is usually associated with the state and government.[142]

The governance conception – in its narrow sense of controlling policyholders' behaviour – is more difficult to apply to offering insurance for climate change mitigation technologies, where the availability of cover supports their economic viability. In this example, the insurer influences the conditions that allow these technologies to develop and become more widely adopted, but the link to the policyholder's behaviour is more tenuous, and there is no coercion or control from the insurer. The governance conception also becomes attenuated with respect to insurance products that shift policyholders'

137 Ibid 47–49; as summarised by K.S. Abraham (n 115) Sec IV, fn.74.

138 Ericson and Doyle (n 48); and Caroline A. Heimer, 'Insuring More, Ensuring Less: The Costs and Benefits of Private Regulation through Insurance' in Tom Baker and Jonathan Simon (eds.) *Embracing Risk* (Chicago University Press 2002), 116–145; Anja Shortland, *Kidnap: Inside the Ransom Business* (OUP 2019); Omri Ben-Shahar and Kyle D. Logue, 'Outsourcing Regulation: How Insurance Reduces Moral Hazard' (2012) 111 *Mich Law Rev*, 197; Peter Kochenburger, 'Liability Insurance and Gun Violence' (2013–2014) 46 *Conn Law Rev*, 1265.

139 Conversation between Thomas Reagan, Cyber Practice Lead at Marsh, and Ed Amoroso, CEO of TAG Cyber, about cyber insurance. TAG Cyber TV (20 January 2023) <https://www.youtube.com/watch?app=desktop&v=PfFdr_Jop5g> accessed on 1 June 2023.

140 Ericson and Doyle (n 48) 45, 361.

141 See Tom Baker, Kyle D. Logue, and Chaim Saiman, *Insurance Law and Policy* (5th ed, Aspen Publishing 2022).

142 K.S. Abraham (n 115) Sec IV A.

behaviour and processes towards reducing their GHG emissions because an insurer's influence is unlikely to be 'controlling.' As will be discussed in Chapter 7, Section 7.5.2, in most types of policies there will be no causal link between the risk insured and the GHG emissions of the policyholder, as a result of which insurers are more likely to rely on 'nudge terms,' rather than imposing exclusions or terms that obligate policyholders to reduce GHG emissions.[143]

The governance conception has been criticised for requiring that insurers assume regulatory functions that could be performed by a governmental body through private law contracts but without being subject to the standards we expect from, and the limitations placed upon, governmental authority,[144] such as transparency, due process, and acting intra vires and reasonably. Moreover, insurers are not sovereign quasi-regulators as they themselves are subject to pressure and influence from their reinsurers,[145] which introduces an additional level of opacity. Some commentators have pointed out that insurers' quasi-regulatory functions are not exercised for the purposes of reducing risks to the public, rather insurers only 'regulate' out of self-interest to reduce their own liability[146] and to keep losses insurable.[147] There is also emerging empirical evidence that insurers do not always succeed in preventing loss through quasi-regulatory measures as their means of monitoring and enforcing risk mitigation conduct are limited.[148] The governance conception's focus on the insurance business of insurers also fails to explain insurers' relationships with investee companies and other actors in their value chains.

Given these limitations, in relation to climate-related impact underwriting, this book therefore proposes a novel and expanded conception of insurance as governance which sees insurers as taking on a multi-directional and collaborative enabling role in addressing climate change risk and in the transition to a net-zero economy.

3.4.5 Enabling conception

The enabling conception pictures the insurance industry as supporting policyholders, investee companies, and other stakeholders in their net-zero transition. As risk carriers and investors, insurers can enable actors in their value chain and in the wider community to take climate mitigation action and to adopt climate change adaptation measures. Based on their contractual relationship, the policyholder and the insurer can take collaborative climate action, and the insurer's support of any climate action taken by the policyholder can be delivered through that contractual relationship. The notion of 'enabling' envisages some engagement between the insurer and the policyholder: rather than being told what to do, a (prospective) policyholder is included in the decision-making process on taking

143 The effect of s 11(2) of the Insurance Act 2015 is that insurers may not be able to rely on a non-compliance with a risk mitigation term to decline liability if the insured can show 'that the non-compliance with the term could not have increased the risk of the loss which actually occurred in the circumstances in which it occurred.' Also see Chapter 7, Section 7.6.1.

144 K.S. Abraham (n 115) Sec IV A.

145 Aviva Abramovsky, 'Reinsurance: The Silent Regulator' (2008) 15 *Conn Ins LJ*, 345.

146 Kenneth S. Abraham and Daniel Schwarcz, 'The Limits of Regulation by Insurance' (2023) 98(1) *Ind Law Journal* (Art.5); and also see literature review in pt I.A. of this article.

147 Tom Baker and Anja Shortland, 'How Crime Shapes Insurance and Insurance Shapes Crime' (March 10, 2023) U of Penn, Inst for Law and Econ Research Paper No. 23-10, *Journal of Legal Analysis* <https://ssrn.com/abstract=4390802> accessed on 1 June 2023.

148 Abraham and Schwarcz (n 146), in particular see the literature review in Sec I.B. of this article.

certain climate change mitigation or adaptation measures. Similarly, insurers in their role as investors can engage with their investees.

The inclusion of, and communication with, different actors and stakeholders in complex risk decision-making is, according to van Asslet and Renn, a hallmark of good risk governance.[149] Some scholars and the IPCC emphasise that the inclusion of different actors and stakeholders is beneficial to CRD approaches because decisions will be based on knowledge pluralism among actors, each of whom may contribute different knowledge, whether technical, experiential, cultural, or a combination thereof.[150]

Accordingly, the contractual design discussed in Chapter 7 envisages that policyholders are incentivised and supported, rather than coerced, by insurers towards emission-reducing or carbon-neutral activities, and that insurers directly engage with existing and prospective policyholders on climate change risk mitigation, adaptation, and loss prevention in the context of their insurance contracts. By offering innovative risk transfer solutions, insurers enable the scaling up of new climate technologies.[151] Their 'enabling' is likely to involve other actors in the insurance value chain, such as reinsurers, brokers, and repair and rebuild services providers. In Chapter 8, the enabling role of insurers as investors is explored by reference to the existing scholarship on green finance, stewardship, and using contract law as a 'green pill' to incentivise and enforce net-zero commitments of their investee companies.[152] Stewardship, in particular, is likely to require co-ordination with other investors and shareholders, as well as dialogue with decision-makers at the investee company and an insurer's own shareholders.

The insurance industry can also make enabling contributions to climate change mitigation and adaptation to the wider community grounded in its core expertise of risk assessment, risk management, and loss response. Insurers can seek to influence public policies that may decrease aggregate physical climate risk and losses by sharing their expertise, raising awareness of climate change risk, and developing socially useful information for society to understand climate change risk and to build greater resilience – including through insurance – to manage better the impact of climate change.[153] The insurance industry can support community-based risk transfer and financing strategies geared towards climate action.[154] Enabling contributions on a wider societal level is dependent on collective action by the insurance industry inter se, and engagement with communities, governments, scientists, and other experts. This has been recognised by the Glasgow Financial Alliance for Net-Zero ("GFANZ") whose recommendations include for financial institutions to adopt a strategy to engage with external stakeholders in support of the net-zero objectives.[155] Two of the most ambitious examples of this type of enabling contribution are the 'Global Shield against Climate Risks' and the 'InsuResilience Global

149 Van Asselt (n 51) sec 5; IPCC 2022 Sixth Assessment Report [4.4].

150 Ibid.

151 The Geneva Association, 'Climate Change Risk Assessment for the Insurance Industry' (February 2021) 8 <http://doc.genevaassociation.org/publication/climate-change-and-environment/climate-change-risk-assessment-insurance-industry> accessed on 1 June 2023.

152 John Armour, Luca Enriques, and Thom Wetzer, 'Green Pills: Making Corporate Climate Commitments Credible' (2023) 65 *Ariz L Rev*, 285 Pt 3.

153 Abraham and Schwarcz (n 146) Sec III.B.

154 See Chapter 8, Section 8.5.1.

155 GFANZ, 'Financial Institution Net-Zero Transition Plans' (November 2022), Pt C <https://assets.bbhub.io/company/sites/63/2022/09/Recommendations-and-Guidance-on-Financial-Institution-Net-zero-Transition-Plans-November-2022.pdf> accessed on 1 June 2023.

Partnership Vision 2025' initiatives for climate and disaster risk finance and insurance.[156] Chapter 9 will explore public-private partnerships for climate action between insurers, public authorities, and other stakeholders.

The enabling conception of insurance builds upon the governance conception: when insurers help implement government policy (achieving the objective of the Paris Agreement and national net-zero targets) and support people and businesses in their transition to a net-zero economy, they are arguably exercising a quasi-governmental function by providing public good services. The enabling conception also builds upon the 'relational model' of insurance put forward by Merkin and Steele which considers insurance in terms of the party relations of which it is an inherent part.[157] As noted above, these relations are not just the contractual relationship between the insurer and the insured but also include relations with other actors in the insurance value chain, investee companies, fellow investors and shareholders, other insurers and reinsurers, public authorities, and stakeholders in the wider community. The role of multi-lateral and collaborative stakeholderism in combating climate change – in a manner that is just and inclusive – is explicitly recognised in the SHIP[158] and is anticipated in the Paris Agreement.[159] The enabling conception develops further the investor stewardship model of engaging with and influencing investee companies, on ESG issues,[160] to apply stewardship notions of 'engagement' and 'influencing' in the underwriting context. It is aligned to the broader concept of 'environmental stewardship' which can be defined as 'the actions taken by individuals, groups or networks of actors, with various motivations and levels of capacity, to protect, care for or responsibly use the environment in pursuit of environmental and/or social outcomes in diverse social-ecological contexts.'[161]

The UK government pursues a 'Green Finance Strategy' that sees the alignment and support of the financial sector as a vital part of environmentally sustainable and resilient growth.[162] The enabling role of insurers is also implicit in statements by the IAIS,[163] by EIOPA,[164] and by the UK's FCA.[165] The role of insurers as 'enablers' is in line with the stakeholder model of corporate social responsibility,[166] emerging theoretical frameworks

156 See Chapter 9, Section 9.5.2.

157 Rob Merkin and Jenny Steele, *Insurance and the Law of Obligations* (OUP 2013), ch 2 and 3.

158 SHIP sec VIII art 28 and sec IX art 30–31.

159 Paris Agreement art 2(1)(c), 9(3).

160 See Chapter 8, Section 8.1.3.

161 Nathan J. Bennett et al., 'Environmental Stewardship: A Conceptual Review and Analytical Framework' (2018) 61(4) *Environ Manag*, 597, text to Fig.1. The article also contains a literature review on the definition of 'environmental stewardship.'

162 HM Government, 'Mobilising Green Investment – 2023 Green Finance Strategy' (April 2023) <https://www.gov.uk/government/publications/green-finance-strategy> accessed on 1 June 2023.

163 IAIS, 'IAIS Commitment to Amplify Response to Climate Change' (28 October 2021) <https://www.iaisweb.org/uploads/2022/01/211028-IAIS-Statement_Commitment-to-amplify-response-to-climate-change_October-2021.pdf> accessed on 1 June 2023.

164 EIOPA, 'Opinion on Sustainability within Solvency II,' EIOPA-BoS-19/241, s 4.

165 FCA, 'A Strategy for Positive Change: Our ESG Priorities,' Introduction (November 2021) <https://www.fca.org.uk/publications/corporate-documents/strategy-positive-change-our-esg-priorities> accessed on 1 June 2023.

166 R. Edward Freeman, *Strategic Management: A Stakeholder Approach* (Cambridge University Press 2015; first published in 1984).

on 'stakeholder capitalism,'[167] 'environmental stewardship,'[168] and a wider meaning of 'corporate purpose,'[169] which see the role of corporations as not just optimising short-term profits for shareholders, but maximising long-term shareholder value creation, by taking into account the needs of all their stakeholders, and society at large, including by taking responsibility for protecting the environment. This will be examined further in Chapter 6.

The enabling conception also harks back to the contract conception if one is reminded of the 'hold harmless' obligation of an insurer under an indemnity insurance contract: while in reality, the parties' understanding of the insurer's obligation is likely to be that it is a promise to compensate the insured in the event of a loss,[170] the primary obligation of the insurer is to **hold the insured harmless** against loss by an insured peril. A policyholder's best chance of being held harmless from climate risk is to implement climate change adaptation measures in relation to the insured property, and there is therefore an argument that insurers, in order to hold policyholders harmless, should enable and support such measures.

3.5 Conclusion

The legal relationship between an individual policyholder and an insurer is based on a contract of insurance which is an agreement to transfer risk from the policyholder (the insured) to the insurer. Some climate change risks are insurable, some are uninsurable, and some are becoming uninsurable as a result of their increase in frequency and severity and their complexity. Uninsurability and other factors can create protection gaps that leave climate-related losses uninsured. Climate change risks have an inward impact on insurers' underwriting business and investment activities, while insurers through their operations, underwriting business, and investment activities can have a positive or negative outward impact on the environment by counteracting or contributing to climate change. Insurers can increase their positive outward impact by adopting climate-related impact underwriting and investment strategies that enable their policyholders and investees in their transition to a net-zero economy.

Although insurers have not yet widely adopted the role of 'climate action enablers,' they will be motivated to do so as and when customer demand for products with positive environmental impact rises. In addition, as voluntary sustainability and climate disclosure frameworks harden into mandatory disclosure requirements,[171] there will be growing pressure from investors, shareholders, and other stakeholders on insurers to engage in climate-related impact underwriting and investment. Increasingly, an enabling role will go hand in hand with managing insurers' own exposure to climate change risk, mid-

167 World Economic Forum, 'Davos Manifesto 2020: The Universal Purpose of a Company in the Fourth Industrial Revolution' (2019) <https://www.weforum.org/agenda/2019/12/davos-manifesto-2020-the-universal-purpose-of-a-company-in-the-fourth-industrial-revolution/> accessed on 1 June 2023; Klaus Schwab, *Stakeholder Capitalism* (Wiley 2021).

168 Bennett (n 161).

169 British Academy, 'The Future of the Corporation: Principles for Purposeful Business' (November 2019) <https://www.thebritishacademy.ac.uk/publications/future-of-the-corporation-principles-for-purposeful-business> accessed on 1 June 2023.

170 See the criticism of the 'hold harmless' obligation as legal fiction in: Neill Campbell, 'The Nature of an Insurer's Obligation' (2000) *LMCLQ*, 42, 63–64.

171 See Chapter 5.

and long-term, and preventing and minimising protection gaps. In the following chapters, the enabling conception of insurance will be tested against the existing laws, regulatory regimes, and industry initiatives and will inform the discussion on future regulation of climate-related impact underwriting and investment as well as the contractual features of insurance products with positive climate impact.

CHAPTER 4

Climate change risk assessment and regulation

How is inward impact – the financial risks stemming from climate change on insurers – and outward impact – the impact of an insurer's operations on climate change – regulated? This chapter maps to what extent insurance regulators in the UK and the EU have integrated climate change risks and combating climate change into their regulatory frameworks. Tracing regulatory developments it will be shown that UK and EU regulators were initially focused on inward impact by seeking to ensure that insurers properly identify, measure, monitor, manage, control, and report on the financial risk posed by climate change and to take that risk into account in their assessment of their solvency needs. More recently, their regulatory mandates were expanded to take climate change and environmental issues into account in discharging their responsibilities but the regulation of outward impact remains selective and fragmented.

This chapter is organised as follows: Section 4.1 provides an introduction to insurance regulation and the insurance regulatory bodies that have been chosen for comparison: the International Association of Insurance Supervisors ('IAIS'), the UK Prudential Regulation Authority ('PRA'), the Financial Conduct Authority ('FCA'), and the European Insurance and Occupational Pensions Authority ('EIOPA'). Section 4.2 explains why climate change should be considered a regulatory issue, and Section 4.3 analyses the extent to which regulators can make and enforce rules, or take supervisory action, in relation to climate change within the scope of their respective mandates. Section 4.4 compares the regulatory approaches to climate change risk and climate impact of the IAIS, the PRA, the FCA, and EIOPA. It also examines anti-ESG legislation developments in the US.

4.1 Insurance regulation and regulators

Most jurisdictions have some form of licensing requirements for insurance companies and impose rules relating to insurance activities that insurance companies are required to comply with on an ongoing basis. The need for insurance regulation is readily explained:

- **policyholder protection**: under most contracts of insurance, the policyholder pays the premium upfront, but the insurer may not be called upon to pay any claims until some unidentifiable point in the future. Insurance regulation aims to ensure that the insurer will have the financial resources to pay out claims as they arise. In addition, recognising that policyholders may have limited bargaining power and lack a detailed understanding of insurance, insurance regulation may

 DOI: 10.4324/b23081-4

require insurers to conduct their business in a way that treats policyholders fairly and does not cause them harm;

- **ensure fair, safe, and stable financial markets**: through their underwriting and investment activities, insurers and reinsurers are connected to other re/insurers, other actors in the financial markets, and the real economy. Insurance regulation aims to ensure the safety and soundness of insurance entities and thus contributes to the overall stability of the financial market. Insurance regulation is also concerned with the fairness and efficiency of the insurance market, and the financial market more generally, and therefore also aims to prevent market abuse and unfair competition.

Insurance regulation is the process of the imposition of rules by government or government agencies that apply to insurers and insurance activities. The term 'insurance regulation' is also frequently used interchangeably with 'insurance supervision' which is a key function of any insurance regulatory authority and may include:

> monitor[ing] (re)insurer and intermediary behaviour, and implement[ing] insurance rules (including legislation and regulation) through on-site and off-site supervision of (re)insurers that operate in its market to verify compliance with the requirements for engaging in financial activities and by issuing administrative measures and enforcement actions based on relevant legislation and non-legislative regulation.[1]

Insurance regulation can be divided into two types of regulation: (1) prudential regulation – the regulation pertaining to prudential requirements, and the oversight of insurers' observance of prudential requirements, including capital and technical provisions, to contribute to their financial safety and soundness; and (2) market conduct regulation – the elements of regulation and supervision to protect consumers, focusing on insurers' behaviour in the market.[2]

4.1.1 IAIS

The IAIS is not a regulator. It is a voluntary membership organisation of insurance regulators from more than 200 jurisdictions acting as the global standard-setting body responsible for developing and assisting in the implementation of principles, standards, and guidance as well as supporting material for the supervision of the insurance sector.[3] The IAIS promotes globally consistent supervisory approaches and develops principles and standards for the supervision of the insurance industry 'in order to develop and maintain fair, safe and stable insurance markets for the benefit and protection of policyholders and to contribute to global financial stability.'[4] The implementation of IAIS standards is not mandatory for national regulators but they frequently help shape regulatory approaches at the national level. The IAIS's standard-setting strength and effectiveness rest on its

1 OECD, 'Policy Guidance on the Structure of Insurance Regulation and Supervision' (2020) 10 <https://www.oecd.org/daf/fin/insurance/Policy-Guidance-on-the-Structure-of-Insurance-Regulation-and-Supervision.pdf> accessed on 1 June 2023.

2 Ibid 11.

3 See: IAIS, 'About the IAIS' <https://www.iaisweb.org/home> accessed on 1 June 2023.

4 Ibid.

relationships with member state regulators and international organisations such as the IMF and the World Bank.[5]

4.1.2 UK: PRA and FCA

The PRA and the FCA are the regulators for insurers carrying on insurance business in the UK ('UK insurers'). The PRA is part of the Bank of England, and its remit is prudential regulation and supervision. Under FSMA 2000, the PRA is responsible for the authorisation, in conjunction with the FCA, and prudential supervision of individual deposit takers, insurers, and certain designated investment firms. Its objective is to promote the safety and soundness of PRA-authorised firms, and it is required to advance this objective primarily by seeking to minimise any adverse effects of firm failure on the UK financial system and to ensure that firms carry on their business in a way that avoids adverse effects on the system.[6] In the case of insurers, the PRA has the additional objective of contributing, through its prudential supervision of insurers, to securing an appropriate degree of protection for policyholders.[7]

The FCA's general duties are to ensure through rules and supervision that the financial markets function well,[8] to secure an appropriate degree of protection for consumers,[9] to protect and enhance the integrity of the UK financial system,[10] and to promote effective competition in the interests of consumers in the markets for financial services.[11] Broadly, under FSMA 2000, the FCA is responsible for (1) regulating standards of conduct in retail and wholesale markets; (2) supervising trading infrastructures that support those markets; (3) the prudential supervision of firms that are not PRA-regulated (including insurance brokers); and (4) the functions of the UK Listing Authority.[12]

Both the PRA and the FCA are bound by regulatory principles that apply to the discharge of their respective functions, including:

- the principle that a burden or restriction which is imposed on a person, or on the carrying on of an activity, should be proportionate to the benefits, considered in general terms, which are expected to result from the imposition of that burden or restriction;
- the desirability of sustainable growth in the UK economy in the medium or long term;
- the general principle that consumers should take responsibility for their decisions;

5 Louise Steinberg, 'The International Regulation of Systemic Risk: The Role of the Leading International Organizations, Groups and Standard-Setting Bodies in Shaping the Post-Crisis Reform of Insurance Regulation' in Andromachi Georgosouli and Miriam Goldby, *Systemic Risk and the Future of Insurance Regulation* (Routledge 2015) 153.

6 FSMA 2000, s.2B(2).

7 Ibid s 2C(2).

8 Ibid s 1B(2).

9 Ibid s 1C(1).

10 Ibid s 1D(1).

11 Ibid s 1E(1).

12 Memorandum of Understanding between the Financial Conduct Authority (FCA) and the Prudential Regulation Authority (PRA) cl 3 <https://www.fca.org.uk/publication/mou/mou-pra.pdf> accessed on 1 June 2023.

- the responsibilities of the senior management of regulated firms in relation to compliance with any regulatory requirements under FSMA 2000;
- the principle that the regulators should exercise their functions as transparently as possible.[13]

The PRA and the FCA are both under a duty to co-operate and co-ordinate the exercise of their respective functions[14] and are signatories to a Memorandum of Understanding which describes the role of each regulator and how they intend to discharge their duty to co-operate.[15]

Following HM Treasury's 'Future Regulatory Framework Review'[16] in 2021/2022, the Financial Services and Markets Bill 2022–23 was introduced into Parliament last year and received Royal Assent on 29 June 2023. FSMA 2023 makes important updates to the UK's regulatory framework for financial services. Amongst other changes, the FSMA 2023 revokes retained EU law relating to financial services and enables HM Treasury, and the PRA and FCA, to replace it with legislation designed specifically for UK markets.[17] The FSMA 2023 also introduces a new secondary 'competitiveness and growth objective' pursuant to which the PRA and the FCA would be required to advance that objective when discharging their general functions.[18] The FSMA 2023 also introduces an additional regulatory principle applicable to the discharge of the PRA's and FCA's respective functions: namely, to consider the need to contribute towards achieving compliance with section 1 of the Climate Change Act 2008 (UK net-zero emissions target) and other environmental targets.[19] Separately, HM Treasury has proposed specific changes[20] to the UK insurance prudential regulatory regime (which derives from the EU Solvency II Directive[21]). Some of these changes will be implemented by direct legislation,[22] while other reforms will be implemented through changes to the PRA's rules.[23]

---

13 FSMA 2000, s 3B(b),(c), (d), (e), and (h).

14 Ibid s 3D.

15 Ibid s 3E.

16 HM Treasury, 'Future Regulatory Framework Review' (2021) <https://assets.publishing.service.gov.uk/government/uploads/system/uploads/attachment_data/file/1032075/FRF_Review_Consultation_2021_-_Final_.pdf> accessed on 1 June 2023.

17 FSMA 2023, s 1.

18 FSMA 2023, s 25.

19 FSMA 2023, s 27; and see Section 4.3.2.

20 HM Treasury, 'Review of Solvency II: Consultation – Response' (November 2022) <https://www.gov.uk/government/consultations/solvency-ii-review-consultation> accessed on 1 June 2023.

21 The UK transposed the Directive 2009/138/EC of the European Parliament and of the Council of 25 November 2009 on the taking up and pursuit of the business of Insurance and Reinsurance (Solvency II) (recast) ('Solvency II Directive') into national law with amendments to the FSMA 2000, the PRA Rulebook and FCA Handbook, and secondary legislation which came into force on 1 January 2016. The UK is now in the process of making its own UK Solvency rules as anticipated in HM Treasury (n 20) and the Edinburgh Reforms – see HM Treasury, 'Financial Services: The Edinburgh Reforms' (announcement dated 9 December 2022) <https://www.gov.uk/government/collections/financial-services-the-edinburgh-reforms> accessed on 1 June 2023. Also see Section 4.4.3.

22 HM Treasury has published drafts of (1) The Insurance and Reinsurance Undertakings (Prudential Requirements) Regulations, and (2) The Insurance and Reinsurance Undertakings (Prudential Requirements) (No. 2) Regulations, which are expected to come into force by end of 2023 and end of 2024 respectively.

23 For the first instalment of the consultation see: PRA, 'Review of Solvency II: Adapting to the UK Insurance Market' CP12/23 (June 2023). A second consultation paper is planned for September 2023.

4.1.3 EU: EIOPA

EIOPA is an independent advisory body to the European Commission, the European Parliament and the Council of the European Union, and one of three European Supervisory Authorities that supervise the financial system within the EU.[24] EIOPA's objective is to protect the public interest by contributing to the short-, medium-, and long-term stability and effectiveness of the financial system in the fields of insurance and occupational pensions, for the European Union economy, its citizens, and businesses,[25] paying particular attention to any potential systemic risk posed by financial institutions.[26] EIOPA does not itself have rule-making powers, rather it assists the European Commission with providing proposals and technical standards for primary EU legislation.[27] EIOPA's functions include:

- contributing to the establishment of common regulatory and supervisory standards and practices;
- improving the functioning of the internal market, including in particular a sound, effective, and consistent level of regulation and supervision;
- ensuring the integrity, transparency, efficiency, and orderly functioning of financial markets;
- strengthening international supervisory co-ordination;
- preventing regulatory arbitrage and promoting equal conditions of competition;
- ensuring the taking of risks related to insurance, reinsurance, and occupational pensions activities is appropriately regulated and supervised;
- enhancing customer protection.[28]

EIOPA does not have a direct supervisory relationship with EU insurers and generally relies on national regulators in the EU member states to implement and enforce regulatory standards.[29] In relation to these national regulators, EIOPA has powers to intervene where a national regulator has acted in breach of EU law,[30] in emergency situations jeopardising the orderly functioning and integrity of financial markets or the stability of the whole or part of the financial system in the EU,[31] and where there is a disagreement between national regulators in cross-border situations.[32] Following Brexit, the UK regulators no longer have a formal relationship with EIOPA, UK insurers without any presence or dealings in the EU are no longer within the remit of EIOPA, and EU laws are no longer applicable in the

24 The other two European Supervisory Authorities are the European Banking Authority ('EBA') and the European Securities and Markets Authority ('ESMA').

25 Regulation (EU) No 1094/2010 of the European Parliament and of the Council of 24 November 2010 establishing a European Supervisory Authority (European Insurance and Occupational Pensions Authority) art 1(6).

26 Ibid.

27 Ibid art 8.

28 Ibid art 1(6) and art 8(1).

29 Ibid ch III.

30 Ibid art 17.

31 Ibid art 18.

32 Ibid art 19.

UK unless they have been implemented into domestic law, or have been 'onshored.'[33] However, there are many insurers that carry on business in the UK and the EU through group structures and branches and therefore fall under two regulatory regimes.

4.2 Climate change as a regulatory issue

Although there is a general acceptance that 'climate change is a common concern of humankind'[34] that poses a global threat, why is it an issue that falls within the remit of insurance regulators? Chapter 3 set out in detail the impact of climate change risk on insurers. The inward impact of physical, transition, and liability risks manifests itself in significant financial risk on both the liability side and the asset side of an insurer's balance sheet, which in turn can have an impact on the financial resilience of individual insurers, as well as the stability of financial systems.[35] Insurance regulators across the world have turned their attention to how insurers should assess, manage, and disclose the financial risk stemming from climate change.[36] The IAIS and the SIF[37] recognised that climate change risk calls for strategic regulatory response and identified several areas for regulatory involvement:[38]

- on a microprudential level, if climate risks are not identified, accurately quantified, and managed, an individual insurer's solvency may be endangered as it may not hold sufficient capital to meet its liabilities;
- on a macroprudential level, climate change risks can have systemic implications on the financial stability of the insurance sector, the financial services industry, and the wider economy if a significant number of insurers, or a global systemically important insurer, fails or fails as a result of unexpectedly high climate change-related losses;
- there could also be a systemic risk to the financial services industry and the wider economy if certain climate change risks are becoming uninsurable and transcend sectors and jurisdictions.[39] Uninsurable climate change risks lead to protection gaps that can disrupt the economy more widely because they can have second order impacts on supply chains, the availability of loans and investment capital,

33 This process of 'onshoring' was effected by the European Union (Withdrawal) Act 2018 (as amended by the European Union (Withdrawal Agreement) Act 2020). This Act retains directly effective legislation as domestic UK legislation and confers powers on Government ministers to make changes to EU-derived legislation so that it continues to operate effectively after the UK's withdrawal from the EU.

34 Paris Agreement, Preamble.

35 IAIS and SIF, 'Application Paper on the Supervision of Climate-Related Risks in the Insurance Sector' (May 2021) [1.1.2] <https://www.iaisweb.org/uploads/2022/01/210525-Application-Paper-on-the-Supervision-of-Climate-related-Risks-in-the-Insurance-Sector.pdf> accessed on 1 June 2023.

36 The Geneva Association, 'Insurance Industry Perspectives on Regulatory Approaches to Climate Risk Assessment' (June 2021) <https://www.genevaassociation.org/sites/default/files/research-topics-document-type/pdf_public/climate_regulation_web.pdf> accessed on 1 June 2023.

37 The SIF is a leadership group of insurance supervisors convened by the United Nations Environment Programme.

38 IAIS and SIF, 'Issues Paper on Climate Change Risks to the Insurance Sector' (July 2018) sec 5 <https://www.iaisweb.org/page/supervisory-material/issues-papers> accessed on 1 June 2023.

39 Financial Stability Board, 'Supervisory and Regulatory Approaches to Climate-Related Risks: Final report' (October 2022) ch 3 <https://www.fsb.org/2022/10/supervisory-and-regulatory-approaches-to-climate-related-risks-final-report/> accessed on 1 June 2023.

and the profitability of investments. Protection gaps place additional financial burdens on individuals, enterprises, and governments;

- insurers must give adequate disclosure of the inward climate change risks they are facing to their regulators and the public.

In addition, there is growing acceptance that insurers' outward impact – the impact of insurers on the climate and climate change – is a matter for regulatory scrutiny. Outward impact on the environment is an externality that is not automatically integrated into markets and may therefore require regulatory intervention.[40] Where national net-zero targets have been set, regulators should discharge their responsibilities consistent with such targets.[41] For example, the European Commission has acknowledged that an understanding of an insurer's outward impact will be of interest to an increasing number of that insurer's (prospective) shareholders and investors in order to measure the climate impact of their investment portfolios.[42] The IAIS notes that the outward impact of an insurer's investments on the environment, and an insurer's investment strategy of impact underwriting and stewardship, may have an impact on the investment risk profile and its asset management liability.[43] In addition, there may be a growing appetite for insurance products with environmental characteristics or objectives. This raises insurance conduct of business questions as to what extent prospective policyholders should be advised of the environmental characteristics of insurance products, and how they should be protected from 'green-washing.'[44] Insurance regulation is also relevant to supporting, and not hindering, insurance product innovation and climate-related investment to contribute towards achieving national net-zero emissions targets.[45]

4.3 Regulatory mandate

The extent to which regulators can make and enforce rules, or take supervisory action, in relation to climate change depends on the scope of their mandates.

4.3.1 IAIS

The IAIS's mandate to engage in standard-setting in relation to climate change risks, promoting a globally consistent supervisory response to climate change, and providing supervisors with the necessary tools to monitor, assess, and address climate change risks to the insurance sector, is based on its Strategic Plan 2020–2024.[46]

40 Nicholas Stern, '*The Economics of Climate Change: The Stern Review*' (Cambridge University Press, 2007), ch. 2.

41 See Section 4.3.2.

42 Communication from the Commission, 'Guidelines on Non-Financial Reporting: Supplement on Reporting Climate-Related Information' (2019) 2019/C 209/01.

43 IAIS and SIF (n 35) 6.

44 FCA, 'Sustainability Disclosure Requirements (SDR) and Investment Labels' CP22/20 (October 2022) ('FCA Sustainability Disclosure Proposals') [1.2] <https://www.fca.org.uk/publication/consultation/cp22-20.pdf> accessed on 1 June 2023, and see Chapter 5.

45 FSMA 2023, s 27.

46 IAIS, 'Strategic Plan 2020–2024' (June 2019) 7 <https://www.iaisweb.org/uploads/2022/01/190613-2020-2024-Strategic-Plan.pdf> accessed on 1 June 2023.

4.3.2 PRA and FCA

The starting point for considering the PRA's and FCA's mandates is their respective regulatory objectives and functions.[47] The PRA's objectives – the safety and soundness of PRA-authorised firms and the protection for policyholders – are engaged because the inward impact of physical, transition, and liability risks manifests itself in significant financial risk which can have an impact on the financial resilience of individual insurers, as well as the stability of financial systems.[48] The PRA is part of the Bank of England which has set itself a climate change objective to:

> [p]lay a leading role, through our policies and operations, in ensuring the financial system, the macroeconomy, and the Bank are resilient to the risks from climate change and supportive of the transition to a net-zero economy.[49]

The FCA's overarching strategic objective is to ensure that the relevant markets function well. Climate change, and society's response to it, are likely to cause disruption to the economy and financial markets. Further to its market integrity objective, the FCA seeks to ensure that 'the UK's financial markets can both respond to and support the transition in a stable and orderly way.'[50] This includes reporting and disclosures on climate-related risks and the outward impact of insurers and their products. The FCA's competition objective provides the mandate for supporting product innovation, regulating environmental stewardship, and prohibiting green-washing.[51] Regulating insurance product disclosures and prohibiting green-washing also fall within the FCA's consumer protection objective.[52] The FCA has been consulting on whether it should seek to regulate the governance, remuneration, and competence structures with regulated firms in relation to sustainable finance under its overarching strategic objective and its consumer protection objective.[53]

For the first few years of their engagement with climate change, the PRA and the FCA were almost exclusively focused on inward impact – the impact of the financial risk from climate change – on regulated firms. This is not surprising given that neither the PRA nor the FCA has an 'environmental objective,' and they had no mandate to ensure that the UK financial markets operate with outward impact. This is now changing. In March 2021, the then-Chancellor of the Exchequer Rishi Sunak wrote to the Prudential Regulation Committee (on behalf of the PRA) and the FCA requesting that each:

> should have regard to the government's commitment to achieve a net-zero economy by 2050 under the Climate Change Act 2008 (Order 2019) when considering how to advance its objectives and discharge its functions.[54]

---

47 See Section 4.1.2.

48 Also see PRA, 'Enhancing Banks' and Insurers' Approaches to Managing the Financial Risks from Climate Change,' Supervisory Statement SS3/19 (April 2019) ('PRA SS3/19') [1.2].

49 Bank of England, 'Our Response to Climate Change' <https://www.bankofengland.co.uk/climate-change> accessed on 1 June 2023.

50 FCA, 'Climate Change and Green Finance' DP18/8 (October 2018) ch 3.

51 FSMA 2000, s 1E(1); FCA DP18/8 (n 50) ch 3; FCA, 'Building a Regulatory Framework for Effective Stewardship' DP19/1 (January 2019) [1.13] and [1.14].

52 FCA, Sustainability Disclosure Proposals [1.5].

53 FCA, 'Finance for Positive Sustainable Change: Governance, Incentives and Competence in Regulated Firms' DP23/1 (February 2023).

54 Letters from the then-Chancellor of the Exchequer Rishi Sunak to the PRC and the FCA, dated 23 March 2021 (PRC:

The effect of these letters is that the remit of the PRA and the FCA has now been extended to take into account the UK's net-zero goal to enable a financial system which supports a net-zero economy. In the most recent remit letters, the Chancellor of the Exchequer Jeremy Hunt wrote to the Prudential Regulation Committee (on behalf of the PRA) and the FCA that the regulators should have regard to the government's economic policy to 'delivering Net-Zero' and the 'provision of sustainable finance.'[55]

Under the FSMA 2023, the PRA and the FCA will also be under a statutory requirement to consider the need to contribute towards achieving compliance with section 1 of the Climate Change Act 2008 (UK net-zero emissions target) and the environmental targets set in section 5 of the Environment Act 2021.[56] The requirement does not, however, have the status of a regulatory objective – it is a regulatory principle applicable to the discharge of the PRA's and FCA's respective functions within the confines of their respective objectives. The difference in 'status' is important: regulatory objectives must be actively promoted through rules and supervisory measures, while regulatory principles are merely matters to 'have regard to.'[57] Regulatory principles cannot themselves be the basis for the regulators' policy and rule-making. Moreover, on a literal reading of the statutory provision, it is not clear whether the FCA and PRA would be permitted to take into account climate change adaptation and CRD which are approaches that go beyond meeting net-zero targets.[58] Thus, the scope for regulating insurers' outward impact remains limited, although HM Treasury considers that embedding the UK's net-zero targets into the regulatory principles is sufficient to demonstrate the government's long-term commitment to transform the economy.[59]

In addition, when making rules or issuing guidance in connection with disclosure concerning matters relating to sustainability, the regulators must have regard to any Sustainability Disclosure Requirement Policy Statement that HM Treasury has published and not withdrawn.[60] The limitations to the PRA's and FCA's respective mandates recognise that they are financial services regulators, not climate policymakers and that their rules and guidance affecting environmental matters must be aligned to national net-zero and environmental policies.

<https://assets.publishing.service.gov.uk/government/uploads/system/uploads/attachment_data/file/972443/CX_Letter_-_PRC_Remit_230321.pdf>; FCA: <https://assets.publishing.service.gov.uk/government/uploads/system/uploads/attachment_data/file/972445/CX_Letter_-_FCA_Remit_230321.pdf> both accessed on 1 June 2023.

55 Letters from the Chancellor of the Exchequer Jeremy Hunt to the Prudential Regulation Committee and the FCA, dated 8 December 2022 (Prudential Regulation Committee: <https://www.gov.uk/government/publications/recommendations-for-the-prudential-regulation-committee-december-2022>; FCA: <https://www.gov.uk/government/publications/recommendations-for-the-financial-conduct-authority-december-2022> both accessed on 1 June 2023).

56 FSMA 2023, s 27.

57 Ibid s 3B and ss. 1B(5)(a) and 2H(2).

58 See Chapter 2, Sections 2.3.3 and 2.4.1.

59 HM Treasury, 'Financial Services Future Regulatory Framework Review: Proposals for Reform' CP 548 (November 2021) [3.26].

60 FSMA 2023, s 21.

4.3.3 EIOPA

Since 1 January 2020, EIOPA's authority has been expressly extended in relation to issues not directly covered by the Solvency II Directive and other legislative acts covering the supervision of insurance and occupational pensions,

> … including matters of corporate governance, auditing and financial reporting, taking into account sustainable business models and the **integration of environmental**, social and governance-related **factors**, provided that such actions are necessary to ensure the effective and consistent application of those acts[61] (emphasis added).

EIOPA's mandate will be extended again to include 'sustainability risks' in due course. [62]

This extended remit reflects the wider EU environmental and sustainability objectives in the European Green Deal[63] and the European Climate Law which incorporates the 2050 climate neutrality target into binding legislation.[64] EIOPA plays an 'important role in identifying and reporting risks that environmental, social and governance-related factors pose to financial stability, and in rendering financial markets activity more consistent with sustainability objectives,' and 'should provide guidance on how sustainability considerations can be effectively embodied in relevant Union financial legislation and promote coherent implementation of those provisions upon adoption.'[65]

Compared to the PRA and FCA, EIOPA has a wider sustainability and environmental remit for discharging its functions supported by substantive EU legislation (the European Climate Law). However, as noted in Section 4.1.3, EIOPA does not itself have rule-making powers. Therefore, the integration of environmental factors is focused on its advisory and technical contributions to the establishment of common regulatory and supervisory standards and practices within the EU.

4.4 Regulatory approaches

4.4.1 Challenges of regulating inward impact and outward impact

Inward impact: the inward impact from climate change presents insurers and their regulators with a number of challenges. Climate change risks are complex risks that span multiple lines of insurance business, a variety of geographies, and insureds from all different

61 Regulation (EU) 2019/2175 of the European Parliament and of the Council of 18 December 2019 amending Regulation (EU) No 1093/2010 establishing a European Supervisory Authority (European Banking Authority), Regulation (EU) No 1094/2010 establishing a European Supervisory Authority (European Insurance and Occupational Pensions Authority), Regulation (EU) No 1095/2010 establishing a European Supervisory Authority (European Securities and Markets Authority), Regulation (EU) No 600/2014 on markets in financial instruments, Regulation (EU) 2016/1011 on indices used as benchmarks in financial instruments and financial contracts or to measure the performance of investment funds, and Regulation (EU) 2015/847 on information accompanying transfers of funds, art 1(3).

62 European Commission: Proposal for a Directive of the European Parliament and of the Council amending Directive 2009/138/EC as regards proportionality, quality of supervision, reporting, long-term guarantee measures, macroprudential tools, sustainability risks, group and cross-border supervision (COM/2021/581) art 1(91) and see below.

63 European Commission, Communication from the Commission – The European Green Deal COM(2019) 640.

64 Regulation (EU) 2021/1119 of the European Parliament and of the Council of 30 June 2021 establishing the framework for achieving climate neutrality and amending Regulations (EC) No 401/2009 and (EU) 2018/1999 ('European Climate Law').

65 Regulation (EU) 2019/2175 (n 61), Preamble (8).

sectors and markets.[66] Different types of climate change risks can combine with secondary effects and create interlinkages to other sectors resulting in losses of unpredictable magnitude[67] and giving rise to systemic risk.[68] While acute physical climate risks can materialise within a known short-term time horizon, other climate change risks have an uncertain and extended time horizon.[69] The severity and magnitude of the mid-term and long-term inward impact of climate change are determined by policy decisions and actions taken now and in the short term and, therefore, multiple potential pathways have to be considered for risk management and business strategy purposes.[70] There is limited statistical data on climate change risks and, where available, that data is likely to be historical and of limited use to assess the evolving inward impact on insurers going forward. In the absence of robust and consistent financial and regulatory accounting, there is a risk that insurers do not hold sufficient capital to absorb unexpected losses from climate change risks.[71]

For these reasons, climate change risk assessment strategies require a forward-looking perspective that captures future climate change events. In contrast to the statistical probabilistic (actuarial) approaches traditionally used by insurers to model short-term future risk exposure, the emerging tools for a forward-looking assessment of climate change risk are:[72]

- scenario analysis: a tool in risk analysis for the forward-looking assessment of risks and opportunities for multiple possible but uncertain pathways. Scenario analysis can be quantitative (the potential impact of a pathway of action, or inaction, by society to address climate change risk measured in monetary or percentage terms), qualitative (formulating the potential consequences of a pathway), or a mix of both;
- stress-testing: a quantitative projection of outcomes from assumed changed circumstances – e.g. the effect on the financial stability of an insurer under a specific set of severely adverse conditions as a result of one or more climate change risks impacting on the insurer over multiple periods of time or one specific climate change risk having a catastrophic impact that is short in duration;
- sensitivity analysis: a predominantly quantitative assessment of the effect of a set of alternative assumptions regarding a future environment, such as a relatively small change in these risk factors or their likelihood of occurrence.

66 See Chapter 3, Table 3.1.

67 The Geneva Association, 'Climate Change Risk Assessment for the Insurance Industry' (February 2021) 18–19 <https://www.genevaassociation.org/research-topics/climate-change-and-emerging-environmental-topics/climate-change-risk-assessment> accessed on 1 June 2023.

68 PRA, 'Climate-Related Financial Risk Management and the Role of Capital Requirements – Climate Change Adaptation Report 2021' (October 2021) ('PRA Role of Capital Requirements Report') 7 <https://www.bankofengland.co.uk/-/media/boe/files/prudential-regulation/publication/2021/october/climate-change-adaptation-report-2021.pdf?la=en&hash=FF4A0C618471462E10BC704D4AA58727EC8F8720> accessed on 1 June 2023.

69 PRA SS3/19 2-3.

70 Ibid.

71 Bank of England, 'Report on Climate-Related Risks and the Regulatory Capital Frameworks' (March 2023) ('BoE Climate and Capital Frameworks Report') [25].

72 The Geneva Association (n 67) 14.

As will be shown below, the insurance regulatory response to climate change has focused on identifying, assessing, and disclosing the inward impact of climate change risks.

Outward impact: one of the challenges of regulating outward impact is the lack of or limited mandate and appetite of regulators to do so.[73] In a 2022 survey conducted by the Geneva Association, only two out of eleven regulators responded that they were pursuing 'environmental stewardship' objectives.[74] The PRA considers that the responsibility for driving the transition to net-zero sits with the government through setting climate policy.[75] Regulators have also been relatively cautious in their approach to outward impact due to actual and perceived barriers. The FCA in particular has sought to engage with the financial services industry and other stakeholders to gather market intelligence on the development of 'green finance products' – i.e. financial products with outward impact. Industry feedback raised concerns that introducing regulatory measures too fast and too soon could create additional transition risks. It was also noted that a 'short-term results culture' in finance, and limited customer interest in green finance products, were commercial barriers to growth. Moreover, without standards and metrics for defining green characteristics of financial products, firms are reluctant to invest in the development of green products. While this feedback was provided in relation to 'green finance products,' and some of these issues are starting to be addressed, some of these commercial barriers are relevant to insurance products and impact investment by insurers.

Lack of harmonisation: a key challenge in regulating climate change is that there are diverging national regulatory approaches and inconsistent regulatory approaches across sectors. Diverging and inconsistent regulatory approaches cannot effectively address the financial risk from climate change and set the market incentives for outward impact, leading to harmful market fragmentation.[76]

4.4.2 IAIS

In a 2021 Application Paper[77] jointly published with the SIF, the IAIS provided guidance on how insurance regulators can integrate climate risk into the supervision of the insurance sector. The implementation of IAIS guidance is not mandatory for national regulators but such guidance is influential as 'soft standards' that help shape regulatory approaches at the national level. The IAIS's key recommendations included:

1. **supervisory review and reporting**: insurance regulators should gather and review quantitative and qualitative information on the inward impact on individual insurers and the insurance sector as a whole. This information could be gathered from existing reporting requirements. In addition, insurance regulators

---

73 See Section 4.3.

74 The Geneva Association, 'Anchoring Climate Change Risk Assessment in Core Business Decisions in Insurance' (September 2022) s 3.2 <https://www.genevaassociation.org/publication/climate-change-and-environment/climate-change-risk-3-report> accessed on 1 June 2023.

75 PRA Role of Capital Requirements Report Sec IV.

76 See: Financial Stability Board (n 39) ch 1, and in relation to banking regulation of climate change, see: Kern Alexander and Rosa Lastra, 'International Banking Regulation and Climate Change,' Queen Mary Law Research Paper No. 401/2023.

77 IAIS and SIF (n 35).

could ask insurers to carry out forward-looking scenario analysis and stress testing exercises in relation to the inward impact of climate change risk;[78]

2. **corporate governance**: each insurer should allocate responsibility for the management of climate change risk to a dedicated function or committee which is overseen by, and accountable, to the board and senior management;[79]
3. **risk management and internal controls**: each insurer should review its risk-management system and policies and ensure that they take into account appropriately the inward impact of climate change risks. Each of an insurer's Control Functions[80] should integrate the consideration of climate change risks into the performance of their duties;[81]
4. **enterprise risk management for solvency purposes**: climate change risks and their inward impacts should be integrated into an insurer's underwriting policy and underwriting processes, while the underwriting exposure to climate change risks should be continuously monitored to take appropriate and timely steps to mitigate and manage any potential build-up in the concentration of exposure. As part of an insurer's Own Risk and Solvency Assessment ('ORSA'), an insurer should continuously analyse its ability to manage its risk and meet its capital requirements, including forward-looking stress testing and scenario analysis;[82]
5. **investments**: insurers should carry out a risk assessment on their investments as to the extent to which climate change risk impacts the security and availability of assets matching their liabilities for capital adequacy purposes;
6. **disclosure**: as part of their existing regulatory, financial, and corporate disclosure obligations, insurers should give public disclosure in relation to climate change risks, including their exposure, targets to manage these risks (underwriting and investments), their performance against those targets, and the corporate governance framework in place.[83]

This guidance is helpful as it connects climate change risks and their inward impacts to existing IAIS Insurance Core Principles ('ICPs') which are already part of a globally accepted and recognised framework for insurance supervision. Guidance given in an Application Paper is of a high-level nature and does not include any new requirements, but merely provides advice, illustrations, recommendations, or examples of good practice to national regulators on how supervisory material may be implemented.[84] Detailed implementation is left to national regulators within their mandate and to be integrated into existing regulatory regimes and structures.

---

78 Ibid sec 2.

79 Ibid sec 3.

80 Control Functions: Risk Management Function, Compliance Function, Actuarial Function, and Internal Audit Function (see IAIS, 'Insurance Core Principles and Common Framework for the Supervision of Internationally Active Insurance Group' (November 2019 update) Insurance Core Principle 8, <https://www.iaisweb.org/page/supervisory-material/insurance-core-principles-and-comframe//file/91154/iais-icps-and-comframe-adopted-in-november-2019> accessed on 1 June 2023).

81 IAIS and SIF (n 35) sec 4.

82 Ibid sec 5.

83 Ibid 6.

84 Ibid 2.

The IAIS Application Paper has self-acknowledged limitations in scope: it does not address regulatory capital,[85] conduct of business issues (including green-washing), systemic risk to the insurance sector, and the (un)insurability of assets vulnerable to climate change risks.[86] In addition, the IAIS Application Paper is limited to inward impact – i.e. the financial risk from climate change on insurers. No guidance is given on, and there is no consideration of, the outward impact of insurers. While it is disappointing that the IAIS has not yet taken greater leadership on regulating and supervising outward impact, its introspective perspective focusing on inward impact is understandable given its limited mandate, possibly a lack of appetite amongst the majority of its members, and considering that at the time of its publication, standards and methodologies for identifying and measuring outward impact were still in their infancy.

4.4.3 PRA

In 2014, the PRA accepted an invitation from the Department for Environment, Food and Rural Affairs (Defra) to examine the impact of climate change on the PRA's objectives in relation to insurers.[87] The resulting 2015 Report, and especially its theoretical analysis of physical, transition, and liability risks stemming from climate change, led the way in climate risk assessment not just for insurers, but also for banks and other financial institutions in the UK and abroad. Building on this report, and a 2018 Report for the Banking Sector,[88] the PRA became the first regulator to set supervisory expectations – in its Supervisory Statement 3/19[89] – for insurers and banks on the management of climate-related financial risks, covering governance, risk management, scenario analysis, and disclosure.

Governance: for UK-authorised insurers, the 'Fundamental Rule' on governance is that a 'firm must organise and control its affairs responsibly and effectively.'[90] It must have in place an effective system of governance which provides for sound and prudent management of its business.[91] The system of governance must include a clear allocation of responsibilities segregated into different Senior Management Functions, a Risk Management Function, an Internal Control Function, an Internal Audit Function, and an Actuarial Function, with an effective system for ensuring the transmission of information.[92] The board of directors of an insurance company is ultimately responsible for compliance with all applicable laws and regulations.[93]

Further to SS3/19, the PRA expects insurance companies to have clear roles and responsibilities for their boards of directors and their relevant sub-committees in managing the financial risks from climate change. The board and the highest level of executive

85 The IAIS is currently undertaking work on the interlinkage on regulatory capital and climate change.

86 IAIS and SIF (n 35) 10 and 11.

87 PRA, 'The Impact of Climate Change on the UK Insurance Sector – A Climate Change Adaptation Report by the PRA' (September 2015) [1.1] <https://www.bankofengland.co.uk/prudential-regulation/publication/2015/the-impact-of-climate-change-on-the-uk-insurance-sector> accessed on 1 June 2023.

88 PRA, 'Transition in Thinking: The Impact of Climate Change on the UK Banking Sector' (September 2018).

89 PRA SS3/19.

90 PRA Rulebook, Solvency II Firms ('PRA SII'), Fundamental Rules, 2.6.

91 PRA SII, Conditions Governing Business, General Governance requirements, 2.2(1).

92 Ibid 2.2(2) and (3).

93 Ibid 2.1.

management should identify and allocate responsibility for identifying and managing financial risks from climate change to the relevant existing senior management functions most appropriate within an insurer's organisational structure and risk profile. The PRA expects to see evidence that the board and its relevant sub-committees exercise effective oversight of risk management and controls and ensure that adequate resources and sufficient skills and expertise are devoted to managing the financial risks from climate change.[94]

The PRA expects the board of directors of an insurance company to understand and assess the financial risks from climate change that affect the company, and to be able to address and oversee these risks within its overall business strategy and risk appetite, as well as long-term business planning.[95] The PRA also expects to see evidence of how an insurer monitors and manages inward impact in line with its risk appetite statement. The risk appetite statement should include the risk exposure limits and thresholds for the financial risks that the insurer is willing to bear and should take into account factors such as

- long-term financial interests of the insurer, and how decisions today affect future financial risks;
- results of stress and scenario testing, for shorter and longer time horizons;
- uncertainty around the timing and the channels through which inward impact materialises;
- sensitivity of the balance sheet to changes in key risk drivers and external conditions.[96]

Risk management: for UK-authorised insurers, the 'Fundamental Rule' on risk management is that '[a] firm must have effective risk strategies and risk management systems.'[97] This means that an insurer must have in place an effective risk-management system comprising strategies, processes, and reporting procedures necessary to identify, measure, monitor, manage, and report on a continuous basis the risks, at an individual and at an aggregated level, to which it is or could be exposed, and their interdependencies.[98] That risk-management system must be effective and well-integrated into the organisational structure and decision-making processes of the firm, and cover (1) the risks to be included in the calculation of the Solvency Capital Requirements (underwriting risk, market risk, credit risk, and operational risk),[99] as well as other risks which are not included in that calculation; (2) underwriting and reserving; (3) asset-liability management; (4) investments; (5) liquidity risk and concentration risk management; (6) operational risk management; and (7) reinsurance and other risk-mitigation techniques.[100] As part of its risk-management

94 PRA SS3/19 [3.4].

95 Ibid [3.2].

96 Ibid [3.3].

97 PRA SII, Fundamental Rules, 2.5.

98 PRA SII, Conditions Governing Business, Risk Management, 3.1(1).

99 PRA SII, Solvency Capital Requirements – General Provisions, 3.3(1): 'all quantifiable risks to which the firm is exposed are taken into account, including at least the non-life underwriting risk, life underwriting risk, health underwriting risk, market risk, credit risk, and operational risk.'

100 PRA SII, Conditions Governing Business, Risk Management, 3.1(2).

system and business strategy planning, insurers must conduct a regular ORSA,[101] in which they identify their material exposures and demonstrate that they are holding adequate capital.

The PRA expects insurers to address the financial risks from climate change through their existing risk management frameworks, in line with their board-approved risk appetite, while recognising that the nature of the risks requires a strategic approach. In a manner proportionate to their business, insurers should identify, measure, monitor, manage, and report on their exposure to these risks and, where appropriate, update existing risk management policies.[102]

Risk identification and measurement: the PRA expects insurers to understand the financial risks of climate change and the inward impact on their business model. Insurers should use scenario analysis and stress testing to inform the risk identification process and understand the short- and long-term financial risks to their business model from climate change. Firms are also expected to go beyond using only historical data to inform their risk assessment, for example by considering future trends in catastrophe modelling.[103] The ORSA should include an assessment of (1) all material exposures relating to the financial risks from climate change; and (2) how insurers have determined the material exposure(s) in the context of their business.[104]

Risk monitoring: where appropriate, the PRA expects insurers to consider a range of quantitative and qualitative tools and metrics to monitor their exposure to financial risks from climate change.[105] Insurers should also use these metrics to monitor progress against their overall business strategy and risk appetite.[106]

Risk management and mitigation: where inward impact is material, the PRA expects insurers to evidence how they will mitigate the financial risks and to have a credible plan or policies in place for managing exposures.[107] Under the 'Prudent Person Principle' ('PPP') an insurer should only invest in assets for which risks can be identified, measured, monitored, managed, controlled, and reported.[108] If there is an excessive accumulation of financial risks from climate change in their investment portfolio, insurers must consider whether it is necessary to diversify their assets or use other mitigants.[109] To inform their risk assessment and management, insurers should seek to understand the potential current and future impacts of the physical and transition risk factors on their clients, counterparties, and organisations in which the firm invests or may invest. To the extent that insurers do not have the necessary information and cannot obtain it using data from public

101 Ibid 3.8 and 3.9.
102 PRA SS3/19 [3.5].
103 Ibid [3.6].
104 Ibid [3.7].
105 Ibid [3.8].
106 Ibid [3.9].
107 Ibid [3.10].
108 PRA SII, Investments, 2.1, and see below in this section.
109 PRA SS3/19 [3.11].

resources, firms are expected to engage with clients and counterparties where this information is considered material to a firm's own risks.[110]

Risk reporting and management information: the PRA expects insurers to provide their boards and relevant sub-committees with management information on their exposure to the financial risks from climate change, to enable them to discuss, challenge, and make decisions relating to the management of the financial risks from climate change.[111]

Scenario analysis: UK insurers must have in place sound, effective, and comprehensive strategies, processes, and systems that enable them adequately to set an impact tolerance for each of their 'important business services.'[112] As part of its obligation to do so, an insurer carries out regular scenario testing of its ability to remain within its impact tolerance for each of its important business services in the event of a severe but plausible disruption of its operations.[113] Where proportionate, the PRA expects insurers to conduct scenario analysis to inform their strategic planning and determine the inward impact of climate change on their overall risk profile and business strategy, and to explore the resilience and vulnerabilities of an insurer's business model to a range of outcomes.[114] An insurer's scenario analysis should address a range of outcomes relating to different transition paths to a low-carbon economy and a path where no transition occurs. The scenario analysis should, where appropriate, include

- a short-term assessment which sets out the firm's exposure to the financial risks from climate change within its existing business planning horizon, including, where appropriate, the quantification of these risks;
- a longer-term assessment of the firm's exposure, based on its current business model, to a range of different climate-related scenarios.[115]

The PRA expects insurers to use these scenarios to understand the inward impact of climate change on their solvency, their liquidity, and their ability to pay policyholders. Where an insurer relies on management actions to mitigate the financial risks from a scenario, it should consider (1) whether these are realistic, credible, consistent with regulatory expectations, and achievable, and (2) whether any of the actions identified should be taken in advance as precautionary measures, or whether they would be relevant or desirable only if the scenario emerges.[116]

The PRA considers ORSAs to be useful frameworks within which to consider the financial risks deriving from climate change. A consideration of the long-term inward impact is essential to insurers being able to assess their ability to continue as a going

110 Ibid [3.12].

111 Ibid [3.13].

112 PRA SII, Insurance – Operational Resilience, 3.1. An 'important business service' in this context means a service provided by an insurer 'which, if disrupted, could pose a risk to: (1) … the stability of the UK financial system; (2) the firm's safety and soundness; or (3) an appropriate degree of protection for those who are or may become the firm's policyholders' (PRA Rulebook, Glossary).

113 PRA SII, Insurance – Operational Resilience, 5.1.

114 PRA SS3/19 [3.14].

115 Ibid [3.15]. For different climate-related scenarios, see Chapter 2, Section 2.2.3.

116 PRA SS3/19 [3.16].

concern. Scenario analysis is a key tool that the PRA expects firms to employ as part of that assessment;[117] however qualitative scenario analysis has been criticised as failing to provide 'decision-useful information' given that the results are highly dependent on initial but speculative assumptions.[118] The Geneva Association suggests that, instead, insurers should move towards an exploratory, holistic, iterative, and adaptive process of climate change risk assessment, leveraging their experiences to date and using quantitative data where available, with a view to both sides of the balance sheet.[119] In a recent report, the Bank of England conceded that the scenario analysis and stress tests 'have been necessarily exploratory, partial, and are limited by some of the capability gaps' but elaborated that ORSAs should now provide 'sufficient contextual information to allow a reader to understand the firm's analysis of climate risk and capital,' including methodologies and underlying assumptions, judgements, proxies, and consequent uncertainties.[120] The Geneva Association (an insurance industry body)[121] and the UN Environment Programme's PSI Initiative[122] have started to develop frameworks and templates for assessing climate change risks with methodologies that aim to create transparency and consistency.

Disclosure: UK-authorised insurers have wide-ranging disclosure obligations to their regulators and the public. They must regularly provide information to the PRA which is necessary for the purposes of the PRA's supervision[123] and disclose publicly, on an annual basis, a solvency and financial condition report.[124] In addition, the PRA expects insurers to consider disclosing how climate-related financial risks are integrated into governance and risk management processes[125] and to develop and maintain an appropriate approach to disclosure, reflective of the distinctive elements of the financial risks from climate change.[126] In particular, the PRA expects insurers to engage with the Taskforce for Climate-related Financial Disclosures ('TCFD') framework[127] and other disclosure initiatives, as well as encouraging others to engage with such disclosures through their investment relationships.[128] For a full analysis of regulatory disclosure obligations reference is made to Chapter 5.

Regulatory capital: an important area in which the PRA is working on further guidance is the interlinkage between climate change risk and regulatory capital. The capital regime for UK insurers is based on the EU Solvency II Directive,[129] which sets forward-looking, risk-based capital requirements to ensure that an insurer has sufficient resources

---

117 Ibid [3.17].

118 The Geneva Association (n 67) 10.

119 Ibid 40.

120 BoE Climate and Capital Frameworks Report [26] and [22].

121 The Geneva Association (n 67).

122 UN Environment Programme's Principles for Sustainable Insurance Initiative, 'Insuring the Climate Transition – Enhancing the Insurance Industry's Assessment of Climate Change Futures' (January 2021) <https://www.unepfi.org/psi/wp-content/uploads/2021/01/PSI-TCFD-final-report.pdf> accessed on 1 June 2023.

123 PRA SII, Reporting, 2.1.

124 Ibid 3.1.

125 PRA SS3/19 [3.19].

126 Ibid [3.20].

127 Taskforce for Climate-Related Financial Disclosures, 'Recommendations of the Task Force on Climate-Related Financial Disclosures' (June 2017) <https://www.fsb-tcfd.org/recommendations/> accessed on 1 June 2023, and see Chapter 5, Section 5.1.

128 PRA SS3/19 [3.21].

129 See n 21.

to absorb an appropriate degree of financial losses in stress, supporting its safety and soundness, and protect policyholders, and in the case of systemically important insurers, safeguarding the stability of the financial system as a whole. Following Brexit, the UK Solvency II regime is still largely equivalent to the EU Solvency regime in respect of key prudential principles, but reforms have been announced by HM Treasury.[130] The PRA has recently published a consultation paper setting out its first instalment of Solvency II reform proposals,[131] and a second consultation paper is planned for September 2023. Reforms on risk margins are expected to be implemented by late 2023, and the remainder of the new regime will come into force by the end of 2024.[132]

Summary of Solvency II regime: the Solvency II regime is complex in substance and is implemented through numerous layers of legislation and instruments. A very brief summary of the basic principles is attempted in order to provide the context for the regulatory issues discussed in this book. An insurer is required to hold technical provisions to cover all of their expected future insurance or reinsurance contractual liabilities (that is, their liabilities to policyholders and beneficiaries).[133] The value of the technical provisions is to be equal to the sum of both (1) a 'best estimate,' and (2) an additional risk margin.[134] The 'best estimate' corresponds to the probability-weighted average of future cash-flows relating to the insurance or reinsurance obligations of the insurer, taking account of the time value of money (the expected present value of future cash-flows), using the relevant risk-free interest rate term structure.[135] With the permission of the PRA, an insurer can apply a 'matching adjustment' to the best estimate which allows for recognition upfront as capital a part of the income it expects to earn on its assets in the future, but only as long as it can show that the cash-flows it expects to receive from those assets closely match the payments it has undertaken to make to its policyholders (hence 'matching' adjustment).[136] The matching adjustment benefits insurers who hold long-term assets which match the cash flows of similarly long-term insurance liabilities.[137] The risk margin is necessary to ensure that the value of the technical provisions is equivalent to the amount that a UK insurer would be expected to require in order to take over and meet the insurance and reinsurance obligations over their lifetime.[138] The methodology used to calculate the risk margin is referred to as the 'cost-of-capital method' which is the cost of holding the capital related to the liabilities a third party may require to take on the insurer's liabilities.[139] Both matching adjustments and risk margins are subject to the forthcoming reforms.[140]

In addition to having sufficient capital to cover technical provisions, an insurer also needs to have capital to cover both the 'minimum capital requirement' ('MCR') and the

130 HM Treasury (n 20).

131 PRA, 'CP12/23' (n 23).

132 HM Treasury, 'Draft Insurance and Reinsurance Undertakings (Prudential Requirements) Regulations' (n 22).

133 PRA SII, Technical Provisions, 2.1; Solvency II Directive.

134 PRA SII, Technical Provisions, 2.4.

135 Ibid 3.1.

136 Ibid 7.2.

137 HM Treasury (n 20).

138 PRA SII, Technical Provisions, 4.2.

139 Bank of England, 'DP2/22 – Potential Reforms to Risk Margin and Matching Adjustment within Solvency II,' DP2/22 (April 2022) [29].

140 For further discussion, see Chapter 8, Section 8.3.1.

'solvency capital requirement' ('SCR').[141] The regulatory capital a firm is required to hold is referred to as 'Own Funds.' Own Funds are the sum of 'basic own funds' and 'ancillary own funds.'[142] Basic own funds are the excess of assets over liabilities (less the amount of own shares held by the firm) and subordinated liabilities.[143] Ancillary own funds are items that could be called on to absorb losses (i.e. off balance sheet funds such as unpaid share capital, letters of credit, and guarantees).[144] There are certain eligibility requirements for Own Funds to ensure that insurers have the right quality of capital in place to cover the technical provisions, MCR and SCR.[145]

The MCR and the SCR together act as trigger points for varying levels of supervisory intervention and are the basis on which the amount of regulatory capital is determined. The MCR denotes a level of capital below which policyholders would be exposed to an unacceptable level of risk and is calibrated to achieve a level of 85% probability of adequacy over one year.[146] The SCR is the quantity of capital that is intended to provide protection against unexpected losses, over the following year, up to the statistical level of 99.5% (or a '1 in 200-year event').[147] An insurer can calculate its SCR using either a 'standard formula' or apply to the PRA for approval to customise its calculation of the SCR using an 'internal model' that aims to reflect that insurer's specific circumstances and risks.[148] An insurer can propose, or the PRA can impose, a 'capital add-on' for significant deviations in its risk profile or governance from that expected under Solvency II.[149]

An insurer's investments are subject to the PPP which requires an insurer to:

- only invest in assets and instruments the risks of which it can properly identify, measure, monitor, manage, control, and report and appropriately take into account in the assessment of its overall solvency needs;[150]
- invest in assets (1) in such a manner as to ensure the security, quality, liquidity, and profitability of the portfolio of assets of the firm as a whole; and (2) that are localised such as to ensure their availability;[151]
- in the case of a conflict of interest, ensure that any third party which manages its assets will ensure that the investment of assets is made in the best interest of policyholders;[152]
- ensure that assets held to cover its technical provisions[153] are invested in a manner appropriate to the nature and duration of the firm's insurance and reinsurance

141 PRA SII, Solvency Capital Requirement – General Provisions, 2.1.

142 PRA SII, Own Funds, 2.1.

143 Ibid 2.2.

144 Ibid 2.3.

145 Ibid 3 and 4.

146 PRA SII, Minimum Capital Requirement, 3.1.

147 PRA SII, Solvency Capital Requirement – General Provisions, 3.3. Some firms calculate their SCR using a 'standard formula' – a standardised calculation intended to capture the risk profile of most firms. Alternatively, firms may use an internal model to calculate the SCR, subject to prior supervisory approval.

148 PRA SII, Solvency Capital Requirement – Standard Formula, and PRA SII, Solvency Capital Requirement – Internal Models.

149 PRA SII, Solvency Capital Requirement – General Provisions, 5.

150 PRA SII, Investments, 2.1(1).

151 Ibid 2.1(2).

152 Ibid 2.1(3).

153 Technical provisions are the current amount the insurer would have to have to pay for an immediate transfer of its liabilities to another UK insurer (PRA Rulebook, SII Firms, Technical Provisions, r.2.2).

liabilities and in the best interests of all policyholders, taking into account any disclosed policy objectives (the 'technical provisions requirement').[154]

Interlinkage with climate change: noting that work is being done on this issue at an international level, the PRA and more recently the Bank of England have provided some initial findings on the interlinkage with climate change risk: capital requirements are useful to address the inward impact of climate change.[155] However, there are material gaps in both the application (capability gaps) and the design (regime gaps) of the current Solvency II regime in relation to the inward impact of climate change that create uncertainty about whether insurers are sufficiently capitalised for future climate-related losses.[156] Regulators will need to consider measures to address them (e.g. by asking insurers to adjust their modelling or by imposing capital add-ons).[157]

The Bank of England and the PRA have ruled out extending the existing twelve-month time horizon over which risks are capitalised by insurers: they argue that there are already tools within the existing regulatory frameworks that could be used to test firms' resilience to the risks in a given year over longer time horizons (for example, stress testing, long-term scenario analysis, recognising long-term expected losses through accounting and market valuations that feed into capital resources).[158] In addition, there are concerns that extending the time horizon could introduce challenges and extra costs for insurers, such as the likely increase of regulatory capital requirements in the short term, a potential widening of protection gaps, amplifying regime gaps and introducing greater complexity into the overall prudential framework.[159] However, the Bank of England has acknowledged that 'protection gaps' are a wider prudential issue that falls within the PRA's policyholder protection objective.[160]

Neither the Bank of England nor the PRA see a convincing case for capital requirements being used for addressing the causes of climate change – either by introducing 'carbon penalising factors' and/or 'green supporting factors' for exposures to assets or counterparties that are respectively more or less carbon-intensive.[161] The PRA's initial conclusion relies on research in the banking sector that shows that the use of capital requirements as a tool to stimulate outward impact – i.e. affect investment decisions directly – is not likely to be effective.[162] Moreover, using capital requirements in that way could give rise to unintended consequences, such as a deterioration of safety and soundness, given that regulatory capital – calibrated on outward impact – may not necessarily be reflective of the investment risk.[163] Regulatory capital requirements in the context of investments will be discussed further in Chapter 8, Section 8.3.1.

154 PRA Rulebook SII Firms, Investments, 3.1.

155 PRA Role of Capital Requirements Report Pt B.

156 BoE Climate and Capital Frameworks Report, Finding 1.

157 PRA Role of Capital Requirements Report Pt B: the PRA is still considering potential approaches and policy measures for addressing gaps and will be formally consulting on this for banks in the near future.

158 BoE Climate and Capital Frameworks Report [35]; also see: PRA, 'CP12/23' (n 23).

159 BoE Climate and Capital Frameworks Report [36].

160 Ibid [39].

161 Ibid, Finding 5; PRA Role of Capital Requirements Report Pt B.

162 PRA Role of Capital Requirements Report Pt B.

163 Ibid.

Continuing supervision: in 2019, the PRA asked insurers for the first time to include in their biannual stress-testing exercise an exploration of climate change scenarios and their impacts on insurers' liabilities and investments stemming from physical and transition risks.[164] The climate change stress testing exercise highlighted gaps in capabilities, data, and tools to evaluate climate-related scenarios.[165] In a 'Dear CEO letter' dated 1 July 2020, the PRA asked insurers to implement the expectations set out in SS3/2019 by the end of 2021 as fully as possible.[166] Since 2022, the PRA has switched its supervisory approach to climate-related supervisory expectations from one of assessing implementation to actively supervising against them. Insurers are expected to demonstrate effective management of climate-related financial risks, including in relation to capital adequacy, through regular supervisory engagements and reviews.[167] Where progress is insufficient and assurance or remediation is needed, the PRA will request clear plans and consider exercising its powers and making use of its wider supervisory toolkit.[168]

In a 'Dear CEO letter' dated 21 October 2022, the PRA reported that 'insurers across the sector have taken concrete and positive steps to implement our expectations ... [but] levels of embedding [climate risk management practices] vary.'[169] Although the PRA recognises that insurers face technical challenges such as the lack of high-quality climate data and disclosure, complexities in scenario analysis and risk management, and governance structures which may not lend themselves well to long-term strategic risk management,[170] an insurer who is not meeting any element of the PRA's expectations should be able to explain why that is the case and how it is planning to address any climate risk assessment gaps.[171]

Most recently, the Bank of England published a 'Report on Climate-Related Risks and the Regulatory Capital Frameworks,' in which it noted that the Bank of England will need to do further work to explore whether there may be any material regime gaps in microprudential capital requirements for insurers that need to be addressed.[172] In particular, the Bank of England will consider whether any of the calibrations and/or definitions in the Standard Formula calculation for capital requirements need to be adjusted to take account of climate risks over time,[173] and whether the way insurers assess risks within

164 PRA, 'Dear CEO Letter – IST 2019' (17 June 2019) <https://www.bankofengland.co.uk/prudential-regulation/letter/2019/insurance-stress-test-2019> accessed on 1 June 2023.

165 PRA, 'Dear CEO Letter – Insurance Stress Test 2019 and Covid-19 Stress Testing: Feedback for General and Life Insurers' (17 June 2020) Annex 4 <https://www.bankofengland.co.uk/-/media/boe/files/prudential-regulation/letter/2020/insurance-stress-test-2019-feedback.pdf?la=en&hash=BF3DF52210D9CBAF6FED788E35DB8530A74B5337> accessed on 1 June 2023.

166 PRA, 'Dear CEO Letter – Managing Climate-Related Financial Risk – Thematic Feedback from the PRA's Review of Firms' SS3/19 Plans and Clarifications of Expectations (1 July 2020) <https://www.bankofengland.co.uk/prudential-regulation/letter/2020/managing-the-financial-risks-from-climate-change> accessed on 1 June 2023.

167 PRA Role of Capital Requirements Report 21–22.

168 Ibid.

169 PRA , 'Dear CEO Letter – Thematic Feedback on the PRA's Supervision of Climate-Related Financial Risk and the Bank of England's Climate Biennial Exploratory Scenario Exercise' (21 October 2022) <https://www.bankofengland.co.uk/-/media/boe/files/prudential-regulation/letter/2022/october/managing-climate-related-financial-risks.pdf?la=en&hash=D0D7E6F305C448D503EA385E20E0683E734696A0> accessed on 1 June 2023.

170 PRA Role of Capital Requirements Report 12.

171 PRA, 'Dear CEO Letter' (n 169).

172 BoE Climate and Capital Frameworks Report [59].

173 Ibid [60].

the matching adjustment adequately allows for the capture of climate risks.[174] Finally, the Report states that the Bank of England will also consider wider prudential issues such as the vulnerability to protection gaps in relation to climate change risks. The Bank of England and the PRA have not yet commented in detail on the interlinkage between capital requirements and impact underwriting.[175] The Bank of England is participating in the ongoing international discussions with the Basel Committee on Banking Supervision, the Task Force on Climate-related Financial Risks, and the IAIS, and advocates for an internationally co-ordinated response to how regulatory frameworks and supervisory practices need to be adjusted to account for climate risks.

The Climate Financial Risk Forum, an industry forum jointly convened by the PRA and FCA to build capacity and share best practices across the financial industry's responses to the financial risks from climate change, has published a series of guides to help the financial sector develop its approach to addressing climate-related financial risks and opportunities,[176] and the PRA has also published guidance for assessing physical climate change risks.[177]

4.4.4 FCA

The FCA's regulatory approach to climate change and sustainability is organised around five themes:

1. **transparency** – promoting transparency on climate change and wider sustainability along the value chain: the FCA has already introduced requirements for TCFD-aligned disclosure for listed commercial companies and for asset managers, life insurers, and FCA-regulated pension providers.[178] These disclosure requirements will be discussed in Chapter 5;
2. **trust** – building trust and integrity in ESG-labelled instruments, products, and the supporting ecosystem: in October 2022, the FCA published proposals for sustainable disclosure requirements and for sustainable investment labels, which would initially apply to asset managers (including to insurers providing IBIPs) in respect of their UK fund products and portfolio management. The proposals would also extend to combating 'green-washing' by requiring firms to back up the sustainability claims they make. These proposals – to the extent applicable to insurers and insurance products – will be discussed in Chapter 5. In addition,

174 Ibid [61].

The matching adjustment is a mechanism that allows life insurers to recognise, upfront, a proportion of the spread (in excess of the risk-free rate) they project to earn over the future lifetime on the assets matching their matching adjustment liabilities as capital requirements. Also see Chapter 8, Section 8.3.1.

175 See Chapter 6, Section 6.3.3.

176 Bank of England, 'Climate Financial Risk Forum, Climate Financial Risk Forum (CFRF) Guides' <https://www.bankofengland.co.uk/climate-change/climate-financial-risk-forum> accessed on 1 June 2023.

177 PRA, 'A Framework for Assessing Financial Impacts of Physical Climate Change' (May 2019) <https://www.bankofengland.co.uk/-/media/boe/files/prudential-regulation/publication/2019/a-framework-for-assessing-financial-impacts-of-physical-climate-change.pdf?la=en&hash=7DE2A5E0442752ED910CF01F36BC15AA661AD1D9> accessed on 1 June 2023.

178 Listing Rules (Disclosure of Climate-Related Financial Information) Instrument 2020 amending the FCA Listing Rules Sourcebook; and Disclosure of Climate-Related Financial Information.

(Asset Manager and Asset Owner) Instrument 2021 introducing the FCA Environmental, Social and Governance sourcebook (ESG).

the FCA are considering bringing ESG data and rating providers within their regulatory oversight to ensure that ESG data and rating services are transparent, well-governed, independent, objective, and based on reliable and systematic methodologies and processes, and to support a globally consistent regulatory approach informed by the recommendations on ESG data and ratings developed by the International Organization of Securities Commission (IOSCO) in 2021;[179]

3. **tools** – working with others to enhance industry capabilities and support firms' management of climate-related and wider sustainability risks, opportunities, and impacts: together with the PRA, the FCA established the Climate Financial Risk Forum.[180] In addition, the FCA supports the development of new products and solutions to address climate change through innovation programmes and sandboxes;[181]
4. **transition** – supporting the role of finance in delivering a market-led transition to a more sustainable economy: the FCA consulted on a regulatory framework for 'stewardship' by investors who are FCA-regulated asset management firms and life insurers.[182] However, following industry feedback, the FCA decided not to introduce new regulatory measures that prescribe how asset owners and asset managers should exercise stewardship for the time being,[183] relying instead on existing measures such as the revised Shareholder Rights Directive[184] and endorsing compliance with the voluntary standards set in the UK Stewardship Code 2020.[185] These measures will be discussed in Chapter 8;
5. **team** – developing strategies, organisational structures, resources, and tools to support the integration of ESG into the FCA's regulatory activities: in February 2023, the FCA published a Discussion Paper to seek finance industry-wide views on financial services firms' sustainability-related governance, incentives, and competencies.[186] The FCA is consulting on potential regulatory measures and good practices that would stimulate positive sustainable change in the financial services industry.

---

179 FCA, 'ESG Integration in UK Capital Markets' FS22/4 (June 2022) [4.1]. On 30 March 2023, HM Treasury published a Consultation Paper on the future regulatory regime for environmental, social, and governance (ESG) ratings providers (<https://www.gov.uk/government/consultations/future-regulatory-regime-for-environmental-social-and-governance-esg-ratings-providers> accessed on 1 June 2023).

180 See Section 4.4.3.

181 FCA, 'Climate Change and Sustainable Finance' <https://www.fca.org.uk/firms/climate-change-sustainable-finance> accessed on 1 June 2023.

182 FCA, 'Discussion Paper, Building a Regulatory Framework for Stewardship' DP19/1 (January 2019).

183 FCA, 'Feedback Statement, Building a Regulatory Framework for Effective Stewardship' FS19/7 (October 2019) [1.5].

184 Directive (EU) 2017/828 of the European Parliament and of the Council of 17 May 2017 amending Directive 2007/36/EC as regards the encouragement of long-term shareholder engagement; adopted into UK law through the Occupational Pension Schemes (Investment and Disclosure) (Amendment) Regulations 2019 and the Pension Protection Fund (Pensionable Service) and Occupational Pension Schemes (Investment and Disclosure) (Amendment and Modification) Regulations 2018.

185 Financial Reporting Council, 'UK Stewardship Code 2020' <https://www.frc.org.uk/getattachment/5aae591d-d9d3-4cf4-814a-d14e156a1d87/Stewardship-Code_Final2.pdf> accessed on 1 June 2023.

186 FCA, DP23/1 (n 53).

It is evident from the FCA's 'Strategy for Positive Change,'[187] and in particular from DP23/1,[188] that the FCA is moving towards a regulatory approach that embraces outward impact through supporting product innovation and that develops good practices that foster outward impact opportunities that will ultimately benefit consumers. The FCA has explicitly acknowledged the enabling role of financial institutions on environmental issues:

> Institutions large and small can use their business decisions, their innovation and creativity, and their voice and their influence, to encourage positive change.[189]

In contrast, the PRA's focus remains for now on the prudential regulation of inward impact – the financial risks from climate change – and, as has been noted above, the PRA is not supportive of using capital requirements to stimulate outward impact of investments, and to date has not commented on the interlinkage between capital requirements and impact underwriting. The PRA considers that the responsibility for driving the transition to net-zero sits with the government through setting climate policy.[190] This position disregards that (1) as will be argued in Chapter 6, Section 6.2.3, impact underwriting is a strategy to ensure the long-term availability and affordability of non-life insurance products covering climate risk, that builds financial resilience to climate change risks and contributes to the stability of the financial system as a whole, and (2) as will be argued in Chapter 8, Section 8.3.1, the regulatory framework needs to be supportive of impact investment to channel finance into green infrastructure and the green economy. The PRA's approach is not in line with an enabling conception of insurers as outlined in Chapter 3, Section 3.4.5.

4.4.5 EU and EIOPA

The European Green Deal[191] is the EU's ambitious plan to make Europe the first climate-neutral continent in the world by 2050 and to reduce greenhouse gas emissions by at least 55% by 2030 compared to 1990 levels.[192] It provides the framework for this transformational change in all sectors, including financial services. The EU's strategy for the role of the financial services sector in reaching these targets and supporting a sustainable recovery from the COVID-19 pandemic is set out in the 'Strategy for Financing the Transition to a Sustainable Economy.'[193] Its strategy recognises the role of insurance in building financial resilience to climate change risks,[194] and for the regulatory framework to support investment flows towards economic activities that are already environmentally sustainable and towards plans to make them environmentally sustainable.[195] The Commission has proposed to strengthen insurers' management of climate and sustainability risks, in line with the European Green Deal by amending the Solvency II Directive by introducing:

187 FCA, 'A Strategy for Positive Change: Our ESG Priorities' <https://www.fca.org.uk/publications/corporate-documents/strategy-positive-change-our-esg-priorities> accessed on 1 June 2023.

188 FCA DP23/1 (n 53).

189 FCA, 'A Strategy for Positive Change' (n 187) Introduction.

190 PRA Role of Capital Requirements Report.

191 European Commission (n 63).

192 These targets have now been passed into law: see European Climate Law, art 2(1).

193 Communication from the Commission to the European Parliament, the Council, the European Economic and Social Committee, and the Committee of the Regions, 'Strategy for Financing the Transition to a Sustainable Economy' COM/2021/390 (July 2021).

194 Ibid Sec II.

195 Ibid Sec I.

- a new Article 45a into the Solvency II Directive on climate scenario analysis. Insurers will have to identify any material exposure to climate change risks and, where relevant, assess the impact of long-term climate change scenarios on their business. This analysis will take into account climate change-related risks that may not always be captured when insurers are calculating their regulatory capital requirements. However, insurers classified as low-risk profile undertakings will be exempt from the scenario analysis. In addition, EIOPA will conduct centralised climate stress tests in the insurance sector;[196]
- a new Article 304a into the Solvency II Directive. This provision will give mandates to EIOPA relating to sustainability risks, including considering whether a dedicated prudential treatment of exposures related to assets or activities associated substantially with environmental or social objectives is justified, and reviewing the scope and calibration of the standard parameters of the non-life catastrophe sub-module of the SCR with respect to natural catastrophe risk.[197]

EIOPA recognises that insurers have an active role to play in increasing the European market and its citizens' resilience to climate change by developing new products addressing risks stemming from climate change and promoting risk mitigation behaviour, and by engaging with public authorities to promote mitigation and adaptation strategies.[198] The key areas of activity on sustainable finance for 2022–2024 are: (1) integrating ESG risks in the prudential framework of insurers, (2) consolidating the macro/microprudential risk assessment of ESG risks, (3) promoting sustainability disclosures and a sustainable conduct of business framework, (4) supporting the supervision of ESG risks and supervisory convergence in the EU, (5) addressing protection gaps, (6) promoting the use of open-source modelling and data in relation to climate change risks, and (7) contributing to international convergence for the assessment and management of sustainability risks.[199] In addition, EIOPA has been requested by the European Commission to advise on greenwashing risks and the supervision and enforcement of sustainable finance policies,[200] and the European Commission has now issued a proposal for a directive on the substantiation and communication of explicit environmental claims ('Green Claims Directive').[201]

Integrating ESG risks in the prudential framework: in its 2019 Opinion addressed to the European Commission, the European Parliament, and the Council, EIOPA concluded

196 European Commission: Proposal for a Directive of the European Parliament and of the Council amending Directive 2009/138/EC as regards proportionality, quality of supervision, reporting, long-term guarantee measures, macro-prudential tools, sustainability risks, group, and cross-border supervision (COM/2021/581) art 1(25).

197 Ibid art 1(91).

198 EIOPA, 'Opinion on Sustainability within Solvency II' EIOPA-BoS-19/241' (30 September 2019) [4.12] and [4.16] European Commission: Proposal (COM/2021/581) (n 196) [4.19].

199 EIOPA, 'Sustainable Finance Activities 2022–2024' <https://www.eiopa.europa.eu/system/files/2021-12/eiopa-sustainable-finance-activities-2022-2024.pdf> accessed on 1 June 2023.

200 European Commission, 'Request for Input to the European Banking Authority (EBA), the European Insurance and Occupational Pensions Authority (EIOPA) and the European Securities and Markets Authority (ESMA) Related to Greenwashing Risks and Supervision of Sustainable Finance Policies' August 2022 <https://www.eiopa.europa.eu/publications/european-commissions-call-advice-esas-greenwashing-risks-and-supervision-sustainable-finance_en> accessed on 1 June 2023.

201 European Commission, 'Proposal for a Directive of the European Parliament and of the Council on Substantiation and Communication of Explicit Environmental Claims (Green Claims Directive)' COM/2023/166.

that under the existing Solvency II regime 'climate change-related risks bring considerable challenges to the valuation of assets and liabilities, underwriting and investment decisions and risk measurement.'[202] While the Pillar 1 (quantitative requirements) valuation principles were largely flexible enough to capture the inward impact of climate change,[203] Pillar 2 (qualitative requirements) needed to be more explicitly extended to integrate the assessment and management of climate change risks.[204] EIOPA recommended that insurers take into account the impact of their underwriting and investment activity on sustainability factors.[205]

Following EIOPA's recommendations,[206] the European Commission adopted delegated regulations[207] that amend the Solvency II Delegated Regulation[208] to integrate sustainability considerations into the Solvency II regime. Thus, EU insurers must now assess and manage in relation to their underwriting activities the risk of loss or of adverse change in the values of insurance and reinsurance liabilities, resulting from inadequate pricing and provisioning assumptions, including sustainability risks.[209] In addition, EU insurers must take into account sustainability risk when identifying, measuring, monitoring, managing, controlling, reporting, and assessing risks arising from investments (= inward impact), and the potential long-term impact of their investment strategy and decisions on sustainability factors (= outward impact).[210] An insurer's investment strategy and decisions on sustainability factors must reflect the sustainability preferences of its customers taken into account in the product approval process.[211] 'Sustainability risk' is defined as 'an environmental, social or governance event or condition that, if it occurs, could cause an actual or a potential negative impact on the value of the investment or on the value of the liability,'[212] and 'sustainability factors' mean environmental, social, and employee matters, respect for human rights, anti-corruption, and anti-bribery matters.[213]

EIOPA is now planning to deepen its analysis of the capital treatment of natural catastrophe liabilities, investments associated with environmental and/or social objectives, or associated substantially with harm to such objectives, and climate-resilient insurance products.[214] EIOPA has already published:

---

202 EIOPA (n 198) [1.11].

203 Ibid [4.1] and [4.6].

204 Ibid [1.13].

205 Ibid [4.12] and [4.16].

206 EIOPA, 'EIOPA's Technical Advice on the Integration of Sustainability Risks and Factors in the Delegated Acts under Solvency II and IDD' EIOPA-BoS-19/172, (30 April 2019) s 3 and 4 <https://register.eiopa.europa.eu/Publications/EIOPA-BoS-19-172_Final_Report_Technical_advice_for_the_integration_of_sustainability_risks_and_factors.pdf> accessed on 1 June 2023.

207 Commission Delegated Regulation (EU) 2021/1256 of 21 April 2021 amending Delegated Regulation (EU) 2015/35 as regards the integration of sustainability risks in the governance of insurance and reinsurance undertakings.

208 Commission Delegated Regulation (EU) 2015/35 of 10 October 2014 supplementing Directive 2009/138/EC of the European Parliament and of the Council on the taking up and pursuit of the business of Insurance and Reinsurance (Solvency II).

209 Commission Delegated Regulation (EU) 2021/1256 (n 207) art 1(2).

210 Ibid art 1(6).

211 Ibid art 1(6).

212 Ibid art 1(1).

213 Ibid art 1(1).

214 EIOPA, 'Sustainable Finance Activities 2022–2024' (n 199).

- a Methodology Paper for the potential inclusion of climate change in the Solvency II standard formula when calculating natural catastrophe underwriting risk,[215] proposing a formalised approach to re-assess current natural catastrophe solvency capital requirement parameters on a regular basis and to regularly re-calibrate the relevant risks for specific geographical regions with latest data and models available every three to five years;
- a Discussion Paper that examines the prudential treatment of certain assets exposed to transition risk, and the prudential treatment of climate change adaptation measures.[216]

Consolidating the macro/microprudential risk assessment of ESG risks and supporting the supervision of ESG risks and supervisory convergence in the EU: climate risk assessment, including using climate change scenarios and stress testing, is essential to assess the insurance sector's resilience to climate risks. EIOPA has already provided an Opinion on the use of climate change risk scenarios in ORSAs,[217] and guidance on the sensitivity analysis of climate change-related transition risk.[218]

EIOPA is planning to develop further methodological principles of stress testing for climate change risks. They propose a Supervisory Handbook on the supervision of climate-related risk to provide further guidance on climate risk materiality assessment and scenario analysis in the ORSAs. EIOPA is also looking to give further guidance on the supervision of ESG conduct risks, including green-washing, and will start monitoring the offer of sustainable products.[219]

Promoting sustainability disclosures: the EU's main regulatory focus to date in relation to the financial services has been on disclosure, namely providing investors with information to make informed sustainable investment decisions, underpinned by a science-based taxonomy system providing a common definition of sustainability and thereby protecting against green-washing. This will be discussed in Chapter 5, Section 5.4.

Insurance advice on sustainable IBIPs: in relation to IBIPs,[220] the EU has sought to integrate sustainability factors, risks, and preferences into the product oversight and governance requirements for EU insurers and insurance intermediaries and into the existing conduct of business rules arising under the Insurance Distribution

215 EIOPA, 'Methodology Paper on Potential Inclusion of Climate Change in the Nat Cat Standard Formula' EIOPA-BoS-21/253.

216 EIOPA, 'Prudential Treatment of Sustainability Risks – Discussion Paper' EIOPA-BoS-22-527, and see Chapter 6, Section 6.3.3 and Chapter 8, Section 8.3.1.

217 EIOPA, 'Opinion on the Supervision of the Use of Climate Change Risk Scenarios in ORSA' EIOPA-BoS-21-12.

218 EIOPA, 'Sensitivity Analysis of Climate-Change Related Transition Risks' (December 2020) <https://www.eiopa.europa.eu/publications/sensitivity-analysis-climate-change-related-transition-risks_en> accessed on 1 June 2023.

219 EIOPA, 'Sustainable Finance Activities 2022–2024' (n 199).

220 For the purposes of EU insurance regulation, an IBIP means an insurance product which offers a maturity or surrender value and where that maturity or surrender value is wholly or partially exposed, directly or indirectly, to market fluctuations (Regulation (EU) No 1286/2014 of the European Parliament and of the Council of 26 November 2014 on key information documents for packaged retail and IBIPs (PRIIPs) art 4(2)).

> Directive ('IDD')[221] and IDD-related Delegated Regulations.[222] Accordingly, insurers and insurance intermediaries who create, develop, and/or design IBIPs must consider sustainability factors in (1) the product approval process, and (2) other product governance and oversight arrangements, for each such product that is intended to be distributed to customers seeking insurance products with a sustainability-related profile.[223] 'Sustainability factors' are environmental, social, and employee matters, respect for human rights, anti-corruption, and anti-bribery matters.[224]

Insurers and insurance intermediaries who advise on IBIPs must first assess a customer's or potential customer's investment objectives and individual circumstances, and then also ask questions to identify their individual sustainability preferences. They must ensure that any recommendations to customers or potential customers reflect both the financial objectives and any sustainability preferences expressed by those customers.[225] 'Sustainability preferences' means a customer's or potential customer's choice as to whether and, if so, to what extent, financial products that promote social or environmental characteristics and/or financial products that have 'sustainable investment' as their objective should be integrated into his or her investment.[226] At this point, the advice requirements interlink with the pre-contractual disclosure requirements for IBIPs under the EU Regulation (EU) 2019/2088 on sustainability-related disclosures in the financial services sector ('SFDR').[227] An insurer and insurance intermediary must not recommend IBIPs as meeting a customer's or potential customer's sustainability preferences where those IBIPs do not meet those preferences, in which case they must explain the reasons for not doing so and keep records of those reasons.[228]

Regulatory requirements on the integration of sustainability factors, risks, and preferences into the product oversight and governance requirements is a recognition of insurers' (and insurance intermediaries') enabling role: manufacturing, offering, and advising on sustainable IBIPs encourages (potential) customer demand for such products and enables them to invest in products they can trust to have the sustainable features they claim to have. It is important to note that these regulatory requirements are limited to IBIPs, and do not extend to other insurance products.

---

221 Directive (EU) 2016/97 of the European Parliament and of the Council of 20 January 2016 on insurance distribution (recast).

222 Commission Delegated Regulation (EU) 2017/2358 of 21 September 2017 supplementing Directive (EU) 2016/97 of the European Parliament and of the Council with regard to product oversight and governance requirements for insurance undertakings and insurance distributors; and Commission Delegated Regulation (EU) 2017/2359 of 21 September 2017 supplementing Directive (EU) 2016/97 of the European Parliament and of the Council with regard to information requirements and conduct of business rules applicable to the distribution of IBIPs.

223 Commission Delegated Regulation (EU) 2021/1257 of 21 April 2021 amending Delegated Regulations (EU) 2017/2358 and (EU) 2017/2359 as regards the integration of sustainability factors, risks, and preferences into the product oversight and governance requirements for insurance undertakings and insurance distributors and into the rules on conduct of business and investment advice for IBIPs, art 1.

224 Ibid art 2.

225 Ibid art 2.

226 Ibid arts 8 and 9.

227 See Chapter 5, Section 5.4.2.

228 Commission Delegated Regulation (EU) 2021/1257 (n 223) art 2.

Addressing protection gaps: as noted in Chapter 3, protection gaps can lead to hardship at the individual policyholder level, they may have a cascading effect on economic activities, supply chains, and the performance of loans and investments across the financial system,[229] and they are consequently costly to society as a whole. EIOPA's work on protection gaps aims to raise risk awareness and inform the discussion on measures to improve risk assessment, risk prevention, and adaptation measures, as well as incentives for appropriate product design and risk transfer, for climate change risks.[230] Its report on non-life underwriting and pricing in light of climate change highlights the challenges associated with short-term non-life contracts and annual re-pricing in the context of climate change, and identifies how insurers could address the insurance protection gap and contribute to climate change mitigation and adaptation.[231] EIOPA is also developing a pilot EU-wide dashboard on insurance protection gaps which shows current and historical protection gaps by country and, going forward, will enable evidence-based decision-making on insurance protection and other measures to improve society's resilience against natural catastrophes.[232]

Promoting the use of open-source modelling and data in relation to climate change risks: EIOPA aims to support the modelling and management of climate change risks by positioning itself as a relevant open-source data hub providing relevant aggregate data, such as for example natural catastrophe insured loss data, in a transparent and easily accessible manner.[233]

Contributing to international convergence for the assessment and management of sustainability risks: EIOPA recognises the need for global convergent practices on the supervision and management on sustainability risk, and as a member of the Network for the Greening of the Financial System, the SIF, and the IAIS, seeks to build synergies and contribute to global standard-setting.[234] EIOPA is also involved in the EU–US dialogue on climate-related projects on climate risk financial oversight and climate risk and resilience.[235]

Corporate social responsibility: the European Commission has adopted a proposal for a directive on corporate sustainability due diligence ('CSDDD') which would establish a corporate due diligence duty for certain companies to identify, bring to an end, prevent, mitigate, and account for negative human rights and environmental impacts in the company's own operations, their subsidiaries, and business relationships in their value chains.[236] Providing insurance to fossil fuel businesses could be seen as a harmful environmental impact on an insurer's value chain.[237] The CSDDD, if adopted and implemented into the national laws of EU member

229 IAIS and SIF (n 38) 14.

230 EIOPA, 'Sustainable Finance Activities 2022–2024' (n 199).

231 EIOPA, 'Report on Non-Life Underwriting and Pricing in Light of Climate Change' EIOPA-BoS-21/259 01.

232 EIOPA, 'Dashboard on Insurance Protection Gap for Natural Catastrophes' <https://www.eiopa.europa.eu/tools-and-data/dashboard-insurance-protection-gap-natural-catastrophes_en> accessed on 1 June 2023.

233 EIOPA, 'Sustainable Finance Activities 2022–2024' (n 199).

234 Ibid.

235 Ibid.

236 Proposal for a Directive of the European Parliament and of the Council on Corporate Sustainability Due Diligence and amending Directive (EU) 2019/1937 COM/2022/71, arts 6–8.

237 Proposal for CSDDD, art 3(e) – the definition of 'business relationship' refers to providing insurance.

states, will apply to companies incorporated in the EU with (1) 500+ employees and a net EUR 150 million+ turnover worldwide; and/or (2) 250+ employees, a net EUR 40+ million turnover worldwide, and operating in defined high-impact sectors, e.g. textiles, agriculture, extraction of minerals. Those companies will also be required to have a plan to ensure that their business model and strategy are compatible with limiting global warming to 1.5°C in line with the Paris Agreement.[238] Directors of in-scope companies will be required to set up and oversee the implementation of the due diligence processes and integrate due diligence into the corporate strategy.[239] The CSDDD could also become applicable to any UK insurers that generate a net turnover of EUR 150 million in the EU.[240] It is not yet settled to what extent the CSDDD would apply to financial services firms, including insurers: the European Commission proposal envisages that the CSDDD apply to regulated financial undertakings, whereas the Council has adopted the position that the financial sector should be exempted from most of the rules, giving discretion to the member states to decide whether or not to include the financial sector when implementing the directive.[241] The European Parliament agreed with the proposal to apply the CSDDD to regulated financial undertakings but proposed to limit the scope in that obligations would only extend to activities of a direct client and its corporate group that has linked activities to the contract in question. The Commission, Council, and Parliament are hoping to be able to reach a final agreement on the scope of the CSDDD by the end of 2023.

ESG rating activities: the European Commission has put forward a proposal for regulating ESG rating services to improve their reliability and transparency and foster trust and confidence in those services.[242] The proposed regulation aims to enhance the quality of information about ESG ratings, by (1) improving transparency of ESG ratings characteristics and methodologies, and by (2) ensuring increased clarity on operations of ESG rating providers and the prevention of risks of conflict of interest at ESG rating providers' level. The general objective of the initiative is to improve the quality of ESG ratings to enable investors to make better-informed investment decisions in regard to sustainability objectives, and to enable rated entities to make informed decisions about managing ESG risks and the impact of their operations.

4.4.6 USA: anti-ESG legislation

This section does not discuss the insurance supervisory approaches to climate risk assessment and regulation taken in the US. The main reason for this exclusion is that pursuant to the McCarran–Ferguson Act (15 U.S.C. §1012), insurance law is the subject of state law and the analysis would therefore require a review of the laws of 50 states in a fast

238 Ibid art 15.

239 Ibid art 25.

240 Ibid art 2(2)(a).

241 Council of the European Union, 'Proposal for a Directive of the European Parliament and of the Council on Corporate Sustainability Due Diligence and Amending Directive (EU) 2019/1937 – General Approach' 6533/22.

242 Proposal for a Regulation on the transparency and integrity of Environmental, Social and Governance (ESG) rating activities 2023/0177 (COD) COM/2023/314.

and diversely developing area. Instead, this section draws brief attention to a counter-development that is of relevance to insurers: anti-ESG legislation. While liberal-leaning state governments have started to embrace ESG-focused investing,[243] conservative-led states have passed or are planning to pass legislation that prohibits the state from (1) doing business with financial institutions that 'boycott' or 'discriminate against' companies in certain (e.g. fossil fuel) industries, and/or (2) investing the state's assets (including pension plan assets) through such financial institutions.[244] The reasons cited for such 'Boycott Bills' are concerns that ESG investing is putting policy and social objectives ahead of financial objectives, can negatively impact local economies,[245] and is, according to Florida Governor Santos, one of the ways legislators 'can protect individual freedom from stridently ideological private actors.'[246]

Boycott Bills are already in place, or about to come into force, in Kentucky, Oklahoma, Tennessee, Texas, West Virginia, Wyoming, Iowa, and Florida.[247] Some of these measures (Kentucky, Oklahoma, Texas, West Virginia, and Florida) authorise state regulators to blacklist financial entities that engage in boycotts of fossil fuel companies for divestment purposes.[248] Texas has already published a banking and funds blacklist (including Blackrock, Inc, HSBC, and UBS), and there is now a push to expand the blacklist regime to insurers.[249] In addition, some of these measures compel companies entering into contracts with state entities to attest, as a condition of doing business with public entities, that they do not and will not engage in boycotts against fossil fuel companies during the life of the contract.[250] Whether insurers and their underwriting and investment activities are within the scope of these measures will depend on each instrument, including the application of exceptions and thresholds. Moreover, in May 2023, a group of 23 US AGs wrote a letter to US insurers who are members of the NZIA raising concerns about the legality of their commitments to collaborate with other insurers and asset owners in order to 'advance an activist climate agenda.'[251]

243 Illinois and Maryland laws promote the consideration of ESG factors in state investment strategies, and Maine laws require the state to divest itself of assets invested in the fossil fuel industry by a specified date. See: Leah Malone, Emily Holland, and Carolyn Houston from Simpson Thacher & Bartlett LLP, 'ESG Battlegrounds: How the States Are Shaping the Regulatory Landscape in the U.S.,' Harvard Law School Forum on Corporate Governance (11 March 2023) <https://corpgov.law.harvard.edu/2023/03/11/esg-battlegrounds-how-the-states-are-shaping-the-regulatory-landscape-in-the-u-s/> accessed on 1 June 2023.

244 *Reuters*, 'The Challenge of Investing in the Face of State Anti-ESG Legislation' (24 August 2022). A second group of anti-ESG legislation are measures that restrict states from considering ESG factors in their investment strategies.

245 Ibid.

246 Florida Governor Ron DeSantis, *The Courage to Be Free: Florida's Blueprint for America's Revival* (Harper Collins 2023) cited in CBC News, 'Biden to Use Veto to Keep ESG Investing Rule. What Is It, and Why Do Most Republicans Hate It?' (2 March 2023).

247 Simpson Thacher & Bartlett LLP (n 243).

248 Ibid.

249 Shelly Hagan and Nic Querolo, 'Texas Anti-ESG Push Is Coming for Insurers and Pensions in New Bills' (*Insurance Journal*, 6 March 2023).

250 Simpson Thacher & Bartlett LLP (n 243).

251 Letter from the State Attorney Generals of Utah, Louisiana, Alabama, Alaska, Arkansas, Georgia, Idaho, Indiana, Iowa, Kansas, Kentucky, Mississippi, Missouri, Montana, New Hampshire, Ohio, Oklahoma, South Carolina, South Dakota, Texas, Virginia, West Virginia, and Wyoming to NZIA insurers, dated 16 May 2023 <https://attorneygeneral.utah.gov/wp-content/uploads/2023/05/2023-05-15-NZIA-Letter.pdf> accessed on 1 June 2023. This letter and its implication will be considered further in Chapter 6, Section 6.4.5.

The US House Financial Services Committee has set up an ESG Working Group which has recently held hearings on the impact of ESG policies on capital markets. In a preliminary report, it set out a number of 'key priorities,' including to

- Strengthen oversight and conduct thorough investigations into federal regulatory efforts that would contort [the] financial system into a vehicle to implement climate policy;
- Demand transparency, responsibility, and adherence to statutory limits from financial and consumer regulatory agencies;
- Protect US companies from burdensome EU regulations, safeguarding American interests in global markets.[252]

In contrast, the US Senate Committee on the Budget recently wrote to seven US insurers (State Farm, Liberty Mutual, Berkshire Hathaway, AIG, Travelers Insurance, Chubb, and Starr), stating that continuing to underwrite and invest in fossil fuel projects was inconsistent with the goals of the Paris Agreement to which the US is a signatory, harmful to policyholders who are increasingly facing protection gaps, and potentially creating systemic risk for the economy. The Committee has launched an investigation into Berkshire Hathaway to account for their plans to phase out underwriting and investing in fossil fuel projects.[253] The rise of anti-ESG legislation in some states, and pro-ESG measures in other states[254] and at the federal government level,[255] poses significant legal, operational, reputational, and financial concerns for insurers that integrate ESG factors into their investment and underwriting policies and disclosures, especially where a company is operating across different states and/or internationally.[256] The anti-ESG legislation in the US also stands in stark contrast to the EU proposals for the CSDDD. Insurance companies that have EU and US operations may be caught by conflicting policy approaches to corporate purpose and corporate social responsibility.

4.5 Conclusion

The preceding discussion on the regulatory approaches of the IAIS, PRA, FCA, and EIOPA indicates that the regulation of the inward impact of climate change risks and the outward impact on climate change by insurance regulators is circumscribed by their mandate and regulatory objectives, as well the wider environmental policies of the jurisdiction or legal

252 Memorandum from the SG Working Group of the House Committee on Financial Services to Republican Members of the House Committee on Financial Services regarding 'Preliminary Report on ESG Climate Related Financial Services Concerns' (dated 23 June 2023) <https://financialservices.house.gov/uploadedfiles/hfsc_esg_working_group_memo_final.pdf> accessed on 10 August 2023.

253 Letter from the United States Senate Committee on the Budget to State Farm, Liberty Mutual, Berkshire Hathaway, AIG, Travelers Insurance, Chubb, and Starr dated 9 June 2023 launching investigation into Berkshire Hathaway for continuing to insure and invest in fossil fuel projects, dated 9 June 2023 <https://www.budget.senate.gov/imo/media/doc/Budget%20Committee%20Letters%20to%20Insurance%20Companies.pdf> accessed 9 June 2023.

254 Simpson Thacher & Bartlett LLP (n 243).

255 See e.g. US Department of Labor: Final Rule on Prudence and Loyalty in Selecting Plan Investments and Exercising Shareholder Rights (22 November 2022) <https://www.dol.gov/agencies/ebsa/about-ebsa/our-activities/resource-center/fact-sheets/final-rule-on-prudence-and-loyalty-in-selecting-plan-investments-and-exercising-shareholder-rights> accessed on 1 June 2023 – now subject to a challenge by the US Senate. Also see the Letter from the United States Senate Committee on the Budget (n 253).

256 Simpson Thacher & Bartlett LLP (n 243).

framework in which they operate. A common theme is that the initial regulatory focus was on inward impact – the financial risks stemming from climate change on individual insurers' balance sheets and the financial stability of the financial system as a whole – and how this inward impact could be assessed and integrated into existing risk governance and management structures. A second focus of activity has been the disclosure and reporting of climate-related financial risks, and increasingly also the disclosure of sustainability-related issues, and these matters will be closely examined in the following chapter.

There is a more fragmented picture and a number of unresolved questions in relation to outward impact, including to what extent and how regulation should be supporting and incentivising impact underwriting and impact investment (e.g. through regulatory capital treatment). It seems that the FCA and EIOPA recognise the role of insurers as net-zero enablers and are prepared to consider regulatory tools to bolster outward impact. The most progress in that respect has been made in relation to IBIPs. As will be discussed further in Chapters 6 to 8 there is not yet sufficient consensus and science-based evidence on how this should be done and scaled up so that the insurance industry – through underwriting and investment – can support an orderly and equitable net-zero transition in the real economy. There are not yet any norms that mandate substantive standards of behaviour in relation to impact underwriting and impact investment, although with the CRDDD and the US anti-ESG legislation we see polarised developments in opposite directions.

Importantly, the IAIS, the Bank of England, and EIOPA recognise that climate change is a global issue that requires co-ordinated regulatory approaches and standard-setting at the international level across the financial services sector and consultation with the financial services industry. This multi-lateral and multi-sectoral approach has already been tested in relation to disclosure and reporting. The Financial Stability Board ('FSB') is going to issue guidance on supervisory and regulatory approaches across borders and sectors to address market fragmentation and potential sources of systemic risk.[257] One of the key action points that the President-Designate of COP28, Dr. Sultan Ahmed Al Jaber, is proposing to for the forthcoming COP28 meeting is to progress the harmonisation of regulatory systems in order to enable the deployment of private sector financial solutions consistent with the Paris Agreement.[258]

Returning to regulatory mandates and the integration of financial regulation into environmental policy at the national, regional, and international levels, it is suggested that convergence on clear regulatory objectives, a common commitment to the implementation of the objectives of the Paris Agreement, and consensus on the role of the insurance industry are key steps towards international regulatory standards that support outward impact.

257 FSB, 'FSB Roadmap for Addressing Climate-Related Financial Risks' (June 2021) Block 4 <https://www.fsb.org/wp-content/uploads/P070721-2.pdf#:~:text=The%20FSB%20roadmap%20sets%20out%20for%20G20%20endorsement,and%20Central%20Bank%20Governors%20meeting%20in%20July%202021.> accessed on 1 June 2023.

258 Message from the President-Designate of COP28/CMP18/CMA5, and UAE Special Envoy for Climate Change, Dr. Sultan Ahmed Al Jaber, 'COP 28 Vision' (13 July 2023) https://unfccc.int/documents/630572 accessed on 13 July 2023.

CHAPTER 5

Climate-related disclosures

There is a growing demand for climate-related information about enterprises, their products, and value chains.[1] Insurers need information and data on climate change risks and their financial impacts for their underwriting processes and investment decisions to support robust risk assessments and valuations. Insurers also need this information to be able to assess climate change risk and their exposures to climate-related losses for the purposes of their regulatory risk management processes, including the impact on their regulatory capital requirements and the value of their investments. In addition, insurers are facing public demand, as well as an increasing number of legal and regulatory requirements, for disclosing information on their inward and outward impacts and their risk governance and management practices in relation to those impacts. Bowman and Wiseman explain the logic of climate-related disclosures at three levels: (1) at the macro-economic level, such disclosures allow the markets to price in climate change risk; (2) at the meso-market level, investors can use the disclosed information to inform their investment and divestment decisions; and (3) at the micro individual company level, the relevant information helps companies to identify and manage climate change risk.[2]

Public disclosure of inward impact – how climate change risks have already impacted, and can affect, an enterprise – is important because it provides investors and the financial markets with information to make informed decisions and investment choices.[3] In the financial sector, the disclosure of outward impact on financial institutions also assists regulators in assessing the financial stability of a firm and the systemic risk posed by climate change to the financial sector.[4]

The need for public disclosure on outward impact – what impact an enterprise has on the environment – is gaining traction. Proponents stress that corporate disclosure of outward impacts creates transparency and, through standardisation, introduces a greater

1 TCFD, 'Implementing the Recommendations of the Task Force on Climate-Related Financial Disclosures' (June 2017) sec A <https://assets.bbhub.io/company/sites/60/2020/10/FINAL-TCFD-Annex-Amended-121517.pdf> accessed on 1 June 2023.

2 Megan Bowman and Daniel Wiseman, 'Finance Actors and Climate-Related Disclosure Regulation: Logic, Limits and Emerging Accountability' in Cameron Holley, Liam Phelan and Clifford Shearing (eds), '*Criminology and Climate Insurance, Finance and the Regulation of Harmscapes*' (Routledge, 2020) ch.9.

3 See e.g. Communication from the European Commission to the European Parliament, the Council, the European Economic and Social Committee, and the Committee of the Regions, 'Strategy for Financing the Transition to a Sustainable Economy' (COM/2021/390) [8] and TCFD, 'Implementing Recommendations' (n 1) s A.1.

4 TCFD, 'Implementing Recommendations' (n 1), and see Chapter 4, Section 4.4.

DOI: 10.4324/b23081-5

degree of comparability.[5] Giving disclosure on outward impact creates transparency as to the extent to which an enterprise's operations, products, and value chains are aligned to the Paris Agreement goals, the national and international net-zero targets, or pursue other environmental objectives. This information will be important to (potential) investors, customers, and other stakeholders in value chains who seek to integrate environmental factors into their relationships with business partners and suppliers (including suppliers of financial services). Disclosures on outward impacts introduce better comparability and create competition (1) as some institutional investors have adopted (environmental) stewardship principles[6] and thus require that information for their investment and divestment decisions and their proxy voting decisions; and (2) as such disclosures can create negative or positive publicity which in turn can give rise to reputational risk and opportunities.

In addition, public disclosure of positive outward impact can increase awareness of climate action and set an example for others to act. The FCA considers that transparency through disclosure drives positive change.[7] In the financial services industry, there is a parallel development concerning product disclosure regulations relating to the provision of information on environmental and sustainability-related characteristics of a financial product to a prospective customer at the pre-contractual stage so that the prospective customer can make an informed decision on whether or not to buy that product. The European Commission sees reporting on 'outward impact' as a pre-requisite to re-orient capital flows towards sustainable investments in order to achieve a socially just transition to a sustainable net-zero economy.[8] Public disclosures on outward impact are essential to taking CRD approaches that are informed by data and measure complex trade-offs and synergies among different actions.[9]

The growing demand for decision-useful, climate-related information has resulted in the ongoing development of several climate-related disclosure, reporting, and accounting standards, including the Greenhouse Gas Protocol in 2001,[10] TCFD Recommendations,[11] and the climate-related disclosures standards from the International Sustainability Standards Board ('ISSB').[12] These climate-related disclosure standards started off as voluntary frameworks but are now hardening into law in several key jurisdictions.

Customers and investors will only be able to trust corporate and product disclosures if they can rest assured that certain labels and descriptions relating to environmental impact, environmental objectives, and environmental outcomes are meaningful and are not used to green-wash products and corporate identities. Therefore, to achieve transparency, consistency, and comparability, disclosure reporting needs to be standardised in format and

5 SFDR (Regulation (EU) 2019/2088 on sustainability-related disclosures in the financial services sector), Recitals.

6 See Chapter 8, Section 8.3.2.

7 FCA, 'Finance for Positive Sustainable Change: Governance, Incentives and Competence in Regulated Firms' DP23/1 (February 2023) [1.4].

8 Communication from the Commission, 'Action Plan: Financing Sustainable Growth' (COM/2018/97).

9 See Chapter 2, Section 2.4.1.

10 The World Business Council for Sustainable Development and the World Resources Institute, 'The Greenhouse Gas Protocol: A Corporate Accounting and Reporting Standard' (now in a revised edition, 2004) <https://ghgprotocol.org/corporate-standard> accessed on 1 June 2023; also see Chapter 3, Section 3.3.2.

11 TCFD, 'Recommendations of the Task Force on Climate-Related Financial Disclosures' (June 2017) <https://www.fsb-tcfd.org/recommendations/> accessed on 1 June 2023.

12 ISSB, 'IFRS Sustainability Standards Navigator' <https://www.ifrs.org/issued-standards/ifrs-sustainability-standards-navigator/> accessed on 10 August 2023.

contents, and any labels used need to have prescribed criteria and clear classifications, and key terms ought to have precise definitions. Finally, for quality assurance and credibility purposes, the underlying data used for corporate and product disclosures should be verifiable and verified.[13]

This chapter critically examines the TCFD Recommendations (Section 5.1), the IFRS Sustainability Disclosure Standards (Section 5.2), the emerging UK sustainability-related disclosure regimes (Section 5.3), and the EU sustainability-related disclosure regime and taxonomy framework (Section 5.4), as they apply to insurance companies. Given the technical detail of the various disclosure regimes and frameworks, it has been necessary to summarise their provisions and methodologies and to focus on key requirements relevant to insurers. Reference is made to the full texts cited. This chapter does not address climate-related disclosure requirements applicable to insurers in the US for two reasons: the fragmented ESG disclosure landscape at the state and federal levels in the US[14] (1) would have added considerable volume to an already lengthy chapter, and (2) is a 'political battleground'[15] characterised by rapid developments that would quickly render any discussion obsolete.

5.1 The TCFD Recommendations

There are numerous initiatives on climate-related disclosures. They all have in common the aim to create transparent reporting standards that would allow an enterprise's performance on environmental matters to be measured and compared to others. The TCFD Recommendations are the most widely referenced framework. They have been adopted as standards in regulations at the national level, and subsequent frameworks and proposals build upon the TCFD's work.[16] It is for this reason that a discussion of the TCFD Recommendations serves as the cornerstone of this chapter.

5.1.1 The Task Force

The Task Force on Climate-Related Financial Disclosures ('Task Force') was set up by the FSB in 2015 to improve and increase the reporting of climate-related financial information. The FSB called on the Task Force to develop climate-related disclosures that 'could promote more informed investment, credit [or lending], and insurance underwriting decisions' and, in turn, 'would enable stakeholders to understand better the concentrations of carbon-related assets in the financial sector and the financial system's exposures to climate-related risks,' as well as assisting the financial services sector with 'foster[ing] an early assessment of these risks' and 'facilitate[ing] market discipline.'[17]

13 Bowman and Wiseman (n 2).

14 See Chapter 4, Section 4.4.6.

15 See Leah Malone, Emily Holland, and Carolyn Houston from Simpson Thacher & Bartlett LLP, 'ESG Battlegrounds: How the States Are Shaping the Regulatory Landscape in the U.S.,' Harvard Law School Forum on Corporate Governance (11 March 2023) <https://corpgov.law.harvard.edu/2023/03/11/esg-battlegrounds-how-the-states-are-shaping-the-regulatory-landscape-in-the-u-s/> accessed on 1 June 2023.

16 See Sections 5.2 and 5.3.

17 FSB, 'Proposal for a Disclosure Task Force on Climate-Related Risks' (9 November 2015) <https://www.fsb.org/wp-content/uploads/Disclosure-task-force-on-climate-related-risks.pdf> accessed on 1 June 2023.

In 2017, the Task Force published the TCFD Recommendations 'designed to help companies provide better information to support informed capital allocation.'[18] The TCFD Recommendations provide a foundational framework for climate-related disclosures which is built around four core themes – governance, strategy, risk management, and metrics and targets – that are intended to help investors and others understand how reporting organisations assess climate-related risks and opportunities.[19]

The TCFD Recommendations distinguish between climate-related risks (divided into two sub-categories: (1) transition risks, and (2) physical risks),[20] and climate-related opportunities. Both climate-related risk and climate-related opportunities can have financial impacts on an organisation's revenue, expenses, the value of its assets and liabilities, and its access to finance. The 'opportunity' category recognises that efforts to mitigate and adapt to climate change also produce positive outcomes for organisations as a result of improving resource efficiency and making cost savings, the adoption of low-emission energy sources, the development of new products and services, access to new markets, and building resilience along the supply chain.[21]

The Task Force is not a standard-setting body and compliance with the TCFD Recommendations is voluntary. However, the TCFD Recommendations have been widely adopted as reporting standards for enterprises across different industries and jurisdictions and have been implemented as binding rules. According to the TCFD Status Report 2022, 3,723 companies and 237 other organisations (e.g., industry associations, governments, regulators) from around the world have expressed their support of the TCFD recommendations.[22] For fiscal year 2021 reporting, 80% of companies disclosing TCFD-aligned information disclosed in line with at least one of the eleven recommended disclosures; however, only 4% disclosed in line with all eleven recommended disclosures and only around 40% disclosed in line with at least 5.[23] The level of implementation varies significantly across jurisdictions, sectors, and sizes of organisations.[24]

Information reported under the TCFD Recommendations is frequently included in companies' public annual filings. Most information in such filings is subject to a 'materiality assessment,' i.e. information that is deemed to be material in terms of level of detail, and in terms of errors and omissions. The TCFD Recommendations apply a materiality threshold – that is materiality of financial impacts from climate-related risks and opportunities – in relation to strategy, metrics, and targets. However, in relation to governance and risk management, the TCFD recognises that context and background are important and that is reflected in the detail of the governance TCFD Recommendations.[25]

18 TCFD, 'Our Work' <https://www.fsb-tcfd.org/about/> accessed on 1 June 2023.

19 TCFD, 'Recommendations of the Task Force' (n 11) Figure 2.

20 Ibid Sec.B.1; and see Chapter 3, Section 3.2.2 and Table 3.2.

21 TCFD, 'Recommendations of the Task Force' (n 11) Sec.B.2.

22 TCFD, 'Task Force on Climate-Related Financial Disclosures 2022 Status Report' (October 2022) 98 <https://assets.bbhub.io/company/sites/60/2022/10/2022-TCFD-Status-Report.pdf> accessed on 1 June 2023.

23 Ibid, Key Takeways and Findings, 5.

24 Ibid.

25 TCFD, 'Recommendations of the Task Force' (n 11) s C.2.b.

5.1.2 The 'all sector' recommendations

Table 5.1 reproduces the TCFD Recommendations for all sectors.[26]

5.1.3 The insurance guidance

The TCFD Recommendations are supplemented with more detailed Guidance applicable to all sectors (which is not reproduced).[27] In addition, the TCFD has issued Supplemental Guidance for the financial sector. That Guidance, as it applies to insurers, asset owners, and asset managers (the latter two being relevant to insurers as investors), has been reproduced in Table 5.2.[28]

Table 5.1 TCFD Recommendations for all sectors

Area	*Recommended disclosures*
Governance: Disclose the organisation's governance around climate-related risks and opportunities.	1. Describe the board's oversight of climate-related risks and opportunities. 2. Describe management's role in assessing and managing climate-related risks and opportunities.
Strategy: Disclose the actual and potential impacts of climate-related risks and opportunities on the organisation's businesses, strategy, and financial planning where such information is material.	3. Describe the climate-related risks and opportunities the organisation has identified over the short, medium, and long term. 4. Describe the impact of climate-related risks and opportunities on the organisation's businesses, strategy, and financial planning. 5. Describe the resilience of the organisation's strategy, taking into consideration different climate-related scenarios, including a 2°C or lower scenario.
Risk management: Disclose how the organisation identifies, assesses, and manages climate-related risks.	6. Describe the organisation's processes for identifying and assessing climate-related risks. 7. Describe the organisation's processes for managing climate-related risks. 8. Describe how processes for identifying, assessing, and managing climate-related risks are integrated into the organisation's overall risk management.
Metrics and targets: Disclose the metrics and targets used to assess and manage relevant climate-related risks and opportunities where such information is material.	9. Disclose the metrics used by the organisation to assess climate-related risks and opportunities in line with its strategy and risk management process. 10. Disclose Scope 1, Scope 2, and, if appropriate, Scope 3 GHG emissions and the related risks. 11. Describe the targets used by the organisation to manage climate-related risks and opportunities and performance against targets.

26 Ibid s 3.

27 The Guidance for all sectors has not been reproduced in this chapter but the latest version can be accessed from: TCFD, 'Implementing Recommendations' (n 1).

28 Ibid s D.

Table 5.2 TCFD Guidance for the insurers, asset owners and asset managers

Area	*Supplemental Guidance for Insurance Companies, Asset Owners, and Asset Managers*
Strategy – insurers	In relation to Recommendation 4: insurance companies should describe the potential impacts of climate-related risks and opportunities as well as provide supporting quantitative information where available, on their core businesses, products, and services, including: • information at the business division, sector, or geography levels; • how the potential impacts influence client or broker selection; • whether specific climate-related products or competencies are under development, such as insurance of green infrastructure, speciality climate-related risk advisory services, and climate-related client engagement. In relation to Recommendation 5: insurance companies that perform climate-related scenario analysis on their underwriting activities should provide the following information: • description of the climate-related scenarios used, including the critical input parameters, assumptions and considerations, and analytical choices. In addition to a 2°C scenario, insurance companies with substantial exposure to weather-related perils should consider using a greater than 2°C scenario to account for physical effects of climate change; • time frames used for the climate-related scenarios, including short-, medium-, and long-term milestones.
Strategy – asset owners and asset managers	In relation to Recommendation 4: asset owners and asset managers should describe how climate-related risks and opportunities are factored into relevant investment strategies. For asset owners, this could be described from the perspective of the total fund or investment strategy or individual investment strategies for various asset classes. Asset managers should also describe how each product or investment strategy might be affected by the transition to a low-carbon economy. In relation to Recommendation 5: asset owners that perform scenario analysis should consider providing a discussion of how climate-related scenarios are used, such as to inform investments in specific assets.
Risk management – insurers	In relation to Recommendation 6: insurance companies should describe the processes for identifying and assessing climate-related risks on re-/insurance portfolios by geography, business division, or product segments, including the following risks: • physical risks from changing frequencies and intensities of weather-related perils; • transition risks resulting from a reduction in insurable interest due to a decline in value, changing energy costs, or implementation of carbon regulation; • Click here to enter text. • liability risks that could intensify due to a possible increase in litigation. In relation to Recommendation 7: insurance companies should describe key tools or instruments, such as risk models, used to manage climate-related risks in relation to product development and pricing. Insurance companies should also describe the range of climate-related events considered and how the risks generated by the rising propensity and severity of such events are managed.

(*Continued*)

Table 5.2 Continued

Area	*Supplemental Guidance for Insurance Companies, Asset Owners, and Asset Managers*
Risk management – asset owners and asset managers	In relation to Recommendation 6: asset owners and managers should describe, where appropriate, engagement activity with investee companies to encourage better disclosure and practices related to climate-related risks in order to improve data availability and asset owners' and managers' ability to assess climate-related risks. Asset owners and asset managers should also describe how they identify and assess material climate-related risks for each product or investment strategy. This might include a description of the resources and tools used in the process. In relation to Recommendation 7: asset owners should describe how they consider the positioning of their total portfolio with respect to the transition to a low-carbon energy supply, production, and use. This could include explaining how asset owners actively manage their portfolios' positioning in relation to this transition. Asset managers should describe how they manage material climate-related risks for each product or investment strategy.
Metrics and targets – insurers	In relation to Recommendation 9: insurance companies should provide aggregated risk exposure to weather-related catastrophes of their property business (i.e., annual aggregated expected losses from weather-related catastrophes) by relevant jurisdiction. Insurance companies should describe the extent to which their insurance underwriting activities, where relevant, are aligned with a well below 2°C scenario, using whichever approach or metrics best suit their organisational context or capabilities. Insurance companies should also indicate which insurance underwriting activities (e.g., lines of business) are included. In relation to Recommendation 10: insurance companies should disclose weighted average carbon intensity or GHG emissions associated with commercial property and specialty lines of business where data and methodologies allow.
Metrics and targets – asset owners and asset managers	In relation to Recommendation 9: asset owners and asset managers should describe metrics used to assess climate-related risks and opportunities in each fund or investment strategy. Where relevant, asset owners and asset managers should also describe how these metrics have changed over time. Where appropriate, asset owners and asset managers should provide metrics considered in investment decisions and monitoring. Asset owners should describe the extent to which assets they own and their funds, and asset managers should describe the extent to which their assets under management and products, and investment strategies, where relevant, are aligned with a well below 2°C scenario, using whichever approach or metrics best suit their organisational context or capabilities. Asset owners and asset managers should also indicate which asset classes are included. In relation to Recommendation 10: asset owners should disclose GHG emissions for assets they own and the weighted average carbon intensity (WACI) for each fund or investment strategy, where data and methodologies allow. In addition to WACI, asset owners should consider providing other carbon foot printing metrics they believe are useful for decision-making.

5.1.4 Disclosures on outward impact?

The TCFD Recommendations have a clear focus on financial disclosures relating to the inward impact of climate change risks at a corporate level, namely their financial impacts on the organisation's governance, business, strategy, and finances; and the organisation's structures and processes for managing climate change risks. It is less obvious to what extent the TCFD Recommendations capture 'outward impact,' but on a detailed review of the Recommendations and Guidance there are a few disclosures that would require information on an insurer's impact on the environment:

- **strategy disclosures on climate-related opportunities**: climate-related opportunities are the potential positive impacts related to climate change on an organisation.[29] While the emphasis is still on 'inward impact,' climate change opportunities are the result of efforts by the organisation to mitigate or adapt to climate change, such as operational GHG reductions by adopting renewable energy sources and taking steps towards resource efficiency, the development of new products and services, and the implementation of investment strategies transitioning to a low-carbon economy. To the extent that the impact of such climate-related opportunities on the organisation's businesses, strategy, and financial planning are material, they should be disclosed (Recommendation 4). Specifically for insurers, this means that they should report on climate-related insurance product innovations, climate-related risk advisory services, and climate-related client engagement.[30] However, this reporting recommendation does not on its face extend to reporting on the insurer's current position and performance in relation to impact underwriting, or whether the previously identified opportunities have been developed or realised, or what research and processes they have used to positively identify potential opportunities or conclude that there are none;
- **metrics and targets disclosure on GHG emissions for insurers**: organisations should disclose their Scope 1, Scope 2, and, if appropriate, Scope 3 greenhouse gas (GHG) emissions and the related risks (Recommendation 10). Further to the TCFD Guidance for Insurers, the Scope 3 emission disclosure requirements for insurers lack ambition: insurance companies are only asked to disclose weighted average carbon intensity or GHG emissions associated with commercial property and speciality lines of business where data and methodologies allow.[31] As discussed in Chapter 3, Section 3.3.2, there is now a drive towards introducing more stringent reporting and accounting standards for 'insurance-associated emissions'[32] which have already been adopted as an in-scope emission in

29 See above and TCFD, 'Recommendations' (n 11) s B.2.

30 TCFD Guidance for Insurers – see Table 4.

31 Ibid.

32 Partnership for Carbon Accounting Financials, 'Insurance-Associated Emissions' (November 2022), 8 <https://carbonaccountingfinancials.com/files/downloads/pcaf-standard-part-c-insurance-associated-emissions-nov-2022.pdf> accessed on 1 June 2023.

the Target-Setting Protocol[33] published by the NZIA. No specific disclosure is required for GHG emission reduction targets;

- **metrics and targets disclosure on GHG emissions for asset owners**: asset owners should disclose GHG emissions for assets they own and the weighted average carbon intensity for each fund or investment strategy, where data and methodologies allow. These emissions should be calculated in line with the Global GHG Accounting and Reporting Standard for the Financial Industry developed by the Partnership for Carbon Accounting Financials[34] or a comparable methodology. Currently, there is no guidance or recommendation on disclosing whether the weighted average carbon intensity is increasing or decreasing year-on-year;
- **disclosure on commitments to reduce GHG emissions**: organisations that have made GHG emissions reduction commitments, operate in jurisdictions that have made such commitments, or have agreed to meet investor expectations regarding GHG emissions reductions, should describe their plans for transitioning to a low-carbon economy, which could include GHG emissions targets and specific activities intended to reduce GHG emissions in their operations and value chain or to otherwise support the transition.[35] However, there is no recommended disclosure on the past and present trajectory – how much progress an organisation has already made;
- **disclosure of stewardship activities**: asset owners and asset managers should disclose any engagement activity with investee companies to encourage better disclosure and practices related to climate-related risks to improve data availability and asset owners and managers' ability to assess climate-related risks.[36] This is aimed at engagement in relation to the investee company's TCFD disclosures, not engagement to influence the investee company to take climate action.

Overall, the TCFD Recommendations and Guidance on disclosures relating to outward impact are limited and relatively vague. The main reason for the limited scope of the TCFD Recommendations is that the Task Force's remit has been to improve and increase the reporting of climate-related financial information with a focus on the impacts of climate change on an organisation's financial performance and financial positions. The TCFD Recommendations pre-date the concept of 'double materiality' which has now gained recognition by the EU and is gaining momentum with the FCA and with industry associations such as the NZIA.[37] With their focus on financial impacts, the TCFD Recommendations have been criticised for prioritising risk management of climate change risk over outcomes that contribute to the Paris Agreement goals and the national and international

33 NZIA, 'Target-Setting Protocol 1.0' (January 2023) <https://www.unepfi.org/industries/insurance/launch-of-nzia-target-setting-protocol-version-1-0/> accessed on 1 June 2023 and see Chapter 6, Section 6.4.4.

34 Partnership for Carbon Accounting Financials, 'The Global GHG Accounting and Reporting Standard for the Financial Industry' (2020) <https://ghgprotocol.org/sites/default/files/standards/The%20Global%20GHG%20Accounting%20and%20Reporting%20Standard%20for%20the%20Financial%20Industry_0.pdf> accessed on 1 June 2023.

35 General Guidance on Recommendation 5 – see TCFD, 'Implementing Recommendations' (n 1) s C.

36 Ibid.

37 See Sections 5.3.5, 5.4.2, and 5.4.3.

net-zero targets, thereby giving entities that are making TCFD disclosures the misleading impression that they are making a difference to climate change.[38]

5.1.5 Metrics and targets

The Metrics and Targets Recommendations envisage that the reporting entity should provide the key metrics used to measure and manage climate-related risks and opportunities. The metrics must be detailed enough for investors and other stakeholders 'to assess the organization's potential risk-adjusted returns, ability to meet financial obligations, general exposure to climate-related issues, and progress in managing or adapting to those issues.'[39] However, in the absence of standardised metrics and targets, it can be difficult for reporting entities to implement those recommendations, while to users of the disclosures (e.g. investors and underwriters) non-standardised metrics and targets mean that there is limited consistency or direct comparability between different organisations.

Following a consultation on standardised metrics, the Task Force published additional 'Guidance on Metrics, Targets, and Transition Plans'[40] in 2021. The Metrics Guidance sets out cross-sector climate-related metric categories (and examples of key data points that could be measured by those metrics) that can be used as a framework for metrics reporting:[41]

- GHG emissions: absolute Scope 1, Scope 2, and Scope 3 under the Greenhouse Gas Protocol;[42] emissions intensity;
- transition risks: amount and extent of assets or business activities vulnerable to transition risks;
- physical risks: amount and extent of assets or business activities vulnerable to physical risks;
- climate-related opportunities: proportion of revenue, assets, or other business activities aligned with climate-related opportunities;
- capital deployment: the amount of capital expenditure, financing, or investment deployed towards climate-related risks and opportunities;
- internal carbon prices: price of each ton of GHG emissions used internally by an organisation;
- remuneration: proportion of executive management remuneration linked to climate considerations.

38 Ben Caldecott, 'Achieving Alignment in Finance' (October 2020) 13 <https://www.unepfi.org/wordpress/wp-content/uploads/2020/08/200915_J932-CKIC-UNEP-ThoughtLeadershipSeries-DrBenCaldecott-11.pdf> accessed on 1 June 2023.

39 TCFD, 'Recommendations of the Task Force' (n 11) 22, and see 'Principles for Effective Disclosure' (June 2017) <https://www.fsb-tcfd.org/recommendations/> accessed on 1 June 2023.

40 TCFD, 'Guidance on Metrics, Targets, and Transition Plans' (October 2021) <https://assets.bbhub.io/company/sites/60/2021/07/2021-Metrics_Targets_Guidance-1.pdf> accessed on 1 June 2023.

41 Ibid Table C1.

42 The World Business Council for Sustainable Development and the World Resources Institute, 'The Greenhouse Gas Protocol: A Corporate Accounting and Reporting Standard' (n 9) and see Chapter 3, Section 3.3.2.

In addition, there is guidance on 'portfolio alignment metrics' for the financial sector in the form of tools that can be used to measure the extent to which investment portfolios are aligned with a net-zero GHG emissions reduction ambition that would limit average temperature rise to 1.5°C by 2050.[43] This is relevant to insurers as asset owners who should report on 'portfolio positioning' under Recommendation 7. The Task Force has not given equivalent recommendations or guidance on underwriting portfolio positioning, measuring underwriting portfolio alignment to the Paris goals, although such guidance is now emerging from the NZIA Target-Setting Protocol.[44] The key challenges of reporting on the GHG emissions of their underwriting portfolios under Scope 3 of the Greenhouse Gas Protocol are that (1) an insurer would be reliant on primary data on the GHG emissions of a policyholder's operations and assets, (2) only a 'proportional share' of those emissions should be attributed to the insurer, and (3) there is potential for double-counting as between the insurer and the policyholders, between the insurer and reinsurers, and between an insurer's underwriting portfolio emissions and emissions from its investments.[45]

In relation to Targets and Transition Plans, the Metrics Guidance sets out criteria for effective climate-related forward-looking Targets and Transition Plans, such as their alignment with strategic and risk management goals, their linkage to relevant metrics, measurability, clear time lines, and providing for governance and review processes.[46] While the Metrics Guidance goes some way towards harmonising approaches to metric and target methodologies, the Task Force has not (and has no authority to) set reporting standards and does not provide globally consistent methodologies and taxonomies of terms. The TCFD Recommendations have been criticised for being limited as 'largely principles-based recommendations [that] may not result in consistent and comparable disclosures that fully meet investors' needs for decision-useful information.'[47] The IFRS Sustainability Disclosure Standards discussed in Section 5.2 seek to address this by introducing detailed industry-specific disclosure requirements and metrics.

5.1.6 Data assurance

The Task Force does not give recommendations or guidance on data assurance processes except that disclosures made should be reliable, verifiable, and objective.[48] To the extent climate-related financial disclosures are included in an entity's public annual filings, they should be subject to the same scrutiny and auditing processes as other information included in those filings. As TCFD Recommendations remain voluntary in many jurisdictions, even where such disclosures are made, they may not be subject to consistent data assurance processes.

---

43 Ibid.

44 NZIA, 'Target-Setting Protocol 1.0' (n 31) (January 2023).

45 Partnership for Carbon Accounting Financials (n 32) Box 4-2.

46 TCFD, 'Guidance on Metrics, Targets, and Transition Plans' (n 40) s D and E.

47 FCA, 'ISSB Exposure Drafts on IFRS S1 (General Requirements for Disclosure of Sustainability-Related Financial Information) and IFRS S2 (Climate-Related Disclosures): FCA response' <https://www.ifrs.org/content/dam/ifrs/project/general-sustainability-related-disclosures/exposure-draft-comment-letters/f/financial-conduct-authority-a0a3de76-6b2e-4f9b-bdfc-d1e6a8c466d7/fca-response-to-issb-exposure-drafts.pdf> accessed on 1 June 2023.

48 TCFD, 'Recommendations of the Task Force' (n 11) Figure 6.

The TCFD Recommendations have been a ground-breaking development. They help the reporting entity to identify financial risks from climate change and these insights can help in managing these risks and informing strategic decision-making within organisations, as well as helping investors to make informed choices. There is, however, a gap in that the TCFD Recommendations do not focus on disclosures on outward impact. The forthcoming IFRS Sustainability Disclosure Standards will raise the bar by introducing disclosure baseline standards and more detailed guidance in relation to climate-related opportunities and outward impact, and by developing global reporting standards, to increase transparency for stakeholders, enable better transition risk management, and stimulate the development of new products and services.

5.2 IFRS International Sustainability Disclosure Standards

At COP26 in Glasgow, the International Financial Reporting Standards Board ('IFRSB') announced the formation of a new International Sustainability Standards Board ('ISSB') tasked with developing a comprehensive global baseline of standards for sustainability disclosure.[49] The new IFRS Sustainability Disclosure Standards aim to enable companies to provide comprehensive sustainability information focused on the information needs of investors and the financial markets.[50] Given the fragmented landscape of voluntary, sustainability-related recommendations and standards already in place, the IFRS Sustainability Disclosure Standards also seek to facilitate interoperability with disclosures that are jurisdiction-specific or aimed at broader stakeholder groups, and to deliver standards that are cost-effective, decision-useful, and market-informed.[51]

The ISSB's work builds on the work of market-led investor-focused reporting initiatives, including the TCFD Recommendations, the Climate Disclosure Standards Board, the Value Reporting Foundation's Integrated Reporting Framework and industry-based Sustainability Accounting Standards Board ('SASB') Standards,[52] and the World Economic Forum's Stakeholder Capitalism Metrics.[53]

In March 2022, the ISSB published its first proposed standards: one sets out general sustainability-related disclosure requirements and the other specifies climate-related disclosure requirements. Following consultation and the consideration of feedback received, the ISSB issued IFRS S1 General Requirements for Disclosure of Sustainability-Related Financial Information ('IFRS S1') and IFRS S2 Climate-related Disclosures ('IFRS S2') in June 2023.[54] The UK government has announced the creation of 'UK Sustainability

49 IFRS, 'IFRS Foundation Announces International Sustainability Standards Board' (November 2021) <https://www.ifrs.org/news-and-events/news/2021/11/ifrs-foundation-announces-issb-consolidation-with-cdsb-vrf-publication-of-prototypes/> accessed on 1 June 2023.

50 IFRSB, 'About the International Sustainability Standards Board' <https://www.ifrs.org/groups/international-sustainability-standards-board/> accessed on 1 June 2023.

51 Ibid.

52 The SASB Standards are a set of 77 industry-specific sustainability accounting standards designed to help entities disclose material, decision-useful information to investors. As of August 2022, the International Sustainability Standards Board (ISSB) of the IFRS Foundation assumed responsibility for the SASB Standards (<https://sasb.org/standards/> accessed on 1 June 2023).

53 IFRSB, 'About the International Sustainability Standards Board' (n 50).

54 IFRS S1 <https://www.ifrs.org/issued-standards/ifrs-sustainability-standards-navigator/ifrs-s1-general-requirements.html/content/dam/ifrs/publications/html-standards-issb/english/2023/issued/issbs1/> and IFRS S2 <https://www.ifrs.org/issued-standards/ifrs-sustainability-standards-navigator/ifrs-s2-climate-related

Disclosure Standards' by assessing and endorsing the global corporate reporting baseline of IFRS Sustainability Disclosure Standards, and aims to make endorsement decisions on the first IFRS 1 and IFRS 2 by July 2024.[55]

5.2.1 IFRS S1

IFRS S1 sets out the core content for a complete set of sustainability-related financial disclosures. Sustainability-related disclosures are 'about sustainability-related risks and opportunities that are useful to users of general purpose financial reporting when they assess an entity's enterprise value, including information about its governance, strategy and risk management, and related metrics and targets.'[56] A reporting entity would need to disclose material information about significant sustainability-related risks and opportunities to which it is exposed,[57] and a complete, neutral, and accurate depiction of its sustainability-related financial information.[58]

Sustainability-related financial information is defined as:

> information that gives insight into sustainability-related risks and opportunities that affect enterprise value, providing a sufficient basis for users of general purpose financial reporting to assess the resources and relationships on which an entity's business model and strategy for sustaining and developing that model depend.[59]

There is as yet little commentary or guidance on the scope of 'resources and relationships' but it appears to refer to an entity's relationship with natural resources, its workforce, and local communities.[60] In particular, it is unclear whether sustainability-related information includes or excludes climate-related information which is more particularly covered in IFRS S2. The established understanding of 'sustainability' would extend to combating climate change and protecting the environment and biodiversity,[61] but the definitions for sustainability-related risks, sustainability-related opportunities, and sustainability-related financial information do not reference 'climate-related' or the 'environment.' Instead, 'sustainability' seems to be more limited referencing 'relationships' and 'resources.' In practice, this may not matter as it is envisaged that IFRS S1 and IFRS S2 disclosures are reported together.[62]

The core content of disclosures is organised around the same key themes as in the TCFD Recommendations: governance, strategy, risk management, and metrics and targets. IFRS

-disclosures.html/content/dam/ifrs/publications/html-standards-issb/english/2023/issued/issbs2/> accessed on 10 August 2023.

55 HM Government Department for Business and Trade, 'UK Sustainability Disclosure Standards' (August 2023) <https://www.gov.uk/guidance/uk-sustainability-disclosure-standards> accessed on 10 August 2023.

56 IFRS S1, Appendix A, definition for 'Sustainability-related financial disclosures.'

57 IFSR S1, [2]. The materiality judgement is made in the context of the sustainability-related information necessary for users of general purpose financial reporting (investors) to assess enterprise value. Enterprise value is the total value of an entity's equity and net debt and reflects expectations of the amount, timing, and uncertainty of future cash flows over the short, medium, and long term and the value attributed to those cash flows (reflecting the cost of capital).

58 IFRS S1 [3].

59 Ibid, Appendix A, definition for 'Sustainability-related information.'

60 Ibid, Introduction.

61 See Chapter 2, Section 2.4.2.

62 IFRS S2 [2] and see Section 5.2.3.

S1 is breaking new ground in expressly recognising that a company's outward impact can give rise to sustainability-related risks and opportunities:

> An entity's sustainability-related risks and opportunities arise from its dependencies on resources and **its impacts on resources**, and from the **relationships it maintains that may be positively or negatively affected by those impacts** and dependencies. When an entity's business model depends, for example, on a natural resource—like water—it is likely to be affected by changes in the quality, availability and pricing of that resource. When an **entity's activities result in adverse, external impacts**—on, for example, local communities—it could be subjected to stricter government regulation and consequences of reputational effects—for example, negative effects on the entity's brand and higher recruitment costs.[63] *(emphasis added)*

Although reporting sustainability-related outward impact is only required under IFRS S1 where it materially impacts the enterprise value, this is nevertheless a step towards double materiality which acknowledges the need for reporting on the impact of a company's operations on the wider community. For insurers, this means that they must consider the impact of providing insurance for assets and projects that have an impact on natural resources, its workforce, and/or local communities. Whether this would cover providing insurance for coal extraction projects is a question of materiality: the impact on resources is indirect (insurance may make the project commercially viable) and the impact on local communities may depend on the context and location.

In relation to metrics and targets, IFRS S1 is more explicit about the metrics an entity can use: there is a hierarchy of the IFRS's own metrics, industry-based SASB Standards, the Climate Disclosure Standard Board Framework, and an entity's own metrics.[64] Additional disclosure requirements on the methodology and use of metrics apply if an entity uses its own metrics.[65] Where metrics are used that have significant estimation uncertainty, this must be identified in the disclosure, together with the sources and nature of the estimation uncertainties and the factors affecting the uncertainties.[66] Moreover, an entity will be required to disclose comparative information in respect of the preceding period for all metrics disclosed in the current period.[67] For targets, there are detailed disclosure requirements on the metrics and time period used for measuring progress, performance against targets and analysis of trends in performance, as well as revisions to any targets and the explanation for those revisions.[68]

IFRS S1 aims for greater comparability and consistency between sustainability-related disclosures from different entities. There are general provisions relating to 'decision useful information' applicable to both IFRS S1 and S2 which are discussed in Section 5.2.3. Appendix A to IDRS S1 provides a set of definitions, but some key concepts are broad and remain vague – e.g. 'sustainability-related risks and opportunities' and 'sustainability-related financial information,' 'trade-offs,' and 'value chains.' There is a need for further

63 IFRS S1 [17].

64 Ibid [28] and [54]. The Climate Disclosure Standard Board Framework is an initiative to advance and align disclosure of environmental and social information in mainstream reports (<https://www.ifrs.org/content/dam/ifrs/groups/cdsb/cdsb-framework-2022.pdf> accessed on 1 June 2023).

65 Ibid [28]–[31].

66 Ibid [79].

67 Ibid, [63].

68 Ibid [32]–[33].

guidance on their meaning, as well as their interoperability with other terminology frameworks such as the EU Taxonomy.[69]

5.2.2 IFRS S2

IFRS S2 builds on the TCFD Recommendations and adopts its framework on the disclosure of climate-related information on the four core themes of governance, strategy, risk management, and metrics and targets. A reporting entity is required 'to disclose information about its exposure to significant climate-related risk and opportunities' which should be useful to users of general purpose financial reporting when they assess an entity's enterprise value.[70] 'Climate-related risks' include physical risk ('the potential negative effects of climate change on an entity') and transition risk ('risks … associated with the transition to a lower-carbon global economy').[71] 'Climate-related opportunities' are defined as 'the potentially positive climate-change generated outcomes for an entity' produced by global efforts to mitigate and adapt to climate change.[72]

Similarly to the TCFD Recommendations, the main body of IFRS S2 is almost exclusively focused on inward impact – specifically how climate-related risks and opportunities affect:

- an entity's financial position and financial performance;
- an amount, timing, and certainty of the entity's future cash flows over the short, medium, and long term and, therefore, the assessment of enterprise value by users of general purpose financial reporting;
- an entity's strategy and business model.[73]

The most substantial additions, compared to the TCFD Recommendations, are under the 'Strategy' theme. For example, there are additional and more granular requirements for inward and outward impact disclosures aimed at providing information on (1) how the reporting entity is addressing climate-related risk and opportunities in its strategy to adjust its business model to respond to, or in anticipation of, climate-related risk and opportunities, (2) transition planning, and (3) GHG emission reduction targets:

- information about direct and indirect adaptation and mitigation efforts it is undertaking (e.g. in relation to customers and supply chains);[74]
- information regarding climate-related targets, including the entity's GHG emission targets and carbon offset plans;[75]
- metrics that show the entity assesses its performance, including progress towards the targets it has set, including GHG emissions in Scope 1, 2, and 3[76]

69 See Section 5.4.1.
70 IFRS S2 [1].
71 Ibid [2] and Appendix A, definition of 'climate-related risks.'
72 Ibid, Appendix A, definition of 'climate-related opportunities.'
73 Ibid [1], [4], and [7].
74 Ibid [13(a)(i)(2) and (3)].
75 Ibid [13(b)(ii) and (iii)].
76 Ibid [21(a)].

and the amount and percentage of assets or business activities aligned with climate-related opportunities.[77]

IFRS S2 provides for a range of metrics without setting a clear hierarchy: cross-industry metrics, industry-based metrics, and a reporting entity's own metrics.[78] The industry-based metrics for the insurance industry are contained in 'Volume B17—Insurance' ('IFRS Insurance Disclosures').[79] They present an extensive set of climate-related disclosures on inward and outward impact in relation to insurance underwriting and investment activities. Although presented separately in Annex B, industry-specific disclosure requirements for climate-related disclosures such as the IFRS Insurance Disclosures, derived from the SASB Standards, will form part of the IFRS S2 requirements. It is not entirely clear whether industry-specific requirements are mandatory, but IFRS S2 para.20(b) ('shall disclose … industry-based metrics (as set out in Appendix B)') suggests that they are.

Table 5.3 reproduces a summary of the IFRS Insurance Disclosures, but attention is drawn to the rich details on the metrics contained in FN-IN-410a, FN-IN-410b, FN-IN-450a, FN-IN-1 to 5, and FN-IN-000.A.

The required disclosures relating to 'Incorporation of ESG Factors in Investment Management' and 'Policies Designed to Incentivize Responsible Behaviour' would capture impact investment and impact underwriting respectively and thus help raise the bar for insurers taking an enabling role as outlined in Chapter 3, Section 3.4.5. However, it has been pointed out that insurers would need to exercise fair judgement (including on materiality) on whether standard insurance products with incidental effects on environmentally responsible behaviours should be reported.[80]

One omission in the otherwise comprehensive IFRS Insurance Disclosures is that the GHG emissions to be reported do not include emissions associated with an insurer's underwriting portfolio.[81] Scope 3 emission accounting under the GHG Protocol is optional for insurance contracts.[82] A recent initiative by the Partnership for Carbon Accounting Financials is introducing reporting and accounting standards for 'insurance-associated emissions,'[83] and their recommendations could have been incorporated into the IFRS Insurance Disclosures, especially as they have already been adopted as an in-scope emission in the NZIA Target-Setting Protocol.[84] Another gap is that the requirements do not extend to information on any underwriting guidelines for carbon-intensive assets and projects.

77 Ibid [21(d)].

78 Ibid [20].

79 Ibid, Appendix B, Volume B17—Insurance <https://www.ifrs.org/content/dam/ifrs/project/climate-related-disclosures/industry/issb-exposure-draft-2022-2-b17-insurance.pdf> accessed on 1 June 2023.

80 Letter from QBE Insurance Group Limited to the ISSB dated 15 July 2022 <https://www.ifrs.org/content/dam/ifrs/project/climate-related-disclosures/exposure-draft-comment-letters/q/qbe-insurance-group-7768be16-6310-4076-a782-ceaec46cfe1d/qbe-letter-on-issb-proposals-v.f-issb.pdf> accessed on 1 June 2023.

81 IFRS S2, Appendix A, definition for 'Scope 3 emissions.'

82 The World Business Council for Sustainable Development and the World Resources Institute, 'The Greenhouse Gas Protocol: Corporate Value Chain (Scope 3) Accounting and Reporting Standard' (2011) ch 5 <https://ghgprotocol.org/sites/default/files/standards/Corporate-Value-Chain-Accounting-Reporing-Standard_041613_2.pdf> accessed on 1 June 2023.

83 Partnership for Carbon Accounting Financials (n 32).

84 NZIA, 'Statement of Commitment by Signatory Companies' <https://www.unepfi.org/psi/wp-content/uploads/2021/07/NZIA-Commitment.pdf> accessed on 1 June 2023.

Table 5.3 IFRS Insurance Disclosures

Topic	*Metric*	*Category*	*Unit of measure*	*Code*
Incorporation of ESG factors in investment management	Description of approach to incorporation of ESG factors in investment management processes and strategies	Discussion and analysis	n/a	FN-IN-410a.2
Policies designed to incentivise responsible behaviour	Net premiums written related to energy efficiency and low-carbon technology	Quantitative	Reporting currency	FN-IN-410b.1
	Discussion of products and/or product features that incentivise health, safety, and/or environmentally responsible actions and/or behaviours	Discussion and analysis	n/a	FN-IN-410b.2
Physical risk exposure	Probable Maximum Loss (PML) of insured products from weather-related natural catastrophes. Description of climate-related scenarios used, including the critical input parameters, assumptions and considerations, analytical choices, and time frames, in calculation of the PML	Quantitative and discussion and analysis	Reporting currency for quantitative	FN-IN-450a.1
	Total amount of monetary losses attributable to insurance payouts from (1) modelled natural catastrophes and (2) non-modelled natural catastrophes, by type of event and geographic segment (net and gross of reinsurance). Discussion of how climate change-related impacts and variability of weather-related losses impact the cost of reinsurance and the entity's approach to transferring risk through reinsurance	Quantitative and discussion and analysis	Reporting currency for quantitative	FN-IN-450a.2

(Continued)

Table 5.3 Continued

Topic	*Metric*	*Category*	*Unit of measure*	*Code*
	Description of approach to incorporation of environmental risks into (1) the underwriting process for individual contracts and (2) the management of firm-level risks and capital adequacy	Discussion and analysis	n/a	FN-IN-450a.3
Transition risk exposure	(1) Gross exposure to carbon-related industries, by industry, (2) total gross exposure to all industries, and (3) percentage of total gross exposure to each carbon-related industry	Quantitative	Presentation currency, percentage %	FN-IN-1
	Percentage of gross exposure included in the financed emissions calculation	Quantitative	Percentage %	FN-IN-2
	For each industry by asset class: (1) absolute gross (a) Scope 1 emissions, (b) Scope 2 emissions, and (c) Scope 3 emissions, and (2) gross exposure (i.e., financed emissions)	Quantitative	Metric tons (t) CO_2-e, presentation currency	FN-IN-3
	For each industry by asset class: (1) gross emissions intensity of (a) Scope 1 emissions, (b) Scope 2 emissions, and (c) Scope 3 emissions, and (2) gross exposure (i.e., financed emissions)	Quantitative	Metric tons (t) CO_2-e per unit of physical or economic output	FN-IN-4
	Description of the methodology used to calculate financed emissions	Discussion and analysis	n/a	FN-IN-5
Activity metrics	Number of policies in force, by segment: (1) property and casualty, (2) life, (3) assumed reinsurance	Quantitative	Number of policies	FN-IN-000.A

Appendix A contains an extensive set of definitions for climate-related terms forming the basis of a terminology framework necessary to ensure consistency and comparability of disclosures between reporting entities and between one entity's yearly filings. This set of definitions is also intended to serve as the basis for a wider 'IFRS Sustainability Disclosures Taxonomy' that is being developed to facilitate digital reporting in the future.[85] Yet, as there are other emerging terminology frameworks, most notably the EU Taxonomy,[86] and, given the IFRS Sustainability Disclosure Standards' aim to facilitate interoperability with jurisdiction-specific disclosure requirements, more clarity is needed on how the IFRS S2 definitions align to, and how they could work in conjunction with, other frameworks.

5.2.3 Joint provisions and boundaries

The architecture of the IFRS Sustainability Disclosure Standards is that IFRS S1 addresses general sustainability disclosure, and IFRS S2 is dedicated to climate-related disclosures. IFRS S2 para.2 provides that the IFRS S2 disclosures shall be prepared in accordance with IFRS S1. This is important because IFRS S1 contains a number of general provisions relating to 'decision useful information,' including:

- a provision on the identity of the reporting entity (including in relation to group reporting where consolidated financial statements are provided);[87]
- a requirement to disclose by presenting 'connected information' (assessing the connections between various sustainability-related risks and opportunities, and their link to information in the general purpose financial statements) – this is to prevent 'silo reporting';[88]
- provisions on 'fair presentation'[89] and 'materiality';[90]
- a requirement to disclose comparative information on metrics used in the previous reporting period;[91]
- a requirement to report sustainability-related financial disclosures at the same time, and for the same reporting period, as related financial statements,[92] and as part of an entity's general purpose financial reporting,[93]

which will also be of application to IFRS S2 mutatis mutandis. Moreover, the IFRS Insurance Disclosures under IFRS S2 cover broader ESG issues that go beyond 'climate-related' and would fall within 'sustainability-related information' disclosable under IFRS

85 IFRS S1 and S2, Question 15—Digital reporting.
86 See Section 5.4.1.
87 IFRS S1 [37]–[39].
88 Ibid [42].
89 Ibid [45] and [46].
90 Ibid [56].
91 Ibid [63].
92 Ibid [66].
93 Ibid [72].

S1.[94] Other content overlaps have been noted.[95] It is envisaged that disclosures under IFRS S1 and S2 are reported together to avoid double-reporting and to present holistic and connected narrative information on governance, strategy, and risk management to related metrics and targets. While IFRS S2 expressly links to IFRS S1, it is odd that the IFRS S1 provisions on 'connected information' do not specifically link to (draft) IFRS S2.[96] However, both sets are required to be presented as connected information with the general purpose financial statements.[97]

Given that the required disclosures are of 'material information about all of the significant [sustainability-related/climate-related] risks and opportunities to which it is exposed,' it has been noted that further guidance is required on how the materiality requirement interacts with the additional qualifier of 'significant,'[98] and on how reporting entities should carry out that materiality assessment.[99] In addition, further clarification would also be helpful on the status of the industry-related disclosure requirements, such as the IFRS Insurance Disclosures.

To enhance accountability and data assurance, the IFRS Sustainability Disclosure Standards envisage a 'compliance statement.' Only an entity whose sustainability-related financial disclosures comply with all of the relevant requirements of the IFRS Sustainability Disclosure Standards (i.e. IFRS S1 and S2) is permitted to include an explicit and unqualified statement of compliance.[100] As an entity and its directors could be held liable for false reporting in the event of a material misrepresentation, this is likely to focus the minds of the board of directors and a company's auditors and advisers on the accuracy, veracity, and completeness of the IFRS Sustainability Disclosure Standards. The inclusion of standardised and granular metrics will facilitate the performance of quality assurance audits as and when they become a requirement.[101]

The IFRS Sustainability Disclosure Standards introduce for the first time a global baseline for sustainability and climate-related disclosures which in itself will raise the bar for such disclosure. Further work needs to be done on the interoperability with other jurisdiction and industry-specific disclosure frameworks and reporting standards. Working towards interoperability and convergence is important to increase transparency and comparability, and to reduce complexity and costs associated with a fragmentation of standards and recommendations. The IFRS Sustainability Disclosure Standards are investor-focused because (1) they connect sustainability and climate-related information and financial information in an entity's financial statements so that investors can assess a reporting entity's enterprise value, (2) they provide industry-specific content, and (3) they introduce greater accountability for disclosures made.

---

94 See Table 5.5, in particular FN-IN-410a.2, FN-IN-410b.1, and FN-IN-410b.2.

95 See e.g. Letter from the Financial Reporting Council to the ISSB dated 22 June 2022 <https://www.ifrs.org/projects/completed-projects/2023/general-sustainability-related-disclosures/#consultation-feedback> accessed on 1 June 2023.

96 IFRS S1 [42]–[44].

97 Ibid [42].

98 See e.g. Letter from Deloitte to the ISSB dated 20 July 2022 <https://www.ifrs.org/projects/completed-projects/2023/general-sustainability-related-disclosures/#consultation-feedback> accessed on 1 June 2023.

99 See e.g. FCA, 'ISSB Exposure Drafts on IFRS S1' (n 47).

100 IFRS S1 [91].

101 See e.g. Letter from the International Auditing and Assurance Standards Board to the ISSB dated 26 July 2022 <https://www.ifrs.org/projects/completed-projects/2023/general-sustainability-related-disclosures/#consultation-feedback> accessed on 1 June 2023.

5.3 UK climate-related and sustainability disclosure requirements

The landscape of climate-related disclosure requirements applicable to insurers in the UK is fragmented: there are climate-related disclosure requirements that are specific to UK-authorised insurers as regulated firms, listing reporting requirements for those insurers that are listed companies, disclosure requirements that apply to insurers that provide IBIPs, corporate reporting requirements that apply to all companies, and corporate reporting requirements that apply to specific categories of companies. There are climate-related disclosures in relation to the reporting entity itself and there may be additional requirements in relation to its products. Yet, despite the wide-ranging requirements, disclosure of the outward impact of insurer's operations and their product is sparsely covered.

5.3.1 PRA regulatory disclosure requirements

UK-authorised insurers must regularly provide information to the PRA which is necessary for the purposes of the PRA's supervision,[102] and disclose publicly, on an annual basis, a solvency and financial condition report ('SFCR').[103] The SFCR must contain, inter alia, a description of any material risks, including their risk exposure, risk concentration, risk mitigation, and risk sensitivity.[104] The SFCR should include information on financial risks from climate change (i.e. inward impact) to the extent they are material.[105] In addition, the PRA expects insurers to consider disclosing how climate-related financial risks are integrated into governance and risk management processes,[106] and to develop and maintain an appropriate approach to disclosure, reflective of the distinctive elements of the financial risks from climate change.[107] In particular, the PRA expects insurers to engage with the TCFD Recommendations and other disclosure initiatives, as well as encouraging others to engage with such disclosures through their investment relationships.[108] An insurer who is not meeting the PRA's expectations should be able to explain why that is the case and how it is planning to address gaps.[109]

5.3.2 FCA regulatory disclosure requirements

The sustainability and climate-related disclosure requirements under the FCA's regulatory umbrella are extensive and growing. The following sections examine the disclosure requirements for (1) listed insurers (Section 5.3.3), (2) life insurers (Section 5.3.4), (3) life insurers who provide IBIPs or operate certain types of pension schemes (Section 5.3.5), and (4) UK-regulated insurers generally (Section 5.3.6).

102 PRA Rulebook SII Firms, Reporting, 2.1.
103 Ibid 3.1.
104 Ibid 3.3(3).
105 PRA SS3/19 [3.18].
106 Ibid [3.19].
107 Ibid [3.20].
108 Ibid [3.21].
109 PRA, 'Dear CEO Letter – Thematic Feedback on the PRA's Supervision of Climate-Related Financial Risk and the Bank of England's Climate Biennial Exploratory Scenario Exercise' (21 October 2022) <https://www.bankofengland.co.uk/-/media/boe/files/prudential-regulation/letter/2022/october/managing-climate-related-financial-risks.pdf?la=en&hash=D0D7E6F305C448D503EA385E20E0683E734696A0> accessed on 1 June 2023.

5.3.3 FCA: listed insurers

5.3.3.1 The TCFD Listing Rules statement

With effect from 1 January 2021, the FCA introduced a rule for commercial companies with a UK premium listing to disclose, on a comply or explain basis, against the TCFD Recommendations.[110] This rule was extended to issuers of standard listed shares with effect from 1 January 2022.[111] In particular, the Listing Rules require that a listed company must include a statement (the '**TCFD LR statement**') in its annual financial reports setting out:

- whether it has made disclosures consistent with the TCFD Recommendations in its annual financial report;[112]
- where it has included some, or all, of its disclosures consistent with the TCFD Recommendations in a document other than its annual financial report, an explanation of why and a reference to where the disclosures can be found;[113]
- where it has not made disclosures consistent with the TCFD Recommendations, an explanation of why, and a description of any steps it is taking or plans to take to be able to make consistent disclosures in the future – including relevant time frames.[114]

Many UK insurance companies are listed companies: those of them who are premium listed (e.g. Aviva, Beazley, Direct Line Insurance Group, Legal & General, RSA) would have already been required to report in 2022 on their 2021 compliance with the TCFD Recommendations. The FCA and the Financial Reporting Council ('FRC') jointly carried out a review of the first round of TCFD LR statements from 171 premium-listed commercial companies in 2022 (of which 14 were insurance companies).[115] The FCA found that:

- over 90% of premium-listed companies self-reported that they had made disclosures consistent with the TCFD's Governance and Risk Management pillars, but this dropped to below 90% for the Strategy and Metrics and Targets pillars;[116]
- in some instances, reporting companies indicated that they had made disclosures consistent with the TCFD Recommendations, but the disclosures themselves appeared to be very limited in content;[117]
- large insurance companies were among the most compliant performers;[118]

110 Listing Rules (Disclosure of Climate-Related Financial Information) Instrument 2020 amending the FCA Listing Rules Sourcebook.

111 Listing Rules (Disclosure of Climate-Related Financial Information) (No 2) Instrument 2021 amending the FCA Listing Rules Sourcebook.

112 FCA Handbook, Listing Rules Sourcebook (LR) ('LR') 9.8.6.8(a).

113 LR 9.8.6.8(b)(i).

114 LR 9.8.6.8(b)(ii).

115 FCA, 'Review of TCFD-Aligned Disclosures by Premium Listed Commercial Companies' (July 2022) <https://www.fca.org.uk/publications/multi-firm-reviews/tcfd-aligned-disclosures-premium-listed-commercial-companies> accessed on 1 June 2023.

116 Ibid, Table 1.

117 Ibid, Summary.

118 Ibid, Figure 21(a).

- 80% of reporting companies included net-zero statements (expressed as a 'goal,' 'target,' or 'commitment').[119]

In addition, the FRC observed that the 2021 TCFD disclosures reviewed needed to be better integrated with other narrative disclosures in the annual financial report (which could be challenging given that the Listing Rules require a separate TCFD statement), and should provide more specificity and granularity of information.[120] Given that the disclosures requirements for listed companies do not go beyond the requirements of the TCFD Recommendations, reference is made to Section 5.1.6 on the limited scope of the TCFD Recommendations.

5.3.3.2 Other requirements for listed insurers and insurer issuers

Listed insurer issuers, other insurer issuers with securities admitted to trading on regulated markets, and insurers in the scope of the requirements under the Prospectus Regulation[121] and the Market Abuse Regulation:[122] the FCA has highlighted a number of other more general disclosure requirements in relation to ESG matters, including climate change risks that can have a financial impact on issuers,[123] and thus apply to insurers that are listed companies. Issuers trading on regulated markets must make disclosures under the Listing Rules and the Disclosure Guidance and Transparency Rules that could extend to climate-related information: Listing Principle 1, LR 7.2.2G, LR 7.2.3G, LR 9.8.6(5) to (7)R, and LR 13.3.1R;[124] and DTR 4.1.7R-4.1.9R and DTR 7.2.[125]

When issuers of transferable securities, such as shares, are required to produce a prospectus, it must contain the necessary information which is material to an investor for making an informed assessment of (among other things) the assets and prospects of the issuer and of the reasons for the issuance and its impact on the issuer, including ESG-related matters.[126] Recital 54 of the Prospectus Regulation specifically notes that 'environmental, social and governance circumstances can also constitute specific and material risks for the issuer and its securities and, in that case, should be disclosed.'

An issuer must also publicly disclose inside information that directly concerns them as soon as possible, including any inside information that relates to climate change and other

119 Ibid s 2.3(c).

120 FRC, 'CRR Thematic Review of TCFD Disclosures and Climate in the Financial Statements' (July 2022) <https://www.frc.org.uk/getattachment/65fa8b6f-2bed-4a67-8471-ab91c9cd2e85/FRC-TCFD-disclosures-and-climate-in-the-financial-statements_July-2022.pdf> accessed on 1 June 2023.

121 Prospectus Regulation (Regulation (EU) No 2017/1129 of the European Parliament and of the Council of 14 June 2017 on the prospectus to be published when securities are offered to the public or admitted to trading on a regulated market, and repealing Directive 2003/71/EC). The UK version of the Prospectus Regulation is part of UK law by virtue of the European Union (Withdrawal) Act 2018.

122 The Market Abuse Regulation (Regulation (EU) No 596/2014 of the European Parliament and of the Council of 16 April 2014 on market abuse (market abuse regulation) and repealing Directive 2003/6/EC of the European Parliament and of the Council and Commission Directives 2003/124/EC, 2003/125/EC and 2004/72/EC). The UK version of the market abuse regime is part of UK law by virtue of the European Union (Withdrawal) Act 2018.

123 FCA, 'Primary Market Technical Note: Disclosures in Relation to ESG Matters, Including Climate Change' (December 2020) <https://www.fca.org.uk/publication/primary-market/tn-801-1.pdf> accessed on 1 June 2023.

124 Ibid and LR.

125 Ibid and FCA Handbook, Disclosure Guidance and Transparency Rules Sourcebook.

126 Prospectus Regulation (n 121), art 6; and FCA Prospectus Regulation Rules Sourcebook, PRR 2.1.1.

ESG-related matters.[127] When disclosing climate-related and other ESG-related information, an issuer must not do so in a way (for example by omitting information) that breaches the prohibition of market manipulation,[128] such as the dissemination or suppression of information which is likely to give false or misleading signals as to the supply of, demand for, or price of a financial instrument.[129]

5.3.4 FCA: life insurers

UK life insurers are required to disclose on their website on an annual basis their 'engagement policy' which sets out details of its engagement with investee companies, including how it monitors investee companies on social and environmental impact.[130] In addition, a UK life insurer which is managing investments for a professional client that is not a natural person must disclose on its website the nature of its commitment to the UK Stewardship Code (or where it does not commit to the Code, its alternative investment strategy).[131]

5.3.5 FCA: in-scope life insurers

5.3.5.1 ESG Sourcebook

In December 2021, the FCA introduced climate-related disclosure rules set out in a new part of the FCA Handbook: the Environmental, Social and Governance Sourcebook ('ESG Sourcebook').[132] In addition to the TCFD disclosures, the ESG Sourcebook also sets out, and is intended to set out, rules and guidance for the disclosure of environmental, social, and governance matters.[133] The ESG Sourcebook applies to asset managers, insurers providing IBIPs or operating certain types of pension schemes, and FCA-regulated pension providers.[134] As IBIPs can only be provided by life insurers, insurers providing such products will be referred to as 'in-scope life insurers' by way of shorthand in this chapter, although not all life insurers do provide such products. The in-scope financial firms have in common that they are regulated asset owners and asset managers with investments that may be sensitive to climate-related risks and opportunities.

The ESG Sourcebook requires the publication of disclosures by 30 June of each calendar year at two levels: (1) at entity level in the TCFD entity report; and (2) at product level for each product in a public TCFD product report.[135] These reports must be available in a prominent place on the entity's main website.[136] The public TCFD product report must

---

127 Market Abuse Regulation (n 122) art 17 and FCA Handbook, Market Conduct (MAR).

128 Market Abuse Regulation (n 122) art 15 and see Chapter 8, Section 8.3.4.

129 Market Abuse Regulation (n 122) art 12 and see Chapter 8, Section 8.3.4.

130 FCA Handbook, Senior Management Arrangements, Systems and Controls sourcebook (SYSC) ('SYSC') 3.4; and see Chapter 8, Section 8.3.2.

131 FCA Handbook, Conduct of Business Sourcebook (COBS) ('COBS') 2.2.3R; and see Chapter 8, Section 8.3.2.

132 Disclosure Of Climate-Related Financial Information (Asset Manager and Asset Owner) Instrument 2021 introducing the FCA Environmental, Social and Governance Sourcebook. The rules come into effect for the largest firms on 1 January 2022 and one year later for smaller firms.

133 ESG Sourcebook 1.1.1G.

134 Ibid 1.2.1R.

135 Ibid 2.1.1R.

136 Ibid 2.1.3R. 'Prominence' may be achieved by adding hyperlinks to the reports which are accessible via the landing page of the main website for the business of the firm (ESG Sourcebook 2.1.4G).

also be included or cross-referenced in an in-scope life insurer's annual report to its with-profits policyholders.[137] In addition, after 1 July 2023, the in-scope life insurer must provide an on-demand TCFD product report within a reasonable period of time if requested by a client who itself needs to satisfy a legal or regulatory requirement for climate-related financial disclosure obligations.[138] Any climate-related financial disclosures in the TCFD entity report and the TCFD product report (whether public or on-demand) must be consistent with the TCFD Recommendations, including the 'Guidance for All Sectors'[139] and the guidance for asset owners and asset managers in the 'Supplemental Guidance for the Financial Sector,'[140] as well as other technical TCFD guidance.[141]

The **TCFD entity report** must contain climate-related financial disclosures regarding the overall assets managed or administered by the in-scope life insurer in relation to its IBIPs and any of its in-scope pension schemes business ('TCFD products').[142] In-scope life insurers are encouraged to assess the extent to which they have considered the UK's commitment to transition to a net-zero economy[143] in developing and disclosing their transition plans.[144] In relation to TCFD Recommendation 7 (description of the resilience of the organisation's strategy), an in-scope life insurer must also explain (1) its approach to climate-related scenario analysis; and (2) how the firm applies climate-related scenario analysis in its investment and risk decision-making process.[145] In relation to TCFD Recommendation 11 (description of the targets used by the organisation to manage climate-related risks and opportunities and performance against targets), an in-scope life insurer must also describe any targets it has set to manage climate-related risks and opportunities, including the key performance indicators it uses to measure progress against these targets, in a manner consistent with the TCFD Recommendations and Recommended Disclosures.[146]

The TCFD entity report may cross-reference to relevant climate-related financial disclosures contained in a third party's climate reporting, where such information enables the in-scope life insurer to make climate-related financial disclosures consistent with the TCFD Recommendations.[147] If an in-scope life insurer is a member of a group, it may rely on climate-related financial disclosures consistent with the TCFD Recommendations made by its group or a member of its group when producing its TCFD entity report, but only to the extent that those group disclosures are relevant to that life insurer and cover the assets it administers or manages as part of its IBIPs and any of its in-scope pension schemes business.[148] These provisions are useful where the relevant information and data can be obtained from third parties (such as investee companies or group companies) as such information can be cross-referenced and recycled.

Any public or on-demand **TCFD product report** must contain for each of its TCFD products:

137 Ibid 2.3.1R and COBS 20.4.7R.
138 ESG Sourcebook 2.1.1R(2) and 2.3.5R.
139 Ibid 2.1.5R and see Section 5.1.
140 Ibid 2.1.6R and see Section 5.1.
141 Ibid 2.1.7G.
142 Ibid 2.2.1R.
143 Climate Change Act 2008 (2050 Target Amendment) Order 2019, and see Chapter 2, Section 2.3.4.
144 ESG Sourcebook 2.2.2G.
145 Ibid 2.2.3R.
146 Ibid 2.2.4R.
147 Ibid 2.1.14R.
148 Ibid 2.2.5R.

1. information on the following metrics:
   - Scope 1 and 2 GHG emissions;
   - Scope 3 GHG emissions;
   - total carbon emissions;
   - total carbon footprint;
   - weighted average carbon intensity;[149]
2. relevant contextual information (such as explaining how the metrics should be interpreted; any assumptions);[150]
3. after the first year of preparing a TCFD product report, historical annual calculations of the metrics listed above;[151]
4. material deviations from the TCFD Recommendations 1 to 8;[152]
5. a qualitative summary of how climate change is likely to impact the assets underlying the relevant TCFD product under 'orderly transition,' 'disorderly transition,' and 'hothouse world' scenarios;[153]
6. a discussion of the most significant drivers of impact on that TCFD product;[154]
7. in relation to any of its TCFD products that have concentrated exposures or high exposures to carbon-intensive sectors, a quantitative analysis of 'orderly transition,' 'disorderly transition,' and 'hothouse world' scenarios;[155]
8. calculations for climate value-at-risk, and metrics that show the climate warming scenario with which a TCFD product is aligned, such as using an implied temperature rise metric.[156]

The ESG Sourcebook disclosure requirements for asset managers, in-scope life insurers, and FCA-regulated pension providers add further fora and formats – TCFD entity reports and public TCFD product reports published on the entity's website, and on-demand TCFD product reports – for a target audience of a reporting entity's institutional clients and end-user consumers. They do not extend to general insurers and life insurers that do not offer in-scope products. In their current format, these disclosure requirements are based on the TCFD Recommendations with a few additional or more specific requirements, none of which require disclosure of 'outward impact' or 'ESG' matters other than climate-related issues. Given that 'ESG' is in its title, the currently limited scope of the ESG Sourcebook might appear disappointing. However, the FCA has put forward proposals to extend the current scope of the ESG Sourcebook to rules and guidance which will introduce for in-scope insurers sustainable investment labels in relation to their in-scope products, and

149 Ibid 2.3.9(1)R.

150 Ibid 2.3.9(2)(a)R.

151 Ibid 2.3.9(2)(b)R.

152 Ibid 2.3.9(2)(c)R, and for the TCFD Recommendations see Section 5.1.2.

153 Ibid 2.3.11.(1)(a)R and 2.3.11(2). 'Orderly transition' scenarios assume climate policies are introduced early and become gradually more stringent, reaching global net-zero CO2 emissions around 2050 and likely limiting global warming to below 2°C on pre-industrial averages. 'Disorderly transition' scenarios assume climate policies are delayed or divergent, requiring sharper emissions reductions achieved at a higher cost and with increased physical risks in order to limit temperature rise to below 2°C, and 'hothouse world' scenarios assume only currently implemented policies are preserved, current commitments are not met, and emissions continue to rise, with high physical risks and severe social and economic disruption and failure to limit temperature rise (ESG Sourcebook 2.3.11(3)).

154 Ibid 2.3.11.(1)(b)R and 2.3.11(2).

155 Ibid 2.3.11.(1)(c)R.

156 Ibid 2.3.13.

sustainability-related disclosure at both entity and product levels, to come into effect in the third quarter of 2023.[157]

5.3.5.2 Sustainable investment labels

The **sustainable investment label regime** proposed by the FCA in their 'Sustainability Disclosure Requirements (SDR) and Investment Labels' Consultation Paper will apply to an in-scope life insurer that provides IBIPs and any of its in-scope pension schemes business ('in-scope investment products').[158] The FCA has consulted on the sustainable investment label regime and is currently preparing a response and Policy Statement.[159] The regime distinguishes between three different types of sustainable products according to whether they aim to invest:

1. in assets that are environmentally and/or socially sustainable ('sustainable focus');
2. to improve the environmental and/or social sustainability of assets over time, including in response to the stewardship influence of the firm ('sustainable improvers');
3. in solutions to environmental or social problems, to achieve positive, real-world impact ('sustainable impact').[160]

The sustainable investment labels are aimed at protecting consumers from green-washing, namely claims that in-scope investment products seek to pursue sustainable objectives when they do not. The labels will be underpinned by a set of principles and criteria (general and category-specific).[161] However, these principles and criteria do not define 'environmentally sustainable' and 'socially sustainable,' and the sustainability objective is determined by the firm itself.[162] A product's sustainability objective must have a plausible, purposeful, and credible link to an environmental and/or social outcome[163] (but 'environmental and/or social outcome' is not defined either) which needs to be demonstrated by credible, rigorous, and evidence-based key performance indicators ('KPIs') that measure a sustainable investment product's ongoing performance towards achieving its sustainability objective.[164] The principles and criteria are process and governance-driven, rather than prescriptive on the sustainable merits of the objective the product seeks to achieve. The approach contrasts with the EU Taxonomy[165] approach which is based on a classification of activities that are labelled as 'sustainable.'

157 The implementation timetable has been pushed back from July 2023 following consultation: see 'FCA Updates on Its Sustainability Disclosure Requirements (SDR) and Investment Labels Consultation' (29 March 2023) <https://www.fca.org.uk/news/news-stories/fca-updates-sustainability-disclosure-requirements-and-investment-labels-consultation> accessed on 1 June 2023.

158 FCA Sustainability Disclosure Proposals [3.5].

159 The Policy Statement was planned for Q3 2023 but has been delayed: FCA, 'FCA updates on its Sustainability Disclosure Requirements (SDR) and investment labels consultation' <https://www.fca.org.uk/news/news-stories/fca-updates-sustainability-disclosure-requirements-and-investment-labels-consultation> accessed on 5 November 2023.

160 Ibid [3.2].

161 Ibid [4.49].

162 Ibid [4.55] (Principle 1).

163 Ibid [4.55] (Principle 1).

164 Ibid [4.60] (Principle 3).

165 See Section 5.4.1.

In deciding whether to use a sustainable investment label, the in-scope insurer must ensure that the in-scope product meets the criteria in full and continues to meet them on an ongoing basis.[166] No application for the use of such a label is necessary, and there is no requirement for independent verification that the criteria have been met.[167] The FCA has stated that there will be no hierarchy between the proposed categories: each type of product is designed to deliver a different profile of assets, and to meet different consumer preferences.[168] Under the FCA's proposals, where insurance distributors offer in-scope products that use a sustainable investment label, they must display the label prominently on a relevant digital medium (such as a product website or page on a mobile application).[169]

As the sustainable investment labels are dependent on a sustainability objective that is linked to the prescribed outcomes, they cannot be used for investment products that merely integrate ESG factors into the investment strategy and management, or only use negative or positive screening as an investment approach.[170] However, such investment approaches would still be the subject of the sustainability disclosure requirements discussed below.

To ensure that in-scope products that do not qualify for a sustainable investment label will not name or market products in a way that may suggest that they are sustainable, the FCA is also proposing to introduce restrictions around names and marketing of investment products: life insurers providing in-scope products to retail investors that do not qualify for any of the sustainable investment labels will be prohibited from using sustainability-related terms including, but not limited to, 'ESG' (or 'environmental,' 'social,' or 'governance'), 'climate,' 'impact,' 'sustainable' or 'sustainability,' 'responsible,' 'green,' 'SDG' (sustainable development goals), 'Paris-aligned,' or 'net-zero' in their product names and marketing. In addition, the FCA also proposes that 'sustainable focus' or 'sustainable improvers' labelled products should be prohibited from using the term 'impact' in the naming and marketing of these products.[171]

The FCA's proposals on labels do not extend to general insurance products and life insurance products that are not IBIPs. This has several unfortunate consequences: (1) insurance products that have an environmentally sustainable focus, improve the environmental sustainability of assets, or offer solutions to climate change cannot use the sustainable investment labels to signal the product's environmental features to potential customers in an accessible way; (2) the naming and marketing restrictions on using environmental tags do not apply so that they can continue to be used without meeting specific criteria (subject to the general anti-green-washing rule explained below and misrepresentation-based claims); and (3) as the label criteria do not apply, insurers may down-play or under-report on the environmental features of an insurance product so as not to fall foul of green-washing (a practice referred to as 'green-blushing').[172] The FCA has indicated that the sustainable investment label regime will be expanded in scope over time.

166 FCA Sustainability Disclosure Proposals [4.68].

167 Ibid [4.79].

168 Ibid [3.2].

169 Ibid [7.8].

170 Ibid [2.3], [4.24], and [4.25].

171 Ibid [6.12].

172 See e.g.: World Economic Forum, 'What Is "Greenhushing" and Is It Really a Cause for Concern?' (18 November 2022) <https://www.weforum.org/agenda/2022/11/what-is-greenhushing-and-is-it-really-a-cause-for-concern/> accessed on 1 June 2023.

Such an extension will need to be mindful of any forthcoming Sustainability Disclosure Requirement Policy Statement to be published by HM Treasury.[173]

Moreover, on its wording, it is not clear whether the FCA's proposed sustainable investment label regime would cover climate change adaptation objectives and measures. The FCA has also said that the labels would not cover negative screening investment approaches, so it should be assumed that, even if the labelling regime were to be extended to insurance products, any insurance products that sought to reduce or exclude cover for fossil fuel projects would not be eligible.[174]

5.3.5.3 Sustainability-related disclosure regime

The **sustainability-related disclosure regime** proposed by the FCA is targeted at institutional investors and those consumers who seek information beyond (the absence of) a sustainable investment label, consisting of:

1. consumer-facing disclosures and a sustainability product report providing ongoing sustainability-related performance information;
2. pre-contractual disclosures of key sustainability-related features of products using a sustainable investment label;
3. a sustainability entity report covering how firms are managing sustainability-related risks and opportunities.

The FCA proposes that life insurers using a sustainable investment label provide **consumer-facing disclosures** for all in-scope products are produced in a standalone document (alongside the Key Information Document)[175] that is made available in a prominent place on the relevant digital medium for the firm (i.e. the main product webpage, page on a mobile application, etc.).[176] Insurance distributors will need to provide access to the consumer-facing disclosures and keep disclosed information up-to-date.[177] The FCA is considering a template but for now, they are proposing that firms must make disclosures in the following categories:

- basic information: the firm's name, product name, International Securities Identification Number (ISIN; where applicable), or any other unique identifier, and date;
- if the product has a sustainable investment label, this should be prominently displayed towards the beginning of the disclosure and include a brief description of what the label means;
- sustainability goal: the product's sustainability objective, signposted as 'sustainability goal,' highlighting if there is an impact or expected impact on the financial return; and description of progress towards the sustainability objective;

173 FSMA 2023, s 21.

174 FCA Sustainability Disclosure Proposals [2.3], [4.24], and [4.25].

175 Regulation (EU) No 1286/2014 of the European Parliament and of the Council of 26 November 2014 on key information documents for packaged retail and IBIPs (PRIIPs) art 13(1), as onshored into UK law by the European Union (Withdrawal) Act 2018.

176 FCA Sustainability Disclosure Proposals [5.25] and [5.26].

177 Ibid [7.8].

- sustainability approach: summary of key elements of the product's investment strategy to pursue the objective, clearly signposted as 'sustainability approach'; key sustainability characteristics of assets in which the product will and will not invest and the firm's approach to stewardship;
- unexpected investments: summary of the types of holdings that the firm would reasonably expect consumers of the product to find 'surprising' (i.e. inconsistent with the sustainability objective), clearly signposted as 'unexpected investments';
- sustainability metrics: relevant metrics/KPIs linked to achieving the sustainability objective and, where relevant, any other metrics that would help consumers to further understand the approach that the firm has taken, clearly signposted as 'sustainability metrics';
- signposting to other disclosures: cross refer/hyperlink to further information in the detailed product-level disclosures (Part A and Part B – see below), entity-level disclosures, and relevant documents that set out non-sustainability-related information for the product.[178]

The consumer-facing disclosures will need to be reviewed and updated at least annually and must be reviewed, and if necessary revised, prior to any proposed change to the in-scope product.[179]

The FCA is also proposing that life insurers that offer in-scope products that use a sustainable investment label make **pre-contractual disclosures** available in a sustainability product report ('Part A').[180] The Part A disclosures are aimed at institutional investors and other stakeholders and are to be published in a prominent place on a relevant digital medium for the firm, where the product is offered. The contents of Part A include disclosures on the firm's sustainability objective, its investment policy and strategy, its stewardship strategy, unexpected investments (i.e. those an investor may not typically associate with the sustainability objective), and sustainable investment label category-specific criteria.[181]

In addition, the FCA is proposing that life insurers that offer in-scope products that use a sustainable investment label produce disclosures on the sustainability-related performance of their products on an ongoing basis, in a dedicated **sustainability product report** ('Part B'). The Part B disclosures are aimed at institutional investors and other stakeholders and are to be published in a prominent place on a relevant digital medium for the firm, where the product is offered. The contents of Part B include disclosures on the firm's sustainability objective, its progress towards that objective, its stewardship strategy, unexpected investments, its ongoing reporting on sustainability metrics/KPIs, and sustainable investment label category-specific criteria.[182] Part B must also incorporate or hyperlink to the TCFD product report.[183] The first disclosures under 'Part B' of the sustainability product report must be published no later than 24 months after the rules enter

178 Ibid [5.38].
179 Ibid [6].
180 Ibid [5.44] to [5.46].
181 Ibid [5.50].
182 Ibid [5.67].
183 ESG Sourcebook 2.1.1R and see this section above; FCA Sustainability Disclosure Proposals [5.64].

into force, and thereafter annually.[184] The FCA will also allow for on-demand sustainability product reports if requested by a client who itself needs to satisfy a legal or regulatory requirement for sustainability disclosure obligations.[185]

Further, the FCA will require life insurers that offer in-scope products that use a sustainable investment label to produce a **sustainability entity report**, with a phased implementation from 30 June 2025 or later,[186] and thereafter to be published annually. The sustainability entity report will need to be published in a prominent place on a relevant digital medium for the firm and incorporate or hyperlink to the TCFD entity report.[187] At this stage, the FCA is only proposing to introduce core entity-level disclosure requirements based on the core themes in the TCFD Recommendations:

- the governance around sustainability-related risks and opportunities;
- the actual and potential impacts of sustainability-related risks and opportunities on their businesses, strategy, and financial planning, where such information is material;
- how the firm identifies, assesses, and manages sustainability-related risks;
- the metrics and targets used to assess and manage relevant sustainability-related risks, where such information is material;

but it may extend the scope of disclosures in the future.[188] The FCA's sustainability-related disclosure regime is extensive, comprising three different sets of product-related disclosures and one entity report. However, it only applies to a limited circle of in-scope firms and in-scope products. As regards insurance, this means that a large constituency of general insurers and life insurers will not be required to report on their 'outward impact' as firms and in relation to their products.

5.3.6 FCA: all UK-regulated insurers

The FCA proposes to introduce a general 'anti-green-washing' rule, requiring all regulated firms (including insurers and insurance distributors) to ensure that the naming and marketing of financial products and services in the UK is clear, fair and not misleading, and consistent with the sustainability profile of the product or service (i.e. proportionate and not exaggerated).[189] This rule would apply immediately upon the FCA's sustainability-related disclosure rules coming into effect (anticipated for late 2023).[190] In addition, the FCA is considering updating the sustainability disclosure rules in the future to include further disclosures against the UK Green Taxonomy intended to help investors compare the environmental performance of investment products. The UK Green Taxonomy – to be applicable across industries – is still under development by the Green Technical Advisory

184 FCA Sustainability Disclosure Proposals [5.77].

185 Ibid [5.74].

186 Ibid [5.87]. The FCA reported that the timeline might slip due to the large volume of responses received to CP22/20 <https://www.fca.org.uk/news/news-stories/fca-updates-sustainability-disclosure-requirements-and-investment-labels-consultation> accessed on 1 June 2023.

187 FCA Sustainability Disclosure Proposals [5.89].

188 Ibid [5.97].

189 Ibid [6.9].

190 Ibid [1.18]. The implementation timetable has been pushed back following consultation: see n 155.

Group established by the UK government.[191] Once available, it would also be useful to link the sustainable investment label regime to generally applicable definitions, rather than letting firms self-define the sustainable objectives of their investment products. Moreover, the FCA's proposed regime, which is focused on entity- and product-level disclosures, does not capture and could indeed encourage 'brown-spinning,'[192] a practice used to move business parts with heavy negative externalities for the environment or other stakeholders within legal structures that are beyond the reach of public scrutiny or subject to fewer disclosures.

In summary, the main building blocks of the FCA's climate-related disclosure requirements applicable to UK-regulated insurers are TCFD-aligned disclosures for listed insurers and in-scope life insurers, and the proposed sustainability-related disclosures that are limited to in-scope life insurers and IBIPs and specified pension schemes business. The FCA's existing and proposed sustainability disclosure regime takes a patchwork approach that creates complexity and a proliferation of different reporting documents, reporting media, and reporting cycles, as highlighted in Table 5.4. The sustainable investment label regime allows firms to self-determine the sustainable object of an investment product.

As noted above, the TCFD Recommendations focus on inward impact – the financial risk from climate change – and, with some exceptions, do not require disclosure of outward impact. The FCA's proposed sustainability disclosure requirements do not extend to information on the outward impact of general insurers and not in-scope life insurers, and their products. The concept of 'double materiality' therefore only applies to a very limited group of insurers and insurance products. In that respect, the FCA's climate-related disclosure requirements appear to be a step back from the IFRS Sustainability Disclosure Standards, and in particular IFRS S2, Appendix B-17.[193] The FCA regime fails to enable customers to make better-informed decisions and to create competition between insurers in relation to insurance products with outward impact. This limited approach is not supportive of the enabling role of insurers. The FCA intends to expand the disclosure requirements in the future, so that a wider circle of insurers and a wider range of insurance products may be added going forward as and when more reliable data (including on GHG emissions) becomes available in respect of insurer's policyholders and supply chains.[194]

It should also be noted that this is an area where the FCA is closely monitoring international developments, including the EU and US sustainability disclosure regimes, as many firms will need to make disclosures under other regimes internationally. This means that

191 HM Government, 'Greening Finance: A Roadmap to Sustainable Investing' (October 2021) <https://www.gov.uk/government/publications/greening-finance-a-roadmap-to-sustainable-investing> accessed on 1 June 2023; and HM Government, 'Mobilising Green Investment – 2023 Green Finance Strategy' (April 2023) 10 <https://www.gov.uk/government/publications/green-finance-strategy> accessed on 1 June 2023.

192 Suren Gomtsiam, 'Debtholder Stewardship' (2023) 86(2) *MLR*, 395, at 411.

193 See Section 5.2.2.

194 A recent survey carried out by the Lloyd's Market Association indicated that the integration of ESG factors, including GHG emissions, into underwriting decisions is hampered by a lack of quality data – see LMA, 'Why Is Collaboration Key to Improving ESG Data for Underwriting?' (March 2023) <https://www.lmalloyds.com/LMA/News/Blog/why_090323.aspx> accessed on 1 June 2023.

the FCA needs to balance coherence in relation to other regimes and international developments, with the needs and competitiveness of the UK market.[195]

5.3.7 Companies Act 2006 corporate disclosure requirements

There are various levels of corporate reporting in relation to environmental matters depending on the type and size of a company. All UK companies (except for small companies that are exempt from preparing annual accounts and reports)[196] must prepare an annual 'Strategic Report' as part of their annual accounts and report.[197] The purpose of the Strategic Report – which is prepared by the directors – is to inform members (i.e. shareholders) of the company and help them assess how the directors have performed their duty under s.172 of the Companies Act 2006 (the directors' duty to promote the success of the company).[198] The Strategic Report must contain a fair review of the company's business and a description of the principal risks and uncertainties facing the company.[199] The Strategic Report must be approved by the board of directors and signed on behalf of the board by a director or the secretary of the company.[200] If a Strategic Report is approved but does not comply with the requirements of the Companies Act 2006, every director who (1) knew that it did not comply, or was reckless as to whether it complied, and (2) failed to take reasonable steps to secure compliance with those requirements or, to prevent the report from being approved, commits an offence and may be liable to a fine.[201] Earlier in 2023, the UK government put forward – but has now withdrawn – a draft Companies (Strategic Report and Directors' Report) (Amendment) Regulations that would have required companies with at least 750 employees and an annual turnover of £750 million or more to include in their Strategic Report an annual resilience statement which sets out how a company manages risk over the short, medium, and long term.[202] In-scope companies will need to explain how they are managing the impact of climate-related risks and sustainability-related risks on the company's business model.

5.3.7.1 Strategic Report

All UK companies required to prepare a Strategic Report, except for a company which qualifies as medium-sized in relation to that financial year,[203] must include a 'Section 172(1) statement' which describes how the directors have had regard to the matters set

195 FCA Sustainability Disclosure Proposals, Annex 1 [7]; and see Chapter 4, Section 4.3.2.

196 Companies Act 2006, s 381 and 382.

197 Ibid s 414A.

198 Ibid s 414C(1); for the directors' duty to promote the success of the company, see discussion in Chapter 6, Section 6.2.1.

199 Ibid s 414C(2).

200 Ibid s 414D(1).

201 Ibid s 414D(2).

202 HM Government Department for Business and Trade, 'New Transparency over Resilience and Assurance for Big Business' (July 2023) <https://www.gov.uk/government/publications/new-transparency-over-resilience-and-assurance-for-big-business> accessed on 10 August 2023. The UK government has now withdrawn the draft regulations after consultation with companies raised concerns about imposing additional burdensome reporting requirements (https://www.gov.uk/government/news/burdensome-legislation-withdrawn-in-latest-move-to-cut-red-tape-for-businesses accessed on 3 November 2023).

203 Ibid ss 465–467.

out in s.172(1)(a)–(f) of the Companies Act 2006 when performing their duty to promote the success of the company.[204] As will be discussed in more detail in Chapter 6, Section 6.2.1, Companies Act 2006 s.172(1)(d) requires directors, in discharging their s.172 duty, to have regard to the impact of the company's operations on the environment. Therefore, the Strategic Report should contain, where relevant and material, a narrative on how the directors have promoted the success of the company having regard (among other matters) to the impact of the company's operations on the community and the environment. Although this could give rise to disclosures on outward impact, it is a general requirement that could be addressed with a high-level description addressing all matters in s.172(1)(a)–(f) of the Companies Act 2006 in the round. There is a more specific disclosure requirement that applies to quoted companies[205] who must also include information on environmental matters, including information on the impact of the company's business on the environment, in their Strategic Reports.[206]

5.3.7.2 Non-financial and sustainability information statement

In addition, for any UK-authorised insurance company and any company carrying on insurance market activity, each with 500 or more employees, the Strategic Report must also contain a 'non-financial and sustainability information statement' ('NFSIS').[207] The NFSIS is based on non-financial reporting requirements that were originally introduced to implement the EU Non-Financial Reporting Directive ('NFRD'),[208] and which have now been amended to include additional disclosures in line with the TCFD Recommendations.[209] The NFSIS must contain information, to the extent necessary for an understanding of the company's development, performance, and position and the impact of its activity, relating to (among other matters) environmental matters, including the impact of the company's business on the environment.[210] The NFSIS must also contain the climate-related financial disclosures of the company,[211] defined as follows:

1. a description of the company's governance arrangements in relation to assessing and managing climate-related risks and opportunities;
2. a description of how the company identifies, assesses, and manages climate-related risks and opportunities;
3. a description of how processes for identifying, assessing, and managing climate-related risks are integrated into the company's overall risk management process;

---

204 Ibid s 414CZA.

205 A 'quoted company' means a company whose equity share capital has been included in the official list in accordance with the provisions of Part 6 of the Financial Services and Markets Act 2000 (c. 8), or is officially listed in an EEA State, or is admitted to dealing on either the New York Stock Exchange or the exchange known as Nasdaq – see Companies Act 2006 s 385(2).

206 Ibid s 414C(7)(b)(i).

207 Ibid ss414CA (A1) and (1).

208 Directive 2014/95/EU of the European Parliament and of the Council of 22 October 2014 amending Directive 2013/34/EU as regards disclosure of non-financial and diversity information by certain large undertakings and groups.

209 The Companies (Strategic Report) (Climate-Related Financial Disclosure) Regulations 2022.

210 Companies Act 2006 s 414CB(1)(a).

211 Ibid s 414CB(A1).

4. a description of:
   a. the principal climate-related risks and opportunities arising in connection with the company's operations, and
   b. the time periods by reference to which those risks and opportunities are assessed;
5. a description of the actual and potential impacts of the principal climate-related risks and opportunities on the company's business model and strategy;
6. an analysis of the resilience of the company's business model and strategy, taking into consideration different climate-related scenarios;
7. a description of the targets used by the company to manage climate-related risks and to realise climate-related opportunities and of performance against those targets; and
8. a description of the key performance indicators used to assess progress against targets used to manage climate-related risks and realise climate-related opportunities and of the calculations on which those key performance indicators are based.[212]

If the company does not pursue policies in relation to one or more of the climate-related financial disclosures mentioned above, the NFSIS must provide a clear and reasoned explanation for the company's not doing so.[213] Where the directors of a company reasonably believe that, having regard to the nature of the company's business, and the manner in which it is carried on, the whole or a part of a climate-related financial disclosure required by (5)–(8) is not necessary for an understanding of the company's business, the directors may omit the whole or (as the case requires) the relevant part of that climate-related financial disclosure. This is unlikely to be the case in relation to insurance companies to which the NFSIS requirement applies.[214]

While the climate-related financial disclosures under s.414(CB) of the Companies Act 2006 introduced by the Companies (Strategic Report) (Climate-related Financial Disclosure) Regulations 2022 have achieved better alignment with the TCFD Recommendations, they are inward impact focused. In fact, the 2022 Regulations amendments have deleted from s.414CB a reporting requirement on outward impact, including a requirement for the company to disclose 'a description of its business relationships, products and services which are likely to cause adverse impacts on the environment.'[215] The climate-related financial disclosure requirements and other relevant disclosure requirements under the Companies Act 2006 also introduce additional layers of complexity to the disclosure obligations of different types of companies and companies of different sizes. Table 5.4 contains a simplified representation of the disclosure requirements relevant to climate-related information, consolidating regulatory and corporate disclosure requirements.

212 Ibid s 414CB(2A).

213 Ibid s 414CB(4).

214 See Chapter 3, Section 3.3, which explains the inward impact of climate change risks on insurance companies, and an insurance company's outward impact on climate change.

215 Companies Act 2006 s CA 414CB(2) prior to its amendment by the Companies (Strategic Report) (Climate-Related Financial Disclosure) Regulations 2022.

Table 5.4 Summary of existing and proposed climate-related disclosures applicable to UK-regulated insurers

Document, frequency, and location	*Listed/ quoted insurers*	*Life insurers*	*In-scope life insurers*	*In-scope life insurer using sustainable investment label*	*Authorised insurers with 500+ employees*
Solvency and financial condition report (annually, public disclosure – publication on insurer's website)	√	√	√	√	√
TCFD LR statement (annually, published in annual accounts and reports)	√				
TCFD entity report (annually, published in a prominent place on the entity's main website)			√	√	
Public TCFD product report (annually, published in a prominent place on the entity's main website)			√	√	
On-demand TCFD product report (on demand within a reasonable period of time from request by an eligible client)			√	√	
Engagement policy (on website, must be annually updated)		√			
Commitment to UK Stewardship Code (on website, must be annually updated)		√[a]			
Sustainable investment label (from 30.6.2024 or later – to be reviewed regularly; displayed prominently on a relevant digital medium, such as product website or page on a mobile application)				√	
Consumer sustainability disclosure document (from 30.6.2024 or later, to be reviewed and updated at least annually; displayed prominently on a relevant digital medium, such as product website or page on a mobile application)				√	

(*Continued*)

Table 5.4 Continued

Document, frequency, and location	*Listed/ quoted insurers*	*Life insurers*	*In-scope life insurers*	*In-scope life insurer using sustainable investment label*	*Authorised insurers with 500+ employees*
Sustainability product report Part A (pre-contractual disclosure) (from 30.6.2024 or later, to be reviewed and updated at least annually; displayed prominently on a relevant digital medium, such as product website or page on a mobile application)				√	
Sustainability product report Part B (to be published annually from 30.6.2025 or later; displayed prominently on a relevant digital medium, such as product website or page on a mobile application)				√	
On-demand sustainability product report (on demand within a reasonable period of time from request by an eligible client)				√	
Sustainability entity report (to be published annually from 30.6.2025 or later; displayed prominently on a relevant digital medium, such as product website or page on a mobile application)			√	√	
Strategic Report (annually, in annual accounts and report)	√	√	√	√	√
Strategic Report with information on environmental matters, including information on the impact of the company's business on the environment (annually, in annual accounts and report)	√				
Non-financial and sustainability information statement (annually, in Strategic Report in annual accounts and report)					√

[a]Applies only to life insurers that manage investments for professional clients (not for a natural person) – COBS 2.2.3R.

5.3.8 Data assurance

As regards regulatory climate-related disclosures in the SFCR, the insurer must ensure that it has in place the systems and processes to fulfil all the requirements in relation to the SFCR and a written policy ensuring the ongoing appropriateness of any information disclosed.[216] The SFCR must be approved by the insurer's board of directors.[217] Contraventions of the PRA's and FCA's rules can attract regulatory sanctions.[218] Under FSMA 2000, s.138D(2), a contravention by an authorised insurer of an FCA Handbook rule would also generally be actionable by a policyholder who is a private person and who has suffered a loss as a result of the contravention, subject to defences and certain exceptions.

The TCFD LR statement, the Strategic Report, and the NFSIS are all part of the annual accounts, which must be approved by the board of directors and signed on behalf of the board by a director of the company.[219] The Strategic Report, including the NFSIS where applicable, also must be approved in its own right by the board of directors and signed on behalf of the board by a director or the secretary of the company.[220] External auditors are required to report on the company's annual accounts;[221] in doing so, an auditor must:

(a) state whether, in his opinion, based on the work undertaken in the course of the audit –
   (i) the information given in the strategic report (if any) and the directors' report for the financial year for which the accounts are prepared is consistent with those accounts; and
   (ii) any such strategic report and the directors' report have been prepared in accordance with applicable legal requirements;
(b) state whether, in the light of the knowledge and understanding of the company and its environment obtained in the course of the audit, he has identified material misstatements in the strategic report (if any) and the directors' report; and
(c) if applicable, give an indication of the nature of each of the misstatements referred to in paragraph (b).[222]

Thus, auditors carry out a limited review of the Strategic Report (consistency and compliance) based on a limited data set (based on their audit). A 2020 review by the FRC highlighted that investors were already expecting auditors to review climate-related information, and also to challenge appropriately the company's management on climate-related risks.[223] At that time, FRC concluded that 'auditors need to improve their consideration of climate-related risks when planning and executing their audits.'[224] The FRC has now

216 PRA Rulebook, SII Firms, Reporting, r.6.1.

217 Ibid r.6.2.

218 FSMA 2000, Part XIV.

219 Companies Act 2006 s 414.

220 Ibid s 414D.

221 Ibid s 495.

222 Ibid s 496.

223 FRC, 'Climate Thematic Review – Audit' (November 2020) 5 <https://www.frc.org.uk/getattachment/0ef2c94a-9028-4efa-ac80-3b8c2e0d9a11/Audit-FINAL.pdf> accessed on 1 June 2023.

224 Ibid.

issued further guidance on 'Auditor responsibilities under ISA (UK) 720'[225] in respect of climate-related reporting by companies required by the FCA.[226] Their responsibilities depend on whether the climate-related information is considered 'other information' – i.e. financial or non-financial information other than the financial statements in the auditor's report which is being considered in the audit. The TCFD LR statement is 'other information' for the auditor's purpose as the LR requires it to be included in the company's annual account and report.[227] Whether climate-related disclosures constitute other information in accordance with ISA (UK) 720 will depend on the placement of that material, and/or the integration of that material with other climate-related material in the company's annual accounts and report.[228] If the information is in the annual accounts and report or in the Strategic Report it will be covered by ISA (UK) 720.[229] The UK government has indicated that it is likely to adopt the IFRS Sustainability Disclosure Standards as a basis for a single set of reporting standards for corporate and regulatory climate-related and sustainability disclosures.[230]

An in-scope life insurer's TCFD entity report must include a statement, signed by a member of senior management of the firm, confirming that the disclosures in the report, including any third-party or group disclosures cross-referenced in it, comply with the disclosure requirements in the ESG Sourcebook, chapter 2. The same requirement will apply, mutatis mutandis, to the sustainability entity report.[231] For the product-related disclosures, the existing rules relating to the accuracy of financial promotions will apply. The applicability of a sustainable investment label does not require independent verification.[232]

In connection with data assurance, it should also be noted that the FCA is planning to bring ESG data and rating providers within their regulatory oversight to ensure that ESG data and rating services should be transparent, well-governed, independent, objective, and based on reliable and systematic methodologies and processes.[233]

5.3.9 Is the UK disclosure regime supporting an enabling role?

Taking stock, the current UK disclosure regime on climate-related matters has been built up over the last three years and is to expand again over the next two years. The incremental

225 ISA (UK) 720 requires that 'auditors must read and consider the other information because other information that is materially inconsistent with the financial statements or the auditor's knowledge obtained in the audit may indicate that there is a material misstatement of the financial statements or that a material misstatement of the other information exists, either of which may undermine the credibility of the financial statements and the auditor's report thereon.' (See FRC, 'International Standard On Auditing (UK) 720 (revised November 2019) The Auditor's Responsibilities Relating to Other Information' [3].)

226 FRC, 'Auditor Responsibilities under ISA (UK) 720 in Respect of Climate-Related Reporting by Companies Required by the FCA' (February 2022) <https://www.frc.org.uk/getattachment/b6e1b51c-4dc8-413f-8a83-ae051e4d000e/FRC-Staff-Guidance-Auditor-responsibilities-under-ISA-(UK)-720-in-respect-of-climate-related-reporting.pdf> accessed on 1 June 2023.

227 LR 9.8.6.8; and FRC (n 223).

228 FRC (n 226) 3.

229 Ibid.

230 HM Government, 'Mobilising Green Investment – 2023 Green Finance Strategy' (n 191) 43.

231 FCA Sustainability Disclosure Proposals [5.92].

232 Ibid [4.79].

233 FCA, 'ESG Integration in UK Capital Markets,' FS22/4 (June 2022) [4.1]. On 30 March 2023, HM Treasury published a Consultation Paper on the future regulatory regime for environmental, social, and governance (ESG) ratings providers (<https://www.gov.uk/government/consultations/future-regulatory-regime-for-environmental-social-and-governance-esg-ratings-providers> accessed on 1 June 2023).

extension of these disclosure requirements in scope and applicability has led to a (temporarily) complex and fragmented system that seems to run counter to the sentiment behind the reform proposals to ease the reporting burden of insurers.[234]

The UK disclosure regime raises the bar for insurers taking an enabling role as outlined in Chapter 3, Section 3.4.5, but falls short of being supportive. The focus thus far has been on climate-related and sustainability disclosures that pose financial risks and opportunities for insurers, and disclosure requirements in relation to outward impact have been much more limited for both regulatory and corporate disclosures. To improve transparency as to which insurers take an enabling role, the FCA's sustainability-related disclosure regime should be expanded beyond the limited circle of in-scope firms and in-scope products. To improve the comparability of disclosed information, the UK must proceed with the development of the UK Green Taxonomy to define the 'sustainability' or 'net-zero' characteristics of financial products and underlying investments. To improve data assurance, auditors should have a clear mandate to review all of a company's sustainability and climate-related reporting and should be required to acquire the skills necessary to carry out such a review.

5.4 EU climate-related and sustainability disclosure requirements

Since Brexit, the EU has been pushing ahead with the European Green Deal – the EU's plan launched in 2019 to transform the EU into a 'modern, resource-efficient and competitive economy' without the UK's input. The European Green Deal sets a net-zero target for 2050, and also aims to reverse biodiversity loss and the broader degradation of the environment, while leaving nobody behind in the process.[235] To reach these targets, the European Commission seeks to mobilise private financial flows into relevant economic activities underpinned by its 2018 'Action Plan: Financing Sustainable Growth' ('EU Action Plan')[236] and its 2021 'Strategy for Financing the Transition to a Sustainable Economy' ('EU Finance Strategy').[237]

The EU Action Plan had three major components: (1) a 'taxonomy' of sustainable activities, (2) a sustainability disclosure framework, and (3) investment tools, including benchmarks, standards, and labels.[238]

5.4.1 The EU Taxonomy

The EU Taxonomy Regulation ('EU Taxonomy'),[239] which entered into force in July 2020, provides a science-based classification and definition system for environmentally sustainable economic activities for the purposes of establishing whether an investment is environmentally sustainable. With this catalogue of economic activities that are considered environmentally sustainable, the EU hopes to create more transparency for investors,

234 PRA, 'Review of Solvency II: Adapting to the UK Insurance Market,' CP12/23 (June 2023).

235 Communication from the Commission, 'The European Green Deal' (2019) COM/2019/640.

236 European Commission, 'Action Plan: Financing Sustainable Growth' (COM/2018/97).

237 Communication from the European Commission (COM/2021/390) (n 3).

238 EU Action Plan and EU Finance Strategy.

239 Regulation (EU) 2020/852 of the European Parliament and of the Council of 18 June 2020 on the establishment of a framework to facilitate sustainable investment, and amending Regulation (EU) 2019/2088.

protect retail customers from green-washing, and help companies to shift their activities towards environmental sustainability.[240]

5.4.1.1 Environmentally sustainable economic activities

For an economic activity to qualify as environmentally sustainable, four **overarching conditions** have to be met:

1. it contributes substantially to one or more of the six environmental objectives (see below);
2. it does not significantly harm any of the six environmental objectives (see below);
3. it is carried out in compliance with the specified minimum safeguards;[241]
4. it complies with technical screening criteria that have been established by the European Commission.[242]

The six **environmental objectives** are:

1. climate change mitigation;
2. climate change adaptation;
3. the sustainable use and protection of water and marine resources;
4. the transition to a circular economy;
5. pollution prevention and control;
6. the protection and restoration of biodiversity and ecosystems.[243]

For each environmental objective, there are detailed but non-exhaustive definitions,[244] and provisions that set out what constitutes 'significant harm' in relation to each.[245] It should be noted that only economic activities that make a substantial, rather than a marginal, contribution to reaching the environmental objectives qualify. This could exclude certain impact underwriting and impact investment activities designed to support the transition to environmentally sustainable activities that do not make a sufficient or measurable impact. The conditions under which a specific economic activity qualifies as making a substantial contribution are or will be set out in the technical screening criteria.

5.4.1.2 Technical screening criteria

The **technical screening criteria** are intended to provide further detail on which economic activities make a substantial contribution to the EU's environmental goals and are set by the European Commission through delegated acts. The first Delegated Act on sustainable activities for climate change adaptation and mitigation objectives[246] came into force on 1 January 2022. For each economic activity considered, this Delegated Act speci-

240 EU Taxonomy, Recitals.

241 Essentially, these safeguards are ensuring the alignment with the OECD Guidelines for Multinational Enterprises and the UN Guiding Principles on Business and Human Rights, including the principles and rights set out in the eight fundamental conventions identified in the Declaration of the International Labour Organisation on Fundamental Principles and Rights at Work and the International Bill of Human Rights.

242 EU Taxonomy, art 3.

243 Ibid art 9.

244 Ibid arts 10–15.

245 Ibid art 17.

246 Commission Delegated Regulation (EU) 2021/2139 of 4 June 2021 supplementing Regulation (EU) 2020/852 of the European Parliament and of the Council by establishing the technical screening criteria for determining the conditions under which an economic activity qualifies as contributing substantially to climate

fies environmental performance requirements that ensure the activity makes a substantial contribution to climate change mitigation[247] and climate change adaptation,[248] and does no significant harm to the other environmental objectives. Non-life insurance that covers climate-related perils has been included as an economic activity that can make a substantial contribution to climate change adaptation if it meets some or all of the following technical screening criteria:

- leadership in modelling and pricing of climate risks: the re/insurer uses (1) modelling techniques that incorporate climate risk and forward-looking scenarios, (2) incentives for risk reduction by setting out the (pre)-conditions for the insurance coverage of risk and by acting as a price signal of risk;
- product design: the insurer (1) offers risk-based rewards for preventive actions taken by policyholders or (2) provides to customers measures in relation to an asset, an activity, or people that prevent or protect against natural catastrophes. The reinsurer supports the development and supply of enabling non-life reinsurance products;
- innovative insurance coverage solutions: the re/insurer offers coverage for the climate-related perils, including (where appropriate) protection against business interruption, contingent business interruption, other non-physical damage-related loss factors, cascading effects and interdependencies of hazards (secondary perils), cascading impacts of interacting natural and technological hazards, critical infrastructure failures;
- data sharing: a significant share of loss data related to the re/insurer's activity is made available, free of charge, to one or several public authorities for the purpose of analytical research;
- high level of service in post-disaster situations: claims from large-scale loss events resulting from climate risks are processed fairly and in a timely manner;
- the re/insurance activity does not include insurance of the extraction, storage, transport, or manufacture of fossil fuels or insurance of vehicles, property, or other assets dedicated to such purposes.[249]

No technical screening criteria have been provided for insurance in relation to climate change mitigation yet. This is because sectors with the highest contribution to CO_2 emissions (energy, manufacturing, transport, buildings), as well as activities enabling their transformation, have been prioritised. The EU Taxonomy technical screening criteria are however clear evidence that the EU envisages an enabling role for insurers in relation to climate change adaptation. The EU Taxonomy is also relevant to insurers' mandatory disclosures in relation to investment strategies and investment products.[250] Moreover, for insurers, the EU Taxonomy is also a tool to assess whether their clients, investee

change mitigation or climate change adaptation and for determining whether that economic activity causes no significant harm to any of the other environmental objectives.

247 Ibid art 1 and Annex I.

248 Ibid art 2 and Annex II.

249 Ibid, Annex II, s 10.

250 EU Taxonomy art 5–7, and see Section 5.4.2.

companies, and other actors in their value chains engage in environmentally sustainable economic activities.

A Delegated Act supplementing Article 8 of the Taxonomy Regulation (in force since 1 January 2022) specifies the content, methodology, and presentation of information to be disclosed by financial and non-financial undertakings concerning the proportion of environmentally sustainable economic activities in their business, investments, or lending activities.[251] A Complementary Climate Delegated Act has been in force since 1 January 2023.[252] This Delegated Act is controversial since it includes, under strict conditions, specific nuclear and gas energy activities in the list of environmentally sustainable economic activities covered by the EU Taxonomy on the basis that nuclear and gas activities are part of the transition from coal and oil towards a net-zero economy.[253]

The intention is that the technical screening criteria as contained in the delegated acts will be 'living documents' that will be added to over time and updated as necessary.[254] In 2021, the European Commission announced plans for another Delegated Act that would cover activities making a substantial contribution to the other four environmental objectives as set out in the EU Taxonomy (sustainable use and protection of water and marine resources, transition to a circular economy, pollution prevention and control, protection and restoration of biodiversity and ecosystems),[255] and for an extension of the EU Taxonomy to include a 'social taxonomy' and to recognise activities with an intermediate level of environmental performance.[256] These plans have not been implemented yet.

5.4.1.3 Key obligations

The EU Taxonomy imposes three **key obligations**:

1. on member states and at EU level to apply the EU Taxonomy when regulating how environmentally sustainable financial products or corporate bonds are made available (art.4);
2. on 'financial market participants' (including insurers offering IBIPs) to make statements about the alignment of investments with the Taxonomy when making available financial products, including when these products are not considered to be environmentally sustainable (art.5–7);

251 Commission Delegated Regulation (EU) 2021/2178 of 6 July 2021 supplementing Regulation (EU) 2020/852 of the European Parliament and of the Council by specifying the content and presentation of information to be disclosed by undertakings subject to Articles 19a or 29a of Directive 2013/34/EU concerning environmentally sustainable economic activities, and specifying the methodology to comply with that disclosure obligation.

252 Commission Delegated Regulation (EU) 2022/1214 of 9 March 2022 amending Delegated Regulation (EU) 2021/2139 as regards economic activities in certain energy sectors and Delegated Regulation (EU) 2021/2178 as regards specific public disclosures for those economic activities.

253 Ibid, Recitals.

254 European Commission, 'FAQ: What Is the EU Taxonomy and How Will It Work in Practice?' (April 2021) <https://ec.europa.eu/info/sites/default/files/business_economy_euro/banking_and_finance/documents/sustainable-finance-taxonomy-faq_en.pdf> accessed on 1 June 2023.

255 Communication from the Commission, 'EU Taxonomy, Corporate Sustainability Reporting, Sustainability Preferences and Fiduciary Duties: Directing Finance towards the European Green Deal' (COM2021/188).

256 Communication from the European Commission (COM/2021/390) (n 3).

3. on large undertakings[257] and public-interest entities[258] to include information about how their activities align with the EU Taxonomy in the non-financial disclosure part of their financial statements (art.8).

The disclosure obligations for financial market participants (including insurers offering IBIPs) in art.5 to 7 of the EU Taxonomy supplement the SFDR (discussed in Section 5.4.2). The disclosures under art.8 of the EU Taxonomy apply to all EU insurers (except for micro insurers)[259] and require the insurer to include its non-financial statement in the annual accounts and report information on how and to what extent its activities are associated with economic activities that qualify as environmentally sustainable under the EU Taxonomy, articles 3 and 9.

The EU Taxonomy is not a mandatory list of economic activities for investors to invest in. Nor does it set mandatory requirements on environmental performance for companies or for financial products. Conversely, economic activities that are not recognised by the EU Taxonomy Delegated Acts as substantially contributing to one of the EU's climate and environmental objectives are not necessarily environmentally harmful or unsustainable. There are, however, many possible voluntary uses of the EU Taxonomy by market participants, which are not referenced in the EU Taxonomy. For example, insurers could use the criteria for screening their underwriting activities, or for identifying investment opportunities aiming to achieve a positive environmental impact.

The EU Taxonomy Regulation is an ambitious project which is far from being completed. However, it already provides a useable baseline in the discourse on what is 'environmentally sustainable' and its technical screening criteria for insurance serve as a blueprint for how insurers can take an enabling role in relation to climate change adaptation.

5.4.2 SFDR: sustainability-related disclosures in the financial services sector

The SFDR has been directly applicable in EU Member States since 10 March 2021 and all of its provisions are in force now. It is currently undergoing a review with targeted consultation (targeted at public bodies and stakeholders) and a public consultation on its implementation and operation.[260] The SFDR has introduced disclosure requirements for EU 'financial market participants' and 'financial advisers,' including EU insurers that make

257 Large undertaking: balance sheet total: EUR 20,000,000; net turnover: EUR 40,000,000; average number of employees during the financial year: 250 (Directive 2013/34/EU of the European Parliament and of the Council of 26 June 2013 on the annual financial statements, consolidated financial statements and related reports of certain types of undertakings, amending Directive 2006/43/EC of the European Parliament and of the Council and repealing Council Directives 78/660/EEC and 83/349/EEC, art 3(4)).

258 Public-interest entity: there is a wide-ranging list of different types of entities, including EU insurers (Directive 2013/34/EU (n 255) art 2).

259 A micro undertaking is an entity which on its balance sheet dates does not exceed the limits of at least two of the three following criteria: (a) balance sheet total: EUR 350,000; (b) net turnover: EUR 700,000; (c) average number of employees during the financial year: 10 (Directive 2013/34/EU (n 255) art 3(1)).

260 European Commission, 'Targeted consultation on the implementation of the Sustainable Finance Disclosures Regulation (SFDR)' and 'Public consultation on the implementation of the Sustainable Finance Disclosures Regulation (SFDR)' (September 2023) <https://finance.ec.europa.eu/sustainable-finance/disclosures/sustainability-related-disclosure-financial-services-sector_en> accessed on 5 November 2023)

available or advise on,[261] and insurance intermediaries that advise on,[262] IBIPs. The SFDR does not apply to insurers and intermediaries that do not provide or advise on IBIPs.

The aim of the SFDR is to provide more transparent information to buyers of investment products (referred to as 'end investors') in relation to (1) the integration of sustainability risks and the consideration of adverse sustainability impacts in the provider's processes, and (2) any adverse sustainability impacts or environmental or social characteristics of the products. Accordingly, the SFDR extends to 'outward impact' disclosures. The SFDR distinguishes between disclosure requirements:

- at entity level and at product level;
- on an entity's website, as part of its pre-contractual information, in its remuneration policy and its annual report to policyholders.

Table 5.5 sets out disclosures under the SFDR that are applicable to EU insurers that make available or advise on, and insurance intermediaries that advise on IBIPs, to be made on that insurer's website, pre-contractual, and annual accounts.[263] The references to articles are provisions in the SFDR, except where expressly stated otherwise.

Key definitions in the SFDR include:

- 'sustainable investment': an *investment in an economic activity that contributes to an environmental objective, as measured, for example, by key resource efficiency indicators on the use of energy, renewable energy, raw materials, water and land, on the production of waste, and greenhouse gas emissions, or on its impact on biodiversity and the circular economy*, or an investment in an economic activity that contributes to a social objective, in particular an investment that contributes to tackling inequality or that fosters social cohesion, social integration and labour relations, or an investment in human capital or economically or socially disadvantaged communities, provided that such investments do not significantly harm any of those objectives and that the investee companies follow good governance practices, in particular with respect to sound management structures, employee relations, remuneration of staff, and tax compliance;
- 'sustainability risk': an *environmental*, social, or governance event or condition that, if it occurs, could cause an actual or a potential material negative impact on the value of the investment;
- 'sustainability factors': *environmental*, social, and employee matters, respect for human rights, anti-corruption, and anti-bribery matters.[264] [emphasis added to highlight environmental aspects]

The European Supervisory Authorities (which include EIOPA) have clarified that, in order to qualify as 'sustainable investment,' it must not significantly harm any of the environmental or social objectives and, therefore, referring to a transition plan aiming to achieve

261 SFDR art 2(1)(a) and art 2(11)(b)).

262 Ibid art 2(11)(a).

263 Table 7 does not include disclosures of remuneration policies in relation to the integration of sustainability risks (art 5).

264 SFDR, art 2(17), (22), and (24).

Table 5.5 Disclosure obligations under the SFDR

	Website	*Pre-contractual information to be provided to end investors in key information document (IDD, art.29)*	*Annual report to policyholders (Solvency II Directive, art.185)*
Entity-level disclosures for in-scope EU insurers and intermediaries	Information about its policies on the integration of sustainability risks in their investment decision-making process, and their investment advice or insurance advice (art.3(1) and (2))	Descriptions of the manner in which sustainability risks are integrated into its investment decisions (art.6(1)(a)) and/or its investment or insurance advice (art.6(2)(a))	
	Where it considers principal adverse impacts of investment decisions on sustainability factors, a statement on due diligence policies with respect to those impacts, taking due account of their size, the nature and scale of their activities, and the types of financial products they make available (and where it does not do so, clear reasons why not) (art.4(1))		
	Information as to whether or not it considers in their investment advice or insurance advice the principal adverse impacts on sustainability factors (and if not when it intends to do so) (art.4(5))		
Product-level disclosures for in-scope EU insurers and intermediaries	Explanation of whether, and, if so, how a financial product considers principal adverse impacts on sustainability factors (art.7(1)(a))	Results of the assessment of the likely impacts of sustainability risks on the returns of the financial products it makes available (art.6(1)(b)), and/or the returns of the financial products it advises on (art.6(2)(b))	
	Statement that information on principal adverse impacts on sustainability factors is available in SFDR section in annual accounts (art.7(2))		
	For each product that promotes sustainable characteristics or has a sustainable investment objective: a description of the environmental or social characteristics or the sustainable investment objective, information on the methodologies used to assess these characteristics or the impact of the sustainable investments (art.10(1))	Where a financial product promotes, among other characteristics, environmental or social characteristics, or a combination thereof, information on how those characteristics are met; and if an index has been designated as a reference benchmark, information on whether and how this index is consistent with those characteristics (art.8(1))	For a financial product that promotes, among other characteristics, environmental or social characteristics, or a combination of those characteristics, the extent to which environmental or social characteristics are met (art.11(1)(a))

(Continued)

Table 5.5 Continued

	Website	*Pre-contractual information to be provided to end investors in key information document (IDD, art.29)*	*Annual report to policyholders (Solvency II Directive, art.185)*
		Where a financial product has sustainable investment as its objective and an index has been designated as a reference benchmark, information on how the designated index is aligned with that objective; and an explanation as to why and how the designated index aligned with that objective differs from a broad market index (art.9(1)). If no index has been set, an explanation why not (art.9(2))	For a financial product that has sustainable investment as its objective and an index has been designated as a reference benchmark, the overall sustainability-related impact of the financial product by means of relevant sustainability indicators; or where an index has been designated as a reference benchmark, a comparison between the overall sustainability-related impact of the financial product with the impacts of the designated index and of a broad market index through sustainability indicators (art.11(1)(b))
		Where a financial product has a reduction in carbon emissions as its objective, the objective of low-carbon emission exposure in view of achieving the long-term global warming objectives of the Paris Agreement (art.9(3))	
Additional EU Taxonomy disclosures for in-scope EU insurers and intermediaries		Where a financial product has sustainable investment as its objective (see art.9), a description of how and to what extent the investments underlying the financial product are in economic activities that qualify as environmentally sustainable under the EU Taxonomy (EU Taxonomy, art.5)	
		Where a financial product promotes, among other characteristics, environmental or social characteristics, or a combination thereof (see art.8), a description of how and to what extent the investments underlying the financial product are in economic activities that qualify as environmentally sustainable (EU Taxonomy, art.6) and 'do no significant harm' statement (EU Taxonomy, art.7)	
		For financial products that do not fall with art.8 or 9, a statement: 'The investments underlying this financial product do not take into account the EU criteria for environmentally sustainable economic activities' (EU Taxonomy, art.6)	

that the whole investment does not significantly harm any environmental and social objectives in the future could not be considered as sufficient.[265] This is likely to exclude from 'sustainable investments' under the SFDR investments in projects or assets associated with coal and gas activities but where there is a plan to transition them into sustainable activities (and indeed the investment is needed for implementing the transition).

The SFDR's focus on 'outward impact' is evident from the required disclosures (as set out in Table 5.7) on the integration of sustainability risks, on the consideration of adverse sustainability impacts, on sustainable investment objectives, or on the promotion of environmental or social characteristics, in investment decision-making and in advisory processes. It also introduces a classification of financial products into financial products that promote social or environmental characteristics (art.8; also referred to as 'light green' financial products), and financial products that have 'sustainable investment' as their objective (art.9; also referred to as 'dark green' financial products).

Another innovation of the SFDR is that it extends disclosures to financial advisers, including insurance intermediaries that advise on insurance-based investment products. This is important, given that the ultimate purpose of the SFDR is to provide more transparent information to buyers of investment products, including IBIPs. On this point, the SFDR interlinks with the Commission Delegated Regulation (EU) 2021/1257)[266] which integrates sustainability factors, risks, and preferences into the rules on product oversight for, and on advising on, IBIPs. The SFDR does not expressly cross-reference to EU Taxonomy (because it predates the EU Taxonomy), but the EU Taxonomy seeks to ensure consistency between both instruments by supplementing the disclosure requirements in the SFDR in respect of 'financial market participants' (including insurers offering investment-based insurance products): articles 5 and 6 of the EU Taxonomy align the information required to be disclosed under articles 9 and 8 of the SFDR respectively to the definition/classification of 'environmentally sustainable economic activity.' In accordance with the SFDR provisions,[267] EIOPA, the European Banking Authority, and the European Securities and Markets Authority have jointly developed further details and technical standards on the content, methodologies, and presentation of the relevant information to be disclosed under the SFDR by insurers.[268]

The SFDR disclosure requirements require EU insurers that make available or advise on, and insurance intermediaries that advise on, IBIPs to disclose specific information regarding their approaches to the integration of sustainability risks and the consideration of adverse sustainability impacts. This information should enable end investors to make informed decisions to invest in products they can trust to have the sustainable features they claim to have, and to deal with insurers and insurance intermediaries that have

265 ESMA, 'Q&As on the Interpretation of Regulation (EU) 2019/2088 SFDR' Q3 <https://www.esma.europa.eu/document/qas-interpretation-regulation-eu-20192088-sfdr> accessed on 1 June 2023.

266 Commission Delegated Regulation (EU) 2021/1257 of 21 April 2021 amending Delegated Regulations (EU) 2017/2358 and (EU) 2017/2359 as regards the integration of sustainability factors, risks, and preferences into the product oversight and governance requirements for insurance undertakings and insurance distributors and into the rules on conduct of business and investment advice for IBIPs.

267 See SFDR, art 4(6), 8(3), 9(5), 10(2).

268 Joint Committee of the three European Supervisory Authorities (EBA, EIOPA, and ESMA) ESA, 'Final Report on Draft Regulatory Technical Standards' (February 2021) <https://www.eba.europa.eu/sites/default/documents/files/document_library/Publications/Draft%20Technical%20Standards/2021/962778/JC%202021%2003%20-%20Joint%20ESAs%20Final%20Report%20on%20RTS%20under%20SFDR.pdf> accessed on 1 June 2023. These technical standards apply from 1 January 2022.

sustainable investment strategies. It is important to note that the SFDR disclosure requirements are limited to specified investment products, including IBIPs, but do not extend to other insurance products. This self-limiting approach is not supportive of the enabling role of insurers in relation to other types of insurance products. It has also been noted that the SFDR does not contain any provisions that address non-compliance and, depending on the EU member state, there could be significant uncertainty as to the legal classification of violations, and consequently, the sanctions and remedies that would be available.[269]

5.4.3 Corporate disclosures on sustainability

The Corporate Sustainability Reporting Directive ('CSRD')[270] came into force in January 2023 and must be implemented into the national laws of EU member states in time for its requirements to be phased in from January 2024. The CSRD seeks to strengthen the existing rules[271] about the social and environmental information that companies have to report. The CSRD will broaden the range of companies that are required to report, as well as the scope of the information that needs to be provided. The CSRD also puts in place measures to achieve greater transparency and to improve data assurance. Ironically, the CSRD itself is not a model of transparency – it is almost impenetrable to read – as it is drafted as an amending text to several preceding pieces of legislation, rather than presenting a consolidated text.

5.4.3.1 Scope and phasing in

The CSRD requirements should become applicable – through national implementing legislation – to insurers as follows:

- European insurance companies with more than 500 employees that are already reporting in line with the current rules under the NFRD must apply the CSRD rules for the first time in the financial year 2024, for reports published in 2025;[272]
- European insurance companies with fewer than 500 employees that were not required to comply with the NFRD and meet at least two of the following criteria (more than 250 employees, gross written premiums ('GWP') in excess of €40 million, or more than €20 million in total assets) must apply the CSRD rules for the first time in the financial year 2025, for reports published in 2026;[273]
- certain European captive insurers that meet at least two of the following criteria (more than ten employees, GWP in excess of €700,000, or more than €350,000

269 See Manfred Wandt and Gerrit Lüders, 'Nachhaltigkeitsregulierung des Finanzbereichs im Allgemeinen und produktbezogene Offenlegungspflichten im Versicherungsbereich im Besonderen' (2023) 13 VersR 829, sec. IV. The authors argue that, in the absence of directions in the SFDR, it is up to the EU member states to determine the legal consequences in accordance with their national legal systems and with general principles of EU law.

270 Directive (EU) 2022/2464 of the European Parliament and of the Council of 14 December 2022 amending Regulation (EU) No 537/2014, Directive 2004/109/EC, Directive 2006/43/EC, and Directive 2013/34/EU, as regards corporate sustainability reporting.

271 In particular the non-financial reporting requirements under the Directive 2014/95/EU (n 205).

272 CSRD art 5(2)(a).

273 Ibid art 5(2)(b).

in total assets) must apply the CSRD rules for the first time in the financial year 2026, for reports published in 2027;[274]

- non-European insurance subsidiaries of EU corporate groups are, subject to materiality, potentially caught by CSRD-reporting requirements at a group level;[275]
- non-European corporate groups with substantial activity in the EU will be caught by the CSRD requirements. 'Substantial activity' is defined as generating GWP of more than €150 million in the EU for each of the last two consecutive years and owning at least one subsidiary that meets the general scoping criteria or at least one branch that generated more than €40 million in the preceding year. This will potentially apply at a group level, not just to the EU subsidiary, with such groups required to report in relation to the financial year 2028 onwards.[276]

Given the global nature of the commercial insurance market and the need to have an EU-authorised insurer to access the EU Single Market, as well as the CSRD group reporting requirements, UK insurers may find themselves subject to the CSRD requirements. To reduce the reporting burden for globally active companies, the CSRD provides for an equivalence regime that will permit reporting under the sustainability reporting standards of a non-EU disclosure regime determined to be 'equivalent' by the European Commission.[277] However, at present it is not known whether the Commission is minded to grant equivalence status to the UK and/or the IFRS Sustainability Disclosure Standards. The CSRD which, over time, would extend to most EU insurers is an important addition to the SFDR which, as noted above, only applies to EU financial market participants (which exclude insurers that do not provide IBIPs).

5.4.3.2 What needs to be disclosed?

A CSRD-reporting insurer must disclose, in a dedicated section of its annual management report, information necessary to understand the undertaking's impacts on sustainability matters, and information necessary to understand how sustainability matters affect the undertaking's development, performance, and position.[278] This information must contain:

1. a brief description of the undertaking's business model and strategy, including
    a. the resilience of the undertaking's business model and strategy in relation to risks related to sustainability matters;
    b. the opportunities for the undertaking related to sustainability matters;
    c. the plans of the undertaking, including implementing actions and related financial and investment plans, to ensure that its business model and strategy are compatible with the transition to a sustainable economy and with the limiting of global warming to 1.5°C in line with the Paris Agreement and the European Green Deal;
    d. how the undertaking's business model and strategy take account of the interests of the undertaking's stakeholders and of the impacts of the undertaking on sustainability matters;

274 Ibid art 5(c)(iii).
275 Ibid art 1, point (7).
276 Ibid art 5(3).
277 Ibid art 3, point (3).
278 Ibid art 1, point (4).

   e. how the undertaking's strategy has been implemented with regard to sustainability matters;
2. a description of the time-bound targets related to sustainability matters set by the undertaking, including, where appropriate, absolute GHG emission reduction targets at least for 2030 and 2050, a description of the progress the undertaking has made towards achieving those targets, and a statement of whether the undertaking's targets related to environmental factors are based on conclusive scientific evidence;
3. a description of the role of the administrative, management, and supervisory bodies with regard to sustainability matters, and of their expertise and skills in relation to fulfilling that role or the access such bodies have to such expertise and skills;
4. a description of the undertaking's policies in relation to sustainability matters;
5. information about the existence of incentive schemes linked to sustainability matters which are offered to members of the administrative, management, and supervisory bodies;
6. a description of:
   a. the due diligence process implemented by the undertaking with regard to sustainability matters and, where applicable, in line with Union requirements on undertakings to conduct a due diligence process;
   b. the principal actual or potential adverse impacts connected with the undertaking's own operations and with its value chain, including its products and services, its business relationships, and its supply chain, actions taken to identify and monitor those impacts, and other adverse impacts which the undertaking is required to identify pursuant to other EU requirements on undertakings to conduct a due diligence process;
   c. any actions taken by the undertaking to prevent, mitigate, remediate, or bring an end to actual or potential adverse impacts, and the result of such actions;
7. a description of the principal risks to the undertaking related to sustainability matters, including a description of the undertaking's principal dependencies on those matters, and how the undertaking manages those risks;
8. relevant indicators to the disclosures referred to above.[279]

These disclosure requirements remove any ambiguity as regards double materiality: point 6 clearly requires reporting on 'outward impact.' In addition, disclosures must, as appropriate, include forward-looking, retrospective, qualitative, and quantitative information.[280]

5.4.3.3 European Sustainability Reporting Standards

CSRD-reporting companies will have to report according to European Sustainability Reporting Standards ('ESRS').[281] The ESRS were developed by EFRAG, previously known as the European Financial Reporting Advisory Group, an independent body gathering various stakeholders, and were adopted by the European Commission on 31 July

279 Ibid art 1, point (4).
280 Ibid art 1, point (8).
281 Ibid art 1, point (8).

2023.[282] The European Commission is currently preparing a Delegated Act that would supplement the CSRD with the ESRS. There are twelve sector-agnostic ESRSs that will be supported by sector-specific and entity-specific ESRSs. Draft ESRS 1 and 2 address general requirements and general disclosures, respectively. Draft ESRS E1 covers sector-agnostic climate change disclosures including on the following matters:

- integration of sustainability-related performance in incentive schemes;
- transition plan for climate change mitigation;
- information on material impacts, risks and opportunities and their interaction with strategy and business model(s);
- description of the processes to identify and assess material climate-related impacts, risks, and opportunities;
- impact, risk, and opportunity management in relation to climate change;
- policies related to climate change mitigation and adaptation;
- actions and resources in relation to climate change policies;
- metrics and targets;
- targets related to climate change mitigation and adaptation;
- energy consumption and mix;
- energy intensity based on net revenue;
- gross Scopes 1, 2, 3 and total GHG emissions;
- GHG intensity based on net revenue;
- GHG removals and GHG mitigation projects financed through carbon credits;
- internal carbon pricing;
- potential financial effects from material physical and transition risks and potential climate-related opportunities.[283]

No insurance or financial services sector-specific ESRS have been published yet. EFRAG has reported on how the SFDR disclosure requirements and the EU Taxonomy alignment disclosure requirement[284] have been incorporated into the ESRS but there is no discussion of their interoperability with other initiatives, such as the IFRS Sustainability Disclosure Standards. By June 2024, the European Commission is planning to adopt delegated acts to provide for sustainability reporting standards proportionate and relevant to the capacities and the characteristics of small and medium-sized companies.[285]

5.4.3.4 Single electronic reporting format

CSRD-reporting companies will have to prepare their report electronically in XHTML format and mark up their sustainability reporting in accordance with the electronic reporting format which is to be specified under Delegated Regulation (EU) 2019/815.[286] It is

282 EFRAG, 'First Set of Draft ESRS' (November 2022) <https://www.efrag.org/lab6> accessed on 1 June 2023; European Commission, 'The Commission adopts the European Sustainability Reporting Standards' (Press Release 31 July 2023) <https://finance.ec.europa.eu/news/commission-adopts-european-sustainability-reporting-standards-2023-07-31_en> accessed on 5 November 2023

283 EFRAG, 'ESRS E1.'

284 EU Taxonomy art 8 and see Section 5.4.1.

285 CSRD art 1, point (8).

286 Ibid art 1, point (9).

envisaged that a forthcoming ESRS on digital reporting will require information to be electronically 'tagged' so that it is machine-readable and easily searchable and comparable.[287] These requirements go alongside the creation of a European single access point for public corporate information.[288]

5.4.4 Data assurance

The EU Taxonomy and the SFDR do not address to what extent reported disclosures must be subject to any independent assurance or audit process to ensure the reliability of data and avoid green-washing and double-counting. The CSRD introduces an audit requirement for sustainability disclosures made under its provisions, the ESRS and article 8 of the EU Taxonomy.[289] By October 2026, the Commission must adopt delegated acts to provide for limited assurance standards setting out the procedures that the auditor(s) and the audit firm(s) shall perform in order to draw his, her, or its conclusions on the assurance of sustainability reporting, including engagement planning, risk consideration, and response to risks and type of conclusions to be included in the assurance report on sustainability reporting or, where relevant, in the audit report.[290] A limited assurance audit means that the auditor performs fewer tests on a smaller set of defined data, and that the auditor's report is provided in a negative form of expression (i.e. by stating that no matter has been identified by the auditor to conclude that the subject matter is materially misstated).[291] While a limited assurance audit is a lower standard than a reasonable assurance audit and does not require that information is verified, it represents a step up for sustainability information which is currently frequently excluded from audits.

The CSRD also envisage that auditors who carry out sustainability reporting audits must have the relevant qualification, training, and professional competencies in sustainability analysis.[292]

Many of the CSRD provisions are sketchy, pending further delegated acts and ESRS, and leaving room for discretion for national implementing legislation. The CSRD is also almost impenetrable to read as it is drafted as an amending text to several preceding pieces of legislation. Yet, together with the SFDR and the CSDDD, the CSRD is an example of the EU's strong commitment to double materiality disclosures on sustainability, including climate-related matters, applicable to large and medium-sized enterprises. The EU has started to build a disclosure framework that is comprehensive in its width of application and contents. By introducing the EU Taxonomy, sustainability reporting standards, electronic machine-readable reporting, and an auditing requirement, the path has been set for reported information to become more consistent, comparable, accessible, and reliable.

287 Ibid Recital (55).

288 Communication from the Commission 'A Capital Markets Union for People and Businesses – New Action Plan' COM (2020) 590.

289 CSRD art 3, point (15).

290 Ibid art 3, point (15).

291 Ibid, Recital (60).

292 Ibid art 3, points (4) and (7).

5.4.5 Benchmarks, standards, labels, and green-washing

The third building component of the EU Action Plan is a set of benchmarks and labels, that make it easier for investors to align their investment strategies with the EU's climate and environmental goals.[293] The EU has already introduced the labels 'EU Climate Transition Benchmark' and 'EU Paris-aligned Benchmark.' The 'EU Climate Transition Benchmark' can be used by a 'benchmark administrator'[294] for a financial instrument or investment portfolio if its underlying assets are selected, weighted, or excluded in such a manner that the resulting benchmark portfolio is on a measurable, science-based and time-bound trajectory towards alignment with the objectives of the Paris Agreement by reducing Scope 1, 2, and 3 GHG emissions.[295]

The 'EU Paris-aligned Benchmark' can be used by a benchmark administrator for a financial instrument or investment portfolio if its underlying assets are selected, weighted, or excluded in such a manner that the resulting benchmark portfolio's carbon emissions are aligned with the objectives of the Paris Agreement, and it complies with the minimum standards laid down in the delegated acts, and the activities relating to its underlying assets do not significantly harm other ESG objectives.[296] For the 'EU Paris-aligned Benchmark,' the benchmark administrator must prepare and publish a document containing information on the methodology used for the calculation of the benchmark.

The European Commission proposed a regulation on a voluntary European green bond standard,[297] on which the European Parliament and Council have now reached a political agreement.[298] This regulation lays down uniform requirements for issuers of bonds that wish to use the designation 'European green bond' or 'EuGB' for their environmentally sustainable bonds that are aligned with the EU Taxonomy. It also establishes a registration system and supervisory framework for external reviewers of European green bonds. To prevent green-washing in the green bonds market in general, the regulation also provides for some voluntary disclosure requirements for other environmentally sustainable bonds and sustainability-linked bonds issued in the EU.[299] The EU Climate Transition Benchmark,' the 'EU Paris-aligned Benchmark,' and the 'European green bond' or 'EuGB' labels do not apply to any insurance products but could be relevant to insurers in

293 EU Action Plan and EU Finance Strategy.

294 A 'benchmark administrator' is a natural or legal person that has control over the provision of a benchmark, and in particular administers the arrangements for determining the benchmark, collects and analyses the input data, determines the benchmark, and either directly publishes or outsources the publication or the calculation of the benchmark to a third party (Regulation (EU) 2016/1011 of the European Parliament and of the Council of 8 June 2016 on indices used as benchmarks in financial instruments and financial contracts or to measure the performance of investment funds and amending Directives 2008/48/EC and 2014/17/EU and Regulation (EU) No 596/2014, art 3(6)).

295 Regulation (EU) 2019/2089 of the European Parliament and of the Council of 27 November 2019 amending Regulation (EU) 2016/1011 as regards EU Climate Transition Benchmarks, EU Paris-aligned benchmarks, and sustainability-related disclosures for benchmarks, art 1, point (1).

296 Ibid.

297 Commission, 'Proposal on European Green Bonds' COM/2021/391.

298 European Parliament, 'Legislators Strike Deal on a New Standard to Fight Greenwashing in the Bond Markets' (Press Release 28 February 2023) <https://www.europarl.europa.eu/news/en/press-room/20230227IPR76596/legislators-strike-deal-on-new-standard-to-fight-greenwashing-in-bond-markets> accessed on 1 June 2023.

299 Council of the EU 'Sustainable Finance: Provisional Agreement Reached on European Green Bonds' (Press Release dated 28 February 2023) <https://www.consilium.europa.eu/en/press/press-releases/2023/02/28/sustainable-finance-provisional-agreement-reached-on-european-green-bonds/> accessed on 1 June 2023.

their capacity as investors: the labels signal that the underlying assets meet specific (externally assessed or reviewed) environmental criteria and this information can be used for the sustainability and climate-related disclosures that the insurer has to provide.

The EU is developing an 'EU Ecolabel for Retail Financial Products' aimed at retail investors. The Ecolabel will define the minimum environmental performance of in-scope products with the objective of awarding the best environmentally performing financial products.[300] From initial proposals it appears that the Ecolabel would be available for IBIPs but not for other insurance products. The EU Action Plan also envisages ESG benchmarks for financial products but no proposals have been published yet.[301] The European Commission has put forward a proposal for regulating ESG rating services to improve their reliability and transparency and foster trust and confidence in those services.[302]

In addition, the European Commission has issued a proposal for a Green Claims Directive.[303] The proposals include a list of commercial practices which will be considered unfair and which are associated with green-washing:

- displaying a sustainability label which is not based on a certification scheme or not established by public authorities;
- making a generic environmental claim for which the trader is not able to demonstrate recognised excellent environmental performance relevant to the claim;
- making an environmental claim about the entire product when it concerns only a certain aspect of the product;
- presenting requirements imposed by law on all products in the relevant product category on the Union market as a distinctive feature of the trader's offer.

The Green Claim Directive is intended to stop companies from making misleading claims about the environmental merits of their products and services and allow consumers to make informed environmental choices. It would apply to all industries (but excludes 'green claims' that are covered by existing EU rules) and provide for a system of independent verification for the use of environmental labels.[304]

5.4.6 EU: further developments

The EU is building a two-pronged disclosure framework with the SFDR (applicable to 'financial market participants') and the CSRD (applicable to all companies meeting the size thresholds). By introducing the EU Taxonomy, sustainability reporting standards, electronic machine-readable reporting, and an auditing requirement, the path has been set for reported information to become more consistent, comparable, accessible, and reliable. Many of the CSRD provisions are sketchy, pending further delegated acts and ESRS, and leaving room for discretion for national implementing legislation. Similarly, the EU

300 EU Action Plan and EU Finance Strategy.

301 EU Finance Strategy.

302 European Commission, 'Proposal for a Regulation on the Transparency and Integrity of Environmental, Social and Governance (ESG) Rating Activities 2023/0177' (COD) COM/2023/314.

303 European Commission, 'Proposal for a Directive of the European Parliament and of the Council on Substantiation and Communication of Explicit Environmental Claims' COM/2023/166.

304 Proposal for Green Claims Directive.

Taxonomy's technical screening criteria are still incomplete. The SFDR introduces extensive sustainability disclosure requirements but only for a limited group of financial market participants and a limited set of investment products. The SFDR leaves a gap for insurers and insurance intermediaries who do not offer or advise on IBIPs. The European Supervisory Authorities, including EIOPA, are currently reviewing the SFDR but their proposals do not include an extension of the SFDR disclosures to other financial market participants and insurance products.[305]

While the EU is working on an internally coherent taxonomy and disclosure framework, unanswered questions remain about its interoperability with other national and international frameworks. Important questions remain to be answered as to whether the EU will accept the IFRS Sustainability Disclosures Standards (once they are finalised and issued) and the UK sustainability disclosure regime as 'equivalent,' and vice versa, and how internationally active groups of companies can manage their sustainability disclosure obligations in an efficient and transparent manner without having to prepare multiple sets of disclosure. If insurers are to take an enabling role, regulators across the world should strive for converging or equivalent status disclosure regimes to ease the reporting burden for insurers who operate in a number of jurisdictions.

As noted in Chapter 4, Section 4.4.5, the European Commission has adopted a proposal for the CSDDD which would establish a corporate due diligence duty for certain companies to identify, bring to an end, prevent, mitigate, and account for negative human rights and environmental impacts in the company's own operations, their subsidiaries, and business relationships in their value chains.[306] The corporate due diligence duty itself would be a substantive duty to which civil liability attaches, but there would also be associated disclosure and reporting requirements.[307] There is also a proposal for a regulation on ESG rating services to improve their reliability and transparency and foster trust and confidence in those services.[308]

5.5 Conclusion

From the ground-breaking TCFD Recommendations, the IFRS Sustainability Disclosure Standards, the FCA's proposed sustainability disclosure regime, and the EU's disclosures and taxonomy regime, we have seen how climate-related disclosures have grown in the scope of required information, the standardisation of presentation, methodologies and data sets for disclosure, and the growing acceptance of double materiality and outward impact reporting.

As regards insurers and their insurance products, there are still only few disclosure requirements that relate directly and specifically to the outward impacts of their underwriting business, decision-making processes, and any insurance products on the environment. The SFDR and the FCA's proposed sustainability disclosure regime do not apply to general insurers and their products. As the existing sustainability disclosure requirements

305 European Supervisory Authorities, 'Joint Consultation Paper – Review of SFDR Delegated Regulation Regarding PAI and Financial Product Disclosures' JC 2023 09 (12 April 2023).

306 Proposal for a Directive of the European Parliament and of the Council on Corporate Sustainability Due Diligence and amending Directive (EU) 2019/1937 COM/2022/71, art 6–8.

307 Ibid art 11 and 23.

308 Proposal for a Regulation on ESG Rating Activities (n 302).

embed, and reporting companies, regulators, auditors and users become familiar with the contents and methodologies, it is to be hoped that the SFDR and the FCA's ESG Sourcebook will be extended to a wider range of insurers and insurance products. Most importantly, the labelling system contemplated by the FCA for investment products should be replicated for insurance products. This would help potential policyholders to identify and make informed choices in relation to (environmentally) sustainable insurance products and protect them further from green-washing. As noted above, approved and protected labels can increase consumer trust in the characteristics of the product and could thus support the take up of (environmentally) sustainable insurance products. The technical screening criteria for the EU Taxonomy envisage insurance products that provide incentives and set price signals for risk reduction through climate change adaptation measures. Another missing piece in the UK regime is the UK Green Taxonomy which is still under development. Once available, it would also be useful to link the sustainable investment label regime to generally applicable definitions, rather than letting firms self-define the sustainable objectives of their financial products.

Making climate-related disclosures can increase awareness of climate action, set an example to other insurers, and serve as an invitation for customers to act on climate change. In that sense, a more comprehensive climate-related disclosure regime that extends to inward and outward impacts of all insurers and all insurance products would better support the enabling role of insurers. It would also achieve a better alignment with the UK government's commitment to achieve a net-zero economy by 2050 (which the FCA is required to take into account when considering how to advance its objectives and discharge its functions).[309] On the other hand, both the UK and the EU have already created complex and multi-layered disclosure regimes that not only create a regulatory and compliance burden but can also lead, anecdotally, to 'green-blushing' and 'green-hushing' – the deliberate underreporting of environmentally sustainable activities so as not to fall foul of green-washing, and anti-ESG legislation and sentiments, respectively.[310] Regulators across the world should now strive for converging or equivalent status disclosure regimes to ease the reporting burden for insurers who operate in a number of jurisdictions. To improve data assurance, auditors should have a clear mandate to review all of a company's sustainability and climate-related reporting and should be required to acquire the skills necessary to carry out such a review.

One must not lose sight of the fact that the mere process of making disclosures and reporting does not contribute directly to the Paris Agreement goals or the national and international net-zero targets or respond to the adverse effects of climate change that are already felt around the world. As the UK Climate Change Committee pointed out recently 'Better transparency is no substitute for real delivery' and it is the latter where the UK is falling short.[311] For insurers to take an enabling role in the transition to a net-zero economy, they must consider impact underwriting and impact investment strategies, which will be discussed in the next three chapters.

309 See Chapter 4, Section 4.3.2.

310 See e.g.: World Economic Forum (n 172).

311 Climate Change Committee, 'Better Transparency Is No Substitute for Real Delivery' (Press Release 23 June 2023) <https://www.theccc.org.uk/2023/06/28/better-transparency-is-no-substitute-for-real-delivery/> accessed on 24 June 2023, and see Chapter 2, Section 2.3.4.

CHAPTER 6

Insuring green and not insuring brown

Although insurers are not seen as direct polluters, climate activists have sought to highlight the role of the insurance industry in fuelling the climate crisis by continuing to insure coal and oil projects. In 2021, Extinction Rebellion dumped fake coal outside Lloyd's of London and held up banners reading 'climate criminals' and 'insuring fossil fuels = ensuring climate breakdown.'[1] Meanwhile, there is recognition that the insurance industry must be part of the joint global effort to meet the Paris Agreement objectives of climate change mitigation, climate change adaptation, and climate resilience.[2]

To date, insurance has been primarily viewed as an instrument to foster loss resilience as insurance cover can absorb the financial impact of losses from physical and liability climate change risks.[3] However, improving loss resilience does not prevent or reduce such losses and does not reduce global GHG emissions to stem climate change. In Chapter 3 it was therefore argued that, as risk carriers and investors, insurers can and should enable actors in their value chain and in the wider community to take climate mitigation action and to adopt climate change adaptation measures. This chapter and Chapter 7 are concerned with how insurers – in their capacity as risk carriers – could take this role by engaging in climate-related impact underwriting.

This chapter is organised in four sections: in Section 6.1, the term 'impact underwriting' is examined and a definition for 'climate-related impact underwriting' derived from the literature and the disclosure requirements discussed in Chapter 5 will be put forward. Section 6.2 is concerned with the justifications for climate-related impact underwriting and how it can be reconciled with a company's corporate purpose to create value for shareholders. Section 6.3 looks at how insurers can insure 'green' by providing insurance cover for technologies and infrastructure projects aimed at climate change mitigation and adaptation. Section 6.4 examines legal and practical issues that can arise when insurers cease to insure 'brown.' Given the volume of materials, the discussion of 'greening insurance' – insurance products and services that shift policyholders' behaviour and processes towards taking climate change mitigation and adaptation measures – is dealt with in Chapter 7. Concluding remarks on both chapters can be found at the end of Chapter 7.

1 Matt Mathers, 'Extinction Rebellion Activists Dump Fake Coal outside Lloyd's of London in Fossil Fuel Protest' (*The Independent*, 23 April 2021).

2 See Chapter 3, Section 3.4.

3 For example, see IPCC 2022 Mitigation Report [15.6.4] which discusses insurance exclusively in terms of financial resilience.

DOI: 10.4324/b23081-6

6.1 What is climate-related impact underwriting?

The technical meaning of the term 'underwriting' is the process of evaluating and defining risks to be transferred (or where appropriate rejecting the risk) and calculating a premium that is reflective of the specific risk and the underwriting pool as a whole.[4] In this chapter and Chapter 7, the term 'underwriting' as a component of 'climate-related impact underwriting' is used in a wider sense to include (1) the whole value chain of insurance products, including insurance product development, marketing and sales, risk management and underwriting (in its narrower technical sense), and claims management, and (2) the whole range of activities in which insurers in their capacity as underwriters and risk carriers are involved. 'Climate-related impact underwriting' is concerned with an insurer's climate-related outward impact on the 'liability side' of the insurance business.

EIOPA pioneered the term 'impact underwriting' in 2019,[5] and has subsequently put forward a refined definition:

> Consistently with actuarial risk-based principles, (re)insurers, as risk managers and underwriters, can contribute to climate adaptation and mitigation by applying their data, expertise and risk assessment capacity to incentivise policyholders to mitigate insured risks via risk-based pricing and contractual terms, and consider in their underwriting strategy measures that contribute to climate change adaptation and/or mitigation.[6]

The notable features of this definition are that the desired impact encompasses climate change mitigation and climate change adaptation, and that the contractual relationship between the insurer and the policyholder is seen as the mechanism for delivering that impact.

The PSI extend to all three ESG components aiming for:

> a strategic approach where all activities in the insurance value chain, including interactions with stakeholders, are done in a responsible and forward-looking way by identifying, assessing, managing and monitoring risks and opportunities associated with environmental, social and governance issues.[7]

Given that 'climate-related issues' are a sub-set of 'environmental issues,'[8] some guidance of what climate-related impact underwriting entails can be derived from the recommended actions under Principle 1, including the following:

> *Risk management and underwriting*
>
> - establish processes to identify and assess ESG issues inherent in the portfolio and be aware of potential ESG-related consequences of the company's transactions;

4 Lloyd's of London, 'Glossary and Acronyms of Insurance Terms' <https://www.lloyds.com/help/glossary-and-acronyms> accessed on 1 June 2023.

5 EIOPA, 'Opinion on Sustainability within Solvency II' EIOPA-BoS-19/241, [4.17].

6 EIOPA, 'Report on Non-Life Underwriting and Pricing in Light of Climate Change' EIOPA-BoS-21/259, [2.40].

7 UNEP FI, 'Principles for Sustainable Insurance – What Is Sustainable Insurance?' <https://www.unepfi.org/insurance/insurance/> accessed on 1 June 2023.

8 See Chapter 2, Section 2.4.

- integrate ESG issues into risk management, underwriting and capital adequacy decision-making processes, including research, models, analytics, tools and metrics.

Product and service development

- develop products and services which reduce risk, have a positive impact on ESG issues and encourage better risk management;
- develop or support literacy programmes on risk, insurance and ESG issues.

Claims management

- respond to clients quickly, fairly, sensitively and transparently at all times and make sure claims processes are clearly explained and understood;
- integrate ESG issues into repairs, replacements and other claims services.

Sales and marketing

- educate sales and marketing staff on ESG issues relevant to products and services and integrate key messages responsibly into strategies and campaigns;
- make sure product and service coverage, benefits and costs are relevant and clearly explained and understood.[9]

Thus, the PSI actions go beyond underwriting in its narrow technical sense and also cover other aspects of the value chain, such as product development, marketing and sales, and claims management. Compared to the EIOPA notion of 'impact underwriting' which is result-oriented (climate change mitigation and adaptation), the PSI actions are drafted more vaguely (e.g. 'positive impact on ESG issues') and with a greater focus on the process of promoting and achieving sustainable insurance. Similarly, the SFDR draws a distinction between financial products that promote social or environmental characteristics (= light green),[10] and financial products that have 'sustainable investment' as their objective (= dark green).[11]

Although the FCA Sustainability Disclosure Proposals on sustainable investment labels will initially only apply to specified investment products,[12] they provide an insight into the FCA's approach to classifying financial products as 'sustainable.' These labels distinguish between products with 'sustainable focus,' 'sustainable improver' products, and 'sustainable impact' products.[13] Applied mutatis mutandis to insurance products that promote or have as their objective climate action, the labels could serve as a basis for the classification of insurance products that (1) provide insurance cover for green assets (= focus), (2) promote the net-zero transition of policyholders and their assets over time (= improver), and (3) provide insurance cover for technologies and other solutions to combat climate

9 PSI Prin 1.
10 SFDR, art 8 – 'light green financial products' – and see Chapter 5, Section 5.4.2.
11 Ibid art 9 – 'dark green financial products.'
12 See Chapter 5, Section 5.3.5.2.
13 FCA Sustainability Disclosure Proposals [3.2].

change (= impact). Even if the FCA's proposed sustainable investment label regime were to be extended in this way, it is not clear whether it would cover climate change adaptation measures and underwriting approaches that screen out fossil fuel projects.[14]

The FCA has also said that the labels would not cover negative screening investment approaches, so it should be assumed that, even if the labelling regime were to be extended to insurance products, any insurance products that sought to reduce or exclude cover for fossil fuel projects would not be eligible.[15]

Should climate-related impact underwriting encompass both climate change mitigation and climate change adaptation? The objectives of the Paris Agreement clearly consider both mitigation and adaptation as integral parts of the global response to the threat of climate change.[16] Climate change mitigation is concerned with measures to reduce GHG emissions and improve GHG sinks to stem global warming.[17] Thus, the NZIA members' commitment relates specifically to climate change mitigation, namely to '[t]ransitioning all operational and attributable [GHG] emissions from its insurance and reinsurance underwriting portfolios to net-zero emissions by 2050.'[18]

In contrast, climate change adaptation is concerned with the process of adjustment to actual or expected climate change and its effects, in order to moderate harm or exploit beneficial opportunities.[19] Adaptive action and interventions do not address the main cause of climate change: past and continuing GHG emissions and impact underwriting aimed at climate change adaptation cannot reduce the risk of weather-related impacts resulting from climate change.[20] Climate change adaptation measures (e.g. such as flood defences and early warning systems) can reduce the impact of losses caused by physical climate change risks. Adaptation measures have been linked to climate justice and are considered necessary to ensure the safety of populations and the security of property and to minimise destabilising effects on the economy, as a result of climate change effects that are already occurring or will occur.[21]

The IPCC has adopted the concept of CRD, which is a strategy of co-ordinated and integrated implementation of adaptation and mitigation solutions, to support sustainable development for all and achieve better results by leveraging their interdependence.[22] Similarly, the EU Taxonomy considers that both economic activities that have a climate change mitigation objective and those that have a climate change adaptation objective can be 'environmentally sustainable.'[23] The UK government's 2023 Green Finance Strategy now explicitly incorporates climate change adaptation into the government's green finance

14 Ibid [2.3], [4.24], and [4.25] and see Chapter 5, Section 5.3.5.

15 Ibid [2.3], [4.24], and [4.25].

16 Paris Agreement art 4; and see Chapter 2, Section 2.3.3.

17 IPCC 2022 Adaptation Report, Summary for Policymakers, Glossary 'Mitigation.'

18 NZIA, 'Target-Setting Protocol 1.0' (January 2023) <https://www.unepfi.org/industries/insurance/launch-of-nzia-target-setting-protocol-version-1-0/> accessed on 1 June 2023.

19 IPCC 2022 Adaptation Report, Summary for Policymakers, Glossary 'Adaptation.'

20 See Chapter 2, Section 2.2.

21 See Paris Agreement art 7; and United Nations, 'Transforming Our World: The 2030 Agenda for Sustainable Development' (25 September 2015) A/RES/70/1.

22 IPCC 2022 Adaptation Report, Summary for Policymakers and ch 18; and see Chapter 2, Section 2.4.1.

23 EU Taxonomy art 9. The technical screening criteria for insurance related to climate change adaptation. See Chapter 5, Section 5.4.1.2.

policy framework.[24] The Sharm-El-Sheikh Adaptation Agenda expressly references the role of the insurance sector in supporting climate change adaptation solutions.[25]

For these reasons, it is suggested that 'impact underwriting' should embrace both climate change mitigation and climate change adaptation approaches. In relation to 'impact underwriting' two additional requirements are discussed in the literature: 'additionality' and 'intentionality.'[26] Applied to climate-related impact underwriting, this means that insurers provide insurance cover with the intention to have a positive and measurable impact. With all of the above criteria in mind, the following definition – adapted from the EIOPA definition – is proposed as a working definition for 'climate-related impact underwriting':

> Insurers, as risk managers and underwriters, can contribute to climate change adaptation and mitigation by applying their data, expertise and risk assessment capacity to influence policyholders to mitigate and adapt to insured risks via risk-based pricing and contractual terms, and consider in their product design, underwriting strategy and claims management measures that contribute to climate change adaptation and/or mitigation.

This working definition is aligned to the Paris Agreement objectives and follows the IPCC's CRD approach (as it includes impact on climate change mitigation and adaptation measures). It extends an insurer's potential contribution to the whole value chain of an insurance product as envisaged by the PSI. It is wide enough to cover light green and dark green insurance products by analogy to the SFDR, and to cover both underwriting processes in the technical sense and wider engagement strategies. As it is impossible to discuss all permutations, this chapter and Chapter 7 will discuss examples of and legal issues relating to 'climate-related impact underwriting' organised into three categories: (1) 'insuring green' (Section 6.3), (2) 'not insuring brown' (Section 6.4), and (4) 'greening insurance' (Chapter 7). Before doing so, the next section addresses whether climate-related impact underwriting is consistent with the corporate governance principle of shareholder value maximisation which is relevant to all types of climate-related impact underwriting.

6.2 Corporate purpose and environmental objectives[27]

Whether or not, and to what extent, an insurer should engage in climate-related impact underwriting requires complex strategic decisions based on a detailed assessment of its existing inward and outward impacts and the climate change risks and opportunities that are specific to that insurer's business.[28] Companies are not (yet) under a positive legal duty to engage in climate action, and directors are not yet under a duty to the company to

24 HM Government, 'Mobilising Green Investment – 2023 Green Finance Strategy' (April 2023) 8 <https://www.gov.uk/government/publications/green-finance-strategy> accessed on 1 June 2023.

25 United Nations Climate Change, 'Sharm-El-Sheikh Adaptation Agenda' (November 2022) <https://climatechampions.unfccc.int/wp-content/uploads/2022/12/SeS-Adaptation-Agenda_Complete-Report_COP27-.pdf> accessed on 1 June 2023.

26 See Chapter 8, Section 8.1.2.

27 The discussion in this section builds upon materials in Franziska Arnold-Dwyer, 'A Legal Framework for Net-Zero Aligned Insurance Products' (2023) 29(2) *Conn Ins LJ*, 1, and text passages have been reproduced with permission of the *Conn Ins LJ*.

28 The Geneva Association, 'Anchoring Climate Change Risk Assessment in Core Business Decisions in Insurance' (September 2022) Sec. 4 <https://www.genevaassociation.org/publication/climate-change-and-environment/climate-change-risk-3-report> accessed on 1 June 2023.

prevent environmental harm caused by the company.[29] This section cannot make a business case for impact underwriting by any particular insurer but it examines the arguments for and against climate-related impact underwriting in light of an insurance company's corporate purpose and directors' fiduciary duties.

6.2.1 Corporate purpose

The predominant view in Anglo-American scholarship is that the purpose of a company is to create value for its shareholders.[30] A corporate purpose framed in that way is indifferent to climate change, climate change mitigation, and adaptation in so far as they do not affect value creation. Regulating harmful impacts on society is not part of corporate decision-making but is left to legislative frameworks set by governments that prescribe the 'rules of the game.'[31] Milton Friedman famously said that 'The social responsibility of business is to increase its profits.'[32] The common law fiduciary duty of the directors of a company to act in a way to promote the success of the company is reflective of a corporate purpose that focuses on valuation creation. Under the Companies Act 2006, s.172(1), a director of a UK (insurance) company has a statutory duty to:

> act in the way he considers, in good faith, to be most likely to promote the success of the company for the benefit of its members as a whole;

however, that duty is qualified so that directors, in exercising the duty, must have regard to (among other matters):

> (d) the impact of the company's operations on the community and the environment,
> *(the 's.172 duty').*

The s.172 duty raises questions as to the extent to which directors of an insurance company would be permitted to forego higher profits of the company by engaging with climate-related impact underwriting. The s.172 duty is owed by the directors to the company for the benefit of its members as a whole, but not to other stakeholders (such as policyholders). Promoting the success of the company means primarily to create value from which shareholders will benefit.[33] The directors have discretion to act in what they believe – in good faith – to be in the best interests of the company, and this could, in principle, accommodate short- or longer-term approaches to promoting the success of the company.[34]

---

29 But note the EU proposals for the CSDDD: discussed in Section 6.2.2 and Chapter 4, Section 4.4.5.

30 Paul Davies, Sarah Worthington, and Chris Hare, *Principles of Modern Company Law* (11th ed, Sweet & Maxwell 2021) ch 10; Beate Sjåfjell, Andrew Johnston, Linn Anker-Sørensen, and David Milton, 'Shareholder Primacy: The Main Barrier to Sustainable Companies' in Beate Sjåfjell, *Company Law and Sustainability Legal Barriers and Opportunities* (Cambridge University Press 2015), ch 3; Martin Gelter, 'The Dark Side of Shareholder Influence: Managerial Autonomy and Stakeholder Orientation in Comparative Corporate Governance' (2009) 50 *Harvard International Law Journal*, 129, 131; and Mathias M. Siems, *Convergence in Shareholder Law* (Cambridge University Press 2008) 176–178.

31 Milton Friedman, *Capitalism and Freedom* (University of Chicago Press, 2002); also see: John Armour, Luca Enriques, and Thom Wetzer, 'Green Pills: Making Corporate Climate Commitments Credible' (2023) 65 *Ariz L Rev*, 285 Pt 3.

32 Milton Friedman, 'A Friedman Doctrine – The Social Responsibility of Business Is to Increase Its Profits' (*New York Times*, 13 September 1970).

33 Davies and Worthington (n 30) ch 10.

34 This is a subjective test – see *In Re Smith and Fawcett* [1942] Ch. 304, at 306 per Lord Greene; *Regentcrest Plc v Cohen* [2001] 2 BCLC 80 at [120] per Jonathan Parker J. There is no officially recognised

Climate-related impact underwriting does not necessarily mean foregone profits and can in fact create value through new business opportunities. The UK government considers that the net-zero transition is not only an environmental imperative, but a growth opportunity,[35] and Mark Carney, the former Governor of the Bank of England and UN Special Envoy on Climate Action and Finance, considers it the 'greatest commercial opportunity' for banks, insurers, and fund managers.[36] For example, there are business opportunities in providing insurance cover to new carbon capture technologies and renewable energy projects.[37] With these impact underwriting examples, the directors of an insurance company would be able to justify their decisions using a conventional business case, fully aligned with traditional shareholder value maximisation norms. On the other hand, engagement with climate-related impact underwriting can (1) create additional costs for insurers incurred in relation to insuring green (such as research and development costs, marketing costs) and greening insurance (higher reinstatement costs), and (2) reduce premium income by ceasing to insure brown or giving premium discounts and rebates to incentivise policyholders to take climate change mitigation or adaptation actions.[38]

The success of an insurance company can be impacted by climate change: Table 3.1 in Chapter 3 describes how climate change risks (whether they are physical, transition, or liability risks) pose a threat to an insurer's financial stability and ultimately its ability to provide insurance cover and pay claims. On a simplistic level, it could therefore be argued that in order to avert the threat of climate change and the associated financial risks that could impact negatively on the success of the company, its directors should incorporate climate-related impact underwriting in its strategy. However, there are a number of reasons that discourage taking a longer-term view on value creation, First, there is a timing disconnect in that climate-related underwriting costs incurred now may not translate into immediate benefits (on any of the pathways modelled by the IPPC global warming will not slow down until mid-century).[39] Directors may be disincentivised from longer-term value creation as investors and board remuneration structures frequently favour short-term shareholder value.[40] Secondly, there is a distribution disconnect in that net benefits of climate-related impact underwriting may not, or only marginally accrue, to the insurer,[41] while allowing other insurers and stakeholders to free-ride. Thirdly, climate action is held back by the 'tragedy of the commons,'[42] a perception that individual mitigation or adaptation measures can neither reverse climate change nor increase resilience. Mann refers to 'climate doomism' – an attitude of disengagement founded on the belief that 'there is

'business judgment rule' in English law but the approach of this rule – to defer to the judgement of the directors – has been adopted in a broad range of cases. For an overview, see Andrew Keay and Joan Loughrey, 'The Concept of Business Judgment' (2019) 39(1) *LS*, 36.

35 HM Government (n 24) 8.

36 Alastair Marsh and Benjamin Robertson, 'Carney Calls Net-Zero Greenhouse Ambition "Greatest Commercial Opportunity"' (*Bloomberg*, 9 November 2020).

37 See Section 6.3.2.

38 See Sections 6.3 and 6.4 and Chapter 7.

39 See Chapter 2, Section 2.2.3.

40 EY, 'Study on Directors' Duties and Sustainable Corporate Governance,' Report for the European Commission (29 July 2020) <https://op.europa.eu/en/publication-detail/-/publication/e47928a2-d20b-11ea-adf7-01aa75ed71a1/language-en> accessed on 1 June 2023.

41 IPCC 2022 Mitigation Report [4.27]; and OECD Insurance and Adaptation Paper 19.

42 Garrett Hardin, 'The Tragedy of the Commons' [1968] 162 *Science*, 1243; Nigar Hashimzade, Gareth Myles, and John Black, *Oxford Dictionary of Economics* (5th ed, OUP 2017) entry for 'Tragedy of the Commons.'

nothing we can do.'[43] Fourthly, insurers do not currently need to account for 'insurance-associated emissions' (GHG emissions in connection with assets they insure),[44] so that there is little financial and reputational incentive to incur additional costs to reduce those GHG emissions through climate-related impact underwriting. Yet, there are a number of interrelated reasons why the board of directors of an insurance company should not ignore climate-related impact underwriting strategies.

6.2.2 Consideration of the impact on the environment

The s.172 duty requires directors to have regard, among other matters, to the impact of the company's operations on the community and the environment.[45] A director of an insurance company is expected to consider the company's approach to environmental impacts, but this is just one factor among many. The factors to which directors must have regard, as set out in s.172(1)(a) to (f), are not separate stand-alone duties, but instead:

> The weighing of all these considerations [as set out in s.172] is essentially a commercial decision, which the court is ill-equipped to take, except in a clear case.[46]

In *ClientEarth v Shell Plc*, an application for permission to bring a derivative action, the shareholder's substantive case was that the directors of Shell were in breach of duty for failing to set an appropriate GHG emissions target and to ensure that Shell had a measurable and realistic pathway to meeting the net-zero target. The judge agreed with Shell's argument that the s.172 factors do not constitute separate duties and that it is for the directors themselves to determine the weight to be attached to the non-exhaustive list of factors to which each director must have regard in the performance of their duty to promote the success of the company.[47] While ClientEarth (qua shareholder) was unsuccessful in trying to force the directors to take specific climate actions, the case also shows that there is substantial discretion in how much weight a director can attribute to considerations of the company's impact on the environment.

The impact of an insurer's operations on the community and on the environment, and whether an insurer seeks to reduce such impacts that are harmful through climate-related impact underwriting, should be part of its defensive strategy to avert reputational harm and reduce litigation risk.[48] Positive impacts of an insurer's operations on the community or the environment should also be part of its offensive strategy to build a competitive advantage by developing new insurance products that meet environmental objectives, to enhance customer choice and loyalty, to expand its customer base to climate-conscious customers, to attract talented employees, and to attract and retain climate-conscious shareholders and other investors.[49] UK insurers who are already required to report in line

---

43 Michael Mann, *The New Climate War: The Fight to Take Back Our Planet* (PublicAffairs 2021).

44 Scope 3 emissions do not include 'underwriting emissions' under the Greenhouse Gas Protocol (see Chapter 3, Section 3.3.2).

45 Companies Act 2006, s 172(1)(d).

46 *Iesini v Westrip Holdings Ltd* [2009] EWHC 2526 (Ch) at [85] per Lewison J, cited in *ClientEarth v Shell Plc* [2023] EWHC 1137 at [19] per Trower J.

47 *ClientEarth v Shell Plc* (n 46) at [19] per Trower J.

48 See Chapter 3, Table 3.1.

49 Ramon Mullerat, *Corporate Social Responsibility: The Corporate Governance Responsibility of the 21st Century* (2nd ed, Wolters Kluwer Law and Business 2011).

with the TCFD Recommendations[50] should already identify and develop their strategies and transition plans in light of the climate change risks and opportunities that they are facing.[51]

Insurers who fail to put in place strategies for climate action in their operations and through their products and services may suffer reputational harm, compare unfavourably to their competitors, and be the subject of negative publicity, resulting in loss of market share and creating a strategic risk to overall business viability.[52] Ultimately, these reputational, operational, and strategic risks could reflect negatively on the value of a company and thus affect the shareholders' return on equity. Emerging theoretical research and empirical evidence suggest that 'greeniums' – a higher share or securities price that climate-conscious investors are prepared to pay – are already priced into the value of companies that commit to reducing GHG emissions.[53] Hart and Zingales show that, to the extent that a company has a comparative advantage relative to individuals in producing a public good (or avoiding a public bad), its shareholders may wish it to pursue some social goals at the expense of profit.[54] In contrast, 21 US State Attorney Generals recently asserted that investments and votes for environmental purposes 'are not financially justified' on the basis that the pathway to achieving the Paris Agreement objectives and a global transition to net-zero GHG emissions is far from inevitable.[55]

The s.172 duty does not permit directors to promote environmental goals at the expense of shareholders. Thus, authorising premium discounts and rebates that are not risks-based but given to encourage technologies and infrastructure projects aimed at climate change mitigation and adaptation could be inconsistent with the s.172 duty. Nor does s.172 take a 'pluralist' approach whereby the directors must balance the interests of the members with those of the stakeholders.[56] The literature describes the s.172 duty as representing a philosophy of 'enlightened shareholder value' where shareholders' interests are paramount, but the interests of stakeholders (including communities and the environment) are to be taken into account when determining the best way of promoting the company's success.[57]

Public debate and scholarship are starting to shift the corporate focus from 'shareholder primacy' to a wider view of engagement with stakeholders and society.[58] The UK Corporate Governance Code defines the role of the board of directors 'to promote the

50 See Chapter 5, Section 5.1.

51 See Chapter 5, Section 5.1.2.

52 IAIS and SIF, 'Issues Paper on Climate Change Risks to the Insurance Sector' (July 2018) 16–17 and Table 1 <https://www.iaisweb.org/page/supervisory-material/issues-papers> accessed on 1 June 2023; and The Geneva Association, 'Climate Change Risk Assessment for the Insurance Industry' (February 2021) 16–19 <https://www.genevaassociation.org/research-topics/climate-change-and-emerging-environmental-topics/climate-change-risk-assessment> accessed on 1 June 2023.

53 Armour (n 31) 18–20.

54 Oliver Hart and Luigi Zingales, 'Companies Should Maximize Shareholder Welfare Not Market Value' (2017) *Journal of Law, Finance and Accounting*, 247.

55 Letter from the State Attorney Generals of Montana, Louisiana, Utah, Alabama, Arkansas, Georgia, Idaho, Indiana, Iowa, Kansas, Kentucky, Mississippi, Missouri, New Hampshire, Ohio, South Carolina, Tennessee, Texas, Virginia, West Virginia, and Wyoming, to asset managers, dated 30 March 2023, 17 <https://attorneygeneral.utah.gov/wp-content/uploads/2023/03/2023-03-30-Asset-Manager-letter-Press-FINAL.pdf> accessed on 1 June 2023.

56 Davies and Worthington (n 30) 420.

57 Ibid.

58 For an overview of the public, political, and academic debate on 'corporate purpose' see: Edward B. Rock, 'For Whom Is the Corporation Managed in 2020? The Debate over Corporate Purpose' (2021) 76(2) *Business Lawyer*, 363. Also see Sjåfjell, Johnston, Anker-Sørensen, and Milton (n 30); Frederick H. Alexander,

long-term sustainable success of the company, generating value for shareholders and contributing to wider society.'[59] A survey carried out by the FCA revealed that '79% of consumers think businesses have a wider social responsibility than simply to make a profit.'[60] Advocates of a wider corporate purpose argue that societal issues such as climate change cannot be addressed, and can even be made worse, by companies that solely focus on (short-term) financial performance since they ignore the longer-term, economy- and society-wide negative externalities that result, by placing them outside the realm of their business decisions.[61]

Corporate social responsibility ('CSR') theories seek to position social and ethical demands within a company's responsibilities: Carroll's Pyramid of CSR distinguishes philanthropic responsibility (pure giving) and ethical responsibility (to avoid harm) from a company's legal (to comply with laws) and economic responsibilities (to make money) – the former two are expected, whereas the latter two are required, by society.[62] Many companies engage in philanthropy and embrace ethical responsibility to enhance their reputation and because they recognise that, in order to maximise profits, they must take into account the needs of stakeholders and wider society. Similarly, Elkington's 'triple bottom line' theory holds that a company must seek social, environment, and economic impact to be sustainable on a long-term basis.[63] Stakeholder-focused CSR theories highlight that companies have responsibilities towards the individuals and groups on whom the company depends, and who can affect or be affected by the company's operations.[64] The emerging concept of 'stakeholder capitalism' expands the understanding of a company's 'corporate purpose':

> to engage all its stakeholders in shared and sustained value creation. In creating such value, a company serves not only its shareholders, but all its stakeholders – employees, customers, suppliers, local communities and society at large. The best way to understand and harmonize the divergent interests of all stakeholders is through a shared commitment to policies and decisions that strengthen the long-term prosperity of a company.[65]

The Davos Manifesto 2020 puts forward a vision of a company that serves society, including 'as a steward of the environmental and material universe for future generations,'

Benefit Corporation Law and Governance Pursuing Profit with Purpose (Berrett-Koehler Publishers, Inc 2017).

59 FRC, 'UK Corporate Governance Code 2018' Prin 1A.

60 FCA, 'Finance for Positive Sustainable Change: Governance, Incentives and Competence in Regulated Firms' DP23/1 (February 2023) [2.5].

61 British Academy, 'The Future of the Corporation: Principles for Purposeful Business' (November 2019) <https://www.thebritishacademy.ac.uk/publications/future-of-the-corporation-principles-for-purposeful-business> accessed on 1 June 2023, and Marco Rubio, 'American Investment in the 21st Century: Project for Strong Labor Markets and National Development' (15 May 2019) 22 <https://www.rubio.senate.gov/public/%5Fcache/files/94fcb79e-eedd-4496-a262-7091647563e6/B68DE3EF858700E482305C9ED26AEC72.5.14.2019.-final-project-report-american-investment.pdf> accessed on 1 June 2023.

62 Archie B. Carroll, 'Carroll's Pyramid of CSR: Taking Another Look' (2016) 1 *Int J Corporate Soc Responsibility*, 3.

63 John Elkington, 'Cannibals with Forks: The Triple Bottom Line of 21st Century Business' (2000) 23 *Journal of Business Ethics*, 229.

64 Edward Freeman, *Strategic Management: A Stakeholder Approach* (Cambridge University Press 2015; first published in 1984).

65 World Economic Forum, 'Davos Manifesto 2020: The Universal Purpose of a Company in the Fourth Industrial Revolution' (2019) <https://www.weforum.org/agenda/2019/12/davos-manifesto-2020-the-universal-purpose-of-a-company-in-the-fourth-industrial-revolution/> accessed on 1 June 2023; Klaus Schwab, *Stakeholder Capitalism* (Wiley, 2021).

where '[p]erformance must be measured not only on the return to shareholders, but also on how it achieves its environmental, social and good governance objectives.'[66] Some jurisdictions legally recognise benefit corporations – companies whose corporate form and constitution allow them to consider social responsibility interests.[67]

The European Commission has adopted its version of stakeholder capitalism in its CSDDD proposal: the CSDDD is a directive which would establish a corporate due diligence duty to identify, bring to an end, prevent, mitigate, and account for negative human rights and environmental impacts in the company's own operations, their subsidiaries, and their value chains.[68] Directors of in-scope companies will have additional duties that include setting up and overseeing the implementation of the due diligence processes and integrating due diligence into the corporate strategy. In addition, when fulfilling their duty to act in the best interest of the company, directors must take into account the human rights, climate change, and environmental consequences of their decisions in the short, medium, and long term.[69] The CSDDD will move the dial significantly away from a pure value maximisation focus to a more pluralist and long-term perspective for those companies to which the duty will apply.[70] The CSDDD proposal stands in stark contrast to the anti-ESG legislation in the US.[71] Insurance companies that have EU and US operations may be caught by conflicting policy approaches to corporate purpose and corporate social responsibility.

Yet, even if the corporate purpose debate is moving towards a more pluralist view that envisages a link between benefitting society more widely and long-term corporate growth, this is not the legal position under the s.172 duty. Moreover, there are market practices and company constitutional issues that put pressure on directors to maximise shareholder value within a short-term horizon, rather than engaging with sustainable corporate governance practices.[72] A study carried out by EY for the European Commission identi-

66 World Economic Forum (n 65).

67 A company can register as a benefit corporation in some of the US states (see: US Chamber of Commerce, A Complete Guide to Starting a B Corp <https://www.uschamber.com/co/start/strategy/b-corp-advantages-and-requirements#:~:text=What%20is%20a%20B%20corp%3F%20According%20to%20the,as%20well%20as%20some%20sort%20of%20public%20benefit> accessed on 1 June 2023. In France, a company can register as, or change its status to, 'Société à Mission' under the *Loi PACTE* 2019 <https://www.economie.gouv.fr/loi-pacte-croissance-transformation-entreprises> accessed on 1 June 2023. In the UK, a company can register as a community interest company (Companies Act 2006, s 6) – a special type of limited company which exists to benefit the community rather than private shareholders. In addition, a mainstream company can formulate its corporate purpose more widely, to promote the success of the company for the benefit of its members by achieving those wider or other purposes (Companies Act 2006, s 172(2)) – this may protect to some extent against liability in shareholder actions.

68 Proposal for a Directive of the European Parliament and of the Council on Corporate Sustainability Due Diligence and amending Directive (EU) 2019/1937 COM/2022/71, and see Chapter 4, Section 4.4.5.

69 Proposal for CSDDD, art 25 and 26, and see Chapter 4, Section 4.4.5, in relation to whether and to what extent the CSDDD would apply to insurance companies.

70 Large EU-based companies: Group 1 – 500+ employees and net EUR 150 million+ turnover worldwide; Group 2 – 250+ employees and net EUR 40+ million turnover worldwide, and operating in defined high-impact sectors, e.g. textiles, agriculture, extraction of minerals. For this group, the rules start to apply two years later than for Group 1. The CSDDD could also become applicable to any UK insurers that generate a net turnover of EUR 150 million in the EU (Proposal for CSDDD art 2).

71 See Chapter 4, Section 4.4.6.

72 For a discussion of the pressures of 'corporate culture' and market forces counter-acting ESG considerations, see: Jonathan Macey, 'ESG Investing: Why Here? Why Now?' Yale Law & Economics Research Paper (forthcoming) Law & Economics Center at George Mason University Scalia Law School Research Paper Series No. 22-013.

fied a number of key drivers for board short-termism, including pressure from investors with short-term investment goals, board remuneration structures that incentivise the focus on short-term shareholder value rather than long-term value creation for the company, current corporate governance frameworks and practices that do not sufficiently voice the long-term interests of stakeholders, and the limited enforcement of directors' duties in the long-term interest of the company.[73] The FCA is currently consulting on whether and how executive remuneration should be linked to sustainability-related objectives and KPIs.[74] A draft of the Companies (Strategic Report and Directors' Report) (Amendment) Regulations was introduced in Parliament – but has now been withdrawn – which would have required larger companies to include in their annual reports an annual resilience statement which sets out how a company manages risk over the short, medium, and long term.[75] But the board of directors of an insurance company cannot ignore short-term performance as its regulatory solvency capital requirements are calibrated at a level to ensure that their assets will be able to cover liabilities over the following 12-month period.[76] Insurers must therefore be careful to limit costs associated with climate-related impact underwriting to levels, and incur such costs for reasons, that are consistent with promoting the success of the company and their solvency capital requirements.

Insurers must engage with their shareholders to foster stewardship and to ensure their support for the creation of sustainable value for shareholders that takes into account the wider interests of society in stemming climate change. Such engagement rests on appropriate disclosures on net-zero targets, climate strategy and transition planning, and the prevention of green-washing.[77] It has been noted that a growing number of investors are 'prosocial' and would prefer their investee companies to reduce socially harmful activities connected to their businesses even if this might reduce profits.[78] There is a body of literature that suggests that companies that address ESG factors can outperform those companies that do not,[79] or at least offer competitive returns,[80] and that climate-conscious investors see value in their investee companies reducing GHG emissions.[81] However, other studies suggest that investors only account for climate risk in some contexts and to a limited extent.[82]

73 EY (n 40).

74 FCA DP23/1 (n 60) Q8.

75 HM Government Department for Business and Trade, 'New Transparency over Resilience and Assurance for Big Business' (July 2023) <https://www.gov.uk/government/publications/new-transparency-over-resilience-and-assurance-for-big-business> accessed on 10 August 2023, and see Chapter 5, Section 5.3.7. The UK government has now withdrawn the draft regulations after consultation with companies which raised concerns about imposing additional burdensome reporting requirements. <https://www.gov.uk/government/news/burdensome-legislation-withdrawn-in-latest-move-to-cut-red-tape-for-businesses> accessed on 3 November 2023.

76 PRA SII, Solvency Capital Requirement – General Provisions, [3.3], and see Chapter 4, Section 4.4.3.

77 See Chapter 5.

78 Hart and Zingales (n 54).

79 For an overview, see Alexander Dyck, Karl V. Lins, Lukas Roth, and Hannes F. Wagner, 'Do Institutional Investors Drive Corporate Social Responsibility? International Evidence' (2019) 131(3), *Journal of Financial Economics*, 693.

80 Quinn Curtis, Jill E. Fisch, and Adriana Z. Robertson, 'Do ESG Mutual Funds Deliver on Their Promises?' ECGI Working Paper Series in Law, Working Paper N° 586/2021 (May 2021).

81 Armour (n 31) 18–30.

82 Irene Monasterolo and Luca de Angelis, '2020: Blind to Carbon Risk? An Analysis of Stock Market Reaction to the Paris Agreement' (2019) 170 *Ecol Econ*, 106571; Lucia Alessi, Elisa Ossola, and Robert Panzica, 'What Greenium Matters in the Stock Market? The Role of Greenhouse Gas Emissions and Environmental

There will come a tipping point where the maximisation of shareholder value is aligned to insurance business models that have clear net-zero targets and adaptation projects to be achieved with climate-related impact underwriting and investments. This tipping point will be reached when the rising costs of climate change risks compared to the business opportunities of product innovation and decarbonised or decarbonising investments can no longer be ignored.[83]

6.2.3 Protection gaps and financial stability

Table 3.1 in Chapter 3 shows how physical risk, transition risk, and liability risk can have negative financial impacts on both the liability side and the asset side of an insurer's balance sheet. As climate-related extreme weather events are expected to become more frequent and severe, insured losses can be expected to increase. For insurers, this means that claims costs, capital costs, and the costs of reinsurance are likely to increase as a result of climate change.[84] Thus, where insurers provide cover for climate-related losses, they have an incentive to control their policyholders' exposure to, and help them in their efforts to protect themselves from losses resulting from, these risks.[85]

Projections by the Bank of England show a rise in average annualised losses for general insurers of around 50% and 70% via a build-up in climate risk for general insurers in a 'No Additional Action' scenario where governments around the world fail to enact policy responses to global warming and no additional action is taken to address climate change.[86] General insurers might either pass on the cost of higher claims into premiums, or otherwise refuse to renew insurance for some customers. It also finds that, if banks and insurers do not respond effectively, climate risks could cause a persistent and material drag on their profitability of around 10–15% on average.[87] Losses of this magnitude could make individual firms, and the financial system overall, more vulnerable to other future shocks.

The prevalent practice among property and casualty insurers to respond to increasing physical climate change risk is to re-price premiums annually (which is possible as non-life insurance contracts typically have a duration of twelve months).[88] In re-pricing annually, climate change would be implicitly reflected gradually by including recent events in the risk analysis based on historical data. Climate change is also reflected by gradual adjustments to policy terms and conditions.[89] EIOPA has found evidence that the annual re-pricing may lead to insurance becoming unaffordable over a longer term period or disincentivise consumers from buying insurance, which, in turn, can create and increase protection gaps.[90] For example, a study by Schwarze and Wagner shows that, following the

---

Disclosures' (2021) 54 *J Financ Stab*, 54, 100869; Patrick Bolton and Marcin Kacperczyk, 'Do Investors Care about Carbon Risk?' (2021) 142(2) *J Financ Econ*, 517.

83 Armour (n 31) 11.

84 EIOPA Non-Life Underwriting and Climate Change Report, Table 1.

85 Caroline Heimer, *Reactive Risk and Rational Action: Managing Moral Hazard in Insurance Contracts* (University of California Press, 1985).

86 Bank of England, 'Results of the 2021 Climate Biennial Exploratory Scenario' [4.2] (24 May 2022) <https://www.bankofengland.co.uk/stress-testing/2022/results-of-the-2021-climate-biennial-exploratory-scenario> accessed on 1 June 2023.

87 Ibid, Summary.

88 EIOPA Non-Life Underwriting and Climate Change Report [2.16].

89 Ibid [2.17].

90 Ibid [2.32].

'Flood of the Century' in 2002 in Saxony (Germany), insurers responded by increasing premiums by up to 60% and reducing coverage in some regions of Saxony.[91] A study by Tesselaar et al. (2020) on the impacts of climate change on EU flood insurance markets shows that in the context of climate change, annual re-pricing will not be sustainable as, by 2080, the increase of premiums for flood insurance could quadruple, and the proportion of the population which cannot afford flood insurance could increase by around 40%.[92] In its 'Report on Climate-Related Risks and the Regulatory Capital Frameworks,' the Bank of England acknowledged that 'protection gaps' are a wider prudential issue that falls within the PRA's policyholder protection objective.[93] The US Senate Committee on the Budget suggested that insurance companies must consider phasing out their underwriting of and investment in fossil fuel projects generating the GHG emissions that are causing climate change, given that the impacts of climate change had already led to widening protection gaps, as well as posing risks to insurers, and potentially creating systemic risk to the economy.[94]

EIOPA has already made the addressing of 'protection gaps' one of its regulatory priorities for 2022–2024;[95] the Bank of England has acknowledged that 'protection gaps' are a wider prudential issue that falls within the PRA's policyholder protection objective.[96] To ensure the availability and affordability of insurance in light of climate change, EIOPA argues, insurers must consider climate-related impact underwriting.[97] The EU Commission set up a Climate Resilience Dialogue to bring together insurers, reinsurers, risk managers, public authorities, and consumer representatives, among others, to intensify efforts for narrowing the protection gap from climate-related disasters, and to identify how the insurance industry can contribute more to climate adaptation, ranging from actions that increase the penetration of climate risk insurance for all of society to making the conditions right for more investment in good adaptation solutions.[98]

The gradual premium increase and the erosion of insurance cover leading to protection gaps can have cascading effects on economic activities, supply chains, and the performance of loans and investments across the financial system.[99] The current property and casualty insurance business model of annually increasing premiums to accommodate climate risks could also lead to a gradual contraction of market share and business volume. The

91 Reimund Schwarze and Gert Wagner, 'The Political Economy of Natural Disaster Insurance: Lessons from the Failure of a Proposed Compulsory Insurance Scheme in Germany' (2007) 17 *Eur Env*, 403, cited in EIOPA Non-Life Underwriting and Climate Change Report [2.24].

92 Max Tesselaar, 'Impacts of Climate Change and Remote Natural Catastrophes on EU Flood Insurance Markets: An Analysis of Soft and Hard Reinsurance Markets for Flood Coverage' (2020) 11(2) *Atmosphere*, 146, cited in EIOPA Non-Life Underwriting and Climate Change Report [2.33]–[2.35].

93 BoE Climate and Capital Frameworks Report [39].

94 Letter from the United States Senate Committee on the Budget to State Farm, Liberty Mutual, Berkshire Hathaway, AIG, Travelers Insurance, Chubb, and Starr dated 9 June 2023 launching investigation into Berkshire Hathaway for continuing to insure and invest in fossil fuel projects <https://www.budget.senate.gov/imo/media/doc/Budget%20Committee%20Letters%20to%20Insurance%20Companies.pdf> accessed on 1 June 2023.

95 EIOPA, 'Sustainable Finance Activities 2022–2024' <https://www.eiopa.europa.eu/system/files/2021-12/eiopa-sustainable-finance-activities-2022-2024.pdf> accessed on 1 June 2023.

96 BoE Climate and Capital Frameworks Report [39].

97 EIOPA Non-Life Underwriting and Climate Change Report [2.32] and [2.38].

98 A mid-term report is due in summer 2023 – see: European Commission, 'Climate Resilience Dialogue' <https://climate.ec.europa.eu/eu-action/adaptation-climate-change/climate-resilience-dialogue_en> accessed on 1 June 2023.

99 IAIS and SIF (n 52) 14.

ever-increasing frequency and severity of climate risks could lead to limited reinsurance capacity and create reinsurance protection gaps, and catastrophic claims could deplete an insurer's financial resources. Catastrophic climate risks will become uninsurable.[100] Ultimately, protection gaps at the insurance and reinsurance levels, increasing uninsurability, and catastrophic claims can have a negative impact on the financial stability of individual insurers. Insurers are required to have effective risk strategies and risk management systems in relation to climate change risk.[101] The complexity of climate risk in conjunction with the high degree of concentration in climate risk exposures in some geographical areas and in some industries, exacerbated by existing vulnerabilities,[102] mean that climate risks could even pose a systemic threat to the stability of the financial system as a whole.[103] The US Senate Committee on the Budget recently wrote to seven US insurers (State Farm, Liberty Mutual, Berkshire Hathaway, AIG, Travelers Insurance, Chubb, and Starr), stating that continuing to underwrite and invest in fossil fuel projects was inconsistent with the goals of the Paris Agreement to which the US is a signatory, harmful to policyholders who are increasingly facing protection gaps, and potentially creating systemic risk for the economy.[104]

Climate-related impact underwriting is already considered by some insurers as 'an important and effective approach for maintaining the long-term availability and affordability of non-life insurance products covering climate-related hazards.'[105] Climate-related impact underwriting can lower an insurer's exposures to climate risks and reduce climate risk losses by incentivising policyholders to take climate change mitigation and adaptation measures,[106] as well as contributing to climate change mitigation.[107] On these grounds, it is arguable that the s.172 duty requires directors of an insurance company to consider climate-related impact underwriting strategies.

6.2.4 Disclosure, reputational implications, and litigation risk

As noted in Chapter 5, the disclosure requirements relating to UK and EU insurers' outward impact are limited at this stage but are likely to grow. The EU Taxonomy already classifies non-life insurance that covers climate-related perils as an economic activity that can make a substantial contribution to climate change adaptation,[108] the ISSB Insurance Disclosures provide for disclosure on climate-related impact underwriting,[109] and there are developments to include 'insurance-associated emissions' in Scope 3 GHG emission reporting.[110]

---

100 See Chapter 3, Section 3.2.2.

101 See Chapter 4, Sections 4.4.3and 4.4.5.

102 See Section 3.2.4.

103 PRA SS3/19 [2.5]–[2.6]; Domenico Curcio, Igor Gianfrancesco, and Davide Vioto, 'Climate Change and Financial Systemic Risk: Evidence from US Banks and Insurers' (2023) 66 *Journal of Financial Stability*, 101132.

104 Letter from the United States Senate Committee on the Budget (n 94).

105 EIOPA Adaptation and Insurance Report EIOPA [7] and [38].

106 EIOPA Non-Life Underwriting and Climate Change Report [3.31].

107 See Sections 6.3 and 6.4.

108 See Chapter 5, Section 5.4.1.2.

109 See Chapter 5, Section 5.2.2 and Table 5.

110 Partnership for Carbon Accounting Financials, 'Insurance-Associated Emissions' (November 2022) <https://carbonaccountingfinancials.com/files/downloads/pcaf-standard-part-c-insurance-associated-emissions-nov-2022.pdf> accessed on 1 June 2023 and see Chapter 3, Section 3.3.2.

The growing body of climate-related disclosures aims to create transparency and a greater degree of comparability, enabling prospective customers and investors to make informed decisions factoring in climate-related objectives of financial products and the climate-related impact of different providers. Regulators hope that this will enhance competition between providers, increase customer interest in green products, and encourage the flow of funds towards green assets and activities.[111] Increasingly, the disclosure regime will allow investors and customers to distinguish between insurers who do and who do not engage in climate-related impact underwriting. Studies have noted that there is an evolution in customer expectations, especially among younger customers, that insurance products should not just deliver financial protection but should also engage with social impact and risk prevention.[112] An insurer who does not engage in climate-related impact underwriting may compare unfavourably to its competitors. It could lose market share if it does not offer green insurance products, and it may become the subject of negative publicity and suffer reputational harm (e.g. if it continues to insure coal and gas projects), all of which could have negative impacts on its business and ultimately the profits distributable to shareholders.[113] Thus, as envisaged in Carroll's CSR Pyramid,[114] insurers should consider their philanthropic and ethical responsibilities in order to enhance their reputation.

To date, climate change litigation risk for insurers has been primarily considered through the lens of their increasing exposure under environmental liability and general liability policies to their policyholders who seek indemnification for compensation claims they have to pay to third parties, and for their defence costs.[115] However, actions could also be brought against insurers directly in relation to their underwriting activities that are harmful to the environment. Investors have already been sued for not taking climate change considerations into account in their investment decisions.[116] Although it would be difficult to conceive of tortious actions by third parties, and the *ClientEarth v Shell Plc* case has clarified that directors do not owe any specific climate change duties to their shareholders,[117] the CSDDD proposal as currently drafted would allow for complaints against companies who fail in their corporate due diligence duty to identify, bring to an end, prevent, mitigate, and account for negative environmental impacts in the company's own operations, their subsidiaries, and their value chains.[118] Breaches of the duty could attract civil liability claims against the company itself,[119] and actions for breach of the directors' duties in relation to integrating due diligence into the corporate strategy, and in

111 See e.g. FCA, 'A Strategy for Positive Change: Our ESG Priorities' (3 November 2021) <https://www.fca.org.uk/publications/corporate-documents/strategy-positive-change-our-esg-priorities> accessed on 1 June 2023; and SFDR, Recitals.

112 Carlo Pugnetti, Thomas Gebert, Miriam Hürster, Edward Huizenga, Markus Moor, Lukas Stricker, Herbert Winistörfer, and Angela Zeier Röschmann, 'Leading the Green Insurance Revolution' (Winterthur: ZHAW Zürcher Hochschule für Angewandte Wissenschaften, Working Paper no. 1, 2022) sec. 2.1.

113 IAIS and SIF (n 52) 16–17; The Geneva Association (n 52) 16–19.

114 Carroll (n 62); and see Section 6.2.2.

115 Climate Financial Risk Forum, 'Climate Financial Risk Forum Guide 2022 Disclosures – Managing Legal Risk' (December 2022) <https://www.fca.org.uk/cfrf> accessed on 1 June 2023; and see Chapter 3, Section 3.3.1.

116 See Chapter 8, Section 8.2.2.

117 *ClientEarth v Shell Plc* (n 46) [19] per Trower J; and see Section 6.2.2.

118 Proposal for CSDDD, art 9 and 19; and see Chapter 4, Section 4.4.5.

119 Ibid art 22.

relation to taking into account climate change and environmental consequences in their decisions in the short, medium, and long term.[120]

6.2.5 Environmental stewardship

Stakeholder theories focus on protecting and balancing the interests of individuals and groups impacted by decision-making. The s.172 duty is an example of a legislative attempt to take the interests of different stakeholders, such as employees, customers, suppliers, and the wider community, into account in corporate decision-making. Environmental stewardship can be broadly defined as 'the actions taken by individuals, groups or networks of actors, with various motivations and levels of capacity, to protect, care for or responsibly use the environment in pursuit of environmental and/or social outcomes in diverse social-ecological contexts.'[121] Macro stewardship develops the idea of stakeholder capitalism recognising that financial institutions have a responsibility to engage with governments, regulators, policymakers, and other key influencers to correct material market failures on sustainability issues in order to help preserve the integrity of the whole financial system.[122] Within the financial services industry, there is a tendency to limit the understanding of 'stewardship' to the micro investment and asset management contexts. For example, the UK Stewardship Code 2020 defines 'stewardship' as 'the responsible allocation, management and oversight of capital to create long-term value for clients and beneficiaries leading to sustainable benefits for the economy, the environment and society.'[123] For a more detailed discussion of stewardship activities by investors reference is made to Chapter 8, Section 8.1.3.

It is suggested that the understanding of the environmental and macro stewardship should be extended to insurers in their capacity as underwriters and risk carriers. Through climate-related impact underwriting, they have the ability to influence and challenge the behaviour and activities of prospective and existing policyholders, steering or incentivising them towards emission-reducing or carbon-neutral activities and adaptation measures. The enabling role of insurers – as envisaged in Chapter 3 – is a form of environmental stewardship. Just like investment stewardship, insurance stewardship can contribute to wider societal benefits when insurers contribute to, and support their policyholders in taking, climate change adaptation and mitigation measures. Longer term, environmental stewardship by insurers would support the real economy and the stability of the financial system. Macro stewardship – working together with governments, regulators, and other policymakers to promote wide-spread action across society on environmental issues – is

120 Ibid art 25 and 26.

121 Nathan J. Bennett et al., 'Environmental Stewardship: A Conceptual Review and Analytical Framework' (2018) 61(4) *Environ Manag*, 597, text to Fig.1. The article also contains a literature review on the definition of 'environmental stewardship.'

122 Mark Versey, 'Redefining Stewardship – Why Stakeholder Capitalism Needs to Wake up' AIQ Aviva Investors (April 2023) 11–16 <https://www.avivainvestors.com/en-gb/views/aiq-investment-thinking/2022/08/redefining-stewardship/> accessed on 1 June 2023.

123 FRC, 'UK Stewardship Code 2020' <https://www.frc.org.uk/getattachment/5aae591d-d9d3-4cf4-814a-d14e156a1d87/Stewardship-Code_Final2.pdf> accessed on 1 June 2023; also see PRI, 'Principles for Responsible Investment' which define 'Stewardship' as 'the use of influence by institutional investors to maximise overall long-term value including the value of common economic, social and environmental assets, on which returns and clients' and beneficiaries' interests depend' (<https://www.unpri.org/about-us/about-the-pri> accessed on 1 June 2023).

an important channel of communication for insurers as risk carriers, and one that insurers are familiar with from other contexts. It recognises that market forces cannot fix all market failures (in time), that regulators and policymakers sometimes need prompting, and that governments need signalling that they must strengthen their commitments under the Paris Agreement. Macro stewardship is also recognised in PSI Principle 3.

Ewart carried out interviews with senior representatives from ten (re)insurance companies to inquire into the motivation for engaging with commercial customers in relation to their net-zero transition.[124] He found that most insurers had multiple motivations broadly falling within the following four categories:

1. system leaders who are motivated by social responsibility (driven by leaders and employees within the company);
2. reactive leaders who are driven by regulatory requirements aimed at financial stability, and are motivated their policyholders and investors to engage with environmental sustainability;
3. strategic managers who take a strategic approach to risk management and business opportunities;
4. stakeholder managers who are steered towards managing their net-zero transition by investors, who are motivated by competition and peer pressure, and respond to customer demands.

This is a helpful analysis to which further dimensions could be added, such as the maintenance of the insurability of assets exposed to climate-related risks and the prevention and reduction of protection gaps,[125] and the operation of climate-related disclosure regimes.[126]

6.3 Insuring green

The global transition to a resilient net-zero economy is dependent on investment into new technologies, services, and infrastructure that reduce or neutralise GHG emissions and improve resilience to climate-related physical risks.[127] Between 2023 and 2050, US$150 trillion of total investment in the energy transition will be required for the world to align with a 1.5°C pathway, requiring current levels of investment to quadruple.[128] The UK government estimates that in 2022 alone, £23 billion of new low-carbon investment was delivered in the UK – ranging from renewables, hydrogen, carbon capture and storage, nuclear, sustainable materials, energy storage, and electrified transport, to clean heat.[129] While the majority of tracked climate finance is targeted at mitigation,[130] investment is

124 Tom Ewart, 'Net-Zero Insurance: Engaging Businesses in the Low-Carbon Transition through Insurance Underwriting & Risk Management' (28 February 2023) <https://medium.com/@tom.ewart/net-zero-insurance-engaging-businesses-in-the-low-carbon-transition-through-insurance-underwriting-9e83efd-c0a7f> accessed on 1 June 2023.

125 See Section 6.2.3 and Chapter 3, Section 3.2.4.

126 See Section 6.2.4 and Chapter 5.

127 See e.g.: SHIP sec IX, art 61 and 62.

128 International Renewable Energy Agency, 'World Energy Transitions Outlook 2023: 1.5°C Pathway' (March 2023) <https://www.irena.org/Publications/2023/Mar/World-Energy-Transitions-Outlook-2023> accessed on 1 June 2023.

129 HM Government (n 24) 18.

130 Climate adaptation finance only represents 0.05% of total tracked private climate finance in 2018 – see: IPCC 2022 Sixth Assessment Report [C.3.2] and [TS.D.1.6]. Adaptation measures in natural and managed

also needed for climate change adaptation measures. Reference is made to Chapter 8 for a discussion of how insurers can make a contribution in their capacity as investors. This section is concerned with insurers providing insurance cover for technologies and infrastructure projects that provide climate change mitigation and adaptation solutions.

6.3.1 Insuring infrastructure projects

For infrastructure projects – including green infrastructure projects – the project parties (the employer/owner, the operator, the main contractor, sub-contractors, and any government authorities) are exposed to a number of risks – such as loss or damage to assets, legal liability, loss of earnings, and political risks – in the construction phase and operational phase of the project. Banks providing finance and other investors are indirectly exposed to the same risks via credit risk: their likelihood of being repaid and making a return on their investment diminishes when the project's earning capacity becomes impaired. Risks are primarily allocated through the main contractual documents by assigning responsibilities and obligations to the project parties (usually, to the party who is best able to manage the risk).

Insurance is needed because the project parties' risk appetite or tolerance may be exceeded (usually measured by what risks could be absorbed by a party's balance sheet), and/or because some risks may be outside any parties' control. Moreover, taking out co-insurance is also a way to prevent costly litigation between the project parties.[131] Without insurance and appropriate security arrangements over the insurance contracts and proceeds, banks would be unwilling to lend money to finance the project on affordable terms, or at all, and many projects would not be able to go ahead. Insuring green thus often goes hand-in-hand with 'green investment.'

There are different types of insurance for the construction phase and the operational phase of a project. The main types of construction phase insurance are:

- **Construction (or Contractors) All Risks (CAR) or Erection All Risks (EAR)**: these policies primarily cover physical loss or damage to the project itself, building materials, machinery, and equipment, subject to the terms, conditions, and exclusions of the policy. Historically, CAR was used for general building and civil engineering risks, whereas EAR was mostly used for industrial process construction sites including the installation of related engineering works,[132] but there is not much difference between them now. CAR cover may extend to the defects liability period to cover loss or damage in that period. Some CAR policies contain construction third-party liability cover, or such cover can be obtained

ecosystems include earlier planting and changes in crop varieties, soil improvement and water management for livestock and crops, aquaculture, restoration of coastal and hydrological processes, introduction of heat- and drought-adapted genotypes into high-risk populations, increasing the size and connectivity of habitat patches, agroecological farming, agroforestry, and managed relocations of high-risk species.

131 *Gard Marine & Energy Ltd v China National Chartering Co Ltd (The Ocean Victory)* [2017] UKSC 35. In this case a majority of the Supreme Court held that the commercial purpose of maintaining co-insurance arrangements was not only to provide a joint fund to make good the loss, but to avoid litigation, or the bringing of a subrogation claim by one against the other. Co-insurance schemes contained an implicit understanding that there would be no separate liability for the project or asset.

132 A crude distinction between CAR and EAR is CAR involves mud and dirt, EAR steel and bolts.

under a separate policy: it covers accidental damage to property of third parties or injury to third parties;

- **delay in start-up insurance (DSU)**: this type of policy is often part of a programme with CAR or EAR, either as a separate schedule of CAR or EAR or as a separate policy but which will usually only be issued in conjunction with the property insurance. DSU cover is designed to cover the portion of revenue that the project is not generating as a result of late completion which itself is caused by damage to the works or materials. Essentially, DSU cover ensures that any loan from lenders that becomes due upon scheduled completion can be serviced.

Once the construction phase is completed, and the project becomes operational, the following types of insurance are essential:

- **property all risk**: property all risk insurance covers accidental loss or damage to specified buildings and specified machinery and contents, subject to the terms, conditions, and exclusions of the policy;
- **business interruption (BI)**: BI is usually sold alongside some kind of property insurance. The reason for this is that standard BI insurance covers lost revenue that is the result of property damage. BI can be extended to other situations that do not require physical damage to the insured property: e.g. denial of access to the property due to insured damage to a neighbouring property;
- **equipment breakdown (EB)**: EB covers the loss of income and/or additional costs resulting from failing equipment or machinery;
- **public liability (PL)**: PL insurance protects against legal liability (not voluntarily assumed) to pay civil damages to third parties for injury or property damage caused on the project site once the works have been completed.

Throughout the project's construction and operational phases, depending on the project's location, political risk insurance may be advisable. Political risk cover is provided by commercial insurers and state-run export credit agencies. It covers asset-based risks, such as expropriation, nationalisation, forced abandonment, etc., but also trade-related risks such as currency exchange risks and contract frustration.

For green assets and technologies, there are many specialist types of property insurance that are designed for the risk profile of specific types of property. Where the asset generates earnings, BI insurance may be available. Asset owners or operators can be exposed to legal liability on account of the asset for which some form of liability insurance will be available (or could indeed be mandatory).[133] For example, product liability insurance protects a manufacturer or supplier of goods against legal liability (not voluntarily assumed) to pay civil damages to third parties for injury or property damage caused on the project site once the works have been completed. All these insurances transfer risk to insurers and therefore 'de-risk' the asset.

There are already many examples of 'insuring green' where traditional insurance products are used for green projects and assets. Due to insufficient data for risk modelling and pricing, the risk assessment can be complex where the underlying insured subject-matter

133 For mandatory insurance in the UK, see Chapter 3, Section 3.1.

is innovative and untested or prototypical technology is used.[134] Moreover, the physical characteristics of the insured subject-matter can display higher risk characteristics for example because of its location in vulnerable geographies, because the materials used are more susceptible to physical damage, and because there is significant reliance on emerging technologies. All these risk factors can have an effect on premium pricing and can make insurance for green projects and assets more expensive compared to their conventional equivalents. Insurers must still carry out a risk-based assessment in order to price the risk appropriately.

In addition to adapting traditional lines to green projects and assets, innovative insurance products that support green energy resources are also emerging. The FCA product governance regime imposes rigorous internal approval and testing requirements for new insurance products or where existing insurance products are changed with significant adaptations.[135] This may add to research and development costs that are likely to be reflected in insurance premium rates. Any insurance product innovation carries the risk of 'free riders,' that is, other insurers that may benefit from the product innovation (e.g. by adopting it into its offering) without contributing to its development or implementation. The FCA supports the development of new products and solutions to address climate change through innovation programmes and sandboxes.[136]

6.3.2 Insuring green: examples

Providing insurance cover that protects against climate change risks is not 'insuring green.' The English common law analysis for indemnity insurance that the insurer undertakes to hold the insured harmless against loss by an insured peril or perils specified in the policy[137] is a legal fiction. The insurer has no intention, or ability, to prevent loss or damage by an insured peril.[138] Insurance against climate change risks can build the resilience of individuals and government budgets to the financial impact of climate change risks, but it does not prevent the loss from climate change risks and it does not address the root cause of climate change (i.e. GHG emissions). Insuring green is concerned with climate change mitigation and adaptation.

Carbon capture, utilisation, and storage technologies ('CCUS') are an example that insuring green cannot necessarily be equated with a lower risk profile for insurance purposes. CCUS entails the **capture** of CO_2 at the source and storing of it, to stop it from entering the atmosphere. First, the CO_2 produced by power creation or industrial activity is separated from other gases. It is then captured, compressed, transported, and injected into geological formations deep underground where, in this state, it can be **stored** for

134 The Geneva Association, 'Investing in Climate-Resilient Decarbonised Infrastructure to Meet Socio-Economic and Climate Change Goals' (December 2019) <https://www.genevaassociation.org/sites/default/files/research-topics-document-type/pdf_public/infrastructure_investment_gap_4-pager_091219.pdf> accessed on 1 June 2023.

135 See Chapter 7, Section 7.2.

136 FCA, 'Climate Change and Sustainable Finance' <https://www.fca.org.uk/firms/climate-change-sustainable-finance> accessed on 1 June 2023.

137 *Secony Mobil Oil Inc v West of England Shipowners Mutual Insurance Association (The Padre Island)* [1991] 2 AC 1; *Sprung v Royal Insurance (UK) Ltd* [1997] C.L.C. 70 (CoA); *Ventouris v Mountain (The Italia Express) (No.3)* [1992] 2 Lloyd's Rep. 281 (Comm Ct).

138 Neil Campbell, 'The Nature of an Insurer's Obligation' (2000) *LMCLQ*, 42, 63–64.

millions of years. The extracted CO_2 can be **used** to produce hydrogen (a clean energy source) or converted into materials such as plastic, concrete, and biofuels.[139] Global insurance and risk adviser Marsh has identified several key risks in CCUS operations:

- **technical hazards**: the construction of the plants needed to capture and process CO_2 can be complex. Whether this construction is of new facilities or those that are being retrofitted, the plants require dedicated tanks and technologies, enabling the separation of CO_2 from other gases. There are inherent technical exposures in the CO_2 separation process, related to the compression and cooling of gases flowing through pipes and the use of chemical solvents, for instance;
- **fire and explosion**: there are lifting, handling, or accidental damage risks at carbon capture plants, as is the case at any construction site. When carbon capture technology is retrofitted to operational industrial plants or facilities in typically high-hazard locations, such as power stations, the risk of accidental damage and subsequent fire and explosion risk to existing assets may be enhanced;
- **leaks**: during the operational phase, there is a risk that CO_2 causes cracks in steel pipes, tanks, and vessels when they reach low temperatures. Moreover, where CO_2 comes into contact with water, or liquids containing water, it forms carbonic acid, which can cause corrosion in metals. If carbonic acid escapes into water sources, it can also cause relatively local environmental liability;
- **business interruption and failure to meet carbon goals**: in order to treat CO_2 and ready it for transportation, pure carbon dioxide gas can be compressed so that it reaches its dense or supercritical phase. In some cases, it can instead be cooled, which transforms it into a liquid state. Mechanical failures or breakdowns affecting this stage of the process could lead to lengthy business interruptions for clients. If the captured CO_2 cannot be transported, this may affect emissions targets and carbon credits committed to by clients.

In light of these risks, CCSU would require a complex insurance programme during the construction phase and the operational phase, involving bespoke EAR insurance, property and BI insurance, and liability insurance that covers environmental risks. This will add transaction costs to the premium costs.

Examples of innovative insurance products that support green energy resources are:

- **energy efficiency insurance** covers material damage (including equipment breakdown) of the installed systems; business interruption; protecting against loss of revenue in the event of equipment failure; and asset performance insurance covering a shortfall in energy savings;[140]
- **home-owner alternative energy insurance** provides cover for homeowners who generate their own geothermal, solar, or wind power electricity in relation to extra expenses incurred from temporarily buying electricity from another source

139 See: Marsh, 'Carbon Capture in the UK: Risk Considerations' (March 2021) <https://www.marsh.com/uk/industries/energy-and-power/insights/carbon-capture-in-uk-risk-considerations.html> accessed on 1 June 2023.

140 See e.g. Munich Re, 'Energy Efficiency Insurance' <https://www.munichre.com/hsbeil/en/products/energy-efficiency-insurance.html> accessed on 1 June 2023.

and for lost income from not being able to sell surplus during a power outage due to an insured peril;[141]

- **photovoltaic warranty insurance** covers manufacturers with respect to excessive warranty claims on modules for a period of 20+ years. In the event of the manufacturer's insolvency, the policy is seamlessly transferred to a registered buyer, ensuring that his warranty claims remain covered.[142]

Would these examples fall within the scope of climate-related impact underwriting? Insuring assets and projects that have the objective to contribute to climate change adaptation or mitigation clearly has a positive impact. In terms of 'intentionality,' one might query whether insurers who simply see 'insuring green' as a sound business opportunity and who are not specifically motivated by also achieving an 'environmental or social good' have the required intention but, given the climate-related and sustainability disclosure requirements, many insurers will wish to give clear expression to such an intention. As will be further argued in Chapter 8, Section 8.1.2, 'intentionality' should not be a necessary pre-condition to impact investment or impact underwriting.

6.3.3 Prudential treatment of insuring green

In the banking and capital markets sector, there is an ongoing discussion about whether 'investing green' should attract favourable capital treatment to incentivise banks to channel funding into green infrastructure projects and assets. Bowman describes the concept of "legal readiness for climate finance" which entails the development of a coherent regulatory system to attract and mobilise finance at scale to address climate change and its impacts: regulation must create the "facilitative modalities" that enable an environment where climate finance can thrive, and regulation must be a coherent part of the wider climate finance policies.[143] Arguably, therefore, if signatory countries to the Paris Agreement seek to make finance flows consistent with lowering GHG emissions and climate-resilient development, their regulatory approaches to green finance should reflect that goal. In the EU, Regulation (EU) 2019/876[144] amending the Capital Requirements Regulation ('CCR')[145] introduced limited preferential treatment of loan exposures to corporates specifically set up to fund public infrastructure where the assets being financed contribute to certain environmental and sustainability objectives (including climate change mitigation

141 See e.g. Insurance Information Institute, 'Green Insurance' <https://www.iii.org/article/green-insurance#:~:text=For%20homeowners%20who%20generate%20their%20own%20geothermal%2C%20solar,the%20outage%20is%20caused%20by%20a%20covered%20peril%29> accessed on 1 June 2023.

142 See e.g. Munich Re, 'Photovoltaic Warranty Insurance' <https://www.munichre.com/en/solutions/for-industry-clients/pv-warranty-insurance-backing-your-solar-investment.html> accessed on 1 June 2023.

143 Megan Bowman, 'Turning Promises into Action: "Legal Readiness for Climate Finance' and Implementing the Paris Agreement' (2022) 16 CCLR 41.

144 Regulation (EU) 2019/876 of the European Parliament and of the Council of 20 May 2019 amending Regulation (EU) No 575/2013 as regards the leverage ratio, the net stable funding ratio, requirements for own funds and eligible liabilities, counterparty credit risk, market risk, exposures to central counterparties, exposures to collective investment undertakings, large exposures, reporting and disclosure requirements, and Regulation (EU) No 648/2012.

145 Regulation (EU) No 575/2013 of the European Parliament and of the Council of 26 June 2013 on prudential requirements for credit institutions and investment firms and amending Regulation (EU) No 648/2012.

and adaptation) and satisfy various other tests.[146] EBA is mandated to assess whether exposures related to assets or activities associated substantially with environmental and/ or social objectives require a bespoke (banking) prudential treatment and must submit a report on its findings by mid-2025.[147] In a 2022 Discussion Paper, EBA expressed the preliminary view that there was not yet strong and granular enough evidence to show the connection between lower credit risk and 'green projects.'[148] EBA noted that any preferential capital treatment must be anchored in a risk-based assessment and recommended that further empirical evidence on risk differentials should be collected prior to proposing any amendments.[149]

Should the solvency framework for insurers reward 'insuring green' with preferential solvency capital treatment? It could be argued that such a preferential treatment would stimulate climate-related impact underwriting by insurers and thereby enable policyholders to adapt to climate risk and to transition to a net-zero economy. The Bank of England and the PRA see no convincing case for capital requirements being used for addressing the causes of climate change – either by introducing 'carbon penalising factors' and/or 'green supporting factors' for exposures to assets or counterparties that are respectively more or less carbon-intensive.[150] Their initial conclusion relies on research in the banking sector that shows that the use of capital requirements as a tool to stimulate outward impact – i.e. affect investment decisions directly – is not likely to be effective.[151] Moreover, there is a concern that giving preferential capital treatment based on environmental considerations is not necessarily reflective of the financial risk associated with the project or asset and could thus lead to a deterioration of the safety and soundness of the firm.[152]

While it is accepted by most commentators that 'green' does not necessarily mean lower risk,[153] and that capital treatment must be based on a risk-based assessment, the Bank of England's and EBA's consideration has been focused on the banking sector. In contrast to banks, for insurers, in their capacity as risk carriers and underwriters, 'insuring green' does not represent a credit risk but an underwriting liability and underwriting risk. 'Insuring green' means that the insurer incurs a liability to pay valid claims under the relevant insurances. An insurer is required to hold technical provisions to cover all of their expected future insurance or reinsurance contractual liabilities.[154] Liabilities must be valued at the amount for which they could be transferred or settled between knowledgeable willing parties in an arm's length transaction.[155] Thus, the valuation of a liability is based on its hypothetical market value; there is no discretion to discount the liability just for being 'green.' Whether a knowledgeable willing party would put a lower value on a

---

146 CCR art 501a.

147 Ibid art 501c.

148 European Banking Authority, 'The Role of Environmental Risks in the Prudential Framework' Discussion Paper EBA/DP/2022/02 (2 May 2022) [96].

149 Ibid [101].

150 BoE Climate and Capital Frameworks Report [35]; PRA Role of Capital Requirements Report Pt B.

151 PRA Role of Capital Requirements Report Pt B.

152 Ibid Pt B.

153 See e.g. Sini Matikainen, 'Green Doesn't Mean Risk-Free: Why We Should Be Cautious about a Green Supporting Factor in the EU,' Grantham Research Institute on Climate Change and the Environment blog (December 2017) <https://www.lse.ac.uk/granthaminstitute/news/eu-green-supporting-factor-bank-risk/> accessed on 1 June 2023.

154 PRA SII, Technical Provisions, 2.1.

155 PRA SII, Valuation, 2.1(2).

'green' liability depends on whether they would consider that the relevant insurance cover in respect of a green project or asset represents a lower risk of losses and claims and then a comparable insurance cover in respect of a standard (non-green) project or asset.

Similarly, for the SCR[156] to be reduced, it would be necessary to show that the underwriting risk has been reduced on account of the insured subject-matter being 'green.' This will depend on data and modelling that can evidence that correlation in actuarial terms. There is no in-built risk weighing for 'green' underwriting risks. As noted above, insuring green projects and green assets can in fact be more risky because there is no historical data, they rely on unproven technology, they are located in vulnerable geographies, and/or they use materials that are more susceptible to physical damage. However, there may be green projects that have a specific climate change adaptation objective which could in fact reduce the risk of loss once implemented. Climate-related adaptation measures may smooth the claim distribution by reducing the frequency or intensity of climate-related losses. As a result, the risk of mispricing insurance policies (and not having enough premium income to cover claims) due to climate change might be reduced.[157] There is currently no specific mechanism in the SCR standard formula that would recognise a risk reduction effect. EIOPA are currently assessing the potential for a dedicated prudential treatment of climate-related adaptation measures in non-life insurance, and have conducted a quantitative study on the influence of climate-related adaptation measures on premium risk.[158] The analysis of this data will feed into EIOPA's analysis of and proposals for the prudential treatment of climate-related adaptation measures.

EIOPA is planning to deepen its analysis of the capital treatment of natural catastrophe liabilities, investments associated with environmental and/or social objectives, or associated substantially with harm to such objectives, and climate-resilient insurance products.[159] It may be that EIOPA is more willing to entertain favourable prudential treatment for 'insuring green' (1) as a quid pro quo for the proposed inclusion of climate change in the Solvency II standard formula when calculating natural catastrophe underwriting risk,[160] and (2) because of parallel developments in the EU banking sector.

A credible case for preferential solvency capital treatment for green insurance could be made if it could be shown that there is a risk reduction evidenced by empirical data and credible models, including data that knowledgeable willing parties in an arm's length transaction would favourably price green liabilities, and data and modelling that show an underwriting risk reduction. More consideration should also be given to whether there are potential correlations between insuring green and a reduction in market risk, credit risk, or operational risk. As the climate-related disclosure regimes and labelling regimes take hold, there is going to be more publicly available data which could serve as base evidence for further studies on the link between prudential risk and outward impact which in turn could inform the regulatory course of action. This is an

156 See Chapter 4, Section 4.4.3.

157 EIOPA, 'Prudential Treatment of Sustainability Risks – Discussion Paper' EIOPA-BoS-22-527 (November 2022) [257].

158 Ibid ch 3.

159 EIOPA (n 95).

160 EIOPA, 'Methodology Paper on Potential Inclusion of Climate Change in the Nat Cat Standard Formula' EIOPA-BoS-21/253 29 June 2021; and see Chapter 4, Section 4.4.5.

area to watch over the next two years, with potentially diverging routes being taken by the EU and the Bank of England/PRA.

6.4 Not insuring brown

The definition of climate-related impact underwriting adopted in this chapter envisages that insurers consider underwriting strategies that contribute to climate change mitigation. Those strategies could include a withdrawal from insuring fossil fuel assets and activities. Climate activists argue that, without insurance, almost no new coal mines could be developed, and most existing projects would have to be phased out.[161] This view holds that by deriving profits from harmful activities, insurers are complicit in such harms. Insurers have been branded 'climate criminals' by Extinction Rebellion protestors for continuing to do so. The UN General Secretary, Antonio Guterres, has said that insurers who insure polluting carbon assets must be held to account:

> We need to hold fossil fuel companies and their enablers to account. That includes the banks, private equity, asset managers and other financial institutions that continue to invest and underwrite carbon pollution.[162]

6.4.1 Impact of not insuring brown

What are insurers required, and expected, to do? There are currently no UK laws that require insurance companies to cease underwriting fossil fuel assets and activities. As and when the proposed CSDDD comes into force and is implemented into law, large EU insurers will be under a due diligence duty to identify, bring to an end, prevent, mitigate, and account for negative environmental impacts in the company's own operations, their subsidiaries, and business relationships in their value chains.[163] Providing insurance to fossil fuel businesses could be regarded as creating a negative environmental impact that falls within the scope of that duty.[164] The US Senate Committee on the Budget recently wrote to seven US insurers stating that continuing to underwrite and invest in fossil fuel projects was inconsistent with the goals of the Paris Agreement, harmful to policyholders who are increasingly facing protection gaps, and potentially creating systemic risk for the economy. The Committee has launched an investigation into Berkshire Hathaway to account for their plans to phase out underwriting and investing in fossil fuel projects.[165]

Yet, as long as the underlying carbon-related activities remain legal, there are no legitimate grounds on which insurance for such assets and activities should be prohibited. Such a blanket prohibition could even be counter-productive since the absence of insurance could leave protection gaps and could lead to tort victims and employees of fossil fuel companies being left uncompensated for injury and damage to their property.

161 See e.g. Peter Bosshard, 'Making Coal Uninsurable' <https://www.fairplanet.org/op-ed/making-coal-uninsurable/> accessed on 1 June 2023.

162 UN General Secretary Antonio Guterres, 'Our World Is in Big Trouble,' opening speech to the UN General Assembly on 22 September 2022 (SG/SM/21466) <https://press.un.org/en/2022/sgsm21466.doc.htm> accessed on 1 June 2023.

163 Proposal for CSDDD art 6–8 and see Chapter 4, Section 4.4.5.

164 Ibid art 3(e) – the definition of 'business relationship' makes reference to providing insurance.

165 Letter from the United States Senate Committee on the Budget (n 94); and see Chapter 4, Section 4.4.6.

Without insurance, coal and other fossil fuel projects cannot be financed, built, or operated on affordable terms, or at all. Conversely, the availability of insurance enables the financing and operation of fossil fuel projects. A 2022 report by Harvard Business School observed that coal power plants owned by firms exposed to bank loan issuance restriction policies are more likely to close down.[166] Without the necessary project and operational insurance cover that protects the lenders' interests, banks are less likely to provide loans to fossil fuel projects. It could therefore be said that 'not insuring brown' disables the owners and operators of fossil fuel projects from carrying on. While this looks like a development to be welcomed, there is increased transition risk to other industries that are still reliant on coal and fossil fuels, which in turn could impact other businesses along supply chains in key industries, and ultimately consumers. The energy crisis triggered by Russia's invasion of Ukraine and subsequent sanctions have shown the precarity of energy supplies and the cascading effect on supply chains and the energy security of countries that cannot fall back on their own or alternative energy resources. To stabilise its energy supplies, the UK government agreed to open a new coal mine in Cumbria, a decision that has raised global attention and undermined the UK's climate leadership role.[167]

For now, there are still enough insurers that continue to underwrite coal projects.[168] The coal industry has contemplated setting up self-insurance schemes.[169] However, insurers that do not have a policy on reducing their underwriting activities in the fossil fuel sector may find that some of their own investors may challenge that approach by withdrawing their investment,[170] or challenging the board by resolutions asking the company to stop insuring fossil fuel assets.[171]

On the other hand, insurers that do pursue 'not insuring brown' strategies lose out on premiums from the fossil fuel industry. They could also be at risk of falling foul of anti-ESG legislation in some US states.[172] This is relevant to insurers who consider ceasing to 'insure brown' since anti-ESG legislation may prohibit the relevant US state from doing business with financial institutions that 'boycott' or 'discriminate against' companies in certain (e.g. fossil fuel) industries.[173] Some of these measures authorise state regulators to blacklist financial entities that engage in boycotts of fossil fuel companies for divest-

166 Daniel Green and Boris Vallee, 'Can Finance Save the World? Measurement and Effects of Coal Divestment Policies by Banks' (8 April 2022) <https://papers.ssrn.com/sol3/papers.cfm?abstract_id=4090974> accessed on 1 June 2023.

167 Climate Change Committee, 'Better Transparency Is No Substitute for Real Delivery' (Press Release 23 June 2023) <https://www.theccc.org.uk/2023/06/28/better-transparency-is-no-substitute-for-real-delivery/> accessed 24 June 2023.

168 Insure Our Future, '2022 Scorecard on Insurance, Fossil Fuels and the Climate Emergency' 15 <https://insure-our-future.com/wp-content/uploads/2023/02/SP-IOF-2022-Scorecard-v0.8-online-3.pdf> accessed on 1 June 2023; and also see Letter from the United States Senate Committee on the Budget (n 94).

169 Nick Toscano and Mike Foley, 'Coal Miners in Talks to Self-Insure as Climate Pressure Heats up' (*Sydney Morning Herald*, 13 August 2021).

170 See e.g. Alastair Marsh, 'Legal & General Divests from U.S. Insurer AIG over Climate Policies' (*Bloomberg*, 15 June 2021). AIG has since introduced a policy that they will no longer provide underwriting services and investments for the construction of any new coal-fired power plants, thermal coal mines, or oil sands – see *Reuters*, 'Insurer AIG Steps back from Coal, Arctic Energy Underwriting' (1 March 2022).

171 In the US, shareholders started to engage insurers and filed resolutions asking Chubb, The Hartford, and Travelers to stop insuring new fossil fuel projects. Though ultimately unsuccessful, these resolutions received stronger support than expected, with all three passing the threshold required for resolutions to be filed again next year. (Reported in: Insure Our Future (n 168) 14.)

172 See Chapter 4, Section 4.4.6.

173 *Reuters*, 'The Challenge of Investing in the Face of State Anti-ESG Legislation' (24 August 2022).

ment purposes.[174] In addition, some of these measures compel companies entering into contracts with state entities to attest, as a condition of doing business with public entities, that they do not and will not engage in boycotts against fossil fuel companies during the life of the contract.[175]

At this stage, many jurisdictions only require, or even just encourage, insurance companies to disclose their GHG emissions, their exposure to carbon-related industries, and their strategies for managing climate-related risks.[176] The public disclosure approach does hold insurance companies accountable to investors, policyholders, and the general public to the extent that it can create transparency and comparability as to how their operations, products, and value chains are aligned to the Paris Agreement goals, national and international net-zero targets, or pursue other environmental objectives. Insurance companies that wish to publicise their green credentials need to be mindful that continuing to underwrite fossil fuel assets and activities is likely to be inconsistent with an environmental sustainability profile at entity level and could lead to allegations of green-washing. The EU Taxonomy technical screening criteria expressly exclude from economic activities that are 'environmentally sustainable' any activities that 'include insurance of the extraction, storage, transport or manufacture of fossil fuels or insurance of vehicles, property or other assets dedicated to such purposes.'[177] In contrast, the FCA has indicated that it would exclude 'negative screening' (such as an investment approach that excludes investments in fossil fuel projects) from the scope of its proposed sustainable investment labelling regime on the grounds that such an approach 'would not plausibly contribute to positive sustainable outcomes.'[178]

Disclosure requirements also force insurance companies to identify and assess the risks associated with insuring carbon-intense assets and develop strategies for managing those risks.[179] Thus, disclosure requirements can create the basis for expectations held by stakeholders and the general public that insurance companies develop plans for reducing, and ultimately withdrawing from, underwriting activities in relation to fossil fuel assets. However, one significant impediment to raising expectations through disclosures is that the TCFD Recommendations and the ISSB Insurance Disclosures do not require emissions associated with an insurer's underwriting portfolio to be reported[180] – therefore, unless voluntarily disclosed, this information is not readily available. A recent initiative by the Partnership for Carbon Accounting Financials is introducing reporting and

174 Ibid.

175 Leah Malone, Emily Holland, and Carolyn Houston, Simpson Thacher & Bartlett LLP, 'ESG Battlegrounds: How the States Are Shaping the Regulatory Landscape in the U.S.,' Harvard Law School Forum on Corporate Governance (11 March 2023) <https://corpgov.law.harvard.edu/2023/03/11/esg-battlegrounds-how-the-states-are-shaping-the-regulatory-landscape-in-the-u-s/> accessed on 1 June 2023.

176 See Chapter 5.

177 Commission Delegated Regulation (EU) 2021/2139 of 4 June 2021 supplementing Regulation (EU) 2020/852 of the European Parliament and of the Council by establishing the technical screening criteria for determining the conditions under which an economic activity qualifies as contributing substantially to climate change mitigation or climate change adaptation and for determining whether that economic activity causes no significant harm to any of the other environmental objectives, Annex II, s 10.

178 FCA Sustainability Disclosure Proposals [2.3], [4.24], and [4.25]. For further discussion, also see Chapter 8, Section 8.1.2.

179 See: PRA SS3/19 [3.18] and see Chapter 5, Introduction.

180 TCFD, 'Implementing the Recommendations of the Task Force on Climate-Related Financial Disclosures' (October 2021) sec D <https://assets.bbhub.io/company/sites/60/2021/07/2021-TCFD-Implementing_Guidance.pdf> accessed on 1 June 2023, and see Chapter 5.1.

accounting standards for 'insurance-associated emissions,'[181] which have already been adopted as an in-scope emission in the NZIA Target-Setting Protocol (although reporting remains voluntary).[182] For meaningful disclosures on an insurer's GHG emissions, 'insurance-associated emissions' should be included in Scope 3 emissions.[183]

6.4.2 Prudential treatment of insuring brown

An insurer is required to hold technical provisions to cover all of their expected future insurance or reinsurance contractual liabilities.[184] Liabilities must be valued at the amount for which they could be transferred or settled between knowledgeable willing parties in an arm's length transaction.[185] Whether a knowledgeable willing party would put a higher value on a 'brown' liability depends on whether they would consider that the relevant insurance cover in respect of a fossil fuel project or asset represents a greater risk of losses and claims on account of the insured subject-matter (e.g. higher vandalism risk or business interruption risk from climate activists). An insurer's SCR[186] could increase since insuring coal, gas, and oil could introduce additional market risk (from fluctuations in the value of the insured asset) and operational risk (legal and reputational risk from supporting fossil fuels) which should be reflected in the market risk and operational risk components in the SCR Standard Formula[187] (or an approved internal model).

As noted above, the Bank of England and the PRA do not see a convincing case for capital requirements being used for addressing the causes of climate change by introducing 'carbon penalising factors' for exposures to assets or counterparties that are carbon-intensive.[188] While the EU has introduced limited preferential treatment for specific green investments,[189] neither EBA nor EIOPA are considering a penalising prudential treatment for investing in or insuring fossil fuel assets and activities.[190]

6.4.3 Individual voluntary commitments

In the absence of mandatory targets, some insurance companies have set themselves targets for reducing their 'insurance-associated emissions' and transitioning their underwriting portfolios to net-zero. These targets could include any or a combination of the following:

- prohibition or restriction on coverage for new coal/gas/oil projects of new clients;
- prohibition or restriction on coverage for new coal/gas/oil projects of existing clients;

181 Partnership for Carbon Accounting Financials (n 110); and see Chapter 3, Section 3.3.2.
182 NZIA (n 18), and see Section 6.4.4.
183 See Chapter 3, Section 3.3.2.
184 PRA SII, Technical Provisions, 2.1.
185 PRA SII, Valuation, 2.1(2).
186 See Chapter 4, Section 4.4.3.
187 PRA SII, Solvency Capital Requirement – Standard Formula, 3.1.
188 BoE Climate and Capital Frameworks Report [36] and Finding 5; PRA Role of Capital Requirements Report Pt B.
189 Regulation (EU) 2019/876 (n 144).
190 European Banking Authority (n 147); EIOPA (n 156).

- phasing out of coverage for existing coal/gas/oil projects;
- prohibition, restrictions, or phasing out of coverage for coal/gas/oil companies;
- engagement with coal/gas/oil companies to ask them to commit to phasing out targets;
- development of products that support climate solutions (insuring green[191] and greening insurance[192]).

Public commitments can be phrased as 'targets,' 'goals,' 'commitments,' or 'pledges.' Any mid- and long-term commitments that do not set out plans for how these targets are to be achieved and do not describe KPIs to assess progress against those targets year-on-year are relatively meaningless as it would be difficult to hold current company directors and managers to account for vague targets in the future when those decision-makers will no longer be in office. A UK insurer providing IBIPs must produce a TCFD entity report – to be made available in a prominent place on the entity's main website[193] – in which it is 'encouraged' to assess and disclose the extent to which it has considered the UK's commitment to transition to a net-zero economy[194] in developing and disclosing its transition plan.[195] The NFSIS (the non-financial and sustainability information statement in the Strategic Report)[196] that all UK-authorised insurance companies must produce as part of their annual corporate filings does not require reporting on net-zero commitments, but must contain:

- a description of the targets used by the company to manage climate-related risks and to realise climate-related opportunities and of performance against those targets;
- a description of the key performance indicators used to assess progress against targets used to manage climate-related risks and realise climate-related opportunities and of the calculations on which those key performance indicators are based.[197]

In contrast, as and when EU insurers must start reporting in line with the CSRD,[198] they will be required to disclose information on net-zero targets and implementing plans, such as

- the plans of the undertaking, including implementing actions, to ensure that its business model and strategy are compatible with the transition to a sustainable economy and with the limiting of global warming to 1.5°C in line with the Paris Agreement and the European Green Deal;

191 See Section 6.3.

192 See Chapter 7.

193 ESG Sourcebook 2.1.1 and 2.1.3, and see Chapter 5.3.5.

194 Climate Change Act 2008 (2050 Target Amendment) Order 2019.

195 ESG Sourcebook 2.2.2G.

196 Companies Act 2006 ss 414CA (A1) and (1); and see Chapter 5.3.7.

197 Ibid s 414CB(2A) and see Chapter 5.3.7.

198 CSRD (Directive (EU) 2022/2464 of the European Parliament and of the Council of 14 December 2022 amending Regulation (EU) No 537/2014, Directive 2004/109/EC, Directive 2006/43/EC and Directive 2013/34/EU, as regards corporate sustainability reporting), and see Chapter 5, Section 5.4.3.

- a description of the time-bound targets related to sustainability matters set by the undertaking, including, where appropriate, absolute GHG emission reduction targets at least for 2030 and 2050, a description of the progress the undertaking has made towards achieving those targets, and a statement of whether the undertaking's targets related to environmental factors are based on conclusive scientific evidence;
- a description of the principal actual or potential adverse impacts connected with the undertaking's own operations and with its value chain, including its products and services, its business relationships, and its supply chain, actions taken to identify and monitor those impacts, and other adverse impacts which the undertaking is required to identify pursuant to other EU requirements on undertakings to conduct a due diligence process.[199]

Without specific mandatory disclosure on net-zero targets, pathways, and KPIs, there is little transparency as to what measures insurance companies have taken and are taking.

Rather than relying on publicly available information, the Insure Our Future Campaign, constituted of a number of NGOs including Greenpeace, publishes annual 'Scorecards' of leading insurers and reinsurers, assessing their policies on insuring and investing in coal, oil, and gas based on questionnaires sent to insurers.[200] Reporting on the 2022 round of Scorecards,[201] they noted that most large insurers have now backed away from insuring new coal projects. Forty-one insurers have withdrawn or reduced cover for coal, representing 39.3% of the market for primary insurance and 62.1% of the market for reinsurance. However, only 14 of the 41 insurers have committed to phasing out cover for existing coal operations, and many still underwrite the operations of coal companies that are not aligned with a pathway to limit global warming to 1.5°C. The top scorers on coal withdrawal are Allianz, Axa, and Axis Capital with a 9/10 score each. Withdrawal from oil and gas underwriting is much more limited: only 13 insurers have put in place restrictions on underwriting oil and gas but they tended to be limited in scope or contained exceptions. The top scorers on oil and gas withdrawal – but still with low scores – are Aviva with a 4/10 score, and Munich Re with a score of 3/10. The relative lack of enthusiasm for withdrawing from oil and gas underwriting is grounded in continuing business appetite for the premium income from the oil and gas sector,[202] as well concerns about anti-ESG legislation in the US,[203] and competition issues that can arise where insurers are acting or seen to be acting together.[204]

As a result of restricted underwriting capacity following a growing number of insurers withdrawing from the coal market, coal companies are already facing premium rate

199 CSRD, art 1, point 4.

200 Their methodology consists of sending questionnaires with questions on fossil fuel underwriting and divestment policies to insurers. The responses are then analysed and scored with a points system (scale 1–10) by Reclaim Finance (a research and campaign organisation) in collaboration with Insure Our Future. Each participating insurer receives its score for publication.

201 Insure Our Future (n 168) 11–19.

202 Ibid 19.

203 See Chapter 4, Section 4.4.6.

204 See Section 6.4.5.

increases of up to 40%.[205] In contrast, but unsurprisingly, Insure Our Future says that the very limited withdrawal from oil and gas underwriting has had little impact.[206] Individual voluntary commitments on 'not insuring brown' have had limited impact in practice because of patchy adoption and insufficient transparency as regards implementation. Game theory suggests that individual insurers may engage in strategic behaviours that seek to anticipate other insurers' actions and potential rewards from taking the same or a different course of action.[207] A key concept in game theory is the'Nash Equilibrium' where no player has an incentive to change their strategy given the strategies chosen by the other players.[208] Thus, unless a critical mass of insurers withdraw from fossil fuel underwriting, an individual insurer may not be incentivised to do so. The 'Stag Hunt Theory' has it that players involved must all work together in order to successfully hunt the stag and reap the rewards.[209] These game theory concepts raise the question of whether collaborative approaches to net-zero commitments can be more effective.

6.4.4 The Net Zero Insurance Alliance (NZIA)

Even before the NZIA was founded, leading insurance think-tank Geneva Association recognised that:

> [r]obust intra- and inter-sectoral collaboration is the only way to expedite the development and convergence of good practices, meaningful baseline requirements for decision-useful climate change risk assessments and disclosures that would allow for cross-company comparisons.[210]

The UN-convened NZIA was set up in July 2021 and is a member-led group of insurers and reinsurers that supports its members as they work towards decarbonising their underwriting portfolios by individually setting science-based intermediate targets and reporting on their progress annually. Its signatory members make the following 'Commitment':

> Transitioning all operational and attributable greenhouse gas (GHG) emissions from its insurance and reinsurance underwriting portfolios to net-zero emissions by 2050 consistent with a maximum temperature rise of 1.5°C above pre-industrial levels by 2100 in order to contribute to the implementation of the COP21 Paris Agreement.[211]

The NZIA suggests a number of approaches to how the Commitment to the 2050 net-zero target can be achieved, including

205 Willis Towers Watson, 'Managing the Transition: Mining Risk Review 2020' (2020) <https://willistowerswatson.turtl.co/story/mining-risk-review-2020-ungated/page/1> accessed on 1 June 2023.

206 Insure Our Future (n 168) 19.

207 For an application of game theory in the context of ESG and insurance, see David Cabral, 'Mastering ESG Transition Risks: Utilising Game Theory's Strategic Power' <https://www.linkedin.com/pulse/mastering-esg-transition-risks-utilising-game-theorys-david-v-cabral/> accessed on 1 June 2023.

208 Nigar Hashimzade, Gareth Myles, and John Black, *Oxford Dictionary of Economics* (5th ed, OUP 2017) entry for 'Nash Equilibrium.'

209 Douglas G. Baird, Robert H. Gertner, and Randal C. Picker, *Game Theory and the Law* (Harvard University Press 1998) 35–36.

210 The Geneva Association (n 52) 9.

211 NZIA, 'Statement of Commitment by Signatory Companies' <https://www.unepfi.org/psi/wp-content/uploads/2021/07/NZIA-Commitment.pdf> accessed on 1 June 2023.

- setting independently underwriting criteria and guidelines for activities, particularly the most GHG-intensive and GHG-emitting activities within an insurer's underwriting portfolios;
- engaging with clients and potential clients, particularly those with the most GHG-intensive and GHG-emitting activities, on their decarbonisation strategies and net-zero transition pathways;
- developing and offering insurance and reinsurance products, solutions, and arrangements for low-emission and zero-emission technologies and nature-based solutions that are key to the net-zero transition;
- improving claims management in an environmentally sustainable manner to promote a net-zero economy;
- integrating independently determined, company-specific net-zero and decarbonisation-related risk criteria into risk management frameworks (e.g. ESG/sustainability risk management frameworks) applicable to underwriting portfolios;
- advocating for and engaging in governmental policies for a science-based and socially just transition of economic sectors to net-zero.[212]

However, it is left to each NZIA member's individual discretion, using any of the re/insurance-relevant approaches listed above and taking into consideration the latest available scientific knowledge and associated social impacts, how they transition their underwriting portfolios to net-zero GHG emissions by 2050. The NZIA has published a 'Target-Setting Protocol' which sets out the recommended approach to target setting and reporting.[213] The Protocol suggests five target types, split into three differentiated target categories:

1. a GHG emissions reduction target, which can be:
   a. an overarching emissions reduction target for re/insurers' own insurance-associated emissions reduction targets of between 34 and 60% by 2030; or
   b. a sectoral decarbonisation target that seeks to converge an individual re/insurance portfolio's physical carbon intensity to a given decarbonisation pathway at the sector level;
2. an engagement target, which can be:
   a. a portfolio coverage approach (PCA) that seeks to increase the share of clients in a re/insurer's portfolio who have set their own science-based targets; or
   b. a focused engagement target type under which a re/insurer engages with selected clients regarding their transition plans and decarbonisation strategies;
3. a target for re/insuring the transition, that is by offering re/insurance solutions to activities that avoid, reduce, or remove emissions, or that help cope with the negative impacts of climate change (= insuring green[214] and greening insurance[215]).

212 Ibid.
213 NZIA (n 18) and (n 211).
214 See Section 6.3.
215 See Chapter 7.

The Protocol envisages that each NZIA member selects at least one of the five target types by 31 July 2023, and at least one target type in each of the three target categories by 31 July 2024, and reports on its progress on an annual basis.

The NZIA Commitment and Protocol have been criticised by climate activists, insurers, and US lawmakers. Climate activists have pointed out that the Commitment is vague and discretionary so that it does not commit NZIA members to 'not insuring brown' – i.e. withdrawing from underwriting coal, oil, and gas projects.[216] Moreover, the Protocol does not require NZIA members to set a GHG emission reduction target; instead they can use engagement strategies to influence their clients' decarbonisation strategies, or they can develop green insurance products or insure green assets. Even the two types of GHG emission reduction targets do not explicitly recommend that insurers start excluding coal, gas, and oil from their underwriting portfolios. The inclusion of 'insurance-associated emissions'[217] in GHG emission reporting and accounting is voluntary under the Protocol.[218] As a result, insurers could decide to disregard any GHG emissions produced by the companies which they insure, along their value chains and by their products.[219] For example, insurers would only have to measure the GHG emissions produced from the operation of an oil well they insure, but not those produced when the oil is burned.[220] In addition, various key lines relevant to the coal, oil, and gas sector and carbon-intense industries have been designated to be out of the scope of the Protocol, such as construction all risks insurance, erection all risks insurance, and trade credit and surety insurance.[221]

While the NZIA initially attracted a membership of the world's leading insurance companies, since its publication of the Protocol it has imploded with high-profile departures including Munich Re, Zurich, Hannover Re, Swiss Re, Allianz, Scor, Sompo, Axa, Mapfe, and Lloyd's. While some of these insurers have withdrawn quietly, others have been outspoken, stating that the reason for leaving the NZIA has been the increased risk of anti-trust (competition) issues arising from a collective approach to decarbonisation.[222] This risk has become acute since a group of 23 US Attorney Generals wrote a letter to insurers who are members of the NZIA raising concerns about the legality of their commitments to collaborate with other insurers in order to 'advance an activist climate agenda.'[223] Similar concerns that the co-ordinated industry actions could give rise to competition issues have

216 Insure Our Future (n 168) 20.

217 Partnership for Carbon Accounting Financials (n 110); and see Chapter 3, Section 3.3.2.

218 NZIA (n 18).

219 Peter Boshardt, Finance Programme Director at the Sunrise Project, quoted in: Kenza Bryan and Ian Smith, 'Activists Criticise Insurance Industry's First Attempt to Measure Carbon Emissions' (*Financial Times*, 17 January 2023).

220 Insure Our Future (n 168) 20.

221 NZIA (n 18).

222 Munich Re, 'Munich Re Discontinues NZIA Membership' (Press Release 31 March 2023) <https://www.munichre.com/en/company/media-relations/media-information-and-corporate-news/media-information/2023/media-release-2023-03-31.html> accessed on 1 June 2023.

223 Letter from the State Attorney Generals of Utah, Louisiana, Alabama, Alaska, Arkansas, Georgia, Idaho, Indiana, Iowa, Kansas, Kentucky, Mississippi, Missouri, Montana, New Hampshire, Ohio, Oklahoma, South Carolina, South Dakota, Texas, Virginia, West Virginia, and Wyoming to NZIA insurers, dated 16 May 2023 <https://attorneygeneral.utah.gov/wp-content/uploads/2023/05/2023-05-15-NZIA-Letter.pdf accessed 23 May 2023> accessed on 1 June 2023; and see below in this section.

been expressed across the financial services industry which has led to (threatened) departures by members of the GFANZ.[224]

6.4.5 Competition issues

What are the anti-trust or competition issues that arise from collaborative initiatives to tackle climate change, including by seeking to decarbonise underwriting portfolios?

In the **UK, the Competition Act 1998** prohibits agreements between undertakings, decisions by associations of undertakings, or concerted practices which may affect trade within the United Kingdom, and have as their object or effect the prevention, restriction, or distortion of competition within the United Kingdom (the 'Chapter 1 prohibition').[225] Prima facie, an alliance of insurers to work towards decarbonising their underwriting portfolios by ceasing to provide insurance cover to coal, oil, and gas projects could prevent and restrict competition since the number of insurers that still offer such cover is diminishing, and as a result insurance capacity becomes restricted and premium prices rise.[226]

The Competition Act 1998 recognises situations where agreements that restrict competition are beneficial and for this reason provides for exemptions, either by way of block exemption order for particular categories of agreements,[227] or for specific agreements that meet the following conditions (whereby the burden of proof is on the undertaking or association of undertakings wishing to rely on the exemption):

1. the agreement contributes to (i) improving production or distribution, or (ii) promoting technical or economic progress, while allowing consumers a fair share of the resulting benefit;
2. the agreement does not (i) impose on the undertakings concerned restrictions which are not indispensable to the attainment of those objectives; or (ii) afford the undertakings concerned the possibility of eliminating competition in respect of a substantial part of the products in question.[228]

The UK Competition and Markets Authority ('CMA') has issued draft guidance for consultation on the treatment of agreements between competitors or potential competitors in relation to environmental sustainability ('environmental sustainability agreements') and agreements which combat or mitigate climate change ('climate change agreements').[229] Environmental sustainability agreements are agreements or concerted practices between competitors and potential competitors which are aimed at preventing, reducing, or mitigating the adverse impact that economic activities have on environmental sustainability or assessing the impact of their activities on environmental sustainability.[230] 'Climate change

224 Mike Scott, 'ESG Watch: Is It Curtains for Mark Carney's Green Alliance, or Just Teething Problems?' (*Reuters*, 6 April 2023).

225 Competition Act 1998 s 2.

226 See Sections 6.4.1 and 6.4.3.

227 Competition Act 1998 s 6.

228 Ibid s 9.

229 Competition & Markets Authority, 'Draft Guidance on the Application of the Chapter I Prohibition in the Competition Act 1998 to Environmental Sustainability Agreements – Draft Guidance' CMA177 (28 February 2023).

230 Ibid [2.1].

agreements' – a sub-set of environmental sustainability agreements – cover agreements which contribute towards the UK's binding climate change targets under domestic or international law, such agreements relating to the reduction of GHG emissions.[231] One example of a climate change agreement provided by the CMA is an agreement not to provide insurance to fossil fuel producers.[232]

Recognising that tackling climate change is a major public concern and that industry collaboration is likely to be necessary to meet the UK's binding international commitments and legislative obligations to achieve a net-zero economy, the CMA is keen to ensure that businesses are not unnecessarily or erroneously deterred from lawfully collaborating in this space due to fears about competition law compliance.[233] The CMA's draft guidance states that agreements to phase out particular non-environmentally sustainable processes are unlikely to have an appreciable negative impact on competition where it does not involve an appreciable increase in price for consumers or an appreciable reduction in product choice.[234] Phasing out insurance cover for coal has already increased premiums and reduced the availability of cover,[235] and if more insurers were to exclude gas and oil from their underwriting portfolios this could also have a similar effect of premium increases and restricted choice and capacity. Although the premium price increases affect the fossil fuel companies in the first instance, the cost could be passed on to consumers through increased energy prices.

However, it is suggested that the NZIA Commitment and Protocol do not constitute an agreement between its members: the 'commitments' are not binding among the NZIA inter se and each NZIA member has individual discretion on whether and how it transitions its underwriting portfolio to net-zero emissions by 2050. The Protocol gives non-binding recommendations for targets and methodologies for unilateral and voluntary actions by the NZIA members. The CMA's draft guidance states that:

> setting of non-binding targets or ambitions for the whole industry with regard to environmental sustainability objectives are unlikely to have an appreciable negative effect on competition. Such an industry wide ambition might concern the reduction of carbon dioxide emissions, but where such targets are not binding on the participating businesses (which remain free to determine their own contribution and the way in which the targets are realised) ...[236]
>
> Similarly, the establishment of a common framework for target setting, including which emissions and business activities are within the scope of the common framework and the duration and timing of the targets, would be unlikely to infringe the Chapter I prohibition. Such a common framework could allow for the unilateral setting, disclosure and reporting of the participants' targets, as well as how – in broad terms – the participants intend to meet their targets and the participants' progress towards meeting those targets.[237]

These paragraphs from the draft guidance indicate that the CMA considers industry frameworks and alliances such as the NZIA to be outside the Chapter 1 prohibition since there is no binding agreement between its members.

231 Ibid [2.4].
232 Ibid.
233 Ibid [1.5].
234 Ibid [3.13].
235 See Section 6.4.1.
236 Competition and Markets Authority (n 228) [3.15].
237 Ibid [3.18].

Prior to the publication of the CMA's draft guidance, it was reported in the press that the NZIA had received legal advice that an explicit commitment to withdrawing from underwriting coal projects could infringe competition rules, and that this is indeed the reason for the vague and discretionary approach of the NZIA Commitment and Protocol.[238]

If the view was taken that there is an agreement, it would need to be assessed whether such agreement has the 'object' or 'effect' to restrict competition. The object of the NZIA is to support its members as they work towards decarbonising their underwriting portfolios 'to the extent permissible by applicable laws and regulation,'[239] not to restrict competition. In contrast, as has been noted above, the NZIA Commitment and Protocol could have a negative effect on competition because of premium increases and restricted capacity ultimately leading to increased energy prices for consumers. The CMA's draft guidance states that even if an agreement has such an effect, it may still benefit from exemption from the Chapter 1 prohibition if the parties to the agreement can demonstrate that it meets the following conditions:

1. the agreement must contribute to certain **benefits**, namely improving production or distribution or contributing to promoting technical or economic progress (Condition 1);
2. the agreement and any restrictions of competition within the agreement must be **indispensable** to the achievement of those benefits (Condition 2);
3. **consumers must receive a fair share** of the benefits (Condition 3); and
4. the agreement must **not eliminate competition** in respect of a substantial part of the products concerned (Condition 4).[240]

The benefit (Condition 1) of an agreement to withdraw from underwriting coal projects is that less coal is mined and burned resulting in a reduction of GHG emissions.[241] Arguably, such an agreement is indispensable (Condition 2) in the sense that there is no less restrictive, but equally effective, alternative given the limitations of individual commitments that have been highlighted above. The NZIA Protocol engagement target and the target for re/insuring the transition are complementary alternatives but arguably less effective in reducing GHG emissions. In assessing whether consumers would receive a fair share of the benefits (Condition 3), the CMA's draft guidance sets out a more permissive approach for climate change agreements by taking into account the benefits to all UK consumers, instead of only the consumers in the relevant market, when balancing the harm to competition against the benefits that result from the agreement.[242] The benefit of the NZIA to all UK consumers would be the reduction in GHG emissions. The NZIA parties would need to be able to demonstrate that the benefits are substantial enough to offset any harm caused (i.e. the restriction of competition), e.g. by showing the monetary value of the reduction in GHG emissions compared to the costs of the restrictive practice.[243] This could be problematic if e.g. the price increases exceed the monetary value of the GHG emissions from

238 Alastair Marsh, 'Net-Zero Insurers' Climate-Friendly Plans to Exit Coal Impeded by Antitrust Laws' (*Insurance Journal*, 19 January 2023).

239 NZIA (n 210).

240 Competition & Markets Authority (n 229) [5.1] and [5.2].

241 Ibid [5.4].

242 Ibid Sec 6.

243 Ibid [5.23] and [5.25].

coal projects that are attributable to insurers.[244] However, 'fair share' does not mean a full share, so on the wording of Condition 3 full compensation is not necessary. Finally, there must be some remaining competition in the relevant market (Condition 4) – this could be problematic if the market is defined narrowly (the market for insuring coal projects) but should not be an issue if the market is defined more widely (e.g. the energy insurance market).

In summary, the NZIA Commitment and Protocol are drafted with a view to taking them outside the Chapter 1 prohibition. However, if they do fall within its scope, it is by no means clear whether the NZIA members could avail themselves of the exemption. The CMA has said that it would give informal guidance before an environmental sustainability initiative is set up and there is a proposed protection from fines where advance guidance has been obtained.[245] As the NZIA is already set up this protection from fines is not applicable. Prior to the publication of the CMA's draft guidance, the NZIA asked the CMA to consider a formal blanket exemption for climate change agreements provided that they pursue a legitimate objective, that they do not go beyond what is necessary, and that any consequential restrictive competitive effects are inherent in the pursuit of that (legitimate) objective.[246] Given that this suggestion has not been incorporated into the draft guidance, it is unlikely that the CMA is willing to consider a blanket exemption or block exemption order for climate change agreements.

Similar concerns arise under **Art.101 of the Treaty on the Functioning of the European Union** ('TFEU'),[247] and its EU member state counterparts. EU guidance has also rejected a blanket approach for sustainability co-operation agreements (including those that pursue a reduction in GHG emissions).[248] Instead, the EU has issued guidance in which the exemption conditions have been customised for sustainability agreements.[249] The term 'sustainability agreement' used in the EU draft guidance refers to any type of horizontal co-operation agreement that genuinely pursues one or more sustainability objectives, irrespective of the form of co-operation.[250] Sustainability agreements that have the 'object' of restricting competition are prohibited.[251] If a sustainability agreement has a competition restricting effect, it will fall outside Art.101 if it meets a number of soft safe harbour conditions, including that the agreement 'should not lead to a significant increase in price or to a significant reduction in the choice of products available on the market.'[252] The NZIA Commitment and Protocol are unlikely to meet the soft safe harbour conditions

244 The GHG emission attributable to an insurer would be the 'insurance-associated emissions' – see Partnership for Carbon Accounting Financials (n 110); and see Chapter 3, Section 3.3.2.

245 Competition & Markets Authority (n 229) Sec 7.

246 UNEP FI NZIA, 'Net-Zero Insurance Alliance: Response to CMA Call for Inputs on Environmental Sustainability and the Competition and Consumer Regimes' (Letter from the NZIA to the CMA dated 18 November 2021) <https://assets.publishing.service.gov.uk/government/uploads/system/uploads/attachment_data/file/1061316/Net-Zero_Insurers_Alliance.pdf> accessed on 1 June 2023.

247 Art.101 TFEU is similarly structured to the UK Chapter 1 prohibition and the exemption conditions in s.9 of the Competition Act 1998. Insurance Block Exemption Regulation 267/2010 which applied to (1) joint compilations, tables, and studies, and (2) co-(re)insurance pools, expired on 31 March 2017.

248 European Commission, 'Draft Guidelines on the Applicability of Art 101 of the Treaty on the Functioning of the EU to Horizontal Co-Operation Agreements' 1 March 2022 C(2022) 1159 [548].

249 Ibid [548].

250 Ibid [547].

251 Ibid [570].

252 Ibid [572].

since, as noted above, they could cause premium increases and restricted capacity leading to energy price increases for consumers.

The EU guidance indicates that sustainability agreements that set standards, guidelines, or frameworks among the subscribing parties in relation to possibly a wide range of sustainability metrics such as the environmental impacts (including GHG emissions) can raise competition concerns through price co-ordination, foreclosure of alternative standards, and/or the exclusion of or discrimination against certain competitors.[253] However, such sustainability agreements could still be exempted from the prohibition if certain conditions (similar to Conditions 1–4 above) are met. The EU guidance has clarified the indispensability condition[254] (similar to Condition 2 above) that such agreements can be necessary to overcome the 'first mover disadvantage' – i.e. the lost premium income of those insurers who are the first to cease underwriting coal projects, and to concentrate the parties' efforts to achieve scale.[255] The EU guidance has also expanded the understanding of the consumer benefit condition[256] (similar to Condition 3 above) for exemption: to assess whether consumers have been allowed a fair share of the benefit of the agreement, collective consumer benefits, that 'occur irrespective of the consumers' individual appreciation of the product,' can be taken into account.[257] The concept of 'collective consumer benefits' is similar to the UK CMA's notion of 'benefits to all UK consumers' but the test remains an economic test that compares the benefit with the costs of the restriction in monetary terms. The EU guidance also indicates that the residual competition condition[258] (similar to Condition 4 above) is satisfied even if the agreement covers an entire industry, as long as the parties to the agreement continue 'to compete vigorously' on at least one important aspect of competition, such as price or the availability of product variants.[259] In the example of an agreement to withdraw from underwriting coal projects, satisfaction of the residual competition condition could depend on whether insurance for other energy sources and projects would be considered as product variants in relation to which competition is maintained.

In contrast to the CMA's draft guidance which locates the 'establishment of a common framework for target setting' outside the Chapter 1 prohibition, the EU draft guidance indicates that such frameworks would be prima facie caught by the prohibition and would need to rely on exemption. Writing extra-judicially, Judge Simon Holmes said that competition law need not stand in the way of urgent action and co-operation by the private sector to fight climate change.[260] He argues that EU competition law can be part of the solution if legal and economic advisers, and competition regulators, take a more robust approach to interpreting competition law in line with EU constitutional treaty principles (such as 'sustainable development' and the 'protection of the environment')[261] and do not shy away from giving clear guidance on what does and does not infringe the competition provisions.

253 Ibid [569].
254 TFEU art 101(3).
255 European Commission, Draft Guidelines (n 248) [584]–[586].
256 TFEU art 101(3).
257 European Commission, Draft Guidelines (n 248) [601].
258 TFEU art 101(3).
259 European Commission, Draft Guidelines (n 248) [611].
260 S. Holmes, 'Climate Change, Sustainability, and Competition Law' (2020) 8 *JAE*, 354.
261 Treaty on European Union art 3.

In the **US, s.1 of the Sherman Antitrust Act, s.5 of the Federal Trade Commission Act** and equivalent state laws prohibit horizontal agreements and combinations that unreasonably restrain trade. In a highly politicised atmosphere, there have been a series of official and semi-official communications from State Attorney Generals, US senators, and members of Congress that have suggested that co-ordinated ESG measures, and in particular joint action initiatives on net-zero commitments, could violate the Sherman Antitrust Act and/or other anti-trust instruments.[262] An investigative demand issued by 19 State Attorney Generals in October 2022 to the six largest US banks seeking documents relating to their membership in the Net-Zero Banking Alliance on the grounds of anti-trust concerns ultimately led to GFANZ dropping its requirement that members must phase out fossil fuel support.[263] Co-ordinated ESG and net-zero initiatives are not per se illegal, but it has become a contentious point whether agreements between industry participants not to invest in, or not to insure, fossil fuels that have an anticompetitive effect of raising prices for consumers could violate anti-trust laws.[264] In March 2023, a group of 21 US State Attorney Generals wrote a letter to various asset managers to express concerns that participation in ESG initiatives could constitute collusive behaviour in violation of the anti-trust laws.[265] They noted that participants in Climate Action 100+,[266] an investor-led initiative to ensure the world's largest corporate GHG emitters take action on climate change:

> **exert coordinated pressure** to seek 'commitments from boards and senior management' to 'reduce greenhouse gas emissions across the value chain' consistent with the Paris Agreement and achieving net-zero by 2050.' Members of Climate Action 100+ commit to forcing portfolio companies to 'align political lobbying with the Paris Agreement,' without allowance for whether such an alignment would be in the financial best interests of the company. **Potential unlawful coordination** appears throughout Climate Action 100+'s documents. **Despite boilerplate disclaimers**, initiative members clearly speak for the group as they commit to communicate 'a central message' to companies: '[I]naction by companies following engagement may result in investors taking further action.' None of this is financially defensible.[267] *(emphasis added; footnotes omitted)*

Notably, the Attorney Generals said that Climate Action 100+'s documentation pointed to potential unlawful co-ordination, 'despite boilerplate disclaimers,' indicating that the disclaimer language on the website of Climate Action 100+ (which stresses that Climate Action 100+ does not require or seek collective decision-making and that signatories are independent fiduciaries responsible for their own investment and voting decisions and must always act completely independently to set their own strategies)[268] is not effective to qualify or override any co-ordinated action. On 16 May 2023, a group of 23 US Attorney Generals also wrote a letter to insurers who are members of the NZIA raising concerns

262 For an overview, see: Debevoise and Plimpton, 'ESG and Antitrust: More Focus but No Consensus – Recent Developments, Pitfalls and Mitigating Risk' (3 March 2023) <https://www.debevoise.com/insights/publications/2023/03/esg-and-antitrust-more-focus-but-no-consensus> accessed on 1 June 2023.

263 *Reuters*, 'Carney Defends Dropping U.N. Climate Initiative over Antitrust Concerns' (3 November 2022).

264 Debevoise and Plimpton (n 262).

265 Letter from the State Attorney Generals to asset managers (n 55).

266 Climate Action 100+ <https://www.climateaction100.org/> accessed on 1 June 2023.

267 Letter from the State Attorney Generals to asset managers (n 55) 3.

268 Climate Action 100+, 'Disclaimer' <https://www.climateaction100.org/> accessed on 1 June 2023.

about the legality of their commitments to collaborate with other insurers and asset owners in order to 'advance an activist climate agenda.'[269] The letter stated:

> The push to force insurance companies and their clients to rapidly reduce their emissions has led not only to increased insurance costs, but also to high gas prices and higher costs for products and services across the board, resulting in record-breaking inflation and financial hardships for the residents of our states ...
>
> While this protocol insists that it is 'nonbinding' and that you are 'free' to meet the protocol's requirements 'independently and unilaterally,' it goes on to instruct that NZIA members must follow its directions on a 'comply-or-explain basis.'[270]

The Attorney Generals' letter suggests that all directions in the NZIA Target Setting Protocol are mandatory on a 'comply or explain basis' because they require 'concrete action.' In fact, very few processes are expressed to be mandatory ('shall') and those few tend to relate to procedural steps and disclosures, rather than substantive targets. The implication of the letter is that the relevant Attorney Generals see any disclaimer language and language that stresses non-binding and individual commitments as inconsistent with any kind of climate-agenda collaboration that is more than 'aspirational.'[271] The Attorney Generals indicate that they see potential anti-trust law violations as a result of a collective agreement to illegally (1) boycott fossil fuel businesses, and (2) restrict production of fossil fuels, 'ultimately rais[ing] prices for customers.' If the clear language on voluntariness, individual and discretionary decision-making is brushed aside as 'boilerplate' and ineffective to show that there is no collective agreement, there is clearly a significant legal risk that NZIA members who are active in the US will be subject to further anti-trust investigations, litigation, and potentially liability to pay fines.

Although the allegations of anti-trust violations are reportedly considered weak by commentators and insurers alike,[272] the political pressure, litigation, and reputational issues in connection with such allegations are risks that need to be managed and which must be balanced against the directors' duty to act in the best interest of the company as a whole taking into account other stakeholders' interests and factors such as the impact on the environment.[273] Even for those insurers who do not do business in the US, in the absence of clear competition guidance, it may be advisable to collaborate loosely and transparently on frameworks aimed at decarbonising the insurance industry, and on the basis of individual and non-binding commitments. Yet, such loose collaborations may lead to a lack of ambition and increased legal risk aversity even in respect of individual insurer actions, ultimately slowing down the pathway to net-zero. In response to the Attorney Generals' letter to NZIA members UNEP stated that it:

269 Letter from the State Attorney Generals to NZIA insurers (n 223).

270 Ibid 1–3.

271 Ibid 4.

272 See Ian Smith and Kenza Bryan, 'Lloyd's and Five Big Insurers Quit Sector's Net-Zero Initiative' (*Financial Times*, 26 May 2023) and 'Insurance Industry Turmoil over Climate Alliance Exodus' (*Financial Times*, 30 May 2023).

273 Martin Lipton, 'Navigating the Current ESG Landscape: Recommendations for the Board and Management' (23 May 2023) Harvard Law School Forum on Corporate Governance <https://corpgov.law.harvard.edu/2023/05/23/navigating-the-current-esg-landscape-recommendations-for-the-board-and-management/> accessed on 1 June 2023.

> reaffirms its conviction ever since it initiated, convened, and launched the NZIA—that in order to successfully tackle the climate emergency, there is a fundamental and urgent need for collaboration, not just individual action.[274]

As many insurers operate in multiple jurisdictions, clarity and convergence on the competition law treatment of industry collaborations to tackle climate change would be a key step towards insurers taking an enabling role in the net-zero transition. Such convergence is, however, unlikely to be forthcoming in the near future given the politicisation of ESG issues in the US. While the EU is pushing the Green Deal, it has been reported that European governments have privately expressed concerns that insurers in the NZIA could cause the cost of energy to rise if they collectively stopped underwriting fossil fuels.[275] It may not be coincidental that two of the first NZIA quitters were Munich Re and Hannover Re, both headquartered in Germany where coal plants have been brought back temporarily to deal with the energy security crisis caused by the Russia war in Ukraine.[276] For now, given these unresolved and unharmonised competition/anti-trust issues, combined with the anti-ESG legislation in some US states, it is not surprising that insurers want to err on the side of caution. The politicised legal environment is a significant hurdle to impact underwriting strategies that screen out insurance for fossil fuel projects. Insurers must consider macro stewardship approaches – working together with governments, regulators, their fossil fuel policyholders, and other stakeholders – to find workable and equitable solutions to these issues.

274 Public statement by the United Nations Environment Programme on the UN-Convened Net-Zero Insurance Alliance (24 May 2023) <https://www.unepfi.org/industries/insurance/public-statement-by-the-united-nations-environment-programme-on-the-un-convened-net-zero-insurance-alliance/> accessed on 1 June 2023.

275 See Ian Smith and Kenza Bryan, 'Lloyd's and Five Big Insurers Quit Sector's Net-Zero Initiative' (*Financial Times*, 26 May 2023).

276 Valentina Romei and Martin Arnold, 'Germany Turns to Coal for a Third of Its Electricity' (*Financial Times*, 7 September 2022).

CHAPTER 7

Greening insurance[1]

This chapter contains the second part of climate-related impact underwriting. It is concerned with 'greening insurance' – insurance products and services that shift policyholders' behaviour and processes towards taking climate change mitigation and adaptation measures. The enabling conception pictures the insurance industry as supporting policyholders in their net-zero transition. Green insurance products can incentivise policyholders to reduce their GHG emissions and take climate change adaptation measures that make them more resilient to climate change effects that are already felt. Insurers can assume and deliver their enabling role through the pre-contractual and contractual relationship between an insurer and its policyholder. Green insurance products are not newly invented types of cover but introduce green features and objectives to established insurance products.

This chapter will analyse different stages and activities in the value chain of non-life insurance products – product development, marketing and sale, pre-contractual risk management, the pricing of the risk, contract terms, and claims – that could integrate features to incentivise policyholders to take climate change mitigation action (i.e. reduce GHG emissions) or climate change adaptation measures. The value chain model is introduced in Section 7.1. It is significant because the insurer's activities at different stages overlap and are interconnected through many cross-cutting legal and regulatory issues.[2] It will be argued that it is important to take a holistic strategic approach to climate-related impact underwriting where all stages and activities are considered together for how they can enable policyholders in their net-zero transition. Using a value chain methodology highlights that the underwriting decision-making process and the claims process are important points of contact for engagement with (prospective) policyholders. The value chain methodology also flags the role of insurance intermediaries in arranging and advising on green insurance products.

Section 7.2 considers the product design, target market, and fair value requirements that do, and should, apply to green insurance products. Section 7.3 examines the regulatory requirements in the UK and the EU that seek to ensure that green insurance products are suitable for the policyholder, and that prospective policyholders are provided with

1 The discussion in this chapter builds upon materials in Franziska Arnold-Dwyer, 'A Legal Framework for Net-Zero Aligned Insurance Products' (2023) 29(2) *Conn Ins LJ*, 1 and text passages have been reproduced with permission of the *Conn Ins LJ*.

2 For a similar approach, see the discussion in: Lukas Stricker, Carlo Pugnetti, Joël Wagner, and Angela Zeier Röschmann, 'Green Insurance: A Roadmap for Executive Management' (2022) 15 *Journal of Risk and Financial Management*, 221.

DOI: 10.4324/b23081-7

sufficient and accurate information about the green insurance product so that they can make an informed decision about whether to buy. Section 7.4 argues that existing information exchanges between the insurer (or an insurance intermediary) and a prospective policyholder at the pre-contractual stage is a point of engagement that could be utilised to provide prospective policyholders with information on climate risk, climate risk assessments, and advice on climate change mitigation and adaptation measures. Section 7.5 considers risk-reflective pricing as a tool to signal risk and to incentivise policyholders to take climate change mitigation and adaptation measures. Section 7.6 discusses different strategies, and their implications, for contractual terms that oblige or incentivise policyholders to take climate action. Green claims and green reinstatement – and legal issues in connection with them – will be considered in Section 7.7. Section 7.8 explains how the unfair contract terms legislation may impact green terms and green claims.

This chapter will also make some suggestions on how the existing legal and regulatory frameworks can be harnessed, or could be improved, to support the development of green insurance products while creating safe and fair market conditions, ensuring the protection of policyholders, and maintaining broad access to insurance.

7.1 The insurance value chain

The concept of a 'value chain' was first introduced by Porter in his book *Competitive Advantage: Creating and Sustaining Superior Performance*.[3] A value chain is a series of consecutive steps that go into the creation of a product, from its initial design to its end use by customers and beyond.[4] The value chain concept takes a full life-cycle perspective and identifies each step in the process at which value is added, including the sourcing, design, manufacturing, and marketing and after-sale service stages of its products, by internal and external stakeholders.[5]

The insurance value chain includes insurance product development, marketing, distribution and sales, risk management and underwriting (in its narrower technical sense), claims management, and renewals. On the asset side, the value chain extends to asset and investment management. The main actors involved are insurers and their policyholders, but other actors include insurance intermediaries and other insurance professionals who may be involved in the market, distribution, and sale processes and claims management. These steps and activities throughout the life cycle of an insurance policy give rise to engagement opportunities between those stakeholders which can be used to incentivise policyholders to take climate change mitigation or adaptation action.

The legal relationship between an individual policyholder and an insurer is based on a contract of insurance,[6] but this relationship pre-dates the point of entering into the contract. As will be explained in Sections 7.2 and 7.3, the FCA Handbook sets out detailed requirements about the process for developing insurance products and information that

3 Michael E. Porter, *Competitive Advantage: Creating and Sustaining Superior Performance* (Free Press 2004), originally published in 1985.

4 Investopedia, 'Value Chain: Definition, Model, Analysis, and Example' <https://www.investopedia.com/terms/v/valuechain.asp> accessed on 1 June 2023.

5 Cambridge Institute for Sustainability Leadership, 'What Is a Value Chain? Definitions and Characteristics' <https://www.cisl.cam.ac.uk/education/graduate-study/pgcerts/value-chain-defs> accessed on 1 June 2023.

6 See Chapter 3, Section 3.1.

an insurer must provide to the prospective policyholder about itself, its services, and the insurance product in question before a contract is concluded. The insurer will ask a prospective consumer policyholder questions about the risk to be insured in order to determine whether to take the risk and, if so, on what terms. Non-consumer policyholders must give a fair presentation of the risk to be insured to the insurer before entering into the contract.

At the pre-contractual stage, insurers can influence prospective policyholders' behaviour by offering different levels of covers and different levels of premium depending on the existing risk management measures and risk attitude of the prospective policyholder. Risk-based premiums can signal to policyholders what risks they are exposed to, and what adaptation and resilience measures they could take to reduce the risk of loss.

Once the insurer has accepted the risk, it wants to ensure the risk – as presented at the pre-contractual stage – does not increase and that the insured does not adopt a reckless attitude towards the risk in the knowledge that it has insurance cover. Typically, the contract of insurance will therefore contain 'risk mitigation terms' which, if complied with by the policyholder, would tend to reduce the risk of loss of a particular kind, at a particular location, or at a particular time.[7] The contract of insurance will also contain other terms that impose continuing obligations, describe or limit the risk, and deal with the administration of the contract.

If there has been an insured event, an insurer can also exert influence at the claims stage. An insurer's obligation in relation to claims is generally limited to paying the insured's loss proximately caused by an insured peril.[8] Therefore, in economic terms, an insurer's interest in supporting the policyholder at the claims stage does not usually extend beyond reducing its own liability. However, there is scope for insurers to take on a wider role at the claims stage by influencing policyholders to adapt to and mitigate potential future losses.

Standard consumer and business property policies have a twelvemonth policy period. At the end of the policy period, a policyholder may renew with the same insurer, may choose to insure with another insurer, or may choose not to insure. As will be explained in Section 7.5.4, the short-term nature of the contract gives an insurer a rather limited timeframe for engagement and makes it difficult for both parties to make upfront investments from which they may not benefit unless the contract is renewed.

7.2 Product development

The question of how green insurance products can be designed, or how existing insurance products can be adapted to become green insurance products, has received little public, regulatory, and scholarly attention so far outside the context of IBIPs.[9] EIOPA notes that the European insurance market appears to be 'at an early stage regarding non-life insurance products implementing climate-related adaptation measures, particularly in

---

7 Insurance Act 2015 s 11(1).

8 Marine Insurance Act 1906 s 55(1) (marine insurance contracts). This provision is treated by the courts as also stating the law applicable to non-marine insurance (*FCA v Arch Insurance (UK) Ltd and Ors* [2021] UKSC 1, [163]).

9 IBIPs where the premium is invested in environmentally sustainable investments are already available. See Chapter 5 for disclosure requirements applicable to IBIPs. It is suggested that they are an example of 'impact investment,' rather than 'impact unwriting.'

the context of the retail insurance business.'[10] Caldecott argues that for a financial product to make a difference in the real economy's transition to environmental sustainability, the product must make a clear and measurable difference by either enabling the customer to adopt sustainable practices, reducing the cost of capital for green activities, or increasing the cost of capital for polluting activities.[11] This reflects the concept of 'additionality' discussed in Chapter 8, Section 8.1.2. If the FCA's proposed sustainable investment labels were to be applied, mutatis mutandis, to general insurance products, the most pertinent category for 'greening insurance' would be 'sustainable improver' products that promote the net-zero transition of policyholders and their assets over time.[12]

7.2.1 Product design and target market

UK-regulated insurers must comply with the product design requirements in the FCA Product Intervention and Product Governance Sourcebook ('PROD'). Primarily, this means that the insurer is required to have in place an internal product approval process to ensure that the design of insurance products or the adaptation of existing insurance products (1) takes into account the objectives, interests, and characteristics of customers; (2) does not adversely affect customers; and (3) prevents or mitigates customer detriment.[13] Moreover, the product approval process must identify whether the product provides fair value to customers in the target market including whether it will continue to do so for a reasonably foreseeable period (including following renewal).[14] In addition, insurers must test their insurance products appropriately, by assessing whether the insurance product over its lifetime meets the identified needs, objectives, and characteristics of the target market, before bringing that product to the market.[15]

Thus, if the target markets for a green insurance product are consumers and small businesses, insurers need to consider their respective needs, objectives, interests, and characteristics as they relate to the type of insurance (e.g. home and content, property, motor, business insurance). It may be necessary to granularise the target market further to focus on shared characteristics in relation to the risk profile, experience and expertise, expectations, and needs of specific market segments.

The PROD rules and guidance do not require insurers to consider whether the insurance product as a whole has beneficial or detrimental impacts on the environment. There is no explicit requirement that an insurer must take into account the target market's environmental objectives, if any, at the product design stage. If insurers are not prompted to consider environmental design features and the target market's appetite for insurance products with an environmental objective, they are less likely to explore the design of, and demand for, green insurance products, and consequently are less likely to bring green

10 EIOPA, 'Impact Underwriting – Report on the Implementation of Climate-Related Adaptation Measures in Non-Life Underwriting Practices' EIOPA-BoS-22-593 (February 2023) ('EIOPA Adaptation and Insurance Report') [4].

11 Ben Caldecott, 'Achieving Alignment in Finance' (October 2020) <https://www.unepfi.org/wordpress/wp-content/uploads/2020/08/200915_J932-CKIC-UNEP-ThoughtLeadershipSeries-DrBenCaldecott-11.pdf> accessed on 1 June 2023.

12 FCA Sustainability Disclosure Proposals [3.2]; and see Chapter 5, Section 5.3.5.2.

13 PROD 4.2.8.

14 Ibid 4.2.14AR.

15 Ibid 4.2.22.

insurance products to market. Lack of customer access to, and awareness of, green insurance products will hamper the development of market appetite.

This vicious circle of lack of supply and demand is aggravated further by the absence of any labelling system for green insurance products. As noted in Chapter 5, the FCA's proposed sustainable investment label regime and the SFDR's product disclosure regime only apply to an in-scope life insurer that provides IBIPs. Green insurance products other than IBIPs cannot use sustainable investment labels to signal the product's environmental features to potential customers in an accessible way. Without a transparent and comparable system of definitions and classification, there is yet little customer trust and confidence in green financial products.[16] This lack of confidence affects market appetite. Insurers are not permitted to bring insurance products to the market if the results of the product testing show that the products do not meet the identified needs, objectives, and characteristics of the target market.[17]

The PROD rules could be amended to integrate into the product design and approval process environmental sustainability factors and consideration of the target market's environmental objectives. By way of comparison, EU insurers and insurance intermediaries who create, develop, and/or design IBIPs are already required to consider sustainability factors[18] in (1) the product approval process, and (2) the other product governance and oversight arrangements, for each such product that is intended to be distributed to customers seeking insurance products with a sustainability-related profile.[19] If the PROD rules were to be amended to contain similar rules applicable to all insurance products, there would also be a need for definitions or labels that indicate which environmental factors and attributes qualify. The UK does not yet have a 'Green Taxonomy' to classify (environmentally) sustainable economic activities.[20]

7.2.2 Fair value

Determining whether a green insurance product would provide 'fair value' entails looking at the relationship between the overall price to the customer, the quality of the product and services provided, and the overall costs to the insurer.[21] Where the difference between the risk price to the insurer and the total price paid by the customer bears no reasonable relationship to the actual costs incurred by the insurer (or any other person involved in the distribution arrangements), the quality of any benefits, or the quality of any other services provided, there is a presumption that the product does not provide 'fair value.'[22] Thus, the contractual design of the green insurance product must be considered as a whole: what benefit does the policyholder receive, what are the premium costs to the policyholders, and

16 FCA Sustainability Disclosure Proposals ch 1.

17 PROD 4.2.22R and 4.2.24R.

18 'Sustainability factors' are environmental, social, and employee matters, respect for human rights, anti-corruption, and anti-bribery matters (see Commission Delegated Regulation (EU) 2021/1257 of 21 April 2021 amending Delegated Regulations (EU) 2017/2358 and (EU) 2017/2359 as regards the integration of sustainability factors, risks, and preferences into the product oversight and governance requirements for insurance undertakings and insurance distributors and into the rules on conduct of business and investment advice for insurance-based investment products, art 2).

19 Commission Delegated Regulation (EU) 2021/1257 (n 18), art 1.

20 See Chapter 5, Section 5.3.6.

21 PROD 4.2.14ER.

22 Ibid 4.2.14M.

what are the overall costs to the insurer of carrying out its obligations, under the terms of the contract of insurance in question?

The 'fair value' assessment is inextricably linked to the policy premium rates and its terms.[23] If insurance products are too heavily reliant on exclusions[24] that erode the cover they may not provide fair value. Similarly, if the level of GHG emissions of the policyholder is made a pricing factor, but the increase in premium for higher GHG emissions cannot be linked to the risk insured, there is a risk that to do so would be contrary to the 'fair value' principle. An insurance product that contains a term that imposes obligations on the policyholder to implement certain climate change mitigation or adaptation measures for which the policyholder will incur significant costs in addition to the premium is unlikely to provide fair value since the total costs to the policyholder are unlikely to bear a reasonable relationship to the benefits provided by the policy. Higher premium rates for green insurance products compared to the equivalent type of conventional insurance might still provide 'fair value' if the green insurance product cover provides additional benefits and services, such as green reinstatement and risk management and advice on climate change risks and reducing emissions.[25] However, 'fighting climate change' or 'reducing GHG emissions' are not in themselves (non-financial) factors relevant to the 'fair value' principle.

7.2.3 Modular design

Where the green insurance product design takes a modular approach to coverage – by including cover for additional risks for additional premium – the product design and product information should make this clear.[26] In addition, distribution channels and distributors must be appropriate for policyholders in the target market and be monitored by insurers accordingly.[27] However, as this chapter is concerned with contractual design, the governance of distribution is beyond its scope.

7.2.4 Compliance with the consumer duty

The product design requirements are underpinned by a new consumer duty which requires insurers to deliver good outcomes for consumers, including ensuring that consumers (1) receive fair prices and quality, (2) receive suitable products and good treatment, and (3) have access to products that meet their needs.[28] In relation to outcomes relating to products and fair value,[29] the FCA has acknowledged that there is an overlap with the existing rules and guidance in PROD.[30] Evidence of compliance by insurance manufacturers and insurance distributors with PROD 4 will demonstrate that the firm is not in contravention of the products and services outcome and the fair value outcome.[31] However, the consumer

23 'Pricing' is considered in Section 7.5, and 'Terms' are considered in Section 7.6.
24 See Section 7.6.1.
25 See Sections 7.7 and 7.3.
26 PROD 4.2.25(2)R.
27 Ibid 4.3.
28 See Section 7.4.5.
29 FCA Handbook, Principles of Business (PRIN) ('PRIN') 2A.3.
30 FCA, 'Final Non-Handbook Guidance for Firms on the Consumer Duty' FG22/5 (July 2022) [6.82].
31 Ibid [6.86] and [7.53].

duty is broader in that it also requires the delivery of good outcomes with respect to customer support for their product or service, and appropriate regard to the nature and scale of characteristics of vulnerability that exist in the target market.[32] This means that when insurers design green insurance products, they should also consider how they can enable retail customers to realise the benefits and ensure that they can act in their own interest,[33] including those with characteristics of vulnerability.

7.3 The marketing and sale of green insurance products

In the UK, the marketing and sale of non-IBIPs is governed by rules and guidelines in ICOBS, and for IBIPs in the FCA Conduct of Business Sourcebook ('COBS'). IBIPs and COBS will be considered in Chapter 8. The key marketing and sale requirements are that the insurance product must be suitable for the policyholder (product suitability), and that prospective policyholders are provided with sufficient and accurate information about the insurance product so that they can make an informed decision about whether to buy it (product disclosure). ICOBS does not apply to insurance of 'large risks.'[34] The marketing stage is crucial to the enabling role of insurers as it represents one of the 'moments for green choices'[35] where insurers can promote climate-related mitigation and adaptation measures to influence or incentivise their customers' decision-making.

7.3.1 Product suitability

An insurer must take reasonable steps to ensure that a customer (whether the customer is a consumer or business insured) only buys an insurance policy under which he is eligible to claim benefits.[36] For example, a motor policy providing cover for an electric vehicle would be unsuitable for an owner of a petrol fuel vehicle. If the insurance product is not sold by the insurer directly, the insurer must carefully select distribution channels that are appropriate to the target market,[37] and ensure that any insurance distributor (brokers and other insurance intermediaries) selected has the necessary knowledge, expertise, and competence to understand the features of an insurance product and the identified target market.[38] The insurance distributor must be provided with all the necessary product information and target market information.[39]

---

32 See Section 7.4.5.

33 FCA FG22/5 (n 30) [9.2].

34 A 'large risk' as defined in the FCA Handbook is a contract of insurance for the following: (1) railway rolling stock, aircraft, ships (sea, lake, river and canal vessels), goods in transit, aircraft liability, and liability of ships (sea, lake, river, and canal vessels); (2) credit and suretyship, where the policyholder is engaged professionally in an industrial or commercial activity or in one of the liberal professions, and the risks relate to such activity; or (3) land vehicles (other than railway rolling stock), fire and natural forces, other damage to property, motor vehicle liability, general liability, and miscellaneous financial loss, in so far as the policyholder exceeds the limits of at least two of the following three criteria: (i) balance sheet total: €6.2 million; (ii) net turnover: €12.8 million; (iii) average number of employees during the financial year: 250.

35 Carlo Pugnetti, Thomas Gebert, Miriam Hürster, Edward Huizenga, Markus Moor, Lukas Stricker, Herbert Winistörfer, and Angela Zeier Röschmann, 'Leading the Green Insurance Revolution' (Winterthur: ZHAW Zürcher Hochschule für Angewandte Wissenschaften, Working Paper no. 1, 2022) sec. 2.2.2.

36 ICOBS 5.1.1G.

37 PROD 4.2.27.

38 Ibid 4.2.28.

39 Ibid 4.2.29.

Prior to the conclusion of a contract of insurance, an insurance distributor (whether it is the insurer selling insurance directly to a customer or an insurance intermediary selling insurance on behalf of an insurance company) must obtain information from the customer in order to establish the customer's demands and needs for insurance.[40] The insurance distributor must then ensure that the contract of insurance offered is consistent with these demands and needs.[41] In an advised sale, the insurance distributor must take reasonable care to ensure the suitability of its advice for any customer who is entitled to rely upon its judgement.[42] The customer's demands and needs with respect to their environmental preferences may be obvious from the subject matter to be insured. For example, if the customer wants to buy motor insurance for an electric car, the insurance cover must be suitable for that risk. Conversely, if the asset to be insured is a coal plant, a business property insurance that excludes cover for carbon-intense activities would be unsuitable. In other instances, the prospective customer's demands and needs with respect to environmental objectives may not be apparent, and more likely, there may be a lack of awareness that green insurance products are available or what benefits they offer.

Yet, under the current ICOBS product suitability rules, there is no requirement to make a suitability assessment on the customer's demands and needs in relation to environmental objectives. If consideration of the customer's environmental objectives and preferences is not part of the sales process, there is a risk that such preferences are not explored and are ignored. EU insurance distributors are already required to ascertain, as part of the suitability assessment in relation to IBIPs, the (potential) customer's 'sustainability preferences' which includes asking questions about whether they wish to invest in an economic activity that contributes to an environmental objective as defined by the EU Taxonomy.[43]

The FCA consulted on whether there should be an equivalent UK requirement that advisers should consider sustainability matters in their investment advice and ensure their advice is suitable and reflects consumer sustainability-related needs and preferences,[44] but this suggestion has not been included in the finalised proposals.[45] The reason for this omission may be that there are not yet enough sustainable insurance products that would meet the sustainability-related needs and preferences of customers. Yet, ascertaining such preferences at the marketing stage – e.g. by asking the customer questions in person or by way of a questionnaire prior to any contract of insurance being proposed[46] – could assist in testing market appetite, collecting information on potential target markets for sustainable insurance products (which would be useful for new green insurance product design[47]), and providing an opportunity for insurance distributors to raise customer awareness of green insurance products and climate change mitigation and adaptation measures. EIOPA has noted that the current lack of awareness is limiting market demand for green insurance products.[48]

40 ICOBS 5.2.2R.
41 Ibid 5.2.2R.
42 Ibid 5.3.1R.
43 Commission Delegated Regulation (EU) 2021/1257 (n 18) art 2.
44 FCA Sustainability Disclosure Proposals [5.5] and Q18.
45 Ibid.
46 ICOBS 5.2.2.
47 See Section 7.2.1.
48 EIOPA Adaptation and Insurance Report [9].

The California Department of Insurance has developed a searchable 'Climate Smart Insurance Products' database to help the public access these products and encourage further innovation.[49] No information has been made available on which criteria have to be met to be included in the database, and the California Department of Insurance has disclaimed liability for the accuracy of any data.

7.3.2 Product disclosure

An insurer is responsible for producing, and an insurance distributor (an insurance intermediary selling insurance on behalf of an insurance company, or an insurer selling insurance directly to a customer) is responsible for providing a prospective customer, information about the insurance policy before the contract of insurance is concluded.[50] The customer must be given appropriate information about a policy in good time and in a comprehensible form, taking into account the complexity of the policy and the type of customer, so that the customer can (1) make an informed decision about the arrangements proposed,[51] and (2) compare the insurance product to the insurance products of other providers.

The FCA's proposals for specific sustainability product disclosures are limited to investment products (including IBIPs but excluding general insurance products).[52] ICOBS provides for different sets of general pre-contractual product information requirements for different types of insurance contracts,[53] but they do not contain specific product disclosure requirements to provide information on whether the policy pursues environmental objectives, or contains any other green or sustainability-related features. However, some of the more general information categories may be relevant to green insurance products:

- significant features and benefits[54] or a summary of the insurance cover, including its main terms:[55] this could be the basis for including information on premium rebates, green terms, or green reinstatement;[56]
- significant or unusual exclusions or limitations:[57] this disclosure requirement could be relevant to an exclusion that places specified carbon-intense activities outside the scope of the policy cover, or deductions or sub-limits of liability relating to losses caused by carbon-intense activities. Either kind of term might be considered 'unusual' if it is not one that is not normally found in comparable

49 California Department of Insurance, 'Climate Smart Insurance Products' <https://interactive.web.insurance.ca.gov/apex_extprd/f?p=142:1:341076167753> accessed on 1 June 2023.

50 ICOBS 6.-1; 6.1; 6.2.

51 Ibid 6.1.5R; 6.1.6.

52 See Chapter 5.

53 ICOBS 6.1.7 – a policy summary for commercial customers; and 6.1.10 – an insurance product information document (IPID) for consumers in relation to general insurance contracts; ICOBS 6.3.1R – a disclosure statement for pure protection contracts; FCA Handbook, Conduct of Business Standards (COBS) ('COBS') 13 Annex 1 and 14.2.1R – a disclosure statement for life insurance contracts.

54 ICOBS 6 Annex 2 and s 2 (pure protection contracts and/or commercial customers) and COBS 13 Annex 1 (life insurance).

55 ICOBS 6, Annex 3 and s 2 (consumer contracts other than pure protection contracts and life insurance).

56 See Sections 7.5, 7.6, and 7.7.

57 ICOBS 6, Annex 2, s 2 (pure protection contracts and/or commercial customers) and Annex 3 and s 2 (consumer contracts other than pure protection contracts and life insurance).

contracts, and also 'significant' if it would tend to affect the decision of customers generally to buy;

- obligations at the start and during the term of the contract:[58] this disclosure requirement might be relevant to terms imposing a contractual obligation on the policyholder to put in place a particular GHG emission-reducing measure or adaptation measure at the start of the contract (e.g. installation of better insulation or flood doors) or a continuing obligation to take such measures;
- obligations in the event claims are made:[59] this disclosure requirement could be relevant to green reinstatement terms. For example, if property damage claims are settled by way of sustainable repairs and reinstatement, this would require the property owner's co-operation and it is therefore important that the customer is provided with information on these matters before the contract is concluded;
- pricing information:[60] it has already been noted that as 'manufacturers of insurance products,' insurers must consider a product's pricing structure and the value it provides to customers. Where an insurance policy has modular coverage sections, they should be priced separately so that it is transparent to the customer what s/he is being charged for. If a premium discount is available, there should be information as to when and to whom it applies. However, factors that are part of the general risk assessment for pricing the premium do not need to be priced and disclosed separately.

The FCA's proposed general 'anti-green-washing' rule would require all UK-regulated financial firms (including insurers) to ensure that the naming and marketing of their financial products and services 'is clear, fair and not misleading, and consistent with the sustainability profile of the product or services.'[61] Any sustainability-related claims must be proportionate to the sustainability profile of the product or services, and not exaggerated. The FCA has stated that it will use this new rule to challenge firms that it considers to be potentially green-washing their products or services, and to take enforcement action, if necessary, in order to ensure better outcomes for consumers, in line with the new consumer duty.[62]

It is suggested that, in the absence of specific sustainability disclosure requirements for green insurance products that are not IBIPs, an inclusive and proportionate approach to providing information on environmental objectives and green product features would be in line with the spirit of the general requirement that, when insurance distributors communicate information to a customer, they must ensure that it is clear, fair, and not misleading.[63] Any claims that a green insurance product facilitates the reduction of GHG emissions or supports climate change adaptation must be evidence-based and proportionate. This approach may also be advisable to reduce the risk that green terms in consumer

58 ICOBS 6, Annex 3, s 2 (consumer contracts other than pure protection contracts and life insurance).

59 ICOBS 6, Annex 3, s 2 (consumer contracts other than pure protection contracts and life insurance).

60 ICOBS 6, Annex 2, s 2 (pure protection contracts and/or commercial customers) and ICOBS, 6, Annex 3, s 2 (consumer contracts other than pure protection contracts and life insurance).

61 FCA Sustainability Disclosure Proposals [6.9].

62 See Section 7.4.5.

63 ICOBS 2.2.2R.

insurance contracts are found to be unfair under the Consumer Rights Act 2015 ('CRA 2015'), ss.62 and 64.[64]

Yet, given that the sustainable investment label regime does not apply to general insurance products and that there is not yet a UK Green Taxonomy that defines the meaning of 'net-zero,' 'environmentally sustainable,' or 'green' in a consistent, transparent, and comparable way, insurers may be reluctant to label an insurance product in that way or provide information that suggests that the product pursues environmental objectives so as not to be accused of 'green-washing.' Could the proposed 'sustainable investment labels' give guidance on, or be adapted to, insurance products by analogy? The category description and criteria for each of the three 'sustainable investment labels' are centred around investments with a sustainable objective and are therefore not directly transferrable to insurance products. However, some of the 'Principles' that have to be met to qualify for the sustainable investment labels could be applied mutatis mutandis to insurance products; for example:

- Principle 1, Sustainability Objective: 'A sustainable investment product must have an explicit environmental and/or social sustainability objective'[65] – could be applied to insurance products that have an explicit environmental and/or social sustainability objective;
- Principle 3, Key Performance Indicators: 'A firm must specify credible, rigorous and evidence-based KPIs that measure a sustainable investment product's ongoing performance towards achieving its sustainability objective'[66] – could be applied to insurance products if the key performance indicators are adjusted appropriately;
- Principle 4, Resources and Governance: 'A firm must apply and maintain appropriate resources, governance and organisational arrangements commensurate with the delivery of the sustainable investment product's sustainability objective'[67] – could be applied to insurance products.

As insurers develop green insurance products, it would be useful to extend the FCA's sustainability labels regime to insurance products other than IBIPs. This would help customers to understand better, and develop trust in, insurance products with sustainable characteristics. The FCA's own research indicates that consumers were hypothetically more likely to choose a sustainable financial product with a sustainability grading or label, and if provided with product information on the sustainable goals of the product.[68] In line with the new 'consumer duty,'[69] insurers should take responsibility for establishing an environment in which consumers can act in their own interests and make informed choices. Good product design, a more probing product suitability assessment, and more informative product disclosure should all be considered together to ensure good outcomes

64 See Section 7.8.
65 FCA Sustainability Disclosure Proposals [4.55].
66 Ibid [4.57].
67 Ibid [4.61].
68 Ibid, Box 2.
69 See Section 7.4.5.

for consumers and to enable all customers to make informed choices suited to their own interests.

7.4 Pre-contractual risk management and information

The information flow at the pre-contractual stage is two-way: the prospective policyholder needs information about the product to make an informed decision on whether or not to buy it,[70] and the insurer needs information about the insured subject matter and the prospective policyholder in order to determine whether to insure the risk and, if so, on what terms, and how much premium it will charge. The prospective consumer policyholder is under a pre-contractual duty to take reasonable care not to make a misrepresentation to the insurer.[71] A prospective non-consumer policyholder owes the insurer a pre-contractual duty to give a fair presentation of all circumstances material to the risk.[72] A circumstance or representation is material if it would influence the judgement of a prudent insurer in determining whether to take the risk and, if so, on what terms.[73]

7.4.1 Climate risk as part of the policyholder's risk presentation

As mandatory climate-related disclosures become more prevalent for companies,[74] it is suggested that that kind of information may be material for the purposes of a company's risk presentation in relation to property, business interruption, directors and officers, and certain liability insurances.

Flood Re[75] – the UK public-private partnership flood reinsurers – commissioned WPI Economics to scope out the feasibility of a system of Flood Performance Certificates ('FPCs') and develop a framework for how they could be implemented effectively in the UK. WPI Economics recommended the introduction of FPCs on the grounds that they would help to provide relevant and actionable information that creates a roadmap for household flood resilience and improve the property sales process by providing more information at the outset of any transaction.[76] They also recommended that, while FPCs should be universal, only households at significant flood risk should be required to have a detailed physical survey to inform the risk rating and the recommendations.[77] FPCs have not been introduced yet,[78] but when they become applicable, insurers should be asking for copies as part of the risk presentation process for household property insurance.

---

70 See Section 7.2.

71 Consumer Insurance (Disclosure and Representations) Act 2012 s 2(2).

72 Insurance Act 2015 s 3(1) and s 3(4).

73 Ibid s 7(3).

74 See Chapter 5, Section 5.3.7 and Section 5.4.3.

75 See Chapter 9, Section 9.4.2.

76 WPI Economics, 'Flood Performance Certificates – Developing a Blueprint for How They Can Support Household Climate Resilience' (December 2020) 2 <https://www.floodre.co.uk/wp-content/uploads/Flood-Performance-Certificates.pdf> accessed on 1 June 2023.

77 Ibid 3: which households would require a survey would need to be determined by publicly available data, such as that of the Environment Agency (EA), the Scottish Environment Protection Agency (SEPA), and Natural Resources Wales.

78 Flood Re, 'Annual Report and Financial Statements 2022' 14 <https://www.floodre.co.uk/about-us/reports/> accessed on 1 June 2023.

GeoSmart, a UK company specialising in environmental reports and data, can produce instant flood risk reports for individual properties covering tidal, fluvial, pluvial, and groundwater flood risk with quantified event loss and damage calculations for the next 20 years at an affordable price point.[79] Such a report would enable informed decision-making on appropriate flood resilience measures and allow property insurers to price more accurately the risk they are assuming. With government endorsement, flood risk reports could be expected to become part of the conveyancing or rental process for residential property in the same way as energy performance certificates are already used.[80] Commercial property developers and their lenders are already using professional flood risk assessments. Where such assessments and reports do exist, they should be part of the pre-contractual risk presentation to their property insurers.

7.4.2 Risk assessment as part of the underwriting process

How can an insurer influence policyholder behaviour at the pre-contractual stage? Based on the pre-contractual information provided by the prospective policyholder, an insurer can integrate environmental issues in the underwriting decision-making process[81] by offering different levels of cover, applying or disapplying exclusions, and setting different levels of premium, deductibles, and limits, depending on the existing risk management measures and risk attitude of the prospective policyholder. This may cause the prospective policyholder to make positive risk adjustments at that stage in order to secure more comprehensive cover or a lower premium.

For example, in Germany, a number of insurers are reportedly requiring property-level flood risk reduction measures without which policyholders at high risk of flooding will be denied cover.[82] This type of requirement is relatively rare as it would likely be difficult to impose in a competitive market, and it could also lead to protection gaps for those unable to take such measures (e.g. because they are too costly).[83]

For larger businesses, some brokers and insurers have already started to use pre-contractual ESG risk assessments that seek to identify the ESG issues faced by prospective policyholders that are material to the insurance cover to be provided. For example, leading insurance broker Marsh offers an ESG risk assessment on the basis of which the prospective policyholder is awarded an ESG rating which then informs the scope of cover for directors' and officers' insurance and in particular eligibility for add-on cover for investigation costs related to climate-related financial disclosures.[84] The ESG risk assessment and rating might prompt the policyholder to choose pathways for mitigating ESG risks and to set targets for improving its ESG rating. FM Global offer 'Climate Risk Reports' that

79 GeoSmart, 'FloodSmart Analytics' <https://geosmartinfo.co.uk/risk-management-for-financial-services/floodsmart-analytics/> accessed on 1 June 2023.

80 HM Government, 'Buying or Selling Your Home – Energy Performance Certificates' <https://www.gov.uk/buy-sell-your-home/energy-performance-certificates> accessed on 1 June 2023.

81 See PSI Prin 1.

82 Isabel Seifert-Dähnn, 'Insurance Engagement in Flood Risk Reduction – Examples from Household and Business Insurance in Developed Countries' (2018) 18/9 *Natural Hazards and Earth System Sciences*, 2409.

83 OECD Insurance and Adaptation Paper 16.

84 Marsh, 'Delta Side D: Cover for Investigation Costs Related to TCFD Reporting' <https://www.marsh.com/uk/services/financial-professional-liability/products/delta-side-d-cover-investigation-costs-tcfd-reporting.html> accessed on 1 June 2023.

identify climate change risks in specific locations by peril and information on potential adaptation actions, as well as a 5% premium credit to eligible clients to fund identified adaptation measures.[85] Anecdotally, the author is also aware of aviation insurance products that give premium rebates for meeting GHG emission reduction targets.

In relation to consumers and small businesses, insurers are less willing to incur the expense of a tailored ESG/environmental assessment of property and business operations since premium levels in retail insurances tend to be lower and are therefore less likely to absorb the costs of a tailored risk assessment.[86] There is also a risk that a prospective policyholder who benefitted from a pre-contractual risk assessment from insurer A decides to insure with insurer B, or not insure at all. Moreover, if a risk assessment and corresponding recommendations are made for consumer and small business policyholders, insurers have found it difficult to generalise the risk-reducing effects of any measures for standardised insurance contracts since they typically depend on multiple influencing factors, such as the spatial and climate-resilient characteristics of the insured property, and the effectiveness of any measures taken to reduce risk exposures.[87] Nevertheless, there are US examples that show that insurers are carrying out (increasingly standardised) risk assessments and give recommendations which, if taken up, can be reflected in premium discounts.[88]

For insurers, it may be advisable to link any risk assessment to the pre-contractual information duties owed by the prospective policyholder as well as ongoing warranties to maintain any risk-reducing measures, as this may give an insurer remedies if the information provided is incorrect or incomplete, or if the policyholder fails or ceases to comply with specific recommendations.[89] Insurance intermediaries too may be willing to become involved in designing and/or administering environmental risk assessments in order to secure better terms for customers and add value to their services.

For consumers and small businesses, contracts of insurance are contracts of adhesion that are offered with standardised terms on a 'take it or leave it' basis. If the terms are too onerous or premium levels are uncompetitive, a prospective policyholder's only other option are to buy insurance from another insurer who offers better terms or not insure at all. Many consumers buy standardised insurance products over the Internet or apps without any interaction with an insurance distributor who can provide a risk assessment and discuss risk reduction options that could be reflected in the terms and pricing.[90] However, there is potential in harnessing insurance distribution technology to offer (1) risk assessments and advice on risk reduction, as well as (2) modularised insurance cover that responds to risk levels. For example, Zurich Resilience Solutions has developed a free risk management app 'Zurich Risk Advisor' for its corporate policyholders which enables them to carry out a risk self-assessment on the basis of which the app then offers

85 FM Global, 'Climate Resilience Product Suite' <https://www.fmglobal.com/products-and-services/products/climate> accessed on 1 June 2023.

86 Seifert-Dähnn (n 82).

87 EIOPA Adaptation and Insurance Report [63]; also see Kenneth Abraham and Daniel Schwarcz 'The Limits of Regulation by Insurance' (2023) 98 *Indiana Law Journal*, sec II.A.1.

88 For a number of US examples see: EIOPA Adaptation and Insurance Report [65].

89 For consumer insureds, see: Consumer Insurance (Disclosure and Representations) Act 2012 ss 2(2), 4(1) and sch 1; for business insureds, see: Insurance Act 2015 ss 3(1), 8(1) and sch 1.

90 EIOPA, 'Report on Non-Life Underwriting and Pricing in Light of Climate Change' EIOPA-BoS-21/259 (July 2021) ('EIOPA Non-Life Underwriting and Climate Change Report') [2.47].

actionable risk management insights and can connect the user to Zurich professionals who can carry out a more in-depth risk assessment.[91] EIOPA has stated that it will do further research into web-based tools and databases to enhance climate-related risk awareness and understanding of related prevention measures among society and industry.[92] A modular approach to coverage – including cover for additional risks for additional premium – is a concept that is already widely used in the insurance industry and one that could be used for green insurance products sold online.

There are also opportunities for insurers to co-operate with insurance brokers and other actors to carry out climate risk assessments and disseminate risk management advice. As noted above, insurers are responsible for ensuring that their distributors have all the necessary product information and target market information.[93] Some of the global broker and risk management firms, such as Marsh, Aon, and WTW, have been developing their own climate risk advisory and risk assessment capabilities for their corporate customers,[94] which could be or are already used for insurers' risk assessments. Where lenders require their mortgagors to obtain (1) climate risk assessments on the mortgaged property (e.g. a GeoSmart flood report), and (2) property insurance, that climate risk assessment should be disclosed to the insurer.

7.4.3 *Information on risk management*

The pre-contractual stage is a point of engagement where insurers or an insurance intermediary could also provide general or semi-tailored[95] climate change risk information on climate change mitigation and adaptation measures with prospective policyholders. To do so was one of the key recommendations of a recent OECD Report,[96] and a recent EIOPA Study shows that some insurers already do so.[97] In the UK, flood back-stop reinsurer Flood Re in partnership with the UK Environment Agency recently launched the 'Be Flood Smart' campaign encouraging householders to adapt their homes with property flood resilience measures to protect against the impact of future floods while also helping with speeding up repair work, and helping people move back into their properties quicker after a flood.[98] Some studies have shown that clear information about people's local climate-related risk exposures and corresponding socio-economic consequences can

91 Zurich Resilience Solutions, 'Zurich Risk Advisor' <https://www.zurich.com/en/products-and-services/tools-for-business/zurich-risk-advisor> accessed on 1 June 2023.

92 EIOPA Adaptation and Insurance Report [74].

93 PROD 4.2.29.

94 Marsh, 'Delta Side D: Cover for Investigation Costs Related to TCFD Reporting' <https://www.marsh.com/uk/services/financial-professional-liability/products/delta-side-d-cover-investigation-costs-tcfd-reporting.html> accessed on 1 June 2023; Aon, 'The Climate Service – Climanomics' <https://www.aon.com/unitedkingdom/commercial-risk/climate-risk/capabilities.jsp> accessed on 1 June 2023; and WTW, 'Climate' <https://www.wtwco.com/en-gb/solutions/climate> accessed 1 June 2023.

95 Semi-tailored risk climate change risk information and information on risk reduction measures would be information that is specific to a line of business, a type of insurance, and/or a wider geographical location.

96 OECD Insurance and Adaptation Paper 26.

97 EIOPA Adaptation and Insurance Report [59].

98 Saumya Jain, 'Flood Re Launches 'Be Flood Smart' Campaign in Partnership with Environment Agency' (*Reinsurance News*, 23 May 2023).

effectively increase climate risk awareness and stimulate the take-up of risk prevention measures,[99] while another (earlier) study found that it has little impact.[100]

Abraham and Schwarcz have argued that general loss reduction information is only likely to have a very limited effect because (1) policyholders have limited incentives to take up any recommendations as they derive no financial benefit from taking them up, and (2) such information can be counterproductive for insurers because it could reduce demand for insurance.[101] That insurers do have strong incentives for engaging in climate-related impact underwriting has already been shown above. While Abraham and Schwarcz may be taking too bleak a view on policyholders' attitudes, it may increase the effectiveness of generalised advice if it is linked to potential consequences that can have personal implications for policyholders (e.g. premium rises and protection gap in the mid-term future). Rapidly developing artificial intelligence technologies may soon extend to diagnosing risk, and generating tailored advice, on the basis of a wide range of risk factors and characteristics of the insured subject matter. Climate risk-management information that is tailored to specific insurance products (albeit not tailored to individual customers) could also be produced by insurers and be disseminated through their existing distribution channels, alongside the relevant product information, at the pre-contractual stage.[102]

The OECD has suggested that the following information could be provided:

- information on local climate-related risk exposures and corresponding socio-economic consequences;
- information indicating how policyholders' premiums might be impacted in the future by a changing climate;
- information on risk reduction and adaptation measures that policyholders could take to reduce their risk (and premiums), based on current as well as future climate conditions;
- information on potential sources of funding or financing for risk reduction and adaptation investments (e.g. from government grants);
- specific information on available premium discounts for risk reduction and adaptation measures, including any conditions that must be met in order to receive that discount;
- information on (local) trusted contractors to implement such adaptation measures.[103]

99 Jennifer K. Poussin, W.J. Wouter Botzen, and Jeroen C.J.H. Aerts, 'Factors of Influence on Flood Damage Mitigation Behaviour by Households' (2014) 40 *Environmental Science & Policy*, 69; Joop de Boer, W.J. Wouter Botzen, and Teun Terpstra, 'Flood Risk and Climate Change in the Rotterdam Area, The Netherlands: Enhancing Citizen's Climate Risk Perceptions and Prevention Responses Despite Skepticism' (2016) 16 *Regional Environmental Change*, 1613; Susanne Hanger, Joanne Linnerooth-Bayer, Swenja Surminski, Cristina Nenciu-Posner, Anna Lorant, Radu Ionescu, and Anthony Patt, 'Insurance, Public Assistance, and Household Flood Risk Reduction: A Comparative Study of Austria, England, and Romania'(2018) 38(4) *Risk Analysis*, 680.

100 Renato Miceli, Igor Sotgiu, and Michele Settanni, 'Disaster Preparedness and Perception of Flood Risk: A Study in an Alpine Valley in Italy' (2008) 28/2 *Journal of Environmental Psychology*, 164.

101 Kenneth S. Abraham and Daniel Schwarcz, 'The Limits of Regulation by Insurance' (2023) 98(1) Ind Law Journal (Art.5).

102 See Section 7.3.2.

103 OECD Insurance and Adaptation Paper 21–22.

As the OECD Report is climate change adaptation focused, it does not address information on climate change mitigation measures. Information on the latter is much more likely to be available – or should be made available – in standardised form from government authorities and official sources but insurers could use the pre-contractual point of contact to act as a transmission channel. Such information might include:

- the likely GHG emissions of the property by reference to its size, type of heating, and EPC rating;
- reducing GHG emissions of buildings and in transport, for example by reference to the recommendations of the UK's Climate Change Committee;[104]
- available government schemes and grants aimed at reducing GHG emissions.[105]

By raising awareness on these matters, insurers can enable consumer and small business policyholders to make better-informed choices on these matters. There is a free-rider issue where insurers who do not provide information (and do not incur the expense from doing so) would still benefit from raised awareness levels among prospective policyholders. It is also important to consider that raising awareness of climate change mitigation and adaptation cannot be reached through the sole contribution of insurance but must go hand in hand with public information campaigns and public standards such as developing and enforcing public building codes adapted to the dynamics of climate change.[106] However, there are a number of legal and regulatory issues that need to be considered.

7.4.4 Restrictions on non-insurance business

In the UK, insurers must not carry on any commercial business other than insurance business and activities directly arising from that business.[107] Other jurisdictions have similar restrictions,[108] the purpose of which is to ensure that financial resources do not get side-tracked into other activities and are exposed to additional risks. Could providing information and risk management advice on climate change mitigation and adaptation measures to prospective policyholders fall within the scope of the restriction? It is suggested that this is an activity that directly arises from the insurance business – because it is concerned with the mitigation and adaptation of the very risk to be insured – and that it is therefore not caught by the restriction. It could even be argued further that, in relation to consumers, the new UK consumer duty (which comes into force for all new products in July 2023, and for all products and services from July 2024) demands that insurers act to deliver good outcomes including in relation to the pricing (which could be positively affected by climate change mitigation and adaptation measures) and value (in addition to

104 Committee on Climate Change, 'Sixth Carbon Budget Report – Sector Summary for Buildings and Sector Summary for Surface Transport' (December 2020) <https://www.theccc.org.uk/wp-content/uploads/2020/12/Sector-summary-Buildings.pdf and https://www.theccc.org.uk/wp-content/uploads/2020/12/Sector-summary-Surface-transport.pdf> accessed on 1 June 2023.

105 See Section 7.7.2.

106 EIOPA Adaptation and Insurance Report [5].

107 PRA Rulebook, Solvency II Firms, General Conditions Governing Business, 9.1.

108 All EU member states were required to transpose into national law the Solvency II Directive, including art 18(1)(a) which requires EU insurers 'to limit their objects to the business of insurance and operations arising directly therefrom, to the exclusion of all other commercial business.'

claims payments) of insurance products, as well as enhancing consumer understanding and support.[109]

In the United States, the provision of information and risk management advice on climate change mitigation and adaptation measures to prospective policyholders at no cost would need to comply with any anti-rebate laws applicable at US state level in some US states.[110] In its model Unfair Trade Practices Act in 2021, the National Association of Insurance Commissioners has clarified that 'value-added products or services' at no or reduced cost are not considered to be impermissible rebates where they relate to the insurance coverage and are primarily designed to (inter alia) provide loss mitigation or loss control, or education about liability risks or risk of loss to persons or property.[111] However, it would need clarification at US state level whether information and risk management advice on climate change mitigation and adaptation measures can be provided.

7.4.5 The consumer duty

A new package of measures under the umbrella of the 'consumer duty' came into force for new regulated financial products and services from 31 July 2023, and must be implemented for all existing regulated financial products and services by 31 July 2024.[112] The measures include:

1. a new Consumer Principle that requires firms to act to deliver good outcomes for retail customers.[113] 'Retail customers' include prospective and existing customers who are consumers, and small and medium-sized enterprises when acting outside their trade, business, or profession;[114]
2. cross-cutting rules provide further detail on the FCA's expectations under the new Consumer Principle and help firms interpret the four outcomes (see below). The cross-cutting rules require firms to:
   a. act in good faith towards retail customers;
   b. avoid causing foreseeable harm to retail customers;
   c. enable and support retail customers to pursue their financial objectives;[115]
3. there are rules and guidance that codify proactive obligations in relation to four outcomes under the consumer duty:
   a. products and services;
   b. price and value;
   c. consumer understanding;
   d. consumer support;
4. the consumer duty applies throughout the life cycle of the insurance product.[116]

---

109 FCA, 'A New Consumer Duty – Feedback to CP21/36 and Final Rules' FS 22/9 (July 2022).

110 OECD Insurance and Adaptation Paper 13.

111 National Association of Insurance Commissioners, 'Unfair Trade Practices Act' (Spring 2021) <https://content.naic.org/sites/default/files/inline-files/MDL-880_0.pdf> accessed on 1 June 2023.

112 Consumer Duty Instrument 2022 (FCA 2022/31); FCA, 'A New Consumer Duty – Feedback to CP21/36 and Final Rules' (n 109) [1.34].

113 PRIN 2.1.1R Prin 12.

114 Ibid 2A.1.

115 Ibid 2A.2.

116 Ibid 2A.3.

The provision of information and risk management advice on climate change mitigation and adaptation measures to prospective policyholders is not itself a regulated activity. However, the Consumer Principle extends to 'ancillary activities' in relation to certain regulated activities, including insurance distribution activities. These are activities carried on in connection with a regulated activity or held out as being for the purposes of a regulated activity.[117] Any information and risk management advice on climate change mitigation and adaptation measures to prospective retail policyholders would be provided in connection with insurance distribution activities and is therefore likely to be caught by the Consumer Principle.

If the information or advice is incorrect, this may foreseeably cause harm to a retail policyholder. On the other hand, it could also be argued that not providing information on certain climate change mitigation and adaptation measures could be contrary to the Consumer Principle and in breach of the cross-cutting rules. For example, to achieve good consumer outcomes in relation to homeowner property insurance that covers flood risks, it is arguable that:

- acting in good faith, being a standard of conduct characterised by honesty, fair and open dealing, and acting consistently with the reasonable expectations of retail customers,[118] requires an insurer to share flood risk exposure information on the insured property held by the insurer;
- to avoid causing foreseeable harm to retail customers, an insurer should provide information on flood resilience measures to retail customers that are exposed to flood risk, so that they can take informed decisions on whether and what action to take to ensure that they continue to be insurable at affordable prices;[119]
- enabling and supporting retail customers to pursue their financial objectives means that insurers must empower retail customers to make good choices in their interests, including by making sure retail customers have the information and support they need, when they need it, to make and act on informed decisions.[120]

The standard of care in discharging the consumer duty is that which could reasonably be expected of a prudent firm (1) carrying on the same activity in relation to the same product; and (2) taking appropriate account of the needs and characteristics of retail customers based on the needs and characteristics of retail customers in the relevant target market or of individual retail customers as the context requires.[121] The FCA has said it will:

> take robust action where [it] see[s] firms' failure to implement the Duty causing actual or potential harm to consumers. This could include holding senior managers to account where they have failed to act to implement the Duty and prevent such harm.[122]

However, a breach of the Consumer Principle is unlikely to give rise to action in damages by the retail customer who has suffered a harm. Although, under FSMA 2000, s.138D(2),

117 FCA FG22/5 (n 30) [2.42].

118 PRIN 2A.7.2.2R.

119 Ibid 2A.2.10G.

120 Ibid 2A.2.20(2)G.

121 Ibid 2A.7.1R.

122 FCA, 'Consumer Duty Firm Survey – Spring 2023' (June 2023) <https://www.fca.org.uk/data/consumer-duty-firm-survey-spring-2023> accessed on 29 June 2023.

a contravention by an authorised insurer of an FCA Handbook rule would generally be actionable by a policyholder who is a private person and who has suffered a loss as a result of the contravention, such an action is not available:

- to business insureds, including small and medium-sized enterprises.[123] Even certain categories of individuals may not fall within the categories of 'private person';[124]
- upon contraventions of FCA guidance,[125] and the rules in PRIN.[126] Accordingly, a policyholder would not be able to establish a right of action in reliance on contraventions of Principle 12 in PRIN 2.1.1, and the cross-cutting rules in PRIN 2A.2.

7.4.6 Duty of care

Is there a risk that insurers could incur liability under the tort of negligence for providing information on climate change mitigation and adaptation measures if any of the information is incorrect? The risk of tort liability has been used as an argument against informational engagement by insurers with policyholders by Logue,[127] and Abrahams and Schwarcz.[128] Under English law, the tort of negligence has four elements to be proven, namely:

1. the existence in law of a duty of care situation, i.e. one in which the law attaches liability to carelessness;
2. breach of the duty of care by the defendant, i.e. that there was a failure to measure up to the standard set by law;
3. a causal connection between the defendant's careless conduct and the damage;
4. that the particular kind of damage to the particular claimant is not so unforeseeable as to be too remote.[129]

The defendant must owe a notional duty of care in relation to the general class within which the claimant and the type of damage that has arisen fall before there can be any question of liability to the claimant in question.[130] This will be decided by reference to (1) existing categories of duty of care, or (2) in novel cases, whether there is (i) foreseeability of harm to the claimant; (ii) proximity of relationship between claimant and defendant; and (iii) whether imposing a duty would be fair, just, and reasonable.[131] There are no reported cases that have established a duty of care owed by an insurer to the insured. There is no contract for the provision of information on climate change mitigation and adaptation measures

123 Financial Services and Markets Act 2000 (Rights of Action) Regulations 2001, SI 2001/2256 (amended by SI 2013/472), reg.3(1).

124 *Sivagnanam v Barclays Bank Plc* [2015] EWHC 3985 (Comm).

125 FSMA 2000, s.138D(2). See also: *R (British Bankers Association) v FSA* [2011] EWHC 999 (Admin), [71]-[94] per Ouseley J.

126 FSMA 2000, s.138D(3); PRIN 3.4.4R.

127 Kyle D. Logue, 'Encouraging Insurers to Regulate: The Role (If Any) for Tort Law' (2015) 5(6) *UC Irvine L Rev*, 1355.

128 Abraham and Schwarcz (n 101).

129 Micheal Jones, Anthony Dugdale, Mark Simpson QC, *Clerk & Lindsell on Torts* (23rd ed.; Sweet & Maxwell, 2020) [7-04].

130 *Donoghue v Stevenson* [1932] AC 562, at 580 per Lord Atkins (HL).

131 *Caparo Industries plc v Dickman* [1990] 2 AC 605, 617–618 per Lord Bridge (HL).

from which a contractual duty of care could be derived, although it is arguable that such a duty comes into existence once a contract of insurance is entered into.[132] Where a defendant makes a statement which is reasonably relied upon by a claimant in the way intended by the defendant, there may be an assumption of responsibility sufficient to give rise to liability for economic loss flowing from the reliance.[133] A (prospective) policyholder may regard an insurer to have 'professional knowledge' on risk management matters and it is therefore arguably reasonably foreseeable that a policyholder may rely on the information communicated to him by the insurer and that economic loss may be caused if the insurer does not exercise reasonable skill and care in providing correct information.

The existence and scope of a notional duty of care may also be informed by regulatory requirements.[134] As noted in Section 7.4.5, the consumer duty imposes upon an insurer or insurance intermediary a duty to deliver good outcomes for retail customers. ICOBS rule 2.2.2 requires UK insurers to ensure that information communicated to customers is 'clear, fair and not misleading.' The definition of 'customer' includes existing and prospective policyholders, and 'information' includes, but is not limited, to financial promotions and marketing materials, as long as it was communicated. Therefore, it is arguable that an insurer providing information on climate change mitigation and adaptation measures to prospective or existing policyholders owes a duty of care that the information is clear, fair, and not misleading. The IDD, Art.17(2) from which ICOBS r.2.2.2 derives is narrower: it only applies to information 'related to subjects of [the IDD].'[135] The customer information requirements in the IDD relate to corporate details of an insurance intermediary and insurer,[136] transparency and conflict of interest issues relating to an insurance intermediary,[137] insurance product information,[138] and costs and charges arising in relation to IBIPs.[139] Thus, arguably, the Art.17(2) requirement does not extend to information not captured in those categories.

Even if a notional duty of care can be established, there would need to be a breach. The legal standard or care is objective – i.e. that which might be expected from a person of ordinary prudence, or person of ordinary care and skill, engaged in the type of activity in which the defendant was engaged.[140] As risk advisory and risk management services are frequently provided by insurance brokers, it is likely that a court would set the standard by reference to the skill and care exercised by a reasonable or prudent broker. To the extent that information can be backed up by government recommendations and scientific evidence from reputable sources, the standard is likely to be met. In relation to the consumer duty, the standard of care is an objective one, but also takes into account specific characteristics, vulnerabilities, and biases of retail customers.[141]

Pursuant to the Social Action, Responsibility and Heroism Act 2015 ('SARHA'), the court will take into account whether the alleged negligence occurred when the person was

132 CRA 2015, s 49 and Supply of Goods and Services Act 1982, s 13.

133 *Hedley Byrne & Co Ltd v Heller & Partners Ltd* [1964] AC 465, [1963] 2 All ER 575 (HL).

134 *Dunlop Haywards (DHL) Ltd v Barbon Insurance Group Ltd* [2009] EWHC 2900 (Comm).

135 IDD art 17(2).

136 Ibid art 18.

137 Ibid art 19.

138 Ibid art 20.

139 Ibid art 29.

140 See further: *Clerk & Lindsell on Torts* (n 129) [7-157]–[7-159].

141 PRIN 2A.7.1R and 2A.7.4G.

acting for the benefit of society or any of its members.[142] The Explanatory Notes clarify that this provision can apply to individuals and organisations, but there are no reported cases under SARHA. It is at least arguable that providing information on climate change mitigation measures at no cost to policyholders is also for the benefit of society given that according to the Paris Agreement climate change is a global endeavour.

Additional hurdles for a negligence action would be to show a causal connection between the defendant's careless conduct and the damage, whereby the particular kind of damage to the particular claimant is foreseeable and not too remote. Especially for generalised information, it is unlikely that the causal link and the remoteness test can be satisfied. Although it seems doubtful that a negligence action would succeed in the English courts, there are measures that insurers could take to protect themselves, such as verifying any information against government and scientific advice and using disclaimer language. Another option might be that the information is produced by the government (or jointly by the government and the insurance industry), and insurers and brokers merely act as distribution channels for that information.

Overall, pre-contractual risk assessments tailored to the prospective policyholder that may affect premium levels are more likely to be an effective approach with which policyholder behaviour can be meaningfully influenced. The main hurdles are the potential costs that cannot be easily absorbed in premium rates in competitive markets, and the fact that retail customers frequently do not directly engage with insurers or brokers. Insurers should invest in insurance distribution technology that is capable of offering (1) risk assessments and advice on risk reduction based on input data, as well as (2) modularised insurance cover that responds to risk levels. Conversely, any climate risk assessments on the property to be insured (e.g. flood risk assessments) that the policyholder has obtained from third parties should be disclosed to their prospective insurers. Generalised information should be produced by, or be based on, government information and be verifiable or evidence-based. While generalised information may be less effective, it should still be part of a holistic climate-related impact underwriting strategy.

7.5 Pricing

Pricing in insurance means primarily the level of premium payable by policyholders, but also intersects with policy terms that provide for the application of deductibles and coverage limits which have the effect that policyholders remain uninsured for part of their losses. The premium is calculated by the insurer by reference to the level of risk that is transferred and the costs of the insurer associated with assuming the risk.

7.5.1 Pricing factors and considerations

In non-life insurance, premium pricing should take into account:

1. risk profile analysis (e.g. risk appetite, levels of risk tolerance), including
    - the risk profile of policyholders ('feature-rating');

142 Social Action, Responsibility and Heroism Act 2015, s 1.

- expected cost of claims, in terms of frequency and severity, based on past loss experience ('experience-rating');
- the way risks are diversified in the insurer's portfolio;
- the relative risk premium of different policyholders (to avoid anti-selection) but allowing for regulatory restrictions;

2. business strategies, including capital management strategies, business planning, and product development programme:

   - the overall level of premium for the various risks covered including the product design (e.g. incentives, mitigation measures, exclusions, and/or deductibles);
   - the expected profit margins, taking into account costs borne by the insurers;
   - the cost of reinsurance;
   - the cost of capital required to support the business;
   - the time value of money (investment return, claims time lag).[143]

Given the crowded retail insurance market, premium levels need to be competitive and yet be capable of generating a profit for insurers. If premiums are too high so as to become unaffordable, policyholders may decide to remain uninsured, and this will create protection gaps.[144] While pricing is primarily an actuarial and commercial matter, there are also some legal considerations. For example, insurers must not discriminate on account of race, religion, sex, sexual orientation, gender, or marital status,[145] but are allowed to take into account age and disability where it is relevant to the risk assessment.[146] In relation to retail motor and home insurance, insurers must not set a renewal premium price that is higher than the equivalent it would give to new customers.[147] The product design requirement for 'fair value,' and whether premium discounts are consistent with an insurer's 'corporate purpose' have already been discussed.[148]

In some countries (not in the UK), premiums are fixed for some climate-related (and other catastrophe) perils (e.g. for flood risk in France) and/or insurers may not be allowed to provide discounts (or lower deductibles) for risk reduction or adaptation investments made by policyholders.[149] In the US, some states heavily regulate premium rates for household property insurance, while others regulate premium rates more lightly.[150] A recent study shows that this leads to insurers in more regulated states adjusting premium rates less frequently and by a lower magnitude after experiencing losses, while making compensating premium adjustments in less regulated states, so that policyholders in less regulated states are effectively cross-subsidising policyholders in heavily regulated states.[151] Under

143 Adapted from: EIOPA Non-Life Underwriting and Climate Change Report [2.2] and [2.7].

144 See Chapter 6, Section 6.3.2.

145 Equality Act 2010 s 29.

146 Ibid Sch 3 pt 5, paras 20A and 21.

147 The practice of 'price walking' – giving premium discounts to new customers but not to existing customers – has been banned for consumer motor and home insurance from 1 January 2022 – see ICOBS 6B.2R.

148 See Section 7.2.2 and Chapter 6, Section 6.2.

149 OECD Insurance and Adaptation Paper 17.

150 Sangmin Oh, Ishita Sen, and Ana-Maria Tenekedjieva, 'Pricing of Climate Risk Insurance: Regulation and Cross-Subsidies' (22 December 2022) <https://ssrn.com/abstract=3762235> accessed on 1 June 2023, Sec. 1.2.

151 Ibid Sec. 5.

the UK insurance solvency regulatory regime,[152] an insurer must set premiums at a level that is consistent with actuarial risk-based principles so that, together with other income streams, the insurer continues to have enough funds for its technical provisions[153] and to match or exceed its solvency capital requirements.[154]

How can premium pricing incentivise policyholders to take climate change mitigation measures or make them engage in climate change adaptation measures? Feature-rating can incentivise the prospective policyholder to alter their activities or adopt risk reduction measures prior to the inception of the policy on the expectation that doing so will decrease the premium. Experience-rating can incentivise policyholders to put in place risk or loss reduction measures so as to avoid or minimise losses while they are insured, so that they can secure favourable premium rates in the future.[155] In contrast, decoupling premium rates from risk can undermine the extent to which insurance prices can influence policyholders to take climate change adaptation measures. Non-risk reflective premium rates do not signal to policyholders the level of risk they are exposed to and do not provide incentives to take steps to mitigate or adapt to the risk.[156] Premium rates that do not reflect the risk of the policyholder can also give rise to moral hazard, namely that a policyholder will adopt a reckless attitude towards the risk in the knowledge that insurance cover is available.

Risk-reflective premium rates are conceptually similar to the mechanism of 'green pills' proposed by Armour et al.[157] in relation to investment strategies that pursue environmental objectives. Green pills are contractual obligations on the investee company to reduce GHG emissions by meeting specified milestones coupled with an undertaking by the investee company to make a payment or sell discounted debt upon the non-compliance with a target. Thus, a green pill would make it costly for the investee company to deviate from its transition path.

Setting premium levels is interlinked with deciding on the terms of the insurance contract that define the scope of the cover (such as defining the insured property, identifying the insured perils, exclusions and limits of liability) but also with terms that seek to mitigate the insured risk and control the extent of potential insured losses.

7.5.2 Pricing climate change mitigation

Insurers could use pricing structures that penalise carbon-intense activities or reward net GHG emission-reducing activities. Coal companies are already facing premium rate increases of up to 40%,[158] although the increase is more likely to be the result of restricted underwriting capacity following a growing number of insurers withdrawing from the coal market. In relation to policyholders with carbon-intense businesses, there will be a correlation between the risk that the policyholder poses and certain insured perils – such

152 See Chapter 4, Section 4.4.3.

153 PRA Rulebook, SII Firms, Technical Provisions, 2.

154 PRA Rulebook, SII Firms, Solvency Capital Requirements – General Provisions, 2.

155 Abraham and Schwarcz (n 87) sec II.A.

156 Oh and Sen (n 150) Sec. 7.

157 John Armour, Luca Enriques, and Thom Wetzer, 'Green Pills: Making Corporate Climate Commitments Credible' (2023) 65 *Ariz L Rev*, 285 Pt 3; and see Chapter 8, Section 8.1.4.

158 Willis Towers Watson, 'Managing the Transition: Mining Risk Review 2020' (2020) <https://willistowerswatson.turtl.co/story/mining-risk-review-2020-ungated/page/1> accessed on 1 June 2023.

as litigation risk, the risk of government intervention, the risk of vandalism, the risk of supply chain interruptions – that would warrant feature-rating premium increases.

However, in many other cases, the GHG emissions of the prospective policyholder will have little relevance to its risk profile, and it will be difficult to causally connect any climate change mitigation measure (some form of GHG emission reduction) to a risk reduction, for the purposes of a particular insurance.[159] This would require that an evidence-based link between GHG emissions and the (twelve -month) insured risk can be established for actuarial purposes. Even if a risk reduction can be established, its benefit may not materialise in the twelve month policy term that is customary for general insurance. Adding a 'penal element' for GHG emissions to the premium where GHG emissions are not part of the feature- or experience-rating could suggest that the product does not provide 'fair value.'[160] Reducing premium, or giving a premium rebate, for reasons unrelated to the insured risk itself, could still be consistent with the directors' s.172 duty if there are other good business reasons for doing so.[161] Insurers routinely take into account wider business considerations, such as reputation, competition, and business models, in setting premiums. However, it has been noted by EIOPA and the OECD that the additional costs of supporting climate change mitigation and adaptation measures are of concern to insurers and that different funding models need to be considered.[162]

In the US, some home insurers already offer premium discounts for LEED-certified homes.[163] In the UK, an Energy Performance Certificate (EPC) is already required when a property is being built, sold, or rented. The UK government is consulting on plans that would require mortgage lenders to take a property's EPC rating into account in their lending decision and offer financial rewards (lower interest rates, cash-backs, and extended mortgages) to facilitate improvements to a home's energy efficiency.[164] These plans could be extended to property insurers, so that premium rebates might be offered in relation to insured properties that improve their energy performance in prescribed ways (e.g. carrying out energy efficiency retrofit or installing low-carbon heating) during the policy term. Yet, it is by no means clear whether improved energy efficiency reduces the risk of damage to property: it may be possible to identify a causal connection between improved energy efficiency and reduced fire risk, or a reduced risk of burst pipes, and it may also be possible to show a correlation between the policyholders who are likely to adopt such measures and a lower likelihood of claims because that kind of policyholder is more likely to take care to prevent losses in a variety of ways.[165]

159 EIOPA Adaptation and Insurance Report [21].

160 PROD 4.2.14M and see Section 7.2.2.

161 Companies Act 2006 s 172, and Chapter 6, Section 6.2.

162 OECD Insurance and Adaptation Paper 24-2, and see Section 7.5.4, Chapter 8, Section 8.5, and Chapter 9, Section 9.3.

163 LEED (Leadership in Energy and Environmental Design Green Building Rating System) is a system, developed by the US Green Building Council, that is a recognised environmental standard in the building world and has high efficiency and sustainability standards. See: Insurance Information Institute, 'Green Insurance' <https://www.iii.org/article/green-insurance> accessed on 1 June 2023.

164 The UK government is proposing the annual disclosure of portfolio-wide Energy Performance Certificate (EPC) data and the gross value of lending for energy performance improvement works by mortgage lenders. See: Department for Business, Energy and Industrial Strategy, 'Improving Home Energy Performance through Lenders' Consultation Paper (November 2020) <https://www.gov.uk/government/consultations/improving-home-energy-performance-through-lenders> accessed on 1 June 2023.

165 EIOPA Non-Life Underwriting and Climate Change Report [2.57].

Could motor insurers discount premiums for hybrid and electric cars? Until recently, motor insurance for hybrid and electric cars has been more expensive compared to petrol or diesel cars as insurers have had scant historic data to price repairs.[166] The risk of injuring third parties is the same, but it has been reported that electric cars are considered to be a lower theft risk because of their limited range and still limited charging infrastructure.[167] As more data has become available and technology and infrastructure for hybrid and electric cars have advanced, premium levels have been adjusted.[168] Generali is already offering a 20% premium discount for 'environmentally friendly vehicles' (electric and hybrid cars).[169] Motor insurers could consider a one-off premium discount for existing customers switching from a petrol or diesel car to an electric or hybrid car. For businesses, insurers could consider packages at attractive premium rates for electric and hybrid car fleets. However, such discounts would not necessarily be risk-based. In contrast, motor policies that offer 'Pay as You Drive' coverage could incentivise a policyholder to drive less: a telematic device installed in the car tracks the miles driven in the car, and the policyholder is charged a premium on a per-mile basis.[170] Driving fewer miles means less risk which in turn means paying less premium, less fuel consumption, and reduced GHG emissions. Although this is an example of incidentally enabling an environmental goal, usage-based premium mechanisms could be marshalled to reduce GHG emissions on a cost-effective basis.

7.5.3 Pricing climate change adaptation

It is more straightforward to establish a causal link between a specific climate change adaptation measure and a reduction in the risk of loss that can be reflected in a premium discount or premium.[171] These measures can be public projects, such as dikes against flood risks, or they can be smaller scale privately implemented measures such as specific household-level building improvements like flood-resistant windows and doors or external building measures like sandbags and domestic protection walls against flood risk, heat- and fire-resistive construction materials for buildings against wildfires, using tempered glass against hail risk, elevation of ground floor electrical installations against flood risk, or forecasting and warning systems to enable policyholders to protect their goods in advance of severe weather events.[172] The focus here is on private measures and private insurance.

Several studies have shown that a majority of policyholders would be willing to invest in climate change adaptation measures to benefit from a premium reduction, but there is limited evidence that demonstrates whether risk-based pricing has actually led to

166 Aviva, 'Choosing an Electric Car' <https://www.aviva.co.uk/insurance/motor/car-insurance/electric-and-hybrid-cars/> accessed on 1 June 2023.

167 What Car, 'Are Electric Cars More Expensive to Insure?' (4 November 2019) <https://www.whatcar.com/advice/owning/are-electric-cars-more-expensive-to-insure/n18043> accessed on 1 June 2023.

168 What Car, 'Are Electric Cars More Expensive to Insure?' (4 November 2019) <https://www.whatcar.com/advice/owning/are-electric-cars-more-expensive-to-insure/n18043> accessed on 1 June 2023.

169 Generali, 'Car Insurance' <https://www.generali.ch/en/privatkunden/fahrzeuge-reisen/autoversicherung> accessed on 1 June 2023.

170 See e.g. By Miles Car Insurance <https://www.bymiles.co.uk/> accessed on 1 June 2023.

171 EIOPA Adaptation and Insurance Report [21].

172 EIOPA Adaptation and Insurance Report [18] and [45].

significant policyholder investment in adaptation measures.[173] A recent survey carried out by EIOPA found that to date only a minority of those EU-based insurers surveyed used premium discounts and deductibles to incentivise the take-up of adaptation measures by policyholders,[174] but there are some US examples:

- a number of insurance companies, particularly in hurricane-exposed states, offer discounts to households that make investments to meet construction standards under the IBHS Fortified Home Program;[175]
- the US National Flood Insurance Program offers discounts of up to 45% for the implementation of adaptation measures against flood risk;[176]
- several US states require insurance premium discounts for buildings implementing wind- and storm-resistant features.[177]

The Quinquennial Review of UK-based government-sponsored Flood Re Scheme[178] proposed offering discounted premiums for households that proactively install flood resistance and resilience measures.[179] Flood Re considered that:

> [t]hrough lower inward insurance premiums, Flood Re will reward those who have taken active steps to reduce the impact and costs of future flooding events on their property. This will help to support a market for resilience products and help to change attitudes and behaviours.[180]

This proposal was not supported by the UK government on the grounds of ambiguous feedback from the insurance industry on the proposal's effectiveness and concerns about creating a two-tier premium system that would exacerbate inequality.[181]

7.5.4 Barriers to risk-based pricing

There are a number of obstacles that hinder the more wide-scale use of premium discounts and rebates to incentivise or reward the implementation of climate change adaptation measures by policyholders.

7.5.4.1 Costs and fairness of distribution

Climate change adaptation measures can be costly: for example, anti-flood shutters can cost EUR 1,300, anti-flood doors EUR 3,000, and soil rehydration systems and micropiles to counter-act subsidence can cost between EUR 15,000 and EUR 100,000.[182] However, there are also measures that are less costly yet effective in reducing loss, such as using

---

173 For an overview, see: OECD Insurance and Adaptation Paper 14.

174 EIOPA Adaptation and Insurance Report [49].

175 OECD Insurance and Adaptation Paper 14.

176 EIOPA Adaptation and Insurance Report [70].

177 Ibid [70].

178 See Chapter 9, Section 9.4.2.

179 Flood Re, 'Quinquennial Review' (July 2019) 50 <https://www.floodre.co.uk/wp-content/uploads/QQR_FINAL.pdf> accessed on 1 June 2023.

180 Ibid 52.

181 Department for Environment, Food and Rural Affairs, 'Consultation on Amendments to the Flood Re Scheme Summary of Responses' (July 2021) 7–20 <https://www.gov.uk/government/consultations/amendments-to-the-flood-re-scheme> accessed on 1 June 2023; and Flood Re (n 78) 24.

182 EIOPA Adaptation and Insurance Report [48].

sandbags as water barriers and raising sockets.[183] If premium discounts and rebates are not large enough to cover those costs, policyholders may not be able to afford the investment, or even if they can, they may not be willing to do so. The policyholder may compare the immediate costs of the adaptation measure to the potential future premium savings and decide that the future premium savings are too uncertain and, in any event, delayed. Risk-based premiums also shift responsibility for climate change mitigation and adaptation in relation to the insured subject matter onto individuals rather than placing it on the government. This may or may not be a responsibility that individuals can reasonably bear: for those who cannot afford to take such measures, risk-based premiums could act as a multiplier of inequality both in terms of affordability of insurance and improving resilience.[184] As noted in the Flood Re consultation, the unintended consequences of premium discounts for implementing property flood resilience measures could be:

- growing inequality in affordability and those benefitting from such measures, creating a two-tier system between those who can afford such measures and those who cannot;
- potential inflation for premiums to compensate for discounts;
- the added costs for homeowners who would be paying for such measures (and tenants who would be paying for such measures indirectly via increased rents);
- potential rising prices of property flood resilience measures as the market is unable to respond to a sudden rise in demand;
- homeowners' disappointment with the extent of financial gains (costs vs savings).[185]

One option for UK insurers for funding additional costs could be to utilise some of the capital that will be released on the forthcoming reforms of the risk margins levels.[186] Some potential funding and financing solutions will be considered in Chapters 8 and 9.

7.5.4.2 Lack of policyholders' awareness about climate change and related adaptation measures

Studies show that people in Europe tend to consider climate change as not having any immediate consequences that require any action.[187] It is only when they have had personal experience with climate change-related natural catastrophes that they become more risk-aware and are inclined to consider risk adaptation measures.[188] Section 7.4 discussed how

183 Jennifer K. Poussin, W.J. Wouter Botzen, and Jeroen C.J.H. Aerts, 'Effectiveness of Flood Damage Mitigation Measures: Empirical Evidence from French Flood Disasters' (2015) 31 *Global Environmental Change*, 74.

184 Paula Jarzabkowski, Konstantinos Chalkias, Eugenia Cacciatori, and Rebecca Bednarek, *Disaster Insurance Reimagined* (OUP 2023) 95.

185 Department for Environment, Food and Rural Affairs (n 181) 15–16.

186 See Chapter 8, Section 8.3.1, and HM Treasury, 'Review of Solvency II: Consultation – Response' (November 2022) <https://assets.publishing.service.gov.uk/government/uploads/system/uploads/attachment_data/file/1118359/Consultation_Response_-_Review_of_Solvency_II_.pdf> ch 2.

187 Manuel Frondel, Michael Simora, and Stephan Sommer, 'Risk Perception of Climate Change: Empirical Evidence for Germany' (2017) 137 *Ecological Economics*, 173; and also see the 'tragedy of the commons' explained in Section 7.6.2.

188 Ibid.

insurers could provide information on climate change mitigation and adaptation to raise awareness.

7.5.4.3 Lack of pricing signal

The OECD has noted that premium discounts and rebates may not be sufficiently reflective of (longer-term) climate risk to provide the necessary price signal to incentivise policyholders to take an adaptation measure for a number of reasons: (1) the coverage for climate perils is bundled with coverage for other perils without a clear allocation of premium cost for climate perils; (2) there is a reliance on the possibility for frequent re-pricing to account for changes in climate conditions or excessive uncertainty about future climate conditions; or (3) other (non-risk) factors are incorporated into pricing.[189]

7.5.4.4 Measuring risk reduction

Isolating the effect of a climate change adaptation measure could be difficult as frequently climate-related perils will be bundled into insurance contracts that cover a range of risks. Some surveyed insurers commented that within the constraints of standardised insurance contracts in retail insurance, it is difficult to recognise the risk reduction effect of an adaptation measure individually implemented by a policyholder. Its effectiveness can be influenced by multiple factors, such as (1) the spatial characteristics of the insured object or the type of climate-related hazard, (2) the existing physical condition of the insured object in terms of climate resilience (e.g. existence of damage-resistant structures and materials), and (3) the effectiveness of adaptation measures to reduce risk exposures (e.g. dependence on human interaction in case of alert systems).[190] EIOPA considers that possible approaches to tackling this problem could be to improve risk-based modelling of the effects of climate change adaptation measures, and improvements in standardising adaptation measures and underwriting practices.[191] Risk-based modelling could be made more sensitive to a greater variety of factors and their weighting across a pool of policyholders, although this would require more granular data including on the above-mentioned factors. Standardising adaptation measures could entail using industry-wide frameworks; for example in the US insurance market, the IBHS Fortified Home Program provides recommendations on climate-related risk prevention measures related to wind, hail, or wildfire risks, and in certain US states, policyholders are eligible to receive premium discounts for their property insurance if houses meet the required standards.[192] The insurance industry could also contribute to official or government-sponsored development planning guides and building codes[193] that integrate climate change adaptation measures. These could then serve as a baseline for their underwriting assessment.

7.5.4.5 Verification and monitoring continuing compliance

If a premium reduction or rebate is given for a particular adaptation measure, the insurer may wish to be provided with some evidence or confirmation that the measure has been

189 OECD Insurance and Adaptation Paper 15.

190 EIOPA Adaptation and Insurance Report [50] and [63].

191 Ibid [64].

192 Ibid [65].

193 Swenja Surminski, Jonathan Barnes, and Katharine Vincent, 'Can Insurance Catalyse Government Planning on Climate? Emergent Evidence from Sub-Saharan Africa' (2022) 153 *World Development*, 105830.

implemented. Some adaptation measures may be reversible or dependent on continuing input from the policyholder in which case the insurer ought to make continuing compliance a warranty in the insurance contract or allow for an adjusting premium payment at the end of the policy period. Although compliance may be costly or difficult to monitor in retail business, this is not an issue unique to climate change adaptation measures and insurance contracts frequently include a variety of ongoing risk mitigation terms.

7.5.4.6 Twelve-month policy term

A commonly cited obstacle to greater involvement by insurers in supporting climate change adaptation measures taken by policyholders is the 12-month policy period that is standard for most retail (non-life) policies. The policyholder cannot be certain that a premium discount will be available on renewal with the same insurer, or if it subsequently insures with a different insurer. An insurer who has given a premium discount to enable an investment in an adaptation measure that reduces risk over a longer time frame cannot take full advantage of the benefit if the policyholder changes insurers at the end of the 12-month policy period. It has therefore been suggested that multi-year policies should be considered: they could be used to give a larger premium discount upfront to enable the policyholder to make the investment in the adaptation measure, while providing certainty to both parties that insurance cover is placed over the longer (i.e. beyond twelve months) policy term.[194] Multi-year contracts do however restrict the policyholder's choice and may attract higher capital requirements for insurers since they cannot re-price annually.[195]

7.5.4.7 Uncertain prudential treatment

The risk-reducing effect of an adaptation measure could be relevant to an insurer's technical provisions which need to cover all of its expected future insurance or reinsurance contractual liabilities.[196] Liabilities must be valued at the amount for which they could be transferred or settled between knowledgeable willing parties in an arm's length transaction.[197] The valuation of a liability is based on its hypothetical market value which would be capable of pricing in any factors that reduce its liabilities, such as adaptation measures that reduce the risk of loss. For the SCR[198] to be reduced, it would be necessary to recognise the adaptation measures somewhere within the SCR Standard Formula (or an approved internal model). There is currently no particular component in the Standard Formula that gives explicit recognition. An adaptation measure is not a 'risk-mitigation technique' as no risk transfer to another party is taking place. EIOPA has stated its plans to assess the potential for a dedicated prudential treatment of climate-related adaptation measures in non-life insurance,[199] but there are no corresponding plans of the Bank of England/PRA.[200] Taking account of adaptation measures requires them to be measurable (see above), and double-counting (e.g. by giving credit to the technical provisions and the SCR) should be avoided.

194 EIOPA Non-Life Underwriting and Climate Change Report [2.64].
195 Ibid [2.65].
196 PRA Rulebook, Solvency II Firms, Technical Provisions, 2.1.
197 PRA Rulebook, Solvency II Firms, Valuation, 2.1(2).
198 See Chapter 4, Section 4.4.3.
199 EIOPA Adaptation and Insurance Report [74].
200 BoE Climate and Capital Frameworks Report [59].

7.5.5 *Other pricing mechanisms*

It is apparent from this considerable list of obstacles that there is still a lot of work to be done at the individual insurer level, by the insurance industry as a whole, and by the regulators and policymakers to make risk-based premium pricing an effective tool to incentivise policyholders to implement climate adaptation measures. It has also been noted – and this will be discussed in more detail in Chapter 9 – that public funding is likely to be required for certain climate change adaptation measures.

Other pricing benefits that could be considered – depending on their suitability in the policy context – are lowering deductibles and increasing (sub-)limits of liability that become applicable if the policyholder takes specified adaptation measures. Some commentators have argued that risk-reflective deductibles are more effective than premium discounts since they can make the cost-effectiveness of the investment in the adaptation measure more obvious,[201] while others have argued that deductibles are uncertain future costs for policyholders, and that they will not appreciate the cost-effectiveness of adaptation measures in comparison to the deductible when entering into the contract and before a loss (to which the deductible applies) has occurred.[202] The benefit of a raised limit of liability could be even less obvious to a policyholder at the outset and may therefore not be an effective incentive.[203] Deductibles and limits must be documented as contractual terms in the insurance policy.

7.6 Terms (other than pricing and claims)

The definition of 'climate-related impact underwriting' adopted in this chapter extends to influencing policyholders to mitigate and adapt to insured risks via contractual terms. The terms of a contract of insurance govern the obligations of the parties during the term of the contract but, in addition, they can also have a prospective effect on the policyholder at the pre-contractual stage. The prospective effect has already been alluded to above: an insurer can influence a prospective policyholder's behaviour by offering different levels of covers and different levels of premium depending on the existing risk management measures and risk attitude of the prospective policyholder. This may cause the prospective policyholder to make positive risk adjustments in order to secure better cover or a lower premium. The flipside is, however, that if the terms are too onerous, or less onerous terms are available from other insurers, a prospective insured is likely to buy insurance from another insurer (or not at all).

201 Michael Bräuninger, Sonja Butzengeiger-Geyer, Andrew Dlugolecki, Stefan Hochrainer, Michel Köhler, Joanne Linnerooth-Bayer, Reinhard Mechler, Axel Michaelowa, and Sven Schulze, 'Application of Economic Instruments for Adaptation to Climate Change, Final Report' (2011) CLIMA.C.3./ETU/2010/0011 Perspectives Climate Change <https://www.researchgate.net/publication/248399515_Application_of_economic_instruments_for_adaptation_to_climate_change_Final_report> accessed on 1 June 2023.

202 Sally J. Priest, Edmund C. Penning-Rowsell, and Cathy Suykens, 'Promoting Adaptive Flood Risk Management: The Role and Potential of Flood Recovery Mechanisms' (2016) 7 E3S Web Conf 17005.

203 EIOPA Non-Life Underwriting and Climate Change Report [2.58].

7.6.1 Existing landscape

Contractual terms are one of the established 'steering tools' (besides pricing) used by insurers to control the moral hazard during the term of the contract, namely that, in the knowledge that insurance cover is available, an insured could engage in behaviours that increase the risk of loss or even be incentivised to produce a loss.

A frequently used contractual device to ensure that the risk accepted by the insurer at the outset does not deteriorate is the insurance warranty – an undertaking by the insured 'that some particular thing shall or shall not be done, or that some condition shall be fulfilled.'[204] Traditionally, an insurance warranty incentivised (or coerced) the insured to comply since upon a breach of warranty the insurer used to be automatically discharged from liability.[205] Since the Insurance Act 2015 has been in force, a breach of warranty only suspends the insurer's liability while the breach is ongoing, but the insurer's liability is restored as and when a breach has been remedied.[206] Moreover, further to s.11(2) of the Insurance Act 2015, an insurer can no longer rely on a breach of warranty to discharge its liability for a loss if the insured can show that the breach of warranty could not have increased the risk of the loss which actually occurred in the circumstances in which it occurred. Section 11 limits the incentivising effect of any warranties (and other risk mitigation terms)[207] that are not material to the risk of insured loss.

An exclusion in an insurance contract means that the excluded risk remains outside the scope of the cover.[208] Exclusions can have the capacity to put the insured on notice not to engage in certain activities, or to take certain measures, as otherwise there will be no insurance cover. For example, an exclusion in a home and contents policy that excludes from coverage the 'escape of water' from domestic water and heating installations while the home has not been lived in for more than [x] consecutive days and where the mains supply has not been shut off,[209] signals to the insured that it must turn off its mains supply when going away for an extended period of time. More often, however, exclusions are used for risks that are outside the control of the insured (e.g. losses deriving from war, nuclear incidents, communicable diseases) or losses that are inevitable (e.g. wear and tear). That type of exclusion cannot therefore be said to incentivise the insured. Exclusions can also be used as a pricing lever, where specified risks are excluded from a standard form of cover, but can be 'written back in' for an additional premium. For example, this technique is used for terrorism[210] and cyber-attack[211] coverage.

More recently, insurers started introducing terms that promise rewards, or provide upfront benefits, for certain policyholder behaviours considered conducive to reducing the risk insured. For example, many motor insurance policies contain a 'no claims bonus'

---

204 Marine Insurance Act 1906 s 33(1).

205 Ibid s 33(3) – now deleted.

206 Insurance Act 2015 s 10(2).

207 Ibid s 11(1): a risk mitigation term is a term (express or implied) of a contract of insurance, other than a term defining the risk as a whole, if compliance with it would tend to reduce the risk of one or more of the following (a) loss of a particular kind, (b) loss at a particular location, or (c) loss at a particular time.

208 John Birds, Ben Lynch, KC, and Simon Paul, *MacGillivray on Insurance Law* (15th ed, Sweet & Maxwell 2022) 10-009.

209 See e.g. Aviva, 'Aviva Private Client – High Net Worth Home Insurance Policy' 17 <https://connect.avivab2b.co.uk/broker/personal/high-net-worth/> accessed on 1 June 2023.

210 See e.g. IUA clause 'JS2018 001 Cyber Attack Exclusion Clause and Writeback.'

211 See e.g. IUA clause 'JL2011 004 JLC Terrorism Write Back Clause.'

clause further to which the insurer promises to reduce the premium by a set percentage upon renewal if the policyholder has not made any claims under the policy in the current year. Some health insurance products operate a 'reward system' where the policyholder can earn credits by leading an active lifestyle (tracked by a fitness tracker that provides relevant data to the insurer). The credits can then be used for benefits – such as gym memberships, Pelotons, or Fitbits – that promote healthy lifestyles.[212] Thus, an insurer can incentivise policyholders to adopt behaviours that reduce the risk of loss (e.g. driving more carefully and living more healthily). Some commentators have pointed out that the purpose of influencing policyholder behaviour is to reduce an insurer's own liability (or 'damage control'), rather than a more altruistic motivation to prevent loss and reduce the risk to the public.[213] Yet, these reward terms do enable policyholders to make behavioural adjustments that are considered positive by signalling to them what these beneficial behaviours are and incentivising adjustments. In contrast, insurance warranties are more 'coercive' in nature since there is the threat of losing the right to be indemnified if they are breached.

What type of term it is, and what its meaning is, is a matter of contractual construction. A contract of insurance, like any other contract, must be interpreted objectively by asking what a reasonable person, with all the background knowledge which would reasonably have been available to the parties when they entered into the contract, would have understood the language of the contract to mean.[214] In *FCA v Arch Insurance (UK) Ltd and others*[215] the Supreme Court took a construction approach that was more favourable to policyholders by reframing the identity of the 'reasonable person' (from whose perspective the term's meaning is assessed) as 'a reasonable policyholder' rather than an objective or disinterested person, and by resolving any ambiguity in the meaning of a term against the insurer.[216] This means that, in relation to terms that confer benefits on the policyholder, any ambiguity in the meaning of such a term is likely to be resolved by giving the term a more generous meaning vis-à-vis the policyholder, while terms that impose obligations on the policyholder and non-compliance with which may entitle the insurer to decline liability for a claim will be construed narrowly.

In relation to consumer (insurance) contracts,[217] the CRA 2015, s.69(1) provides that where a term could have different meanings, the meaning that is most favourable to the consumer is to prevail. This means that, in relation to green terms that confer benefits on the policyholder, any ambiguity in the meaning of such a term is likely to be resolved to give the term a more generous meaning vis-à-vis the policyholder, while terms that impose obligations on the policyholder and non-compliance with which may entitle the insurer to decline liability for a claim will be construed narrowly. In relation to consumer (insurance) contracts, the CRA 2015, s.69(1), provides that where a term could have different meanings, the meaning that is most favourable to the consumer is to prevail.

212 See e.g. Vitality Health Insurance, 'Reward Yourself, You've Earned It' <https://www.vitality.co.uk/rewards/> accessed on 1 June 2023.

213 Abraham and Schwarcz (n 87).

214 *FCA v Arch Insurance (UK) Ltd and Ors* [2021] UKSC 1, [Lord Hamblen] and [Lord Leggatt JJSC] at [47].

215 Ibid.

216 See e.g. [121] and [227].

217 A consumer for the purposes of the CRA 2015 is an individual acting for purposes that are wholly or mainly outside that individual's trade, business, craft, or profession (s 2(3)).

Further to the new consumer duty, insurers must also consider contractual terms in light of delivering good outcomes for retail customers.[218] The ICOBS pre-contractual product disclosure requirements include the disclosure of significant or unusual exclusions or limitations,[219] and of obligations at the start and during the term of the contract.[220]

7.6.2 Terms for green insurance products

The enabling conception discussed in Chapter 3, Section 3.4.5, pictures insurers as supporting, rather than coercing, policyholders to take climate mitigation action and to adopt climate change adaptation measures. What kind of contractual terms can influence a policyholder's behaviour and enable it to mitigate and adapt to climate-related risks ('green term' will be used as shorthand)? Before discussing specific examples, it is useful to establish some drafting criteria:

- if the green term imposes an obligation on the policyholder, it should be an action or inaction within the control of the policyholder and an obligation that the policyholder is realistically able to fulfil without imposing a disproportionate burden;
- the substance of the green term (whether it is an obligation or an exclusion) must have a degree of salience – it has to be relevant to the commercial purpose of the insurance contract in question which is the risk transfer in relation to the insured subject matter. As noted above in relation to pricing, in property insurance there can be a link between a specific climate change adaptation measure and a reduction in the risk of loss – therefore relevance can be established. By contrast, it is more difficult to translate a climate change mitigation action (e.g. reducing GHG emissions) into a meaningful green term given that climate change mitigation measures (some form of GHG emission reduction) cannot be straightforwardly connected to a reduction of an insured risk;
- if the term is an exclusion from coverage, the excluded risks must be well-defined and must not obliterate the cover.[221] If the insurance policy wording is too heavily reliant on exclusions, it may not meet the 'fair value' requirement;[222]
- terms in consumer (insurance) contracts are required to be fair.[223] Any term compliance with which would require a consumer policyholder to incur additional costs is at risk of being unfair, as well as likely to be inconsistent with the 'fair value' requirement;
- the green term has to be one that is broadly acceptable to a policyholder. It has already been noted that consumers and small businesses buy insurance on standard terms that are not open for negotiation. If any of the terms by themselves or the terms in the round are too onerous, a prospective policyholder may decide

218 PRIN 2.1.1R Prin 12; and see Section 7.4.5.

219 ICOBS 6, Annex 2, s 2 (pure protection contracts and/or commercial customers) and ICOBS, 6 Annex 3 and s 2 (consumer contracts other than pure protection contracts and life insurance); and see Section 7.3.2.

220 ICOBS 6, Annex 3 and s 2 (consumer contracts other than pure protection contracts and life insurance); and see Section 7.3.2.

221 *FCA v Arch Insurance (UK) Ltd and ors* [2021] UKSC 1, [78] per Lord Hamblen and Lord Leggatt; and also note the 'good faith' cross-cutting rule which is part of the new consumer duty (discussed in Section 7.4.5).

222 See Section 7.2.2.

223 See Section 7.8.

to buy insurance from another insurer who offers better terms, or to not insure at all;

- to prevent contractual construction disputes in relation to, and unfavourable interpretations of, green terms it is important to draft clearly as to what the policyholder must do or must not, whether the policyholder's obligation is absolute or qualified, how and when compliance is assessed or measured, what sanctions are triggered upon a breach or non-compliance, what benefits are available on compliance, and what rights the insurer is entitled to exercise.[224]

Policyholders' motivation to take climate action is undermined by the 'tragedy of the commons'[225]: individual acts by a consumer or a small business do not halt or reverse climate change, so they are likely to act according to their own self-interest, without consideration of the impact on the common good. Behaviour change by individuals and households requires both motivation to change and capacity for change.[226] Motivation for change comes from economic, legal, and social incentives, and/or putting a higher value on climate action over other values.[227] Capacity for change depends on understanding the choices available and the ability and resources to implement changes. Therefore, to influence the policyholder's behaviour effectively, the policyholder must understand the behavioural choices available and their consequences.[228] Bounded rational choice theory holds that a rational decision-maker decides on a preferred course of action that maximises their personal advantage by balancing costs against benefits based on their knowledge and information available to them.[229] Accordingly, good behaviour should be rewarded and facilitated, and bad behaviour should be discouraged and/or penalised. Prospect theory tells us that people's loss aversion tends to be greater than the prospect of a gain.[230] Applied to insurance contract law, compliance with a green term should trigger a contractual benefit to be conferred upon the policyholder by the insurer and/or breach or non-compliance with a green term should trigger a remedy or have other negative contractual consequences.

The primary benefit for the policyholder under an insurance contract is the claims payment in the event of a loss or insured event. What additional benefits could an insurer offer to reward compliance with a green term? Additional benefits could be premium discounts or rebates or, as has been noted in relation to health insurance, credits or vouchers. Nudge theory suggests that incentives should be coupled with good information or feedback

224 See Section 7.6.1 and this section below.

225 Garrett Hardin, 'The Tragedy of the Commons' (1968) 162 *Science*, 1243; Nigar Hashimzade, Gareth Myles, and John Black, *Oxford Dictionary of Economics* (5th ed, OUP 2017) entry for 'Tragedy of the Commons.'

226 Susanne C. Moser and Julia A. Ekstrom, 'A Framework to Diagnose Barriers to Climate Change Adaptation' (2010) 107(51) *Proc Natl Acad Sci*, 22026.

227 IPCC 2022 Mitigation Report, Summary for Policymakers [5.4.1].

228 Also see the consumer duty (Section 7.4.5).

229 Gary S. Becker, *The Economic Approach to Human Behavior* (The University of Chicago Press 1976); Daniel Kahneman, 'Maps of Bounded Rationality: Psychology for Behavioral Economics' (2003) 93 *The American Economic Review*, 1449.

230 Daniel Kahneman and Amos Tversky, 'Prospect Theory: An Analysis of Decision under Risk' (1979) 47 *Econometrica*, 263–291.

to enable better decisions going forward.[231] Thus, to be effective, the additional benefit would not just be a 'perk' for the policyholder but would also be capable of contributing to climate change mitigation or adaptation, as well as providing the policyholder with information on how this is being achieved. For example, this could be a credits system for replacing a fossil fuel appliance or energy source with an electric one,[232] the installation of a thermostat or light sensors, or a voucher for planting trees.[233] Other benefits that could be considered – depending on their suitability in the policy context – are premium discounts and rebates, lowering deductibles, and increasing or reinstating limits of liability upon the policyholder taking or refraining from specified actions.[234] A recent insurance study has shown that 'nudges' lose effectiveness if the content of the nudge is inconsistent with the policyholder's pre-existing beliefs.[235] This demonstrates the need for addressing the lack of policyholder awareness of climate change itself, and climate change mitigation and adaptation,[236] and is a reason for insurers to take a holistic approach to climate-related impact underwriting strategy, including information and risk management strategies.

Whether a green term has been breached may depend on how compliance is assessed or measured, and whether it imposes an absolute obligation on the policyholder (or an obligation to use 'best endeavours' or 'reasonable endeavours') to achieve a specified outcome. Similarly, whether a 'target' for a reward-style term has been met depends on whether the target has been set by reference to measurable KPIs or more subjective criteria. It is unlikely that there exist (yet) any methodologies for measuring GHG emissions from the operation of small businesses or from private households, but it is conceivable to set other GHG emission-related targets such as improving a specific aspect of energy efficiency (e.g. installing better insulation) or reducing a specific carbon-intense activity (e.g. ceasing to use coal in fireplaces). As regards adaptation measures, there is a wider variety of specific actions that could be taken, some of which have been listed above, and whether such measures have been implemented and are being maintained should be easier to ascertain.

The consequences of breach of, or non-compliance with, a term depend on the nature of the term in question. Infamously, English insurance contract law does not use the same classification scheme for contractual terms as general contract law.[237] This is not the place for a detailed exegesis of breach of insurance contract terms and reference is made to the standard textbooks in the field.[238] A remedy in damages for breach of a green term may not be available if that breach itself has not caused any loss to the insurer which meets the contractual remoteness test in *Hadley v Baxendale*.[239] The insurer cannot decline liability

231 Richard H. Thaler and Cass R. Sunstein, *Nudge: Improving Decisions about Health, Wealth and Happiness* (Penguin 2012), ch 2 and 14.

232 It should also be considered how this could be tied in with 'green reinstatement terms' (see Section 7.7).

233 See e.g. 'Plant a tree' vouchers from the National Trust <https://www.nationaltrust.org.uk/features/plant-a-tree> accessed on 1 June 2023.

234 See Section 7.5.

235 Peter John Robinson and W.J. Wouter Botzen, 'Setting Descriptive Norm Nudges to Promote Demand for Insurance against Increasing Climate Change Risk' (2022) 47 Geneva Paper on Risk and Insurance, 3.

236 See Section 7.4.

237 Robert Merkin, *Colinvaux's Law of Insurance* (13th ed, Sweet & Maxwell, 2022) [8-004].

238 Ibid ch 8; *MacGillivray on Insurance Law* (n 208) ch 10; John Birds and Katie Richards, *Birds' Modern Insurance Law* (12th ed, Sweet & Maxwell 2022) ch 9.

239 *Hadley v Baxendale* (1854) 9 Exch 341: the remoteness rule laid down in this case is that losses are recoverable if they flow naturally from the breach or if they are in the contemplation of both parties at the time

for an insurance claim for breach of certain types of green terms, if the breach has been remedied before the insured loss occurred[240] and/or non-compliance with the green term could not have increased the risk of any insured loss which actually occurred in the circumstances in which it occurred.[241] Thus, an insurance warranty in a property insurance policy that the insured shall reduce its GHG emissions by x% per quarter is unlikely to attract a remedy if breached since the failure to reduce its GHG emissions is unlikely to increase the risk of loss or damage to the insured property.

Given the significant costs of (some) climate change mitigation and adaptation measures that policyholders would have to bear, guided by the conception of insurers as enablers, and considering the 'consumer duty' in relation to retail customers and the 'fairness' requirement in consumer insurance contracts,[242] it seems preferable to draft green terms that set policyholders soft targets, upon the implementation or achievement of which the policyholder would be entitled to a reward. Green terms that impose obligations on the policyholder to implement certain climate change mitigation or adaptation measures (or mandate that the policyholder ceases harmful actions) while incurring costs in doing so, and entitle the insurers to a remedy when breached, do not meet the drafting criteria and are less likely to stand up to the fairness test[243] and regulatory[244] scrutiny. It is also worth noting that the EU Taxonomy technical screening criteria for climate change adaptation anticipate that the insurer (1) offers risk-based rewards for preventive actions taken by policyholders or (2) provides to customers measures in relation to an asset, an activity, or people that prevent or protect against natural catastrophes.[245] Arguably, where a policyholder (and not the insurer) is obliged to provide or implement the measure, and there is no risk-based reward, there would be no 'substantial contribution' to climate change adaptation from the insurer and therefore the insurance policy would not qualify as an environmentally sustainable economic activity under the EU Taxonomy.

In contrast, where an insurer has already 'rewarded' the policyholder upfront for implementing a mitigation or adaptation measure, it would seem fair and reasonable to contractually oblige the policyholder – who has accepted the reward – to put that measure in place and maintain it or be liable to return the reward.

Terms that exclude from cover losses in connection with activities that are harmful to the environment and/or contribute to climate change can be effective in making the policyholder cease those activities. However, such exclusions could have a draconian effect where the insured's business depends on carrying out those activities. If the insured carries on with those activities, there will be a protection gap. If the insured cannot for legal

of entry into the contract.

240 Insurance Act 2015 s 10(4). Applies to insurance warranties.

241 Ibid s 11(2). Applies to a term (express or implied) of a contract of insurance, other than a term defining the risk, if compliance with it would tend to reduce the risk of one or more of the following – (1) loss of a particular kind, (2) loss at a particular location, (3) loss at a particular time (Insurance Act 2015, s 11(1)).

242 See Sections 7.4.5 and 7.8.

243 See Section 7.8.1.

244 See Sections 7.2, 7.3, and 7.4.5.

245 Commission Delegated Regulation (EU) 2021/2139 of 4 June 2021 supplementing Regulation (EU) 2020/852 of the European Parliament and of the Council by establishing the technical screening criteria for determining the conditions under which an economic activity qualifies as contributing substantially to climate change mitigation or climate change adaptation and for determining whether that economic activity causes no significant harm to any of the other environmental objectives, Annex II, s 10; and see Chapter 5, Section 5.4.1.

or practical reasons carry on the activities without insurance protection, it may go out of business and jobs and tax revenue may be lost.[246]

7.6.3 Examples

With the above analysis in mind, some green term examples (excluding terms relating to claims and premiums) are set out below:

- the insurer's consent to building works or alterations to the insured property could be made conditional upon using energy-efficient materials and building systems in the new works or alterations (or less stringently, for the policyholder to do so where it is reasonable by reference to costs and efforts);[247]
- a knowledge and information sharing clause that prompts the policyholder to assess climate change risks and impacts and share this information with the insurers and a provision that requires the insurer to provide a report with insights related to climate-related risks and mitigation of those risks that are relevant to the policyholder during the policy year;[248]
- the insurer offers weather alert technologies with the insurance policy, so that policyholders receive an SMS with a warning and a link to the website, where they can find out how to protect themselves against the negative effects of individual weather events;[249]
- setting the policyholder a (soft) GHG emission reduction target in connection with the insured subject matter. When the target is met, the insurer will reward with credits that can be applied towards a premium discount, towards the costs of carrying out an energy efficiency retrofit, or a net-zero activity or project benefitting the public;
- some travel insurance products offer GHG emission 'off-set' extensions for an additional premium investment in carbon sinks that can be purchased by policyholders who will be contributing to GHG emissions through air travel;[250]
- excluding from cover loss or damage caused by, or liability incurred in relation to, specified carbon-intense activities.

Translating 'green term' aspirations into workable contractual terms for green insurance products presents challenges, some of which mirror those discussed in relation to pricing: climate change mitigation and adaptation measures can be costly and may not be affordable by policyholders. Research shows that 'costs' are the main obstacle to greater take-up of adaptation measures,[251] while the availability of funding facilitates such investment

246 Also see Chapter 6, Section 6.4.

247 Insurance Information Institute 'Green Insurance' <https://www.iii.org/article/green-insurance> accessed 1 on 1 June 2023.

248 The Chancery Lane Project, 'Climate Clauses: Insurance' <https://chancerylaneproject.org/practice-areas/insurance/> accessed on 1 June 2023.

249 EIOPA Non-Life Underwriting and Climate Change Report, Table 4.

250 Stricker and Pugnetti (n 2).

251 Priest (n 202); Seifert-Dähnn (n 82).

by policyholders.[252] One possible source of funding would be for UK insurers to make a contribution from those funds that will become available after the forthcoming reforms on risk margins levels come into effect. This will be discussed further in Chapter 8, Section 8.3.1.

Some potential funding and financing solutions will be considered in Chapters 8 and 9. Contracts of general insurance tend to have a 12-month policy period which does not lend itself to committing a policyholder to sustained longer-term action. It is by no means clear whether green terms that mandate or prohibit prescribed conduct or green terms that take a 'nudge approach'[253] are more effective, but the former are more likely to present difficulties in consumer contracts as potentially 'unfair terms.' The substantive content of green terms in relation to climate risk mitigation will evolve as more scientific evidence becomes available as to how GHG can be offset, reduced, or removed from the atmosphere, and technologies to do so become more widely available. Green terms relating to climate change adaptation would benefit from greater standardisation in terms of measures that are suitable and affordable, as well as in the wordings adopted by the insurance industry. Drafting green terms is an integral part of the product design process, and green terms that provide significant benefits or constitute limitations or exclusions must be clearly disclosed at the pre-contractual stage.[254] 'Green terms' is also an area that would benefit from joint research and development by behavioural economists, environmental scientists, climate technology engineers, underwriters, brokers, and lawyers.

7.7 Claims

If the policyholder has made a valid claim under the contract of insurance, the insurer is required to pay the policyholder (or its beneficiary) a sum of money representing its insured loss (in indemnity insurance) or an agreed sum (in contingency insurance). This is also referred to as 'cash settlement.' Subject to the terms of the policy, the policyholder (or beneficiary) can then use the settlement proceeds as it pleases.[255] Instead of a cash settlement, property policies frequently contain 'basis of settlement' clauses which provide for the reinstatement or repair of insured buildings or personal property that have been damaged or the replacement of lost items. These different types of 'basis of settlement' clauses could serve as a powerful precedent for green settlement terms that mandate or encourage the recipient to apply settlement proceeds towards the reinstatement or repair of property with low-carbon materials and lower GHG emission, or the replacement of personal property with recycled or lower emission alternatives ('green reinstatement'). For example:

252 Susanne Hanger, Joanne Linnerooth-Bayer, Swenja Surminski, Cristina Nenciu-Posner, Anna Lorant, Radu Ionescu, and Anthony Patt, 'Insurance, Public Assistance, and Household Flood Risk Reduction: A Comparative Study of Austria, England, and Romania', (2018) 38(4) *Risk Analysis*, 680.

253 Thaler and Sunstein (n 231).

254 See Section 7.3.2.

255 *Rayner v Preston* (1881) 18 Ch D 1 (Ch).

- flood insurance: under the UK Flood Re 'Build Back Better' scheme, homeowners can install property flood resilience measures up to the value of £10,000 when repairing their properties after a flood loss;[256]
- comprehensive motor insurance: after a total loss when a petrol or diesel car is 'written off,' the policyholder replaces it with an electric or hybrid car. The sale of new petrol and diesel cars in the UK will be banned by 2030 as part of the UK government's 'Ten Point Plan for a Green Industrial Revolution,'[257] so insurers could contribute to an earlier phasing out of petrol cars;
- boiler breakdown insurance cover (as separate insurance or as part of home/property insurance): if a gas boiler breaks down, the policyholder replaces it with a greener alternative. A study by UK insurer More Than has found that among homeowners who still have a gas boiler (86%), more than two-fifths (43%) are willing to replace it with an electric one, one in four (27%) want to install a solar water heating system, and almost a fifth (19%) are looking to fit an air source heat pump;[258]
- business insurance and home insurance: upon damage to a building, the policyholder repairs or refits the building to reduce GHG emissions and increase energy efficiency (e.g. carrying out roof repairs with better insulation; replacing single-glazed windows with double-glazed windows), and/or uses sustainable materials to the extent possible. The property is reinstated or repaired with adaptation measures relevant to its location;
- contents cover (as part of business or home insurance) or insurance cover for specific assets: upon loss or damage, the policyholder has the item repaired using sustainable materials to the extent possible or accepts a recycled replacement.

The Global Federation of Insurance Associations published a 'Key Principles for More Resilient and Sustainable Construction' paper which envisages that for claims following a natural disaster, the insured property should be built in a more resilient way with green and recycled materials.[259] These principles could be extended to claims in respect of other insured perils.

7.7.1 Types of green reinstatement terms

There are a number of options for how green reinstatement clauses could be drafted. The key variables are (1) whether there is a reinstatement (or repair or replacement) alternative to a cash settlement, (2) if there is, which party has the right to elect between a cash

256 See Flood Re, 'Build Back Better' <https://www.floodre.co.uk/buildbackbetter/> accessed 1 June 2023.

257 The Prime Minister and the Department for Business, Energy and Industrial Strategy, 'The Ten Point Plan for a Green Industrial Revolution' (18 November 2020) <https://www.gov.uk/government/publications/the-ten-point-plan-for-a-green-industrial-revolution/title> accessed on 1 June 2023.

258 RSA, 'Homeowners Urged to Go Green as Insurance Claims for Heating Breakdowns Surge' (23 March 2021) <https://www.rsagroup.com/news/press-releases/2021/homeowners-urged-to-go-green-as-insurance-claims-for-heating-breakdowns-surge/> accessed on 1 June 2023.

259 Global Federation of Insurance Associations, 'Key Principles for More Resilient and Sustainable Construction' <https://gfiainsurance.org/news/408/cop26-insurers-publish-key-principles-for-more-resilient-and-sustainable-construction> accessed on 1 June 2023.

settlement and reinstatement (or repair or replacement), and (3) if reinstatement (or repair or replacement) applies, whether the insurer is obliged, or can be required, to effect a green reinstatement. Different options might apply to different types of insured assets even within the same property policy.

1. the claim is settled by way of cash settlement. However, where applicable, upon payment the insurer provides information on sustainable reinstatement, replacement, and repair options, including what government schemes and grants (see Section 7.7.2) are available;
2. the insurer has the right to elect between (a) cash settlement and (b) reinstatement. If the insurer elects option (b), the insurer is entitled to elect between conventional or green reinstatement;
3. the insurer has the right to elect between (a) cash settlement and (b) reinstatement. If the insurer elects option (b), the policyholder is entitled to elect between conventional or green reinstatement;
4. the insurer has the right to elect between (a) cash settlement and (b) reinstatement. If the insurer elects option (b), the insurer is required to effect green reinstatement;
5. the insurer is obliged to reinstate but is entitled to elect between conventional or green reinstatement;
6. the insurer is obliged to effect green reinstatement;
7. the policyholder has the right to elect between (a) cash settlement and (b) reinstatement. If the policyholder electschooses option (a), upon payment the insurer provides information on sustainable reinstatement, replacement, and repair options, including what government schemes and grants (see Section 7.7.2) are available. If the policyholder elects option (b), the insurer is entitled to elect between conventional or green reinstatement;
8. the policyholder has the right to elect between (a) cash settlement and (b) reinstatement. If the policyholder elects option (a), upon payment the insurer provides information on sustainable reinstatement, replacement, and repair options, including what government schemes and grants (see Section 7.7.2) are available. If the policyholder elects option (b), the policyholder is entitled to elect between conventional or green reinstatement;
9. the policyholder has the right to elect between (a) cash settlement and (b) reinstatement. If the policyholder elects option (a), upon payment the insurer provides information on sustainable reinstatement, replacement, and repair options, including what government schemes and grants (see Section 7.7.2) are available. If the policyholder elects option (b), the insurer is obliged to effect green reinstatement.

Option 1 is the least onerous for insurers and is also the extent to which insurers have contemplated green reinstatement terms to date.[260] Option 8, which gives the policyholder a choice on (1) cash settlement or reinstatement, and (2) conventional or green reinstate-

260 ABI, 'ABI Climate Change Roadmap' (7 July 2021) <https://www.abi.org.uk/news/news-articles/2021/07/abi-climate-change-roadmap/#:~:text=The%20ABI%E2%80%99s%20Climate%20Change%20Roadmap%20unveiled%20today%20includes%3A,firm%20plans%20to%20reach%20Net%20Zero%20by%202050> accessed on 1 June 2023.

ment, may be the safest option in a consumer contract from an 'unfair terms' perspective (see below) because it gives the policyholder the greatest flexibility to choose a course of action that is most favourable to its circumstances. For all options, except Option 6, one of the parties can opt for a cash settlement and/or conventional reinstatement, in which case there will be no positive net-zero effect. For all options where the insurer can elect reinstatement, the insurer is reliant on the co-operation of the policyholder to give access and control to the asset to be reinstated, replaced, or repaired and, accordingly, the performance of the insurer's reinstatement obligation should be made conditional upon the policyholder's co-operation.

Following a valid election to reinstate the subject matter, the agreement between the insurer and the policyholder is treated as if the policy had been an agreement to reinstate ab initio. The election relates back to the date of the policy, and the contract of insurance becomes enforceable as a building or repair contract,[261] the remedy for breach of which is damages.[262]

7.7.2 Costs

Paying for green reinstatement could be more expensive than making a cash settlement or paying for conventional reinstatement with respect to the materials and construction techniques used. How should additional costs be allocated? In the context of property insurance, the starting point is that the insurer must indemnify the insured for the loss caused by an insured peril to the insured property, but no more than that.[263] However, the parties are, within certain limits, free to agree on how the indemnity is to be calculated.[264] The measure of indemnity can be contractually agreed by way of valued policies,[265] or can be reduced by contractual provisions for deductibles, retentions, and limits of liability. In relation to insurance on real property, the parties may agree that the measure of indemnity is determined by reference to the cost of reinstatement of the property even if the costs of reinstatement are more than the pre-loss value of the property.[266] Policies insuring personal property may offer 'new for old' coverage, even if the new item is more valuable than the (old) insured asset.

Thus, it is not unprecedented that insurers absorb additional costs above their liability to indemnify for the loss once they are contractually committed to reinstatement or replacement. These additional costs would then be reflected in rising premiums for all policyholders in that class of insurance or across different pools. In relation to climate risk mitigation measures, this would be a method of socialising some of the costs of transitioning to a net-zero economy. This could be justified on the basis that slowing down climate change is for the benefit of society as a whole. Arguably, it is a relatively inefficient method given the transaction costs of insurance and its limited and contingent reach (it relies on policyholders choosing an insurance policy offering green reinstatement, that a

261 *Morrell v Irving Fire* (1865) 33 N.Y. 429.

262 *Home District Mutual Insurance v Thompson* (1847) 1 U.C. Er. & App. 247.

263 *Castellain v Preston* (1883) 11 QBD 380 (CA) 386.

264 *North of England Iron Steamship Insurance Asc v Armstrong* (1869–1870) LR 5 QB 244.

265 Subject to that the valuation is not fraudulent or so excessive that the policy is in the nature of a wagering contract (Marine Insurance Act 1906 s 27(2) and (3), and *Lewis v Rucker* (1761) 2 Burr 1167).

266 See *Colinvaux's Law of Insurance* (n 237) [11-159] and [11-160].

policyholder suffers an insured loss and has a valid claim, and that green reinstatement is chosen or applies automatically).

The benefit of adaptation measures at the property level tends to be confined to the property itself and they do not tend to have a wider societal impact. The justification for subsidising adaptation measures with increased premium payment from all policyholders in the pool is that it is a method of socialising the costs and making premiums more affordable for everyone. This is the approach taken by the UK Flood Re scheme: participating insurers pay a levy into the Flood Re pool and that levy can be absorbed by insurers through premium payments from all policyholders who buy home insurance (where flood risk is bundled into the cover).[267] However, the Flood Re scheme is a government-sponsored scheme in which insurers participate and its pooling arrangement is not available for non-flood risks. If additional costs for green reinstatement are reflected in higher premium levels for green insurance products which exceed what policyholders are prepared or can afford to pay, there will be no market for them and they will fail to have an impact.

On the other hand, green reinstatement is an opportunity to 'build back better' with the help of the insurance industry. 'Build Back Better' is the UK government's plan to support growth that, inter alia, enables the transition to a net-zero economy in the UK.[268] Moreover, government schemes and grants available to the policyholder could be used to absorb some of the additional costs. UK environmental schemes currently available to eligible consumers are the Boiler Upgrade Scheme[269] and the ECO4 Scheme (to be replaced by the 'Great British Insulation Scheme'),[270] and to consumers and small businesses the Smart Export Guarantee,[271] the Plug-in Vehicle Grant,[272] and the Plug-in Van and Truck Grant.[273] The Boiler Upgrade Scheme and the Plug-in Grants are one-off direct grants that are applied at the point of sale or installation. If green reinstatement terms apply, they should be supplemented by policy language to the effect that the policyholder must ensure that any rights under those government schemes are preserved and exercised where applicable and that the policyholder will give all necessary consents and assistance to that effect. The reinstatement or replacement costs of the insurer would thus be reduced by the amount of those grants. In contrast, the Smart Export Guarantee and ECO4 schemes pay matching government benefits for renewable energy generated over a number of years. It would be difficult for the insurer to recoup any costs under those schemes, especially as the contractual relationship with the relevant policyholder may be limited to a 12-month policy period. However, there are opportunities for insurers to offer add-on cover for renewable energy sources for extra premium.

Could the government give direct grants to insurers to subsidise green reinstatement in order for insurance policies with green reinstatement clauses to be offered at competitive

267 The Flood Reinsurance (Scheme Funding and Administration) Regulations 2015; and see Chapter 9, Section 9.4.2.

268 HM Treasury, 'Build Back Better: Our Plan for Growth' (March 2021) <https://www.gov.uk/government/publications/build-back-better-our-plan-for-growth/build-back-better-our-plan-for-growth-html#net-zero> accessed on 1 June 2023.

269 Office of Gas and Electricity Markets (Ofgem), 'Environmental and Social Schemes' <https://www.ofgem.gov.uk/environmental-and-social-schemes> accessed on 1 June 2023.

270 Ibid.

271 Ibid.

272 Department for Transport, 'Plug-in Vehicle Grant Port' <https://www.gov.uk/government/publications/plug-in-vehicle-grant-portal-guidance/using-the-plug-in-vehicle-grant-portal> accessed on 1 June 2023.

273 Ibid.

premium rates? Apart from budgetary constraints, such grants could be regarded as state subsidies in conflict with state aid rules. The UK is no longer bound by EU competition rules, and the WTO's General Agreement on Trade in Services[274] applies primarily to cross-border flows of services. The Subsidy Control Act 2022 provides the framework for a new, UK-wide subsidy control regime which will enable public authorities to grant subsidies aimed, inter alia, at achieving net-zero GHG emissions.[275] However, the 'energy and environment principles' with which subsidies need to be consistent do not apply to climate change adaptation measures and do not specifically envisage subsidies that achieve an overall reduction in GHG emissions linked to private households and small businesses.[276] It is suggested that it is more efficient to make grants available to policyholders which an insurer could then take into account when a claim is settled by way of green reinstatement.

The Global Federation of Insurance Associations has recommended that complementary funding should be provided by public authorities, for instance in the form of an interest-free bank loan, if green reinstatement exceeds the insurer's indemnity.[277] As part of delivering the European Green Deal, the European Commission is budgeting EUR 72.2 billion over seven years in funding for the renovation of public and private buildings to use more renewable energy and to provide access to zero- and low-emission mobility.[278] Some of this investment could be delivered through green claims. Further potential financing solutions, including funding from capital releases following the forthcoming risk margins reforms, will be considered in Chapters 8 and 9.

The concept of 'build back better' and green reinstatement terms has wide-spread support, including the OECD,[279] the PSI,[280] the GFIA,[281] the NZIA,[282] and the ABI.[283] On balance, there is a case to be made for insurers to adopt green reinstatement terms in relation to specific categories of assets. At the very least, they raise awareness among policyholders that their homes and business premises can be rebuilt or repaired with low-carbon materials and lower GHG emissions and putting in place adaptation measures, and that certain types of personal property can be replaced or repaired with recycled or lower emission alternatives. At their most effective, green reinstatement terms make a concrete contribution to the net-zero transition by enabling policyholders to remedy the loss of or damage to insured property with greener alternatives and increase their resilience to climate-related risks.

274 World Trade Organisation, 'General Agreement on Trade in Services (GATS)' (in force January 1995).

275 Subsidy Control Act 2022.

276 Ibid sch 2; Prin H is limited to decarbonisation linked to 'industrial activities.'

277 Global Federation of Insurance Associations (n 259).

278 European Commission, 'Delivering the European Green Deal' <https://commission.europa.eu/strategy-and-policy/priorities-2019-2024/european-green-deal/delivering-european-green-deal_en> accessed on 1 June 2023.

279 OECD Insurance and Adaptation Paper 22–25.

280 NZIA, 'Statement of Commitment by Signatory Companies' <https://www.unepfi.org/psi/wp-content/uploads/2021/07/NZIA-Commitment.pdf> accessed on 1 June 2023.

UNEP FI, 'Principles of Sustainable Insurance' <https://www.unepfi.org/psi/the-principles/> accessed on 1 June 2023.

281 Global Federation of Insurance Associations (n 259).

282 NZIA (n 280).

PRI, Prin 1.

283 ABI (n 260).

7.7.3 Prudential treatment of green reinstatement terms

The insurer's liability for claims could be potentially higher where the insurer undertakes to pay for green reinstatement. This would need to be reflected in its technical provisions which need to cover all of its expected future insurance or reinsurance contractual liabilities.[284] Its SCR[285] could increase since an election for reinstatement could introduce additional counter-party risk – that of builders and repairers – which should be reflected in the credit risk and operational risk components in the SCR Standard Formula[286] (or an approved internal model).

7.7.4 Conduct regulation on claims handling

An insurer must (1) handle claims promptly and fairly; (2) provide reasonable guidance to help a policyholder make a claim and appropriate information on its progress; (3) not unreasonably reject a claim; and (4) settle claims promptly once settlement terms are agreed.[287] Although the provisions in FCA Handbook ICOBS Part 8 envisage cash settlements of claims, they do not rule out reinstatement, replacements, and repairs. Two potential issues could arise in relation to green settlement terms: the promptness of the settlement and its fairness. As regards promptness, a repair or reinstatement of property might take longer than a cash settlement. It is submitted that promptness itself should be judged by what is reasonable given the circumstances of the claim. Thus, promptness is not to be assessed by comparing the speed of the settlement process to other claims settled in a different way (by cash), but by reference to the type of insurance, the size and complexity of the claim, compliance with any relevant statutory or regulatory rules or guidance, and factors outside the insurer's control.[288]

As regards fairness, the requirement in ICOBS 8.1.1(1) relates to the handling of the claim, and not the basis on which a claim that has been accepted by the insurer is settled. In contrast, ICOBS 8.1.1(4) is concerned with the settlement of claims but only requires that settlement is made promptly (and there is no reference to 'fairly'). It also refers to 'settlement terms [that] are agreed,' suggesting that it is open to the parties to reach an agreement on how the claim is to be settled. It is suggested that the fairness of any contractual term which sets out the basis of settlement (such as a green settlement term) in a consumer insurance contract is a matter to be considered under the CRA 2015.[289] It is also relevant under the new consumer duty which requires firms to act to deliver good outcomes for retail customers and to enable them to achieve their financial objectives.[290]

In *Parker v The National Farmers Union Mutual Insurance Society Limited* Teare J rejected the contention that a condition precedent requiring the policyholder to provide all information as might be required by the insurers to support his claim was unfair under the

284 PRA Rulebook, Solvency II Firms, Technical Provisions, 2.1.

285 See Chapter 4, Section 4.4.3.

286 PRA Rulebook, Solvency II Firms, Solvency Capital Requirement Standard Formula, 3.1.

287 ICOBS 8.1.1R.

288 These are the factors taken into account to assess whether the insurer has paid the claim within a reasonable time under s.13A of the Insurance Act 2015.

289 See Section 7.8.1.

290 See Section 7.4.5.

Unfair Terms in Consumer Contracts Regulations 1999,[291] on the grounds that it was not unreasonable to reject the claim under ICOBS 8.1.1.(3).[292] The insurer had asked for bank statements as evidence that the policyholder had the funds for a rebuild of the property. The judge said that the request for the bank statements was made reasonably since the documents were relevant to the claim and in the possession of the policyholder.[293] The judge used the insurer's compliance with the ICOBS claims handling provisions as a basis for rejecting the 'unfairness' contention under the Unfair Terms in Consumer Contracts Regulations 1999.

7.8 Unfair contract terms

To what extent could green terms, including green reinstatement terms, be at risk of unenforceability for being 'unfair' to the policyholder? The unfairness of contractual terms is addressed in (1) the CRA 2015, Part 2, which only applies to consumer contracts,[294] and (2) the Unfair Contract Terms Act 1977 which does apply to non-consumer contracts but not to insurance contracts.[295] Accordingly, the discussion below is limited to green terms in consumer contracts.

7.8.1 CRA 2015

Under the CRA 2015, an unfair term of a consumer contract is not binding on the consumer,[296] although the contract will continue to have effect, so far as practicable, without the unfair term.[297] A term is unfair if, contrary to the requirement of good faith, it causes a significant imbalance in the parties' rights and obligations under the contract to the detriment of the consumer.[298] However, core terms – those that deal with the main subject of the contract and the adequacy of the contract price – are not subject to the fairness assessment,[299] provided such core terms are transparent and prominent.[300]

Applied to green insurance products for consumers, the core term exception means that the fairness of the insuring clause, the premium level, deductible and limits, and policy exclusions cannot be challenged, provided those policy terms are transparent and prominent.[301] For the purposes of the unfair terms provisions in the CRA 2015, a term is transparent if it is expressed in plain and intelligible language and (in the case of a written term) is legible; and a term is prominent if it is brought to the consumer's attention in such a way that an average consumer would be aware of the term.[302] Given that green terms are not yet used widely and an average consumer would not be aware of them, green terms

291 A predecessor to the 'unfair terms' provisions in Part 2 of the CRA 2015.

292 *Parker v The National Farmers Union Mutual Insurance Society Limited* [2012] EWHC 2156 (Comm) at [191].

293 Ibid at [176]–[192].

294 CRA 2015 s 61(1).

295 Unfair Contract Terms Act 1977, sch 1 para 1(a).

296 CRA 2015 s 62(1).

297 Ibid s 67.

298 Ibid s 62(4).

299 Ibid s 64(1).

300 Ibid s 64(2).

301 *Van Hove v CNP Assurances SA* [C-96/14], [34], and [35].

302 CRA 2015 s 64(3) and (4).

should not be buried in the policy wording. Green terms that are drafted as exclusions (e.g. excluding losses from specified carbon-intense activities) should define or explain keywords and any ambiguous words in plain and intelligible language as otherwise (1) the exclusion could be subject to the fairness assessment, and (2) the meaning most favourable to the consumer would prevail.[303] A proper description of exclusions must also be provided in the pre-contractual disclosure.[304]

In contrast, green reinstatement terms and terms that oblige a policyholder to take climate change mitigation or adaptation at its own costs are unlikely to be regarded as core terms. Neither is concerned with the main subject matter of the contract – the indemnification for a specified risk. In *Crash Services Ltd v AXA Insurance Ltd*, the court held that a 'preferred repairer clause' in a motor policy, giving the policyholder a choice of having her car repaired by an AXA-approved repairer or an unapproved repairer, but where choosing the latter would mean fewer benefits and a higher excess, was a not a core term because it merely 'sets out some of the detail and practicality as to how the indemnity term [being the core term] is to be satisfied.'[305] Similarly, in *Bankers Insurance Co Ltd v South*,[306] a claims condition was held to be a non-core term.

Core terms that do not meet the 'transparency and prominence' tests and non-core terms are assessed for 'fairness' with the two key ingredients of unfairness being 'contrary to good faith' and 'significant imbalance.' In *Makdessi v Cavendish Square Holdings BV Parking Eye Ltd v Beavis*,[307] the Supreme Court applied the following tests established by the European Court of Justice in *Aziz v Caixa d'Estalvis de Catalunya, Tarragona i Manresa*:[308]

1. the question whether there is a 'significant imbalance in the parties' rights' depends mainly on whether the consumer is being deprived of an advantage which he would enjoy under national law in the absence of the contractual provision. In other words, this element of the test is concerned with provisions derogating from the legal position of the consumer under national law;
2. the imbalance must arise 'contrary to the requirements of good faith.' That will depend on whether the seller or supplier, dealing fairly and equitably with the consumer, could reasonably assume that the consumer would have agreed to such a term in individual contract negotiations.

7.8.2 Application to green reinstatement terms

How would these tests be applied to green reinstatement terms? Green reinstatement terms do not prima facie fall into any of the categories of terms that are potentially unfair set out in the 'grey list' in the CRA 2015, Schedule 2.

303 Ibid s 69.

304 See Section 7.3.2.

305 *Crash Services Ltd v AXA Insurance Ltd* (2018; unreported but judgment available from: <https://www.judiciaryni.uk/judicial-decisions/2018-nicty-3> accessed on 1 June 2023).

306 *Bankers Insurance Company Ltd v South and Another* [2003] EWHC 380.

307 *Makdessi v Cavendish Square Holdings BV Parking Eye Ltd v Beavis* [2015] UKSC 67 [105] per Lord Neuberger and Lord Sumption.

308 *Mohamed Aziz v Caixa d'Estalvis de Catalunya, Tarragona i Manresa (Catalunyacaixa)* (Case C-415/11) [2013] 3 CMLR 89.

Significant imbalance in the parties' rights: in indemnity insurance, the insurer undertakes to hold the insured harmless against loss by an insured peril or perils specified in the policy.[309] Without the green reinstatement terms, the insurer would pay the policyholder (or its beneficiary) a sum of money representing its insured loss and the insured can then use the settlement proceeds as s/he pleases.[310] In that sense, a green reinstatement term is a derogation from (English) insurance contract law, but it is not necessarily a derogation that deprives the consumer policyholder of any advantage s/he would have had. A green reinstatement term is arguably just another way of fulfilling the insurer's primary obligation to indemnify – to 'hold harmless' – for loss. Standard property policies frequently contain basis of settlement clauses providing for the reinstatement or repair of insured buildings or personal property that have been damaged, or the replacement of lost items.

A green reinstatement term where the insured can elect between (1) cash settlement and (2) reinstatement, replacement, and repair (Options 7, 8, and 9 above) does not deprive the policyholder of any advantage that it would have enjoyed in the absence of the provision as the consumer insured has a choice.[311] On the other hand, a green reinstatement term where the insured has no right to elect between (1) cash settlement and (2) reinstatement, replacement, and repair, could be disadvantageous to the consumer insured if s/he has to wait longer for a reinstatement, replacement, or repair of property compared to a cash settlement. If the damaged property is the consumer insured's place of living, s/he may need alternative accommodation during the period the property is reinstated or repaired. Most consumer home insurance policies already contain provisions to that effect. A green reinstatement term could also be disadvantageous if the consumer insured would incur costs as a result of the reinstatement, replacement, or repair that s/he would not have incurred or could have chosen not to incur upon a cash settlement. Thus, a well-drafted green cash settlement provision must not make the consumer insured liable for any part of the costs of reinstatement, replacement, or repair (by way of contribution or by applying a limit of liability) even if the costs exceed the economic loss suffered by the consumer insured.

Good faith: even if the green reinstatement term derogates from the legal position of the consumer insured under insurance contract law it would not necessarily be treated as unfair. The imbalance must arise 'contrary to the requirement of good faith.'[312] Applied to green reinstatement terms, the question is whether an insurer, dealing fairly and equitably with the consumer insured, could reasonably assume that a consumer insured would have agreed to such a term in individual contract negotiations. In determining this question, the courts will take into account whether the term in question is common in that type of contract, whether there is an objective reason for the term, and whether, despite the imbalance it causes, the consumer is not left without protection.[313] Green reinstatement terms are not yet frequently used. 'Dealing fairly and equitably with the consumer' is therefore likely to require that the term is prominently and clearly set out or summarised in the pre-

309 *Sprung v Royal Insurance (UK) Ltd* [1997] C.L.C. 70 (CoA); *Ventouris v Mountain (The Italia Express) (No.3)* [1992] 2 Lloyd's Rep. 281 (Comm Ct).

310 *Rayner v Preston* (1881) 18 Ch D 1 (Ch).

311 This was the reasoning of District Judge Gilipin in *Crash Services Ltd* (n 305) in relation to a preferred repairer clause which gave the insured a choice between approved and unapproved repairers.

312 *Makdessi* (n 307) at [105].

313 Ibid at [106] citing with approval Advocate General Kokott's Opinion in *Mohamed Aziz v Caixa* (n 308).

contractual product information provided to the consumer insured.[314] There is an objective reason for green reinstatement provisions which is to hold policyholders harmless from loss in relation to their insured property, as well as reducing harmful impacts on the environment. The consumer insured is not left without protection as its insured loss is still indemnified, albeit not by way of cash settlement.

Although the concept of a negotiated agreement in relation to standard terms is rather artificial, it is a helpful test by looking at what a reasonable consumer would have done.[315] Objectively, a consumer insured might have reason to accept a green reinstatement term given that any insured loss suffered is still indemnified, and arguably even 'over-compensated' if one subscribes to the view that sustainable reinstatement, replacement, or repair is 'building back better.' However, this may not be the case where a consumer insured might incur additional costs as a result of the reinstatement, replacement, or repair.

If a green reinstatement term was found to be unfair it would not be binding on the consumer insured.[316] In relation to traditional reinstatement clauses, it has been said that if reinstatement is physically or legally impossible before the insurer (or the policyholder, as the case may be) makes his election, any purported election is void and, subject to any other terms of the policy, the insurer's obligation reverts to making a cash settlement.[317] If the effect of a non-binding green reinstatement term is that the insurer's obligation can revert to making a cash settlement, the contract of insurance would still be capable of having effect without the green reinstatement term and would, accordingly, continue to have effect.[318]

7.8.3 Application to terms that mandate climate change mitigation or adaptation measures

Terms that oblige a policyholder to take climate change mitigation or adaptation at its own cost could deprive the policyholder of an advantage which it would have enjoyed under English law in the absence of the provision: the advantage in question is informed by the regulatory requirement that insurance products should provide 'fair value.'[319] An insurance product that contains a term that imposes obligations on the policyholder to implement certain climate change mitigation or adaptation measures for which the policyholder will incur significant costs in addition to the premium is unlikely to provide fair value since total costs of the policyholder are unlikely to bear a reasonable relationship to the benefits provided by the policy. Such a term could clearly introduce a significant imbalance in the parties' rights to the detriment of the policyholder. Taking into account that such a term would not be common in a consumer insurance contract,[320] it could also be contrary to the requirements of good faith as an insurer, dealing fairly and equitably with the consumer policyholder, could not reasonably assume that the consumer policyholder has agreed to such a term in individual contract negotiations. In addition, such a

314 CRA, s 64(2).

315 *Makdessi* (n 307) at [108].

316 CRA 2015 s 62(1).

317 *Anderson v Commercial Union Assurance Corp* (1885) 55 LJQB 146 (CA), 150 (Lord Bowen).

318 CRA 2015 s 67.

319 See Section 7.2.2.

320 *Makdessi* (n 307) at [106] citing with approval Advocate General Kokott's Opinion in *Mohamed Aziz v Caixa* (n 308).

term could be inconsistent with the new 'consumer duty' which will require insurers to deliver good outcomes for consumers, including ensuring that consumers (1) receive fair prices and quality, (2) receive suitable products and good treatment, and (3) have access to products meeting their needs.[321]

From the example of green reinstatement terms and terms that oblige a policyholder to take climate change mitigation or adaptation measures, some more general observations could be made: for terms not to fall foul of the fairness requirements, it is preferable to use green terms that encourage, rather than mandate, climate change mitigation and adaptation measures, and to use rewards (premium rebates or discounts) instead of contractual penalties for non-compliance. Where the policyholder would incur significant additional costs not covered by premium discounts or rebates, other funding and financing models should be considered. Regardless of whether green terms fall within the core terms category, given that they are novel and probably not yet well-known and understood, it would be good practice to draw them to the policyholder's attention before the contract is concluded. That should, in any event, be the course of action of insurance distributors if requirements to ascertain a customer's sustainability preferences and to disclose sustainable product features were to be introduced.[322]

7.9 Conclusion

Chapter 6 and this chapter have contended that insurers in their capacity as risk carriers can take an enabling role by engaging in various forms of climate-related impact underwriting: insuring green, greening insurance, and not insuring brown. Anchored in the contractual framework of insurance policies, there is an enormous potential for insurance companies to provide enabling support to their consumer and business policyholders for making better-informed choices on clean energy sources, energy efficiency, and investing in specific property-level adaptation measures, and to empower them to take ownership of their transition towards a net-zero economy. The key 'enabling' approaches that have been identified are raising awareness of climate risk and climate change mitigation and adaptation measures, scrutinising an insured's climate-related risk profile at the pre-contractual stage, price signalling, exercising influence through terms and conditions, and green claims.

There are a number of legal and regulatory challenges in relation to climate-related impact underwriting that would need to be addressed to support the enabling role of insurers and to achieve a better alignment with the UK government's commitment to achieving a net-zero economy by 2050 (which both the PRA and the FCA are required to take into account when considering how to advance their respective objectives and discharge their functions).[323] Some of these barriers have relatively easy 'fixes,' such as amending the FCA's PROD and ICOBS rules to integrate environmental considerations into the product design process and suitability assessment, to require that clear information on whether (or not) the policy pursues environmental objectives or contains any other green or sustainability-related features is provided in relation to all insurance products, and to

321 See Section 7.4.5.
322 See Section 7.3.
323 See Chapter 4, Section 4.3.2.

extend the FCA's sustainability labels regime to all insurance products. Other barriers require greater international convergence (competition issues) or further research and analysis (regulatory capital treatment of climate-related impact underwriting). The corporate purpose debate has become more polarised at the international level with some US legislators seeking to block companies from adopting certain ESG strategies, while the EU's CSDDD proposals envisage for certain large companies a corporate due diligence duty for certain companies to identify, bring to an end, prevent, mitigate, and account for negative human rights and environmental impacts in the company's own operations, their subsidiaries, and their value chains,[324] and a corporate duty to have a plan to ensure that their business strategy is compatible with limiting global warming to 1.5°C in line with the Paris Agreement.[325]

One of the most significant challenges that has been identified, and one which is inextricably linked to the corporate purpose debate as well as fairness to consumers, is the allocation of costs for climate change mitigation and adaptation measures between insurers (reduced profits), their policyholders (increased premium), and society as a whole (via government subsidies funded by taxation). A number of suggestions have been made as to how insurers could make use of available government grants and subsidies, and further consideration will be given to funding in Chapters 8 and 9. Although further consideration will be given to investment in, and the financial burden of, such measures in the following two chapters, the responsibility for financing climate change mitigation and adaptation measures is not a problem that can be solved in this book. Another overriding concern that must be considered for all types of climate-related impact underwriting activities is whether the activity is likely to close or widen protection gaps. Removing regulatory barriers, spreading costs equitably, and preventing protection gaps are reasons why insurers must act in tandem with government and other stakeholders to tackle climate change, and why climate-related insurance solutions must be integrated into wider environmental and socio-economic policies and systemic measures.

In relation to greening insurance products, it has been argued that it is important to take a holistic approach to the enabling role making use of all stages in the policy value chain to support policyholders to adopt climate change mitigation and adaptation measures. This is necessary in order to develop a consistent strategy between overlapping and interconnected activities. It has also been noted that under the emerging disclosure regimes, isolated acts of climate-related impact underwriting that are not part of a wider strategy could be regarded as 'selective disclosure' and perhaps even green-washing.[326] Insurance industry commentators have therefore recommended the development of 'underwriting roadmaps,'[327] and iterative and adaptive decision-making processes that anchor climate change risk assessment in all core decisions,[328] to ensure a holistic approach. To be truly holistic, an insurer's strategic approach to climate change should also extend to impact investment which is considered in the next chapter.

324 Proposal for a Directive of the European Parliament and of the Council on Corporate Sustainability Due Diligence and amending Directive (EU) 2019/1937 COM/2022/71, arts 6–8.

325 Paris Agreement and see Chapter 2, Section 2.3.3.

326 Pugnetti and Gebert (n 35) Sec 2.2.1.

327 Stricker and Pugnetti (n 2).

328 The Geneva Association, 'Anchoring Climate Change Risk Assessment in Core Business Decisions in Insurance' (September 2022) Sec. 4 <https://www.genevaassociation.org/publication/climate-change-and-environment/climate-change-risk-3-report> accessed 1 June 2023.

CHAPTER 8

Climate-related impact investment and stewardship

The insurance business model is inextricably linked to investment activities by insurers. The main reason for that is that insurance premiums tend to be paid upfront, while the insurer's liability to pay a claim or other benefits is contingent upon the occurrence of an insured loss or a specified event which may not occur until several months or even years later or may not occur at all. Given this time lag – also referred to as an inverted production cycle – the insurer must make provisions for future claims payments under accounting and regulatory standards. They will do so by holding assets matching their technical provisions and their solvency capital requirements.[1] Rather than just setting aside cash, insurers invest the premium into assets that generate a return as a way of protecting the value of the premium against inflation. Depending on the duration and predictability of their exposure, insurers will adopt different investment strategies.

In addition, some life insurers offer IBIPs where the investment return on the premium is a core component of the pay-out to the policyholder or its beneficiaries. In relation to IBIPs, insurers act as asset managers: the insurer invests, or delegates the investment of, (some of) the premium on behalf of the policyholder or beneficiary in specified investment funds that are managed by the insurer or its agents. The pay-out on maturity varies according to the investment performance of the fund (and the underlying assets) in which the premium has been invested.

In light of their wide-ranging investment activities, insurers are major traditional institutional investors. In 2021, the assets of insurance companies globally amounted to approximately 40.3 trillion US dollars.[2] The UK insurance industry is one of the biggest institutional investors in the London stock market and across other asset classes (in 2021 managing over £1.7 trillion worth of assets – equivalent to approximately 25% of the UK's net worth).[3] Their investment activities in equities and bonds provide a key link to the financial and capital markets and ultimately underpin the real economy. It is therefore unsurprising that insurers, in their capacity as investors, have been called upon to engage with impact investment and stewardship.

1 See Chapter 4, Section 4.4.3.

2 Statistica,'Total Assets of Insurance Companies Worldwide from 2002 to 2021' <https://www.statista.com/statistics/421217/assets-of-global-insurance-companies/#:~:text=In%202020%2C%20the%20assets%20of%20insurance%20companies%20globally,by%20around%2024%20trillion%20U.S.%20dollars%20since%202002> accessed on 1 June 2023.

3 ABI, 'UK Insurance & Long-Term Savings Key Facts December 2022' (2022) <https://portfolio.cpl.co.uk/ABI-KeyFacts/2022/top10/> accessed on 1 June 2023.

DOI: 10.4324/b23081-8

The Paris Agreement recognises that finance flows must be made available to respond to the global threat of climate change.[4] The global transition to a resilient net-zero economy is dependent on investment into new technologies, services, and infrastructure that reduce or neutralise GHG emissions and that improve resilience to climate-related physical risks.[5] The UK government estimates that in 2022 alone, £23 billion of new low-carbon investment was delivered in the UK – ranging from renewables, hydrogen, carbon capture and storage, nuclear, sustainable materials, energy storage, and electrified transport, to clean heat.[6] Between 2023 and 2050, US$150 trillion of total investment in the energy transition will be required for the world to align with a 1.5°C pathway, requiring current levels of investment to quadruple.[7] The IPCC has estimated the average annual finance needs between 2020 and 2035 to contain global temperature rises by 2100: US$1.7 trillion for a 2°C pathway, and US$2.4 trillion for a 1.5°C pathway, for the energy sector alone (and three times higher if transport and other sectors were to be included), yet across all sectors and geographies there are significant investment gaps.[8]

In Chapter 3, Section 3.4.5, it was argued that, as risk carriers and investors, insurers can enable actors in their value chain and in the wider community to take climate mitigation action and to adopt climate change adaptation measures. This chapter is concerned with how insurers – in their capacity as investors – could take this role by engaging in climate-related impact investment and stewardship. Section 8.1 looks at the history of impact investment and stewardship and proposes definitions for 'climate-related impact investment' and 'climate-related stewardship' derived from a critical examination of the literature and the disclosure requirements discussed in Chapter 5. Section 8.2 examines the rationales for climate-related impact investment and stewardship. Section 8.3 considers the regulatory requirements that apply to, and legal issues that may arise in respect of, an insurer's own investments. Section 8.4 examines some of the regulatory requirements that apply to IBIPs. Section 8.5 proposes two potential insurance solutions that combine climate-related impact underwriting and investment. This chapter will highlight some significant legal and regulatory barriers with respect to climate-related impact investment and stewardship.

8.1 What are impact climate-related investment and stewardship?

Traditionally, institutional investors have solely focused on making investments that generate a financial return for the investor itself, or its beneficiaries where the institutional investor acts as asset manager, within acceptable levels of risk. To manage the investment risk (the risk of the investment not making the expected return or indeed losing some of the original investment), institutional investors frequently seek to maintain a diversified investment portfolio by allocating their capital to different asset classes with different time

4 Paris Agreement art 2(1)(c).

5 See e.g.: SHIP (UN Framework Convention on Climate Change, Sharm el-Sheikh Implementation Plan (adopted at COP27 in 2022) Decision 1/CP.27) Sec VII, art 50 and sec IX, art 61 and 62.

6 HM Government, 'Mobilising Green Investment – 2023 Green Finance Strategy' (April 2023) 18 <https://www.gov.uk/government/publications/green-finance-strategy> accessed on 1 June 2023.

7 International Renewable Energy Agency, 'World Energy Transitions Outlook 2023: 1.5°C Pathway' (March 2023) <https://www.irena.org/Publications/2023/Mar/World-Energy-Transitions-Outlook-2023> accessed on 1 June 2023.

8 IPCC 2022 Mitigation Report, Summary for Policymakers [15.1] and [15.5.2].

horizons, different risk profiles, in different industries, and in different geographical locations. In contrast, impact investment strategies are intended to 'generate positive, measurable social and environmental impact alongside a financial return.'[9]

8.1.1 Historical background

Making investment decisions motivated by ethical or societal objectives has nevertheless a long history. Some commentators cite the Old Testament as a source for requiring ethical ownership that does not cause harm to oneself and others,[10] while others refer to Quaker and Methodist investors in the later 18th and 19th centuries who actively refrained from investing in enterprises connected with slavery and warfare.[11] Impact investment with a focus on sustainability has been on the horizon since the late 1990s[12] and has been more firmly placed on the agenda of policymakers, regulators, the financial markets, and other stakeholders since the launch of the PRI in 2006[13] and the adoption of the Sustainable Development Goals by the United Nations in 2015.[14] Since 2019, impact investment with environmental objectives has been a specific policy goal of the UK government as part of its 'Green Finance Strategy,'[15] and it remains so in the '2023 Green Investment Strategy.'[16] Pursuing green finance and investment is one of the pillars of the European Green Deal,[17] and the European Commission's 'Strategy for Financing the Transition to a Sustainable Economy' recognises the importance of supporting investment flows towards environmentally sustainable economic activities and for intermediary steps on the pathway towards sustainability. The IPCC has warned that insufficient financing, and a lack of political frameworks and incentives for finance, are key barriers to climate action and cause implementation gaps for both climate change mitigation and adaptation.[18]

Like impact investment, 'stewardship' is not a novel concept, although the label itself is relatively recent. As Talner points out, questions and complaints by shareholders to the board of directors, and discussions with the board on company policies, could be regarded as early forms of shareholder activism.[19] As individual investor holdings declined in the

9 Global Impact Investment Network ('GIIN'), 'Impact investing' <https://thegiin.org/impact-investing/> accessed on 1 June 2023.

10 Céline Louche, Daniel Arenas, and Katinka C. van Cranenburgh, 'From Preaching to Investing: Attitudes of Religious Organisations towards Responsible Investment' (2012) 110(3) *Journal of Business Ethics*, 301; Rabbi Lawrence Troster, 'Beyond the Letter of the Law: The Jewish Perspective on Ethical Investing and Fossil Fuel Divestment' (December 2014) <https://sojo.net/articles/disinvest-reinvest/beyond-letter-law-jewish-perspective-ethical-investing-and-fossil-fuel> accessed on 1 June 2023.

11 Steve Schueth, 'Socially Responsible Investing in the United States' (2003) 43(3) *Journal of Business Ethics*, 189.

12 Louche (n 10).

13 PRI in partnership with UNEP Finance Initiative, 'Principles for Responsible Investment' <https://www.unpri.org/pri/what-are-the-principles-for-responsible-investment> accessed on 1 June 2023.

14 UNGA, 'Resolution Adopted by the General Assembly on: Transforming Our World: The 2030 Agenda for Sustainable Development' (25 September 2015) A/RES/70/1.

15 HM Treasury and Department for Business, Energy and Industrial Strategy, 'Green Finance Strategy' (July 2019) <https://www.gov.uk/government/publications/green-finance-strategy> accessed on 1 June 2023.

16 HM Government (n 6).

17 European Commission, European Green Deal <https://commission.europa.eu/strategy-and-policy/priorities-2019-2024/european-green-deal/delivering-european-green-deal_en> accessed on 1 June 2023.

18 IPCC 2021 Physical Science Report, Summary for Policymakers [2.3.3].

19 Lauren Talner, 'The Origins of Shareholder Activism' (Investor Responsibility Research Center, 1983 – now out of print) cited in Iris Chiu, *The Foundations and Anatomy of Shareholder Activism* (2010, Hart) 2.

post-World War II era, there has been a corresponding rise in the proportion of institutional investment.[20] Into the 1980s, institutional investors in the UK were largely 'sleeping giants' that were relatively passive on exercising voting rights and instead relied on investing and divesting decisions to express (dis)approval of a company's management and strategy.[21] Although institutional investors have become more activist since the 1990s in the UK,[22] fostering more engagement and effective stewardship has been the subject of reviews[23] and is now underpinned by legislation implementing the Shareholder Rights Directive[24] and by FCA-endorsed compliance with the UK Stewardship Code.[25] The role that institutional investors can play in promoting ESG issues was only formally recognised relatively recently in the 2006 Principles of Responsible Investment ("PRI"), which recommend that investors should be 'active owners' that incorporate ESG issues into their ownership policies and practices and engage with their investee companies on ESG issues.[26]

8.1.2 Defining climate-related impact investment

There is a growing body of literature and industry standards on the meaning of 'impact investment.'[27] Clarity on the meaning of 'impact investment' is needed to distinguish between investments that have a genuine impact in relation to a stated objective, and investments where the label 'impact' is used to 'green-wash' its actual impact as a marketing tool or to boost reputations.[28] The Global Impact Investing Network ('GIIN'), a global community of 440 organisations including major institutional investors and investment services providers, define 'impact investments' as:

> investments made with the intention to generate positive, measurable social and environmental impact alongside a financial return.[29]

Intentionality and additionality: the GIIN definition is narrow in two aspects: first, it requires 'intentionality' to achieve social and environmental goals and therefore rules out 'socially neutral investors' who are indifferent to the outcomes of their investments even

20 Paul Myners, 'Institutional Investment in the United Kingdom: A Review' (March 2001), [1.4].

21 Brian Cheffins, *Corporate Ownership and Control: British Business Transformed* (OUP 2009), ch 2, 3, and 4.

22 Louise Gulliver and Jennifer Payne, *Corporate Finance: Principles and Policy* (3rd ed, Hart Publishing 2020) Sec 11.2.2.2.1.

23 UK: Paul Myners (n 20); Sir David Walker, 'A Review of Corporate Governance in UK Banks and Other Financial Industry Entities: Final Recommendations' (November 2009) ch 5; FRC, 'Independent Review of the Financial Reporting Council' (December 2018), Recommendations 42 and 43.

24 Directive (EU) 2017/828 of the European Parliament and of the Council of 17 May 2017 amending Directive 2007/36/EC as regards the encouragement of long-term shareholder engagement ('Shareholders Rights Directive'); adopted into UK law through the Occupational Pension Schemes (Investment and Disclosure) (Amendment) Regulations 2019 and the Pension Protection Fund (Pensionable Service) and Occupational Pension Schemes (Investment and Disclosure) (Amendment and Modification) Regulations 2018.

25 FRC, 'UK Stewardship Code 2020' <https://www.frc.org.uk/getattachment/5aae591d-d9d3-4cf4-814a-d14e156a1d87/Stewardship-Code_Final2.pdf> accessed on 1 June 2023.

26 PRI (n 13) Prin 2.

27 For a useful list of key sources, see: Ben Caldecott, Jakob Thomae, James Mitchell, and Matt Scott, 'How Can Net-Zero Finance Best Drive Positive Impact in the Real Economy' (April 2022) Annex 1 <https://climatechampions.unfccc.int/wp-content/uploads/2022/05/FSEG-report-2_v3.pdf> accessed on 1 June 2023.

28 Timo Busch, Peter Bruce-Clark, Jeroen Derwall, Robert Eccles, Tessa Hebb, Andreas Hoepner, Christian Klein, Philipp Krueger, Falko Paetzold, Bert Scholtens, and Olaf Weber, 'Impact Investments: A Call for (Re)orientation' (2021) 1 SN Bus Econ 33. The authors use the term 'impact washing.'

29 GIIN (n 9).

if they do in fact have a social and environmental impact. Secondly, 'generating a positive and measurable impact' suggests an element of 'additionality' meaning that, without the investment, the social or environmental impact would not occur.[30] This criterion would exclude investments where ESG issues are merely incorporated into the consideration of sustainability-related risks, opportunities, and impacts in the investment processes to assess their implications for enterprise value creation and hence financial returns (**'ESG integration'**) since no 'extra good' is produced by doing so.

Brest and Born argue that impact investing should encompass only affirmative investments but should exclude **'negative screening'** which is an investment approach that excludes certain investments on the basis that they fail to meet positive sustainability-related criteria.[31] This position has been adopted by the FCA, citing Brest and Born, in relation to the proposed sustainable investment label regime.[32] The FCA have said that they cannot be used for investment products that only use negative screening as an investment approach on the grounds that such an approach 'would not plausibly contribute to positive sustainable outcomes.'[33] It is suggested that 'negative screening' can have 'additionality': without the investment, and in particular without debt financing, the cost of capital for targeted companies can increase, then environmentally harmful projects may not go ahead and existing businesses with harmful operations may cease those operations or close down.[34] The 'extra good' is the avoidance of harm that would have been otherwise caused. Arguably, there would then be an impact in the sense that harmful outcomes have been stopped or reduced. On the other hand, if finance and investment are easily available from other sources, the cost of capital may not increase or only increase fractionally,[35] but this is not an argument against additionality of negative screening but a question of fact whether, and to what extent, additionality is material and measurable. It is suggested that excluding negative screening in relation to coal, oil, and gas projects from impact investment (and from impact underwriting) is unattractive in light of the scientific evidence that clearly links GHG emissions to climate change,[36] and is contrary to the Paris Agreement obligations to reduce GHG emissions.[37] Negative screening could amplify peer pressure for other investors to follow suit.[38] On the other hand, negative screening on its own is not an enabling approach – walking away from brown investment does not support the investee company in its transition to net-zero – but is more consistent with a governance (quasi-regulatory) conception of insurance.[39] It is suggested that the better view is that negative

30 Paul Brest and Kelly Born, 'Unpacking the Impact in Impact Investing' [2014] Stanford Social Innovation Review.

31 Ibid.

32 See Chapter 5, Section 5.3.5.2.

33 FCA Sustainability Disclosure Proposals [4.10] and [4.25].

34 Daniel Green and Boris Vallee, 'Can Finance Save the World? Measurement and Effects of Coal Divestment Policies by Banks' (April 2022) <http://dx.doi.org/10.2139/ssrn.4090974> accessed on 1 June 2023; and see Chapter 6, Section 6.4.1.

35 Benjamin J. Richardson, 'Financial Markets and Socially Responsible Investing' in Beate Sjåfjell, *Company Law and Sustainability Legal Barriers and Opportunities* (Cambridge University Press 2015), ch 6, 244.

36 IPCC 2021 Physical Science Report, Summary for Policymakers [A.1].

37 Paris Agreement art 2 and 4.

38 Gomtsiam argues that more investors adjust their investment decisions and divest after observing that many other investors have already exited: see Suren Gomtsiam, 'Debtholder Stewardship' (2023) 86(2) *MLR*, 395 at 403.

39 See Chapter 3, Section 3.4.4.

screening can generate additionality through the reduction of harm, but it is a disabling, rather than an enabling, approach to influencing investee companies.

A '**sustainable focus**' approach – selecting investments on the basis that they fulfil certain sustainability criteria and/or deliver on specific and measurable sustainability outcome(s) – may fall within the GIIN definition if there are measurable sustainability outcomes that provide additionality.[40]

In contrast, the UN-convened PRI require that member investors 'will incorporate ESG issues into investment analysis and decision-making processes.'[41] This is an ESG integration approach that merely requires that ESG issues be taken into account in the investment processes – neither intentionality nor additionality to achieve ESG objectives is necessary. Although the PRI label used is '**responsible** investment' (not impact investment), there is conceptual uncertainty about whether impact investment merely requires that social and environmental issues are taken into account, or whether there is an additionality requirement that the investment be geared towards generating 'social returns,' in addition to financial returns. Busch et al. have sought to re-orientate the discussion by introducing two sub-categories of 'impact investment':

1. **impact-aligned investments**: the investment approach consists of a comprehensive set of exclusion criteria (negative screening) in combination with a sustainable focus approach and stewardship activities to address social or environmental challenges or goals. Impact outcomes must be measurable and verifiable;
2. **impact-generating investments**: the investment approach is focused on impact generation by providing additional capital to actively contribute to social and environmental solutions. Impact outcomes must be measurable and verifiable.[42]

Within this classification, negative screening and sustainable focus investment approaches could be accommodated within 'impact-aligned investment' provided they are part of a more comprehensive approach (including stewardship) and produce measurable outcomes.

To consider what 'impact investment' means for insurance companies, it is useful to distinguish between 'firm-level investment policies' and 'fund-level investment' approaches.[43] The distinction between entity- and product-level sustainability-related activities is a familiar one from the FCA's proposed sustainability-related disclosure regime and the SFDR.[44] This is a useful distinction to adopt for insurers as they invest premiums on their own account, and they make investments on behalf of policyholders in relation to investment-based insurance products.

40 See e.g. The Investment Association, 'IA Responsible Investment – Final Report' (November 2019) Glossary <https://www.theia.org/campaigns/sustainability-and-responsible-investment> accessed on 1 June 2023.

41 PRI (n 13) Prin 1.

42 Busch (n 28) 33, Table 1.

43 The Investment Association (n 40) Sec 4.

44 EU Regulation (EU) 2019/2088 on sustainability-related disclosures in the financial services sector; and see Chapter 5, Section 5.4.2.

At the entity level, the TCFD Supplemental Guidance for the financial sector,[45] the ISSB Insurance Disclosures,[46] the FCA's proposed sustainability-related disclosure regime,[47] and the SFDR[48] envisage disclosures of the extent to which an insurer takes an ESG integration approach to investments. As noted above, an ESG integration approach on its own does not have additionality, but an insurer could adopt an investment policy based on an ESG integration approach and/or negative screening approach, combined with stewardship – such a combined approach would fall within the Busch et al. category of 'impact-aligned investments.'[49] It is unlikely that an exclusive impact investment approach at the entity level would be justifiable under the 'prudent person principle' and it may be inconsistent with an insurer's corporate purpose.[50] However, an exclusive impact investment approach could be applied to specific products.

There is evidence that the EU disfavours investments in environmentally harmful activities: the SFDR requires in-scope insurers to report on whether they consider principal adverse impacts of investment decisions on sustainability factors[51] and is to be interpreted so that it does not capture in the definition of 'sustainable investment' any investments in activities that are harmful to environmental objectives.[52] The CSRD requires reporting companies to describe principal actual or potential adverse impacts connected with the undertaking's own operations and with its value chain.[53] According to the EU Taxonomy, environmentally sustainable economic activities must not significantly harm any of the six environmental objectives.[54] The CSDDD proposals envisage for certain large companies a corporate due diligence duty for certain companies to identify, bring to an end, prevent, mitigate, and account for, inter alia, adverse environmental impacts in the company's own operations, their subsidiaries, and at the level of their direct and indirect business relationships in their value chains. Such adverse impacts could be removed or reduced by adopting a negative screening approach which excludes certain investments on the basis that they are harmful and do not meet specified sustainability-related criteria.[55] This is not suggesting that the SFDR, CSRD, the EU Taxonomy, and CSDDD require negative screening investment approaches but these instruments indirectly support negative screening to prevent potential adverse impacts on the environment at the investee level.

At the product level (i.e. in relation to IBIPs), insurers could adopt an ESG integration approach and/or negative screening approach that is specific to the product's investment

45 TCFD, 'Implementing the Recommendations of the Task Force on Climate-Related Financial Disclosures' (October 2021) s D – see guidance in relation to Recommendation 4 for asset owners and asset managers <https://assets.bbhub.io/company/sites/60/2021/07/2021-TCFD-Implementing_Guidance.pdf> accessed on 1 June 2023, and see Chapter 5, Section 5.1.

46 IFRS S2, Appendix B, Volume B17—Insurance, FN-IN-410a.2; and see Chapter, 5 Section 5.2.2.

47 FCA Sustainability Disclosure Proposals; and see Chapter 5, Section 5.3.2–5.3.6.

48 SFDR, arts 3 and 6 (key information document), and see Chapter 5, Section 5.4.2.

49 Busch (n 28) 33, Table 1; and see this section above.

50 See Sections 8.3.1 and 8.2.2 respectively, and also see Chapter 6, Section 6.2.

51 SFDR, art 4.

52 SFDR art 2(17).

53 CSRD, art 1, point 4.

54 EU Taxonomy (Regulation (EU) 2020/852 of the European Parliament and of the Council of 18 June 2020 on the establishment of a framework to facilitate sustainable investment, and amending Regulation (EU) 2019/2088) art 3.

55 Proposal for a Directive of the European Parliament and of the Council on Corporate Sustainability Due Diligence and amending Directive (EU) 2019/1937 COM/2022/71 6-8, and see Chapter 4, Section 4.4.5, in relation to whether and to what extent the CSDDD would apply to insurance companies.

strategy. Alternatively or in addition, an insurer could adopt a sustainability focus approach or impact investment approach, which may or may not be underpinned by stewardship engagement specific to the product's investment strategy. The product investment approach should be determined at the product development stage and should be part of the pre-contractual suitability assessment and pre-contractual disclosures and consumer-facing disclosures.[56]

The SFDR envisages disclosures in relation to IBIPs that promote social or environmental characteristics[57] (light green), IBIPs that have 'sustainable investment' as their objective[58] (dark green), and information on the principal adverse impacts of an IBIP on sustainability factors (brown).[59]

Light green IBIPs correspond roughly to a sustainable focus approach, and dark green IBIPs are an example of 'impact investment' under the GIIN definition. As noted above, both approaches have additionality. 'Promoting' and 'have as objective' suggest intentionality, rather than indifference to the outcome. Arguably, investment-based insurance products that screen out brown investments have additionality since they seek to avoid or reduce harm. The EU's commitment to additionality at the product level is also apparent from the EU Taxonomy which requires that for an investment to be considered an investment in an environmentally sustainable economic activity it must, inter alia, 'contribute substantially to one or more of the six environmental objectives.'[60]

The FCA's proposed sustainable investment labels for investment-based insurance products clearly require additionality:

- sustainable focus: investment in assets that are environmentally and/or socially sustainable;
- sustainable improvers: investment to improve the environmental and/or social sustainability of assets over time, including in response to the stewardship influence of the firm;
- sustainable impact: investment in solutions to environmental or social problems, to achieve positive, real-world impact.[61]

The FCA's proposed product disclosure requirements relating to investment-based insurance products that will use sustainable investment labels are also indicative of additionality: for example, the pre-contractual product disclosures must include the product's sustainability objective and 'details of the plausible, purposeful, and credible link between the product's sustainability objective's and environmental and/or social outcomes.'[62] As the sustainable investment labels are dependent on a sustainability objective that is linked to the prescribed outcomes,[63] the FCA have said that they cannot be used for investment products that merely take an ESG integration approach, or only use negative or positive

56 See Section 8.4.
57 SFDR art 8.
58 Ibid art 9.
59 Ibid art 7.
60 EU Taxonomy Regulation, art 3.
61 FCA Sustainability Disclosure Proposals [3.2]; and see Chapter 5, Section 5.3.5.
62 Ibid [5.50] Prin 1.3.
63 Ibid [5.67].

screening as an investment approach.[64] While there is no express 'intentionality' requirement, it is suggested that an intention to achieve a social or environmental impact is implicit in the accompanying disclosures requiring that the 'sustainability objective' – an explicit environmental and/or social outcome of the investment – be stated to (prospective) policyholders and investors, and disclosures that require reporting on process and outcomes. ESG integration approaches – while not falling within the scope of 'impact investment' – have been absorbed into the concept of 'stewardship.'[65]

Although 'intentionality' is a moot point where social and environmental goals of the investment are expressly formulated in disclosures, it is queried why it should be a necessary pre-condition of impact investing. Intentions may not be articulated and conceivably there could be more than one motivation for an investment (e.g. to 'do some good,' achieve an investment return, diversify an investment portfolio). In the absence of fraud, motivations behind business decisions are not generally relevant to regulation and contractual agreements. Contract law in particular has adopted an 'objective intent' approach (how a reasonable person would interpret a party's intention) to contract formation[66] and construction.[67] Where 'intention' is relevant in financial services regulation, it is usually connected to a notice or declaration requirement.[68] The investment of an investor who is indifferent to the outcome could still have an impact. However, it is conceded that the absence of an intention to generate a social return could be another factor as to why an ESG integration approach is not 'impact investing' even if there is incidental additionality – an ESG integration approach is no more than a model of analysis in which ESG factors are assessed for materiality and effect on risk and returns.[69] It is therefore suggested that 'intentionality' is indicative, but not conclusive, of impact investing.

As for additionality, it is suggested that this should be a necessary pre-condition for impact investments since it distinguishes impact investing from investment strategies that are purely focused on financial return. Contrary to some of the literature and the FCA's proposals, it is however argued that the prevention or reduction of further harm as a result of negative screening can constitute additionality, and that impact-aligned investments – as described by Busch et al.[70] – should also fall within the scope of 'impact investment.' Under this expanded notion of additionality, which is consistent with the SFDR and the CSRD, negative screening approaches to investment would be captured. This expanded notion of additionality is adopted for this book as it is concerned with inward impact for, and outward impact from, insurers on climate change. It is further posited that ESG integration approaches are unlikely to have additionality since pricing ESG risks and opportunities into the investment is not by itself producing social returns.

Positive climate impact: as can be seen from the brief literature review above, impact investment is often associated with wider ESG and sustainability objectives. The GINN definition provides for social and environmental impact.[71] Similarly, the SFDR definition

64 Ibid [2.3], [4.24], and [4.25] and see the preceding discussion in this section.

65 See Section 8.1.3.

66 *Smith v Hughes* (1871) LR 6 QB 597 (CA).

67 *Arnold v Britton* [2015] UKSC 36, para 15.

68 See e.g. FCA Handbook, Collective Investment Schemes (COLL) 11.6, Registration Function under the Co-operative and Community Benefit Societies (RFCCBS) 8.9, LR 5.2, Investment Funds sourcebook (FUND) 10.5, Prudential Sourcebook for Insurers (INSPRU) 8.2, Supervision Manual (SUP) 11.9.

69 Richardson (n 35) 240.

70 Busch (n 28) 33, Table 1.

71 GIIN (n 9).

of 'sustainable investment' references social and environmental objectives but is more specific. In relation to investments that contribute to an environmental objective, the SFDR gives 'key resource efficiency indicators' (such as the use of energy, renewable energy, raw materials, water and land, on the production of waste, and greenhouse gas emissions, or on its impact on biodiversity and the circular economy) and adds a proviso that such investments do not significantly harm any of those objectives and that the investee companies follow good governance practices.[72] Investments in transition projects (where the investment is intended to turn 'brown' assets/activities into 'green' assets/activities) are excluded from the scope of 'sustainable investments' under the SFDR if they do not meet the 'do no significant harm' criteria from the outset.[73] Under the EU Taxonomy, an 'environmentally sustainable economic activity' must meet the four conditions discussed in Chapter 5, Section 5.4.1.1. To qualify for one of the sustainable investment labels proposed by the FCA, an in-scope life insurer that provides IBIPs would need to invest:

1. in assets that are environmentally and/or socially sustainable ('sustainable focus');
2. to improve the environmental and/or social sustainability of assets over time, including in response to the stewardship influence of the firm ('sustainable improvers');
3. in solutions to environmental or social problems, to achieve positive, real-world impact ('sustainable impact').[74]

This chapter is concerned with climate-related impact investment. Therefore, the outcomes will be framed as investments that make a contribution to climate change mitigation and climate change adaptation. Climate mitigation finance is about investments that aim to reduce global GHG emissions, while climate adaptation investments are concerned with alleviating the consequences of climate change.[75] However, it should be noted that in order to fall within the SFDR definition of 'sustainable investment,' the EU Taxonomy definition of 'environmentally sustainable economic activity,' and the sustainable investment labels proposed by the FCA, the investment must meet the relevant criteria of that regime. It is also important to be mindful that the investment itself will not have a direct positive impact on climate change; rather the impact of the investment will be indirect through the investee company or the project invested in. By providing capital, the investee company may be able to produce goods or provide services, and/or adjust its operations, to contribute to climate change mitigation or adaptation.

Measurability: there are emerging benchmarks, indices, and methodologies for measuring impact and assessing the 'social value' of outcomes in monetary and other metrics.[76]

72 SFDR, art 2(17).

73 ESMA, 'Q&As on the Interpretation of Regulation (EU) 2019/2088 SFDR' Q3 <https://www.esma.europa.eu/document/qas-interpretation-regulation-eu-20192088-sfdr> accessed on 1 June 2023, and see Chapter 5, Section 5.4.2.

74 FCA Sustainability Disclosure Proposals [3.2], and see Chapter 5, Section 5.3.5.

75 IPCC 2022 Mitigation Report, Summary for Policymakers, [4.27]; and OECD Insurance and Adaptation Paper 19 and Box 15.3.

76 See e.g. GIIN, 'Impact Performance Benchmarks' (March 2023) <https://thegiin.org/research/publication/impact-performance-benchmarks-overview/> accessed on 1 June 2023; Brest (n 30); Chris Addy, Maya Chorengel, Mariah Collins, and Michael Etzel, 'Calculating the Value of Impact Investing' (Jan–Feb 2019) *Harvard Business Review*.

The FCA's proposed sustainability-related disclosure regime and the SFDR expect providers of sustainable IBIPs to provide outcome metrics (information on what the sustainability criteria and indicators are) and process metrics (how the product's performance against these criteria and indicators is being assessed).[77] Moreover, if an insurer makes claims about the sustainable impact of its investment that cannot be evidenced by reference to KPIs that assess such impact, such a claim may run the risk of violating forthcoming anti-green-washing rules,[78] as well as being contrary to existing regulatory principles and rules on not making misleading claims.[79] Around 'measurability' there is an emerging ESG data provider industry which is not yet regulated. The EU and the UK want to bring ESG data and rating providers within their regulatory oversight to ensure that ESG data and rating services should be transparent, well-governed, independent, objective, and based on reliable and systematic methodologies and processes.[80]

8.1.3 Defining climate-related stewardship

Hirschmann's model of shareholder influence over corporate decision-making distinguished between Exit and Voice: shareholders can divest of assets and from sectors that have a harmful effect on the environment ('Exit,' but can also include 'Boycott' – taking investment decisions), or they can use their voice by engaging with investee enterprises to promote the creation of sustainable value for beneficiaries, the economy, and society ('Voice' – engagement).[81] The UK Stewardship Code 2020 has redefined 'stewardship' to contain both investment decision elements and engagement elements: 'the responsible allocation, management and oversight of capital to create long-term value for clients and beneficiaries leading to sustainable benefits for the economy, the environment and society.'[82] As the suggested investment approach is 'ESG integration'[83] which has been said to fall outside the definition of impact investment, it is still possible to draw a distinction between 'impact investment' and 'stewardship' but the divide has become blurred.[84] The UN-convened PRI identify the following actions as falling within stewardship (or 'active ownership'):

77 FCA Sustainability Disclosure Proposals [4.56], [4.60] and see Boxes on Prin 2 and 3; SFDR, art 8(1), 9(1), and 10(1)(b).

78 FCA Sustainability Disclosure Proposals [6.9].

79 See e.g. PRIN 2.1, Prin 7; COBS 4.2.1; ICOBS 2.2.2.

80 HM Treasury, 'Consultation Paper on the Future Regulatory Regime for Environmental, Social and Governance (ESG) Ratings Providers' (March 2023) <https://www.gov.uk/government/consultations/future-regulatory-regime-for-environmental-social-and-governance-esg-ratings-providers> accessed on 1 June 2023; Proposal for a Regulation on the transparency and integrity of Environmental, Social and Governance (ESG) rating activities 2023/0177 (COD) COM/2023/314; European Commission Proposal for a Regulation on the transparency and integrity of Environmental, Social and Governance (ESG) rating activities 2023/0177 (COD) COM/2023/314.

81 Albert O. Hirschman, *Exit, Voice, and Loyalty: Responses to Decline in Firms, Organizations, and States. Cambridge* (Harvard University Press 1970).

82 FRC (n 25) Introduction; also see PRI which define 'Stewardship' as 'the use of influence by institutional investors to maximise overall long-term value including the value of common economic, social and environmental assets, on which returns and clients' and beneficiaries' interests depend.'

83 FRC (n 25) Prin 7.

84 Albert O. Hirschman (n 81).

- develop and disclose an active ownership policy consistent with the PRI Principles;
- exercise voting rights or monitor compliance with voting policy (if outsourced);
- develop an engagement capability (either directly or through outsourcing);
- participate in the development of policy, regulation, and standard setting (such as promoting and protecting shareholder rights);
- file shareholder resolutions consistent with long-term ESG considerations;
- engage with companies on ESG issues;
- participate in collaborative engagement initiatives;
- ask investment managers to undertake and report on ESG-related engagement.[85]

Similarly, the Shareholder Rights Directive[86] and FCA requirements[87] consider that:

- monitoring investee companies on relevant matters, including on social and environmental impact and corporate governance;
- conducting dialogues with investee companies;
- exercising voting rights and other rights attached to shares;
- co-operating with other shareholders;
- communicating with other stakeholders of the investee companies,

could be part of a firm's engagement policy. Stewardship is process-orientated – the process of engaging with investees – and there is no 'additionality' requirement in the sense that an activity must produce an outcome (that the investee changes its behaviour or strategy as a result of the engagement). In contrast, 'intentionality' is implicit in the concept of stewardship as it requires the investor to actively engage with the investee. Stewardship activities frequently relate to environmental matters as part of a wider ESG remit,[88] but there are also institutional investor initiatives, such as the UN-convened Net-Zero Asset Owner Alliance,[89] that focus more narrowly on the transition of their members' investment portfolios to net-zero GHG emissions by 2050.

To date, the stewardship discourse has focused on equity investors. In contrast, the role that debt investors can play has received little attention until very recently.[90] Insurers do invest in listed and unlisted equity, but they also invest in debt securities. Direct lenders, such as banks, usually have extensive contractual rights against borrowers under the loan documentation (such as covenants restricting the borrower's activities, negative pledges, termination and acceleration rights, and contractual set-off) and may also take security of the borrower's assets. In contrast, debt securities traded on public bond markets have covenants that do not generally provide debtholders with extensive monitoring and voting

85 PRI (n 13) Prin 2.

86 Shareholders Rights Directive, see in particular art 3g; and see n 24.

87 See e.g. SYSC 3.4.5.

88 PRI (n 13) Prin 2.

89 UNEP Net-Zero Asset Owner Alliance, 'Commitment Document for Participating Asset Owners' (April 2022) <https://www.unepfi.org/wordpress/wp-content/uploads/2022/07/AOA-COMMITMENT-DOC-2022.pdf> accessed on 1 June 2023.

90 The updated UK Stewardship Code 2020 (n 25; p.7) now extends to asset owners and asset managers of different classes of assets, no matter how capital is invested.

rights unrelated to the borrower's credit risk and outside (potential) default scenarios.[91] There are more layers of intermediaries between public debtholders and the managers of the borrower than between shareholders and corporate managers, complicating and increasing the costs of direct engagement by debtholders further.[92] Reference is also made to 'macro stewardship' – the idea that engagement by financial institutions on sustainability issues must extend beyond shareholders to governments, regulators, and policymakers, to preserve the integrity of the financial systems.[93]

8.1.4 Green pills and summary

Straddling impact investment and stewardship is the contractual mechanism of 'green pills' put forward by Armour et al.[94] Green pills are contractual obligations on the investee company to reduce GHG emissions by meeting specified milestones coupled with an undertaking by the investee company to make a payment or sell discounted debt upon the non-compliance with a target. The degree of the investee company's commitment to the GHG emission target can be calibrated to the amount of the payment. Armour et al. argue that a green pill would make it costly for the investee company to deviate from its transition path, thus discouraging its management from doing so. This will increase climate-conscious investors' willingness to pay for the investee company's securities ex ante and avoid the possibility of costly flip-flopping on climate strategy. Moreover, a green pill with a financial penalty for non-compliance will serve to align the ex-post preferences of shareholders who are focused solely on profits with those of climate-conscious investors.[95] Although insurers can be major institutional investors, it is difficult to see how green pills could be adopted for the type of investments that insurers prefer on account of their regulatory requirements.[96]

Although the divide between impact investment and stewardship has become somewhat blurred with the absorption of ESG integration investment approaches into the UK Stewardship Code and the concept of green pills, the main types of climate-related impact investment approaches and stewardship activities are summarised in Table 8.1.

The parallels to climate-related impact underwriting are obvious: stewardship engagement broadly corresponds to greening insurance, insurance policy terms can act as 'green pills,' negative screening as an investment approach has its equivalent in 'not insuring brown,' and investment approaches that focus on investment in climate change solutions are conceptually similar to 'insuring green.'

91 Gulliver (n 22) Sec 3.2.2.3 and 6.3, and Gomtsiam (n 38) 413.

92 Gomtsiam (n 38) 413.

93 See Chapter 6, Section 6.2.5.

94 John Armour, Luca Enriques, and Thom Wetzer, 'Green Pills: Making Corporate Climate Commitments Credible' (2023) 65 *Ariz L Rev*, 285 Pt 3.

95 Ibid Pt 3 Sec 2.

96 See Section 8.3.1.

Table 8.1 Types of climate-related impact investment approaches and stewardship activities.

Impact investment	*Stewardship*
Purpose: climate change mitigation and climate change adaptation measures to be taken by investee	
Impact-generating: • investment approach that has as its objective the investment in assets consistent with the purpose; • investment approach that improves the consistency of assets with the purpose over time; • investment approach that has as its objective the investment in solutions consistent with the purpose. Impact-aligned: negative screening investment approach that excludes investments in fossil fuel assets and projects (in combination with sustainable focus approach and stewardship)	ESG integration investment approach focused on the purpose Engagement: • develop and disclose an engagement policy; • exercise voting rights or monitor compliance with voting policy (if outsourced) consistent with the purpose; • develop an engagement capability (either directly or through outsourcing); • participate in the development of policy, regulation, and standard setting in relation to the purpose; • file shareholder resolutions consistent with the purpose; • engage with companies on issues relating to the purpose; • participate in collaborative engagement initiatives; • ask investment managers to undertake and report on engagement relating to the purpose.
Green pills	
Requires measurable outcome	Requires evidence of policies and compliance with policies

8.2 Rationales for climate-related impact investment and stewardship

8.2.1 Societal rationales

There are important societal reasons for climate-related impact investment and stewardship: as has been noted in several places in this book, public and private investment is necessary to achieve the objectives of the Paris Agreement. Divestment from fossil fuel assets can increase their cost of capital rendering them less profitable or even unviable,[97] so that harmful impacts could be brought to an end. Engagement can be more effective than making investment or divestment decisions since engagement strategies can communicate more clearly what the investee company should change.[98] Moreover, 'investment stewardship' can enhance the quality and integrity of the financial markets, contribute to sustainable, long-term value creation for beneficiaries, and create wider economic and societal benefits.[99] Effective engagement in corporate governance is one of the levers that can help improve the financial and non-financial performance of companies, including

97 See Section 8.1.2.

98 Gomtsiam (n 38) 404.

99 FRC (n 25) Prin 4 and 7; FCA, 'Building a Regulatory Framework for Effective Stewardship' DP 19/1 (January 2019) [1.9].

as regards environmental factors.[100] Davies has noted a shift in investment stewardship objectives in the revised UK Stewardship Code 'from saving the company to saving the planet.'[101]

8.2.2 Financial rationales

But how can insurers as investors justify climate-related impact investment and stewardship to their shareholders, policyholders, stakeholders, and regulators? There are a number of financial rationales: first, climate-related impact investments may produce returns equal to, or better than, conventional investments.[102] Emerging theoretical research and (tentative) empirical evidence suggest that 'greeniums' – a higher share/securities price that climate-conscious investors are prepared to pay – are already priced into the value of companies that commit to reducing GHG emissions.[103] Conversely, according to a survey about climate risk perceptions, institutional investors believe that climate risks have financial implications for their portfolio firms and that these risks, particularly regulatory risks, already have begun to materialise.[104] Secondly, climate-related investment can diversify an insurer's investment portfolio,[105] and divestment from fossil fuel assets can reduce the risk of the portfolio carrying stranded assets.[106] Thirdly, provided there is no green-washing, product- and entity-level disclosures on climate-related impact investment could serve as a marketing tool to attract new customers, shareholders, and investors and retain existing ones.[107] Fourthly, insurers with global investment portfolios should be incentivised to engage on systemic issues, supporting broader sustainability outcomes and well-functioning financial markets, since they will be concerned with both individual asset returns and the overall economic performance impacting on their investments.[108]

Fifthly, both climate-related impact investment and stewardship can reduce an insurer's exposure to reputational damage and environmental litigation risk.[109] Investment decisions to invest in fossil fuel assets have already been challenged in courts for failing to anticipate the risk of stranded assets.[110] In France, BNP Paribas has been sued (in an action

---

100 Shareholders Rights Directive, Recital 14.

101 Paul Davies, ''The UK Stewardship Code 2010–2020: From Saving the Company to Saving the Planet?' (March 2020) Working Paper no. 506/2020 (March 2020).

102 Alexander Dyck, Karl V. Lins, Lukas Roth, and Hannes F. Wagner, 'Do Institutional Investors Drive Corporate Social Responsibility? International Evidence' (2019) 131(3) *Journal of Financial Economics*, 693; Quinn Curtis, Jill E. Fisch, and Adriana Z. Robertson, 'Do ESG Mutual Funds Deliver on Their Promises?' Working Paper no. 586/2021, ECGI Working Paper Series in Law (May 2021).

103 Armour (n 94) Pt 3 18–20.

104 Philipp Krueger, Zacharias Sautner, and Laura T. Starks, 'The Importance of Climate Risks for Institutional Investors' (2020) 33 *Rev Fin Stud*, 1067, 1079–1080.

105 See Section 8.3.1.

106 See Chapter 3, Section 3.3.1 Table 2.

107 Gomtsiam (n 38) 402; Michal Barzuza, Quinn Curtis, and David H. Webber, 'Shareholder Value(s): Index Fund ESG Activism and the New Millennial Corporate Governance' (2020) 93 *Southern California L Rev*, 1243, 1284–1286.

108 For a discussion of stewardship engagement by large institutional investors and asset managers and systemic risk, see Jeffrey N. Gordon, 'Systematic Stewardship,' *Journal of Corporation Law*, 2022 (forthcoming) European Corporate Governance Institute – Law Working Paper No. 566/2021 and Columbia Law and Economics Working Paper No. 640.

109 Richardson (n 35) 240.

110 *Lynn v. Peabody Energy Corp.* United States District Court Eastern District of Missouri Eastern Division (2017, Case No. 4:15CV00916 AGF); *Roe v. Arch Coal, Inc.* United States District Court Eastern

which has now been discontinued) on the grounds that its investments violate the *loi sur le devoir de vigilance* of 2017 (Law on the duty of vigilance, incorporated in articles L. 225-102-4 and L. 225-102-5 of the French Commercial Code), the articles of the Civil Code on the *prejudice écologique* (articles 1246-1252 of the French *Code Civil*), which refers to any 'non-negligible impairment of the components or functions of ecosystems or the collective benefits derived by humans from the environment,' and BNP's 'unilateral commitment of will' to limit and combat climate change.[111] The UK government's approval of an investment made by UK Export Finance (the UK export credit agency) in a liquefied natural gas project in Mozambique was unsuccessfully challenged in judicial review proceedings.[112] Although not many actions have succeeded, they show that activist shareholders and interest groups are willing to challenge investment decisions where investments have been made in environmentally harmful activities. The European Commission's proposal for the CSDDD anticipates that infringements of the corporate due diligence duty can be the subject of enforcement action and sanctions imposed by a member state and give rise to civil liability.[113]

These financial rationales are important arguments for directors of insurance companies who are, as discussed in Chapter 6, Section 6.2.1, under a statutory duty – the s.172 duty – to act in a way they consider, in good faith, to be most likely to promote the success of the company for the benefit of its members as a whole, having regard to (amongst other matters) the impact of the company's operations on the community and the environment. A climate-related impact investment strategy could be problematic if the directors anticipate that investment returns will be reduced as a result. The s.172 duty is about shareholder value creation, not value destruction. However, this is taking a narrow view on 'benefit' and 'value,' defining them purely by reference to short-term profit maximisation. An impact-driven investment strategy – even if reducing returns in the short term – could create value in the long term by making the company's investment portfolio more sustainable. The s.172 duty could, in principle, accommodate short- or longer-term approaches to promoting the success of the company since it is at the discretion of the directors what they, in good faith, consider to be in the best interest of the company.[114]

Insurers must engage with their own shareholders to ensure their support for the creation of sustainable value for shareholders that takes into account the wider interests of society in stemming climate change. Such engagement rests on appropriate disclosures on net-zero targets, climate strategy and transition planning, and the prevention of greenwashing. Armour et al. argue that the adaptation of 'green pills' can bring investors on board and is consistent with the s.172 duty owed by the directors of the investee company on the grounds that they create no apparent issue with the goal of maximising shareholder

District of Missouri Eastern Division (2016, Case No. 4:15-CV-910) – both class actions against pension fund managers – both actions were however unsuccessful.

111 Joana Setzer and Catherine Higham, 'Global Trends in Climate Change Litigation: 2023 Snapshot,' Grantham Research Institute on Climate Change and the Environment and the Centre for Climate Change Economics and Policy (June 2023) 42–43 <https://www.lse.ac.uk/granthaminstitute/wp-content/uploads/2023/06/Global_trends_in_climate_change_litigation_2023_snapshot.pdf> accessed 10 July 2023.

112 *R. (on the application of Friends of the Earth Ltd) v Secretary of State for International Trade/UK Export Finance (UKEF)* [2023] EWCA Civ 14.

113 Proposal for a Directive of the European Parliament and of the Council on Corporate Sustainability Due Diligence and amending Directive (EU) 2019/1937 COM/2022/71, arts 20 and 22.

114 *In Re Smith and Fawcett* [1942] ch 304, 306 (Lord Greene); *Regentcrest Plc v Cohen* [2001] 2 BCLC 80 at [120] (Lord Parker).

value.[115] However, their case for green pills does not consider the position of the directors of the investor company and how they could justify the imposition of a green pill on the investee company.

8.2.3 Policyholder preferences

Policyholders of insurance policies that are not IBIPs have no financial interest in the insurer's investments and stewardship activities as long as the insurer is able to pay any claims (which is a regulated matter).[116] They may however take a non-financial interest in the insurer's ESG performance generally or environmental issues in particular.

Some environmental or climate-conscious policyholders may have a preference for IBIPs that have climate-related impact investment objectives. As discussed below, insurers or insurance intermediaries that offer IBIPs must make the appropriate pre-contractual disclosures on the investment strategy, assess whether an IBIP with a climate-related impact investment strategy is suitable to the prospective policyholder's demands and needs, and record the insurer's mandate to pursue such investment strategies.[117] Conversely, if the policyholder's investment mandate does not permit impact investment strategies, then insurers cannot pursue environmental outcomes to the detriment of maximising returns as to do so could conflict with their contractual duties and regulatory responsibilities.[118]

8.2.4 Regulatory approaches

Regulators welcome stewardship as a governance mechanism that can contribute to well-functioning financial markets and long-term value creation with wider societal benefits.[119] For these reasons, certain stewardship activities are already regulatory requirements for certain insurers. The regulation of climate-related impact investment and stewardship is discussed in Section 8.3.

8.3 Insurer's own investments: regulatory requirements and legal issues

The examination of the regulatory requirements that arise in connection with climate-related impact investment and stewardship is divided into two parts: first, in this section, there is a consideration of the regulatory requirements that apply to, and legal issues that may arise in respect of, an insurer's own investments. Secondly, in Section 8.4, there is a consideration of the regulatory requirements that apply to IBIPs. In the first category, the insurer bears the investment risk, in the second category the insurer invests premium on behalf of the policyholder and the policyholder retains the investment risk.

115 Armour (n 94) Pt 3, Sec 3.

116 PRA SII, Technical Provisions, Minimum Capital Requirement and Solvency Capital Requirement.

117 See Section 8.4.

118 See discussion in FCA, 'Feedback Statement, Building a Regulatory Framework for Effective Stewardship' FS19/7 (October 2019) [3.5]–[3.13] and see Section 8.4.4.

119 Shareholders Rights Directive, Recital 14; FCA DP 19/1 (n 99) [1.9].

8.3.1 Prudential regulation relating to investments

UK: there are currently no prudential rules that mandate that insurers must consider environmental objectives or achieve environmental goals in their investment strategy. UK insurers are free to invest in any category of assets, subject to the 'Prudent Person Principle' ('PPP') which requires insurers to:

- only invest in assets and instruments the risks of which it can properly identify, measure, monitor, manage, control, and report and appropriately take into account in the assessment of its overall solvency needs;[120]
- invest in assets (1) in such a manner as to ensure the security, quality, liquidity, and profitability of the portfolio of assets of the firm as a whole; and (2) that are localised such as to ensure their availability;[121]
- in the case of a conflict of interest, ensure that any third party which manages its assets will ensure that the investment of assets is made in the best interest of policyholders;[122]
- ensure that assets held to cover its technical provisions[123] are invested in a manner appropriate to the nature and duration of the firm's insurance and reinsurance liabilities and in the best interests of all policyholders, taking into account any disclosed policy objectives (the 'technical provisions requirement').[124]

In addition, there are a number of other rules and factors:

- there are restrictions on investing in derivatives, and investments and assets which are not admitted to trading on a regulated market must be kept to prudent levels;[125]
- insurers are required to invest in such a manner that assets are properly diversified;[126]
- insurers must identify, assess, and manage the financial risk from climate change, including their exposure in relation to their investments;[127] the type of investments that life insurers make are also heavily influenced by the limited range of assets that are eligible for the matching adjustment portfolio.[128] For matching adjustments to apply, the investment portfolio must, inter alia, consist of bonds or other assets with similar cash flow characteristics, be in the same currency as the

120 PRA SII, Investments, 2.1(1).

121 Ibid 2.1(2).

122 Ibid 2.1(3).

123 Technical provisions are the current amount the insurer would have to pay for an immediate transfer of its liabilities to another UK insurer (PRA Rulebook, SII Firms, Technical Provisions, 2.2).

124 PRA Rulebook Solvency II Firms, Investments, 3.1.

125 Ibid 5.2.

126 Ibid 5.2.

127 PRA SS3/19 [3.5]–[3.13].

128 PRA Rulebook Solvency II Firms, Technical Provisions 6.3; and The Solvency 2 Regulations 2015 (SI 2015/575), s 42(4). The PRA has presented figures that the total assets in matching adjustment portfolios amount to around £380 billion, and the matching adjustment confers a capital benefit on insurers of around £80 billion – see speech by Sam Wood, 'Solvency II: Striking the Balance' (8 July 2022) <https://www.bankofengland.co.uk/speech/2022/july/sam-woods-speech-given-at-the-bank-of-england-solvency-ii-striking-the-balance> accessed on 1 June 2023.

insurance obligations, and have fixed cash flows in terms of timing and amount (excluding investments with prepayment options and variable income) that match the insurance obligation.[129] The matching adjustment excludes a 'fundamental spread' reflecting the risks retained by the insurer which depends, inter alia, on the credit rating of the investment.[130] Assets rated below BBB in matching adjustment portfolios attract disproportionately severe treatment.[131]

This plethora of requirements has a number of implications for impact investments:

- given the requirement that investments should be made appropriate to the nature and duration of an insurer's insurance liabilities, property and casualty insurers are likely to adopt short-term investment strategies. This would rule out investment in green projects that have a longer-term duration;
- insurers are unlikely to invest any significant amounts in innovative climate solutions and technologies developed by start-ups and/or private companies. The markets for renewable technologies are still in their infancy and can therefore be more volatile, difficult to scale up, and, because there is a limited track record, they cannot be easily risk-assessed. Thus, such an investment may not have an appropriate level of security, its risk may not be fully identifiable and measurable, and there are restrictions on investing in assets which are not admitted to trading on a regulated market;
- an investment strategy that is exclusively, or substantially, climate-related impact-driven or takes a singular sustainable focus approach is likely to be inconsistent with the diversification requirement;
- limited investment opportunities in suitable green investments can lead to a concentration of risk in those developing markets;
- investments in fossil fuel assets are susceptible to transition risk, materialising in lower profitability, higher volatility, or even by becoming stranded assets (that is that they are unexpectedly or prematurely devalued or written down).[132] Their value might be affected due to regulatory changes, the development of new technologies and the increasing use of alternative and greener energy sources, changing investor preferences, high impact physical events, and new developments in climate science.[133] Fossil fuel assets could also pose increased litigation risk in respect of liability for pollution, in negligence, or for breach of statutory duties. Insurers should therefore consider the potentially higher level of market risk of

129 The Solvency II Regulations 2015 (SI 2015/575), s 42(4)(a) and (k).

130 PRA Rulebook SII Firms, Technical Provisions 7.2 and 7.3.

131 HM Treasury, 'Review of Solvency II: Consultation – Response' (November 2022) [4.8] and [4.9] <https://www.gov.uk/government/consultations/solvency-ii-review-consultation> accessed on 1 June 2023.

132 Ben Caldecott, Gerard Dericks, and James Mitchell, 'Stranded Assets and Subcritical Coal: -The Risk to Companies and Investors' (March 2015) <https://www.smithschool.ox.ac.uk/sites/default/files/2022-04/Stranded-Assets-and-Subcritical-Coal.pdf> accessed on 1 June 2023.

133 PRA, 'The Impact of Climate Change on the UK Insurance Sector: - A Climate Change Adaptation Report by the Prudential Regulation Authority' (September 2015) ,[4.14]-–[4.19] <https://www.bankofengland.co.uk/prudential-regulation/publication/2015/the-impact-of-climate-change-on-the-uk-insurance-sector> accessed on 1 June 2023.

mid- and long-term investments in fossil fuel assets and whether prudent risk management requires divestment;

- the current eligibility criteria for matching adjustments are considered to hinder green investments for a number of reasons.[134] They do not easily accommodate green infrastructure projects that go through a construction phase and/or have staggered completion phases because they do not produce fixed cash flows in terms of timing and amount. Green investments do not necessarily have any rating or a rating at BBB or above. The ABI is reported to have said '[i]t is currently much easier to invest in a highly-rated mining company than it is to invest for 30 years in a wind farm.'[135] Green investments that allow for prepayment are not eligible for matching adjustments;
- investments in climate change adaptation projects are most needed in the least developed and developing countries,[136] which makes them more risky, less likely to be admitted to trading on a regulated market, and more likely to be in a currency other than the matching insurance obligations;
- as insurers that seek mid- and long-term investments have a preference for bond investments on account of the matching adjustments, the scope for effective stewardship is limited in the case of commercial bonds (because of the limited contractual rights and the relative remoteness of the debt issuer[137]), or inapplicable in the case of government bonds.

The UK government is proposing to reform the matching adjustment requirements, inter alia in order to release capital for green investments,[138] and has published a draft of the Insurance and Reinsurance Undertakings (Prudential Requirements) (No. 2) Regulations that would effect the necessary legislative changes.[139] It will introduce changes that allow the PRA to broaden matching adjustment eligibility criteria and replace the requirement that all eligible assets must have fixed cash flows with a more flexible requirement that they have highly predictable cash flows.[140] The reforms also seek to introduce a 'notched allowances' approach to the fundamental spread by giving scaled allowances to different credit ratings.[141]

EU: the EU Solvency II regime also makes investments subject to the PPP. However, in contrast to the UK PPP, the EU PPP has been amended to require EU-based insurers to take into account sustainability risk when identifying, measuring, monitoring, managing, controlling, reporting, and assessing risks arising from investments and the potential long-term impact of their investment strategy and

134 See: HM Treasury (n 131) ch 3 and 4.

135 Mona Dohle, 'Solvency II: Insurers Unleashed,' Portfolio Institutional (23 May 2022) <https://www.portfolio-institutional.co.uk/spotlight/solvency-ii-insurers-unleashed/> accessed on 1 June 2023.

136 IPCC 2022 Adaptation Report 2586.

137 See Section 8.1.3.

138 HM Treasury (n 131) ch 3 and 4.

139 HM Treasury, 'Draft Insurance and Reinsurance Undertakings (Prudential Requirements) (No.2) Regulations' <https://www.gov.uk/government/publications/draft-insurance-and-reinsurance-undertakings-prudential-requirements-regulations> accessed 30 June 2023.

140 Ibid s 5.

141 HM Treasury (n 131) ch 3 and 4.

decisions on sustainability factors.[142] An insurer's investment strategy and decisions on sustainability factors must reflect the sustainability preferences of its customers taken into account in the product approval process.[143] Accordingly, EU insurers must consider their investment strategy long-term and in relation to their products, which should include giving consideration to using impact investment strategies. The explicit reference to 'long-term impacts' is also noteworthy as it acknowledges that climate-related risks and opportunities arise beyond the 12-month time horizon used for calculating the SCR.[144]

Prudential treatment of impact investment: should the solvency framework for insurers reward green impact investment by insurers with preferential solvency capital treatment, or penalise brown investments? The IPCC has found that the lack of incentives for providing finance is one of the key causes of the implementation gaps for both mitigation and adaptation.[145] There is already a precedent for preferential capital treatment in the EU banking sector with respect to loan exposures to corporates specifically set up to fund public infrastructure where the assets being financed contribute to certain environmental and sustainability objectives and satisfy various other tests.[146] The key rationale suggested for such interventions is to facilitate a quicker transition to a net-zero economy by channelling funding to more environmentally friendly activities and by increasing the cost of business for carbon-intensive activities.[147]

Neither the Bank of England nor the PRA see a convincing case for capital requirements being used for addressing the causes of climate change – either by introducing 'carbon penalising factors' and/or 'green supporting factors' for exposures to assets or counterparties that are respectively more or less carbon-intensive.[148] Their initial conclusion relies on research in the banking sector that shows that the use of capital requirements as a tool to stimulate outward impact – i.e. affect investment decisions directly – is not likely to be effective.[149] Moreover, there is a concern that giving preferential capital treatment based on environmental considerations is not necessarily reflective of the financial risk associated with the project or asset and could thus lead to a deterioration of safety and soundness of the firm.[150] Although there are recent studies (not considered by the Bank of England and the PRA) that indicate that there is price premium in the valuation of residential properties with a high level of energy efficiency,[151] and that risk of mortgage payment defaults

142 Commission Delegated Regulation (EU) 2021/1256 of 21 April 2021 amending Delegated Regulation (EU) 2015/35 as regards the integration of sustainability risks in the governance of insurance and reinsurance undertakings, art 1(6).

143 Ibid art 1(6).

144 See Chapter 4, Section 4.4.3.

145 IPCC 2022 Sixth Assessment Report [2.3.3].

146 Regulation (EU) No 575/2013 of the European Parliament and of the Council of 26 June 2013 on prudential requirements for credit institutions and investment firms and amending Regulation (EU) No 648/2012, art 501.

147 PRA Role of Capital Requirements Report Pt B.

148 BoE Climate and Capital Frameworks Report [35] and [36].

149 PRA Role of Capital Requirements Report Pt B.

150 Ibid Pt B.

151 Peter Reusens, Frank Vastmans, and Sven Damen, 'The Impact of Changes in Dwelling Characteristics and Housing Preferences on Belgian House Prices' (2022) 2 *NBB Economic Review*.

by borrowers with energy-efficient properties is lower compared to borrowers with energy inefficient properties,[152] the correlation between credit risk and specific environmental characteristics of assets remains to be explored more fully. In a 2022 Discussion Paper, the European Banking Authority expressed the preliminary view that, in the banking context, there was not yet strong and granular enough evidence to show the connection between lower credit risk and 'green projects.'[153]

The UK government has suggested that proposed reforms to increase flexibility in relation to eligible assets for matching adjustments will incentivise insurers to invest in assets supporting the development of new green technologies or to support the adoption of green solutions. This is a speculative approach which may overestimate the impact on insurers' investment decisions.[154] Even with the more flexible criteria, investments in green infrastructure projects and innovative climate solutions may not be suitable since cashflows can be unpredictable or the fundamental spread may be high: infrastructure projects are frequently delivered late and exceed budget. Innovative technologies may fail, be superseded by better technologies, or be difficult to commercialise.

Meanwhile, the Bank of England is considering whether the matching adjustment mechanism could be used to capture climate-related risk in relation to investment assets.[155] This would depend on whether the fundamental spread (the portion of capital excluded from the matching adjustment to reflect the credit risk retained by the insurer) is already sensitive to increases in the riskiness of an asset as a result of climate change over time or could be adjusted to be so. Making the fundamental spread more risk-sensitive to stranded assets as a result of climate change could be a potential microprudential tool to discourage brown investments by insurers.

The UK government is also proposing reforms changing the calculation of the risk margin, including cutting the risk margin by 60–70% for long-term life insurers and 30% for general insurers. It has now published a draft of the Insurance and Reinsurance Undertakings (Prudential Requirements) (No. 2) Regulations which sets the risk tapering factor for calculating risk margins at 0.9 for long-term life insurance obligations and 1.0 for general insurance obligations.[156] This would release capital required to cover an insurer's technical provisions,[157] but it is questionable whether this freed-up capital would be channelled into green investments. In fact, the government envisages that this capital would be used to lower premiums and increase annuity yields in life insurance.[158] A different way to use released capital from lowered risk margins for general insurers might be to channel it into 'greening insurance,' such as climate risk assessments of prospective policyholders, premium discounts and rebates to incentivise or reward the implementation of climate change adaptation measures by policyholders, and green reinstatement.[159] This

152 Benjamin Guin, Perttu Korhonen, and Sidharth Moktan 'Risk Differentials between Green and Brown Assets?' (2022) 213 *Economics Letters*, 110320.

153 European Banking Authority, 'The Role of Environmental Risks in the Prudential Framework' Discussion Paper EBA/DP/2022/02 (2 May 2022) [96].

154 See e.g. PRA, 'FS1/22 – Potential Reforms to Risk Margin and Matching Adjustment within Solvency II' FS1/22 (November 2022).

155 BoE Climate and Capital Frameworks Report [61] and [36].

156 Draft Insurance and Reinsurance Undertakings (Prudential Requirements) (No.2) Regulations (n 139), s 4.

157 See Chapter 4, Section 4.4.3.

158 HM Treasury (n 131) [2.4].

159 See Chapter 7, Sections 7.4 to 7.7.

is, however, not currently part of the reform proposals. When finalising the rules, HM Treasury and the PRA should consider whether the capital released from a proportion of the lowered risk margins should be ringfenced for green investments (life insurers) and greening insurance (general insurers).

EIOPA will be given a specific mandate to consider a dedicated prudential treatment of exposures related to assets or activities associated with environmental objectives.[160] In a 2022 Discussion Paper, EIOPA explores the parameters for a dedicated prudential treatment regarding transition risk for specific asset classes: stocks, bonds, and property investments.[161] No details on the incorporation into the SCR have been provided at this stage, but EIOPA is looking into making adjustments to the market risk component in the Standard Formula and combining a backwards-looking analysis based on historic time series data with a forward-looking model-based assessment to reach a more comprehensive picture on the potential impact of climate change on asset prices.[162] EIOPA refers to research and has been consulting on whether firms with higher levels of transition risk exposures are typically associated with higher levels of GHG emissions, but the opposite relationship does not necessarily hold, as assets with relatively low GHG emission levels can also be exposed to transition risk.[163] Therefore, EIOPA considers it important to assess the potential for a dedicated prudential treatment for the entire range of transition risk exposures, i.e. for assets with a higher exposure to transition risk as well as those with a lower exposure.[164] In sum, the UK and the EU prudential regulatory regimes are currently not actively supportive of insurers channelling investments to finance green infrastructure and the green economy on the grounds that financial risk has not been conclusively linked to the environmental characteristics of investments. In the absence of data and analysis to evidence that link, policymakers and regulators must look for alternative routes to stimulate green investments by insurers. As suggested above, as part of the UK Solvency reforms, HM Treasury and the PRA should consider whether the capital released from a proportion of the lowered risk margins should be ringfenced for green investments (life insurers) and greening insurance (general insurers).

8.3.2 Business conduct regulation of stewardship

Engagement policy: the FCA Handbook Systems and Controls Sourcebook ('SYCS') requires UK life insurers to develop, publicly disclose, and implement an 'engagement policy' which sets out details of its engagement with investee companies or publicly disclose a clear and reasoned explanation of why it has chosen not to comply with the engagement policy requirement.[165] This is a requirement derived from the Shareholder Rights

160 European Commission: Proposal for a Proposal for a Directive of the European Parliament and of the Council amending Directive 2009/138/EC as regards proportionality, quality of supervision, reporting, long-term guarantee measures, macro-prudential tools, sustainability risks, group and cross-border supervision (COM/2021/581), art 1(91).

161 EIOPA, 'Prudential Treatment of Sustainability Risks: Discussion Paper' EIOPA-BoS-22-527 (November 2022) ch 2.

162 Ibid.

163 Ibid; Stefano Battiston, Antoine Mandel, Irene Monasterolo, Franziska Schütze, and Gabriele Visentin, 'A Climate Stress-Test of the Financial System' (2017) 7(4) *Nature Climate Change*, 283.

164 EIOPA (n 161) [15].

165 SYSC 3.4.4R.

Directive,[166] and accordingly, EU-based life insurers will be subject to similar requirements under national laws. There is no equivalent requirement for general insurers.

The engagement policy must describe how the firm:

1. integrates shareholder engagement in its investment strategy;
2. monitors investee companies on relevant matters, including
    a. strategy;
    b. financial and non-financial performance and risk;
    c. capital structure;
    d. social and environmental impact and corporate governance;
3. conducts dialogues with investee companies;
4. exercises voting rights and other rights attached to shares;
5. co-operates with other shareholders;
6. communicates with relevant stakeholders of the investee companies;
7. manages actual and potential conflicts of interests in relation to the firm's engagement.[167]

The annual disclosure must be made on the firm's website and include a general description of voting behaviour, an explanation of the most significant votes and the use of the services of proxy advisers, and information on how the firm has cast votes in the general meetings of companies in which it holds shares, provided that a firm is not required to disclose votes that are insignificant due to the subject matter of the vote or the size of the holding in the company.[168]

Compliance with UK Stewardship Code: a UK life insurer that is managing investments for a professional client that is not a natural person must disclose on its website the nature of its commitment to the UK Stewardship Code.[169] Where it does not commit to the UK Stewardship Code, it must disclose on its website its alternative investment strategy.[170] For now, the FCA is pausing its plans to make the 2020 Code mandatory but it has strongly encouraged voluntary compliance on a 'comply or explain' basis by life insurers.[171] General insurers can voluntarily subscribe to the UK Stewardship Code.

The UK Stewardship Code is a framework of stewardship standards for asset owners and asset managers, and for service providers that support them, set by the FRC. To become a signatory to the 2020 Code, organisations must submit to the FRC a Stewardship Report demonstrating how they have applied the Code's principles in the previous 12 months. The FRC will assess the report and if it meets their reporting expectations, the organisation will be listed as a signatory to the 2020 Code, and this process is repeated on an annual basis. Annual lists of signatories are published on the FRC's website.[172]

The key principles of the 2020 Code relevant to climate-related impact investment and stewardship are:

166 Shareholders Rights Directive, see in particular art 3g, and see n 24.

167 SYSC 3.4.5R and SRD art 3g(1)(b).

168 SYSC 3.4.6R; and SRD art 3g(1)(a).

169 COBS 2.2.3R.

170 COBS 2.2.3R.

171 FCA FS19/7 (n 118) [3.83]–[3.89].

172 FRC, 'UK Stewardship Code Signatories' <https://www.frc.org.uk/investors/uk-stewardship-code/uk-stewardship-code-signatories> accessed on 1 June 2023.

- **Principle 1**: signatories should explain what actions they have taken to ensure their investment beliefs, strategy, and culture enable effective stewardship;
- **Principle 2**: signatories should explain how their governance, resources, and incentive structures and processes support stewardship;
- **Principle 4**: signatories should identify and respond to market-wide and systemic risks to promote a well-functioning financial system;
- **Principle 6**: signatories should take account of client and beneficiary needs and communicate the activities and outcomes of their stewardship and investment to them;
- **Principle 7**: signatories should systematically integrate stewardship and investment, including material environmental, social and governance issues, and climate change, to fulfil their responsibilities. They should disclose the issues they have prioritised for assessing investments, prior to holding, monitoring through holding and exiting. This should include the ESG issues of importance to them. Signatories should explain:
    a. how the integration of stewardship and investment has differed for funds, asset classes, and geographies;
    b. how they have ensured that the design and award of mandates include requirements to integrate stewardship and investment to align with the investment time horizons of clients and beneficiaries;
    c. the processes they have used to integrate stewardship and investment, including material ESG issues, to align with the investment time horizons of clients and/or beneficiaries; and to ensure service providers have received clear and actionable criteria to support the integration of stewardship and investment, including material ESG issues;
    d. how information gathered through stewardship has informed acquisition, monitoring, and exit decisions, either directly or on their behalf, and with reference to how they have best-served clients and/or beneficiaries;
- **Principle 9**: signatories should engage with investee enterprises to maintain or enhance the value of assets and should describe the outcomes of engagement that is ongoing or has concluded in the preceding 12 months, undertaken directly or by others on their behalf;
- **Principle 10**: signatories should disclose what collaborative engagement they have participated in to achieve a specific change or to engage on thematic issues, and why;
- **Principle 12**: signatories should actively exercise their (voting and other) rights and responsibilities to influence the investee enterprise and report on those activities and outcomes.

The SYSC requirements combined with the UK Stewardship Code are a clear endorsement of stewardship, including engagement on environmental issues and ESG integration investment approaches. However, their application is limited to life insurers and compliance remains optional as they operate on a 'comply or explain' basis. This seems unambitious but the FCA gave a number of reasons why further regulation was not appropriate at that time following feedback highlighting the following barriers:

1. investment mandates, voting guidelines, and other arrangements between asset owners and asset managers may not be fully aligned with asset owners' and beneficiaries' investment and stewardship objectives;
2. the information that securities issuers disclose on climate change and other long-term factors may not adequately support investors' long-term decisions;
3. regulatory uncertainties in the Market Abuse Regulation[173] and competition law may discourage engagement between issuers and investors;
4. the information firms disclose on their stewardship may not be detailed enough for investors to distinguish between firms based on the quality of their stewardship – this may weaken market discipline;
5. service providers (including proxy advisers and investment consultants) may not adequately support investors' stewardship;
6. firms' governance arrangements may not put enough emphasis on the value of effective stewardship.[174]

The FCA has left the door open for regulating stewardship in the not-too-distant future and following a series of interim steps and regulation in other areas.[175] Steps are already being taken to overcome some of these barriers: for example, the FCA's proposed sustainability disclosure regime envisages clear and detailed product-level sustainability disclosures that would address Point 1, and entity-level sustainability disclosures that would address Point 4.[176] The Listing Rules now require all issuers of listed shares to make disclosures in line with the TCFD Recommendations[177] – this addresses partially, but not fully, Point 2.[178] Point 3 is discussed below. In the section on 'Regulatory Requirements: IBIPs' below, further proposals that could address some of these barriers will be examined.

8.3.3 US anti-ESG legislation

Reference is made to Chapter 4, Section 4.4.6, which discusses the anti-ESG legislation that some US states have passed or are planning to pass. This is relevant to insurers as investors since anti-ESG legislation may prohibit the relevant US state from (1) doing business with financial institutions that 'boycott' or 'discriminate against' companies in certain (e.g. fossil fuel) industries, and/or (2) investing the state's assets (including pension plan assets) through such financial institutions.[179] Some of these measures authorise state regulators to blacklist financial entities that engage in boycotts of fossil fuel companies for divestment purposes.[180] In addition, some of these measures compel companies enter-

173 Regulation (EU) No 596/2014 of the European Parliament and of the Council of 16 April 2014 on market abuse (market abuse regulation) and repealing Directive 2003/6/EC of the European Parliament and of the Council and Commission Directives 2003/124/EC, 2003/125/EC and 2004/72/EC; and see Section 8.3.3.

174 FCA FS19/7 (n 118) [3.37] to [3.74].

175 Ibid ch 4.

176 FCA Sustainability Disclosure Proposals; and see Chapter 5, Section 5.3.5.

177 LR 9.8.6.8; and see Chapter 5, Section 5.3.3.1.

178 It does not address Point 2 fully because the TCFD Recommendations do not focus on disclosures on outward impact – see Chapter 5, Section 5.1.

179 *Reuters*, 'The Challenge of Investing in the Face of State Anti-ESG Legislation' (24 August 2022). A second group of anti-ESG legislation are measures that restrict states from considering ESG factors in their investment strategies.

180 Ibid.

ing into contracts with state entities to attest, as a condition of doing business with public entities, that they do not and will not engage in boycotts against fossil fuel companies during the life of the contract.[181] Whether insurers and their underwriting and investment activities are in the scope of these measures will depend on each instrument, including the application of exceptions and thresholds. In contrast, in a recent letter to a number of insurers, the US Senate Committee on the Budget suggested that continuing to underwrite and invest in fossil fuel projects was inconsistent with the goals of the Paris Agreement to which the US is a signatory, harmful to policyholders who are increasingly facing protection gaps, and potentially creating systemic risk for the economy. The Committee has launched an investigation into Berkshire Hathaway to account for their plans to phase out underwriting and investing in fossil fuel projects.[182]

8.3.4 Legal issues arising from collective stewardship and collaborative investment practices

Feedback to the FCA[183] highlighted that competition law issues and the Market Abuse Regulation are seen as potentially creating regulatory barriers to engagement between issuers and investors.

Competition issues: the SYSC requirements and the 2020 Code both envisage that investors (either of the same investee enterprise or on the same thematic issue) collaborate in their stewardship activities and engage with other stakeholders.[184] Collective stewardship – where a group of investors collaborate – can be more effective and more cost-efficient in bringing about change,[185] and produce more consistent results. There are already examples of collective engagement on climate change, such as Climate Action 100+, an investor-led initiative to ensure the world's largest corporate greenhouse gas emitters take action on climate change,[186] and the Net-Zero Asset Owner Alliance, an UN-convened group of institutional investors (including a number of UK insurers) committed to collective investor action to align investment portfolios to net-zero GHG emissions by 2050.[187] The NZIA, while primarily focused on transitioning underwriting portfolios to net-zero, also encourages its members to aim to transition their investment portfolios to net-zero GHG emissions by 2050 and to consider joining relevant initiatives (such as the Net-Zero Asset Owner Alliance) in order to achieve a consistent approach to net-zero.[188] The

181 Leah Malone, Emily Holland, and Carolyn Houston, Simpson Thacher & Bartlett LLP, 'ESG Battlegrounds: How the States Are Shaping the Regulatory Landscape in the U.S.,' Harvard Law School Forum on Corporate Governance (11 March 2023) <https://corpgov.law.harvard.edu/2023/03/11/esg-battlegrounds-how-the-states-are-shaping-the-regulatory-landscape-in-the-u-s/> accessed on 1 June 2023.

182 Letter from the United States Senate Committee on the Budget to State Farm, Liberty Mutual, Berkshire Hathaway, AIG, Travelers Insurance, Chubb, and Starr dated 9 June 2023 launching investigation into Berkshire Hathaway for continuing to insure and invest in fossil fuel projects <https://www.budget.senate.gov/imo/media/doc/Budget%20Committee%20Letters%20to%20Insurance%20Companies.pdf> accessed on 1 June 2023.

183 FCA FS19/7 (n 118) ch 4.

184 SYSC 3.4.5(5) and (6)R; UK Stewardship Code (n 25), Prin 10.

185 FCA, 'Discussion Paper, Building a Regulatory Framework for Stewardship' DP19/1 (January 2019) [3.22].

186 Climate Action 100+ <https://www.climateaction100.org/> accessed on 1 June 2023.

187 Net-Zero Owner Alliance <https://www.unepfi.org/net-zero-alliance/> accessed on 1 June 2023.

188 NZIA, 'Statement of Commitment by Signatory Companies' <https://www.unepfi.org/psi/wp-content/uploads/2021/07/NZIA-Commitment.pdf> accessed on 1 June 2023.

ABI published a 'Climate Change Roadmap' in which it sets out how the UK insurance industry can support the delivery of the UK's net-zero target.[189] The non-binding targets set by the ABI Roadmap include for its members to apply the principles set out in the UK Stewardship Code and to engage with collective stewardship.[190]

Potential competition issues (Point 3) arising from collective stewardship activities were one of the specific barriers identified in the feedback that FCA received to its Discussion Paper on stewardship.[191] Competition issues could also arise from collaborative practices involving negative screening investment approaches. Reference is made to the discussion of the general competition law principles, the CMA's draft guidance, and the EU guidance discussed in Chapter 6.

Co-operation between competitors which is made or done to comply with a legal requirement is automatically excluded from the application of the Competition Act 1998 Chapter I prohibition.[192] However, the Chapter I prohibition will still apply if the law merely encourages such co-operation, rather than requiring it. Thus, given the 'comply or explain' approach of the SYSC requirements and the COBS requirements, it is unlikely that collective stewardship approaches would be automatically excluded. The CMA's draft guidance is clear that the CMA considers industry frameworks and alliances to be outside the Chapter 1 prohibition if there is no binding agreement between its members. Thus, alliances such as the Net-Zero Asset Owner Alliance and the NZIA which set non-binding targets that are largely self-determined by its members should not be an issue under UK competition law. It was also highlighted in Chapter 6 that the position is less clear under the EU Guidance, and that there is significant risk that certain collective ESG practices could constitute collusive behaviour in violation of the anti-trust laws in the US.[193] In particular, collective stewardship engagement through voting and by seeking to influence board decisions to reduce GHG emissions could be seen as unlawful co-ordination.[194] Given these unresolved and unharmonised competition/anti-trust issues, combined with the anti-ESG legislation in some US states,[195] it is to be expected that investors in US investee companies will not wish to engage in collective stewardship or in binding collective arrangements that would commit them to divest from US fossil fuel companies. Yet, the UK Stewardship Code and the EU SRD encourage co-operation with other investors. Insurers as investors caught in the crossfire of political battlegrounds face a difficult balancing act between conflicting positions. Clarity and convergence on the competition law treatment of industry collaborations to tackle climate change is needed so that insurers

189 ABI, 'ABI Climate Change Roadmap' (7 July 2021) <https://www.abi.org.uk/about-the-abi/sustainability/climate-change-roadmap/> accessed on 1 June 2023.

190 Ibid.

191 FCA DP19/1 (n 185).

192 Competition Act 1998, sch 3, para 5.

193 Letter from the State Attorney Generals of Montana, Louisiana, Utah, Alabama, Arkansas, Georgia, Idaho, Indiana, Iowa, Kansas, Kentucky, Mississippi, Missouri, New Hampshire, Ohio, South Carolina, Tennessee, Texas, Virginia, West Virginia, and Wyoming, to asset managers, dated 30 March 2023 <https://attorneygeneral.utah.gov/wp-content/uploads/2023/03/2023-03-30-Asset-Manager-letter Press-FINAL.pdf> accessed on 1 June 2023.

194 Ibid 3, and Letter from the State Attorney Generals of Utah, Louisiana, Alabama, Alaska, Arkansas, Georgia, Idaho, Indiana, Iowa, Kansas, Kentucky, Mississippi, Missouri, Montana, New Hampshire, Ohio, Oklahoma, South Carolina, South Dakota, Texas, Virginia, West Virginia, and Wyoming to NZIA insurers, dated 16 May 2023, 1–3 <https://attorneygeneral.utah.gov/wp-content/uploads/2023/05/2023-05-15-NZIA-Letter.pdf accessed 23 May 2023> accessed on 1 June 2023.

195 See Chapter 4, Section 4.4.6.

who operate as underwriters and investors in multiple jurisdictions can take an enabling role.

Market abuse: the market abuse regime sets out a regulatory framework on market abuse, as well as measures to prevent market abuse to ensure the integrity of the financial markets and enhance investor protection and confidence in those markets. The EU Market Abuse Regulation[196] ('EU MAR') came into effect on 3 July 2016 and had a direct effect in the UK until 31 December 2020 when it was onshored into UK law by the European Union (Withdrawal) Act 2018. Changes to EU MAR were made by the Market Abuse Exit Regulations 2019, to ensure that the onshored legislation ('UK MAR') operates effectively in the UK. However, the prohibitions on insider dealing and unlawful disclosure – which are relevant in this context – remain broadly unchanged from that under EU MAR for now.

Broadly speaking, 'inside information' is information of a precise nature, which has not been made public, relating, directly or indirectly, to one or more issuers or to one or more financial instruments, and which, if it were made public, would be likely to have a significant effect on the prices of those financial instruments, on the price of related derivative financial instruments, or GHG emission allowances.[197] Both EU MAR and UK MAR prohibit '**insider dealings**': persons in possession of inside information are prohibited from using that information to deal or attempt to deal in financial instruments or to recommend or induce another person to transact on the basis of inside information.[198] The use of inside information to amend or cancel an existing order also constitutes insider dealing.[199] Both EU MAR and UK MAR also prohibit '**unlawful disclosure**' of inside information which occurs where a person possesses inside information and discloses that information to any other person, except where the disclosure is made in the normal exercise of employment, a profession, or duties.[200]

How could this affect insurers as investors? ESG-related information, including information relating to an issuer's inward and outward impact in relation to climate change, is not 'inside information' if it has already been disclosed publicly, e.g. in a listed company's TCFD LR statement.[201] Thus, if an insurer obtains information about an investee company that is already in the public domain, MAR has no application. Insurers could, however, through their stewardship activities, receive ESG-related information that is not public. Such information would only fall within the scope of 'inside information' if it is (1) precise, and (2) likely to have a significant effect on the prices of relevant securities or financial instruments if it were to be made public. Information is deemed to be of a precise nature if it is specific enough that one could reasonably expect that it could have a significant effect on the price of relevant financial instruments.[202] Information is considered to be likely to have a significant effect on the prices of relevant financial instruments if a reasonable investor would be likely to use it as part of the basis of his or her investment decisions.[203] A reasonable investor is a hypothetical investor and is necessarily assumed

196 Regulation (EU) No 596/2014 (n 173).
197 UK MAR and EU MAR art 7(1).
198 Ibid art 8(1).
199 Ibid art 8(1).
200 Ibid art 10(1).
201 LR 9.8.6.8 and see ch 5.
202 UK MAR and EU MAR art 7(2).
203 Ibid art 7(4); FCA Handbook, Disclosure Guidance and Transparency Rules sourcebook (DTR) 2.2.

to have access to all generally available information and takes account of it where relevant.[204] As noted above, emerging theoretical research and empirical evidence suggest that climate-conscious investors are prepared to pay 'greeniums' that are already being priced into the value of companies that commit to reducing GHG emissions.[205] But are climate-conscious investors reasonable investors within the meaning of art.7(4) of UK and EU MAR? Mülbert and Sajnovits suggest that as real-life investors with ESG preferences gain critical mass in the market as a whole they will be seen as a reflection of the 'reasonable investor.' Until then, they argue, it is by no means clear whether ESG-related information is or can be price-sensitive and the EU should give further guidance on the extent to which ESG-related information could be 'inside information.'

If the ESG-related information is 'inside information,' the issuer is required to inform the public as soon as possible in a manner which enables fast access and complete, correct, and timely assessment of the information by the public.[206] The FCA has highlighted a number of general disclosure requirements in relation to ESG matters, including climate change risks that can have a financial impact on issuers.[207] In contrast, an insurer who has come into the possession of inside information relating to an investee company must not unlawfully disclose that inside information to any other person and must not use that information for insider dealings. It is suggested that this does not put a significant additional compliance burden on insurers who, in their capacity as underwriters and investors, are likely to come into the possession of inside information occasionally (if not frequently) and should already have anti-market abuse procedures in place. To the extent that insurers as investors engage with other shareholders and stakeholders as part of their stewardship activities, they must be careful not to use 'inside information' in their engagement. As the frequency, scope, and level of detail of sustainability-related disclosures are becoming increasingly regulated or subject to industry standards, the realm of inside information (which by definition is not public) should be shrinking.

The FCA have said that investors can comply with the MAR requirements while 'engaging individually and collectively with issuers, as long as they consider how to do this carefully and make appropriate adjustments'[208] but have not specified what these adjustments should be. The Takeover Panel has clarified that 'shareholder activism' may be undertaken without being deemed to be 'acting in concert' in relation to mandatory offer requirements under the Takeover Code.[209]

204 *Hannam v FCA* [2014] UKUT 233 (TCC).

205 Armour (n 94) Pt 3, 18–20.

206 UK MAR and EU MAR art 17(1) and (2); and FCA Handbook, Disclosure Guidance and Transparency Rules sourcebook (DTR) 6.3.2R.

207 FCA, 'Primary Market Technical Note: Disclosures in Relation to ESG Matters, Including Climate Change' (December 2020) <https://www.fca.org.uk/publication/primary-market/tn-801-1.pdf> accessed on 1 June 2023. Issuers trading on regulated markets must make disclosures under the LR and the Disclosure Guidance and Transparency Rules that could extend to climate-related information – see Chapter 5, Section 5.3.3.2.

208 FCA FS19/7 (n 118) [1.27].

209 Takeover Panel, 'Practice Statement No 26: Shareholder Activism' <https://www.thetakeoverpanel.org.uk/wp-content/uploads/2021/07/Practice-Statement-No-26.pdf> accessed on 1 June 2023.

8.4 IBIPs: regulatory requirements

This section considers some of the regulatory requirements and legal issues that arise specifically in connection with IBIPs that pursue impact investment strategies. An IBIP is a contract of insurance which offers a maturity or surrender value and where that maturity or surrender value is wholly or partially exposed, directly or indirectly, to market fluctuations,[210] and **does not include**

- non-life insurance products;
- life insurance contracts where the benefits under the contract are payable only on death or in respect of incapacity due to injury, sickness, or disability;
- pension products which are recognised as having the primary purpose of providing the investor with an income in retirement, and which entitle the investor to certain benefits;
- officially recognised occupational pension schemes;
- individual pension products for which a financial contribution from the employer is required by law and where the employer or the employee has no choice as to the pension product or provider.

Traditionally, the most common form of investment-type life policy has been the with-profits policy commonly used for endowment policies, including mortgage endowments. The policyholder makes regular premium payments during the agreed term. The investment element of the premium is invested in pre-determined funds. At the end of the policy term, or if the policyholder dies, the policyholder or its beneficiary is entitled to a lump sum payment. In addition, during the term of the policy, the policyholders are eligible to receive annual 'bonuses' that are declared by the insurer following an actuarial assessment of its obligations to policyholders and the value of its with-profits funds. The bonuses reflect the policyholders' share in the profit from the fund. The policy documentation must be clear as to whether the bonus entitlement is absolute, contingent, or at the discretion of the insurer.[211] If the fund does not perform well enough to produce a surplus profit, bonuses cannot be declared. The policyholder bears the investment risk in respect of the bonus payments.

Unit-linked insurance products are now the most prevalent form of IBIPs. The policyholder makes regular premium payments during the agreed term. The investment element of the premium is allocated to units. Policyholders can choose how to invest their units from a range of investment options. The value of the units will fluctuate based on the performance of the underlying investment. At the end of the policy term, or if the policyholder dies, the policyholder or its beneficiary is entitled to a benefit payment in the form of units. The size of the payment depends on the number of units held and the value of the units at that point in time. The policyholder bears the investment risk in respect of the units.

For IBIPs, there are a number of regulatory issues that need to be considered if the investment element of the product is to pursue an impact investment strategy.

210 FCA Handbook, Glossary Terms, definition of 'IBIP.'

211 COBS, 20.1A.13.

8.4.1 The client's best interests rule and 'best execution'

An insurer who offers IBIPs must act honestly, fairly, and professionally in accordance with the best interests of its client, i.e. the policyholder (the 'client's best interests rule').[212] In addition, insurers must take all sufficient steps to obtain, when executing orders or passing them to other firms for execution, the best possible result for their clients.[213] This is a *lex specialis* rule to the new consumer duty which requires an insurer to deliver good outcomes for retail customers.[214] Given the nature of IBIPs, all IBIP policyholders will be retail customers. Whenever a client gives a specific instruction about an order, the insurer must execute the order following that specific instruction in order to satisfy its best execution obligations.[215]

Pursuing impact investment strategies for IBIPs may not be in clients' best interests and may not achieve the best possible results, especially for clients who are purely focused on financial results. A group of US State Attorney Generals recently alleged that asset managers who are members of the Net-Zero Asset Managers Initiative could be in breach of their duties to act in the best interests of their clients by making commitments to transition their investment portfolios to net-zero, rather than seeking the best financial returns.[216] In contrast, if a client has expressed its wish to buy an IBIP that pursues an impact investment approach, the best interests of that client would be served by providing a product consistent with that wish.

The FCA has provided guidance that an insurer may take into account non-financial matters (such as 'environmental issues') as part of its investment strategy or investment decision-making for IBIPs if:

(a) the firm has good reason to consider that affected policyholders or relevant policyholders would generally share the views on which the non-financial matters are based; and
(b) taking those matters into account would not involve a risk of a significant financial detriment To any affected investment.[217]

There is not yet any further guidance on what constitutes 'a significant financial detriment,' whether this would be assessed as a percentage or in total terms, and to what extent the financial circumstances of the policyholder in question would be relevant. Rather than relying on 'good reason,' the better approach would be to develop dedicated IBIPs where the contractual terms expressly permit the insurer to pursue an impact investment strategy, and where, at the pre-contractual stage, that investment strategy is appropriately disclosed to prospective policyholders (product disclosure) and the suitability of such a product is explored with a prospective policyholder (product suitability). The latter approach is more likely to produce good outcomes for consumer policyholders in line with the new 'consumer duty' which will require insurers to deliver good outcomes for consumers,

212 Ibid 2.1.1R.
213 Ibid 11.2A.
214 PRIN 2.1.1R Prin 12; and see Chapter 7, Section 7.4.5.
215 COBS 11.2A.12R.
216 Letter from the State Attorney Generals to asset managers (n 193).
217 SYSC 3.2.23(5)G.

including ensuring that consumers (1) receive fair prices and quality, (2) receive suitable products and good treatment, and (3) have access to products meeting their needs.[218]

8.4.2 Product suitability

Prior to the conclusion of a contract, a UK insurance distributor – an insurance intermediary selling IBIPs on behalf of an insurance company, or an insurer selling insurance directly to a client – must obtain information from the client (for example, by asking the client questions in person or by way of a questionnaire) in order to establish the demands and needs of that client,[219] and communicate those demands and needs to the client.[220] If the insurance product is not sold by the insurer directly, the insurer must carefully select distribution channels that are appropriate to the target market[221] and ensure that any insurance distributor (brokers and other insurance intermediaries) selected has the necessary knowledge, expertise, and competence to understand the features of an insurance product and the identified target market.[222] The insurance distributor must be provided with all the necessary product information and target market information.[223] The IBIP proposed by the insurance distributor must be consistent with the client's insurance demands and needs.[224] In an advised sale where the insurance distributor makes a personal recommendation, the insurance distributor is obliged to take reasonable steps to ensure that a personal recommendation is suitable for and consistent with the insurance demands and needs.[225] The client's demands and needs with respect to impact investment strategies are unlikely to be apparent, and that information may not be forthcoming from the client unless specific questions are asked.

Yet, under the current COBS rules, there is no requirement to make a suitability assessment of a customer's demands and needs in relation to environmental investment objectives. If consideration of the customer's environmental objectives and preferences is not part of the sales process, there is a risk that such preferences are not explored and are ignored. EU insurance distributors are already required to ascertain, as part of the suitability assessment in relation to IBIPs, the (potential) customer's 'sustainability preferences' which includes asking questions about whether they wish to invest in an economic activity that contributes to an environmental objective as defined by the EU Taxonomy.[226] It is suggested that enquiring into the customer's environmental objectives and preferences should be part of the process to establish demands and needs with respect to IBIPs in the UK to ensure that insurers comply with the client's best interests rule.

The FCA consulted on whether there should be an equivalent UK requirement that advisers should consider sustainability matters in their investment advice and ensure their

218 See Chapter 7, Section 7.4.5.
219 COBS 7.3.1(1)R.
220 Ibid 7.3.1(3)R.
221 PROD 4.2.27.
222 Ibid 4.2.28.
223 Ibid 4.2.29.
224 COBS 7.3.4R.
225 Ibid 7.3.2G and 9A.
226 Commission Delegated Regulation (EU) 2021/1257 of 21 April 2021 amending Delegated Regulations (EU) 2017/2358 and (EU) 2017/2359 as regards the integration of sustainability factors, risks, and preferences into the product oversight and governance requirements for insurance undertakings and insurance distributors and into the rules on conduct of business and investment advice for IBIPs, art 2.

advice is suitable and reflects consumer sustainability-related needs and preferences,[227] but this suggestion has not been included in the finalised proposals.[228] Yet, ascertaining such preferences at the marketing stage – e.g. by asking the customer questions in person or by way of a questionnaire prior to any contract of insurance being proposed[229] – is likely to be material information necessary to comply with the client's best interests rule and to discharge the best execution obligation, as well as increasing awareness where such products exist.

8.4.3 Product disclosure

Providing fair, clear, and accurate information to a prospective policyholder on the impact investment approach for specific IBIP guards against (1) mis-selling such a product to a policyholder whose interests are exclusively financial returns, and (2) green-washing an IBIP that does not have the environmental investment objectives or characteristics it claims to have.

A UK insurer offering an IBIP must prepare a key information document ('KID') that contains the key information that retail investors need to understand the nature, risks, costs, potential gains, and losses of that product and to assist in comparison with other products.[230] The KID must be expressed in clear and comprehensible language and be presented in a pre-determined sequence of sections with specified headings:

- What is this product?
- What are the risks and what could I get in return?
- What happens if [name of the insurer] is unable to pay out?
- What are the costs?
- How long should I hold it and can I take money out early?
- How can I complain?
- Other relevant information.[231]

The section 'What is the product?' should contain information on the IBIP's objectives and the means for achieving them, in particular whether the objectives are achieved by means of direct or indirect exposure to the underlying investment assets, including, where applicable, specific environmental or social objectives targeted by the product.[232] The KID must be provided to a retail investor in good time before that retail investor becomes bound by the contract.[233] Thus, insurers should already be disclosing to prospective policyholders any climate-related impact investment strategy pursued by an IBIP at the pre-contractual stage.

227 FCA Sustainability Disclosure Proposals [5.5] and Question 18.

228 Ibid.

229 COBS 7.3.3G.

230 Regulation (EU) No 1286/2014 of the European Parliament and of the Council of 26 November 2014 on key information documents for packaged retail and IBIPs (PRIIPs) art 5, as onshored into UK law by the European Union (Withdrawal) Act 2018. Regulation (EU) No 1286/2014 – as onshored – is revoked by the FSMA 2023, s 1 but, at the time of writing, s 1 has not yet come into force.

231 Regulation (EU) No 1286/2014 (n 230) art 8.

232 Ibid art 8.2(c)(ii).

233 Ibid art 13(1).

As and when the FCA's proposed sustainability-related disclosure regime comes into effect,[234] IBIPs meeting the relevant criteria will be able to use one of three sustainable investment labels (sustainable focus, sustainable improvers, or sustainable impact).[235] Insurers using a sustainable investment label for an IBIP will then have to provide additional consumer-facing disclosures in a standalone document (alongside the KID) that are made available in a prominent place on the relevant digital medium for the firm (i.e. the main product webpage, page on a mobile application, etc.).[236] These disclosures would include information on the product's sustainability characteristics:

- sustainability goal: the product's sustainability objective, signposted as 'sustainability goal,' highlighting if there is an impact or expected impact on the financial return; and description of progress towards the sustainability objective;
- sustainability approach: summary of key elements of the product's investment strategy to pursue the objective, clearly signposted as 'sustainability approach'; key sustainability characteristics of assets in which the product will and will not invest and the firm's approach to stewardship. [237]

Within the EU, an extended sustainability-related disclosure regime is already in place for IBIPs under the SFDR.[238] The SFDR requires that pre-contractual disclosures are given in the KID on the environmental characteristics that a product promotes and how those characteristics are met, and/or what sustainable investment objective the product has been set and how that objective is measured or benchmarked.[239] The pre-contractual disclosures contained in the KID pursuant to the SFDR and the EU Taxonomy are more wide-ranging since they also require that explicit information is made available on IBIPs that do not pursue an impact investment strategy:

- the SFDR product disclosure requirements apply to all investment-based insurance products made available in the EU (in contrast, the proposed FCA regime only applies to products which use the sustainable investment label);[240]
- the KID must contain information (1) on the manner in which sustainability risks are integrated into the insurer's investment decisions and (2) the results of the assessment of the likely impacts of sustainability risks on the returns of the product;[241]
- for IBIPs that do not pursue investment strategies in economic activities that qualify as environmentally sustainable under the EU Taxonomy the KID must contain the following express statement: 'The investments underlying this financial product do not take into account the EU criteria for environmentally sustainable economic activities.'[242]

234 See Chapter 5, Section 5.3.5.
235 FCA Sustainability Disclosure Proposals [3.2] and see Chapter 5, Section 5.3.5.2.
236 Ibid [5.25] and [5.26].
237 Ibid [5.38], and see Chapter 5, Section 5.3.5.2.
238 See Chapter 5, Section 5.4.2.
239 SFDR art 8(1) and 9(2); and see Chapter 5, Section 5.4.2.
240 SFDR art 1 and 2(1)(a).
241 Ibid art 6(1).
242 EU Taxonomy art 6.

By adopting an approach that requires IBIPs to expressly spell out whether or not they are 'green' as understood by the EU Taxonomy, the SFDR and EU Taxonomy enable prospective policyholders to make conscious and informed choices, as well as promote awareness of 'green' IBIPs and raising the bar in relation to green-washing.

8.4.4 Business conduct requirements during the term of the IBIP

There are a number of regulatory requirements that apply during the term of the IBIP in relation to investments and investment approaches.

Contractual arrangements: the investment agreement between the insurer and the policyholder must be recorded in a document (which can be part of the policy or in a separate document referenced in the policy) which sets out the rights and obligations of the parties.[243] The investment agreement must be consistent with the pre-contractual information provided on investment approaches and strategies. If the investment agreement provides for a climate-related impact investment strategy, the insurer has the mandate to pursue such a strategy and this mandate informs what investments can be made in accordance with the best interests of the policyholders. If the investment funds are chosen by the policyholder, they should be recorded in the documentation. If investment in particular funds or pursuing a particular investment strategy has become a term of the contract, the contract should specify whether the insurer can make changes with or without the consent of the policyholder, and to what extent to policyholder can switch to different investment options.

Treating 'with profits' customers fairly: in addition to the general principle that a firm must pay due regard to the interests of its customers and treat them fairly,[244] and the COBS client's best interests rule,[245] there are additional rules that apply to insurers offering 'with profits' IBIPs. Such an insurer is expected to manage its with-profits fund so that amounts (whether interest, principal, or other outgoings) payable under an investment included in that insurer's own funds do not impact the with-profits fund's assets or its ability to declare and pay under a with-profits policy discretionary benefits that are consistent with fair treatment and the client's best interest rule.[246]

With-profits business, by virtue of its nature and the extent of discretion applied by firms in its operation, involves numerous potential conflicts of interest that might give rise to the unfair treatment of policyholders. Potential conflicts of interest may arise between shareholders and with-profits policyholders, between with-profits policyholders and non-profit policyholders within the same fund, between with-profits policyholders and the members of mutually-owned firms, between with-profits policyholders and management, and between different classes of with-profits policyholders, for example those with and without guarantees.[247] Conflicts of interest could arise where different interested parties take different views on impact investment. It is therefore of the utmost importance that an impact investment strategy for a with-profits fund is appropriately disclosed to prospective policyholders (product disclosure), the suitability of such a with-profit IBIP is

243 COBS 8.1.4A.
244 PRIN 2.1 6.
245 COBS 2.1.1R and see Section 8.4.1.
246 Ibid 20.1A.14G.
247 Ibid 20.2.1G.

explored with a prospective policyholder (product suitability), and that impact investment strategy is recorded in the contractual documentation, as well as in its 'Principles and Practices of Financial Management' statement.[248]

8.5 Combined insurance and investment solutions with outward impact

The preceding section looked at IBIPs that are pivoted on life insurance policies. Could the 'insurance plus investment' product concept be adapted to general insurance so that there is an investment element which is intended to be used to fund a climate change mitigation or adaptation measure? This section makes a proposal for a community-based insurance scheme and critically examines an EIOPA proposal for an individual policyholder insurance and savings hybrid product while proposing some adjustments. These proposals have not been tested, modelled, and priced, and they present a number of regulatory and funding challenges; they are not perfect and cannot provide more than selective and partial solutions in specific areas.

8.5.1 Climate Resilient Development Bonds

The Climate Resilient Development Bond ('CRD Bond') is an insurance plus investment solution developed by the author and Guy Carpenter.[249] The CRD combines community-based insurance, stacked investment, and advanced funding for loss-prevention measures in an enhanced insurance-linked security structure (Figure 8.1).

Municipality M insures against a specified climate-related risk on behalf of a community with commercial insurer A on a multi-year basis. This could, for example, be a flood risk to which the local community is exposed.

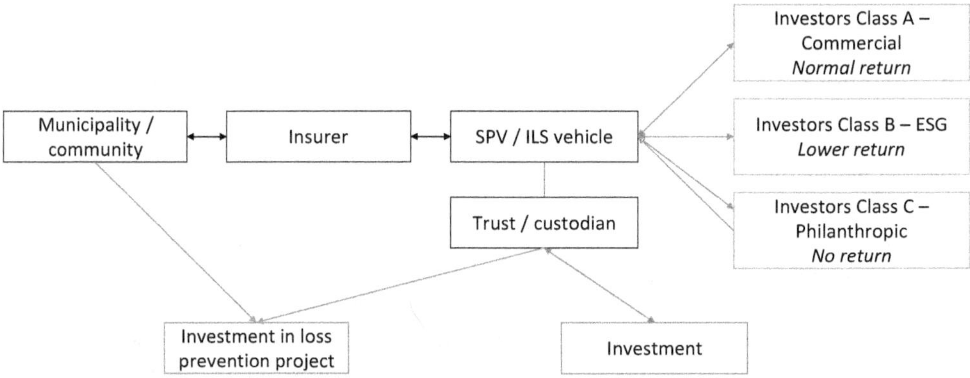

Figure 8.1 CRD Bond structure.

248 Ibid 20.3.1R, 20.3.6(2).

249 Franziska Arnold-Dwyer and Julian Enoizi, 'The Need for a Sea Change in Climate-Related Insurance' (June 2022) <https://www.guycarp.com/insights/2023/06/the-need-for-a-sea-change-in-climate-related-insurance.html> accessed on 15 June 2023. Section 8.5.1 is an adapted version of the article which has been reproduced with the permission of the co-author.

This insurance could operate on a parametric trigger basis. M pays premium to A. The premium becomes more affordable, and the insurance is more accessible, as the scheme is organised on a community-wide basis. In the CRD Bond structure, M has also identified, planned, and approved a public authority-sponsored climate change adaptation project that reduces or prevents losses from the insured climate-related risk. In the examples, this would be a project focused on flood defences, but for other climate-related risks, the project could be an irrigation or water recycling facility, or a housing refurbishment project that boosts windstorm resistance, or another measure. The public project is supported by household-level resilience measures addressing the same risk/s.

Insurer A reinsures the risk with an insurance special purpose vehicle (ISPV) that acts as a risk transformer. The ISPV could be replaced by a vehicle of the World Bank or another development bank. The ISPV passes the risk into the capital markets by issuing bonds or notes to capital market investors. All investors will pay the principal (the purchase price for a note). We envisage that there will be different classes of investors differentiated by their philanthropic and risk appetite – this is the capital stack. Thus, commercial investors (C) and ESG investors (E) will pay principal that is purely risk-based, while philanthropic investors (P) will pay a principal that has a risk-based element but is predominantly project-funding orientated.

In a traditional cat bond structure, both the aggregate principal amount received from the investors and the premium received by the ISPV – and equivalent to or exceeding in amount the anticipated exposure to claims – would be deposited into a collateral account administered by a trustee who would arrange for those funds to be invested. In the CRD Bond structure, the aggregate principal amount received from the investors and the premium received by the ISPV are deposited into two separate accounts administered by a trustee:

1. the risk-based principal amount and the premium are deposited into a collateral account administered by a trustee who would arrange for those funds to be invested;
2. the project-funding elements are allocated to the project fund account for immediate and ongoing funding for the loss-prevention project and the household-level measures.

The E and P investors will receive a lower coupon as a lesser amount of their principal/collateral is invested in return-generating assets. The P investor coupon is fully donated, and the E investor's coupon is partially donated, to the project fund account. If a qualifying event occurs (in this example, flooding meeting the trigger criteria), insurer A pays a claim to M for distribution to the affected households and, where appropriate, for green reinstatement and build-back-better measures. The ISPV will draw on the collateral to make a payment reimbursing insurer A.

As the collateral reduces, coupon payments will reduce too. Upon the implementation of the loss-prevention project, the risk profile of the structure should improve, and the risk of a triggering event and subsequent payment should diminish. The risk reduction could be monetised by offering premium rebates and/or reducing coupon payments to C, E, and P, and such savings would be used as further funding for the project. At the end of the term of the CRD Bond, the remaining collateral is returned to the investors. The order of priority in repayment should be P investors, then E investors, and last C investors, reflecting the fact that the C investors should bear the greatest risk of loss having had the greatest return.

The CRD Bond comes with underwriting, modelling, legal, and logistical challenges. There have been earlier attempts to launch so-called resilience bonds[250] that could not be modelled to scale the savings associated with the risk reduction to the project costs and the time lag associated with the implementation of an infrastructure project. It is suggested that the scale and timing could be improved by community-based insurance schemes that are linked to (1) local climate change adaptation projects that can be implemented within the term of the CRD Bond and (2) household-level measures that can be implemented quickly within the first few months of its term. Projects must be identified on science-based evidence and selected by reference to feasibility criteria that depend on the insured risk, the community, and its location. It is also acknowledged that the funding derived from monetising the risk reduction may not match the full costs of the project. However, it will be a contribution that could make the difference between the project being financially feasible or unaffordable for the relevant community. In addition, it is hoped that there is P and E investor appetite for the CRD Bond as an investment opportunity with clear social and environmental objectives, as well as support from public-private partnerships.[251] Certain types of loss-prevention projects may generate future income streams against which the municipality may be able to borrow. Solutions to the climate crisis and its effects require collaboration at all levels, including from the insurance industry and the financial markets. The CRD Bond is a sustainable solution to combining financial resilience and loss-prevention measures consistent with the principles of equity, sustainable development, co-operation, and the precautionary principle[252] that underpin the Paris Agreement.

The CRD Bond structure has already received a significant amount of insurance media coverage,[253] and the author is working with Guy Carpenter and Fundação Getulio Vargas Brazil on a pilot project.

8.5.2 Green bonus property policies

In its 2021 Report, EIOPA identified products and services that warrant further consideration in the context of impact underwriting a property insurance product that combines 'loss-based insurance indemnification and savings account in a hybrid product, in order

250 M. Muir, 'Resilience Bonds: A Concept Too Ambitious or Ahead of Its Time?' (*Trading Risk*, 7 February 2022).

251 See Chapter 9.

252 The precautionary principle holds that where there is a threat of serious or irreversible damage, lack of full scientific certainty should not be used as a reason for postponing appropriate measure to prevent environmental harm or damage. See Chapter 2, Section 2.3.1.

253 Including in: Artemis <https://www.artemis.bm/news/climate-resilient-development-bond-crd-bond-proposed-with-ils-design/>; Reinsurance News <https://www.reinsurancene.ws/climate-resilient-development-bond-proposed-by-guy-carpenter/>; The Insurer <https://www.esg-insurer.com/news/gc-proposes-resilient-development-bonds-in-paradigm-shift-in-management-of-climate-risk/>; The Insurance Insider <https://www.insuranceinsider.com/article/2brp23q0byjudpx7irxfl/catastrophe-bonds/guy-carpenter-proposes-new-climate-resilience-bonds-mixing-philanthropy-and-ils>; Trading Risk <https://www.trading-risk.com/article/2brow0zh99snxv4gz6nls/catastrophe-bonds/guy-carpenter-proposes-new-climate-resilience-bonds-mixing-philanthropy-and-ils>; and Inside P&C <https://www.insidepandc.com/article/2brp2essle2seqscn28sh/reinsurers-section/guy-carpenter-proposes-new-climate-resilience-bonds-mixing-philanthropy-and-ils> all accessed on 9 June 2023.

to help policyholders finance eco-friendly materials when it is necessary to rebuild after a loss.'[254] EIOPA appears to envisage a consumer property insurance product for which the policyholder pays a premium, part of which is segregated to be used as additional funding for green reinstatement.

There are a number of structural challenges with an insurance and savings account hybrid product: first, insurers are not authorised to accept deposits (which is a regulated activity) and insurers must not carry on any commercial business other than insurance business and activities directly arising from that business.[255] The savings account element would therefore have to be operated by an authorised bank but be linked to the property insurance policy. This model may be feasible in countries in which bancassurance business models are prevalent. Secondly, it would need to be clear what amounts are being paid into the savings account and by whom: is the policyholder making a one-off deposit, or paying in regular amounts? Or is the insurer charging an additional 'premium' which is equivalent to the amount paid into the savings account by the insurer? In whose name is the account, who controls the account, and who can monitor it? Thirdly, the money in the savings account would need to be ringfenced so that it can only be used for specified green reinstatement measures in the event of a claim under the property insurance. Fourthly, what if the savings are insufficient to pay for the extra costs of green reinstatement – who will pay for the shortfall, or would the green reinstatement not go ahead? Fifthly, as most retail property policies only have a 12-month policy period, what happens to the account at the end of the policy period if no claims have been made and/or the policyholder does not renew with the same insurer? The savings account and its associated benefits would need to be transferrable to a property insurance policy with another insurer or be redeemable in another way. Sixthly, it is not clear what would incentivise a policyholder to buy this product: the savings account deposits would be funded by additional premium payments, the money in the account would be illiquid, and any payment from the savings account would be contingent upon the claim that qualifies for green reinstatement. At the same time, policyholders might be disincentivised to make voluntary climate mitigation or adaptation home improvements in the knowledge that they are paying additional premium for green reinstatement in the event of a loss under the policy.

Rather than linking a savings account to the property policy, thought should be given to how an incentive and reward structure can be built into the policy, how the value of accumulated rewards can be increased through investment, and how accumulated rewards can be made transferrable between insurers to allow policyholders to switch insurers. A possible base model could be the no claims bonus discount that is commonly applied in motor insurance. The no claims bonus increases with each year that the policyholder has not made any claims under its motor policy. The no claims bonus represents a monetary value that is applied as a reduction to the premium. Most motor insurers would apply a no claims bonus even if it has accumulated with another insurer (although the discount may vary in size between insurers), even though the new insurer has not had the benefit of the policyholder not having made claims in the preceding year/s, because a policyholder who has not made any claims for a number of years is considered a lower risk. A bonus scheme

254 EIOPA Non-Life Underwriting and Climate Change Report [3.39] and Table 4.
255 PRA SII, General Conditions Governing Business, 9.1.

could be applied to property insurance whereby, instead of giving no claims bonus discounts on the premium, the bonus discounts are converted into bonus points.

For example, Policyholder P insures with Insurer A for four years. During that time P does not make any claims and converts its no claims bonus discounts in Year 2 (10%), in Year 3 (15%), and in Year 4 (20%) into green bonus points (say 10 + 15 + 20 = 45 points). Bonus points could also be accumulated if the policyholder makes voluntary climate mitigation or adaptation improvements to the property. For example, upon installing flood doors, P earns five green bonus points. The monetary value of bonus points is invested by A in a separate green bonus point fund (together with green bonus points from other policies) which itself has an impact investment strategy. In the event of a reinstatement claim, P could choose between 'ordinary reinstatement' or applying the value of its accumulated bonus points towards 'green reinstatement.' If P renews with a different insurer (Insurer B) in Year 5, its bonus point investment remains with A but would be available as an additional payment towards 'green reinstatement'[256] in the event of a claim under its policy with B. B may or may not operate its own green bonus point scheme. Given the transaction costs likely to be involved in setting up a green bonus point fund and operating a green bonus point scheme, insurers might be more willing to contemplate the development of green bonus property policies on a multi-year basis (e.g. three years). Multi-year contracts do however restrict the policyholder's choice and may attract higher capital requirements for insurers since they cannot re-price annually.[257]

It is stating the obvious that both proposals, the CRD Bond and the green bonus property policy, need a lot more analysis, modelling, and testing. The green bonus property policy proposal may be eligible for the FCA's Regulatory Sandbox scheme.[258] Both solutions have the potential to make an impactful contribution from the insurance industry to the implementation of sustainable and just solutions to the climate crisis. The author is appealing to insurers, governments, investors, regulators, philanthropists, and other stakeholders to turn the potential of these proposals into a market reality.

8.6 Conclusion

Insurers in their capacity as investors can take an enabling role by taking various forms of climate-related impact investment approaches and engaging in climate-related stewardship. UK and EU life insurers are already required to develop, publicly disclose, and implement an 'engagement policy' which sets out details of their engagement with investee companies. Yet, insurers face some significant legal and regulatory barriers with respect to climate-related impact investment and stewardship: first, an impact investment approach that foregoes higher returns in order to promote an environmental objective may be inconsistent with the directors' duty to promote the success of the company for the benefit of its members as a whole. Secondly, the PPP imposes limitations on the extent and types of climate-related impact investments and the current regulatory capital treatment of climate-related impact investments is not favourable (although forthcoming UK reforms to the matching adjustment requirements and risk margins may improve that).

256 See Chapter 7, Section 7.7.

257 EIOPA Non-Life Underwriting and Climate Change Report [2.65].

258 See: FCA, 'Regulatory Sandbox' <https://www.fca.org.uk/firms/innovation/regulatory-sandbox> accessed on 1 June 2023.

Thirdly, US anti-ESG legislation and political pressure dressed up as investigations in anti-trust law violations make it difficult for insurers with US business to reduce or fully withdraw from investing in fossil fuel assets and to engage in collaborative stewardship.

As regards IBIPs, regulatory risks can be managed if, at the pre-contractual stage, the impact investment strategy is appropriately disclosed to prospective policyholders (product disclosure), the suitability of such a product is explored with a prospective policyholder (product suitability), and the contractual documentation clearly sets out the insurer's investment mandate. The pre-contractual disclosures are already part of the EU SFDR disclosure regime and the FCA's proposed sustainability-related disclosure regime. Consumer awareness of IBIPs with or without environmental objectives, and thus the potential take-up of those products, could be increased if a prospective policyholder's preferences as regards IBIPs with or without environmental objectives would be more fully considered by insurance distributors. EU insurance distributors are already required to ascertain, as part of the suitability assessment in relation to IBIPs, the (potential) customer's 'sustainability preferences.'

This chapter has highlighted that the extent to which insurers must or can take, or are deterred from taking, an enabling role with impact investment approaches is shaped by government policy and socio-political realities: the spectrum ranges from mandated stewardship engagement (SRD and FCA Handbook) to indirect prohibition of certain types of investment approaches (US anti-ESG legislation) and threats of prosecution in respect of collaborative initiatives (US AG letters). Insurers must work with governments to address legal and regulatory barriers to climate-related impact investment. The CRD Bond proposal is an example of an insurance solution that relies on co-operation with local government and commitments from other stakeholders. Green bonus property policies are a concept that requires the mutual recognition of green bonus points by participating property insurers. CRD Bonds and green bonus property policies are also structures that address funding gaps in relation to climate change mitigation and adaptation measures. The next chapter will consider insurance public-private partnerships between the insurance industry, governments, and international organisations to close climate risk protection gaps and funding gaps and to build resilience.

CHAPTER 9

The role of government and public-private insurance solutions

Insurers cannot act as enablers of policyholders and other stakeholders in their transition to a sustainable net-zero economy in a vacuum. An effective approach requires a multi-stakeholder engagement. The preceding chapters have emphasised that insurers must engage with their policyholders and investee companies to shift behaviours and implement climate change mitigation and adaptation measures. It has also been noted that insurers who use brokers and other insurance intermediaries for the distribution of their insurance products must ensure these insurance distributors have the necessary knowledge, expertise, and competence to understand the features of an insurance product and the identified target market,[1] and are provided with all the necessary product information and target market information.[2] If the current CSDDD proposals are implemented, EU insurers and those insurers who do business generating a net turnover of EUR 150 million in the EU will be required to work with their partners in business relationships to identify, bring to an end, prevent, mitigate, and account for negative environmental impacts in their own operations, their subsidiaries, and business relationships in their value chains.[3]

One of the key findings in the IPCC's 6th Synthesis Report is that effective climate action requires political commitment, well-aligned multi-level governance and institutional frameworks, laws, policies, and funding.[4] Throughout this book, the discussion has identified (1) laws, regulations, and standards that are aligned with, or even supportive of, insurers taking climate action and assuming an enabling role, and (2) legal and regulatory issues that could constitute barriers to climate-related impact underwriting, impact investment, and stewardship. As the example of the US anti-ESG legislation and the letter from a group of US AGs to members of the NZIA shows,[5] the absence of political

1 PROD 4.2.28.

2 Ibid 4.2.29.

3 Proposal for a Directive of the European Parliament and of the Council on Corporate Sustainability Due Diligence and amending Directive (EU) 2019/1937 COM/2022/71, arts. 6–8.

4 IPCC 2022 Sixth Assessment Report [4.7].

5 Letter from the State Attorney Generals of Montana, Louisiana, Utah, Alabama, Arkansas, Georgia, Idaho, Indiana, Iowa, Kansas, Kentucky, Mississippi, Missouri, New Hampshire, Ohio, South Carolina, Tennessee, Texas, Virginia, West Virginia, and Wyoming, to asset managers, dated 30 March 2023, 17 <https://attorneygeneral.utah.gov/wp-content/uploads/2023/03/2023-03-30-Asset-Manager-letter-Press-FINAL.pdf> accessed on 1 June 2023; and Letter from the State Attorney Generals of Utah, Louisiana, Alabama, Alaska, Arkansas, Georgia, Idaho, Indiana, Iowa, Kansas, Kentucky, Mississippi, Missouri, Montana, New Hampshire, Ohio, Oklahoma, South Carolina, South Dakota, Texas, Virginia, West Virginia, and Wyoming to NZIA insurers, dated 16 May 2023, 1–3 <https://attorneygeneral.utah.gov/wp-content/uploads/2023/05/2023-05-15-NZIA-Letter.pdf accessed 23 May 2023> accessed on 1 June 2023; and see Chapter 4, Section 4.4.6, Chapter 6, Section 6.4.5.

DOI: 10.4324/b23081-9

commitment, or even political hostility, towards climate action can result in lowered ambition and scaled-back measures. In contrast, the example of the TCFD Recommendations shows that, in the UK, political support leading to regulatory expectations and regulations mandating TCFD consistent reporting has resulted in wide-spread adoption within the UK insurance industry.[6]

The traditional set-up, that governments design and provide the legal and regulatory framework that underpins any well-functioning private insurance sector while the insurance industry develops cost-efficient and effective risk transfer solutions,[7] requires re-examination considering the challenges presented by climate change-related risks and the enabling role that insurers can play in supporting their policyholders in their transition to a sustainable net-zero economy. In this chapter, it will be argued that insurers must work with governments and a multitude of other stakeholders to address protection gaps, knowledge gaps, and funding gaps. It will be argued that this co-operation may take the form of a public-private partnership ('PPPart') that is designed to close protection gaps, knowledge gaps, and funding gaps and also takes into account resilience building.

This chapter is structured as follows: Section 9.1 will revisit protection gaps and the circumstances in which they can arise. Section 9.2 is concerned with knowledge gaps, while Section 9.3 examines impact underwriting funding gaps. Section 9.4 explores PPPart design for climate change-related risks by reference to the literature and case studies of the UK's Flood Re, the US National Flood Insurance Program, and New Zealand's Toka Tū Ake – Natural Hazards Commission. Section 9.5 reviews government and insurance industry co-operations in relation to climate-related risks and other natural hazard risks at the regional level and the international stage.

9.1 Protection gaps revisited

Reference is made to the discussion of protection gaps in Chapter 3, Section 3.2.4, and Chapters 6 and 7. Climate-related insurance protection gaps already exist for mainly two reasons: (1) uninsurability, and (2) lack of penetration. Climate-related impact underwriting is aimed at reducing protection gaps which are created or exacerbated by climate change. Climate risk mitigation measures that reduce GHG emissions are a key part of slowing down the global surface temperature increase, eventually limiting the frequency of heavy precipitation and flooding and the number of regions where extreme heat can occur.[8] Climate change adaptation measures can reduce policyholders' exposure to losses resulting from climate change risks, which would reduce insurers' exposure to claims and, in turn, could keep premium increases at bay ensuring that insurance remains affordable. Yet, paradoxically, impact underwriting can also create protection gaps and coverage gaps as a result of (1) not insuring brown, and (2) greening insurance.

6 PRA SS3/19 (April 2019) [3.21]; LR 9.8.6.8; FCA, 'Review of TCFD-Aligned Disclosures by Premium Listed Commercial Companies' (July 2022) <https://www.fca.org.uk/publications/multi-firm-reviews/tcfd-aligned-disclosures-premium-listed-commercial-companies#lf-chapter-id-quantitative-review-of-compliance-2-1-summary-of-preliminary-observations> accessed on 1 June 2023.

7 See: The Geneva Association, 'Understanding and Addressing Global Insurance Protection Gaps' (April 2018) 8 <https://www.genevaassociation.org/sites/default/files/research-topics-document-type/pdf_public/understanding_and_addressing_global_insurance_protection_gaps.pdf> accessed on 1 June 2023.

8 See Chapter 2, Section 2.2.3.

9.1.1 Uninsurability

Acute physical risks associated with climate change (flooding, windstorms, wildfires, and droughts) are increasing in frequency and severity.[9] The effect of these acute physical risks can be compounded by the exposure (e.g. hurricanes cause more damage in urban and industrialised areas) and the vulnerability[10] (e.g. the lack of capacity to respond to draughts and wildfires) of affected communities and ecological systems.[11] As insurance pay-outs for weather-related losses have grown significantly over the last 50 years, premiums increase and make insurance less and less affordable, insurers withdraw insurance cover from particular perils or geographical areas because they cannot obtain sufficient reinsurance, and losses are becoming incalculable, too catastrophic, and correlated to other risks. A series of examples illustrating these developments were given in Chapter 3, Section 3.2.4. To date, the prevalent practice among property and casualty insurers in Europe has been to respond to increasing physical climate change risk by re-pricing premium annually (which is possible as non-life insurance contracts typically have a duration of 12 months).[12] EIOPA has found evidence that the annual re-pricing may lead to property insurance becoming unaffordable over a longer term period or disincentivise consumers from buying insurance, both of which can, in turn, create and increase protection gaps.[13]

9.1.2 Lack of access and appetite

Some of the least developed but most vulnerable countries do not have mature insurance markets through which relevant insurance products can be distributed and administered, and their consumers and small businesses lack risk awareness and the financial literacy to understand what insurance has to offer.[14] Concerns about an unstable legal environment and the prospect of small uptake may not justify the set-up and transaction costs for insurers.[15] However, even in developed countries insurance penetration can be low because people may (1) underestimate the likelihood and potential severity of catastrophic weather events and (2) expect governments to step in to provide financial support for uninsured losses.[16] For example, only about 25% of the losses caused by extreme weather and climate-related events in the EU are currently insured, and in several EU member states this share is below 5%.[17] Lack of take-up can also undermine the pooling effect of insurance, so that insurance becomes unavailable or unaffordable.[18]

---

9 Ibid, Section 2.2.2.

10 Vulnerability is defined as the 'propensity or predisposition to be adversely affected and encompasses a variety of concepts and elements, including sensitivity or susceptibility to harm and lack of capacity to cope and adapt' in the IPCC 2022 Adaptation Report, 5 fn.8.

11 IPCC 2022 Adaptation Report, Summary for Policymakers, 5.

12 EIOPA Non-Life Underwriting and Climate Change Report [2.16].

13 EIOPA Non-Life Underwriting and Climate Change Report [2.32].

14 The Geneva Association (n 7) 26; and see Chapter 3, Section 3.2.4.

15 Ibid 29–30.

16 ECB and EIOPA, 'Policy Options to Reduce the Climate Insurance Protection Gap: Discussion Paper' (April 2023) chart 1 <https://www.eiopa.europa.eu/system/files/2023-04/ecb.policyoptions_EIOPA~c0adae58b7.en_.pdf> accessed on 1 June 2023.

17 Ibid 5.

18 Erik Feyen, Rodney Lester, and Roberto de Rezende Rocha, 'What Drives the Development of the Insurance Sector? An Empirical Analysis Based on a Panel of Developed and Developing Countries' (2013)

9.1.3 Not insuring brown

Protection gaps could arise if a critical number of insurers and reinsurers withdraw from underwriting fossil fuel projects. As insurance underwriting capacity decreases, the demand for cover would outstrip supply. Restricted reinsurance capacity would result in further restrictions on insurance capacity and higher costs of capital that would ultimately be reflected in higher premiums that could render the remaining capacity increasingly costly and possibly unaffordable for some fossil fuel businesses.

Although most large insurers have now backed away from insuring new coal projects,[19] only a small number of insurers have committed to phasing out cover for existing coal operations and to restricting oil and gas underwriting.[20] Still, as a result, underwriting capacity has already become more restricted and coal companies are already facing premium rate increases of up to 40%.[21] However, for now, there are still enough insurers in the US and Asia that continue to underwrite coal projects.[22] While climate activists would argue that brown protection gaps are necessary to force companies to phase out their fossil fuel operations,[23] brown protection gaps could be harmful to other stakeholders and wider society as they could lead to (1) tort victims and employees of fossil fuel companies being left uncompensated for bodily injury and damage to their property, and (2) deteriorating credit risk for creditors (suppliers and lenders) of fossil fuel companies which could have knock-on effects on their businesses. A group of US State Attorney Generals have also suggested that 'not insuring brown' also leads 'to high gas prices and higher costs for products and services across the board, resulting in record-breaking inflation and financial hardships for the residents of our states.'[24]

9.1.4 Greening insurance

As discussed in Chapter 7, greening insurance is concerned with introducing green features to established insurance products and services that shift policyholders' behaviour and processes towards taking climate change mitigation and adaptation measures. Protection gaps could arise if losses relating to carbon-intense assets and activities are excluded from cover (e.g. excluding losses from coal fire and heating from property insurance).

If losses relating to carbon-intense assets and activities are excluded from cover (e.g. excluding losses from coal fire and heating from property insurance), policyholders have coverage gaps in their insurance protection. Although conceptually different, coverage gaps can have the same outcome as protection gaps to the extent that the policyholder's cover is less than the amount of insurance that would be economically beneficial. Brown

1(1) *Journal of Financial Perspectives*, 1; Paula Jarzabkowski, Konstantinos Chalkias, Eugenia Cacciatori, and Rebecca Bednarek, *Disaster Insurance Reimagined* (OUP 2023) Sec 1.2.

19 Insure Our Future, '2022 Scorecard on Insurance, Fossil Fuels and the Climate Emergency' 11–19 <https://insure-our-future.com/wp-content/uploads/2023/02/SP-IOF-2022-Scorecard-v0.8-online-3.pdf> accessed on 1 June 2023.

20 Ibid.

21 Willis Towers Watson, 'Managing the Transition: Mining Risk Review 2020' (2020) <https://willistowerswatson.turtl.co/story/mining-risk-review-2020-ungated/page/1> accessed on 1 June 2023.

22 Insure Our Future (n 19) 15.

23 See e.g. Peter Bosshard, 'Making Coal Uninsurable' <https://www.fairplanet.org/op-ed/making-coal-uninsurable/> accessed on 1 June 2023.

24 Letter from the State Attorney Generals to NZIA insurers (n 5) 1–3.

exclusions in retail insurance are a smaller scale version of 'not insuring brown.' Although brown exclusions are unlikely to have negative societal consequences of the same magnitude as 'not insuring brown,' they can have a devastating effect on the policyholder who will not have any insurance protection for excluded losses.

Protection gaps could also proliferate if risk-based premium pricing is used to incentivise the policyholder to take climate risk adaptation measures that reduce the risk of loss or damage to the insured subject matter. A policyholder may not be able to afford (1) to take the climate risk adaptation measures in question to benefit from the premium discount, and (2) any premium increase if those measures are not implemented. For those who cannot afford to take such measures, risk-based premiums could act as a multiplier of inequality both in terms of affordability of insurance and improving resilience.[25] Similarly, if the policy terms require the policyholder to take costly and onerous climate action, a prospective policyholder may decide not to buy insurance, increasing the penetration protection gap. If an insurance contract contains a term that requires the policyholder to take costly and onerous climate action, failing to comply with that term may be a breach of contract that could result in coverage for loss being suspended or impaired.[26] This too could result in a coverage gap.

9.1.5 Different gaps – different solutions?

Protection gaps can have devasting consequences for individuals, on the financial system, and on society as a whole.[27] Distinguishing between different (albeit interrelated) root causes for protection gaps and coverage gaps can inform the approaches that could be taken to address those gaps. Extreme weather events are becoming uninsurable because they are incalculable, too catastrophic, and correlated to other risks. Insurers and reinsurers will be either unable or unwilling to bear the full magnitude of losses from high-impact events with increasing but unpredictable frequency such as natural disasters.[28] Policyholders may be unable to afford increasing premiums. Solutions aimed at reducing protection gaps linked to uninsurability must look at sharing the risk in different ways to create more capacity and keep premiums at affordable levels, as well as ways of mitigating the risk and improving loss resilience. Such solutions may require the support of the government and may need to be delivered through public-private partnerships.[29] Solutions to protection gaps that are caused by the unaffordability of insurance must also be considered in conjunction with the impact underwriting funding gaps identified in Section 9.3.

Protection gaps that arise from a lack of access to suitable insurance products could be reduced by devising new and more effective distribution methods embracing digital technologies, while protection gaps that arise from a lack of policyholder appetite and understanding could be addressed by addressing knowledge gaps.[30]

Protection gaps in relation to fossil fuel assets and activities do not arise because of actuarial uninsurability but because insurers are under political and reputational pressure

25 Jarzabkowski (n18) 95.
26 For breach of warranty see Insurance Act 2015, s 10(2); and see Chapter 7, Section 7.6.1.
27 See Chapter 3, Section 3.2.4.
28 ECB and EIOPA (n 16) 18; Jarzabkowski (n 18) Sec. 1.2.
29 See Sections 9.3 and 9.4.
30 See Section 9.2.

(fuelled by the emerging climate-related disclosure regimes)[31] not to insure fossil fuel assets and activities in order to show that their business strategies and risk management practices are compatible with a transition to a net-zero economy. The US anti-ESG legislation and the letter from a group of US AGs to members of the NZIA are examples of political counter-pressure to prevent or minimise this type of protection gap.[32] How, if at all, this protection gap should be addressed depends on policy decisions, inter alia on (1) whether or not to put pressure on the fossil fuel industry to be phased out, and (2) whether or not to aim for a phase-out as soon as possible and by all means or for an orderly transition. Given the multi-faceted underlying policy decisions, further consideration of this particular protection gap is outside the scope of this book.

Coverage gaps that result from contractual exclusions or a breach of contract are a matter of contractual construction and may depend on the remedies that are available for the breach of a particular contractual term. Any solutions that seek to fill contractually agreed coverage gaps must balance the protection of policyholders from coverage gaps against the freedom of the parties to agree on the terms of their contract. In relation to consumer insurance contracts, consumer protection is frequently prioritised over freedom of contract given that consumer insurance contracts are not freely negotiated and frequently offered on a take-it-or-leave-it basis. Thus, contractual coverage gaps are tempered in relation to consumer policyholders by the Consumer Rights Act 2015, s.62(1) which provides that unfair contract terms are not binding on consumers, the Insurance Act 2015 ss.10 and 11 which have softened the consequences for breach of insurance warranties and risk mitigation terms, and the consumer duty which requires firms to act to deliver good outcomes for retail customers.[33]

9.2 Knowledge gaps

There are a number of knowledge gaps relevant to climate change risks. First, insurers are still filling knowledge gaps relating to the assessment of climate-related risks. The ability to quantify potential losses is critical for establishing the scope of insurance cover and the premium amounts that they need to charge, the technical provisions they need to make, and the regulatory capital they need to keep.[34] For climate-related natural catastrophe events, historical data can be insufficient and needs to be supplemented with forward-looking models that estimate potential financial losses for a given portfolio. However, there are a great number of uncertainties that models cannot capture, including the government policies that determine the pathway to meeting the long-term temperature goal of the Paris Agreement, the impact of climate change on hazard frequency and intensity, and the future exposure and vulnerability of the assets at risk.[35] Insurers, government agencies, the scientific community, and academia must collaborate to fill these knowledge gaps. There are already a number of initiatives in that space, such as:

31 See Chapter 5.

32 Letter from the State Attorney Generals to NZIA insurers (n 5) 1–3; and see Chapter 4, Section 4.4.6, Chapter 6, Section 6.4.5.

33 See Chapter 7, Sections 7.8, 7.6.1, and 7.4.5.

34 OECD Insurance and Adaptation Paper 7.

35 Ibid 8.

- Global Resilience Hub by the Global Resilience Index Initiative: a joint initiative by the UN Office for Disaster Risk Reduction, the Insurance Development Forum, the University of Oxford, and the GEM Foundation to provide open, globally consistent climate risk data for governments and financial institutions to scale-up climate adaptation, resilience, and loss and damage finance and protect exposed communities and economies;[36]
- EIOPA Dashboard on insurance protection gap for natural catastrophes: the dashboard brings together data on economic and insured losses for natural catastrophe risks, current and historic protection gaps, risk estimations as well as insurance coverage from 30 European countries.[37]

Secondly, policyholders have knowledge gaps relating to their exposure to physical climate risks, the availability of insurance to obtain financial protection against some of those risks, and the steps they can take to reduce the risk of loss. Studies show that people in Europe tend to consider climate change as not having any immediate consequences that require any action.[38] It is only when they have had personal experience with climate change-related natural catastrophes that they become more risk-aware and are inclined to consider risk adaptation measures.[39] In contrast, some of the communities most disproportionately affected by climate-related weather will certainly be aware of the impact of climate change but may not know how to protect themselves financially with insurance (if available).[40] Some studies have shown that clear information about people's local climate-related risk exposures and corresponding socio-economic consequences can effectively increase climate risk awareness and stimulate the take up of insurance and risk prevention measures.[41] In Chapter 7, Section 7.4, it was argued that information to fill policyholder knowledge gaps relating to climate change risks and adaptation measures could be provided by property insurers, while knowledge gaps relating to climate change mitigation may be better suited to be distributed through public channels.

Thirdly, governments and public authorities may have climate change risk-related knowledge gaps that insurers can fill with expertise that they have developed in managing their own exposure (1) by making climate risk information available in order to build awareness about exposure to climate risk; (2) by providing advice on potential risk

36 Insurance Development Forum, 'UN, Insurance and Academic Leaders Sign Agreement to Draw upon Insurance Data and Expertise to Advance Climate and Disaster Risk Analytics and Help Mobilise Finance for Adaptation' (Press Release 1 June 2023) <https://www.insdevforum.org/news/> accessed on 1 June 2023.

37 EIOPA, 'Dashboard on Insurance Protection Gap for Natural Catastrophes' <https://www.eiopa.europa.eu/tools-and-data/dashboard-insurance-protection-gap-natural-catastrophes_en> accessed on 1 June 2023.

38 Manuel Frondel, Michel Simora, and Stephen Sommer, 'Risk Perception of Climate Change: Empirical Evidence for Germany' (2017) 137 *Ecological Economics*, 173.

39 Ibid.

40 The Geneva Association (n 7) 26 and see Chapter 3, Section 3.2.4.

41 Jennifer K. Poussin, W.J. Wouter Botzen, and Jeroen C.J.H. Aerts, 'Factors of Influence on Flood Damage Mitigation Behaviour by Households' (2014) 40 *Environmental Science & Policy*, 69; Joop de Boer, W.J. Wouter Botzen, and Teun Terpstra, 'Flood Risk and Climate Change in the Rotterdam Area, The Netherlands: Enhancing Citizen's Climate Risk Perceptions and Prevention Responses Despite Skepticism' (2016) 16 *Regional Environmental Change*, 1613; Susanne Hanger, Joanne Linnerooth-Bayer, Swenja Surminski, Cristina Nenciu-Posner, Anna Lorant, Radu Ionescu, and Anthony Patt, 'Insurance, Public Assistance, and Household Flood Risk Reduction: A Comparative Study of Austria, England, and Romania'(2018) 38(4) *Risk Analysis*, 680

reduction and adaptation investment;[42] and (3) by sharing risk analytical tools that can help governments to identify risks and take resilience-building measures accordingly.[43] For example, insurers can provide climate risk information that informs the development of planning regulations and building codes, and public climate change adaptation projects.[44]

Thus, insurers and governments should work together to fill knowledge gaps among existing and potential policyholders and wider society, while they would also benefit from a two-way information exchange to fill knowledge gaps within their own organisations.

9.3 Impact underwriting funding gap

In addition to different types of protection gaps, it is suggested that there is also an impact underwriting funding gap which (1) consists of the additional costs that arise from climate-related impact underwriting compared to the ordinary and necessary costs incurred by the parties throughout the life cycle of a (non-life) insurance product that does not aim to contribute to climate change adaptation and mitigation (the 'green extra cost'), and (2) cannot be easily and reasonably absorbed by insurers or their policyholders. Impact underwriting funding gaps are not the money needed to fill protection gaps, but they can be a contributing factor to widening protection gaps. Impact underwriting funding gaps can deter (1) insurers from taking an enabling role through impact underwriting and (2) policyholders from taking climate action even if they are prompted to do so, and supported, by insurers.

9.3.1 How do impact insurance funding gaps arise?

Insuring green: as has been noted in Chapter 6, premium pricing for green projects and assets can be more expensive compared to their conventional equivalents if there are additional risk factors (such as the insured subject matter being innovative and untested, being located in vulnerable geographies, using materials more susceptible to physical damage, and/or relying on emerging technologies). However, this does not give rise to an impact underwriting funding gap: the risk profile of the policyholder is a generally accepted factor in premium pricing,[45] and for the policyholder, insurance premium costs for key business insurances are an ordinary and necessary cost of business. Considering the relationship between the overall price to the policyholder, the characteristics of the insurance cover provided, and the overall costs to the insurer, 'insuring green' should still be considered 'fair value,' even if the premium is higher on account of additional

42 Paula Jarzabkowski, Konstantinos Chalkias, Daniel Clarke, Ekhosuehi Iyahen, Daniel Stadtmueller, and Astrid Zwick, 'Insurance for Climate Adaptation: Opportunities and Limitations – Report for the Global Commission on Adaptation' (2019) <https://gca.org/reports/insurance-for-climate-adaptation-opportunities-and-limitations/> accessed on 1 June 2023.

43 Insurance Development Forum, 'The Development Impact of Risk Analytics' (2020) <https://www.insdevforum.org/knowledge/idf-reportspublications/development-impact-of-risk-analytics/> accessed on 1 June 2023.

44 Swenja Surminski, Jonathan Barnes, and Katharine Vincent, 'Can Insurance Catalyse Government Planning on Climate? Emergent Evidence from Sub-Saharan Africa' (2022) 153 *World Development*, 105830.

45 See Chapter 7, Section 7.5.1.

risk factors.[46] Similarly, insurers may incur costs for developing new insurance products for green assets and technologies but research and development costs are a cost of carrying on insurance business whether or not the insurance product is green. It has been noted that there is an ongoing discussion about whether insurers should be rewarded for 'insuring green' with preferential solvency capital treatment.[47] Lowering capital requirements with respect to insurance liabilities for green assets would reduce an insurer's costs of providing insurance. Those savings could be used to lower premiums and/or for research and development costs for 'insuring green.'

Not insuring brown: insurers who are restricting their fossil fuel underwriting activities are foregoing the premium income from fossil fuel assets and activities they could have insured but did not. Foregoing potential profits is not the same as incurring green extra costs. This is a business decision taken by an insurer (albeit possibly under the pressure of public opinion and with an eye on climate-related disclosure obligations). Not underwriting fossil fuel assets frees up capacity for underwriting other business which may be equally or more profitable.

Greening insurance: impact underwriting funding gaps are most likely to arise in this category because green extra costs can be incurred when the insurer goes beyond its role of risk carrier and takes on the role of enabler, and the policyholder is 'influenced' to take climate action. Where insurers carry out climate-related risk assessments and provide climate-related risk management advice for prospective policyholders that go beyond the ordinary underwriting risk assessment process that insurers carry out to decide whether or not to cover a risk and on what terms, green extra costs may be incurred. Green extra costs could be more significant if climate-related risk assessments and risk management advice are bespoke, or semi-tailored to the policyholder and entail repeated engagement. An impact underwriting funding gap could arise if climate-related risk assessments and risk management services are too expensive to be absorbed in the premium charged, and policyholders are not prepared to pay higher premiums for those services.

Impact underwriting funding gaps can also arise in relation to climate change mitigation and adaptation measures. Policyholders may take or contemplate taking climate change mitigation adaptation measures to attract premium discounts or rebates, or because they are under an obligation to take such measures under the terms of their policy. As noted in Chapter 7, Section 7.5.4, the costs of such measures can be significant and may exceed any premium discounts or rebates, which could render the green insurance product unattractive or unaffordable to policyholders which, in turn, could lead to protection gaps. Paying for climate change mitigation or adaptation measures under a green reinstatement term[48] may be significantly more expensive for insurers than paying an indemnity for insured loss, or for traditional reinstatement or replacement of lost or damaged insured property. The costs of climate change mitigation and adaptation measures – whether incurred or borne by the policyholder or the insurer – are green extra costs since (1) these measures are the

46 PROD 4.2.14 E R.
47 See Chapter 6, Section 6.3.3.
48 See Chapter 7, Section 7.7.1.

whole raison d'être of the impact of 'greening insurance' and (2) the costs would not arise in relation to an insurance product that does not aim to contribute to climate change adaptation and mitigation. They represent the difference in costs between (1) a green insurance product and (2) the same insurance product without green features. The impact underwriting funding gap, if left unaddressed, could deter insurers from offering, and policyholders from buying, green insurance products and taking climate action,[49] while the availability of funding would facilitate investments in such measures by policyholders.[50]

9.3.2 Solutions to impact underwriting funding gaps

Solutions aimed at reducing impact insurance funding gaps must look at harnessing technology to keep costs down and sharing costs in different ways. Impact underwriting funding gaps in connection with climate-related risk assessments and the provision of climate-related risk management advice could be (1) addressed by offering such services for a separate fee, (2) reduced by developing risk assessment technologies for risk diagnostics and modelling that can generate (semi-)tailored risk management advice to policyholders, (3) reduced by using third party weather data and weather risk assessment service providers that have already developed databases and risk analytical and modelling tools, and/or (4) (partially) covered by other interested stakeholders such as mortgage lenders who provide loans secured on insured property.

For impact insurance funding gaps in connection with climate change mitigation and adaptation measures, an equitable distribution of costs may entail blended funding with contributions from policyholders, insurers, mortgage lenders, and public finance. As secured creditors, mortgage lenders have an interest in mortgaged property as damage or destruction of the property could impair its value as security for the money lent and increase the credit risk they are exposed to. It is for these reasons that English law recognises that secured lenders have an insurable interest in the secured property.[51] Mortgage lenders in the UK will usually require under the terms of the loan agreement that the mortgagor insures the mortgaged property. Mortgage lenders can benefit from the insurance either by becoming co-insured with their own rights to claim, by taking an assignment of the policy, or by taking an assignment of the rights to recovery under the policy.[52] In each case, they benefit from the insurance protection offered by the insurance contract. If property insurance became unavailable on account of climate risk becoming uninsurable, the credit risk exposure of mortgage lenders would increase significantly and, in some cases, could lead to mortgages becoming unavailable for properties in high-risk areas. There is therefore an argument that mortgage lenders are stakeholders who should be contributing to the funding of climate change mitigation and adaptation measures in relation to mortgaged properties.

49 See Chapter 7, and: Sally J. Priest, Edmund C. Penning-Rowsell, and Cathy Suykens, 'Promoting Adaptive Flood Risk Management: The Role and Potential of Flood Recovery Mechanisms' (2016) 7 E3S Web of Conferences, 17005 <https://doi.org/10.1051/E3SCONF/20160717005> accessed on 1 June 2023; and Isabel Seifert-Dähnn, 'Insurance Engagement in Flood Risk Reduction: Examples from Household and Business Insurance in Developed Countries' (2018) 18/9 *Natural Hazards and Earth System Sciences*, 2409.

50 See Chapter 7; and Hanger (n 41).

51 *P. Samuel & Co v Dumas* [1924] A.C. 431 at 444 (HL).

52 John Birds. Ben Lynch, KC, and Simon Paul, *MacGillivray on Insurance Law* (15th ed, 2022, Sweet & Maxwell) [20-001]–[20-010].

A recent OECD Report on the insurance sector's contribution to climate adaptation recommended that public funding should complement insurance.[53] There are good public policy reasons for public funding of private climate change mitigation and adaptation measures (i.e. measures taken by individuals at the household level):

- climate change is a common concern and fighting climate change requires collective action at all levels;[54]
- from a fiscal perspective financing ex ante climate change adaptation measures that reduce the impact of climate change risk may be more cost-effective and efficient than ex post financial support once a natural catastrophe event has struck;[55]
- national governments have NDCs and many governments set national net-zero targets[56] which are more likely to be met if individual members obtain financial support to take climate change mitigation measures.

The benefits of climate change mitigation measures (reducing GHG emissions to halt and reverse climate change) accrue to society at large. While the kind of private climate change adaptation measures that have been discussed in this book have an immediate benefit (reducing the risk of loss caused by climate change-related risk events) limited to the policyholder, they also have a wider societal impact by increasing physical resilience and reducing financial losses that could otherwise have a cascading effects on economic activities[57] and would put governments under pressure to step in to offer financial relief (with consequential effects on government budgets and tax burden).[58] The financing of such measures may require funding support from governments, and one way of delivering such financial support may be through PPParts discussed in the following section.

9.4 Public-private partnerships

Climate risks are complex risks.[59] The insurance and sociology literature recognises that, given the limits to insurability, complex risks cannot simply be addressed by risk transfer to an insurer but require layered and multi-directional risk governance action by government agencies, the insurance industry, and other stakeholders.[60] Thus, where responsibility and decision-making authority for addressing climate risks are shared, decisions must be negotiated and actions must be co-ordinated between different stakeholders and actors.[61] Some scholars and the IPCC emphasise inclusivity in decision-making: actions that prioritise equity, climate justice, social justice, and inclusion lead to more sustainable

53 OECD Insurance and Adaptation Paper 24–25.

54 See Chapter 2, Section 2.3.

55 ECB and EIOPA (n 16) [2.3.1].

56 See Chapter 2, Section 2.3.3.

57 IAIS and the SIF, 'Issues Paper on Climate Change Risks to the Insurance Sector' (July 2018) 14 <https://www.iaisweb.org/page/supervisory-material/issues-papers> accessed on 1 June 2023.

58 ECB and EIOPA (n 16) [1.1]–[1.3].

59 See Chapter 3, Section 3.2.3.

60 Maureen Essen, Sarah McCaffey, Jesse Abrams, and Travis Paveglio, 'Improving Wildfire Management Outcomes: Shifting the Paradigm of Wildfire from Simple to Complex Risk' (2023) 66(5) *Journal of Environmental Planning and Management*, 909, Sec. 2.1.

61 Andrew Stirling, 'Risk Assessment in Science: Towards a More Constructive Policy Debate' (2007) 8 *EMBO Reports*, 309.

outcomes and advance CRD because decisions will be based on knowledge pluralism among actors, each of whom may contribute different knowledge whether technical, experiential, cultural, or a combination thereof.[62] The management of risk is not separable from social, political, and historic contexts.[63]

Can, and to what extent should, protection gaps, knowledge gaps, and impact investment funding gaps be addressed by PPParts? It is clear from the preceding discussion that the private insurance market cannot by itself provide effective solutions to those gaps: insurers are reliant on government involvement and would benefit from input from other stakeholders and actors. Governments should be incentivised to facilitate the enabling role of insurers and address protection gaps, knowledge gaps, and impact investment funding gaps as it is in the public interest that governments meet their NDCs and national net-zero targets, and that society as a whole and individual members of the public strengthen their financial and physical resilience to climate-related risks. The following sections will consider the nature and design of the collaboration between insurers and the government.

9.4.1 What are PPParts?

The World Bank defines a PPPart as:

> a long-term contract between a private party and a government entity, for providing a public asset or service, in which the private party bears significant risk and management responsibility, and remuneration is linked to performance,

the defining features of which are the contract's long-term nature, that the contract bundles together a number of obligations which are typically delivered through a special purpose vehicle owned or controlled by the private party, and a payment mechanism that allows the private party to collect payments from the government directly or from end users.[64] This definition, and others found in the literature, conceive PPParts as semi-privatising a public service which is carried out by a private entity under a degree of control by the government.[65]

In contrast to the general conception of PPParts in their use for the design and building of infrastructure projects, concessions, and private finance initiatives to name just a few, insurance PPParts have developed differently. Insurance PPParts are generally understood to be insurance schemes which provide public finance support that supplements the losses insured by the private sector, and/or introduce government-sponsored risk redistribution mechanisms, in order to create additional capacity and reduce existing or potential protection gaps.[66] Insurance PPParts are usually deployed in relation to catastrophic risks – such

62 Marjolein van Asselt and Ortwin Renn, 'Risk Governance' (2011) 14(4) *Journal of Risk Research*, 431, sec.5; IPCC 2022 Sixth Assessment Report [4.4].

63 Ortwin Renn, *Risk Governance: Coping with Uncertainty in a Complex World* (Routledge 2008).

64 The World Bank, 'Public Private Partnership Reference Guide' (version 31, 2017), 5–8 <https://ppp.worldbank.org/public-private-partnership/library/ppp-reference-guide-introduction> accessed on 1 June 2023.

65 Also see: Roger Wetenhall, 'The Rhetoric and Reality of Public Private Partnerships' (2003) 3 *Public Organisation Review*, 77–107; Tony Bovaird, 'Public Private Partnerships: From Contested Concepts to Prevalent Practice' (2004) 70(2) *International Review of Administrative Sciences*, 199; Matti Siemiatycki, Eoin Reeves, and Dónal Palcic, 'Editorial: The Unresolved Nature of Public Private Partnerships' (2022) 25(2) *Journal of Economic Policy Reform*, 81–84.

66 ECB and EIOPA (n 16) [2.3.2]; Jarzabkowski (n 18) Sec 1.3.

as weather-related, terrorism, or cyber risk – which without the PPParts are, or would become, uninsurable.

An insurance PPPart usually operates through a not-for-profit special purpose vehicle brought about by legislation which Jarzabkowski et al. have labelled a 'protection gap entity' or 'PGE'[67] (a label which is gratefully adopted in this chapter). The PGE is the corporate embodiment of the partnership between the insurance industry participants and the government. Variable design features include (1) the remit of the PGE, (2) whether the government or the insurance industry has control over the PGE, (3) whether or not the government provides a backstop for insurance liabilities and how the attachment point is set, (4) whether the purchase of the relevant catastrophe cover is made mandatory for policyholders by bundling it into general standard insurance products (such as property insurance), and (5) whether policyholders pay a flat or a risk-based premium. These variables must be tailored to the type of catastrophic risk, the particular market, and the preparedness of the relevant government to subsidise the scheme. PPParts do not just operate at the national level but can also operate at the regional level where several national governments collaborate with the regional and international insurance industry, often supported by additional funding from international development agencies and developed countries.[68]

9.4.2 Examples of insurance PPParts

To illustrate different design features, this section compares insurance PPParts that cover flood losses in the UK and in the US, and the forthcoming revised natural hazards insurance scheme in New Zealand.

UK – Flood Re: the UK insurance industry has adopted a 'bundled' model for flood insurance. Flood risk cover is automatically included in home property insurance.[69] The bundled flood cover is not separately priced and home property policyholders cannot opt-out of the flood risk cover. This ensures wide penetration and the pooling of good and bad flood risks. All insurers that offer home property insurance in the UK can reinsure flood risk through the Flood Reinsurance Scheme. The Flood Reinsurance Scheme was established under Chapter 4, Part 4 of the Water Act 2014 and launched in 2016. The scheme is administered by Flood Re Limited ('Flood Re'), a not-for-profit mutual reinsurance company limited by guarantee.[70] Flood Re offers flood risk reinsurance at a subsidised premium which is not risk-reflective of the ceded flood risk but based on the Council Tax (local property tax) banding for each of the reinsured properties.[71] The scheme is funded from premium receipts and a levy collected from all insurers offering home property insurance in the UK.[72] The bundling approach combined with the availability of

67 Jarzabkowski, (n 18) Sec 1.3.

68 See Section 9.5.

69 Swenja Surminski, 'Flood Re from the United Kingdom' in National Association of Insurance Commissioners and the Center for Insurance and Policy Research, 'Flood Risk and Insurance' (2017) 68 <https://content.naic.org/sites/default/files/inline-files/cipr_study_1704_flood_risk.pdf> accessed on 1 June 2023.

70 Water Act 2014, s 65; and the Flood Reinsurance (Scheme and Scheme Administrator Designation) Regulations 2015.

71 The Flood Reinsurance (Scheme Funding and Administration) Regulations 2015, pt 4.

72 Water Act 2014, s 66; and the Flood Reinsurance (Scheme Funding and Administration) Regulations 2015, pt 3.

subsidised reinsurance from Flood Re allows flood risk insurance to be available at affordable prices to households that had previous claims and are severely exposed to flood risks. Flood Re retrocedes risk into the international reinsurance market.[73]

The remit of Flood Re is to provide flood risk reinsurance to relevant insurers in such a way as to (1) promote the availability and affordability of flood insurance for household premises while minimising the costs of doing so, and (2) manage, over the period of operation of the scheme, the transition to risk-reflective pricing of flood insurance for household premises.[74] Since April 2022, Flood Re has been operating the Build Back Better initiative which is designed to reduce the cost and impact of future floods by paying up to £10,000 to insured homeowners to put in place flood resilience measures as part of flood repairs following a claim.[75] Flood Re partnering with the Environment Agency is also providing generic advice on property flood resilience measures on their website.[76]

The Flood Re Scheme does not benefit commercial property and does not apply to household premises built after 1 January 2009.[77] The scheme is financed and operated entirely by the UK insurance industry. The UK government's role has been limited to passing the relevant legislation (which sets out the remit of the scheme and the terms of its administration and funding) and to taking on an oversight role.[78] The UK government does not provide any backstop reinsurance cover or subsidies. However, the UK government is investing in public flood defences,[79] which together with property-level flood resilience measures should (re)establish the insurability of flood risk in the UK. The Flood Re Scheme is only intended to be temporarily running until 2039, by which time the UK property market is intended to have moved to risk-reflective pricing of flood insurance for household premises.[80] The scheme has been criticised for the premiums and policy structure of home property insurance not being risk-reflective, and thus not incentivising policyholders to take flood prevention measures.[81]

US – NFIP: US Congress established the National Flood Insurance Program ('NFIP') with the passage of the National Flood Insurance Act of 1968. The remit of the NFIP is to enable eligible homeowners and small businesses to buy flood insurance.[82] The NFIP is a federal government-run and backed scheme, managed by the Federal Emergency

73 Flood Re, 'Annual Report 2022,' 17 <https://www.floodre.co.uk/wp-content/uploads/Flood-Re-Annual-Report-2022.pdf> accessed on 1 June 2023.

74 Water Act 2014, s 64.

75 Flood Re (n 73) 17.

76 Flood Re, 'Be Flood Smart' <https://www.floodre.co.uk/be-flood-smart/> accessed on 1 June 2023.

77 Flood Re, 'Qualifying Policies Which May Be Ceded to Flood R' <https://www.floodre.co.uk/find-an-insurer/eligibility-criteria/> accessed on 1 June 2023.

78 Water Act 2014, ss 67, 75, 79.

79 Department for Environment, Food and Rural Affairs, 'Multi-Billion Pound Investment as Government Unveils New Long-Term Plan to Tackle Flooding' (Press Release 14 July 2020) <https://www.gov.uk/government/news/multi-billion-pound-investment-as-government-unveils-new-long-term-plan-to-tackle-flooding> accessed on 1 June 2023.

80 Flood Re, 'What Is Flood Re?' <https://www.floodre.co.uk/about-us/> accessed on 1 June 2023.

81 Swenja Surminski (n 69) 70–71.

82 US National Flood Insurance Act of 1968, §4011.

Management Agency ('FEMA').[83] The US insurance industry has no role in the NFIP other than acting as a distribution channel for selling and servicing NFIP policies.[84]

The NFIP provides flood risk insurance (sold as a voluntary add-on to property insurance) to eligible homeowners and small businesses. Homeowners and small businesses are eligible if they are resident in a 'participating community' that has joined the NFIP. Participating communities must adopt and comply with floodplain management regulations and take risk mitigation measures.[85] The NFIP collects premiums from its policyholders and pays claims to those policyholders for costs associated with covered flood damage. When it was created, the NFIP discounted premiums to maintain property values on structures already built in flood-prone areas, while risk-reflective premiums were charged for newly constructed property.[86] These discounts, combined with several large loss years (most notably Hurricane Katrina in 2005), contributed to revenue shortfalls and resulted in NFIP borrowing from the US government to pay claims in several instances.[87] The NFIP currently owes $20.525 billion to the US Treasury and was projected to make $280 million in interest payments in 2022 alone.[88]

To build a more sound financial framework for the NFIP, the Biggert–Waters Flood Insurance Reform Act of 2012 directed FEMA to remove the discounts for some policyholders with homes insured by the NFIP, so that policyholders would be given flood insurance rates that more accurately reflected their expected flood losses.[89] Because of concerns about rising premiums rendering flood insurance unaffordable in some communities, the Homeowner Flood Insurance Affordability Act of 2014[90] repealed certain parts of the 2012 Act, restoring grandfathering to some of those insured properties that had previously benefitted from premium discounts, putting limits on certain rate increases, and updating the approach to ensuring the fiscal soundness of the fund by applying an annual surcharge to all policyholders.[91] The 2014 Act mandated FEMA to develop an affordability framework aimed at providing targeted assistance for policyholders. FEMA has now developed Risk Rating 2.0, a methodology to address debt and insufficient premium income. Risk Rating 2.0 has been applicable to new policies since 1 October 2022 and all remaining and renewing policies since 1 April 2023.[92] Leveraging technology, industry best practices, catastrophe models, and actuarial science, Risk Rating 2.0 is intended to reflect more accurately an individual property's flood risk and produce premium rates that

83 FEMA, 'An Affordability Framework for the National Flood Insurance Program' 1 <https://www.fema.gov/sites/default/files/2020-05/Affordability_april_2018.pdf> accessed on 1 June 2023.

84 FEMA, 'How to Buy Flood Insurance' <https://www.floodsmart.gov/how-buy-flood-insurance> accessed on 1 June 2023.

85 National Association of Insurance Commissioners and the Center for Insurance and Policy Research, 'Flood Risk and Insurance' (2017) 26–32 <https://content.naic.org/sites/default/files/inline-files/cipr_study_1704_flood_risk.pdf> accessed on 1 June 2023.

86 Ibid.

87 FEMA (n 83) 1.

88 FEMA, 'NFIP Debt' <https://www.fema.gov/case-study/nfip-debt> accessed on 1 June 2023.

89 US Biggert–Waters Flood Insurance Reform Act 2012.

90 US Homeowner Flood Insurance Affordability Act 2014.

91 FEMA, 'The NFIP Affordability Framework' <https://www.fema.gov/flood-insurance/rules-legislation> accessed on 1 June 2023.

92 FEMA, 'Risk Rating 2.0' <https://www.fema.gov/flood-insurance/risk-rating> accessed on 1 June 2023.

are actuarily sound but also equitable by taking property values into account.[93] Existing premium discounts have, however, been largely ring-fenced.[94]

The NFIP has been criticised for the large debt it has incurred, representing an additional burden to US taxpayers. The premium pricing structure prior to Risk Rating 2.0 had been criticised by some for still allowing non-risk reflective discounts to some policyholders and because premium discounts are not means-tested, while others have pointed out that the risk-reflective premiums charged are rendering cover unaffordable for some.[95] As the NFIP cover is sold as a voluntary add-on, there is a high degree of adverse selection (i.e. policyholders with a high exposure to flood risk buy the add-on, whereas low-risk policyholders do not). Although flood prevention measures are an ex ante requirement through the eligibility criteria, there is no program for resilient reinstatement following a flooding event.[96]

New Zealand – Toka Tū Ake – Natural Hazards Commission: in 1945 New Zealand introduced the Earthquake and War Damage Commission which set up and administered a fund to address a protection gap for losses caused by earthquakes that the insurance industry was unable to fill. The fund was built up by levies paid by policyholders as part of their home insurance policies and investment returns from the fund.[97] Its successor, the Earthquake Commission,[98] had an accumulated fund of over NZ$6.1 billion by 2010. Following the Canterbury earthquakes in 2010 and 2011, and the Kaikoura earthquake in 2016, the fund was depleted.[99] A Public Enquiry investigated and reported on the lessons learnt from the Earthquake Commission's operational practices and approaches to claims outcomes in relation to the Canterbury earthquakes: its main findings were that the Earthquake Commission was poorly prepared, was rapidly overwhelmed, did not work effectively together with insurers, and, as a result, the public bore the burden of those shortcomings.[100] Many of the Public Enquiry's recommendations were incorporated into the Natural Hazards Insurance Act 2023 which comes into force on 27 February 2024. The Earthquake Commission will become the Toka Tū Ake – Natural Hazards Commission ('TTA').[101] TTA is a Crown Entity (i.e. public statutory entity).[102] The remit of the TTA is to reduce the impact of natural hazards on people, property, and the community by:

- administering natural hazard cover, in particular by managing and settling claims, in a fair and timely manner;

93 Ibid.

94 Ibid.

95 FEMA (n 91).

96 There are no provisions to that effect in the NFIP Claims Manual (2021) <https://www.fema.gov/sites/default/files/documents/fema_nfip_claims-manual_2021.pdf> accessed on 1 June 2023.

97 Toka Tū Ake Earthquake Commission, 'The Natural Disaster Fund' <https://www.eqc.govt.nz/what-we-do/natural-disaster-fund/> accessed on 1 June 2023.

98 Established under the Earthquake Commission Act 1993.

99 Toka Tū Ake Earthquake Commission (n 97).

100 Public Enquiry into the Earthquake Commission, 'Report of the Public Enquiry into the Earthquake Commission' (March 2020) <https://www.dpmc.govt.nz/sites/default/files/2021-01/report-of-the-public-inquiry-into-the-earthquake-commission.pdf> accessed on 1 June 2023.

101 New Zealand Natural Hazards Insurance Act 2023 s 125.

102 Ibid s 126.

- contributing to the management of the financial risk to the Crown by providing natural hazard cover by managing the fund, collecting the levy, and arranging reinsurance or other risk transfer products;
- improving awareness and understanding of matters relating to natural hazards, improving natural hazard risk management, and improving resilience to natural hazards.[103]

The TTA provides first loss insurance cover for loss and damage to residential buildings and surrounding land caused by natural hazards (including floods) capped at NZ$300,000, and with an excess of NZ$500 per building.[104] TTA cover is automatically available to policyholders who insure their residential building under a fire insurance policy, or property insurance including fire risk cover, with private insurers.[105] Claims payments are made from the Natural Hazard Fund which is owned by TTA on behalf of the Crown.[106] The fund is financed by a levy from each policyholder who insures a residential building under a fire/property insurance policy, and from returns on investments from the fund.[107] The levy is collected by private insurers on behalf of TTA.[108] The levy is charged at a flat rate that applies to all policyholders, regardless of their risk exposure, to support insurance availability and affordability.[109] Given that the lack of co-operation between the Earthquake Commission and insurers was flagged as a major concern by the Public Enquiry, it is surprising that the Natural Hazards Insurance Act 2023 does address the TTA – fire insurer relationship, their respective duties within that relationship, and how boundary issues are to be dealt with. This may be – and should be – covered in secondary legislation.

One innovative feature of the Natural Hazards Insurance Act 2023 is its focus on policyholders: TTA must assess, decide, and settle claims in a timely manner, and in compliance with the 'Code of Insured Persons' Rights.'[110] It is disappointing though that the reinstatement of insured property does not envisage 'BuildBack Better' arrangements or green reinstatement.[111] There are, however, provisions that anticipate that policyholders must take climate risk adaptation measures: TTA is entitled to decline claims if the policyholder has failed to take reasonable steps (1) to mitigate the risk of natural hazard damage to the residential building and residential land; and (2) in the event of loss, to

103 Ibid s 128.

104 Ibid ss 28, 31, 35–37.

105 Ibid s 29.

106 Ibid ss 111 and 109.

107 Ibid ss 110, 116–118.

108 Ibid s 118.

109 See: David Friar and Kate Crichton, 'Natural Hazards Act Passes into Law' (March 2023) <https://www.bellgully.com/insights/natural-hazards-insurance-act-passes-into-law/> accessed on 1 June 2023.

110 Natural Hazards Insurance Act 2023 ss 57 and 88. The Code of Insured Persons' Rights to be prepared by the New Zealand Government has not yet been published but is likely to commit TTA to treating policyholders with fairness, transparency, competence, and respect (following recommendations from the Public Enquiry (n 100)).

111 Ibid s 41(1): the reinstatement cost of residential land is the total cost that would reasonably be incurred to reinstate the damaged residential land in a way that would be reasonably sufficient in the circumstances.

mitigate the risk of any further damage,[112] or if the insured property was of sub-standard construction.[113]

Another noteworthy feature is that the objectives of the TTA go beyond addressing protection gaps and expressly extend to addressing knowledge gaps ('improving awareness and understanding of matters relating to natural hazards') and risk adaptation.[114] Whether the funding structure can refill the fund sufficiently remains to be seen. In any event, TTA is required to make reinsurance and other risk transfer arrangements,[115] while the New Zealand government is required to make top-up payments by way of loan or grant if the assets of the fund are not sufficient to pay the amounts forecast to be due and payable out of the fund.[116]

9.4.3 PPPart design for climate change-related risks

From the preceding discussion and the examples, it can be seen that a number of design choices will have to be made for an insurance PPPart for climate change-related physical risks (a 'Climate Risk PPPart'). These design choices will be dictated by high-level factors such as the specific existing or anticipated protection gaps and any other objectives to be addressed, the maturity of the insurance market and its willingness to collaborate with the government, the level of insurance literacy and climate change awareness of the population, the government's commitment to the goals of the Paris Agreement, and its willingness and ability to implement such commitment with policies, laws, and funding.

What does a well-designed insurance PPPart look like? Jarzabkowski et al. argue that a well-designed PPPart in the form of a PGE seeks to establish a dynamic equilibrium (1) between too much or too little knowledge about the (potentially) uninsurable risk in question, (2) between the private insurance industry and the government in terms of controlling how uninsurability of the risk is addressed, and (3) in respect of paying for the protection.[117] It also integrates into its remit 'physical resilience' (mitigating the effects of the risk ex ante) by working together with the government and other stakeholders so that insurability can be sustained long-term.[118] EIOPA also recognises that a well-designed Climate Risk PPPart must be a 'shared resilience solution,' but the four key elements put a greater emphasis on the PPPart's relationship with the policyholder:

(1) risk assessment: filling the knowledge gap to gain a better understanding of the risk;
(2) risk prevention: the PPPart has a role in risk mitigation and adaptation;
(3) product design: the cover provided addresses the risk and meets the policyholders' reasonable expectations at an affordable premium;

112 Ibid s 73.
113 Ibid s 76.
114 Ibid s 128(2)(c).
115 Ibid s 128(2)(b) and 129.
116 Ibid ss 112 and 113.
117 Jarzabkowski (n 18) ch 2 and 3.
118 Ibid ch 5 and 6.

(4) risk transfer: the risk is shared in a way that the policyholder retains some of the risk and/or pays risk-reflective premium.[119]

Remit: the Climate Risk PPPart must address the protection gaps arising from the uninsurability of physical climate risks by providing insurance or reinsurance cover for those risks. Depending on the territorial coverage of the Climate Risk PPPart, there may be one specific climate-related weather peril (e.g. flood risk in the UK) or a wider range of climate-related weather perils (windstorm, flood, drought, wildfire). Another design choice to be made is whether a wider variety of natural catastrophe risk is included, even if the relevant perils are not necessarily related to climate change (e.g. earthquake or eruption of a volcano).

Following the example of the New Zealand Natural Hazards Insurance Act 2023, addressing the knowledge gap by improving awareness and understanding of physical climate change risks, their impact and climate risk mitigation and adaptation measures, should be an explicit objective of the Climate Risk PPPart. It would need to be clear whether the Climate Risk PPPart PGE itself is tasked with the creation of knowledge and collection of data or whether it merely acts as an interchange, repository, and disseminator of knowledge for insurers, government, and policyholders. The PGE should be well placed to collect underlying data from all participating insurers and, with the input from insurers, can produce standardised information for all policyholders, whereas an insurer would be better placed to produce information that is tailored or semi-tailored to a specific policyholder. If the PGE would be tasked with creating knowledge, it needs the resources to do so: funding to employ internal experts and co-operations for knowledge creation with the insurance industry, commercial data and technology services providers, and the scientific community within academia.[120]

As for 'resilience,' the design choices to be made are whether and how the Climate Risk PPPart contributes to climate change mitigation and adaptation measures taken at the individual policyholder level. Jarzabkowski et al. conceive of 'physical resilience' as limiting insured losses by taking ex ante adaptation measures and, following an insured event, by building back with adaptation measures in place.[121] Arguably, that is not enough in the context of climate change risks where it is key that the root cause of climate change (anthropogenic GHG emissions) is addressed with climate change mitigation measures. Insurers who take an 'enabling role' in supporting their policyholders in their transition to a net-zero economy may therefore also wish to incentivise policyholders to take climate change mitigation measures (using, or replacing existing energy sources in insured property with, clean energy and/or more energy-efficient alternatives).[122] Accordingly, it is suggested that the remit of a Climate Risk PPPart should include both climate change adaptation and climate change mitigation. The Climate Risk PPPart can contribute by

119 EIOPA, 'Issues Paper on Resilience Solutions for Pandemics' (2020) <https://www.eiopa.europa.eu/publications/issues-paper-resilience-solutions-pandemics_en> accessed on 1 June 2023, cited in related to climate risks in ECB and EIOPA (n 16) [2.3.2].

120 Government-industry-academia partnerships are already an established mechanism for technology research and development. See e.g. Henry Etzkowitz, 'Innovation in Innovation: The Triple Helix of University-Industry-Government Relations' (2003) 42(3) *Soc Sci Inf*, 293; L. Rafael Reif (President of the Massachusetts Institute of Technology 2015–2022), 'A Better Way to Deliver Innovation to the World' (*Washington Post*, 24 May 2015).

121 Jarzabkowski (n 18) ch 5.

122 See Chapter 7.

absorbing some of the green extra costs that are incurred by the policyholder or the insurer when the policyholder takes climate change mitigation or adaptation measures envisaged by the insurance policy (e.g. via premium discount or green reinstatement terms).[123] This would (partially) address the impact underwriting funding gap. Detailed consideration would need to be given to a list of climate change mitigation or adaptation measures that would be funded, as this would have implications on the underlying policy design.

Structure of Climate Risk PPPart: the structure of the Climate Risk PPPart determines the contractual relationships between policyholders, insurers, the PGE, and the government. As we have seen, the US NFIP and the New Zealand TTA take a direct insurance approach, whereas UK Flood Re operates at the reinsurance level. It is suggested that there are a number of advantages to the PGE acting as a reinsurer in a mature insurance market. First, if the PGE acts as reinsurer it does not need to engage with policyholders directly or operate under an agency model utilising private insurers for distribution and collecting premiums. This eases the regulatory burden on the PGE and its senior management.[124] Policyholders will not get confused by who their contractual counterparty is.

Secondly, private insurers maintain their sole customer-facing role which they can leverage to require or incentivise policyholders to take climate change mitigation and adaptation measures. They remain in charge of the contractual design of the insurance products they are offering, subject to any requirements of the Climate Risk PPPart design imposed by legislation. Policyholders would only have to claim against their insurer and would not need to get involved in difficult 'demarcation disputes' between different layers of insurance. Insurers can also leverage their existing business relationships with supplies and services providers they use at the claims stage to reinstate, replace, or repair lost or damaged property for implementing climate change mitigation and adaptation measures. If adjustments need to be made to the Climate Risk PPPart, they would not automatically affect the underlying contractual relationship between private insurers and policyholders.[125]

Thirdly, a reinsurance structure allows for flexibility in transferring different types of risk to the PGE. Under the reinsurance contract between private insurers and the PGE, the PGE would indemnify participating insurers in respect of their liability for claims following a specified extreme weather event or climate peril. This should include reimbursement for a proportion of insurers' green extra costs incurred under green reinstatement terms in the underlying policies. Could insurers also be reimbursed for premium discounts and rebates that are given to policyholders if they take in-scope ex ante climate change mitigation or adaptation measures? If the discount or rebate reflects the reduction of risk from which the insurer benefits during that policy year to which the premium relates, the insurer has already been compensated.

If, however, the premium discount or rebate is larger than the monetary value of the reduction of risk during the policy year, and is given to stimulate investment by the policyholder in an in-scope climate risk mitigation or adaptation measure, there is an arguable case that an insurer should be indemnified for a portion of the green extra costs of that

123 See Chapter 7, Sections 7.5 and 7.7.

124 In the UK, ICOBS deals with an insurer's conduct of business obligations vis-à-vis policyholders does not apply to reinsurance contracts (ICOBS 1 Annex 1, Part 2, 1.1R).

125 This is because a contract of reinsurance is separate and independent from the underlying insurance contract (*Wasa International Insurance Co Ltd v Lexington Insurance Co and AGF Insurance Ltd* [2009] UKHL 40).

type to alleviate the '12-month policy term problem,' namely that an insurer who is incurring green extra costs by enabling an ex ante investment in climate change adaptation measures that reduces the risk of loss over a longer time frame cannot take full advantage of the benefit if the policyholder changes insurers at the end of the 12-month policy period.[126] At the reinsurance level, the fact that policyholders change their insurers would be irrelevant as all participating insurers would reinsure with the PGE so that over time the PGE would enjoy the aggregate risk reduction benefit from all in-scope climate change adaptation measures for which participating insurers have given a premium discount. The time lag between giving the premium discount and the risk reduction benefit materialising can be accommodated in the reinsurance contract which would have a long-term policy period or indefinite policy period set by statute.

Fourthly, a reinsurance structure allows for risks to be shared in different ways. In non-proportional reinsurance, the reinsured cedes a layer or horizontal slice of the risk. This layer could be a 'first loss' which applies to aggregate losses incurred below a total amount set in the reinsurance contract, or the layer could be an 'excess of loss' layer located above aggregate losses in excess of a specified amount (the deductible) but below a specified ceiling of aggregate losses, or the layer could be set as 'stop loss' applicable to aggregate losses exceeding a specified amount.[127] Accordingly, there is structural flexibility for a Climate Risk PPPart PGE to take one or more different slices of risk, while other slices could be retained by insurers or transferred to the international reinsurance market (via reinsurance) or to the capital markets (via insurance-linked securities). For example, EIOPA envisages a 'ladder approach' in horizontal layers for natural catastrophe risk with a first loss layer retained by insurers, a second layer transferred into the commercial reinsurance market, a third layer for high-impact and low-frequency events transferred to national Climate Risk PPPart PGEs, and a stop loss layer provided by the EU.[128]

In contrast, in countries that do not have an established property insurance market, it may be better for the Climate Risk PPPart PGE to operate at primary insurance level as existing public sector infrastructure could be used to increase access to and promote the take-up of the relevant insurance products.[129]

Policyholders' responsibilities: insurance PPParts cannot relieve policyholders from their responsibility to pay premium, but they can make premium rates more affordable by redistributing risk from high-risk policyholders across a wider pool of policyholders. Comparing the NFIP design to Flood Re suggests that risk redistribution is more effective when the climate risk peril is bundled into property insurance.[130] This does not make climate risk insurance mandatory for all, but it ensures that those who wish or must insure their property, must also buy the climate risk component. This collectivises the risk and prevents adverse selection where only high-risk policyholders insure against climate risk. Unlike the Flood Re Scheme and the TTA which use a flat rate premium in respect of all policyholders, the

126 See Chapter 7, Section 7.5.4.6.

127 Terry O'Neill, Jan Woloniecki, and Franziska Arnold-Dwyer, *The Law of Reinsurance in England and Bermuda* (5th ed, Sweet & Maxwell 2019) 1-016.

128 ECB and EIOPA (n 16) 16–18.

129 The Geneva Association (n 7) 36.

130 See above, and also see: Jarzabkowski (n 18) ch 3.

Climate Risk PPPart should be designed to use partially risk-reflective premium rates to incentivise policyholders to take climate change mitigation and adaptation measures. In Chapter 7, Section 7.5, it was suggested that this could be done via premium discounts and rebates for policyholders who have taken the prescribed measures.[131]

Involvement of mortgage lenders: as noted above,[132] mortgage lenders are stakeholders who could – and arguably should – be contributing to the funding of climate change mitigation and adaptation measures in relation to mortgaged properties. To the extent mortgage lenders are co-insured, they could be charged a separate premium that could be used by insurers towards green extra costs for green reinstatement. Alternatively, or in addition, mortgage lenders could make direct contributions to, or at least provide loans on favourable terms for, specific household-level climate change mitigation and adaptation measures.

Involvement of government: as can be seen from the PPPart examples (Flood Re, NFIP, and TTA), governments are involved in facilitating the set-up of the insurance PPPart and providing the legal framework for the PGE to operate by passing the necessary laws. In the case of TTA, the New Zealand government is obliged to top up the TTA Fund if it falls short of the amounts forecast to be due and payable out of the Fund.[133] EIOPA too is proposing an ultimate EU-level backstop in their 'ladder approach.' A government guarantee or backstop is likely to go hand in hand with greater government oversight over the PGE as governments and their agencies need to account for their spending of public funds.

For a Climate Risk PPPart that reimburses insurers for green extra costs, it is conceivable that the PGE would need additional funds from the government to cover those costs. These green extra costs derive from insurers giving premium discounts for climate change mitigation and adaptation measures taken by policyholders and green reinstatement. They cannot be absorbed in premium rates if they are to stay affordable and incentivise those measures. Insurers should be compensated for the majority of these green extra costs by the PGE as they do not necessarily derive any risk reduction or other financial benefit in return.[134] It is suggested that insurers should retain a small proportion of those costs to ensure an alignment of interests between the PGE and insurers, and to recognise the wider but less tangible benefits of climate action to insurers that insurability can be maintained or improved, making their business sustainable long-term.[135]

In addition, as suggested by a recent OECD Report, public funding for climate action measures could be delivered via the PGE through insurers to policyholders at the inception of the policy and at the claims stage.[136] In Section 9.3.2, a number of reasons were given why a government should provide funding for private climate change mitigation and adaptation measures (i.e. measures taken by individuals at the household level). There

131 See Chapter 7, Section 7.5.
132 See Section 9.3.2.
133 Natural Hazards Insurance Act 2023, ss.112 and 113.
134 See Section 9.3.
135 See Chapter 6, Section 6.2.
136 OECD Insurance and Adaptation Paper 24–25.

are a number of advantages to providing public funding for such measures in conjunction with insurance:

- the delivery of climate action involves connecting and co-ordinating different stakeholders outside of the traditional boundaries of central or local government and the insurance industry. The PGE can facilitate an interconnected response;[137]
- public funding can be targeted to specific climate change mitigation and adaptation measures at the household level that have been pre-approved by government authorities and insurers;
- insurers can support the delivery of such measures through their networks of approved contractors and suppliers;
- insurers can monitor the application of the funds for the purpose for which they were provided;
- through insurers and the Climate Risk PPPart PGE, the government can access information about the impact of the relevant measures and plan and make adjustments accordingly.

Thus the main benefit of channelling government funding through a Climate Risk PPPart PGE is that insurers can provide administrative technical assistance to the government in relation to the delivery of climate action that will benefit policyholders, insurers themselves, and society as a whole.[138] As noted by Jarzabkowski et al., it is important that the processes of providing financial protection and promoting physical resilience against climate change risks are integrated into the PPPart design, as this will ensure that the Climate Risk PPPart is sustainable long-term and can service the overall resilience of society.[139]

Given the public component of Climate Risk PPParts, a governance-oriented design feature should be **performance and financial accountability** of the PGE: performance accountability would require the PGE to explain its decisions (and the process leading to them) in light of its remit and any objective and targets it has been set, while financial accountability would subject the PGE to a degree of audit control.[140] An interesting point here would be whether the PGE should only be accountable to the relevant government agency, or also to the insurers involved. Given the important protection issues at stake, it is suggested that the PGE should be accountable (1) to the government under the legal framework under which it is set up, (2) to insurers under the reinsurance contract, (3) to the relevant insurance regulator/s under the regulatory framework in which it operates, and (4) in the wider sense, to the public by way of public reporting on its activities in finances.

137 Jarzabkowski (n 18) ch 5.

138 The role of technical co-operation between insurers and governmental agencies for the purpose of risk mitigation has also been recognised by Tom Baker and Anja Shortland, 'How Crime Shapes Insurance and Insurance Shapes Crime' (10 March 2023) U of Penn, Inst for Law & Econ Research Paper No. 23-10, *Journal of Legal Analysis* (forthcoming) <https://ssrn.com/abstract=4390802> accessed on 1 June 2023.

139 Jarzabkowski (n 18) Sec 5.5.

140 For an overview of accountability concepts in the financial sector, see Rosa Lastra and Heba Shams, 'Public Accountability in the Financial Sector' in Eilis Ferrán and Charles Goodhart (eds.), *Regulating Financial Services and Markets in the XXIst Century* (Hart Publishing 2001) ch 12.

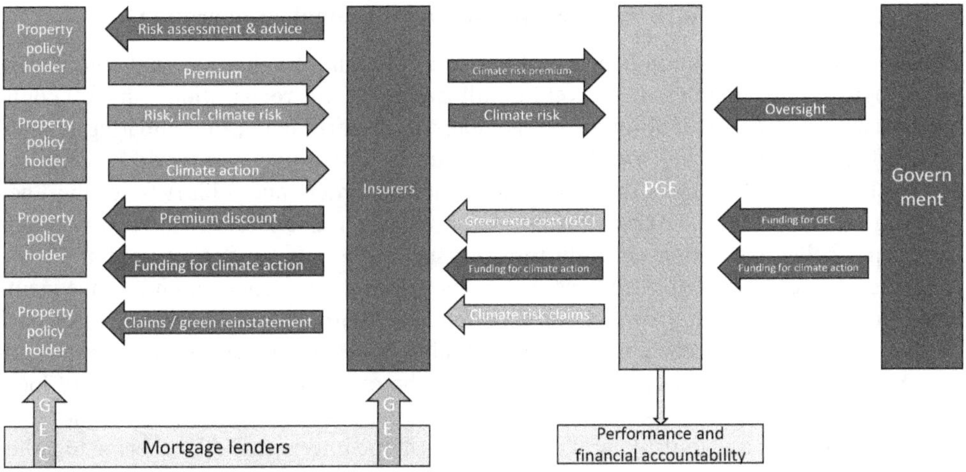

Figure 9.1 Climate risk public-private partnership structure.

Figure 9.1 shows a simplified graphic representation of the Climate Risk PPPart with the design features discussed above.

Disclaimer: it is accepted that the preceding discussion on Climate Risk PPPart design is based on a European-centric perspective and that the suggestions made may not necessarily be suitable for less developed insurance markets. It is also acknowledged that Climate Risk PPParts are not the panacea for insurability, financial protection, and resilience. They present challenges in the process of setting up, requiring extensive dialogue and consensus-building between the insurance industry, different government departments and agencies, and other stakeholders, as well as legislation establishing the scheme and the PGE. They also present operational challenges in co-ordinating actions and maintaining a balance between (1) government oversight, (2) giving insurers sufficient flexibility to manage their risks and pursue business opportunities, and (3) ensuring the availability and affordability of insurance protection to policyholders. Adding climate change mitigation and adaptation measures into the mix creates additional co-ordination and funding challenges. To finance those measures, careful consideration needs to be given to how the costs of those measures are shared equitably between policyholders, insurers, mortgage lenders, and taxpayers generally. Climate Risk PPParts will almost inevitably need additional funding from governments.

Ultimately, the design will be informed by the high-level factors listed at the start of this section, combining local expertise and local best practices to suit local conditions and practicalities.[141] Acting in accordance with the Principles for Sustainable Insurance, insurers should be open to working together with governments and other stakeholders to develop integrated risk management approaches and risk transfer solutions that promote wide-spread climate action across society.[142]

141 Global Risk Modelling Alliance, 'Global and Local, Public and Private: How Climate-Vulnerable Countries Can Have the Best in Understanding Risk' (March 2023) <http://www.insdevforum.org/wp-content/uploads/2023/03/GRMAlaunch_FastTrack_report_10.pdf> accessed on 1 June 2023.

142 PSI Prin 3.

9.5 Regional risk pooling arrangements and international co-operation

Climate change is a common concern of humankind[143] and the international community has recognised – although may not yet be fully acting on this recognition – that all countries must co-operate, and all other stakeholders must participate, in combating climate change.[144] According to the sociologists Beck and Lau, we live in a world risk society that is characterised by risks that transcend national borders and a blurring of the lines between public and private risks.[145] Complex risks, such as climate risk, require multi-directional collective action not only to make such risks more manageable, but also to legitimise the actions taken to address such risks.[146] Developing countries may have insufficient funds to respond to loss and damage associated with the adverse effects of climate change. As a result, natural catastrophes can escalate into humanitarian crises, compounding food and water insecurity, displacement, and the precarity of the livelihoods of local communities,[147] as well as contributing to the growing debt burden of those countries.[148] Regional risk pools and multi-lateral risk solutions at the international level bring together the insurance industry, donor countries, national governments, regional and international organisations, and non-governmental organisations to address the climate risks that affect some of the most vulnerable countries.

9.5.1 Regional risk pools

Some of the countries most vulnerable to climate risks and other natural hazards do not have the financial resources to manage, adapt, and respond to these risks. They are reliant on ad-hoc post-disaster management funded from already fiscally constrained national budgets and international aid. Funds cannot always be mobilised fast enough to prevent humanitarian crises. There are significant protection gaps and knowledge gaps in the developing and least developed countries.

Over the last two decades a number of regional pooling arrangements have been set up: the Caribbean Catastrophe Risk Insurance Facility ('CCRIF')[149] in 2007, the African Risk Capacity ('ARC')[150] in 2012, the Pacific Catastrophe Risk Assessment and Finance Initiative ('PCRAFI')[151] in 2013, and the Southeast Asia Disaster Risk Insurance Facility ('SEADRIF') in 2019.[152] These regional pools are funded from annual premiums paid by the participating countries and from donations from 'donor partners' (G7 countries, EU, World Bank, and philanthropic foundations). Frequently, donor partners and the insurance

---

143 Paris Agreement, Recitals.

144 SHIP (UN Framework Convention on Climate Change, Sharm el-Sheikh Implementation Plan (adopted at COP27 in 2022) Decision 1/CP.27) Sec VIII cl 28 and sec IX cl 30–31.

145 Ulrich Beck and Christoph Lau, 'Second Modernity as a Research Agenda: Theoretical and Empirical Explorations in the "Meta-Change" of Modern Society' (2005) 56 (4) *The British Journal of Sociology*, 525.

146 Van Asselt (n 62) Sec 5.

147 SHIP Sec VI cl 44.

148 SHIP Sec VI cl 45.

149 Caribbean Catastrophe Risk Insurance Facility <https://caricom.org/> accessed on 1 June 2023.

150 African Risk Capacity <https://www.arc.int/> accessed on 1 June 2023.

151 The Pacific Catastrophe Risk Assessment and Finance Initiative was a pilot project initiated and implemented by the World Bank and funded by donor countries Germany, Japan, the UK, and the USA. The pilot has now expired <https://www.worldbank.org/en/results/2012/04/01/pacific-islands-disaster-risk-reduction-and-financing-in-the-pacific> accessed on 1 June 2023.

152 Southeast Asia Disaster Risk Insurance Facility <https://seadrif.org/> accessed on 1 June 2023.

industry provide technical support for establishing and operationalising the facilities.[153] The advantages of a regional pooling arrangement are that (1) it expands the pool so that covariate risk (the same and similar events affecting the whole cohort of participating countries) is lowered and, in the event of an eligible natural catastrophe loss, the affected participating countries can be effectively subsidised by the unaffected participating countries, (2) it can diversify the risk by covering different perils and different countries, and (3) it can pool technical and administrative resources, thereby reducing transaction costs. Premiums are less costly compared to what an individual country would pay in the insurance market.[154] The involvement of the insurance industry as a technical partner contributes to technical expertise.

Two of the key defining features of CCRIF, ARC, PCRAFI, and SEADRIF are that they operate parametric insurance schemes and that the insured is a state, and not an individual policyholder. Conventional insurance pays out on an indemnity basis covering actual financial losses incurred.[155] In contrast, payments under parametric insurance are triggered under a pre-agreed formula – a model – that functions as a proxy for the actual loss. The model calculates an estimated loss based on weather data (e.g. wind speed, rainfall), geophysical data (e.g. strength of earthquake, location), economic data, and population data. If the modelled loss reaches a pre-agreed threshold, the facility will make a payment to the affected participating country, irrespective of whether or not the modelled loss was higher or lower than the actual financial loss.[156] This has the advantage that payments can be made quickly soon after the catastrophic event as there is no need to assess and verify actual losses. It also saves administrative costs which are savings that can be reflected in lowered premiums. A potential disadvantage is that the actual costs of loss and damage suffered may exceed the modelled loss, so that there is a shortfall in the amounts paid. There is no publicly available data, and no existing research, on the extent of that coverage gap in respect of any of these schemes. It should also be noted that traditional indemnity insurance often does not fully cover all insured losses because insurers use deductibles, excess thresholds, and limits of liability to define and limit the sum insured and to ensure that the policyholder has 'skin in the game.'[157]

While the literature acknowledges the value of regional risk pools,[158] it has also pointed out their limitations. As noted above, the pay-outs based on modelled loss may fall short of the actual financial loss suffered. In addition, coverage may be limited to specific perils: CCRIF only covers hurricane, earthquake, and excess rainfall risks; ARC covers droughts; PCRAFI covers tropical cyclones, earthquakes, and tsunamis; and SEADRIF currently only covers flood risks. Despite premiums being more competitive than in the commercial insurance markets, some countries still struggle to pay for premiums and

153 For a detailed comparative study of CCRIF, ARC, and PCRAFI see: Nikolas Scherer, *Insuring against Climate Change: The Emergence of Regional Catastrophe Risk Pools* (Routledge, 2020).

154 IPCC 2022 Mitigation Report, Summary for Policymakers [15.6.4].

155 *Castellain v Preston* (1883) 11 QBD 380 (CA) 386, and see Chapter 7.

156 Scherer 2020 (n 153) 4.

157 Franziska Arnold-Dwyer, *Insurable Interest and the Law* (Routledge 2020), 128–131.

158 IPCC 2022 Mitigation Report, Summary for Policymakers [15.6.4]; Nikolas Scherer, 'How to Advance Regional Climate Risk Insurances,' Climate Diplomacy Policy Brief (June 2017) <https://climate-diplomacy.org/sites/default/files/2020-10/adelphi_2017_climate%20risk%20insurances_policy%20brief_nikolas%20scherer.pdf> accessed on 1 June 2023; Rosemary Forest, 'Climate Risk Insurance: Transparency, Participation and Accountability. An Overview Assessment of Regional Risk Pools' Munich Climate Insurance Initiative' (2018) <https://collections.unu.edu/view/UNU:6705#viewAttachments> accessed on 1 June 2023.

face difficult trade-offs when they divert scarce fiscal resources into premium payments for risks that may or may not materialise.[159] Traditionally, not all of the regional risk pools have provided frameworks or required plans to be in place for how pay-outs are to be applied in a post-disaster situation, and have not been focused on risk management and risk-reducing adaptation measures.[160] This is, however, changing. For example, the ARC has always required post-disaster risk contingency planning as a condition of coverage.[161] CCRIF is using early warning systems that provide alerts to the population prior to severe weather events to inform preparedness activities. This is key to reducing damage and other negative impacts on population, infrastructure, and animals/livestock associated with rainfall and hurricane events. CCRIF is also making contributions to flood walls and other adaptation infrastructure.[162] However, one of the most significant limitations of regional risk pools remains their self-limiting geographical reach, and even within their territorial scope they do not reach all affected households and industry sectors. Many developing and least developed countries vulnerable to climate change risks do not have any or insufficient natural catastrophe insurance protection.

9.5.2 Global initiatives

Could a risk pool operating on a global basis be the answer? As long ago as 2015, Schoenmaker and Zachmann advocated for a global risk pool with contributions from all countries to help countries that are most vulnerable to climate risks to recover from extreme climate events more quickly.[163] The Paris Agreement recognises the importance of insurance instruments in 'addressing loss and damage associated with the adverse effects of climate change.'[164] At COP27, after decades of pressure from climate-vulnerable developing countries, the COP27 parties agreed on the establishment of a Loss and Damage Fund which aims to provide financial assistance, including through catastrophe risk insurance and catastrophe bonds, to those countries.[165] The Loss and Damage Transitional Committee tasked with operationalising the new fund was established 1 March 2023.[166] It will make recommendations on the design of the Loss and Damage Fund and the expanded sources of funding.[167] A number of countries (including Scotland, Denmark, Germany, Austria, Ireland, and Belgium) and philanthropies have already

159 Scherer 2017 (n 158) 4; Sönke Kreft and Laura Schäfer, 'The G20' s Role on Climate Risk Insurance & Pooling: Weathering Climate Change through Climate Risk Transfer Solutions' (2018); cited in IPCC 2022 Mitigation Report, Summary for Policymakers [5.6.4].

160 Scherer 2017 (n 158) 7–8.

161 Ibid 3.

162 CCRIF (n 149).

163 Dirk Schoenmaker and Georg Zachmann, 'Can a Global Climate Risk Pool Help the Most Vulnerable Countries?' (2015) Bruegel Policy Brief <http://aei.pitt.edu/69703/1/pb-2015_041.pdf> accessed on 1 June 2023.

164 Paris Agreement art 8(4)(f).

165 UN Framework Convention on Climate Change, Funding arrangements for responding to loss and damage associated with the adverse effects of climate change (adopted at COP27 in 2022) Decision 2/CP.27 <https://unfccc.int/sites/default/files/resource/cma4_auv_8f.pdf> accessed on 1 June 2023.

166 United Nations Climate Change, 'Transitional Committee on Loss and Damage Begins Work with Successful First Meeting in Egypt' (April 2023) <https://unfccc.int/news/transitional-committee-on-loss-and-damage-begins-work-with-successful-first-meeting-in-egypt> accessed on 1 June 2023.

167 UN Framework Convention on Climate Change (n 165).

made funding pledges but there remains a large (and widening) adaptation finance gap.[168] Estimated annual adaptation costs and needs are in the range of US$160–340 billion by 2030 and US$315–565 billion by 2050, which is currently between five and ten times higher than international adaptation finance flows.[169]

Insurance-based instruments are likely to be an important, but not the only, tool in a multi-layered structure of the Loss and Damage Fund. Although the Transitional Committee has not yet made any recommendation and has not given any indication as to the role of insurance in the Loss and Damage Fund, there are a number of existing initiatives that could be part of an emerging insurance-based solution.

Insurance Development Forum ('IDF'): the IDF is a public-private partnership led by the insurance industry and supported by international organisations. The IDF was first announced at the COP21 in Paris and was officially launched by leaders of the United Nations, the World Bank, and the insurance industry in 2016. The IDF's aim is to improve global risk understanding to create resilience platforms for sustainable growth and human dignity. It is a forum for bringing together the insurance industry and all relevant stakeholders to improve global resilience and address protection gaps.

InsuResilience Global Partnership: the InsuResilience Global Partnership for Climate and Disaster Risk Finance and Insurance Solutions ('InsuResilience') was launched at the 2017 UN Climate Change Conference in Bonn. It is a collaboration led by the V20[170] and G20+ countries and has now more than 120 members from countries, civil society, international organisations, the private sector (including the insurance industry: Allianz, Axa, Europe Re, Munich Re, Nat Re, Scor, Swiss Re, and the IDF), and academia. InsuResilience aims to promote and enable the adoption of climate and disaster risk finance and insurance ('CDRFI') approaches as part of comprehensive disaster risk management strategies and integrated within preparedness, response, and recovery plans that are anchored in national systems through:

- developing a global multi-stakeholder community that can generate and promote best practice in the use of CDRFI;
- facilitating efficient and co-ordinated global action to promote CDRFI solutions;
- empowering governments, businesses, and households to become proactive risk managers through building capability and increasing access to

168 United Nations Environment Programme, 'What You Need to Know about the COP27 Loss and Damage Fund' <https://www.unep.org/news-and-stories/story/what-you-need-know-about-cop27-loss-and-damage-fund> accessed on 1 June 2023; Kate Abnett, 'Factbox: COP27: Which Countries Have Offered "Loss and Damage" Funds?' (*Reuters*, 8 November 2022).

169 United Nations Environment Programme, '2022 Adaptation Gap Report: Too Little Too Slow' (November 2022) <https://www.unep.org/resources/adaptation-gap-report-2022> accessed on 1 June 2023.

170 The V20 countries are countries with climate-vulnerable economies, including Afghanistan, Bangladesh, Barbados, Benin, Bhutan, Burkina Faso, Cambodia, Chad, Colombia, Comoros, Costa Rica, Côte d'Ivoire, the Democratic Republic of the Congo, the Dominican Republic, Eswatini, Ethiopia, Fiji, the Gambia, Ghana, Grenada, Guatemala, Guinea, Guyana, Haiti, Honduras, Kenya, Kiribati, Kyrgyzstan, Lebanon, Liberia, Madagascar, Malawi, the Maldives, the Marshall Islands, Mongolia, Morocco, Nepal, Nicaragua, Niger, Palau, Palestine, Papua New Guinea, the Philippines, Rwanda, Saint Lucia, Samoa, Senegal, South Sudan, Sri Lanka, the Sudan, Tanzania, Timor-Leste, Tunisia, Tuvalu, Uganda, Vanuatu, Vietnam, and Yemen.

knowledge and expertise, services, products, and risk financing linked to disaster prevention, preparedness, and response;
- building a network across sustainable development, social protection, disaster risk reduction, climate services, and climate change adaptation communities to ensure risk financing is embedded within a comprehensive disaster risk management approach – both with respect to international fora as well as to in-country systems;
- taking a pro-poor approach, based on an agreed set of principles, that puts peoples' needs at the centre of risk financing.[171]

Since its inception, InsuResilience has supported 24 implementing programmes (including ARC, CCRIF, PCRAFI, and SEADRIF) with 324 projects in 108 countries.[172]

Global Shield against Climate Risks ('Global Shield'): the Global Shield initiative was launched by Germany with the support of the other G7 countries at COP27. Building upon the work of InsuResilience, Global Shield will bundle activities in the field of climate risk insurance and prevention in close co-operation with the V20. The aim of Global Shield is to provide and facilitate more and better pre-arranged protection against climate and disaster risks.[173] To achieve this, Global Shield aims to close urgent protection gaps in countries by designing, funding, and facilitating interventions, based on the following building blocks:

- strengthened co-ordination within the global CDRFI architecture across G7, V20, and other climate-vulnerable economies to ensure coherence of different institutions' and donors' efforts at global, regional, and national levels;
- a global, flexible, and collaborative financing structure to mobilise and pool respective donor and other funds and enable a more systematic global approach to closing protection gaps;
- sustained protection in the face of increasing climate risks by scaling up existing successful CDRFI programmes and preparing country-specific, needs-based CDRFI support packages, including the scaling up of smart premium and capital support to address affordability barriers.[174]

All interventions will be based on national ownership and will be tailored to local circumstances in 'country support packages': starting with a systematic analysis of a country's

171 InsuResilience Global Partnership, 'Concept Note: Shaping the InsuResilience Global Partnership' (May 2018) <https://www.insuresilience.org/wp-content/uploads/2022/10/20180502_Concept-Note_InsuResilience-Global-Partnership.pdf> accessed on 1 June 2023.

172 InsuResilience Global Partnership, 'Implementation: Programmes & Projects' <https://www.insuresilience.org/implementation/programmes-projects/#projects> accessed on 1 June 2023.

173 Global Shield against Climate Risks, 'Vision & Mission' <https://www.globalshield.org/about/vision-mission/> accessed on 1 June 2023.

174 German Federal Ministry for Economic Cooperation and Development, 'A Joint G7 and V20 Ambition: Working towards a Global Shield against Climate Risks' <https://www.bmz.de/resource/blob/122148/dd6e2de2c73cc601344b1461cf62042b/global-shield-information-note-v20-g7-data.pdf#:~:text=Covering%20support%20gaps%20through%20additional%20GS-focused%20financing%20provided,CVF%20%26%20V20%20Joint%20Multi-Donor%20Fund%20%28V20%20JMDF%293> accessed on 1 June 2023.

protection gaps, Global Shield will facilitate instruments designed to provide rapid financial relief directly to households and businesses to respond to disaster-related losses, or pre-arranged finance instruments for governments, humanitarian agencies, and non-governmental organisations for disaster preparedness and rapid response. Depending on a country's readiness for these instruments, Global Shield will facilitate different types of support from various sources to help countries access the needed instruments sustainably. Technical assistance will be available to support policy reforms, CDRFI strategies, strengthened regulatory frameworks, and capacity building. Financial assistance will be available to build in-country systems like adaptive social safety nets, capitalise risk carriers, and (co)finance insurance premiums.[175] Global Shield envisages a risk tower that consists of a bottom layer for high-frequency/low-severity risks retained by the relevant country (where losses are financed from each country's own budget), a middle layer for which credit-based risk financing instruments can be made available through the Global Shield, and a top layer for catastrophic risks that allows for risk transfer through sovereign risk pools and cat bonds supported by the Global Shield.[176] Global Shield's approach is aligned to CRD because it seeks to integrate the closing of protection gaps with climate change adaptation and loss resilience strategies, leveraging their independence, to support sustainable development in the V20 countries.[177]

The Global Shield received initial funding commitments of around EUR170 million from Germany and more than EUR40 million from other countries.[178] It incorporates three complementary financing vehicles, namely the Global Shield Solutions Platform managed by the Frankfurt School of Finance and Management;[179] the Global Shield Financing Facility managed by the World Bank;[180] and the Climate Vulnerable Forum and V20 Joint Multi-Donor Fund.

Although Global Shield has stated that it will work together with existing CDRFI programmes to seek 'coherence and maximum impact,'[181] the delineation of the respective remits of InsuResilience and Global Shield is not clear-cut. It seems that Global Shield will operate the financing facilities to implement CDRFI projects and subsidise premiums, whereas InsuResilience takes a more technical advice-oriented and facilitative role. Like InsuResilience, Global Shield wants to mobilise the private sector – including the insurance industry – to deliver risk analytics, design products and triggers, and underwrite respective risk transfer solutions.[182] The Global Shield-Solutions Platform is currently

175 Global Shield against Climate Risks, 'FAQ: How Does the Global Shield Work?' <https://www.globalshield.org/resources/faq/> accessed on 1 June 2023.

176 Global Shield against Climate Risks, 'Instruments' <https://www.globalshield.org/activities/instruments/> accessed on 1 June 2023.

177 See Chapter 2, Section 2.4.1.

178 German Federal Ministry for Economic Cooperation and Development, 'V20 and G7 Jointly Launch Global Shield against Climate Risks at COP27' (Press Release 14 November 2022) <https://www.bmz.de/en/issues/climate-change-and-development/global-shield-against-climate-risks> accessed on 1 June 2023.

179 Global Shield Solutions Platform, 'Improving Resilience to Climate Change' <https://global-shield-solutions.org/about/about-global-shield> accessed on 1 June 2023.

180 The World Bank, 'World Bank Group Launches Global Shield Financing Facility to Help Developing Countries Adapt to Climate Change' (Press Release 14 November 2022) <https://www.worldbank.org/en/news/press-release/2022/11/14/world-bank-group-launches-global-shield-financing-facility-to-help-developing-countries-adapt-to-climate-change> accessed on 1 June 2023.

181 Global Shield against Climate Risks (n 175).

182 Ibid.

looking for a variety of 'implementing partners.'[183] The Global Risk Modelling Alliance – an initiative run under the umbrella of the IDF – has already been selected as a key resource to prepare and provide climate and disaster risk information to Global Shield.[184]

The emerging CDRFI landscape relies on technical advisory and implementation support and funding from a variety of sources co-ordinated on a centralised global level but is tailored to and implemented with country-specific packages. This is a development to be welcomed. Some would argue that more or less sporadic donations from developed countries are not enough to sustain InsuResilience and Global Shield if all V20 countries are to have sustained protection against increasing climate risks. As noted above, the 2022 Adaptation Gap Report shows that there is a significant adaptation finance gap. This is why the Loss and Damage Transitional Committee has been tasked to look into a broadened donor base and innovative finance tools. There is an expectation – as can already be seen from the Global Shield and InsuResilience initiatives – that the insurance industry contributes with its expertise in relation to structuring CDRFI projects and underwriting risk transfer solutions. There is no publicly available information confirming whether the insurance sector is already or will be providing additional risk capital or any other funding to Global Shield.[185]

InsuResilience and Global Shield are important initiatives to implement a more co-ordinated global approach to CDRFI driven by the governments of the main donor countries and the V20 countries. Progress is dependent on diplomacy, policies, and international co-operation, balanced against the national interests of the countries that participate. The insurance sector cannot take the driving seat in matters of international relations between countries. Participating insurers cannot leverage their contractual relationships with policyholders at the household level to influence policyholders' behaviours and risk attitudes when they are contracting with countries. In the layered approach envisaged by Global Shield, an insurer may just be a comparatively small risk carrier in a layered CDRFI structure for a V20 country where the overall support package, including any risk reduction measures to be taken, is negotiated and ultimately determined by Global Shield. However, insurers can still lend their technical assistance to inform pre-loss risk management and risk-reducing adaptation measures, as well as structuring products and triggers and underwriting respective risk transfer solutions. With a smaller part to play in the overall scheme, less immediate control over the risks which insurers may be insuring and the measures taken to address uninsurability, the role of insurers in the InsuResilience and Global Shield initiatives is perhaps better described as that of a junior partner supporting the efforts of the governments, rather than an enabling role vis-à-vis policyholders. It may be possible that, once the specific country support packages have been put in place, insurers can regain some control over the ongoing CDRFI process. Insurers can also take the

183 Global Shield Solutions Platform, 'CDRFI Implementing Partners' <https://global-shield-solutions.org/what-we-support> accessed on 1 June 2023.

184 Insurance Development Forum, 'COP27: IDF Media Communique' (21 November 2022) <https://www.insdevforum.org/3888-2/> accessed on 1 June 2023.

185 A meeting note of the InsuResilience Global Partnership 7th High-Level Consultative Group Meeting on 14 October 2022 records: 'The private sector backed the Global Shield by offering quality risk analytics and enhanced public-private coordination of financial protection, and by reaffirming the commitment of providing 5 billion US dollars in additional risk capital by 2025,' but there is no further information on the provenance and payment of this amount.

lead on insurance and resilience structures outside the InsuResilience and Global Shield initiatives, for example by sponsoring CRD Bonds.[186]

9.6 Conclusion

The enabling conception put forward in Chapter 3 pictures the insurance industry as supporting policyholders, investee companies, and other stakeholders in their net-zero transition. This chapter has highlighted that the insurance industry cannot on its own address protection gaps, knowledge gaps, and funding gaps in relation to climate change risks. At national and regional levels, Climate Risk PPParts can be an effective way for insurers and governments to work together to ensure that insurance protection against local climate risks remains available and affordable, as well building resilience against loss at the policyholder level. A Climate Risk PPPart is a mutually beneficial co-operation between a segment of the insurance industry, government, and mortgage lenders to benefit policyholders and society at large. Climate Risk PPParts can close or reduce protection gaps, ensure that property vulnerable to physical climate risk remains insurable, allow government agencies to draw on the insurance industry's distribution and claims services network to reach policyholders, and facilitate the implementation of climate change mitigation and adaptation measures at policyholder level.

Addressing protection gaps affecting the most vulnerable (V20) countries requires a coherent, systematic, and global approach to CDRFI solutions. The InsuResilience and Global Shield initiatives are seeking to strengthen co-ordination within the global CDRFI architecture across G7, V20, and other climate-vulnerable economies to ensure the coherence of different institutions' and donors' efforts at the global, regional, and national levels. The insurance industry is a key, but junior, partner in those initiatives where it is relied upon by governments to provide technical assistance in structuring CDRFI solutions and providing underwriting capacity. Importantly, the emerging global initiatives take a CRD-aligned approach that combines addressing protection gaps with resilience building to support sustainable development in the least developed countries.

186 See Chapter 8, Section 8.5.1.

CHAPTER 10

Conclusion

Insurers as climate action enablers

This book has put forward the case for a new vision of the role of the insurance industry in fighting climate change: insurers are not just risk carriers in relation to climate risks, they can be enablers of climate action who support their policyholders, investees, and other stakeholders in their transition to a net-zero economy. Insurers can enable climate action through climate-related impact underwriting and investments.

Rationales

There are important societal reasons why the insurance industry should participate in combating climate change and its effects:

- climate change is a global emergency that requires international co-operation and the participation of all stakeholders, and in particular the involvement of financial institutions and institutional investors, for a global transition to a net-zero economy;
- climate change risks are complex risks that require multi-directional collective action not only to make such risks more manageable, but also to legitimise the actions taken to address such risks;
- if left unaddressed, climate change risks exacerbate protection gaps which, in turn, can have cascading effects on economic activities, supply chains, the performance of loans and investments across the financial system, and the economy as a whole.

Insurers should be incentivised to engage in climate-related impact underwriting and investments for risk management, business opportunity, competition, and reputational reasons:

- insurers who provide cover for climate-related losses have an incentive to help their policyholders in their efforts to protect themselves from losses resulting from climate risks;
- the ever-increasing frequency and severity of climate risks could lead to limited reinsurance capacity and create reinsurance protection gaps, and catastrophic claims could deplete an insurer's financial resources;

DOI: 10.4324/b23081-10

- as average annualised losses increase as a result of a build-up in climate risk, insurers might either pass on the cost of higher claims into premiums, or refuse to renew insurance for some policyholders. If insurers do not respond effectively, climate risks could cause a persistent and material drag on their profitability which could make individual insurers more vulnerable to other shocks that can impact their financial stability;
- there are new business opportunities in providing insurance cover for green technologies and infrastructure projects and offering insurance products with environmental objectives or other green characteristics;
- climate-related impact investments may produce returns equal to, or better than, conventional investments. Emerging theoretical research and (tentative) empirical evidence suggest that 'greeniums' are already priced into the value of companies that commit to reducing GHG emissions;
- climate-related investment can diversify an insurer's investment portfolio, and divestment from fossil fuel assets can reduce the risk of the portfolio carrying stranded assets;
- the emerging climate and sustainability-related disclosure regimes will allow investors and customers to distinguish between insurers who do and who do not engage in climate-related impact underwriting and investment. An insurer who does not engage in climate-related impact underwriting and investment may compare unfavourably to its competitors and could lose market share as well as investors;
- climate-related impact underwriting and investment can reduce an insurer's exposure to reputational damage and environmental litigation risk. Investment decisions to invest in fossil fuel assets have already been challenged in courts.

Climate-related impact underwriting

Climate-related impact underwriting entails that insurers apply their data, expertise, and risk assessment capacity to influence policyholders to mitigate and adapt to climate change risks via risk-based pricing and contractual terms, and that insurers consider measures that contribute to climate change mitigation and adaptation in product design, underwriting strategy, and claims management. Climate-related impact underwriting can take various forms: insuring green, not insuring brown, and greening insurance. 'Insuring green' is concerned with insurers providing insurance cover for technologies and infrastructure projects that provide climate change mitigation and adaptation solutions. Insuring green has presented new business opportunities which the insurance industry is embracing, and it enables the development and operation of, and investment in, green technologies and infrastructure projects.

'Not insuring brown' is more controversial: a rapid and disorderly withdrawal from insuring fossil fuel assets and activities could endanger energy security and could disrupt supply chains for key industries, such as transport, manufacturing, and construction. On the other hand, continuing to underwrite fossil fuel assets and activities is inconsistent with the goals of the Paris Agreement and harmful to policyholders who are increasingly facing protection gaps as a result of climate change and potentially creating systemic risk for the economy. While a significant proportion of the primary insurance market has withdrawn or reduced cover for coal operations, withdrawal from oil and gas underwriting is much more limited and complicated by political pressure put on insurers in some jurisdictions. Some commentators have argued that negative screening – such as not insuring brown or not investing in fossil fuel projects – lacks additionality because it does not contribute to positive sustainable outcomes. It is suggested that the better view is that negative screening can generate additionality through the reduction of harm, but it is a disabling, rather than an enabling, approach to influencing investee companies.

'Greening insurance' has attracted little attention in the literature to date, and the insurance industry is only just starting to instrumentalise contractual relationships with policyholders to shift their behaviour and processes from generating to reducing GHG emissions, and to encourage them to implement climate risk adaptation measures. Anchored in the contractual relationships between an insurer and its policyholders, there is enormous potential for insurers to provide practical support to their consumer and business policyholders for making better-informed choices aimed at reducing GHG emissions, to engage with policyholders who are involved in environmentally harmful activities about bringing such activities to end, and to incentivise policyholders to take adaptation measures that make their properties more resilient to climate change-related weather risks. Throughout the value chain, there are key points of engagement when the insurer can influence a policyholder. In this book, key 'enabling' approaches and tools for greening insurance have been identified and analysed, including raising policyholder awareness of climate risk and climate change mitigation and adaptation measures, assessing policyholders' climate-related risk profiles at the pre-contractual stage, price signalling, exercising influence through terms and conditions, and green claims. Proposals for insurance products and policy features that can support policyholders to take climate action were made in Chapter 7.

On the international stage, the insurance industry is a key partner in the InsuResilience and Global Shield initiatives where they are relied upon by governments and international organisations to provide technical assistance in structuring CDRFI solutions and providing underwriting capacity.

Climate-related impact investment

Climate-related impact investment consists of investment strategies that generate positive and measurable climate impact by (1) providing additional capital to actively contribute to climate change solutions, and (2) applying positive and exclusionary criteria to the selection of investments to achieve climate goals, alongside achieving an acceptable financial return. Climate change mitigation investment aims to reduce global GHG emissions, while climate change adaptation investments are concerned with alleviating the consequences of climate change. By providing capital to the investee company, an insurer qua investor can enable the investee company to produce goods or provide services, or adjust its operations, so as to contribute to climate change mitigation or adaptation. Conversely, withholding investment or divesting from fossil fuel projects can disable an investee company from pursuing fossil fuel activities and can thus indirectly contribute to the reduction of further harm.

Investor stewardship – seeking to engage with investee companies to promote climate change mitigation and adaptation measures to be taken by the investee – is an effective enabling approach for equity investors who can exercise voting rights and file shareholder resolutions, and for direct lenders who can exert influence through contractual rights against borrowers under loan documentation and security interests over the borrower's assets. Engagement can be more effective than making investment or divestment decisions since engagement strategies can communicate more clearly what the investee company should change. However, insurers will frequently invest through debt securities traded on public bond markets which do not structurally lend themselves to direct engagement and give insurers qua investors little leverage to influence climate-related decisions at the investee entity level. For insurers, stewardship will be most effective in relation to equity investments.

Regulatory landscape

Regulatory approaches to climate change risk, climate-related impact underwriting, and investment are circumscribed by a regulatory authority's mandate and regulatory objectives, as well as the wider environmental policies of the jurisdiction or legal framework in which it operates. A common theme of the IAIS, PRA, and EIOPA has been that the initial regulatory focus was on inward impact – the financial risks stemming from climate change on individual insurers' balance sheets and the financial stability of the financial system as a whole – and how this inward impact could be assessed and integrated into existing risk governance and management structures. This is an important and ongoing process to ensure that individual insurers and the financial system are resilient to climate-related financial risks. This approach indirectly supports the enabling role of insurers as only financially resilient insurers can provide cover for green technologies and infrastructure projects and pay claims for climate-related losses and climate action support to their policyholders, investees, and other stakeholders.

A second focus of regulatory activity has been the disclosure and reporting of climate-related financial risks and sustainability-related issues. Disclosures on these matters are intended to enable policyholders and investors to make better-informed choices and to foster competition between insurers. The emerging disclosure regimes support the enabling role of insurers because making climate-related disclosures (1) can increase awareness of climate action, (2) set an example to other insurers, and (3) in relation to product disclosures, serve as an invitation for customers to act on climate change. The main building blocks of the FCA's climate-related disclosure requirements applicable to UK-regulated insurers are TCFD-aligned disclosures for listed insurers and in-scope life insurers, and the proposed sustainability-related disclosures and investment labels which apply to in-scope life insurers who provide IBIPs and their IBIPs. The disclosure concept of 'double materiality' – disclosure of environmental inward and outward impact – remains of limited application. General insurers and non-IBIP life insurers do not need to make disclosures on their outward impact, such as climate-related impact underwriting and investment activities, and climate action at the operational level, and do not need to green-label their products. Non-financial reporting under the Companies Act 2006 is focused on the inward impact of climate-related financial risks and opportunities. This limited approach to disclosures is not sufficiently supportive of the enabling role of insurers since it fails to enhance transparency in relation to the environmental impact of a large segment of insurers and their products.

In contrast, the EU is building a sustainability disclosure regime (based on the SFDR, the CSRD, and the EU Taxonomy) that is firmly focused on double materiality and thereby raises the bar for insurers to take an enabling role. The SFDR requires, inter alia, disclosure of adverse environmental impacts of in-scope insurers and the environmental characteristics of their in-scope products, but it does not apply to insurers and intermediaries that do not provide or advise on IBIPs. The CSRD applies to all EU companies that meet the size thresholds and requires, inter alia, disclosure of the main actual or potential adverse environmental impacts connected with the company's own operations and with its value chain, including its products and services, its business relationships, and its supply chain, and the actions taken to prevent, mitigate, remediate, or bring an end such adverse impacts. The EU Taxonomy provides a classification and definition system for environmentally sustainable economic activities for the purposes of establishing whether an investment is environmentally sustainable. Non-life insurance that covers climate-related perils has been included as an economic activity that can make a substantial contribution to climate change adaptation if it meets some or all of the technical screening criteria which broadly correspond to insuring green, not insuring brown, and greening insurance.

There is a more fragmented picture with regard to whether and how prudential regulation should be supporting and incentivising impact underwriting and impact investment through favourable regulatory capital treatment. The Bank of England and the PRA see no convincing case for capital requirements being used for addressing the causes of climate change – either by introducing 'carbon penalising factors' and/or 'green supporting factors' for exposures to assets or counterparties that are respectively more or less carbon-intensive. EIOPA is currently assessing the prudential treatment of climate change adaptation measures in non-life insurance, and together with the EBA will give further consideration to the capital treatment of investments associated with environmental and/or social objectives. While favourable prudential treatment of climate-related impact underwriting and investment is likely to boost their uptake by insurers, there is not yet sufficient data and science-based evidence which link environmental considerations to a reduction in the underwriting risk or the financial risk associated with the project or asset to be insured or invested in.

The regulatory landscape is also characterised by diverging developments in different jurisdictions, the most prominent examples of which are the EU's CSDDD proposal and the anti-ESG legislation in some US states. The CSDDD will be seeking to introduce a corporate duty to identify, bring to an end, prevent, mitigate, and account for negative human rights and environmental impacts in a company's own operations, their subsidiaries, and business relationships in their value chains. In stark contrast, the US 'Boycott Bills' seek to curtail negative screening underwriting and investment approaches by prohibiting the relevant US state from (1) doing business with financial institutions that boycott or discriminate against companies in certain (e.g. fossil fuel) industries, and/or (2) investing the state's assets (including pension plan assets) through such financial institutions. Diverging regulatory approaches and standards represent an obstacle to an enabling role for insurers that operate internationally.

The IAIS, the Bank of England, and EIOPA recognise that climate change is a global issue that requires co-ordinated regulatory approaches and standard setting at the international level across the financial services sector and consultation with the financial services industry. This multi-lateral and multi-sectoral approach has already been tested in relation to disclosure and reporting. The FSB is going to issue guidance on supervisory and regulatory approaches across borders and sectors to address market fragmentation and potential sources of systemic risk. It has been argued that convergence on clear regulatory objectives and a common commitment to the implementation of the objectives of the Paris Agreement are key steps towards international regulatory standards that support an enabling role of insurers and the insurance industry.

Challenges and barriers

One of the key findings in the IPCC's 6th Synthesis Report was that effective climate action requires political commitment, well-aligned multi-level governance and institutional frameworks, laws, policies, and funding. There are a number of legal challenges in relation to climate-related impact underwriting and investment that would need to be addressed to enhance the enabling role of insurers and to achieve a better alignment of insurance legal and regulatory frameworks to the goals of the Paris Agreement. Some of them have easy fixes. This is not the place to repeat the discussion from the preceding chapters but it is worth listing the top five legal challenges faced by insurers:

1. the legal uncertainty relating to corporate purpose and the directors' duty to act in good faith in the way most likely to promote the success of the company for the benefit of its members as a whole, and in particular to what extent short-term profit goals can be overridden by mid- and long-term strategic decisions that take into account climate change and environmental considerations;
2. competition law issues arising from collective action by insurers;
3. the potential unfavourable regulatory capital treatment of climate-related impact investments, and the absence of regulatory capital incentives to engage in climate-related impact underwriting and investment;
4. the compliance burden of the complex and diverging sustainability-related disclosure regimes at the UK, EU, and international levels and between different types of insurers and insurance products;
5. staying clear of product green-washing in the absence of sustainability criteria or a labelling regime applicable to insurance products (other than IBIPs).

The corporate purpose and directors' duty issue (Point 1) will be addressed in the EU as and when the CSDDD enters into force and is implemented: the CSDDD would establish a corporate due diligence duty to identify, bring to an end, prevent, mitigate, and account for negative human rights and environmental impacts in the company's own operations, their subsidiaries, and their value chains. Directors of in-scope companies, when fulfilling their duty to act in the best interest of the company, will need to take into account the human rights, climate change, and environmental consequences of their decisions in the short, medium, and long term. However, for an EU insurer with a US subsidiary compliance with the corporate due diligence duty under the CSDDD might be inconsistent with what is in the best interest of the US subsidiary in terms of shareholder value maximisation and in light of the potential consequences of certain ESG activities under the US anti-ESG legislation. International convergence on this matter is unlikely in the short term as the corporate responsibility and corporate purpose debate has become highly politicised, riven by jurisdiction-specific policies and grounded in legal tradition-specific corporate purpose philosophies.

The allegation of competition law issues (Point 2) has diminished the NZIA. Although the legal basis for the allegation is reportedly considered weak, the political pressure, litigation, and reputational issues in connection with such allegations are risks that need to be managed by insurers and it is therefore not surprising that many have taken a cautious view of quitting the NZIA. Yet, in order to raise ambition and implement climate-related underwriting and investment practices, there is a need to collaborate and not just rely on individual action. The UK CMA's draft guidance acknowledges that the setting of non-binding targets or ambitions for the whole industry with regard to environmental sustainability objectives is unlikely to have an appreciable negative effect on competition. However, the EU competition guidance on 'sustainability agreements' is less clear, and, in the US, groups of State Attorney Generals have raised concerns about anti-trust law violations by NZIA members and asset managers. Clarity and convergence on the competition law treatment of industry collaborations to tackle climate change would be a key step towards insurers taking a greater enabling role in the net-zero transition. Such convergence is, however, unlikely to be forthcoming in the near future given the politicisation of ESG issues in the US. US anti-ESG legislation and political pressure dressed up as investigations of anti-trust law violations make it difficult for insurers with US business to reduce or fully withdraw from investing in fossil fuel assets and to engage in collaborative stewardship.

As regards the capital treatment of climate-related impact investment by insurers (Point 3), the PPP imposes limitations on the extent and types of climate-related impact investments. Moreover, the current regulatory capital treatment of climate-related impact investments is not favourable: the current eligibility criteria for matching adjustments are considered to hinder green investments that do not produce a fixed cash flow (which would be the case for green infrastructure projects that go through a construction phase and/or have staggered completion phases) and do not have any rating or a rating below BBB. Forthcoming UK reforms to the matching adjustment requirements are intended to release capital for green investments: they will broaden matching adjustment eligibility criteria and replace the requirement that all eligible assets must have fixed cashflows with a more flexible requirement that they have highly predictable cash flows. The reforms also seek to introduce a 'notched allowances' approach to the fundamental spread by giving scaled allowances to different credit ratings. As noted above, the Bank of England and the PRA see no convincing case for capital requirements being used for rewarding climate-related impact underwriting and investment and penalising the underwriting of, and investments in, carbon-intense assets, whereas the EBA and EIOPA are still assessing the case. This is an area to watch over the next two years, with potentially diverging routes being taken by the EU and the Bank of England/PRA.

Both the UK and the EU have already created complex and multi-layered sustainability-related disclosure regimes that place a heavy compliance burden on insurers, and a double burden on those insurers who operate in the UK and the EU (Point 4). ESG reporting rules and guidance are also emerging in the US at the federal level, in some states, and in key jurisdictions in Asia, which could lead to a further increase in the reporting burden for globally active companies. The ISSB Sustainability Disclosure Standards seek to facilitate interoperability with disclosures that are jurisdiction-specific or aimed at broader stakeholder groups, and to deliver standards that are cost-effective, decision-useful, and market-informed. The UK government has expressed its support of the Sustainability Disclosure Standards and plans to launch a formal assessment to ensure their suitability for use by UK companies. At the EU level, the CSRD envisages an equivalence regime that will permit reporting under the sustainability reporting standards of a non-EU disclosure regime determined to be 'equivalent' by the European Commission. However, at present it is not known whether the Commission is minded to grant equivalence status to the UK and/or the ISSB Sustainability Disclosure Standards. If insurers are to take an enabling role, regulators across the world should strive for converging or equivalent status disclosure regimes to ease the reporting burden for insurers who operate in a number of jurisdictions.

The fear of green-washing (Point 5), exacerbated by the lack of clear criteria for green or sustainability characteristics that apply to insurance products (other than IBIPs), is a potential impediment to the development of green insurance products and the design of green features for existing insurance products, as well as leading to 'green-blushing' – the deliberate underreporting of environmentally sustainable activities so as not to fall foul of green-washing. In the UK, the sustainable investment labels proposed by the FCA will not apply to insurance products other than IBIPs. An extension of the labelling regime is important to send clear signals to potential policyholders as to which insurance products have green characteristics and objectives. Even if the investment label regime were to be extended to all insurance products, the current proposals do not define 'environmentally sustainable' and 'socially sustainable,' and the sustainability objective of the product is determined by the firm itself. Instead, the FCA's investment label regime relies on broad principles and criteria that are process- and governance-driven, rather than prescriptive on the sustainable merits of the objective the product seeks to achieve. The approach contrasts with the EU Taxonomy approach which is based on a classification of activities that are labelled as 'sustainable.' To increase trust in reported sustainability-related information, data assurance and verifications should be enhanced, for example by giving auditors a clear mandate to review all of a company's sustainability and climate-related reporting and to require them to acquire the skills necessary to carry out such a review.

In addition to the legal challenges, one of the most significant barriers to climate-related impact underwriting, and one which is inextricably linked to the corporate purpose debate and to protection gaps as well as to concerns about fairness to policyholders, is the allocation of costs for climate change mitigation and adaptation measures between insurers (reflected in reduced profits), their policyholders (reflected in increased premium), and society as a whole (via government subsidies funded by taxation). This is not the place to consider distributive justice in the delivery of the UK government's net-zero policies and climate justice at an international level, but a few funding sources and structures to cover impact underwriting funding gaps have been suggested throughout the book:

- policyholders should use government environmental schemes and grants that are already available to them to absorb some of the additional costs of green reinstatement (see Chapter 7, Section 7.7.2);

- insurers could channel some of the released capital from lowered risk margins under the forthcoming reforms into 'greening insurance,' such as climate risk assessments of prospective policyholders, premium discounts and rebates to incentivise or reward the implementation of climate change adaptation measures by policyholders, and green reinstatement (see Chapter 8, Section 8.3.1);
- community-based climate change adaptation measures could be financed through a CRD Bond structure (Chapter 8, Section 8.5.1);
- accumulated premium savings could be applied towards green reinstatement through a green bonus point scheme for property insurance policies (Chapter 8, Section 5.1.2);
- blended sources of funding, including from government, mortgage lenders, policyholder levies, and insurer contributions, could be channelled through a Climate Risk Public-Private Partnership risk pool (Chapter 9, Section 9.4.3).

None of these funding sources is a panacea for the impact underwriting funding gap, but they highlight that the costs of climate change mitigation and adaptation measures need to be spread, including to stakeholders – such as mortgage lenders – who are not necessarily a party to the insurance contract. It has also been observed that new technologies can be harnessed for climate-related impact underwriting (such as climate risk assessments, use-based insurance products, enhanced data collection, and risk modelling) to reduce costs and achieve environmental outcomes.

Outlook

This book is concluding more pessimistically than it was begun: the IPCC warned earlier this year that the temperature goal to limit the temperature increase to 1.5°C above pre-industrial levels is unlikely to be met during the 21st century. The UK's Climate Change Committee's confidence in the UK meeting its goals from 2030 onwards is now significantly lower than it was in its previous assessment in 2022. The first-ever global stocktake is set to conclude at the COP28 will show that the we are not on track for meeting the temperature goal of the Paris Agreement. Properties in high-exposure regions are becoming uninsurable as a result of climate risks. The NZIA has lost key members, and insurers in the US are under political and legal pressure not to withdraw from underwriting fossil fuel assets and activities.

Yet there are positive developments: the emerging sustainability-related disclosure regimes have raised awareness amongst insurers inter se, their investors, and (potential) customers of the contributions that insurers can make, and are making, in the global fight against climate change. The insurance market is developing innovative insurance products for new technologies, services, and infrastructure that reduce or neutralise GHG emissions and improve resilience to climate risks. Insurers and insurance brokers have also started to develop insurance products that support the net zero transition. Most large insurers have now withdrawn from insuring new coal projects. The idea that insurers should become more involved in climate resilience building is gaining momentum. Insurance regulators now recognise the relevance of the climate action enabling role of insurers to the integrity of the financial system to closing protection gaps, and have started to consider regulatory tools to bolster this role.

The key challenges and opportunities ahead for the insurance industry are (1) in partnership with governments and other stakeholders, to maintain the insurability of property exposed to climate risks and to reduce climate risk protection gaps, (2) to develop affordable retail insurance products that help policyholders to transition to a net-zero economy and to build resilience against climate risks, (3) to develop business insurance products that foster climate change mitigation and adaptation measures and are aligned to the commercial and financial interests of their policyholders, (4) to raise climate risk awareness and provide information on climate risk management to policyholders in order to mainstream policyholder climate action, (5) to withdraw from fossil fuel underwriting in a sustainable manner that supports fossil fuel customers in their transition to net-zero operations, and (6) to develop and implement investor and macro stewardship approaches to work together with investors, governments, regulators, and other stakeholders on climate change mitigation and adaptation strategies and on financing an equitable transition to a global net-zero economy.

In order to make progress, insurers will need to work together with their policyholders, governments, regulators, non-governmental organisations, the scientific community and academia, and key players in their own value and supply chains (brokers, reinsurers, model and data providers, loss adjusters, and lawyers) and, subject to competition restrictions, with each other. Advances in technology, such as advanced analytics, digitalisation, blockchain, the Internet of Things, and AI, have the potential to drive efficiency and enhance quality throughout the insurance value chain. Effective climate action by insurers and their 'enabled' policyholders is also deeply dependent on factors outside their control: it requires political commitment, adequate funding, and legal and regulatory frameworks that are well-aligned to the goals of the Paris Agreement and convergent across jurisdictions. The prevalent short-termism in corporate governance and risk governance needs to change towards a greater appreciation of long-term value creation and risk management over a long-term time horizon. Across society, we need a cultural shift towards sustainable behaviours and practices that take a longer-term perspective on our own future needs and the needs of future generations.

BIBLIOGRAPHY

Books

Alexander FH, *Benefit Corporation Law and Governance Pursuing Profit with Purpose* (Berrett-Koehler Publishers Inc 2017)
Arnold-Dwyer F, *Insurable Interest and the Law* (Routledge 2020)
Baird DG, Gertner RH, and Picker RC, *Game theory and the law* (Harvard University Press 1998)
Baker T and Simon J (eds.), *Embracing Risk* (Chicago University Press 2002)
Baker T, Logue KD, and Saiman C, *Insurance Law and Policy* (5th edn, Aspen Publishing 2022)
Beck U, *The Risk Society: Towards a New Modernity* (SAGE Publications Ltd 1992)
Becker GS, *The Economic Approach to Human Behavior* (The University of Chicago Press 1976)
Birds J and Richards K, *Birds' Modern Insurance Law* (12th edn, Sweet & Maxwell 2022)
Birds J, Lynch B, and Paul S, *MacGillivray on Insurance Law* (15th edn, Sweet & Maxwell 2022)
Burling J and Lazarus K (eds.), *Research Handbook on International Insurance Law and Regulation* (Edward Elgar Publishing 2011)
Calster G.V and Reins L (eds), *The Paris Agreement on Climate Change: A Commentary* (Edward Elgar Publishing 2021)
Cheffins B, *Corporate Ownership and Control: British Business Transformed* (OUP 2009)
Chiu I, *The Foundations and Anatomy of Shareholder Activism* (Hart 2010)
Cracknell A and Varotsos C, *Understanding Global Climate Change* (2nd edn, CRC Press 2022)
Davies P, Worthington S and Hare C, *Principles of Modern Company Law* (11th edn, Sweet & Maxwell 2021)
DeSantis R, *The Courage to Be Free: Florida's Blueprint for America's Revival* (Harper Collins 2023)
Ericson RV, Doyle A, Ericson D, and Barry D, *Insurance as Governance* (University of Toronto Press 2003)
Ferrán E and Goodhart C (eds.), *Regulating Financial Services and Markets in the XXIst Century* (Hart Publishing 2001)
Freeman RE, *Strategic Management: A Stakeholder Approach* (Cambridge University Press 2015)
Friedman M, *Capitalism and Freedom* (University of Chicago Press 2002)
Georgosouli A, and Goldby M, *Systemic Risk and the Future of Insurance Regulation* (Routledge 2015)
Gulliver L and Payne J, *Corporate Finance: Principles and Policy* (3rd edn, Hart Publishing 2020)
Hashimzade N, Myles G, and Black J, *Oxford Dictionary of Economics* (5th edn, OUP 2017)
Heimer C, *Reactive Risk and Rational Action: Managing Moral Hazard in Insurance Contracts* (University of California Press 1985)
Hirschman AO, *Exit, Voice, and Loyalty: Responses to Decline in Firms, Organizations, and States. Cambridge* (Harvard University Press 1970)

Holley C, Phelan L and Shearing C (eds), '*Criminology and Climate Insurance, Finance and the Regulation of Harmscapes*' (Routledge, 2020)
Jakupec V and Kelly M, and Makuwira J, *Rethinking Multilateralism in Foreign Aid: Beyond the Neoliberal Hegemony* (Routledge 2020)
Jarzabkowski P, Chalkias K, Cacciatori E and Bednarek R, *Disaster Insurance Reimagined* (OUP 2023)
Jepsen H, Lundgren M, Monheim K and Walker H (eds), *Negotiating the Paris Agreement* (Cambridge University Press 2021)
Jones M, Dugdale A, and Simpson M (QC), *Clerk & Lindsell on Torts* (23rd edn, Sweet & Maxwell 2020)
Lowry J and Rawlings P, *Insurance Law: Cases and Materials* (Hart Publishing 2004)
Mann M, *The New Climate War: The Fight to Take Back Our Planet* (PublicAffairs 2021)
Merkin R, *Colinvaux's Law of Insurance* (13th edn, Sweet & Maxwell 2022)
Merkin R and Steele J, *Insurance and the Law of Obligations* (OUP 2013)
Mullerat R, *Corporate Social Responsibility: The Corporate Governance Responsibility of the 21st Century* (2nd edn, Wolters Kluwer Law and Business 2011)
O'Neill PT, Woloniecki J and Arnold-Dwyer F, *The Law of Reinsurance in England and Bermuda* (5th edn, Sweet & Maxwell 2019)
Porter ME, *Competitive Advantage: Creating and Sustaining Superior Performance* (Free Press 2004)
Renn O, *Risk Governance: Coping with Uncertainty in a Complex World* (Routledge 2008)
Sands P and Peel J, *Principles of International Environmental Law* (4th edn, Cambridge University Press 2018)
Scherer N, *Insuring Against Climate Change: The Emergence of Regional Catastrophe Risk Pools* (Routledge 2020)
Schwab K, *Stakeholder Capitalism* (Wiley 2021)
Shortland A, *Kidnap: Inside the Ransom Business* (OUP 2019)
Siems MM, *Convergence in Shareholder Law* (Cambridge University Press 2008)
Simon J (ed), *Embracing Risk: The Changing Culture of Insurance and Insurability* (University of Chicago Press 2002)
Sjåfjell B, *Company Law and Sustainability Legal Barriers and Opportunities* (Cambridge University Press 2015)
Stern N, '*The Economics of Climate Change: The Stern Review*' (Cambridge University Press, 2007)
Thaler RH and Sunstein CR, *Nudge: Improving Decisions About Health, Wealth and Happiness* (Penguin 2012)

Journal articles

Abraham KS, 'Four Conceptions of Insurance' (2013) 161 Univ Penn Law Rev 653
Abraham KS and Schwarcz D, 'The Limits of Regulation by Insurance' (2023) 98(1) Ind LJ Art. 5
Abramovsky A, 'Reinsurance: The Silent Regulator' (2008) 15 Conn Ins LJ 345
Adams J and Brownsword R, 'The Idealogies of Contract Law' (1987) 7 Legal Stud 205
Addy C, Chorengel M, Collins M, and Etzel M, 'Calculating the Value of Impact Investing' (2019) Harvard Business Review 102
Alessi L, Ossola E and Panzica R, 'What Greenium Matters in the Stock Market? The Role of Greenhouse Gas Emissions and Environmental Disclosures' (2021) 54 J Financ Stab 100869
Armour J, Enriques L and Wetzer T, 'Green Pills: Making Corporate Climate Commitments Credible' (2023) 65 Ariz L Rev 285

Arnold-Dwyer F, 'A Legal Framework for Net-Zero Aligned Insurance Products' (2023) 29(2) Conn Ins LJ 1

Asselt MV and Renn O, 'Risk Governance' (2011) 14(4) J Risk Res 431

Avraham R, 'The Economics of Insurance Law: A Primer' (2012) 19 Conn Ins LJ 29, 37

Barzuza M, Curtis Q and Webber DH, 'Shareholder Value(s): Index Fund ESG Activism and the New Millennial Corporate Governance' (2020) 93 Southern California L Rev 1243

Battiston S, Mandel A, Monasterolo I, Schütze F, and Visentin G, 'A Climate Stress-test of the Financial System' (2017) 7(4) Nat Clim Change 283

Beck U and Lau C, 'Second Modernity as a Research Agenda: Theoretical and Empirical Explorations in the 'Meta-Change' of Modern Society' (2005) 56 (4) Br J Sociol 525

Ben-Shahar O and Logue K.D, 'Outsourcing Regulation: How Insurance Reduces Moral Hazard' (2012) 111 Mich Law Rev 197

Bennett NJ et al., 'Environmental Stewardship: A Conceptual Review and Analytical Framework' (2018) 61(4) Environ Manag 597

Berliner B, 'Large Risks and Limits of Insurability' (1985) 10 Geneva Papers on Risk and Insurance: Issues and Practice 313

Bodansky D, 'The Legal Character of the Paris Agreement' (2016) 25(2) Rev Eur Comp Int Environ Law 142

Boer Jd, Botzen WJW and Terpstra T, 'Flood Risk and Climate Change in the Rotterdam Area, The Netherlands: Enhancing Citizen's Climate Risk Perceptions and Prevention Responses Despite Skepticism' (2016) 16 Reg Environ Change 1613

Bolton P and Kacperczyk M, 'Do Investors Care About Carbon Risk?' (2021) 142(2) J Financ Econ 517

Bovaird T, 'Public-Private Partnerships: from Contested Concepts to Prevalent Practice' (2004) 70(2) Int Rev Admin Sci 199–215

Bowman B, '*Turning Promises into Action: 'Legal Readiness for Climate Finance' and Implementing the Paris Agreement*' (2022) 16 CCLR 41

Brest P and Born K, 'Unpacking the Impact in Impact Investing' (August 2014) Stanford Social Innovation Review <https://doi.org/10.48558/7X1Y-MF25>

Busch T, Bruce-Clark P, Derwall J, Eccles R, Hebb T, Hoepner S, Klein C, Krueger P, Paetzold F, Scholtens B and Weber O, 'Impact Investments: A Call for (Re)orientation' (2021) 1 SN Bus Econ 33

Campbell N, 'The Nature of an Insurer's Obligation' (2000) LMCLQ 42

Carroll AB, 'Carroll's Pyramid of CSR: Taking Another Look' (2016) 1 Int J Corporate Soc Responsibility 3

Cohen L.R and Boardman M.R, 'Methodology: Applying Economics to Insurance Law: An Introduction' in Burling J and Lazarus K (eds.), *Research Handbook on International Insurance Law and Regulation* (Edward Elgar Publishing 2011)

Curcio D, Gianfrancesco I and Vioto D, 'Climate Change and Financial Systemic Risk: Evidence from US Banks and Insurers' (2023) 66 J Fin Stab 101132

Dyck A, Lins K.V, Roth L, and Wagner H.F, 'Do Institutional Investors Drive Corporate Social Responsibility? International Evidence' (2019) 131(3) J Fin Econ 693

Elkington J, 'Cannibals with Forks: The Triple Bottom Line of 21st Century Business' (2000) 23 J Bus Ethics 229

Essen M, McCaffey S, Abrams J and Paveglio T, 'Improving Wildfire Management Outcomes: Shifting the Paradign of Wildfire from Simple to Complex Risk' (2023) 66(5) J Environ Plan Manag 909

Etzkowitz H, 'Innovation in Innovation: The Triple Helix of University-Industry-Government Relations' (2003) 42(3) Soc. Sci. Inf 293

Ewald T (Dautrey JM and Stifler C.F), 'Risk in Contemporary Society' (2000) 6 Conn Ins LJ 365
Feiman J, 'What is a Protection Gap? Homeowners Insurance as a Case Study' (2020) 27(1) Conn Ins LJ 82
Ferguson P and Wollersheim L, 'From Sustainable Development to Resilience? (Dis)continuities in Climate and Development Policy Governance Discourse' (2022) 31(1) Sustain Develop 4
Feyen E, Lester R, and Rezende Rocha RD, 'What Drives the Development of the Insurance Sector? An Empirical Analysis Based on a Panel of Developed and Developing Countries' (2013) 1(1) J Fin Perspect 1
Frondel M, Simora M, Sommer S, 'Risk Perception of Climate Change: Empirical Evidence for Germany' (2017) 137 Ecol Econ 173
Gelter M, 'The Dark Side of Shareholder Influence: Managerial Autonomy and Stakeholder Orientation in Comparative Corporate Governance' (2009) 50 Harvard Int Law J 129
Gomtsiam S, 'Debtholder Stewardship' (2023) 86(2) MLR 395
Guin B, Korhonen P, and Moktan S, 'Risk Differentials between Green and Brown Assets?' (2022) 213 Econ Lett 110320
Hanger S, Linnerooth-Bayer J, Surminski S, Nenciu-Posner C, Lorant A, Ionescu R, Patt A, 'Insurance, Public Assistance, and Household Flood Risk Reduction: A Comparative Study of Austria, England, and Romania' (2018) 38(4) Risk Anal 680
Hardin G, 'The Tragedy of the Commons' (1968) 162 Science 1243
Hart O and Zingales L, 'Companies Should Maximize Shareholder Welfare Not Market Value' (2017) J Law Fin Account 247
Holling CS, 'Resilience and Stability of Ecological Systems' (1973) 4(1) Ann Rev Ecol Syst 1
Holmes S, 'Climate change, sustainability, and competition law' (2020) 8 JAE 354
Kahneman D, 'Maps of Bounded Rationality: Psychology for Behavioral Economics' (2003) 93 Am Econ Rev 1449
Kahneman D and Tversky A, 'Prospect Theory: An Analysis of Decision under Risk' (1979) 47 Econometrica, 263–291
Kochenburger P, 'Liability Insurance and Gun Violence' (2013–2014) 46 Conn Law Rev 1265
Krueger P, Sautner Z and Starks L.T, 'The Importance of Climate Risks for Institutional Investors' (2020) 33 Rev Fin Stud 1067
Light SE, 'The Law of the Corporation as Environmental Law' (2019) 71 Stan L Rev 160
Logue KD, 'Encouraging Insurers to Regulate: The Role (If Any) for Tort Law' (2015) 5(6) UC Irvine L Rev 1355
Louche C, Arenas D & Cranenburgh KCV, 'From Preaching to Investing: Attitudes of Religious Organisations Towards Responsible Investment' (2012) 110(3) J Bus Ethics 301
Miceli R, Sotgiu I and Settanni M, 'Disaster Preparedness and Perception of Flood Risk: A Study in an Alpine Valley in Italy' (2008) 28/2 J Environ Psychol 164
Monasterolo I and Angelis L, '2020: Blind to Carbon Risk? An Analysis of Stock Market Reaction to the Paris Agreement' (2019) 170 Ecol Econ 106571
Moser SC, Ekstrom JA, 'A Framework to Diagnose Barriers to Climate Change Adaptation' (2010) 107(51) Proc Natl Acad Sci 22026
Posner E.A and Weyl E.G, 'An FDA for Financial Innovation: Applying the Insurable Interest Doctrine to the 21st Century Financial Markets' (2013) 107 Nw U L Rev 1307
Poussin J.K, Botzen WJW, and Aerts JCJH, 'Factors of Influence on Flood Damage Mitigation Behaviour by Households' (2014) 40 Environ Sci Policy, 69
Priest SJ, Penning-Rowsell EC and Suykens C, 'Promoting Adaptive Flood Risk Management: The Role and Potential of Flood Recovery Mechanisms' (2016) 7 E3S Web Conf 17005
Reusens P, Vastmans F and Damen S, 'The Impact of Changes in Dwelling Characteristics and Housing Preferences on Belgian House Prices' (2022) 2 NBB Econ Rev 1

Robinson PJ and Botzen WJW 'Setting Descriptive Norm Nudges to Promote Demand for Insurance Against Increasing Climate Change Risk' (2022) 47 Geneva Paper on Risk and Insurance 3

Rock EB, 'For Whom Is the Corporation Managed in 2020? The Debate over Corporate Purpose' (2021) 76(2) Bus Law, 363

Scherer N, 'How to Advance Regional Climate Risk Insurances' (June 2017) Climate Diplomacy Policy Brief

Schoenmaker D and Zachmann G, 'Can a Global Climate Risk Pool Help the Most Vulnerable Countries?' (2015) Bruegel Policy Brief

Schueth S, 'Socially Responsible Investing in the United States' (2003) 43(3) J Bus Ethics 189

Schwarcz D, 'A Products Liability Theory for the Judicial Regulation of Insurance Policies' (2007) 48 Wm & Mary L Rev 1389

Schwarze R and Wagner G, 'The Political Economy of Natural Disaster Insurance: Lessons from the Failure of a Proposed Compulsory Insurance Scheme in Germany' (2007) 17 Eur Env 403

Seifert-Dähnn I, 'Insurance Engagement in Flood Risk Reduction: Examples from Household and Business Insurance in Developed Countries' (2018) 18/9 Nat Hazards Earth Syst Sci 2409

Siemiatycki M, Reeves E and Palcic D, 'Editorial: The Unresolved Nature of Public-Private Partnerships' (2022) 25(2) J of EcoPol Ref 81

Spash C, 'The Brave New World of Carbon Trading' (2010) 15(2) New Political Economy 169

Stempel J.W, 'The Insurance Policy as Thing' (2009) 44 Tort Trial Ins. Prac LJ 813

Stirling A, 'Risk Assessment in Science: Towards a More Constructive Policy Debate' (2007) 8 EMBO Reports 309

Stricker L, Pugnetti C, Wagner J, and Röschmann A.Z, 'Green Insurance: A Roadmap for Executive Management' (2022) 15 J Risk Fin Manag 221

Surminski S, Barnes J, and Vincent K, 'Can Insurance Catalyse Government Planning on Climate? Emergent Evidence from Sub-Saharan Africa' (2022) 153 World Develop 105830

Tesselaar M, Botzen WJW, and Aerts JCJH, 'Impacts of Climate Change and Remote Natural Catastrophes on EU Flood Insurance Markets: An Analysis of Soft and Hard Reinsurance Markets for Flood Coverage' (2020) 11 Atmosphere 146

Versey M, 'Redefining Stewardship: Why Stakeholder Capitalism Needs to Wake Up' AIQ Aviva Investors (April 2023) 11

Wandt M and Lüders G, 'Nachhaltigkeitsregulierung des Finanzbereichs im Allgemeinen und produktbezogene Offenlegungspflichten im Versicherungsbereich im Besonderen' (2023) 13 VersR 829

Wetenhall R, 'The Rhetoric and Reality of Public-Private Partnerships' (2003) 3 Pub Organ Rev 77

UK Government and governmental agency materials

Houses of Parliament

UK All-Party Parliamentary Group on Environmental, Social, and Governance Report, 'Defining ESG', Figure 1 (April 2023) <https://appgesg.org/wp-content/uploads/2023/04/20230425-APPG-Defining-ESG-report-final-web.pdf>

Prime Minister

The Prime Minister and the Department for Business, Energy & Industrial Strategy, 'The Ten Point Plan for a Green Industrial Revolution' (18 November 2020) <https://www.gov.uk/government/publications/the-ten-point-plan-for-a-green-industrial-revolution/title>

HM Government

HM Government, 'Greening Finance: A Roadmap to Sustainable Investing' (October 2021) <https://www.gov.uk/government/publications/greening-finance-a-roadmap-to-sustainable-investing>

HM Government, 'Net-zero Strategy: Build Back Greener' (October 2021) <https://assets.publishing.service.gov.uk/government/uploads/system/uploads/attachment_data/file/1033990/net-zero-strategy-beis.pdf>

HM Government, 'Mobilising Green Investment: 2023 Green Finance Strategy' (April 2023) <https://www.gov.uk/government/publications/green-finance-strategy>

HM Government, 'Buying or Selling Your Home: Energy Performance Certificates' https://www.gov.uk/buy-sell-your-home/energy-performance-certificates

HM Treasury

HM Treasury, 'Build Back Better: Our plan for growth' (March 2021) <https://www.gov.uk/government/publications/build-back-better-our-plan-for-growth/build-back-better-our-plan-for-growth-html#net-zero>

HM Treasury, 'Financial Services Future Regulatory Framework Review: Proposals for Reform' CP 548 (November 2021)

HM Treasury, 'Review of Solvency II: Consultation: Response' (November 2022) <https://www.gov.uk/government/consultations/solvency-ii-review-consultation>

HM Treasury, 'Financial Services: The Edinburgh Reforms' (announcement dated 9 December 2022) <https://www.gov.uk/government/collections/financial-services-the-edinburgh-reforms>

HM Treasury, 'Consultation Paper on the Future Regulatory Regime for Environmental, Social and Governance (ESG) Ratings Providers' (30 March 2023) <https://www.gov.uk/government/consultations/future-regulatory-regime-for-environmental-social-and-governance-esg-ratings-providers>

HM Treasury, 'Draft Insurance and Reinsurance Undertakings (Prudential Requirements) Regulations' (22 June 2023) <https://www.gov.uk/government/publications/draft-insurance-and-reinsurance-undertakings-prudential-requirements-regulations>

Other government departments

Department for Business, Energy & Industrial Strategy, 'Improving Home Energy Performance Through Lenders' Consultation Paper (November 2020) <https://www.gov.uk/government/consultations/improving-home-energy-performance-through-lenders>

Department for Business, Energy & Industrial Strategy, 'UK Enshrines New Target in Law to Slash Emissions by 78% by 2035' (2021) <https://www.gov.uk/government/news/uk-enshrines-new-target-in-law-to-slash-emissions-by-78-by-2035>

Department for Business and Trade, 'New Transparency over Resilience and Assurance for Big Business' (July 2023) <https://www.gov.uk/government/publications/new-transparency-over-resilience-and-assurance-for-big-business>

Department for Environment, Food and Rural Affairs, 'Consultation on Amendments to the Flood Re Scheme: Summary of Responses' (July 2021) <https://www.gov.uk/government/consultations/amendments-to-the-flood-re-scheme>

Department for Transport, 'Plug-in Vehicle Grant Port' (December 2018) <https://www.gov.uk/government/publications/plug-in-vehicle-grant-portal-guidance/using-the-plug-in-vehicle-grant-portal>

Governmental agencies

Committee on Climate Change, 'An Independent Assessment of the UK's Clean Growth Strategy, from Ambition to Action' (2018) <https://www.theccc.org.uk/wp-content/uploads/2018/01/CCC-Independent-Assessment-of-UKs-Clean-Growth-Strategy-2018.pdf>

Committee on Climate Change, 'Sixth Carbon Budget Report: Sector Summary for Buildings and Sector Summary for Surface Transport' (December 2020) <https://www.theccc.org.uk/wp-content/uploads/2020/12/Sector-summary-Buildings.pdf and https://www.theccc.org.uk/wp-content/uploads/2020/12/Sector-summary-Surface-transport.pdf>

Competition & Markets Authority, 'Draft Guidance on the Application of the Chapter I Prohibition in the Competition Act 1998 to Environmental Sustainability Agreements -Draft Guidance' CMA177 (28 February 2023)

Office of Gas and Electricity Markets (Ofgem), 'Environmental and Social Schemes' <https://www.ofgem.gov.uk/environmental-and-social-schemes>

Takeover Panel, 'Practice Statement No 26: Shareholder Activism' <https://www.thetakeoverpanel.org.uk/wp-content/uploads/2021/07/Practice-Statement-No-26.pdf>

UK regulatory materials

Bank of England:

Bank of England, 'DP2/22: Potential Reforms to Risk Margin and Matching Adjustment within Solvency II', DP2/22 (April 2022)

Bank of England, 'Results of the 2021 Climate Biennial Exploratory Scenario' (24 May 2022)

Bank of England, 'Report on Climate-related Risks and the Regulatory Capital Frameworks' (March 2023)

Bank of England, 'Our Response to Climate Change' <https://www.bankofengland.co.uk/climate-change>

Bank of England, 'Climate Financial Risk Forum, Climate Financial Risk Forum (CFRF) Guides' <https://www.bankofengland.co.uk/climate-change/climate-financial-risk-forum>

PRA

PRA, 'The Impact of Climate Change on the UK Insurance Sector: A Climate Change Adaptation Report by the PRA' (September 2015)

PRA, 'Transition in Thinking: The Impact of Climate Change on the UK Banking Sector' (September 2018)

PRA, 'Supervisory Statement: Enhancing Banks' and Insurers' Approaches to Managing the Financial Risks from Climate Change' SS3/19 (April 2019)

PRA, 'A Framework for Assessing Financial Impacts of Physical Climate Change' (May 2019)

PRA, 'Dear CEO letter: IST 2019' (17 June 2019)

PRA, 'Dear CEO Letter: Insurance Stress Test 2019 and Covid-19 Stress Testing: Feedback for General and Life Insurers' (17 June 2020)

PRA, 'Climate-related financial risk management and the role of capital requirements: Climate Change Adaptation Report 2021' (October 2021)

PRA, 'Review of Solvency II: Adapting to the UK Insurance Market' CP12/23 (June 2023)

PRA, 'Dear CEO Letter: Managing Climate-related Financial Risk: Thematic Feedback from the PRA's Review of Firms' SS3/19 Plans and Clarifications of Expectations' (1 July 2020)

PRA, 'Dear CEO Letter: Thematic feedback on the PRA's supervision of climate-related financial risk and the Bank of England's Climate Biennial Exploratory Scenario exercise' (21 October 2022)

FCA

FCA, 'Climate Change and Green Finance' DP18/8 (October 2018)
FCA, 'Building a Regulatory Framework for Effective Stewardship' DP19/1 (January 2019)
FCA, 'Feedback Statement, Building a Regulatory Framework for Effective Stewardship' FS19/7 (October 2019)
FCA, 'Primary Market Technical Note: Disclosures in Relation to ESG Matters, Including Climate Change' Primary Markets / TN / 801.2 (December 2021)
FCA, 'ESG Integration in UK Capital Markets' FS22/4 (June 2022)
FCA, 'Final non-Handbook Guidance for Firms on the Consumer Duty' FG22/5 (July 2022)
FCA, 'A New Consumer Duty: Feedback to CP21/36 and Final Rules' FS 22/9 (July 2022)
FCA, 'Sustainability Disclosure Requirements (SDR) and Investment Labels' CP22/20 (October 2022)
FCA, 'Finance for Positive Sustainable Change: Governance, Incentives and Competence in Regulated Firms' DP23/1 (February 2023)
FCA, 'A Strategy for Positive Change: Our ESG Priorities' (November 2021)
FCA, 'Review of TCFD-aligned Disclosures by Premium Listed Commercial Companies' (July 2022)
FCA, 'Consumer Duty Firm Survey: Spring 2023' (June 2023)
FCA, 'Regulatory Sandbox' <https://www.fca.org.uk/firms/innovation/regulatory-sandbox>
FCA, 'Climate Change and Sustainable Finance' https://www.fca.org.uk/firms/climate-change-sustainable-finance

Other

Memorandum of Understanding between the Financial Conduct Authority and the Prudential Regulation Authority
Letters from the then Chancellor of the Exchequer Rishi Sunak to the PRC, dated 23 March 2021 <https://assets.publishing.service.gov.uk/government/uploads/system/uploads/attachment_data/file/972443/CX_Letter_-_PRC_Remit_230321.pdf>
Letters from the then Chancellor of the Exchequer Rishi Sunak to the FCA, dated 23 March 2021 <https://assets.publishing.service.gov.uk/government/uploads/system/uploads/attachment_data/file/972445/CX_Letter_-_FCA_Remit_230321.pdf>
Letters from the Chancellor of the Exchequer Jeremy Hunt to the Prudential Regulation Committee, dated 8 December 2022 <https://www.gov.uk/government/publications/recommendations-for-the-prudential-regulation-committee-december-2022>
Letters from the Chancellor of the Exchequer Jeremy Hunt to the FCA, dated 8 December 2022 <https://www.gov.uk/government/publications/recommendations-for-the-financial-conduct-authority-december-2022>

EU documents

Legislative proposals

European Commission, Proposal for a Directive of the European Parliament and of the Council Amending Directive 2009/138/EC as Regards Proportionality, Quality of Supervision, Reporting, Long-term Guarantee Measures, Macro-prudential Tools, Sustainability Risks, Group and Cross-border Supervision (COM/2021/581)
European Commission, Proposal for a Directive of the European Parliament and of the Council on Corporate Sustainability Due Diligence and amending Directive (EU) 2019/1937 COM/2022/71
European Commission, Proposal for a Directive of the European Parliament and of the Council on substantiation and communication of explicit environmental claims (Green Claims Directive) COM/2023/166

European Commission, Proposal for a Regulation on the Transparency and Integrity of Environmental, Social and Governance (ESG) Rating Activities 2023/0177 (COD) COM/2023/314

European Commission

Communication from the Commission, 'Action Plan: Financing Sustainable Growth' (COM/2018/97)

Communication from the Commission, 'A Clean Planet for all A European Strategic Long-term Vision for a Prosperous, Modern, Competitive and Climate Neutral Economy' (COM/2018/773)

Communication from the Commission, 'The European Green Deal' (COM/2019/640)

Communication from the Commission, 'Guidelines on non-financial Reporting: Supplement on Reporting Climate-related Information' (2019/C 209/01)

Communication from the Commission to the European Parliament, the Council, the European Economic and Social Committee and the Committee of the Regions, 'Stepping up Europe's 2030 Climate Ambition: Investing in a Climate-neutral Future for the Benefit of Our People' (COM/2020/562)

Communication from the Commission 'A Capital Markets Union for People and Businesses: New Action Plan' COM (2020) 590

Communication from the Commission, 'EU Taxonomy, Corporate Sustainability Reporting, Sustainability Preferences and Fiduciary Duties: Directing Finance Towards the European Green Deal' COM (2021) 188

Communication from the Commission to the European Parliament, the Council, the European Economic and Social Committee and the Committee of the Regions, 'Strategy for Financing the Transition to a Sustainable Economy' (COM/2021/390)

Communication from the Commission to the European Parliament, the European Council, the Council, the European Economic and Social Committee and the Committee of the Regions, 'REPowerEU Plan' (COM/2022/230)

European Commission, 'Draft Guidelines on the Applicability of Art 101 of the Treaty on the Functioning of the EU to Horizontal Co-operation Agreements' 1 March 2022 C(2022) 1159

European Commission, '2030 Climate & Energy Framework' <https://ec.europa.eu/clima/eu-action/climate-strategies-targets/2020-climate-energy-package_en>

European Commission, 'EU Emissions Trading System (EU ETS)' <https://ec.europa.eu/clima/eu-action/eu-emissions-trading-system-eu-ets_en>

European Commission, 'Request for input to the European Banking Authority (EBA), the European'

Insurance and Occupational Pensions Authority (EIOPA) and the European Securities and Markets Authority (ESMA) related to greenwashing risks and supervision of sustainable finance policies' August 2022 <https://www.eiopa.europa.eu/publications/european-commissions-call-advice-esas-greenwashing-risks-and-supervision-sustainable-finance_en>

European Commission, 'Climate Resilience Dialogue' <https://climate.ec.europa.eu/eu-action/adaptation-climate-change/climate-resilience-dialogue_en>

EIOPA

EIOPA, 'EIOPA's Technical Advice on the integration of sustainability risks and factors in the delegated acts under Solvency II and IDD' EIOPA-BoS-19/172

EIOPA, 'Opinion on Sustainability within Solvency II' EIOPA-BoS-19/241

EIOPA, 'Report on non-life Underwriting and Pricing in Light of Climate Change', EIOPA-BoS-21/259

EIOPA, 'Opinion on the Supervision of the Use of Climate Change Risk Scenarios in ORSA' EIOPA-BoS-21-12

EIOPA, 'Methodology Paper on Potential Inclusion of Climate Change in the Nat Cat Standard Formula' EIOPA-BoS-21/253

EIOPA, 'Prudential Treatment of Sustainability Risks: Discussion Paper' EIOPA-BoS-22-527

EIOPA, 'Issues Paper on Resilience Solutions for Pandemics' (2020) <https://www.eiopa.europa.eu/publications/issues-paper-resilience-solutions-pandemics_en>

EIOPA, 'Sensitivity Analysis of Climate-change Related Transition Risks' (December 2020) <https://www.eiopa.europa.eu/publications/sensitivity-analysis-climate-change-related-transition-risks_en>

EIOPA, 'Sustainable Finance Activities 2022–2024' <https://www.eiopa.europa.eu/system/files/2021-12/eiopa-sustainable-finance-activities-2022-2024.pdf>

EIOPA, 'Dashboard on Insurance Protection Gap for Natural Catastrophes' https://www.eiopa.europa.eu/tools-and-data/dashboard-insurance-protection-gap-natural-catastrophes_en

Others

Council of the European Union, 'Proposal for a Directive of the European Parliament and of the Council on Corporate Sustainability Due Diligence and amending Directive (EU) 2019/1937: General Approach' 6533/22

ECB, 'The Role of Environmental Risks in the Prudential Framework' Discussion Paper EBA/DP/2022/02 (2 May 2022)

ECB and EIOPA, 'Policy Options to Reduce the Climate Insurance Protection Gap: Discussion Paper' (April 2023) <https://www.eiopa.europa.eu/system/files/2023-04/ecb.policyoptions_EIOPA~c0adae58b7.en_.pdf>

ESMA, 'Q&As on the Interpretation of Regulation (EU) 2019/2088 SFDR' <https://www.esma.europa.eu/document/qas-interpretation-regulation-eu-20192088-sfdr>

European Supervisory Authorities, 'Final Report on Draft Regulatory Technical Standards' JC 2021 03 (February 2021)

European Supervisory Authorities, 'Joint Consultation Paper: Review of SFDR Delegated Regulation Regarding PAI and Financial Product Disclosures' JC 2023 09 (12 April 2023)

Standards, codes, and principles

European Sustainability Reporting Standards ESRS E1 and ESRS E2 (2023)

Financial Reporting Council, 'UK Stewardship Code 2020'

IFRS S1 General Requirements for Disclosure of Sustainability-related Financial Information (July 2023)

IFRS S2 Climate-related Disclosures (July 2023)

Partnership for Carbon Accounting Financials, 'The Global GHG Accounting and Reporting Standard for the Financial Industry' (2020)

Partnership for Carbon Accounting Financials, 'Insurance-Associated Emissions' (November 2022)

PRI in Partnership with the United Nations Environment Programme Finance Initiative, 'Principles for Responsible Investment'

TCFD, 'Recommendations of the Task Force on Climate-related Financial Disclosures' (June 2017)

TCFD, 'Implementing the Recommendations of the Task Force on Climate-related Financial Disclosures' (June 2017)

TCFD, 'Guidance on Metrics, Targets, and Transition Plans' (October 2021)

The World Business Council for Sustainable Development and the World Resources Institute, 'The Greenhouse Gas Protocol: A Corporate Accounting and Reporting Standard' (2004)

The World Business Council for Sustainable Development and the World Resources Institute, 'The Greenhouse Gas Protocol: Corporate Value Chain (Scope 3) Accounting and Reporting Standard' (2011)

United Nations Environment Programme Finance Initiative, 'Principles for Sustainable Insurance'

IPCC reports

IPCC, 'Climate Change 2014: Synthesis Report' (Fifth Assessment Report, Core Writing Team, R.K. Pachauri and L.A. Meyer (eds.) Geneva, Switzerland 2014)

IPCC, '2018 Special Report: Global Warming of 1.5°C' (Masson-Delmotte, V., P. Zhai, H.-O. Pörtner, D. Roberts, J. Skea, P.R. Shukla, A. Pirani, W. Moufouma-Okia, C. Péan, R. Pidcock, S. Connors, J.B.R. Matthews, Y. Chen, X. Zhou, M.I. Gomis, E. Lonnoy, T. Maycock, M. Tignor, and T. Waterfield (eds.), Cambridge University Press 2018)

IPCC, 'Climate Change 2021: The Physical Science Basis' (Masson-Delmotte, V., P. Zhai, A. Pirani, S.L. Connors, C. Péan, S. Berger, N. Caud, Y. Chen, L. Goldfarb, M.I. Gomis, M. Huang, K. Leitzell, E. Lonnoy, J.B.R. Matthews, T.K. Maycock, T. Waterfield, O. Yelekçi, R. Yu, and B. Zhou (eds.), Cambridge University Press 2021)

IPCC, 'Climate Change 2022: Impacts, Adaptation and Vulnerability', (H.-O. Pörtner, D.C. Roberts, M. Tignor, E.S. Poloczanska, K. Mintenbeck, A. Alegría, M. Craig, S. Langsdorf, S. Löschke, V. Möller, A. Okem, B. Rama (eds.) Cambridge University Press 2021)

IPCC, 'Climate Change 2022: Mitigation of Climate Change' (P.R. Shukla, J. Skea, R. Slade, A. Khourdajie, R. van Diemen, D. McCollum, M. Pathak, S. Some, P. Vyas, R. Fradera, M. Belkacemi, A. Hasija, G. Lisboa, S. Luz, J. Malley, (eds.), Cambridge University Press 2022)

IPCC, 'Synthesis Report of the Sixth Assessment Report' (Sixth Assessment Report: Longer Report, Hoesung Lee, Katherine Calvin, Dipak Dasgupta, Gerhard Krinner, Aditi Mukherji, Peter Thorne, Christopher Trisos, José Romero, Paulina Aldunce, Ko Barrett, Gabriel Blanco, William W. L. Cheung, Sarah L. Connors, Fatima Denton, Aïda Diongue-Niang, David Dodman, Matthias Garschagen, Oliver Geden, Bronwyn Hayward, Christopher Jones, Frank Jotzo, Thelma Krug, Rodel Lasco, June-Yi Lee, Valérie Masson-Delmotte, Malte Meinshausen, Katja Mintenbeck, Abdalah Mokssit, Friederike E. L. Otto, Minal Pathak, Anna Pirani, Elvira Poloczanska, Hans-Otto Pörtner, Aromar Revi, Debra C. Roberts, Joyashree Roy, Alex C. Ruane, Jim Skea, Priyadarshi R. Shukla, Raphael Slade, Aimée Slangen, Youba Sokona, Anna A. Sörensson, Melinda Tignor, Detlef van Vuuren, Yi-Ming Wei, Harald Winkler, Panmao Zhai, Zinta Zommers, Cambridge University Press 2022)

Research papers, issues papers, working papers, research reports, and blogs

Alexander K and Lastra R, 'International Banking Regulation and Climate Change', Queen Mary Law Research Paper No. 401/2023

Arnold-Dwyer F and Enoizi J, 'The Need For A Sea Change In Climate-Related Insurance' (June 2022) <https://www.guycarp.com/insights/2023/06/the-need-for-a-sea-change-in-climate-related-insurance.html>

Baker T and Shortland A, 'How Crime Shapes Insurance and Insurance Shapes Crime' (March 10, 2023) U of Penn, Inst for Law & Econ Research Paper No. 23-10 (Journal of Legal Analysis, forthcoming)

Bräuninger M, Butzengeiger-Geyer S, Dlugolecki A, Hochrainer S, Köhler M, Linnerooth-Bayer J, Mechler R, Michaelowa A, Schulze S, 'Application of Economic Instruments for Adaptation to Climate Change, Final Report', (2011) CLIMA.C.3./ETU/2010/0011 Perspectives Climate Change

British Academy, 'The Future of the Corporation: Principles for Purposeful Business' (November 2019) <https://www.thebritishacademy.ac.uk/publications/future-of-the-corporation-principles-for-purposeful-business>

Cabral D, 'Mastering ESG Transition Risks: Utilising Game Theory's Strategic Power' <https://www.linkedin.com/pulse/mastering-esg-transition-risks-utilising-game-theorys-david-v-cabral/>

Caldecott B, 'Achieving Alignment in Finance', (October 2020) <https://www.unepfi.org/wordpress/wp-content/uploads/2020/08/200915_J932-CKIC-UNEP-ThoughtLeadershipSeries-DrBenCaldecott-11.pdf>

Caldecott B, Dericks G, Mitchell J, 'Stranded Assets and Subcritical Coal: The Risk to Companies and Investors' (March 2015) <https://www.smithschool.ox.ac.uk/sites/default/files/2022-04/Stranded-Assets-and-Subcritical-Coal.pdf>

Caldecott B, Thomae J, Mitchell J, and Scott M, 'How Can Net-zero Finance Best Drive Positive Impact in the Real Economy' (April 2022) <https://climatechampions.unfccc.int/wp-content/uploads/2022/05/FSEG-report-2_v3.pdf>

Ceres, 'Inclusive Insurance for Climate-Related Disasters: A Roadmap for the United States' (January 2023) <https://www.ceres.org/sites/default/files/reports/2023-01/Inclusive%20Insurance%20Report.pdf>

Curtis Q, Fisch J.E and Robertson A.Z, 'Do ESG Mutual Funds Deliver on their Promises?' (May 2021) Working Paper No. 586/2021, ECGI Working Paper Series in Law

Davies P, 'The UK Stewardship Code 2010–2020: From Saving the Company to Saving the Planet?' (March 2020) Working Paper No. 506/2020, European Corporate Governance Institute

Debevoise & Plimpton, 'ESG and Antitrust: More Focus but No Consensus: Recent Developments, Pitfalls and Mitigating Risk' (3 March 2023) <https://www.debevoise.com/insights/publications/2023/03/esg-and-antitrust-more-focus-but-no-consensus>

Ewart T, 'Net-Zero Insurance: Engaging Businesses in the Low-Carbon Transition through Insurance Underwriting & Risk Management' (28 February 2023) <https://medium.com/@tom.ewart/net-zero-insurance-engaging-businesses-in-the-low-carbon-transition-through-insurance-underwriting-9e83efdc0a7f>

EY, 'Study on Directors' Duties and Sustainable Corporate Governance', Report for the European Commission (29 July 2020) <https://op.europa.eu/en/publication-detail/-/publication/e47928a2-d20b-11ea-adf7-01aa75ed71a1/language-en>

Financial Reporting Council, 'Climate Thematic Review: Audit' (November 2020) 5 <https://www.frc.org.uk/getattachment/0ef2c94a-9028-4efa-ac80-3b8c2e0d9a11/Audit-FINAL.pdf>

Financial Reporting Council, 'CRR Thematic Review of TCFD Disclosures and Climate in the Financial Statements' (July 2022), <https://www.frc.org.uk/getattachment/65fa8b6f-2bed-4a67-8471-ab91c9cd2e85/FRC-TCFD-disclosures-and-climate-in-the-financial-statements_July-2022.pdf>

Financial Stability Board, 'FSB Roadmap for Addressing Climate-Related Financial Risks' (June 2021)

Financial Stability Board, 'Supervisory and Regulatory Approaches to Climate-related Risks: Final Report' (October 2022) <https://www.fsb.org/2022/10/supervisory-and-regulatory-approaches-to-climate-related-risks-final-report/>

Forest R, 'Climate Risk Insurance: Transparency, Participation and Accountability. An overview Assessment of Regional Risk Pools' Munich Climate Insurance Initiative' (2018) <https://collections.unu.edu/view/UNU:6705#viewAttachments>

Gordon JN, 'Systematic Stewardship' European Corporate Governance Institute: Law Working Paper No. 566/2021 and Columbia Law and Economics Working Paper No. 640 (Journal of Corporation Law, forthcoming)

Green D and Vallee B, 'Can Finance Save the World? Measurement and Effects of Coal Divestment Policies by Banks' (April 8, 2022) <https://papers.ssrn.com/sol3/papers.cfm?abstract_id=4090974>

IAIS, 'Insurance Core Principles and Common Framework for the Supervision of Internationally Active Insurance Group' (November 2019 update)

IAIS and SIF, 'Issues Paper on Climate Change Risks to the Insurance Sector' 15 (July 2018)

IAIS and SIF, 'Application Paper on the Supervision of Climate-related Risks in the Insurance Sector' (May 2021)

Jarzabkowski P, Chalkias K, Clarke D, Iyahen E, Stadtmueller D, and Zwick A, 'Insurance for climate adaptation: Opportunities and limitations: Report for the Global Commission on Adaptation' (2019) <https://gca.org/reports/insurance-for-climate-adaptation-opportunities-and-limitations/>

Lipton M, 'Navigating the Current ESG Landscape: Recommendations for the Board and Management' (23 May 2023) Harvard Law School Forum on Corporate Governance <https://corpgov.law.harvard.edu/2023/05/23/navigating-the-current-esg-landscape-recommendations-for-the-board-and-management/>

LMA, 'Why is Collaboration Key to Improving ESG Data for Underwriting?' (March 2023) <https://www.lmalloyds.com/LMA/News/Blog/why_090323.aspx>

Macey J.R, 'ESG Investing: Why Here? Why Now?' (2021) Yale Law & Economics Research Paper Forthcoming, Law & Economics Center at George Mason University Scalia Law School Research Paper Series No. 22-013

Malone L, Holland E, and Houston C from Simpson Thacher & Bartlett LLP, 'ESG Battlegrounds: How the States Are Shaping the Regulatory Landscape in the U.S.', Harvard Law School Forum on Corporate Governance (11 March 2023) <https://corpgov.law.harvard.edu/2023/03/11/esg-battlegrounds-how-the-states-are-shaping-the-regulatory-landscape-in-the-u-s/>

Matikainen S, 'Green Doesn't Mean Risk-free: Why We Should be Cautious about a Green Supporting Factor in the EU', Grantham Research Institute on Climate Change and the Environment Blog (December 2017) <https://www.lse.ac.uk/granthaminstitute/news/eu-green-supporting-factor-bank-risk/>

Myners P, 'Institutional Investment in the United Kingdom: A Review' (March 2001) <https://www.icaew.com/technical/corporate-governance/codes-and-reports/myners-report>

National Association of Insurance Commissioners and The Center for Insurance and Policy Research, 'Flood Risk and Insurance' (2017) <https://content.naic.org/sites/default/files/inline-files/cipr_study_1704_flood_risk.pdf>

OECD, 'Policy Guidance on the Structure of Insurance Regulation and Supervision' (2020) <https://www.oecd.org/daf/fin/insurance/Policy-Guidance-on-the-Structure-of-Insurance-Regulation-and-Supervision.pdf>

OECD, 'Enhancing the Insurance Sector's Contribution to Climate Adaptation' OECD Business and Finance Policy Papers (OECD Publishing 2023) <https://doi.org/10.1787/0951dfcd-en>

Oh S, Sen I, and Tenekedjieva AM, 'Pricing of Climate Risk Insurance: Regulation and Cross-Subsidies' (22 December 2022) <https://ssrn.com/abstract=3762235>

Pugnetti C, Gebert T, Hürster M, Huizenga E, Moor M, Stricker L, Winistörfer H, and Röschmann AZ, 'Leading the Green Insurance Revolution' (2022), Working Paper No. 1, Winterthur: ZHAW Zürcher Hochschule für Angewandte Wissenschaften

Setzer J and Higham C, 'Global Trends in Climate Change Litigation: 2023 Snapshot' Grantham Research Institute on Climate Change and the Environment and the Centre for Climate Change Economics and Policy (June 2023) <https://www.lse.ac.uk/granthaminstitute/wp-content/uploads/2023/06/Global_trends_in_climate_change_litigation_2023_snapshot.pdf>

The Geneva Association, 'Understanding and Addressing Global Insurance Protection Gaps' (April 2018)

The Geneva Association, 'Investing in Climate-resilient Decarbonised Infrastructure to Meet Socio-economic and Climate Change Goals' (December 2019)

The Geneva Association, 'Climate Change Risk Assessment for the Insurance Industry' (February 2021)

The Geneva Association, 'Insurance Industry Perspectives on Regulatory Approaches to Climate Risk Assessment' (June 2021)

The Geneva Association, 'Anchoring Climate Change Risk Assessment in Core Business Decisions in Insurance' (September 2022)

Troster (Rabbi) L, 'Beyond The Letter of the Law: The Jewish Perspective on Ethical Investing and Fossil Fuel Divestment' (December 2014) <https://sojo.net/articles/disinvest-reinvest/beyond-letter-law-jewish-perspective-ethical-investing-and-fossil-fuel>

UN Environment Programme's Principles for Sustainable Insurance Initiative, 'Insuring the Climate Transition: Enhancing the Insurance Industry's Assessment of Climate Change Futures' (January 2021) <https://www.unepfi.org/industries/insurance/insuring-the-climate-transition/>

Walker D, 'A Review of Corporate Governance in UK Banks and Other Financial Industry Entities: Final Recommendations' (November 2009) <http://image.guardian.co.uk/sys-files/Guardian/documents/2009/11/26/walker-review.pdf>

WPI Economics, 'Flood Performance Certificates: Developing a Blueprint for How They Can Support Household Climate Resilience' (December 2020) 2 <https://www.floodre.co.uk/wp-content/uploads/Flood-Performance-Certificates.pdf>

Newspaper articles and news items

Abnett K, 'Factbox: COP27: Which Countries Have Offered 'Loss and Damage' Funds?' (*Reuters*, 8 November 2022)

Bryan K and Smith I, 'Activists Criticise Insurance Industry's First Attempt to Measure Carbon Emissions' (*Financial Times*, 17 January 2023)

Butler B, 'Suncorp and IAG Temporarily Stop Selling Insurance in Fire-affected Areas of Victoria and NSW' (*The Guardian*, 14 January 2020)

Carrington D, 'The Four Types of Climate Denier, and Why You Should Ignore Them All' (*The Guardian*, 30 July 2020)

CBC News, 'Biden to Use Veto to Keep ESG Investing Rule. What Is it, and Why do Most Republicans Hate It?' (2 March 2023)

Cecco L, 'The Uninsurables: How Storms and Rising Seas Are Making Coastlines Unlivable' (*The Guardian*, 13 October 2022)

Evans S, 'State Farm Stops Writing California Property, Cites Exposure & Reinsurance Challenges' (*Reinsurance News*, 29 May 2023)

Friedman M, 'A Friedman doctrine: The Social Responsibility Of Business Is to Increase Its Profits' (*New York Times*, 13 September 1970)

Hagan S and Querolo N, 'Texas Anti-ESG Push Is Coming for Insurers and Pensions in New Bills' (*Insurance Journal*, 6 March 2023)

Jain S, 'Flood Re launches 'Be Flood Smart' campaign in partnership with Environment Agency' (*Reinsurance News*, 23 May 2023)

Marsh A, 'Legal & General Divests From U.S. Insurer AIG Over Climate Policies' (Bloomberg, 15 June 2021)

Marsh A, 'Net-Zero Insurers' Climate-Friendly Plans to Exit Coal Impeded by Antitrust Laws' (*Insurance Journal*, 19 January 2023)

Marsh A and Robertson B, 'Carney Calls Net-Zero Greenhouse Ambition 'Greatest Commercial Opportunity' (*Bloomberg*, 9 November 2020)

Nuccitelli D, 'Climate Scientists Debate a Flaw in the Paris Climate Agreement' (*The Guardian*, 29 March 2018)

Quiggin J, 'Coal Is on the Road to Becoming Completely Uninsurable' (*The Conversation*, 19 August 2019)

Reuters, 'Insurer AIG Steps Back from Coal, Arctic Energy Underwriting' (1 March 2022)

Reuters, 'The Challenge of Investing in the Face of State anti-ESG Legislation' (24 August 2022)

Reuters, 'Deutsche Bank's DWS Sued by Consumer Group over Alleged Greenwashing' (24 October 2022)

Reuters, 'Carney Defends Dropping U.N. climate initiative over Antitrust Concerns' (3 November 2022)

Romei V and Arnold M, 'Germany Turns to Coal for a Third of Its Electricity' (*Financial Times*, 7 September 2022)

Scott M, 'ESG Watch: Is it Curtains for Mark Carney's Green Alliance, or Just Teething Problems?' (Reuters, 6 April 2023)

Smith I and Bryan K 'Lloyd's and Five Big Insurers Quit Sector's Net-zero Initiative' (*Financial Times*, 26 May 2023)

Smith I and Bryan K 'Insurance Industry Turmoil over Climate Alliance Exodus' (*Financial Times*, 30 May 2023)

The Guardian, 'UN says Climate Change 'Out of Control' after Likely Hottest Week on Record' (7 July 2023)

The Telegraph, 'Households will be Spared £120 Net-zero Levy, says Grant Shapps' (23 June 2023)

Toscano N and Foley M, 'Coal Miners in Talks to Self-insure as Climate Pressure Heats Up' (*Sydney Morning Herald*, 13 August 2021)

Tricks H, 'In Need of a Clean Up' (*The Economist: Special report on ESG investing*, 23 July 2022)

Williams Walsh M, 'How Wildfires Are Making Some California Homes Uninsurable' (*The New York Times*, 20 November 2018)

Speeches, press releases, and other communications

Press releases

Climate Change Committee, 'Better Transparency Is no Substitute for Real Delivery' (Press Release 23 June 2023) <https://www.theccc.org.uk/2023/06/28/better-transparency-is-no-substitute-for-real-delivery/>

Climate Council, 'One In 25 Australian Homes Uninsurable by 2030: Climate Council Launches Cutting Edge Digital Climate-Risk Map' (Press Release 3 May 2022) <https://www.climatecouncil.org.au/resources/australian-homes-uninsurable-2030-climate-risk-map/>

Council of the EU, 'Sustainable Finance: Provisional Agreement Reached on European Green Bonds' (Press Release dated 28 February 2023) <https://www.consilium.europa.eu/en/press/press-releases/2023/02/28/sustainable-finance-provisional-agreement-reached-on-european-green-bonds/>

Department for Environment, Food & Rural Affairs, 'Multi-billion Pound Investment as Government Unveils New Long-term Plan to Tackle Flooding' (Press Release dated 14 July 2020) https://www.gov.uk/government/news/multi-billion-pound-investment-as-government-unveils-new-long-term-plan-to-tackle-flooding

European Commission, 'The Commission adopts the European Sustainability Reporting Standards' (Press Release 31 July 2023) <https://finance.ec.europa.eu/news/commission-adopts-european-sustainability-reporting-standards-2023-07-31_en>

European Parliament, 'Legislators Strike Deal on a New Standard to Fight Greenwashing in the Bond Markets' (Press Release 28 February 2023) <https://www.europarl.europa.eu/news/en/press-room/20230227IPR76596/legislators-strike-deal-on-new-standard-to-fight-greenwashing-in-bond-markets>

German Federal Ministry for Economic Cooperation and Development, 'V20 and G7 Jointly Launch Global Shield against Climate Risks at COP27' (Press Release 14 November 2022) <https://www.bmz.de/en/issues/climate-change-and-development/global-shield-against-climate-risks>

Insurance Development Forum, 'UN, Insurance and Academic Leaders Sign Agreement to Draw upon Insurance Data and Expertise to Advance Climate and Disaster Risk Analytics and Help

Mobilise Finance for Adaptation' (Press Release 1 June 2023) <https://www.insdevforum.org/news/>

Munich Re, 'Munich Re Discontinues NZIA Membership' (Press Release 31 March 2023) <https://www.munichre.com/en/company/media-relations/media-information-and-corporate-news/media-information/2023/media-release-2023-03-31.html>

RSA, 'Homeowners Urged to go Green as Insurance Claims for Heating Breakdowns Surge' (Press Release 3 March 2021) <https://www.rsagroup.com/news/press-releases/2021/homeowners-urged-to-go-green-as-insurance-claims-for-heating-breakdowns-surge/>

SEC, 'SEC Charges BNY Mellon Investment Adviser for Misstatements and Omissions Concerning ESG Considerations' (Press Release 22 May 2022) <https://www.sec.gov/news/press-release/2022-86#:~:text=The%20Securities%20and%20Exchange%20Commission%20today%20charged%20BNY,Adviser%20agreed%20to%20pay%20a%20%241.5%20million%20penalty>

The White House, 'By the Numbers: The Inflation Reduction Act' (Press Release 14 August 2022) <https://www.whitehouse.gov/briefing-room/statements-releases/2022/08/15/by-the-numbers-the-inflation-reduction-act/>

The World Bank, 'World Bank Group Launches Global Shield Financing Facility to Help Developing Countries Adapt to Climate Change' (Press Release 14 November 2022) <https://www.worldbank.org/en/news/press-release/2022/11/14/world-bank-group-launches-global-shield-financing-facility-to-help-developing-countries-adapt-to-climate-change>

US Department of State, On the U.S Withdrawal from the Paris Agreement Press Statement (Press Release 4 November 2019) <https://2017-2021.state.gov/on-the-u-s-withdrawal-from-the-paris-agreement/index.html>

Speeches

Carney M, 'Breaking the Tragedy of the Horizon: Climate Change and Financial Stability' (Speech at Lloyd's of London, September 2015) <https://www.bankofengland.co.uk/speech/2015/breaking-the-tragedy-of-the-horizon-climate-change-and-financial-stability>

Guterres A, 'Closing remarks to Insurance Development Forum' (Speech at the 2021 Insurance Development Forum Summit, 8 June 2021) <https://www.un.org/sg/en/content/sg/speeches/2021-06-08/closing-remarks-insurance-development-forum>

Guterres A, 'Our World Is in Big Trouble' (Opening speech to the UN General Assembly on 22 September 2022 (SG/SM/21466)) <https://press.un.org/en/2022/sgsm21466.doc.htm>

Wood S, 'Solvency II: Striking the Balance' (Speech on 8 July 2022) <https://www.bankofengland.co.uk/speech/2022/july/sam-woods-speech-given-at-the-bank-of-england-solvency-ii-striking-the-balance>

Other

Deloitte, Letter from Deloitte to the ISSB dated 20 July 2022 <https://www.ifrs.org/projects/completed-projects/2023/general-sustainability-related-disclosures/#consultation-feedback>

FRC, Letter from the Financial Reporting Council to the ISSB dated 22 June 2022 <https://www.ifrs.org/projects/completed-projects/2023/general-sustainability-related-disclosures/#consultation-feedback>

IAASB, Letter from the International Auditing and Assurance Standards Board to the ISSB dated 26 July 2022 <https://www.ifrs.org/projects/completed-projects/2023/general-sustainability-related-disclosures/#consultation-feedback>

IAIS, 'IAIS Commitment to Amplify Response to Climate Change' (Statement 28 October 2021) <https://www.iaisweb.org/uploads/2022/01/211028-IAIS-Statement_Commitment-to-amplify-response-to-climate-change_October-2021.pdf>

Insurance Development Forum, 'COP27: IDF Media Communique' (21 November 2022) https://www.insdevforum.org/3888-2/

President-Designate of COP28/CMP18/CMA5, and UAE Special Envoy for Climate Change, Dr. Sultan Ahmed Al Jaber, 'Message on COP 28 Vision' (13 July 2023) <https://unfccc.int/documents/630572>

QBE Insurance Group Limited, Letter from QBE Insurance Group Limited to the ISSB dated 15 July 2022 <https://ifrs-springapps-comment-letter-api-1.azuremicroservices.io/v2/download-file?path=610_64931_qbe-insurance-group-qbe-letter-on-issb-proposals-v-f-issb.pdf>

Reagan T and Amoroso E, Conversation about Cyber Insurance on TAG Cyber TV (20 January 2023) <https://www.youtube.com/watch?app=desktop&v=PfFdr_Jop5g>

United Nations Environment Programme, 'Public Statement by the United Nations Environment Programme on the UN-Convened Net-Zero Insurance Alliance' (24 May 2023) <https://www.unepfi.org/industries/insurance/public-statement-by-the-united-nations-environment-programme-on-the-un-convened-net-zero-insurance-alliance/>

US Department of Labor, 'Final Rule on Prudence and Loyalty in Selecting Plan Investments and Exercising Shareholder Rights' (22 November 2022) <https://www.dol.gov/agencies/ebsa/about-ebsa/our-activities/resource-center/fact-sheets/final-rule-on-prudence-and-loyalty-in-selecting-plan-investments-and-exercising-shareholder-rights>

US Senate Committee on the Budget, Letter from the United States Senate Committee on the Budget to State Farm, Liberty Mutual, Berkshire Hathaway, AIG, Travelers Insurance, Chubb and Starr dated 9 June 2023 launching investigation into Berkshire Hathaway for continuing to insure and invest in fossil fuel projects, dated 9 June 2023 <https://www.budget.senate.gov/imo/media/doc/Budget%20Committee%20Letters%20to%20Insurance%20Companies.pdf>

US SG Working Group, Memorandum from the SG Working Group of the House Committee on Financial Services to Republican Members of the House Committee on Financial Services Regarding 'Preliminary Report on ESG Climate Related Financial Services Concerns' (dated 23 June 2023) <https://financialservices.house.gov/uploadedfiles/hfsc_esg_working_group_memo_final.pdf>

US State Attorney Generals, Letter from the State Attorney Generals of Montana, Louisiana, Utah, Alabama, Arkansas, Georgia, Idaho, Indiana, Iowa, Kansas, Kentucky, Mississippi, Missouri, New Hampshire, Ohio, South Carolina, Tennessee, Texas, Virginia, West Virginia, and Wyoming, to asset managers, dated 30 March 2023, 17 <https://attorneygeneral.utah.gov/wp-content/uploads/2023/03/2023-03-30-Asset-Manager-letter Press-FINAL.pdf>

US State Attorney Generals, Letter from the State Attorney Generals of Utah, Louisiana, Alabama, Alaska, Arkansas, Georgia, Idaho, Indiana, Iowa, Kansas, Kentucky, Mississippi, Missouri, Montana, New Hampshire, Ohio, Oklahoma, South Carolina, South Dakota, Texas, Virginia, West Virginia and Wyoming to NZIA Insurers, dated 16 May 2023 <https://attorneygeneral.utah.gov/wp-content/uploads/2023/05/2023-05-15-NZIA-Letter.pdf>

Websites

ABI, 'Climate Change Roadmap' <https://www.abi.org.uk/about-the-abi/sustainability/climate-change-roadmap/>

ABI, 'UK Insurance & Long-Term Savings Key Facts' <https://portfolio.cpl.co.uk/ABI-KeyFacts/2022/end/>

African Risk Capacity, <https://www.arc.int/>

Artemis, <https://www.artemis.bm/news/climate-resilient-development-bond-crd-bond-proposed-with-ils-design/>

Aviva, 'Aviva Private Client: High Net Worth Home Insurance Policy' <https://connect.avivab2b.co.uk/broker/personal/high-net-worth/>

Aviva, 'Choosing an Electric Car' <https://www.aviva.co.uk/insurance/motor/car-insurance/electric-and-hybrid-cars/>

Bosshard P, 'Making Coal Uninsurable' <https://www.fairplanet.org/op-ed/making-coal-uninsurable/>

By Miles Car Insurance <https://www.bymiles.co.uk/>

California Department of Insurance, 'Climate Smart Insurance Products' <https://interactive.web.insurance.ca.gov/apex_extprd/f?p=142:1:341076167753>

Cambridge Institute for Sustainability Leadership, 'What Is a Value Chain? Definitions and Characteristics' <https://www.cisl.cam.ac.uk/education/graduate-study/pgcerts/value-chain-defs>

Caribbean Catastrophe Risk Insurance Facility <https://caricom.org/>

Chancery Lane Project, 'Climate clauses: Insurance' <https://chancerylaneproject.org/practice-areas/insurance/>

Climate Action 100+, <https://www.climateaction100.org/>

Climate Action 100+, 'Disclaimer' <https://www.climateaction100.org/>

Climate Action Tracker, 'Countries' <https://climateactiontracker.org/countries/>

Climate Action Tracker, 'Glasgow's 2030 Credibility Gap: Net-zero's Lip Service to Climate Action' (2021) 7 https://climateactiontracker.org/documents/997/CAT_2021-11-09_Briefing_Global-Update_Glasgow2030CredibilityGap.pdf

Climate Disclosure Standard Board Framework <https://www.ifrs.org/content/dam/ifrs/groups/cdsb/cdsb-framework-2022.pdf>

Climate Financial Risk Forum, 'Climate Financial Risk Forum Guide 2022 Disclosures: Managing Legal Risk' (December 2022) <https://www.fca.org.uk/cfrf>

Dohle M, 'Solvency II: Insurers Unleashed' Portfolio Institutional' <https://www.portfolio-institutional.co.uk/spotlight/solvency-ii-insurers-unleashed/>

FEMA, 'An Affordability Framework for the National Flood Insurance Program' <https://www.fema.gov/sites/default/files/2020-05/Affordability_april_2018.pdf>

FEMA, 'How to Buy Flood Insurance' <https://www.floodsmart.gov/how-buy-flood-insurance>

FEMA, 'NFIP Claims Manual (2021)' <https://www.fema.gov/sites/default/files/documents/fema_table-of-changes-nfip-claims-manual_2021.pdf>

FEMA, 'NFIP Debt' <https://www.fema.gov/case-study/nfip-debt>

FEMA, 'Risk Rating 2.0' <https://www.fema.gov/flood-insurance/risk-rating>

FEMA, 'The NFIP Affordability Framework' <https://www.fema.gov/flood-insurance/rules-legislation>

Flood Re, 'Annual Report and Financial Statements 2022' <https://www.floodre.co.uk/about-us/reports/>

Flood Re, 'Build Back Better' <https://www.floodre.co.uk/buildbackbetter/>

Flood Re, 'Quinquennial Review' <https://www.floodre.co.uk/wp-content/uploads/QQR_FINAL.pdf>

FM Global, 'Climate Resilience Product Suite' <https://www.fmglobal.com/products-and-services/products/climate>

Friar D and Crichton K, 'Natural Hazards Act Passes into Law' <https://www.bellgully.com/insights/natural-hazards-insurance-act-passes-into-law/>

FRC, 'Auditor Responsibilities under ISA (UK) 720 in Respect of Climate-related Reporting by Companies Required by the FCA' <https://www.frc.org.uk/getattachment/b6e1b51c-4dc8-413f-8a83-ae051e4d000e/FRC-Staff-Guidance-Auditor-responsibilities-under-ISA-(UK)-720-in-respect-of-climate-related-reporting.pdf>

FSB, 'Proposal for a Disclosure Task Force on Climate-related Risks' <https://www.fsb.org/wp-content/uploads/Disclosure-task-force-on-climate-related-risks.pdf>

Generali, 'Car Insurance' <https://www.generali.ch/en/privatkunden/fahrzeuge-reisen/autoversicherung>

GeoSmart, 'FloodSmart Analytics' <https://geosmartinfo.co.uk/risk-management-for-financial-services/floodsmart-analytics/>

German Federal Ministry for Economic Cooperation and Development, 'A Joint G7 and V20 Ambition: Working towards a Global Shield against Climate Risks' <https://www.bmz.de/resource/blob/122148/dd6e2de2c73cc601344b1461cf62042b/global-shield-information-note-v20-g7-data.pdf>

GFANZ, 'Financial Institution Net-zero Transition Plans' <https://assets.bbhub.io/company/sites/63/2022/09/Recommendations-and-Guidance-on-Financial-Institution-Net-zero-Transition-Plans-November-2022.pdf>

Glasgow Financial Alliance for Net-Zero, 'Accelerating the Transition to a Net-zero Global Economy' <https://www.gfanzero.com/>

Glasgow Financial Alliance for Net-Zero, 'Our Mission' <https://www.gfanzero.com/about/>

Global Federation of Insurance Associations, 'Key Principles for More Resilient and Sustainable Construction' <https://gfiainsurance.org/news/408/cop26-insurers-publish-key-principles-for-more-resilient-and-sustainable-construction>

Global Impact Investment Network, 'Impact Performance Benchmarks' <https://thegiin.org/research/publication/impact-performance-benchmarks-overview/>

Global Risk Modelling Alliance, 'Global and Local, Public and Private: How Climate-vulnerable Countries Can Have the Best in Understanding Risk' <http://www.insdevforum.org/wp-content/uploads/2023/03/GRMAlaunch_FastTrack_report_10.pdf>

Global Shield against Climate Risks, 'FAQ: How does the Global Shield work?' <https://www.globalshield.org/resources/faq/>

Global Shield against Climate Risks, 'Instruments' <https://www.globalshield.org/activities/instruments/>

Global Shield against Climate Risks, 'Vision & Mission' <https://www.globalshield.org/about/vision-mission/>

Global Shield Solutions Platform, 'CDRFI Implementing Partners' <https://global-shield-solutions.org/what-we-support>

Global Shield Solutions Platform, 'Improving Resilience to Climate Change' <https://global-shield-solutions.org/about/about-global-shield>

IAIS, 'About the IAIS' <https://www.iaisweb.org/home>

IAIS, 'Strategic Plan 2020–2024' <https://www.iaisweb.org/uploads/2022/01/190613-2020-2024-Strategic-Plan.pdf>

IFRS, 'IFRS Foundation Announces International Sustainability Standards Board' <https://www.ifrs.org/news-and-events/news/2021/11/ifrs-foundation-announces-issb-consolidation-with-cdsb-vrf-publication-of-prototypes/>

IFRSB, 'About the International Sustainability Standards Board' <https://www.ifrs.org/groups/international-sustainability-standards-board/>

IFRSB, 'IFRS Sustainability Standards Navigator' <https://www.ifrs.org/issued-standards/ifrs-sustainability-standards-navigator/>

Inside P&C <https://www.insidepandc.com/article/2brp2essle2seqscn28sh/reinsurers-section/guy-carpenter-proposes-new-climate-resilience-bonds-mixing-philanthropy-and-ils>

Insurance Development Forum, '2022 In Review: A Year of Influence and Implementation' <https://www.insdevforum.org/4118-2/>

Insurance Development Forum, 'The Development Impact of Risk Analytics' <https://www.insdevforum.org/knowledge/idf-reportspublications/development-impact-of-risk-analytics/>

Insurance Information Institute, 'Green Insurance' <https://www.iii.org/article/green-insurance#:~:text=For%20homeowners%20who%20generate%20their%20own%20geothermal%2C%20solar,the%20outage%20is%20caused%20by%20a%20covered%20peril%29>

Insure Our Future, '2022 Scorecard on Insurance, Fossil Fuels and the Climate Emergency' <https://insure-our-future.com/wp-content/uploads/2022/11/SP-IOF-2022-Scorecard-v0.8-online-1.pdf>

InsuResilience Global Partnership, 'Concept Note: Shaping the InsuResilience Global Partnership' <https://www.insuresilience.org/wp-content/uploads/2022/10/20180502_Concept-Note_InsuResilience-Global-Partnership.pdf>

InsuResilience Global Partnership, 'Implementation: Programmes & Projects' <https://www.insuresilience.org/implementation/programmes-projects/#projects>

InsuResilience Global Partnership, 'InsuResilience Global Partnership Vision 2025' <https://www.insuresilience.org/wp-content/uploads/2022/10/vision2025_211022-1.pdf>

International Renewable Energy Agency, 'World Energy Transitions Outlook 2023: 1.5°C Pathway' <https://www.irena.org/Publications/2023/Mar/World-Energy-Transitions-Outlook-2023>

Investopedia, 'Value Chain: Definition, Model, Analysis, and Example' <https://www.investopedia.com/terms/v/valuechain.asp>

IPCC, 'About the IPCC' <https://www.ipcc.ch/about/>

Lloyd's of London, 'Glossary and Acronyms of Insurance Terms' <https://www.lloyds.com/help/glossary-and-acronyms>

Marsh, 'Carbon Capture in the UK: Risk Considerations' <https://www.marsh.com/uk/industries/energy-and-power/insights/carbon-capture-in-uk-risk-considerations.html>

Marsh, 'Delta Side D: Cover for Investigation Costs Related to TCFD Reporting' Which Provides Liability Insurance Cover for Investigations Costs Arising from a Climate Disclosure-Related Investigation, <https://www.marsh.com/uk/services/financial-professional-liability/products/delta-side-d-cover-investigation-costs-tcfd-reporting.html>

Munich Re, 'Energy Efficiency Insurance' <https://www.munichre.com/hsbeil/en/products/energy-efficiency-insurance.html>

Munich Re, 'Photovoltaic Warranty Insurance' <https://www.munichre.com/en/solutions/for-industry-clients/pv-warranty-insurance-backing-your-solar-investment.html>

National Association of Insurance Commissioners, 'Unfair Trade Practices Act' <https://content.naic.org/sites/default/files/inline-files/MDL-880_0.pdf>

National Trust <https://www.nationaltrust.org.uk/features/plant-a-tree>

Net-Zero Owner Alliance <https://www.unepfi.org/net-zero-alliance/>

Net-Zero Tracker <https://zerotracker.net/>

NZIA, 'Statement of Commitment by Signatory Companies' <https://www.unepfi.org/psi/wp-content/uploads/2021/07/NZIA-Commitment.pdf>

NZIA, 'Target-Setting Protocol 1.0' <https://www.unepfi.org/industries/insurance/launch-of-nzia-target-setting-protocol-version-1-0/>

Partnership of the V20 Concept for Consultation and German G7 Presidency, 'Global Shield against Climate Risks' <https://www.bmz.de/resource/blob/127498/global-shield-against-climate-risks-concept-barrierefrei.pdf>

Public Enquiry into the Earthquake Commission, 'Report of the Public Enquiry into the Earthquake Commission' March 2020 <https://www.dpmc.govt.nz/sites/default/files/2021-01/report-of-the-public-inquiry-into-the-earthquake-commission.pdf>

Reinsurance News, <https://www.reinsurancene.ws/climate-resilient-development-bond-proposed-by-guy-carpenter/>

Sabin Center for Climate Change Law (January 2023) <http://climatecasechart.com/about/>

Southeast Asia Disaster Risk Insurance Facility <https://seadrif.org/>

Statistica, 'Total Assets of Insurance Companies Worldwide from 2002 to 2021' <https://www.statista.com/statistics/421217/assets-of-global-insurance-companies/#:~:text=In%202020%2C%20the%20assets%20of%20insurance%20companies%20globally,by%20around%2024%20trillion%20U.S.%20dollars%20since%202002>

Swiss Re Group, 'Global Insured Catastrophe Losses Rise to USD 112 Billion in 2021, the Fourth Highest on Record' <https://www.swissre.com/media/press-release/nr-20211214-sigma-full-year-2021-preliminary-natcat-loss-estimates.html#:~:text=Global%20insured%20catastrophe%20losses%20rise%20to%20USD%20112,given%20increases%20in%20wealth%2C%20urbanisation%20and%20climate%20change>

Swiss Re Institute, 'Natural Catastrophes: The Protection Gap' <https://www.swissre.com/risk-knowledge/mitigating-climate-risk/natcat-country-profiles-infographic.html#/>

TCFD, 'Our work' <https://www.fsb-tcfd.org/about/>

TCFD, 'Task Force on Climate-related Financial Disclosures 2022 Status Report' <https://assets.bbhub.io/company/sites/60/2022/10/2022-TCFD-Status-Report.pdf>

The Insurance Insider, <https://www.insuranceinsider.com/article/2brp23q0byjudpx7irxfl/catastrophe-bonds/guy-carpenter-proposes-new-climate-resilience-bonds-mixing-philanthropy-and-ils>

The Insurer <https://www.esg-insurer.com/news/gc-proposes-resilient-development-bonds-in-paradigm-shift-in-management-of-climate-risk/>

The Investment Association, 'IA Responsible Investment: Final Report' <https://www.theia.org/campaigns/sustainability-and-responsible-investment>

The Merriam-Webster Online Dictionary, <https://www.merriam-webster.com/dictionary/climate>

The World Bank, 'Public Private Partnership Reference Guide' <https://ppp.worldbank.org/public-private-partnership/library/ppp-reference-guide-introduction>

Toka Tū Ake Earthquake Commission, 'The Natural Disaster Fund' <https://www.eqc.govt.nz/what-we-do/natural-disaster-fund/>

Trading Risk, <https://www.trading-risk.com/article/2brow0zh99snxv4gz6nls/catastrophe-bonds/guy-carpenter-proposes-new-climate-resilience-bonds-mixing-philanthropy-and-ils>

United Nations, 'Race to Net-zero Campaign' <https://unfccc.int/climate-action/race-to-zero-campaign>

UNCCC Munich Climate Insurance Initiative, <https://climate-insurance.org/>

United Nation Climate Change, 'Paris Agreement: Status of Ratification' <https://unfccc.int/process/the-paris-agreement/status-of-ratification>

United Nations Climate Change, 'Parties to the United Nations Framework Convention on Climate Change' <https://unfccc.int/process/parties-non-party-stakeholders/parties-convention-and-observer-states?field_partys_partyto_target_id%5B512%5D=512>

United Nations Climate Change, 'Sharm-El-Sheikh Adaptation Agenda' <https://climatechampions.unfccc.int/wp-content/uploads/2022/12/SeS-Adaptation-Agenda_Complete-Report_COP27-.pdf>

United Nations Climate Change, 'Status of Ratification of the Convention' <https://unfccc.int/process-and-meetings/the-convention/status-of-ratification/status-of-ratification-of-the-convention>

United Nations Climate Change, 'Transitional Committee on Loss and Damage Begins Work with Successful First Meeting in Egypt' <https://unfccc.int/news/transitional-committee-on-loss-and-damage-begins-work-with-successful-first-meeting-in-egypt>

United Nations Climate Change, 'What is the Kyoto Protocol?' <https://unfccc.int/kyoto_protocol>

United Nations Environment Programme, 'About the United Nations Environment Programme' <https://www.unep.org/about-un-environment>

United Nations Environment Programme, 'Adaptation Gap Report 2022: Too Little, Too Slow: Climate Adaptation Failure Puts World at Risk' <https://www.unep.org/resources/adaptation-gap-report-2022>

United Nations Environment Programme, 'Emissions Gap Report 2022: The Closing Window' Climate Crisis Calls for Rapid Transformation of Societies (2022) <https://www.unep.org/resources/emissions-gap-report-2022>

United Nations Environment Programme, 'How do Greenhouse Gases Actually Warm the Planet?' <https://www.unep.org/news-and-stories/story/how-do-greenhouse-gases-actually-warm-planet>

United Nations Environment Programme, 'What You Need to Know about the COP27 Loss and Damage Fund' <https://www.unep.org/news-and-stories/story/what-you-need-know-about-cop27-loss-and-damage-fund>

United Nations Environment Programme FI NZIA, 'Net-Zero Insurance Alliance: Response to CMA Call for Inputs on Environmental Sustainability and the Competition and Consumer Regimes' <https://assets.publishing.service.gov.uk/government/uploads/system/uploads/attachment_data/file/1061316/Net-Zero_Insurers_Alliance.pdf>

United Nations Environment Programme FI, 'Principles for Sustainable Insurance: What is Sustainable Insurance?' <https://www.unepfi.org/insurance/insurance/>

United Nations Environment Programme Net-Zero Asset Owner Alliance, 'Commitment Document for Participating Asset Owners' <https://www.unepfi.org/wordpress/wp-content/uploads/2022/07/AOA-COMMITMENT-DOC-2022.pdf>

US Chamber of Commerce, 'A Complete Guide to Starting a B Corp' <https://www.uschamber.com/co/start/strategy/b-corp-advantages-and-requirements#:~:text=What%20is%20a%20B%20corp%3F%20According%20to%20the,as%20well%20as%20some%20sort%20of%20public%20benefit>

Vitality Health Insurance, 'Reward Yourself, You've Earned It' <https://www.vitality.co.uk/rewards/>

What Car, 'Are Electric Cars More Expensive to Insure?' <https://www.whatcar.com/advice/owning/are-electric-cars-more-expensive-to-insure/n18043>

Willis Towers Watson, 'Managing the Transition: Mining Risk Review 2020' <https://willistowerswatson.turtl.co/story/mining-risk-review-2020-ungated/page/1>

World Economic Forum, 'Davos Manifesto 2020: The Universal Purpose of a Company in the Fourth Industrial Revolution' <https://www.weforum.org/agenda/2019/12/davos-manifesto-2020-the-universal-purpose-of-a-company-in-the-fourth-industrial-revolution/>

World Economic Forum, 'What Is "Greenhushing" and Is it Really a Cause for Concern?' <https://www.weforum.org/agenda/2022/11/what-is-greenhushing-and-is-it-really-a-cause-for-concern/>

World Weather Attribution, 'Climate Change-exacerbated Rainfall Causing Devastating Flooding in Eastern South Africa' <https://www.worldweatherattribution.org/climate-change-exacerbated-rainfall-causing-devastating-flooding-in-eastern-south-africa/>

Zurich Resilience Solutions, 'Zurich Risk Advisor' <https://www.zurich.com/en/products-and-services/tools-for-business/zurich-risk-advisor>

INDEX

Note: This index does not have entries for terms that have dedicated chapters and sections. Please refer to the Table of Contents.

For Product Safety Concerns and Information please contact our EU representative GPSR@taylorandfrancis.com
Taylor & Francis Verlag GmbH, Kaufingerstraße 24, 80331 München, Germany

www.ingramcontent.com/pod-product-compliance
Lightning Source LLC
LaVergne TN
LVHW080805011026
849160LV00015B/1538

* 9 7 8 1 0 3 2 3 3 3 0 6 9 *